DATE DUE

~~DE 1 8 99~~			
~~JA 20 01~~			
FE 7 01			
OC 22 01			
~~AG 8 02~~			

DEMCO 38-296

Journal of the Discovery of the Source of the Nile

Engraved by S. Hollyer from a Photograph by Southwell Brothers.

J. H. Speke

Journal of the Discovery of the Source of the Nile

JOHN HANNING SPEKE

Chiefly Illustrated from
Drawings by James Grant

Dover Publications, Inc.
Mineola, New York

Published in Canada by General Publishing Company, Ltd., 30 Lesmill
Road, Don Mills, Toronto, Ontario.
Published in the United Kingdom by Constable and Company, Ltd.,
3 The Lanchesters, 162-164 Fulham Palace Road, London W6 9ER.

Bibliographical Note

This Dover edition, first published in 1996, is an unabridged republi-
cation of the work originally published by Harper & Brothers, Publishers,
New York, in 1868. (Original edition, Edinburgh and London, 1863.)
Several of the illustrations have been repositioned in the present edition.

Library of Congress Cataloging-in-Publication Data

Speke, John Hanning, 1827-1864.
    Journal of the discovery of the source of the Nile / John Hanning
Speke ; illustrations by James Grant.
        p.   cm.
    Originally published: 1863.
    ISBN 0-486-29304-1 (pbk.)
    1. Nile River Valley—Discovery and exploration. 2. Speke, John
Hanning, 1827-1864—Journeys—Nile River Valley. I. Grant, James,
1828-1887. II. Title.
DT117.S74   1996
916.704'3'092—dc20   96-24970
                                                                         CIP

Manufactured in the United States of America
Dover Publications, Inc., 31 East 2nd Street, Mineola, N.Y. 11501

TO

THOSE KIND FRIENDS

WHO THOUGHT OF US, AND RAISED AN EXPEDITION TO SUCCOR US, WHEN
WE WERE SUPPOSED TO BE IN GREAT DANGER IN
THE CENTRE OF AFRICA,

THIS WORK

Is Gratefully Dedicated.

J. H. SPEKE.

JORDANS, *December,* 1863.

CONTENTS.

CHAPTER VII.
USŬI.

CHAPTER VIII.
KARAGŬÉ.

CHAPTER IX.
HISTORY OF THE WAHŬMA.

CHAPTER X.
KARAGŬÉ AND UGANDA.

CHAPTER XI.
PALACE, UGANDA.

CHAPTER XII.
PALACE, UGANDA—Continued.

CHAPTER XIII.
PALACE, UGANDA—Continued.

CHAPTER XX.
MADI.

ILLUSTRATIONS.

MAP OF EASTERN EQUATORIAL AFRICA *(in pocket, inside back cover)*........... *Speke.*

MAP OF THE NILE FROM ITS SOURCE, according to the ancient Hindŭ Books, *page* 30.

INTRODUCTION.

In the following pages I have endeavored to describe all that appeared to me most important and interesting among the events and the scenes that came under my notice during my sojourn in the interior of Africa. If my account should not entirely harmonize with preconceived notions as to primitive races, I can not help it. I profess accurately to describe naked Africa—Africa in those places where it has not received the slightest impulse, whether for good or for evil, from European civilization. If the picture be a dark one, we should, when contemplating these sons of Noah, try and carry our mind back to that time when our poor elder brother Ham was cursed by his father, and condemned to be the slave of both Shem and Japheth; for as they were then, so they appear to be now—a strikingly existing proof of the Holy Scriptures. But one thing must be remembered: While the people of Europe and Asia were blessed by communion with God through the medium of His prophets, and obtained divine laws to regulate their ways and keep them in mind of Him who made them, the Africans were excluded from this dispensation, and consequently have no idea of an overruling Providence or a future state; they therefore trust to luck and to charms, and think only of self-preservation in this world. Whatever, then, may be said against them for being too avaricious or too destitute of fellow-feeling, should rather reflect on ourselves, who have been so much better favored, yet have neglected to teach them, than on those who, while they are sinning, know not what they are doing. To say a negro is incapable of instruction is a mere absurdity, for those few boys who have been educated in our schools have proved themselves even quicker than our own at learning; while, among themselves, the deepness of their cunning and their power of repartee are quite surprising, and are especially shown in their proficiency for telling lies most appropriately in preference to truth, and with an off-handed manner that makes them most amusing.

With these remarks, I now give, as an appropriate introduction to my narrative, (1.) An account of the general geographical features of the countries we are about to travel in, leaving the details to be treated under each as we successively pass through them; (2.) A general view of the atmospheric agents which wear down and so continually help to reduce the continent, yet at the same time assist to clothe it with vegetation; (3.) A general view of the Flora; and, lastly, that which consumes it, (4.) Its Fauna; ending with a few special remarks on the Wangŭana, or men freed from slavery.

GEOGRAPHY.

The continent of Africa is something like a dish turned upside down, having a high and flat central plateau, with a higher rim of hills surrounding it; from below which, exterially, it suddenly slopes down to the flat strip of land bordering on the sea. A dish, however, is generally uniform in shape—Africa is not. For instance, we find in its centre a high group of hills surrounding the head of the Tanganyika Lake, composed chiefly of argillaceous sandstones, which I suppose to be the Lunæ Montes of Ptolemy, or the Soma Giri of the ancient Hindŭs. Farther, instead of a rim at the northern end, the country shelves down from the equator to the Mediterranean Sea; and on the general surface of the interior plateau there are basins full of water (lakes), from which, when rains overflow them, rivers are formed, that, cutting through the flanking rim of hills, find their way to the sea.

ATMOSPHERIC AGENTS.

On the east coast, near Zanzibar, we find the rains following the track of the sun, and lasting not more than forty days on any part that the sun crosses, while the winds blow from southwest or northeast toward the regions heated by its vertical position. But in the centre of the continent, within 5° of the equator, we find the rains much more lasting. For instance, at 5° south latitude, for the whole six months that the sun is in the south, rain continues to fall, and I have heard that the same takes place at 5° north; while on the equator, or rather a trifle to northward of it, it rains more or less the whole year round, but most at the equinoxes, as shown in the table on the following page. The winds, though somewhat less steady, are still very determinable. With an easterly tending, they deflect north and south, following

THE NUMBER OF DAYS ON WHICH RAIN FELL (more or less) during the March of the East African Expedition from Zanzibar to Gondokoro.

1860.	Days on which rain fell.	1861.	Days on which rain fell.	1862.	Days on which rain fell.
......	...	January	19	January	14
......	...	February	21	February*	12
......	...	March	17	March	21
......	...	April	17	April	27
......	...	May	3	May	26
......	...	June	0	June	20
......	...	July	1	July	22
......	...	August	1	August	20
......	...	September	9	September	18
October	2	October	11	October	27
November	0	November	17	November	20
December	20	December	16	December	6

* The equator was crossed on the 8th of February, 1862.

the sun. In the dryer season they blow so cold that the sun's heat is not distressing; and in consequence of this, and the average altitude of the plateau, which is 3000 feet, the general temperature of the atmosphere is very pleasant, as I found from experience; for I walked every inch of the journey dressed in thick woolen clothes, and slept every night between blankets.*

FLORA.

From what has been said regarding the condition of the atmosphere, it may readily be imagined that Africa, in those parts, after all, is not so bad as people supposed it was; for, when so much moisture falls under a vertical sun, all vegetable life must grow up almost spontaneously. It does so on the equator in the most profuse manner; but down at 5° south, where there are six months' drought, the case is somewhat different, and the people would be subject to famines if they did not take advantage of their rainy season to lay in sufficient stores for the fine: and here we touch on the misfortune of the country; for the negro is too lazy to do so effectively, owing chiefly, as we shall see presently, to want of a strong protecting government. One substantial fact has been established, owing to our having crossed over ten degrees of latitude in the centre of the continent, or from 5° south to 5° north latitude, which is this: There exists a regular gradation of fertility, surprisingly rich on the equator, but decreasing systematically from it; and the reason why this great fertile zone is confined to the equatorial regions is the same as that which has

* See climate for one year bordering on the Victoria N'yanza, deduced from the observations of Captain Grant by Francis Galton, F.R.S., in the Appendix.

constituted it the great focus of water or lake supply, whence issue the principal rivers of Africa. On the equator lie the rain-bearing influences of the Mountains of the Moon. The equatorial line is, in fact, the centre of atmospheric motion.*

FAUNA.

In treating of this branch of natural history, we will first take man—the true curly-head, flab-nosed, pouch-mouthed negro—not the Wahŭma.† They are well distributed all over these latitudes, but are not found any where in dense communities. Their system of government is mostly of the patriarchal character. Some are pastorals, but most are agriculturists; and this difference, I believe, originates solely from want of a stable government, to enable them to reap what they produce; for where the negro can save his cattle, which is his wealth, by eating grain, he will do it. In the same way, as all animals, whether wild or tame, require a guide to lead their flocks, so do the negroes find it necessary to have chiefs over their villages and little communities, who are their referees on all domestic or political questions. They have both their district and their village chiefs, but, in the countries we are about to travel over, no kings such as we shall find that the Wahŭma have. The district chief is absolute, though guided in great measure by his "graybeards," who constantly attend his residence, and talk over their affairs of state. These commonly concern petty internal matters, for they are too selfish and too narrow-minded to care for any thing but their own private concerns. The graybeards circulate the orders of the chief among the village chiefs, who are fined when they do not comply with them; and hence all orders are pretty well obeyed.

One thing only tends to disorganize the country, and that is war, caused, in the first instance, by polygamy, producing a family of half-brothers, who, all aspiring to succeed their father, fight continually with one another, and make their chief aim slaves and cattle; while, in the second instance, slavery keeps them ever fighting and reducing their numbers. The government revenues are levied, on a very small scale, exclusively for the benefit of the chief and his graybeards. For instance, as a sort of land-tax, the chief has a right to drink free from the village brews of

* Captain Grant's collection of the flora of Africa will be found in the Appendix.
† The Wahŭma are treated of in Chapter IX.

pombé (a kind of beer made by fermentation), which are made in turn by all the villagers successively. In case of an elephant being killed, he also takes a share of the meat, and claims one of its tusks as his right; farther, all leopard, lion, or zebra skins are his by right. On merchandise brought into the country by traders, he has a general right to make any exactions he thinks he has the power of enforcing, without any regard to justice or a regulated tariff. This right is called Hongo, in the plural Mahongo. Another source of revenue is in the effects of all people condemned for sorcery, who are either burnt, or speared and cast into the jungles, and their property seized by the graybeards for their chief.

As to punishments, all irreclaimable thieves or murderers are killed and disposed of in the same manner as these sorcerers, while on minor thieves a penalty equivalent to the extent of the depredation is levied. Illicit intercourse being treated as petty larceny, a value is fixed according to the value of the woman— for it must be remembered all women are property. Indeed, marriages are considered a very profitable speculation, the girl's hand being in the father's gift, who marries her to any one who will pay her price. This arrangement, however, is not considered a simple matter of buying and selling, but delights in the high-sounding title of "dowry." Slaves, cows, goats, fowls, brass wire, or beads, are the usual things given for this species of dowry. The marriage-knot, however, is never irretrievably tied; for if the wife finds a defect in her husband, she can return to her father by refunding the dowry; while the husband, if he objects to his wife, can claim half price on sending her home again, which is considered fair, because as a second-hand article her future value would be diminished by half. By this system, it must be observed, polygamy is a source of wealth, since a man's means are measured by the number of his progeny; but it has other advantages besides the dowry, for the women work more than the men do, both in and out of doors; and, in addition to the females, the sons work for the household until they marry, and in after life take care of their parents in the same way as in the first instance the parents took care of them.

Twins are usually hailed with delight, because they swell the power of the family, though in some instances they are put to death. Albinos are valued, though their color is not admired. If death occurs in a natural manner, the body is usually either buried in the village or outside. A large portion of the negro races affect nudity, despising clothing as effeminate; but these are chiefly the more boisterous, roving pastorals, who are too lazy either to grow cotton or strip the trees of their bark. Their young women go naked; but the mothers suspend a little tail both before and behind. As the hair of the negro will not grow long, a barber might be dispensed with, were it not that they delight in odd fashions, and are therefore continually either shaving it off altogether, or else fashioning it after the most whimsical designs. No people in the world are so proud and headstrong as the negroes, whether they be pastoral or agriculturists. With them, as with the rest of the world, "familiarity breeds contempt;" hospitality lives only one day; for, though proud of a rich or white visitor—and they implore him to stop, that they may keep feeding their eyes on his curiosities—they seldom give more than a cow or a goat, though professing to supply a whole camp with provisions.

Taking the negroes as a whole, one does not find very marked or much difference in them. Each tribe has its characteristics, it is true. For instance, one cuts his teeth or tattoos his face in a different manner from the others; but, by the constant intermarriage with slaves, much of this effect is lost, and it is farther lost sight of owing to the prevalence of migrations caused by wars and the division of governments. As with the tribal marks, so with their weapons; those most commonly in use are the spear, assegai, shield, bow and arrow. It is true, some affect one, some the other; but in no way do we see that the courage of tribes can be determined by the use of any particular weapon; for the bravest use the arrow, which is the more dreaded, while the weakest confine themselves to the spear. Lines of traffic are the worst tracks (there are no roads in the districts here referred to) for a traveler to go upon, not only because the hospitality of the people has been damped by frequent communication with travelers, but, by intercourse with the semi-civilized merchant, their natural honor and honesty are corrupted, their cupidity is increased, and the show of fire-arms ceases to frighten them.

Of paramount consideration is the power held by the magician (Mganga), who rules the minds of the kings as did the old popes of Europe. They, indeed, are a curse to the traveler; for if it suits their inclinations to keep him out of the country, they have merely to prognosticate all sorts of calamities—as droughts, famines, or wars—in the event of his setting eyes on the soil, and the chiefs, people, and all, would believe them; for, as may be imagined, with men unenlightened, supernatural and imaginary predictions work with more force than substantial reasons. Their implement of divination, simple as it may appear, is a cow's or antelope's horn (Uganga), which they stuff with magic powder, also called Uganga. Stuck into the ground in front of the village, it is supposed to have sufficient power to ward off the attacks of an enemy.

By simply holding it in the hand, the magician pretends he can discover any thing that has been stolen or lost; and instances have been told of its dragging four men after it with irresistible impetus up to a thief, when it belabored the culprit and drove him out of his senses. So imbued are the natives' minds with belief in the power of charms, that they pay the magician for sticks, stones, or mud, which he has doctored for them. They believe certain flowers held in the hand will conduct them to any thing lost; as also that the voice of certain wild animals, birds, or beasts, will insure them good luck, or warn them of danger. With the utmost complacency, our sable brother builds a dwarf hut in his fields, and places some grain on it to propitiate the evil spirit, and suffer him to reap the fruits of his labor, and this, too, they call their Uganga, or church.

These are a few of the more innocent alternatives the poor negroes resort to in place of a "Savior." They have also many other and more horrible devices. For instance, in times of tribulation, the magician, if he ascertains a war is projected by inspecting the blood and bones of a fowl which he has flayed for that purpose, flays a young child, and, having laid it lengthwise on a path, directs all the warriors, on proceeding to battle, to step over his sacrifice and insure themselves victory. Another of these extra barbarous devices takes place when a chief wishes to make war on his neighbor, by his calling in a magician to discover a propitious time for commencing. The doctor places a large earthen vessel, half full of water, over a fire, and over its mouth a grating of sticks, whereon he lays a small child and a fowl side by side, and covers them over with a second large earthen vessel, just like the first, only inverted, to keep the steam in, when he sets fire below, cooks for a certain period of time, and then looks to see if his victims are still living or dead—when, should they be dead, the war must be deferred, but otherwise commenced at once.

These extremes, however, are not often resorted to, for the natives are usually content with simpler means, such as flaying a goat, instead of a child, to be walked over; while, to prevent any evil approaching their dwellings, a squashed frog, or any other such absurdity, when placed on the track, is considered a specific.

How the negro has lived so many ages without advancing seems marvelous, when all the countries surrounding Africa are so forward in comparison; and, judging from the progressive state of the world, one is led to suppose that the African must soon either step out from his darkness, or be superseded by a being superior to himself. Could a government be formed for them like ours in India, they would be saved; but without it, I fear there is very little chance; for at present the African neither can help himself nor will he be helped by others, because his country is in such a constant state of turmoil he has too much anxiety on hand looking out for his food to think of any thing else. As his fathers ever did, so does he. He works his wife, sells his children, enslaves all he can lay hands upon, and, unless when fighting for the property of others, contents himself with drinking, singing, and dancing like a baboon, to drive dull care away. A few only make cotton cloth, or work in wood, iron, copper, or salt; their rule being to do as little as possible, and to store up nothing beyond the necessities of the next season, lest their chiefs or neighbors should covet and take it from them.

Slavery, I may add, is one great cause of laziness, for the masters become too proud to work, lest they should be thought slaves themselves. In consequence of this, the women look after the household work, such as brewing, cooking, grinding corn, making pottery and baskets, and taking care of the house and the children, besides helping the slaves while cultivating, or even tending the cattle sometimes.

Now, descending to the inferior order of creation, I shall commence with the domestic animals first, to show what the traveler may expect to find for his usual support. Cows, after leaving the low lands near the coast, are found to be plentiful every where, and to produce milk in small quantities, from which butter is made. Goats are common all over Africa; but sheep are not so plentiful, nor do they show such good breeding, being generally lanky, with long fat tails. Fowls, much like those in India, are abundant every where. A few Muscovy ducks are imported, also pigeons and cats. Dogs, like the Indian pariah, are very plentiful, only much smaller; and a few donkeys are found in certain localities. Now, considering this goodly supply of meat, while all tropical plants will grow just as well in central equatorial Africa as they do in India, it surprises the traveler there should be any famines; yet such is too often the case; and the negro, with these bounties within his reach, is sometimes found eating dogs, cats, rats, porcupines, snakes, lizards, tortoises, locusts, and white ants, or is forced to seek the seeds of wild grasses, or to pluck wild herbs, fruits, and roots, while at the proper seasons they hunt the wild elephant, buffalo, giraffe, zebra, pigs, and antelopes, or, going out with their arrows, have battues against the Guinea-fowls and small birds.

The frequency with which collections of villages are found all over the countries we are alluding to leaves but very little scope for the runs of wild animals, which are found only in dense jungles, open forests, or prairies, generally speaking, where hills can protect them, and near rivers whose marshes produce a thick growth of vegetation to conceal them from their most dreaded enemy — man. The prowling, restless elephant, for instance, though rarely seen, leaves indications of his nocturnal excursions in every wilderness by wantonly knocking down the forest-trees. The morose rhinoceros, though less numerous, are found in every thick jungle. So is the savage buffalo, especially delighting in dark places, where he can wallow in the mud and slake his thirst without much trouble; and here also we find the wild pig.

The gruff hippopotamus is as wide-spread as any, being found wherever there is water to float him; while the shy giraffe and zebra affect all open forests and plains where the grass is not too long; and antelopes, of great variety in species and habits, are found wherever man will let them alone and they can find water. The lion is, however, rarely heard — much more seldom seen. Hyenas are numerous, and thievishly inclined. Leopards, less common, are the terror of the villagers. Foxes are not numerous, but frighten the black traveler by their ill-omened bark. Hares, about half the size of English ones—there are no rabbits —are widely spread, but not numerous; porcupines the same. Wild-cats, and animals of the ferret kind, destroy game. Monkeys of various kinds, and squirrels, harbor in the trees, but are rarely seen. Tortoises and snakes, in great variety, crawl over the ground, mostly after the rains. Rats and lizards—there are but few mice—are very abundant, and feed both in the fields and on the stores of the men.

The wily ostrich, bustard, and florikan affect all open places. The Guinea-fowl is the most numerous of all game-birds. Partridges come next, but do not afford good sport; and quails are rare. Ducks and snipe appear to love Africa less than any other country; and geese and storks are only found where water most abounds. Vultures are uncommon; hawks and crows much abound, as in all other countries; but little birds, of every color and note, are discoverable in great quantities near water and by the villages. Huge snails and small ones, as well as fresh-water shells, are very abundant, though the conchologist would find but little variety to repay his labors; and insects, though innumerable, are best sought for after the rains have set in.*

THE WA-N-GŬANA, OR FREED MEN.

The Wa-n-gŭana, as their name implies, are men freed from slavery; and as it is to these singular negroes acting as hired servants that I have been chiefly indebted for opening this large section of Africa, a few general remarks on their character can not be out of place here.

Of course, having been born in Africa, and associated in childhood with the untainted negroes, they retain all the superstitious notions of the true aborigines, though somewhat modified, and even corrupted, by that acquaintance with the outer world which sharpens their wits.

Most of these men were doubtless caught in wars, as may be seen every day in Africa, made slaves of, and sold to the Arabs for a few yards of common cloth, brass wire, or beads. They would then be taken to the Zanzibar market, resold like horses to the highest bidder, and then kept in bondage by their new masters, more like children of his family than any thing else. In this new position they were circumcised to make Mussulmans of them, that their hands might be "clean" to slaughter their master's cattle, and extend his creed; for the Arabs believe the day must come when the tenets of Mohammed will be accepted by all men.

The slave in this new position finds himself much better off than he ever was in his life before, with this exception, that as a

---

* The list of my fauna collection will be found in an early number of the "Proceedings of the Zoological Society of London."

slave he feels himself much degraded in the social scale of society, and his family ties are all cut off from him—probably his relations have all been killed in the war in which he was captured. Still, after the first qualms have worn off, we find him much attached to his master, who feeds him and finds him in clothes in return for the menial services which he performs. In a few years after capture, or when confidence has been gained by the attachment shown by the slave, if the master is a trader in ivory, he will intrust him with the charge of his stores, and send him all over the interior of the continent to purchase for him both slaves and ivory; but should the master die, according to the Mohammedan creed the slaves ought to be freed. In Arabia this would be the case, but at Zanzibar it more generally happens that the slave is willed to his successor.

The whole system of slaveholding by the Arabs in Africa, or rather on the coast or at Zanzibar, is exceedingly strange; for the slaves, both in individual physical strength and in numbers, are so superior to the Arab foreigners, that if they chose to rebel, they might send the Arabs flying out of the land. It happens, however, that they are spell-bound, not knowing their strength any more than domestic animals, and they even seem to consider that they would be dishonest if they ran away after being purchased, and so brought pecuniary loss on their owners.

There are many positions into which the slave may get by the course of events, and I shall give here, as a specimen, the ordinary case of one who has been freed by the death of his master, that master having been a trader in ivory and slaves in the interior. In such a case, the slave so freed in all probability would commence life afresh by taking service as a porter with other merchants, and in the end would raise sufficient capital to commence trading himself—first in slaves, because they are the most easily got, and then in ivory. All his accumulations would then go to the Zanzibar market, or else to slavers looking out off the coast. Slavery begets slavery. To catch slaves is the first thought of every chief in the interior; hence fights and slavery impoverish the land, and that is the reason both why Africa does not improve, and why we find men of all tribes and tongues on the coast. The ethnologist need only go to Zanzibar to become acquainted with all the different tribes to the centre of the continent on that side, or to Congo to find the other half south of the equator there.

Some few freed slaves take service in vessels, of which they are especially fond, but most return to Africa to trade in slaves and ivory. All slaves learn the coast language, called at Zanzibar Kisŭahili; and therefore the traveler, if judicious in his selections, could find there interpreters to carry him throughout the eastern half of South Africa. To the north of the equator the system of language entirely changes.

Laziness is inherent in these men, for which reason, although extremely powerful, they will not work unless compelled to do so. Having no God, in the Christian sense of the term, to fear or worship, they have no love for truth, honor, or honesty. Controlled by no government, nor yet by home ties, they have no reason to think of or look to the future. Any venture attracts them when hard-up for food; and the more roving it is, the better they like it. The life of the sailor is most particularly attractive to the freed slave; for he thinks, in his conceit, that he is on an equality with all men when once on the muster-rolls, and then he calls all his fellow-Africans "savages." Still, the African's peculiarity sticks to him; he has gained no permanent good. The association of white men and the glitter of money merely dazzle him. He apes like a monkey the jolly Jack Tar, and spends his wages accordingly. If chance brings him back again to Zanzibar, he calls his old Arab master his father, and goes into slavery with as much zest as ever.

I have spoken of these freed men as if they had no religion. This is practically true, though theoretically not so; for the Arabs, on circumcising them, teach them to repeat the words Allah and Mohammed, and perhaps a few others; but not one in ten knows what a soul means, nor do they expect to meet with either reward or punishment in the next world, though they are taught to regard animals as clean and unclean, and some go through the form of a pilgrimage to Mecca. Indeed, the whole of their spiritual education goes into oaths and ejaculations, Allah and Mohammed being as common in their mouths as damn and blast are with our soldiers and sailors. The long and short of this story is, that the freed men generally turn out a loose, roving, reckless set of beings, quick-witted as the Yankee, from the simple fact that they imagine all political matters affect them, and therefore they must have a word in every debate. Nevertheless, they are seldom wise; and lying being more familiar to their constitution than truth-saying, they are forever concocting dodges with the view, which they glory in, of successfully cheating people.

Sometimes they will show great kindness, even bravery amounting to heroism, and proportionate affection; at another time, without any cause, they will desert and be treacherous to their sworn friends in the most dastardly manner. Whatever the freak of the moment is, that they adopt in the most thoughtless manner, even though they may have calculated on advantages beforehand in the opposite direction. In fact, no one can rely upon them even for a moment. Dog wit, or any silly remarks, will set them giggling. Any toy will amuse them. Highly conceited of their personal appearance, they are forever cutting their hair in different fashions to surprise a friend; or if a rag be thrown away, they will all in turn fight for it, to bind on their heads, then on their loins or spears, peacocking about with it before their admiring comrades. Even strange feathers or skins are treated by them in the same way.

Should one happen to have any thing specially to communicate to his master in camp, he will enter giggling, sidle up to the pole of a hut, commence scratching his back with it, then stretch and yawn, and gradually, in bursts of loud laughter, slip down to the ground on his stern, when he drums with his hands on the top of a box until summoned to know what he has at heart, when he delivers himself in a peculiar manner, laughs and yawns again, and, saying it is time to go, walks off in the same way as he came. At other times, when he is called, he will come sucking away at the spout of a tea-pot, or scratching his naked arm-pits with a table-knife, or, perhaps, polishing the plates for dinner with his dirty loin-cloth. If sent to market to purchase a fowl, he comes back with a cock tied by the legs to the end of a stick, swinging and squalling in the most piteous manner. Then, arrived at the cook-shop, he throws the bird down on the ground, holds its head between his toes, plucks the feathers to bare its throat, and then, raising a prayer, cuts its head off.

But enough of the freed man in camp; on the march he is no better. If you give him a gun and some ammunition to protect him in case of emergencies, he will promise to save it, but forthwith expends it by firing it off in the air, and demands more, else he will fear to venture among the "savages." Suppose you give him a box of bottles to carry, or a desk, or any thing else that requires great care, and you caution him of its contents, the first thing he does is to commence swinging it round and round, or putting it topsy-turvy on the top of his head, when he will run off at a jog-trot, singing and laughing in the most provoking manner, and thinking no more about it than if it were an old stone; even if rain were falling, he would put it in the best place to get wet through. Economy, care, or forethought never enters his head; the first thing to hand is the right thing for him; and, rather than take the trouble even to look for his own rope to tie up his bundle, he would cut off his master's tent-ropes or steal his comrade's. His greatest delight is in the fair sex, and when he can't get them, next comes beer, song, and a dance.

Now this is a mild specimen of the "rowdy" negro, who has contributed more to open Africa to enterprise and civilization than any one else. Possessed of a wonderful amount of loquacity, great risibility, but no stability—a creature of impulse—a grown child, in short—at first sight it seems wonderful how he can be trained to work; for there is no law, no home to bind him: he could run away at any moment; and, presuming on this, he sins, expecting to be forgiven. Great forbearance, occasionally tinctured with a little fatherly severity, is, I believe, the best dose for him; for he says to his master, in the most childish manner, after sinning, "You ought to forgive and to forget; for are you not a big man who should be above harboring spite, though for a moment you may be angry? Flog me if you like, but don't keep count against me, else I shall run away; and what will you do then?"

The language of this people is just as strange as they are themselves. It is based on euphony, from which cause it is very complex, the more especially so as it requires one to be possessed of a negro's turn of mind to appreciate the system, and unravel the secret of its euphonic concord. A Kisŭahili grammar, written by Dr. Krapf, will exemplify what I mean. There is one peculiarity, however, to which I would direct the attention of the reader most particularly, which is, that Wa prefixed to the essential word of a country means men or people; M prefixed means man or individual; U, in the same way, means place or locality; and Ki prefixed indicates the language. Example: Wagogo is the people of Gogo; Mgogo is a Gogo man; Ugogo is the country of Gogo; and Kigogo the language of Gogo.

The only direction here necessary as regards pronunciation of native words refers to the ŭ, which represents a sound corresponding to that of the oo in woo.

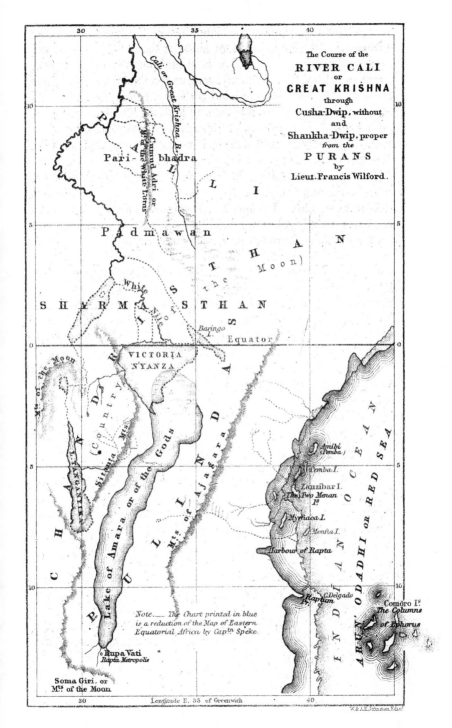

The Course of the
RIVER CALI
or
GREAT KRISHNA
through
Cusha-Dwip, without
and
Shankha-Dwip, proper
from the
PURANS
by
Lieut. Francis Wilford.

Cali or Great Krishna R.

Chand Adri, or M. of the White Lotus

P A L I

Pari-bhadra

Padmawan

the Moon)

White Nile

D R I S T H A N

S H A R M A S T H A N

Baringo L.

Equator

VICTORIA NYANZA

M. of the Moon

CHAN DA

(Country of the Gods

Sirma Ms.

T A N G A N I K A

Lake of Amara or the Gods

Mt. of Ajagara

P U L I

Amibi (Pemba)

Wemba I.

Zanzibar I.

The Two Menan Is.

Myrhaca I.

I. Monfia I.

Harbour of Rapta

Rapta Pr.   C. Delgado

I N D I A N   O C E A N

A R U N' O D A D H I   or   R E D   S E A

Comoro Is.
The Columns
of Ephorus

Note.— The Chart printed in blue
is a reduction of the Map of Eastern
Equatorial Africa by Cap.tn Speke.

Rupa Vati
Rapta Metropolis

Soma Giri, or
M.ts of the Moon

Longitude E. 35 of Greenwich

W. & A.K. Johnston, Edin.

Harper & Brothers, N.Y.

JOURNAL OF THE DISCOVERY

OF

THE SOURCE OF THE NILE.

CHAPTER I.

LONDON TO ZANZIBAR, 1859.

The Design.—The Preparations.—Departure.—The Cape.—The Zúlu Kafirs.—
Turtle-turning.—Capture of a Slaver.—Arrive at Zanzibar.—Local Politics and
News since last Visit.—Organization of the Expedition.

MY third expedition in Africa, which was avowedly for the
purpose of establishing the truth of my assertion that the Victoria
N'yanza, which I discovered on the 30th of July, 1858, would
eventually prove to be the source of the Nile, may be said to
have commenced on the 9th of May, 1859, the first day after my
return to England from my second expedition, when, at the invitation of Sir R. I. Murchison, I called at his house to show him
my map for the information of the Royal Geographical Society.
Sir Roderick, I need only say, at once accepted my views; and,
knowing my ardent desire to prove to the world, by actual inspection of the exit, that the Victoria N'yanza was the source of
the Nile, seized the enlightened view that such a discovery should
not be lost to the glory of England and the society of which he
was president; and said to me, "Speke, we must send you there
again." I was then officially directed, much against my own inclination, to lecture at the Royal Geographical Society on the
geography of Africa, which I had, as the sole surveyor of the
second expedition, laid down on our maps.* A council of the
Geographical Society was now convened to ascertain what proj-

---

* Captain Burton, on receiving his gold medal at the hands of Sir Roderick I.
Murchison, said, "You have alluded, sir, to the success of the last expedition. Justice compels me to state the circumstances under which it attained that success. To
Captain Speke are due those geographical results to which you have alluded in such
flattering terms. While I undertook the history and ethnography, the languages,
and the peculiarity of the people, to Captain Speke fell the arduous task of delinea-
ting an exact topography, and of laying down our positions by astronomical ob-

ects I had in view for making good my discovery by connecting the lake with the Nile, as also what assistance I should want for that purpose.

Some thought my best plan would be to go up the Nile, which seemed to them the natural course to pursue, especially as the Nile was said, though nobody believed it, to have been navigated by expeditions sent out by Mehemet Ali, Viceroy of Egypt, up to 3° 22′ north latitude. To this I objected, as so many had tried it and failed, from reasons which had not transpired; and, at the same time, I said that if they would give me £5000 down at once, I would return to Zanzibar at the end of the year, march to Kazé again, and make the necessary investigations of the Victoria Lake. Although, in addition to the journey to the source of the river, I also proposed spending three years in the country, looking up tributaries, inspecting watersheds, navigating the lake, and making collections on all branches of natural history, yet £5000 was thought by the Geographical Society too large a sum to expect from the government; so I accepted the half, saying that, whatever the expedition might cost, I would make good the rest, as, under any circumstances, I would complete what I had begun, or die in the attempt.

My motive for deferring the journey a year was the hope that I might, in the mean while, send on fifty men, carrying beads and brass wire, under charge of Arab ivory-traders, to Karagué, and fifty men more, in the same way, to Kazé; while I, arriving in the best season for traveling (May, June, or July), would be able to push on expeditiously to my dépôts so formed, and thus escape the great disadvantages of traveling with a large caravan in a country where no laws prevail to protect one against desertions and theft. Moreover, I knew that the negroes who would have to go with me, as long as they believed I had property in advance, would work up to it willingly, as they would be the gainers by doing so; while, with nothing before them, they would be always endeavoring to thwart my advance, to save them from a trouble which their natural laziness would prompt them to escape from.

This beautiful project, I am sorry to say, was doomed from the first; for I did not get the £2500 grant of money or appointment to the command until fully nine months had elapsed, when I

servations—a labor to which, at times, even the undaunted Livingstone found himself unequal."

wrote to Colonel Rigby, our consul at Zanzibar, to send on the
first installment of property toward the interior.

As time then advanced, the Indian branch of the government
very graciously gave me fifty artillery carbines, with belts and
sword-bayonets attached, and 20,000 rounds of ball ammunition.
They lent me as many surveying instruments as I wanted; and,
through Sir George Clerk, put at my disposal some rich presents,
in gold watches, for the chief Arabs who had so generously assisted us in the last expedition. Captain Grant, hearing that I
was bound on this journey, being an old friend and brother
sportsman in India, asked me to take him with me, and his appointment was settled by Colonel Sykes, then chairman of a com-
mittee of the Royal Geographical Society, who said it would only
be a "matter of charity" to allow me a companion.

Much at the same time, Mr. Petherick, an ivory merchant, who
had spent many years on the Nile, arrived in England, and gra-
tuitously offered, as it would not interfere with his trade, to place
boats at Gondokoro, and send a party of men up the White River
to collect ivory in the mean while, and eventually to assist me in
coming down. Mr. Petherick, I may add, showed great zeal for
geographical exploits; so, as I could not get money enough to do
all that I wished to accomplish myself, I drew out a project for
him to ascend the stream now known as the Usŭa River (reported to be the larger branch of the Nile), and, if possible, ascertain
what connection it had with my lake. This being agreed to, I
did my best, through the medium of Earl de Grey (then President of the Royal Geographical Society), to advance him money
to carry out this desirable object.

The last difficulty I had now before me was to obtain a passage
to Zanzibar. The Indian government had promised me a vessel
of war to convey me from Aden to Zanzibar, provided it did not
interfere with the public interests. This doubtful proviso induced me to apply to Captain Playfair, Assistant Political at
Aden, to know what government vessel would be available; and
should there be none, to get for me a passage by some American
trader. The China war, he assured me, had taken up all the
government vessels, and there appeared no hope left for me that
season, as the last American trader was just then leaving for
Zanzibar. In this dilemma, it appeared that I must inevitably
lose the traveling season, and come in for the droughts and famines. The tide, however, turned in my favor a little; for I ob-

tained, by permission of the Admiralty, a passage in the British screw steam-frigate Forte, under orders to convey Admiral Sir H. Keppel to his command at the Cape; and Sir Charles Wood most obligingly made a request that I should be forwarded thence to Zanzibar in one of our slaver-hunting cruisers by the earliest opportunity.

On the 27th of April, Captain Grant and I embarked on board the new steam-frigate Forte, commanded by Captain E. W. Turnour, at Portsmouth; and after a long voyage, touching at Madeira and Rio de Janeiro, we arrived at the Cape of Good Hope on the 4th of July. Here Sir George Grey, the governor of the colony, who took a warm and enlightened interest in the cause of the expedition, invited both Grant and myself to reside at his house. Sir George had been an old explorer himself—was once wounded by savages in Australia, much in the same manner as I had been in the Somali country—and, with a spirit of sympathy, he called me his son, and said he hoped I would succeed. Then, thinking how best he could serve me, he induced the Cape Parliament to advance to the expedition a sum of £300, for the purpose of buying baggage-mules; and induced Lieut. Gen. Wynyard, the commander-in-chief, to detach 10 volunteers from the Cape Mounted Rifle Corps to accompany me. When this addition was made to my force of 12 mules and 10 Hottentots, the admiral

Zŭlŭ Kafir, Delagoa Bay.

of the station placed the screw steam-corvette Brisk at my disposal, and we all sailed for Zanzibar July 16th, under the command of Capt. A. F. de Horsey, the admiral himself accompanying us on one of his annual inspections to visit the east coast of Africa and the Mauritius. In five days more we touched at East London, and, thence proceeding north, made a short stay at Delagoa Bay, where I first became acquainted with the Zŭlŭ Kafirs, a naked set of negroes, whose national costume principally consists in having their hair trussed up like a hoop on the top of the head, and an appendage like a thimble, to which they attach a mysterious importance. They wear additional ornaments, charms, etc., of birds' claws, hoofs and horns of wild animals tied on with strings, and sometimes an article like a kilt, made of loose strips of skin, or the entire skins of vermin strung close together. These things I have merely noticed in passing, because I shall hereafter have occasion to allude to a migratory people, the Watŭta, who, dressing much in the same manner, extend from Lake N'yassa to Uzinza, and may originally have been a part of this same Kafir race, who are themselves supposed to have migrated from the regions at present occupied by the Gallas. Next day (the 28th) we went on to Europa, a small island of coralline, covered with salsolaceous shrubs, and tenanted only by sea-birds, owls, finches, rats, and turtles. Of the last we succeeded in turning three, the average weight of each being 360 lbs., and we took large numbers of their eggs.

We then went to Mozambique, and visited the Portuguese governor, John Travers de Almeida, who showed considerable interest in the prospects of the expedition, and regretted that, as it cost so much money to visit the interior from that place, his officers were unable to go there. One experimental trip only had been accomplished by Mr. Soares, who was forced to pay the Makŭa chiefs $120 footing to reach a small hill in view of the sea, about twenty-five miles off.

Leaving Mozambique on the 9th of August, bound for Johanna, we came the next day, at 11 30 A. M., in sight of a slaver, ship-rigged, bearing on us full sail, but so distant from us that her mast-tops were only just visible. As quick as ourselves, she saw who we were, and tried to escape by retreating. This manœuvre left no doubt what she was, and the Brisk, all full of excitement, gave chase at full speed, and in four hours more drew abreast of her. A great commotion ensued on board the slaver. The sea-pirates threw overboard their colors, bags, and numerous boxes, but would not heave-to, although repeatedly challenged, until a gun was fired across her bows. Our boats were then lowered, and in a few minutes more the "prize" was taken by her crew being exchanged for some of our men, and we learned all about her from accurate reports furnished by Mr. Frere, the Cape Slave Commissioner. Cleared from Havana as "the Sunny South," professing to be destined for Hong-Kong, she changed her name to the Manuela, and came slave-hunting in these regions. The slaver's crew consisted of a captain, doctor, and several sailors, mostly Spaniards. The vessel was well stored with provisions and medicines, but there was scarcely enough room in her, though she was said to be only half freighted, for the 544 creatures they were transporting. The next morning, as we entered Pamoni Harbor by an intricate approach to the rich little island hill Johanna, the slaver, as she followed us, stranded, and for a while caused considerable alarm to every body but her late captain. He thought his luck very bad, after escaping so often, to be taken thus; for his vessel's powers of sailing were so good, that, had she had the wind in her favor, the Brisk, even with the assistance of steam, could not have come up with her. On going on board her, I found the slaves to be mostly Wahiyow. A few of them were old women, but all the rest children. They had been captured during wars in their own country, and sold to Arabs, who brought them to the coast, and kept them half starved until the slaver arrived, when they were shipped in dhows and brought off to the slaver, where for nearly a week, while the bargains were in progress, they were kept entirely without food. It was no wonder, then, every man of the Brisk who first looked upon them did so with a feeling of loathing and abhorrence of such a trade. All over the vessel, but more especially below, old women, stark naked, were dying in the most disgusting "ferret-box" atmosphere, while all those who had sufficient strength were pulling up the hatches, and tearing at the salt fish they found below, like dogs in a kennel.

On the 15th the Manuela was sent to the Mauritius, and we, after passing the Comoro Islands, arrived at our destination, Zanzibar — called Lungŭja by the aborigines, the Wakhadim, and Ungŭja by the present Wasŭahili.

On the 17th, after the anchor was cast, without a moment's delay I went off to the British Consulate to see my old friend Colonel Rigby. He was delighted to see us, and, in anticipation of our arrival, had prepared rooms for our reception, that both Captain Grant and myself might enjoy his hospitality until arrangements could be made for our final start into the interior. The town, which I had left in so different a condition sixteen months before, was in a state of great tranquillity, brought about by the energy of the Bombay government on the Muscat side, and Colonel Rigby's exertions on this side, in preventing an insurrection Sultan Majid's brothers had created with a view of usurping his government.

The news of the place was as follows: In addition to the formerly constituted consulates—English, French, and American—a fourth one, representing Hamburg, had been created. Dr. Roscher, who during my absence had made a successful journey to the N'yinyézi N'yassa, or Star Lake, was afterward murdered by some natives in Uhiyow; and Lieutenant Colonel Baron van der Decken, another enterprising German, was organizing an expedition with a view to search for the relics of his countryman, and, if possible, complete the project poor Roscher had commenced.

Slavery had received a severe blow by the sharp measures Colonel Rigby had taken in giving tickets of emancipation to all those slaves whom our Indian subjects the Banyans had been secretly keeping, and by fining the masters and giving the money to the men to set them up in life. The interior of the continent had been greatly disturbed, owing to constant war between the natives and Arab ivory merchants. Mgŭrŭ Mfŭpi (or Short-legs), the chief of Khoko in Ugogo, for instance, had been shot, and Manŭa Séra (the Tippler), who succeeded the old Sultan Fŭndi

Banyan contemplating his Account-book.

Kira, of Unyanyembé, on his death, shortly after the late expedition left Kazé, was out in the field fighting the Arabs. Recent letters from the Arabs in the interior, however, gave hopes of peace being shortly restored. Finally, in compliance with my request—and this was the most important item of news to myself —Colonel Rigby had sent on, thirteen days previously, fifty-six loads of cloth and beads, in charge of two of Ramji's men, consigned to Mŭsa at Kasé.

To call on the sultan, of course, was our first duty. He received us in his usually affable manner; made many trite remarks concerning our plans; was surprised, if my only object in view was to see the great river running out of the lake, that I did not go by the more direct route across the Masai country

Said Majid, Sultan of Zanzibar.

and Usoga; and then, finding I wished to see Karagŭé, as well as to settle many other great points of interest, he offered to assist me with all the means in his power.

The Hottentots, the mules, and the baggage having been landed, our preparatory work began in earnest. It consisted in proving the sextants; rating the watches; examining the compasses and boiling thermometers; making tents and pack-saddles; ordering supplies of beads, cloth, and brass wire; and collecting servants and porters.

Sheikh Said bin Salem, our late Cafila Bashi, or caravan captain, was appointed to that post again, as he wished to prove his character for honor and honesty; and it now transpired that he had been ordered not to go with me when I discovered the Victoria N'yanza. Bombay and his brother Mabrŭki were bound to me of old, and the first to greet me on my arrival here; while my old friends the Belŭchs begged me to take them again. The Hottentots, however, had usurped their place. I was afterward sorry for this, though, if I ever travel again, I shall trust to none but natives, as the climate of Africa is too trying to foreigners. Colonel Rigby, who had at heart as much as any body the success of the expedition, materially assisted me in accomplishing my object—that men accustomed to discipline and a knowledge of English honor and honesty should be enlisted, to give confidence to the rest of the men; and he allowed me to select from his boat's crew any men I could find who had served in men-of-war, and had seen active service in India.

For this purpose, my factotum, Bombay, prevailed on Baraka, Frij, and Rahan—all of them old sailors, who, like himself, knew Hindŭstani—to go with me. With this nucleus to start with, I gave orders that they should look out for as many Wangŭana (freed men—i. e., men emancipated from slavery) as they could enlist, to carry loads, or do any other work required of them, and to follow me in Africa wherever I wished, until our arrival in Egypt, when I would send them back to Zanzibar. Each was to receive one year's pay in advance, and the remainder when their work was completed.

While this enlistment was going on here, Ladha Damji, the customs' master, was appointed to collect a hundred pagazis (Wanyamŭézi porters) to carry each a load of cloth, beads, or brass wire to Kazé, as they do for the ivory merchants. Meanwhile, at the invitation of the admiral, and to show him some sport in hippopotamus-shooting, I went with him in a dhow over to Kŭsiki, near which there is a tidal lagoon, which at high tide is filled with water, but at low water exposes sand islets covered with mangrove shrub. In these islets we sought for the animals, knowing they were given to lie wallowing in the mire, and we bagged two. On my return to Zanzibar, the Brisk sailed for the Mauritius, but fortune sent Grant and myself on a different cruise. Sultan Majid, having heard that a slaver was lying at Pangani, and being anxious to show his good faith with the English, begged me to take the command of one of his vessels of war and run her down. Accordingly, embarking at noon, as soon as the vessel could be got ready, we lay-to that night at Tombat, with a view of surprising the slaver next morning; but next day, on our arrival at Pangani, we heard that she had merely put in to provision there three days before, and had left immediately afterward. As I had come so far, I thought we might go ashore and look at the town, which was found greatly improved since I last saw it, by the addition of several coralline houses and a dockyard. The natives were building a dhow with Lindi and Madagascar timber. On going ashore, I might add, we were stranded on the sands, and, coming off again, nearly swamped by the increasing surf on the bar of the river; but this was a trifle; all we thought of was to return to Zanzibar, and hurry on our preparations there. This, however, was not so easy; the sea current was running north, and the wind was too light to propel our vessel against it; so, after trying in vain to make way in her, Grant and

I, leaving her to follow, took to a boat, after giving the captain, who said we would get drowned, a letter, to say we left the vessel against his advice.

We had a brave crew of young negroes to pull us; but, pull as they would, the current was so strong that we feared, if we persisted, we should be drawn into the broad Indian Ocean; so, changing our line, we bore into the little coralline island Maziwa, where, after riding over some ugly coral surfs, we put in for the night. There we found, to our relief, some fishermen, who gave us fish for our dinner,-and directions how to proceed.

Next morning, before daylight, we trusted to the boat and our good luck. After passing, without landmarks to guide us, by an intricate channel, through foaming surfs, we arrived at Zanzibar in the night, and found that the vessel had got in before us.

Colonel Rigby now gave me a most interesting paper, with a map attached to it, about the Nile and the Mountains of the Moon. It was written by Lieutenant Wilford, from the "Pŭrans" of the ancient Hindŭs. As it exemplifies, to a certain extent, the supposition I formerly arrived at concerning the Mountains of the Moon being associated with the country of the Moon, I would fain draw the attention of the reader of my travels to the volume of the "Asiatic Researches" in which it was published.* It is remarkable that the Hindŭs have christened the source of the Nile *Amara*, which is the name of a country at the northeast corner of the Victoria N'yanza. This, I think, shows clearly that the ancient Hindŭs must have had some kind of communication with both the northern and southern ends of the Victoria N'yanza.

Having gone to work again, I found that Sheikh Said had brought ten men, four of whom were purchased for one hundred dollars, which I had to pay; Bombay, Baraka, Frij, and Rahan had brought twenty-six more, all freed men; while the Sultan Majid, at the suggestion of Colonel Rigby, gave me thirty-four men more, who were all raw laborers taken from his gardens. It was my intention to have taken one hundred of this description of men throughout the whole journey; but as so many could not be found in Zanzibar, I still hoped to fill up the complement in Unyamŭézi, the land of the Moon, from the large establishments of the Arab merchants residing there. The payment of these men's wages for the first year, as well as the terms of the agreement made with them, by the kind consent of Colonel Rigby were

* I have since learned that the Map here referred to was a forgery practiced upon Lieut. Wilford by his native compiler, and it is therefore omitted from this edition.— J. H. S.

now entered in the Consular Office books as a security to both parties, and a precaution against disputes on the way.* Any one who saw the grateful avidity with which they took the money, and the warmth with which they pledged themselves to serve me faithfully through all dangers and difficulties, would, had he had no dealings with such men before, have thought that I had a first-rate set of followers. I lastly gave Sheikh Said a double-barreled rifle by Blissett, and distributed fifty carbines among the seniors of the expedition, with the condition that they would forfeit them to others more worthy if they did not behave well, but would retain possession of them forever if they carried them through the journey to my satisfaction.

On the 21st, as every thing was ready on the island, I sent Sheikh Said and all the men, along with the Hottentots, mules, and baggage, off in dhows to Bagamoyo, on the opposite main land. Colonel Rigby, with Captain Grant and myself, then called on the sultan to bid him adieu, when he graciously offered me, as a guard of honor to escort me through Uzaramo, one jemadar and twenty-five Belŭch soldiers. These I accepted, more as a government security in that country against the tricks of the natives than for any accession they made to our strength. His highness then placed his 22-gun corvette, " Secundra Shah," at our disposal, and we went all three over to Bagamoyo, arriving on the 25th. Immediately on landing, Ladha and Sheikh Said showed us into a hut prepared for us, and all things looked pretty well. Ladha's hundred loads of beads, cloths, and brass wire were all tied up for the march, and seventy-five pagazis (porters from the Moon country) had received their hire to carry these loads to Kazé, in the land of the Moon. Competition, I found, had raised these men's wages, for I had to pay, to go even as far as Kazé, nine and a quarter dollars a head! as Masŭdi and some other merchants were bound on the same line as myself, and all were equally in a hurry to be off, and avoid as much as possible the famine we knew we should have to fight through at this late season. Little troubles, of course, must always be expected, else these blacks would not be true negroes. Sheikh Said now reported it quite impossible to buy any thing at a moderate rate; for, as I was a "big man," I ought to "pay a big price;" and my men had all been obliged to fight in the bazar before they could get even tobacco at the same rate as other men, because they were the servants of the big

* In Appendix A will be found a detailed list.

man, who could afford to give higher wages than any one else. The Hottentots, too, began to fall sick, which my Wangŭana laughingly attributed to want of grog to keep their spirits up, as these little creatures, the "Tots," had frequently at Zanzibar, after heavy potations, boasted to the more sober free men that they "were strong, because they could stand plenty drink." The first step now taken was to pitch camp under large, shady mango-trees, and to instruct every man in his particular duty. At the same time, the Wangŭana, who had carbines, were obliged to be drilled in their use and formed into companies, with captains of ten, headed by General Baraka, who was made commander-in-chief.

On the 30th of September, as things were looking more order-
Bagamoyo to
Ugéni.   ly, I sent forward half of the property, and all the men I had then collected, to Ugéni, a shamba, or garden, two miles off; and on the 2d of October, after settling with Ladha for my "African money,"* as my pagazis were completed to a hundred and one, we wished Rigby adieu, and all assembled together at Ugéni, which resembles the richest parts of Bengal.

* See Appendix B.

CHAPTER II.

UZARAMO.

The Nature of the Country.—The Order of March.—The Beginning of our Taxation.—Sultan Lion's Claw and Sultan Monkey's Tail.—The Kingani.—Jealousies and Difficulties in the Camp.—The Murderer of M. Maizan.

WE were now in U-zà-Rāmo, which may mean the country of Ramo, though I have never found any natives who could enlighten me on the derivation of this obviously triple word. The extent of the country, roughly speaking, stretches from the coast to the junction or bifurcation of the Kingani and its upper branch, the Mgéta River, westward; and from the Kingani, north, to the Lŭfigi River, south; though in the southern portions several sub-tribes have encroached upon the lands. There are no hills in Uzaramo; but the land in the central line, formed like a ridge between the two rivers, furrow fashion, consists of slightly elevated flats and terraces, which, in the rainy

Mzaramo, or Native of Uzaramo.

season, throw off their surplus waters to the north and south by nullahs into these rivers. The country is uniformly well covered with trees and large grasses, which, in the rainy season, are too thick, tall, and green to be pleasant; though in the dry season, after the grasses have been burnt, it is agreeable enough, though not pretty, owing to the flatness of the land. The villages are not large or numerous, but widely spread, consisting generally of conical grass huts, while others are gable-ended, after the coast-fashion—a small collection of ten or twenty comprising one village. Over these villages certain head men, titled Phanzé, hold

jurisdiction, who take black-mail from travelers with high pre-
sumption when they can.   Generally speaking, they live upon
the coast, and call themselves Diwans, headsmen, and subjects of
the Sultan Majid; but they no sooner hear of the march of a caravan than they transpose their position, become sultans in their
own right, and levy taxes accordingly.

The Wazaramo are strictly agriculturists; they have no cows,
and but few goats.   They are of low stature and thick set, and

Wazaramo, People of Uzaramo.

their nature tends to the boisterous.   Expert slave-hunters, they
mostly clothe themselves by the sale of their victims on the coast,
though they do business by the sale of goats and grain as well.
Nowhere in the interior are natives so well clad as these creatures.
In dressing up their hair, and otherwise smearing their bodies
with ochreish clay, they are great dandies.   They always keep
their bows and arrows, which form their national arm, in excellent order, the latter well poisoned, and carried in quivers nicely
carved.   To intimidate a caravan and extort a hongo or tax, I
have seen them drawn out in line as if prepared for battle; but a
few soft words were found sufficient to make them all withdraw
and settle the matter at issue by arbitration in some appointed
place.   A few men without property can cross their lands fear-
lessly, though a single individual with property would stand no
chance, for they are insatiable thieves.   But little is seen of these
people on the journey, as the chiefs take their taxes by deputy,
partly out of pride, and partly because they think they can extort more by keeping in the mysterious distance.   At the same

time, the caravan prefers camping in the jungles beyond the villages to mingling with the inhabitants, where rows might be engendered. We sometimes noticed albinos with grayish-blue eyes and light straw-colored hair. Not unfrequently we would pass on the track-side small heaps of white ashes, with a calcined bone or two among them. These, we were told, were the relics of burnt witches. The caravan track we had now to travel on leads along the right bank of the Kingani valley, overlooking Uzégŭra, which, corresponding with Uzáramo, only on the other side of the Kingani, extends northward to the Pangani River, and is intersected in the centre by the Wami River, of which more hereafter.

Starting on a march with a large mixed caravan, consisting of 1 corporal and 9 privates, Hottentots—1 jemadar and 25 privates, Belŭchs—1 Arab Cafila Bashi and 75 freed slaves—1 kirangozi or leader, and 100 negro porters—12 mules untrained, 3 donkeys, and 22 goats—one could hardly expect to find every body in his place at the proper time for breaking ground; but, at the same time, it could hardly be expected that ten men, who had actually received their bounty-money, and had sworn fidelity, should give one the slip the very first day. Such, however, was the case. Ten out of the thirty-six given by the sultan ran away, because they feared that the white men, whom they believed to be cannibals, were only taking them into the interior to eat them; and one pagazi, more honest than the freed men, deposited his pay upon the ground, and ran away too. Go we must, however, for one desertion is sure to lead to more; and go we did. Our procession was in this fashion: The kirangozi, with a load on his shoulder, led the way, flag in hand, followed by the pagazis carrying spears or bows and arrows in their hands, and bearing their share of the baggage in the shape either of bolster-shaped loads of cloth and beads covered with matting, each tied into the fork of a three-pronged stick, or else coils of brass or copper wire tied in even weights to each end of sticks which they laid on the shoulder; then helter-skelter came the Wangŭana, carrying carbines in their hands, and boxes, bundles, tents, cooking-pots—all the miscellaneous property on their heads; next the Hottentots, dragging the refractory mules laden with ammunition-boxes, but very lightly, to save the animals for the future; and, finally, Sheikh Said and the Belŭch escort, while the goats, sick women, and stragglers brought up the rear. From

To Bomani, 3d.

first to last, some of the sick Hottentots rode the hospital donkeys, allowing the negroes to tug their animals; for the smallest ailment threw them broadcast on their backs.

In a little while we cleared from the rich gardens, mango clumps, and cocoa-nut-trees, which characterize the fertile coastline. After traversing fields of grass well clothed with green trees, we arrived at the little settlement of Bomani, where camp was formed, and every body fairly appointed to his place. The process of camp-forming would be thus: Sheikh Said, with Bombay under him, issues cloths to the men for rations at the rate of one fourth load a day (about 15 lbs.) among 165; the Hottentots cook our dinners and their own, or else lie rolling on the ground overcome by fatigue; the Belŭchs are supposed to guard the camp, but prefer gossip and brightening their arms. Some men are told off to look after the mules, donkeys, and goats while out grazing; the rest have to pack the kit, pitch our tents, cut boughs for huts and for fencing in the camp—a thing rarely done, by-the-by. After cooking, when the night has set in, the everlasting dance begins, attended with clapping of hands and jingling small bells strapped to the legs, the whole being accompanied by a constant repetition of senseless words, which stand in place of the song to the negroes; for song they have none, being mentally incapacitated for musical composition, though as timists they are not to be surpassed.

What remains to be told is the daily occupation of Captain Grant, myself, and our private servants. Beginning at the foot: Rahan, a very peppery little negro, who had served in a British man-of-war at the taking of Rangoon, was my valet; and Baraka, who had been trained much in the same manner, but had seen engagements at Multan, was Captain Grant's. They both knew Hindŭstani; but while Rahan's services at sea had been short, Baraka had served nearly all his life with Englishmen—was the smartest and most intelligent negro I ever saw—was invaluable to Colonel Rigby as a detector of slave-traders, and enjoyed his confidence completely; so much so, that he said, on parting with him, that he did not know where he should be able to find another man to fill his post. These two men had now charge of our tents and personal kit, while Baraka was considered the general of the Wangŭana forces, and Rahan a captain of ten.

My first occupation was to map the country. This is done by timing the rate of march with a watch, taking compass-bearings along the road or on any conspicuous marks—as, for instance, hills off it—and by noting the watershed—in short, all topographical objects. On arrival in camp every day came the ascertaining, by boiling a thermometer, of the altitude of the station above the sea-level; of the latitude of the station by the meridian altitude of a star taken with a sextant; and of the compass variation by azimuth. Occasionally there was the fixing of certain crucial stations, at intervals of sixty miles or so, by lunar observations, or distances of the moon either from the sun or from certain given stars, for determining the longitude, by which the original-timed course can be drawn out with certainty on the map by proportion. Should a date be lost, you can always discover it by taking a lunar distance and comparing it with the Nautical Almanac, by noting the time when a star passes the meridian if your watch is right, or by observing the phases of the moon, or her rising or setting, as compared with the Nautical Almanac. The rest of my work, besides sketching and keeping a diary, which was the most troublesome of all, consisted in making geological and zoological collections. With Captain Grant rested the botanical collections and thermometrical registers. He also boiled one of the thermometers, kept the rain-gauge, and undertook the photography; but after a time I sent the instruments back, considering this work too severe for the climate, and he tried instead sketching with water-colors, the results of which form the chief part of the illustrations in this book. The rest of our day went in breakfasting after the march was over—a pipe, to prepare us for rummaging the fields and villages to discover their contents for scientific purposes—dinner close to sunset, and tea and pipe before turning in at night.

A short stage brought us to Ikambŭrŭ, included in the district of Nzasa, where there is another small village pre-
To Ikambŭrŭ, 4th. sided over by Phanzé Khombé la Simba, meaning Claw of Lion. He, immediately after our arrival, sent us a present of a basket of rice, value one dollar, of course expecting a return, for absolute generosity is a thing unknown to the negro. Not being aware of the value of the offering, I simply requested the sheikh to give him four yards of American sheeting, and thought no more about the matter, until presently I found the cloth returned. The "sultan" could not think of receiving such a paltry present from me, when on the former journey he got so much; if he showed this cloth at home, nobody would believe

him, but would say he took much more and concealed it from his family, wishing to keep all his goods to himself. I answered that my footing in the country had been paid for on the last journey, and unless he would accept me as any other common traveler, he had better walk away; but the little sheikh, a timid, though very gentlemanly creature, knowing the man, and dreading the consequences of too high a tone, pleaded for him, and proposed as a fitting hongo one dubŭani, one sahari, and eight yards merikani,* as the American sheeting is called here. This was pressed by the jemadar, and acceded to by myself, as the very utmost I could afford. Lion's Claw, however, would not accept it; it was too far below the mark of what he got last time. He therefore returned the cloths to the sheikh, as he could get no hearing from myself, and retreated in high dudgeon, threatening the caravan with a view of his terrible presence on the morrow. Meanwhile the little sheikh, who always carried a sword fully two thirds the length of himself, commenced casting bullets for his double-barreled rifle, ordered the Wangŭana to load their guns, and came wheedling up to me for one more cloth, as it was no use hazarding the expedition's safety for four yards of cloth. This is a fair specimen of tax-gathering, within twelve miles of the coast, by a native who claims the protection of Zanzibar. We shall soon see what they are farther on. The result of experience is, that, ardent as the traveler is to see the interior of Africa, no sooner has he dealings with the natives than his whole thoughts tend to discovering some road where he won't be molested, or a short cut, but long march, to get over the ground.

Quite undisturbed, we packed and marched as usual, and soon passed Nzasa close to the river, which is only indicated by a line of trees running through a rich alluvial valley. We camped at the little settlement of Kizoto, inhospitably presided over by Phanzé Mŭkia ya Nyani, or Monkey's Tail, who no sooner heard of our arrival than he sent a demand for his " rights." One dubŭani was issued, with orders that no one need approach me again, unless he wanted to smell my powder. Two taxes in five miles was a thing unheard of; and I heard no more about the matter until Bombay in the evening told me how Sheikh Said, fearing awkward consequences, had settled to give two dubŭani, one being taken from his own store. Lion's Claw also turned up again, getting his cloths of yesterday—one

To Kizoto, 5th.

* See Appendix B.

more being added from the sheikh's stores—and he was then advised to go off quietly, as I was a fire-eater whom nobody dared approach after my orders had been issued. This was our third march in Uzaramo; we had scarcely seen a man of the country, and had no excessive desire to do so.

Deflecting from the serpentine course of the Kingani a little,

To Kiranga Ranga, 6th. we crossed a small bitter rivulet, and entered on the elevated cultivation of Kiranga Ranga, under Phanzé Mkungŭ-paré, a very mild man, who, wishing to give no offense, begged for a trifling present. He came in person, and his manner having pleased us, I gave him one sahari, four yards merikani, and eight yards kiniki, which pleased our friend so much that he begged us to consider his estate our own, even to the extent of administering his justice, should any Mzaramo be detected stealing from us. Our target-practice, while instructing the men, astonished him not a little, and produced an exclamation that, with so many guns, we need fear nothing, go where we would. From this place a good view is obtained of Uzégŭra. Beyond the flat alluvial valley of the Kingani, seven to eight miles broad, the land rises suddenly to a table-land of no great height, on which trees grow in profusion. In fact, it appeared, as far as the eye could reach, the very counterpart of that where we stood, with the exception of a small hill, very distant, called Phongŭé.

A very welcome packet of quinine and other medicines reached us here from Rigby, who, hearing our complaints that the Hottentots could only be kept alive by daily potions of brandy and quinine, feared our supplies were not enough, and sent us more.

We could not get the sultan's men to chum with the Wangŭana proper; they were shy, like wild animals—built their huts by themselves, and ate and talked by themselves, for they felt themselves inferiors; and I had to nominate one of their number to be their immediate chief, answerable for the actions of the whole. Being in the position of "boots" to the camp, the tending of goats fell to their lot. Three goats were missing this evening, which the goatherds could not account for, nor any of their men. Suspecting that they were hidden for a private feast, I told their chief to inquire farther and report. The upshot was, that the man was thrashed for intermeddling, and came back only with his scars. This was a nice sort of insubordination, which of course could not be endured. The goatherd was pinioned and brought to trial, for the double offense of losing the goats and

rough-handling his chief. The tricking scoundrel — on quietly
saying he could not be answerable for other men's actions if they
stole goats, and he could not recognize a man as his chief whom
the sheikh, merely by a whim of his own, thought proper to ap-
point—was condemned to be tied up for the night, with the prospect of a flogging in the morning. Seeing his fate, the cunning
vagabond said, "Now I do see it was by your orders the chief
was appointed, and not by a whim of Sheikh Said's; I will obey
him for the future;" and these words were hardly pronounced
than the three missing goats rushed like magic into camp, nobody
of course knowing where they came from.

Skirting along the margin of the rising ground overlooking
To Thŭmba the river, through thick woods, cleared in places for
Lhéré, 7th. cultivation, we arrived at Thŭmba Lhéré. The
chief here took a hongo of three yards merikani and two yards
kiniki without much fuss, for he had no power. The pagazis
struck, and said they would not move from this unless I gave
them one fundo or ten necklaces of beads each daily, in lieu of
rations, as they were promised by Ladha on the coast that I
would do so as soon as they had made four marches. This was
an obvious invention, concocted to try my generosity; for I had
given the kirangozi a goat, which is customary, to "make the
journey prosperous"—had suspended a dollar to his neck in recognition of his office, and given him four yards merikani, that he
might have a grand feast with his brothers; while neither the
sheikh, myself, nor any one else in the camp had heard of such
a compact. With high words the matter dropped, African fashion.

The pagazis would not start at the appointed time, hoping to
To Mŭhŭgŭé, enforce their demands of last night; so we took the
8th. lead and started, followed by the Wangŭana. Seeing this, the pagazis cried out with one accord, "The master is
gone, leaving the responsibility of his property in our hands; let
us follow, let us follow, for verily he is our father;" and all came
hurrying after us. Here the river, again making a bend, is lost
to sight, and we marched through large woods and cultivated
fields to Mŭhŭgŭé, observing, as we passed along, the ochreish
color of the earth, and numerous pits which the copal-diggers had
made searching for their much-valued gum. A large coast-bound
caravan, carrying ivory tusks with double-toned bells suspended
to them, ting-tonging as they moved along, was met on the way;

and as some of the pagazis composing it were men who had formerly taken me to the Victoria N'yanza, warm recognitions
passed between us. The water found here turned our brandy
and tea as black as ink. The chief, being a man of small pretensions, took only one sahari and four yards merikani.

Instead of going on to the next village, we halted in this jungly
place for the day, that I might comply with the desire of the Royal Geographical Society to inspect
Mŭhonyéra, and report if there were really any indications of a
"raised sea-beach" there, such as their maps indicate. An inspection brought me to the conclusion that no mind but one prone
to discovering sea-beaches in the most unlikely places could have
supposed for a moment that one existed here. The form and appearance of the land are the same as we have seen every where
since leaving Bomani—a low plateau subtended by a bank cut
down by the Kingani River, and nothing more. There are no
pebbles; the soil is rich reddish loam, well covered with trees,
bush, and grass, in which some pigs and antelopes are found.
From the top of this embankment we gain the first sight of the
East Coast Range, due west of us, represented by the high elephant's-back hill Mkambakŭ, in Usagara, which, joining Uragŭrŭ,
stretches northward across the Pangani River to Usŭmbara and
the Kilimandjaro, and southward, with a westerly deflection,
across the Lŭfiji to Southern N'yassa. What course the range
takes beyond those two extremes the rest of the world knows as
well as I. Another conspicuous landmark here is Kidŭnda (the
little hill), which is the southernmost point of a low chain of hills,
also tending northward, and representing an advance-guard to
the higher East Coast Range in its rear. At night, as we had no
·local "sultans" to torment us, eight more men of Sultan Majid's
donation ran away, and, adding injury to injury, took with them
all our goats, fifteen in number. This was a sad loss. We could
keep ourselves on Guinea-fowls or green pigeons, doves, etc.; but
the Hottentots wanted nourishment much more than ourselves,
and as their dinners always consisted of what we left, "short
commons" was the fate in store for them. The Wangŭana, instead of regarding these poor creatures as soldiers, treated them
like children; and once, as a diminutive Tot—the common name
they go by—was exerting himself to lift his pack and place it on
his mule, a fine Herculean Mgŭana stepped up behind, grasped
Tot, pack and all, in his muscular arms, lifted the whole over his

To Mŭhonyéra, 9th.

head, paraded the Tot about, struggling for release, and put him
down amid the laughter of the camp, then saddled his mule and
patted him on the back.

After sending a party of Belŭch to track down the deserters
To Sagésera, and goats, in which they were not successful, we
10th. passed through the village of Sagésera, and camped
one mile beyond, close to the river. Phanzé Kirongo (which
means Mr. Pit) here paid us his respects, with a presentation of
rice. In return, he received four yards merikani and one dubŭani, which Bombay settled, as the little sheikh, ever done by the
sultans, pleaded indisposition, to avoid the double fire he was always subjected to on these occasions, by the sultans grasping on
the one side, and my resisting on the other; for I relied on my
strength, and thought it very inadvisable to be generous with my
cloth to the prejudice of future travelers, by decreasing the value
of merchandise, and increasing proportionately the expectations
of these negro chiefs. From the top of the bank bordering on
the valley a good view was obtainable of the Uragŭrŭ Hills, and
the top of a very distant cone to its northward; but I could see
no signs of any river joining the Kingani on its left, though on
the former expedition I heard that the Mŭkondokŭa River, which
was met with in Usagara, joined the Kingani close to Sagésera,
and actually formed its largest head branch. Neither could Mr.
Pit inform me what became of the Mŭkondokŭa, as the Wazaramo are not given to traveling. He had heard of it from the
traders, but only knew himself of one river beside the Kingani.
It was called Wami in Uzégŭra, and mouths at Utondŭé, between
the ports of Whindi and Saadani. To try and check the desertions of Sultan Majid's men, I advised—ordering was of no use—
that their camp should be broken up, and they should be amal-
gamated with the Wangŭana; but it was found that the two
would not mix. In fact, the whole native camp consisted of so
many clubs of two, four, six, or ten men, who originally belonged
to one village or one master, or were united by some other family
tie which they preferred keeping intact; so they cooked together, ate together, slept together, and sometimes mutinied together.
The amalgamation having failed, I wrote some emancipation
tickets, called the sultan's men all up together, selected the best,
gave them these tickets, announced that their pay and all rewards
would be placed for the future on the same conditions as those
of the Wangŭana, and as soon as I saw any signs of improvement

in the rest, they would all be treated in the same manner; but, should they desert, they would find my arm long enough to arrest them on the coast and put them into prison.

During this march we crossed three deep nullahs which drain
To Makŭtaniro, the Uzaramo plateau, and arrived at the Makŭtaniro,
11th.   or junction of this line with those of Mboamaji and
Kondŭchi, which traverse central Uzaramo, and which, on my former return journey, I went down. The gum-copal diggings here cease. The dŭm palm is left behind; the large, rich green-leaved trees of the low plateau give place to the mimosa; and now, having ascended the greater decline of the Kingani River, instead of being confined by a bank, we found ourselves on flat, open park-land, where antelopes roam at large, buffalo and zebra are sometimes met with, and Guinea-fowl are numerous. The water for the camp is found in the river, but supplies of grain come from the village of Kipora farther on.

A march through the park took us to a camp by a pond, from
To Matamombo, which, by crossing the Kingani, rice and provisions
12th.   for the men were obtained on the opposite bank.
One can seldom afford to follow wild animals on the line of march, otherwise we might have bagged some antelopes to-day, which, scared by the interminable singing, shouting, bell-jingling, horn-blowing, and other such merry noises of the moving caravan, could be seen disappearing in the distance.

Leaving the park, we now entered the richest part of Uzaramo,
To Dégé la Mho- affording crops as fine as any part of India. Here it
ra, 13th.   was, in the district of Dégé la Mhora, that the first
expedition to this country, guided by a Frenchman, M. Maizan, came to a fatal termination, that gentleman having been barbarously murdered by the sub-chief Hembé. The cause of the affair was distinctly explained to me by Hembé himself, who, with his cousin Darŭnga, came to call upon me, presuming, as he was not maltreated by the last expedition, that the matter would now be forgotten. The two men were very great friends of the little sheikh, and as a present was expected, which I should have to pay, we all talked cheerfully and confidentially, bringing in the fate of Maizan for no other reason than to satisfy curiosity. Hembé, who lives in the centre of an almost impenetrable thicket, confessed that he was the murderer, but said the fault did not rest with him, as he merely carried out the instructions of his father, Mzŭngéra, who, a diwan on the coast, sent him a letter directing

his actions. Thus it is proved that the plot against Maizan was concocted on the coast by the Arab merchants—most likely from the same motive which has induced one rival merchant to kill another as the best means of checking rivalry or competition. When Arabs—and they are the only class of people who would do such a deed—found a European going into the very middle of their secret trading-places, where such large profits were to be obtained, they would never suppose that the scientific Maizan went for any other purpose than to pry into their ivory stores, bring others into the field after him, and destroy their monopoly. The Sultan of Zanzibar, in those days, was our old ally Said Said, commonly called the Imam of Muscat; and our consul, Colonel Hamerton, had been M. Maizan's host as long as he lived upon the coast. Both the imam and consul were desirous of seeing the country surveyed, and did every thing in their power to assist Maizan, the former even appointing the Indian Mŭsa to conduct him safely as far as Unyamŭézi; but their power was not found sufficient to damp the raging fire of jealousy in the ivory-trader's heart. Mŭsa commenced the journey with Maizan, and they traveled together a march or two, when one of Maizan's domestic establishment fell sick and stopped his progress. Mŭsa remained with him eight or ten days, to his own loss in trade and expense in keeping up a large establishment, and then they parted by mutual consent, Maizan thinking himself quite strong enough to take care of himself. This separation was, I believe, poor Maizan's death-blow. His power, on the imam's side, went with Mŭsa's going, and left the Arabs free to carry out their wicked wills.

The presents I had to give here were one sahari and eight yards merikani to Hembé, and the same to Darŭnga, for which they gave a return in grain.

Still following close to the river—which, unfortunately, is so
To Kidŭnda,   enshrouded with thick bush that we could seldom see
14th.   it—a few of the last villages in Uzaramo were passed.
Here antelopes reappear among the tall mimosa, but we let them alone in prosecution of the survey, and finally encamped opposite the little hill of Kidŭnda, which, lying on the left bank of the Kingani, stretches north, a little east, into Uzégŭra. The hill crops out through pisolitic limestone, in which marine fossils were observable. It would be interesting to ascertain whether this lime formation extends down the east coast of Africa from the Somali country, where also, on my first expedition, I found marine

shells in the limestone, especially as a vast continuous band of
limestone is known to extend from the Tagus, through Egypt
and the Somali country, to the Burrampootra. To obtain food,
it was necessary here to ferry the river and purchase from the
Wazaramo, who, from fear of the passing caravans, had left their
own bank and formed a settlement immediately under this pretty
little hill—rendered all the more enchanting to our eyes as it was
the first we had met since leaving the sea-coast. The diwan, or
head man, was a very civil creature; he presented us freely with
two fine goats—a thing at that time we were very much in want
of—and took, in return, without any comments, one dubŭani and
eight yards merikani.

The next day, as we had no farther need of our Belŭch escort,
a halt was made to enable me to draw up a "Progress
Report," and pack all the specimens of natural history collected on the way for the Royal Geographical Society.
Captain Grant, taking advantage of the spare time, killed for the
larder two buck antelopes,* and the Tots brought in, in high excited triumph, a famous pig.

Halt, 15th.

This march, which declines from the Kingani a little, leads
through rolling, jungly ground, full of game, to the
tributary stream Mgéta. It is fordable in the dry
season, but has to be bridged by throwing a tree across it in the
wet one. Rising in the Usagara Hills to the west of the hog-
backed Mkambakŭ, this branch intersects the province of Ukhŭtŭ
in the centre, and circles round until it unites with the Kingani
about four miles north of the ford. Where the Kingani itself
rises I never could find out, though I have heard that its source
lies in a gurgling spring on the eastern face of the Mkambakŭ,
by which account the Mgéta is made the longer branch of the two.

*To thè Mgéta
River, 16th.*

* See Game List, Appendix C.

CHAPTER III.

USAGARA.

Nature of the Country.—Resumption of the March.—A Hunt.—Bombay and Baraka. —The Slave-hunters.—The Ivory-merchants.—Collection of Natural-history Specimens.—A frightened Village.—Tracking a Mule.

UNDER U-Sagara, or, as it might be interpreted, U-sa-Gara—country of Gara—is included all the country lying between the

bifurcation of the Kingani and Mgéta Rivers east, and Ugogo, the first country on the interior plateau west, a distance of a hundred miles. On the north it is bounded by the Mŭkondokŭa, or upper course of the Wami River, and on the south by the Rŭaha, or northern great branch of the Lŭfiji River. It forms a link of the great East Coast Range; but, though it is generally comprehended under the single name Usagara, many sub-tribes occupy and apply their own names to portions of it; as, for instance, the people on whose ground we now stood at the foot of the hills are Wa-Khŭtŭ, and their possessions consequently are

Msagara, or Native of Usagara.

U-Khŭtŭ, which is by far the best producing land hitherto alluded to since leaving the sea-coast line. Our ascent by the river, though quite imperceptible to the eye, has been 500 feet. From this level the range before us rises in some places to 5000 or 6000 feet, not as one grand mountain, but in two detached lines, lying at an angle of 45° from N.E. to S.W., and separated one from the other by elevated valleys, tables, and crab-claw spurs of hill which incline toward the flanking rivers. The whole, having been thrown up by volcanic action, is based on a strong foundation of granite and other igneous rocks, which are exposed in many places in the

shape of massive blocks; otherwise the hill-range is covered in
the upper part with sandstone, and in the bottoms with alluvial
clay. This is the superficial configuration of the land as it strikes
the eye; but, knowing the elevation of the interior plateau to be
only 2500 feet above the sea immediately on the western flank
of these hills, while the breadth of the chain is 100 miles, the
mean slope or incline of the basal surface must be on a gradual
rise of twenty feet per mile. The hill tops and sides, where not
cultivated, are well covered with bush and small trees, among
which the bamboo is conspicuous; while the bottoms, having a
soil deeper and richer, produce fine large fig-trees of exceeding
beauty, the huge calabash, and a variety of other trees. Here, in
certain places where water is obtainable throughout the year, and
wars, or slave-hunts more properly speaking, do not disturb the
industry of the people, cultivation thrives surprisingly; but such
a boon is rarely granted them. It is in consequence of these constantly-recurring troubles that the majority of the Wasagara villages are built on hill-spurs, where the people can the better resist
attack, or, failing, disperse and hide effectually. The normal hab-
itation is the small conical hut of grass. These compose villages,
varying in number according to the influence of their head men.
There are, however, a few mud villages on the table-lands, each
built in a large irregular square of chambers, with a hollow yard
in the centre, known as tembé.

As to the people of these uplands, poor, meagre-looking wretch-
es, they contrast unfavorably with the lowlanders on both sides
of them. Dingy in color, spiritless, shy, and timid, they invite
attack in a country where every human being has a market value,
and are little seen by the passing caravan. In habits they are
semi-pastoral agriculturists, and would be useful members of society were they left alone to cultivate their own possessions, rich
and beautiful by nature, but poor and desolate by force of circumstance. Some of the men can afford a cloth, but the greater
part wear an article which I can only describe as a grass kilt. In
one or two places throughout the passage of these hills a caravan
may be taxed, but if so, only to a small amount; the villagers
more frequently fly to the hill-tops as soon as the noise of the advancing caravan is heard, and no persuasions will bring them
down again, so much ground have they, from previous experience, to fear treachery. It is such sad sights, and the obvious
want of peace and prosperity, that weary the traveler, and make

him ever think of pushing on to his journey's end from the instant
he enters Africa until he quits the country.

Knowing by old experience that the beautiful green park in
the fork of these rivers abounded in game of great
variety and in vast herds, where no men are ever
seen except some savage hunters sitting in the trees with poisoned arrows, or watching their snares and pitfalls, I had all along
determined on a hunt myself, to feed and cheer the men, and also
to collect some specimens for the home museums. In the first
object we succeeded well, as "the bags" we made counted two
brindled gnŭ, four water-boc, one pallah-boc, and one pig—enough
to feed abundantly the whole camp round. The feast was all the
better relished as the men knew well that no Arab master would
have given them what he could sell; for if a slave shot game, the
animals would be the master's, to be sold bit by bit among the
porters, and compensated from the proceeds of their pay. In the
variety and number of our game we were disappointed, partly because so many wounded got away, and partly because we could
not find what we knew the park to contain, in addition to what
we killed—namely, elephants, rhinoceros, giraffes, buffaloes, zebra,
and many varieties of antelopes, besides lions and hyenas. In
fact, "the park," as well as all the adjacent land at the foot of the
hills, is worth thinking of, with a view to a sporting tour as well
as scientific investigation.

A circumstance arose here, which, insignificant though it appeared, is worth noting, to show how careful one must be in understanding and dealing with negro servants. Quite unaccount-
ably to myself, the general of my Wangŭana, Baraka, after showing much discontent with his position as head of Captain Grant's
establishment, became so insolent that it was necessary to displace
him, and leave him nothing to do but look after the men. This
promoted Frij, who enjoyed his rise as much as Baraka, if his pro-
fession was to be believed, enjoyed his removal from that office.
Though he spoke in this manner, still I knew that there was
something rankling in his mind which depressed his spirits as
long as he remained with us, though what it was I could not comprehend, nor did I fully understand it till months afterward. It
was ambition, which was fast making a fiend of him; and had I
known it, he would, and with great advantage too, have been dismissed upon the spot. The facts were these: He was exceedingly clever, and he knew it. His command over men was surpris-

Halt, 17th and
18th.

ing. At Zanzibar he was the consul's right-hand man: he rank-
ed above Bombay in the consular boat's crew, and became a terror even to the Banyans who kept slaves. He seemed, in fact, in
his own opinion, to have imbibed all the power of the British consul who had instructed him. Such a man was an element of dis-
cord in our peaceful caravan. He was far too big-minded for the
sphere which he occupied; and my surprise now is that he ever
took service, knowing what he should, at the time of enlistment,
have expected, that no man would be degraded to make room for
him. But this was evidently what he had expected, though he
dared not say it. He was jealous of Bombay, because he thought
his position over the money department was superior to his own
over the men; and he had seen Bombay, on one occasion, pay a
tax in Uzaramo—a transaction which would give him consequence
with the native chiefs. Of Sheikh Said he was equally jealous,
for a like reason; and his jealousy increased the more that I
found it necessary to censure the timidity of this otherwise worthy
little man. Baraka thought, in his conceit, that he could have
done all things better, and gained signal fame, had he been created chief. Perhaps he thought he had gained the first step toward this exalted rank, and hence his appearing very happy for
the time. I could not see through so deep a scheme, and only
hoped that he would shortly forget, in the changes of the marching life, those beautiful wives he had left behind him, which Bombay in his generosity tried to persuade me was the cause of his
mental distraction.

Our halt at the ford here was cut short by the increasing sick-
To Kirŭrŭ, 19*th* ness of the Hottentots, and the painful fact that Cap-
and 20*th*. tain Grant was seized with fever.* We had to change
camp to the little village of Kirŭrŭ, where, as rice was grown—
an article not to be procured again on this side of Unyamŭézi—
we stopped a day to lay in supplies of this most valuable of all
traveling food. Here I obtained the most consistent accounts of
the river system, which, within five days' journey, trends through
Uzégŭra; and I concluded, from what I heard, that there is no
doubt of the Mŭkondokŭa and Wami Rivers being one and the
same stream. My informants were the natives of the settlement,
and they all concurred in saying that the Kingani above the

---

* It was such an attack as I had on my former journey; but, while mine ceased
to trouble me after the first year, his kept recurring every fortnight until the journey
ended.

junction is called the Rŭfŭ, meaning the parent stream. Beyond it, following under the line of hills, at one days' journey distant, there is a smaller river called Msongé. At an equal distance beyond it, another of the same size is known as Lŭngérengéri; and a fourth river is the Wami, which mouths in the sea at Utondŭé, between the ports of Whindi and Saadani. In former years, the ivory-merchants, ever seeking for an easy road for their trade, and knowing they would have no hills to climb if they could only gain a clear passage by this river from the interior plateau to the sea, made friends with the native chiefs of Uzégŭra, and succeeded in establishing it as a thoroughfare. Avarice, however, that fatal enemy to the negro chiefs, made them overreach themselves by exorbitant demands of taxes. Then followed contests for the right of appropriating the taxes, and the whole ended in the closing of the road, which both parties were equally anxious to keep open for their mutual gain. This foolish disruption having at first only lasted for a while, the road was again opened and again closed, for the merchants wanted an easy passage, and the native chiefs desired cloths. But it was shut again; and now we heard of its being for a third time opened, with what success the future only can determine, for experience *will* not teach the negro, who thinks only for the moment. Had they only sense to 'see, and patience to wait, the whole trade of the interior would inevitably pass through their country instead of Uzaramo; and instead of being poor in cloths, they would be rich and well dressed like their neighbors. But the curse of Noah sticks to these his grandchildren by Ham, and no remedy that has yet been found will relieve them. They require a government like ours in India; and without it, the slave-trade will wipe them off the face of the earth.

Now leaving the open parks of pretty acacias, we followed up To Dŭthŭmi, the Mgazi branch of the Mgéta, traversed large tree-21st. jungles, where the tall palm is conspicuous, and drew up under the lumpy Mkambakŭ, to find a residence for the day. Here an Arab merchant, Khamis, bound for Zanzibar, obliged us by agreeing for a few dollars to convey our recent spoils in natural history to the coast.

My plans for the present were to reach Zungoméro as soon as To Hozŭ, 22d. possible, as a few days' halt would be required there to fix the longitude of the eastern flank of the East Coast Range by astronomical observation; but, on ordering the morning's march, the porters—too well fed and lazy—thought our marching-rate much too severe, and resolutely refused to move. They ought to have made ten miles a day, but preferred doing five. Argument was useless, and I was reluctant to apply the stick, as the Arabs would have done when they saw their porters trifling with their pockets. Determining, however, not to be frustrated in this puerile manner, I ordered the bugler to sound the march, and started with the mules and coast-men, trusting to Sheikh and Baraka to bring on the Wanyamŭézi as soon as they could move them. The same day we crossed the Mgazi, where we found several Wakhŭtŭ spearing fish in the muddy hovers of its banks.

We slept under a tree, and this morning found a comfortable residence under the eaves of a capacious hut. The Zungoméro, 23d. Wanyamŭézi porters next came in at their own time, and proved to us how little worth are orders in a land where every man, in his own opinion, is a lord, and no laws prevail. Zungoméro, bisected by the Mgéta, lies on flat ground, in a very pretty amphitheatre of hills, S. lat. 7° 26′ 53″, and E. long. 37° 36′

Mkambaku Hill, viewed from Zungoméro.

45″. It is extremely fertile, and very populous, affording every thing that man can wish, even to the cocoa and papwa fruits; but the slave-trade has almost depopulated it, and turned its once flourishing gardens into jungles. As I have already said, the people who possess these lands are cowardly by nature, and that is the reason why they are so much oppressed. The Wasŭahili, taking advantage of their timidity, flock here in numbers to live upon the fruits of their labors. The merchants on the coast, too, though prohibited by their sultan from interfering with the natural course of trade, send their hungry slaves, as touters, to entice all approaching caravans to trade with their particular ports, authorizing the touters to pay such premiums as may be necessary for the purpose. Where they came from we could not ascertain; but during our residence, a large party of the Wasŭahili marched past, bound for the coast, with one hundred head of cattle, fifty slaves in chains, and as many goats. Halts always end disastrously in Africa, giving men time for mischief; and here was an example of it. During the target-practice, which was always instituted on such occasions to give confidence to our men, the little pepper-box Rahan, my head valet, challenged a comrade to a duel with carbines. Being stopped by those around him, he vented his wrath in terrible oaths, and swung about his arms, until his gun accidentally went off, and blew his middle finger off.

Baraka next, with a kind of natural influence of affinity when a row is commenced, made himself so offensive to Bombay as to send him running to me so agitated with excitement that I thought him drunk. He seized my hands, cried, and implored me to turn him off. What could this mean? I could not divine; neither could he explain, farther than that he had come to a determination that I must send either him or Baraka to the right-about; and his first idea was that he, and not Baraka, should be the victim. Baraka's jealousy about his position had not struck me yet. I called them both together, and asked what quarrel they had, but could not extract the truth. Baraka protested that he had never given, either by word or deed, the slightest cause of rupture; he only desired the prosperity of the march, and that peace should reign throughout the camp; but Bombay was suspicious of him, and malignantly abused him, for what reason Baraka could not tell. When I spoke of this to Bombay, like a bird fascinated by the eye of a viper, he shrank before the slippery tongue of his opponent, and could only say, "No, Sahib —oh no, that is not it; you had better turn me off, for his tongue is so long, and mine so short, you never will believe me." I tried to make them friends, hoping it was merely a passing ill wind which would soon blow over; but before long the two disputants were tonguing it again, and I distinctly heard Bombay ordering Baraka out of camp, as he could not keep from intermeddling, saying, which was true, he had invited him to join the expedition, that his knowledge of Hindŭstani might be useful to us; he was not wanted for any other purpose, and unless he was satisfied with doing that alone, we would get on much better without him. To this provocation Baraka mildly made the retort, "Pray don't put yourself in a passion; nobody is hurting you; it is all in your own heart, which is full of suspicions and jealousy without the slightest cause."

This complicated matters more than ever. I knew Bombay to be a generous, honest man, entitled by his former services to be in the position he was now holding as fŭndi, or supervisor in the camp. Baraka, who never would have joined the expedition excepting through his invitation, was indebted to him for the rank he now enjoyed—a command over seventy men, a duty in which he might have distinguished himself as a most useful accessory to the camp. Again I called the two together, and begged them to act in harmony like brothers, noticing that there was no cause for entertaining jealousy on either side, as every order rested with myself to reward for merit or to punish. The relative position in the camp was like that of the senior officers in India, Bombay representing the Mulki lord, or governor general, and Baraka the Jungi lord, or commander-in-chief. To the influence of this distinguished comparison they both gave way, acknowledging myself their judge, and both protesting that they wished to serve in peace and quietness for the benefit of the march.

Zungoméro is a terminus or junction of two roads leading to the interior—one, the northern, crossing over the Goma Pass, and trenching on the Mŭkondokŭa River, and the other crossing over the Mabrŭki Pass, and edging on the Rŭaha River. They both unite again at Ugogi, the western terminus on the present great Unyamŭézi line. On the former expedition I went by the northern line and returned by the southern, finding both equally easy, and, indeed, neither is worthy of special and permanent preference. In fact, every season makes a difference in the supply of water and provisions; and with every year, owing to incessant wars, or rather slave-hunts, the habitations of the wretched inhabitants become constantly changed—generally speaking, for the worse. Our first and last object, therefore, as might be supposed, from knowing these circumstances, was to ascertain, before mounting the hill-range, which route would afford us the best facilities for a speedy march now. No one, however, could or would advise us. The whole country on ahead, especially Ugogo, was oppressed by drought and famine. To avoid this latter country, then, we selected the southern route, as by doing so it was hoped we might follow the course of the Rŭaha River from Maroro to Usénga and Usanga, and thence strike across to Unyanyembé, sweeping clear of Ugogo.

With this determination, after dispatching a third set of speci- _{To Kirengŭé,} mens, consisting of large game animals, birds, snakes, _{27th.} insects, land and fresh-water shells, and a few rock specimens, of which one was fossiliferous, we turned southward, penetrating the forests which lie between the greater range and the little outlying one. At the foot of this is the Maji ya Whéta, a hot, deep-seated spring of fresh water, which bubbles up through many apertures in a large, dome-shaped heap of soft lime—an accumulation obviously thrown up by the force of the spring, as the rocks on either side of it are of igneous character. We arrived at the deserted village of Kirengŭé. This was not an easy go-ahead march, for the halt had disaffected both men and mules. Three of the former bolted, leaving their loads upon the ground; and on the line of march, one of the mules, a full-conditioned animal, gave up the ghost after an eighteen hours' sickness. What his disease was I never could ascertain; but, as all the remaining animals died afterward much in the same manner, I may state for once and for all, that these attacks commenced with general swelling, at first on the face, then down the neck, along the belly, and down the legs. It proved so obstinate that fire had no effect upon it; and although we cut off the tails of some to relieve them by bleeding, still they died.

In former days Kirengŭé was inhabited, and we reasonably _{Halt, 28th.} hoped to find some supplies for the jungly march before us. But we had calculated without our host, for the slave-hunters had driven every vestige of humanity away; and now, as we were delayed by our three loads behind, there was nothing left but to send back and purchase more grain. Such was one of the many days frittered away in do-nothingness.

This day, all together again, we rose the first spurs of the well- _{To Camp, 29th.} wooded Usagara Hills, among which the familiar bamboo was plentiful, and at night we bivouacked in the jungle.

Rising betimes in the morning, and starting with a good will, _{To E. Mbŭiga, 30th.} we soon reached the first settlements of Mbŭiga, from which could be seen a curious blue mountain, stand-

ing up like a giant overlooking all the rest of the hills. The
scenery here formed a strong and very pleasing contrast to any
we had seen since leaving' the coast. Emigrant Waziraha, who
had been driven from their homes across the Kingani River by the

Hill View from Eastern Mbŭiga.

slave-hunters, had taken possession of the place, and disposed their
little conical-hut villages on the heights of the hill-spurs in such
a picturesque manner that one could not help hoping they would
here at least be allowed to rest in peace and quietness. The valleys, watered by little brooks, are far richer, and even prettier,
than the high lands above, being lined with fine trees and evergreen shrubs; while the general state of prosperity was such that
the people could afford, even at this late season of the year, to
turn their corn into malt to brew beer for sale; and goats and
fowls were plentiful in the market.

Passing by the old village of Mbŭiga, which I occupied on my
To W. Mŭiga, 31st.   former expedition, we entered some huts on the western flank of the Mbŭiga district; and here, finding a
coast-man, a great friend of the little sheikh's, willing to take back
to Zanzibar any thing we might give him, a halt was made, and
I drew up my reports. I then consigned to his charge three of
the most sickly of the Hottentots in a deplorable condition—one
of the mules, that they might ride by turns—and all the specimens that had been collected. With regret I also sent back the

camera, because I saw, had I allowed my companion to keep
working it, the heat he was subjected to in the little tent while
preparing and fixing his plates would very soon have killed him.
The number of Guinea-fowl seen here was most surprising.

A little lighter and much more comfortable for the good riddance of those grumbling " Tots," we worked up to
and soon breasted the stiff ascent of the Mabrŭki
Pass, which we surmounted without much difficulty. This concluded the first range of these Usagara Hills ; and once over, we
dropped down to the elevated valley of Maketa, where we halted
two days to shoot. As a traveling Arab informed me that the
whole of the Maroro district had been laid waste by the marauding Wahéhé, I changed our plans again, and directed our attention to a middle and entirely new line, which in the end would
lead us to Ugogi. The first and only giraffe killed upon the
journey was here shot by Grant, with a little 40-gauge Lancaster
rifle, at 200 yards' distance. Some smaller animals were killed ;
but I wasted all my time in fruitlessly stalking some wounded
striped eland—magnificent animals, as large as Delhi oxen—and
some other animals, of which I wounded three, about the size of
hartebeest, and much their shape, only cream-colored, with a conspicuous black spot in the centre of each flank. The eland may
probably be the animal first mentioned by Livingstone, but the
other animal is not known.

To Kikobogo, 2d.

Though reluctant to leave a place where such rare animals
were to be found, the fear of remaining longer on the
road induced us to leave Kikobogo, and at a good
stride we crossed the flat valley of Makata, and ascended the higher lands beyond, where we no sooner arrived than we met the
last down trader from Unyamŭézi, well known to all my men as
the great Mamba or Crocodile. Mamba, dressed in a dirty Arab
gown, with coronet of lion's nails decorating a threadbare cutch
cap, greeted us with all the dignity of a savage potentate surrounded by his staff of half-naked officials. As usual, he had been the
last to leave the Unyamŭézi, and so purchased all his stock of
ivory at a cheap rate, there being no competitors left to raise the
value of that commodity; but his journey had been a very trying one. With a party, at his own estimate, of two thousand
souls—we did not see any thing like that number—he had come
from Ugogo to this, by his own confession, living on the products
of the jungle, and by boiling down the skin aprons of his porters

To Ngoto, 5th.

occasionally for a soup. Famines were raging throughout the land, and the Arabs preceding him had so harried the country that every village was deserted. On hearing our intention to march upon the direct line, he frankly said he thought we should never get through, for my men could not travel as his had done, and therefore he advised our deflecting northward from New Mbŭmi to join the track leading from Rŭmŭma to Ugogi. This was a sad disappointment; but, rather than risk a failure, I resolved to follow his advice.

After reaching the elevated ground, we marched over rolling tops, covered with small trees and a rich variety of pretty bulbs, and reached the habitations of Mŭhanda, where we no sooner appeared than the poor villagers, accustomed only to rough handling, immediately dispersed in the jungles. By dint of persuasion, however, we induced them to sell us provisions, though at a monstrous rate, such as no merchant could have afforded; and having spent the night quietly, we proceeded on to the upper courses of the M'yombo River, which trends its way northward to the Mŭkondokŭa River. The scenery was most interesting, with every variety of hill, roll, plateau, and ravine, wild and prettily wooded; but we saw nothing of the people. Like frightened rats, as soon as they caught the sound of our advancing march, they buried themselves in the jungles, carrying off their grain with them. Foraging parties, of necessity, were sent out as soon as the camp was pitched, with cloth for purchases, and strict orders not to use force; the upshot of which was, that my people got nothing but a few arrows fired at them by the lurking villagers, and I was abused for my squeamishness. Moreover, the villagers, emboldened by my lenity, vauntingly declared they would attack the camp by night, as they could only recognize in us such men as plunder their houses and steal their children. This caused a certain amount of alarm among my men, which induced them to run up a stiff bush fence round the camp, and kept them talking all night.

To Mŭhanda and M'yombo, 6th and 7th.

This morning we marched on as usual, with one of the Hottentots lashed on a donkey; for the wretched creature, after lying in the sun asleep, became so sickly that he could not move or do any thing for himself, and nobody else would do any thing for him. The march was a long one, but under ordinary circumstances would have been very interesting, for we passed an immense lagoon, where hippopotami were snorting

To New Mbŭmi, 8th.

as if they invited an attack. In the larger tree-jungles the traces of elephants, buffaloes, rhinoceros, and antelopes were very numerous; while a rich variety of small birds, as often happened, made me wish I had come on a shooting rather than on a long exploring expedition. Toward sunset we arrived at New Mbŭmi, a very pretty and fertile place, lying at the foot of a cluster of steep hills, and pitched camp for three days to lay in supplies for ten, as this was reported to be the only place where we could buy corn until we reached Ugogo, a span of 140 miles. Mr. Mbŭmi, the chief of the place, a very affable negro, at once took us by the hand, and said he would do any thing we desired, for he had often been to Zanzibar. He knew that the English were the ruling power in that land, and that they were opposed to slavery, the terrible effects of which had led to his abandoning Old Mbŭmi, on the banks of the Mŭkondokŭa River, and residing here.

The sick Hottentot died here, and we buried him with Christian honors. As his comrades said, he died because he had determined to die—an instance of that obstinate fatalism in their mulish temperament which no kind words or threats can cure. This terrible catastrophe made me wish to send all the remaining Hottentots back to Zanzibar; but, as they all preferred serving with me to returning to duty at the Cape, I selected two of the *most* sickly, put them under Tahib, one of Rigby's old servants, and told him to remain with them at Mbŭmi until such time as he might find some party proceeding to the coast; and, in the mean while, for board and lodgings I gave Mbŭmi beads and cloth. The prices of provision here being a good specimen of what one has to pay at this season of the year, I give a short list of them: sixteen rations corn, two yards cloth; three fowls, two yards cloth; one goat, twenty yards cloth; one cow, forty yards cloth—the cloth being common American sheeting. Before we left Mbŭmi, a party of forty men and women of the Waquiva tribe, pressed by famine, were driven there to purchase food. The same tribe had, however, killed many of Mbŭmi's subjects not long since, and therefore, in African revenge, the chief seized them all, saying he would send them off for sale to the Zanzibar market unless they could give a legitimate reason for the cruelty they had committed. These Waquiva, I was given to understand, occupied the steep hills surrounding this place. They were a squalid-looking set, like the generality of the inhabitants of this mountainous region.

Halt, 9th, 10th, and 11th.

This march led us over a high hill to the Mdŭnhwi River, an-
To Mdŭnhwi, other tributary to the Mŭkondokŭa. It is all clad in
12th. the upper regions with the slender pole-trees which
characterize these hills, intermingled with bamboo; but the bottoms are characterized by a fine growth of fig-trees of great variety, along with high grasses; while near the villages were found
good gardens of plantains, and numerous Palmyra-trees. The
rainy season being not far off, the villagers were busy in burning
rubble and breaking their ground. Within their reach every
where is the sarsaparilla vine, but growing as a weed, for they
know nothing of its value.

Rising up from the deep valley of Mdŭnhwi, we had to cross
To Tzanzi, 13th. another high ridge before descending to the also deep
valley of Chongŭé, as picturesque a country as the
middle heights of the Himalayas, dotted on the ridges and spur-
slopes by numerous small conical-hut villages, but all so poor that
we could not, had we wanted it, have purchased provisions for a
day's consumption.

Leaving this valley, we rose to the table of Manyovi, overhung
To Manyongé, with much higher hills, looking, according to the ac-
14th. counts of our Hottentots, as they eyed the fine herds
of cattle grazing on the slopes, so like the range in Kafraria, that
they formed their expectations accordingly, and appeared, for the
first time since leaving the coast, happy at the prospect before
them, little dreaming that such rich places were seldom to be met
with. The Wanyamŭézi porters even thought they had found a
paradise, and forthwith threw down their loads as the villagers
came to offer them grain for sale; so that, had I not had the
Wangŭana a little under control, we should not have completed
our distance that day, and so reached Manyongé, which reminded
me, by its ugliness, of the sterile Somali land.

Proceeding through the semi-desert rolling table-land—in one
To Rŭmŭma, place occupied by men who build their villages in
15th. large open squares of flat-topped mud huts, which,
when I have occasion to refer to them in future, I shall call by
their native name tembé—we could see on the right hand the
massive mountains overhanging the Mŭkondokŭa River, to the
front the western chain of these hills, and to the left the high
crab-claw shaped ridge, which, extending from the western chain,
circles round conspicuously above the swelling knolls which lie
between the two main rocky ridges. Contorted green thorn-trees,

"elephant-foot" stumps, and aloes, seem to thrive best here, by
their very nature indicating what the country is, a poor stony

Bugu, Calabash, or Gouty-limbed Trees.

land. Our camp was pitched by the River Rŭmŭma, where, shel-
tered from the winds and enriched by alluvial soil, there ought
to have been no scarcity; but still the villagers had nothing to
sell.

On we went again to Marenga Mkhali, the "Salt Water," to
breakfast, and camped in the crooked green thorns
by night, carrying water on for our supper. This
kind of traveling—forced marches—hard as it may appear, was
what we liked best, for we felt that we were shortening the journey, and in doing so, shortening the risks of failure by disease,
by war, by famine, and by mutiny. We had here no grasping
chiefs to detain us for presents, nor had our men time to become
irritable and truculent, concoct devices for stopping the way, or
fight among themselves.

On again, and at last we arrived at the foot of the western chain,
but not all together. Some porters, overcome by
heat and thirst, lay scattered along the road, while
the corporal of the Hottentots allowed his mule to stray from him,
never dreaming the animal would travel far from his comrades,

To Camp, 16th.

To Inengé, 17th.

and, in following after him, was led such a long way into the bush
that my men became alarmed for his safety, knowing as they did
that the "savages" were out living like monkeys on the calabash
fruit, and looking out for any windfalls, such as stragglers worth
plundering, that might come in their way.   At first the Wangŭana attempted to track down the corporal; but, finding he would
not answer their repeated shots, and fearful for their own safety,
they came into camp and reported the case.   Losing no time, I
ordered twenty men, armed with carbines, to carry water for the
distressed porters, and bring the corporal back as soon as possible.
They all marched off, as they always do on such exploits, in high
good-humor with themselves for the valor which they intended to
show; and in the evening came in, firing their guns in the most
reckless manner, beaming with delight, for they had the corporal
in tow, two men and two women captives, and a spear as a trophy.
Then in high impatience, all in a breath, they began a recital of
the great day's work.   The corporal had followed on the spoor
of the mule, occasionally finding some of his things that had been
torn from the beast's back by the thorns, and, picking up these
one by one, had become so burdened with the weight of them
that he could follow no farther.   In this fix the twenty men came
up with him, but not until they had had a scrimmage with the
"savages," had secured four, and taken the spear which had been
thrown at them.   Of the mule's position no one could give an
opinion, save that they imagined, in consequence of the thickness
of the bush, he would soon become irretrievably entangled in the
thicket, where the savages would find him, and bring him in as a
ransom for the prisoners.

What with the diminution of our supplies, the famished state
of the country, and the difficulties which frowned
upon us in advance, together with unwillingness to
give up so good a mule, with all its gear and ammunition, I must
say I felt doubtful as to what had better be done, until the corporal, who felt confident he would find the beast, begged so hard
that I sent him in command of another expedition of sixteen
men, ordering him to take one of the prisoners with him to pro-
claim to his brethren that we would give up the rest if they returned us the mule.   The corporal then led off his band to the
spot where he last saw traces of the animal, and tracked on till
sundown; while Grant and myself went out pot-hunting, and
brought home a bag consisting of one striped eland, one saltiana

Halt, 18th.

antelope, four Guinea-fowl, four ringdoves, and one partridge—a welcome supply, considering we were quite out of flesh.

Next day, as there were no signs of the trackers, I went again to the place of the elands, wounded a fine male, but gave up the chase, as I heard the unmistakable gun-firing return of the party, and straightway proceeded to camp. Sure enough, there they were; they had tracked the animal back to Marenga Mkhali, through jungle—for he had not taken to the footpath. Then, finding he had gone on, they returned quite tired and famished. To make the most of a bad job, I now sent Grant on to the Robého (or windy) Pass, on the top of the western chain, with the mules and heavy baggage, and directions to proceed thence across the brow of the hill the following morning, while I remained behind with the tired men, promising to join him by breakfast-time. I next released the prisoners, much to their disgust, for they had not known such good feeding before, and dreaded being turned adrift again in the jungles to live on calabash seeds; and then, after shooting six Guinea-fowl, turned in for the night.

Halt, 19th.

Betimes in the morning we were off, mounting the Robého, a good stiff ascent, covered with trees and large blocks of granite, excepting only where cleared for villages; and on we went rapidly, until at noon the advance party was reached, located in a village overlooking the great interior plateau—a picture, as it were, of the common type of African scenery. Here, taking a hasty meal, we resumed the march all together, descended the great western chain, and, as night set in, camped in a ravine at the foot of it, not far from the great junction-station Ugogi, where terminate the hills of Usagara.

To Camp, 20th.

CHAPTER IV.

UGOGO, AND THE WILDERNESS OF MGUNDA MKHALI,

The Lie of the Country.—Rhinoceros-stalking.—Scuffle of Villagers over a Carcass.
—Chief "Short-legs" and his Successor.—Buffalo-shooting.—Getting Lost.—A
Troublesome Sultan.—Desertions from the Camp.—Getting Plundered.—Wilder-
ness March. — Diplomatic Relations with the Local Powers. — Manúa Séra's
Story.—Christmas.—The Relief from Kazé.

THIS day's work led us from the hilly Usagara range into the
more level lands of the interior. Making a double
march of it, we first stopped to breakfast at the quiet

To Camp in the
Bush, 21st & 22d.

little settlement of Inengé, where
cattle were abundant, but grain
so scarce that the villagers were
living on calabash seeds. Proceeding thence across fields
delightfully checkered with
fine calabash and fig trees, we
marched, carrying water through
thorny jungles, until dark, when
we bivouacked for the night,
only to rest and push on again
next morning, arriving at Marenga Mkhali (the saline water)
to breakfast. Here a good view
of the Usagara Hills is obtained.
Carrying water with us, we next
marched half way to the first
settlement of Ugogo, and bivou-

Mgogo, or Native of Ugogo.

acked again, to eat the last of our store of Mbŭmi grain.

At length the greater famine lands had been spanned; but we
were not in lands of plenty, for the Wagogo we
found, like their neighbors Wasagara, eating the seed
of the calabash, to save their small stores of grain.

To E. Ugogo,
23d.

The East Coast Range having been passed, no more hills had
to be crossed, for the land we next entered on is a
plateau of rolling ground, sloping southward to the

Halt, 24th and
25th.

Rŭaha River, which forms a great drain running from west to
east, carrying off all the rain-waters that fall in its neighborhood
through the East Coast Range to the sea.   To the northward can

View of East Coast Range from Marenga Mkhali.

be seen some low hills which are occupied by Wahŭmba, a sub-
tribe of the warlike Masai; and on the west is the large forest-
wilderness of Mgŭnda Mkhali.   Ugogo, lying under the lee side
of the Usagara Hills, is comparatively sterile.   Small outcrops of
granite here and there poke through the surface, which, like the
rest of the rolling land, being covered with bush, principally acacias, have a pleasing appearance after the rains have set in, but
are too brown and desert-looking during the rest of the year.
Large prairies of grass also are exposed in many places, and the
villagers have laid much ground bare for agricultural purposes.

Altogether, Ugogo has a very wild aspect, well in keeping with
the natives who occupy it, who, more like the Wazaramo than
the Wasagara, carry arms, intended for use rather than show.
The men, indeed, are never seen without their usual arms—the
spear, the shield, and the assegai.   They live in flat-topped, square,
tembé villages, wherever springs of water are found, keep cattle
in plenty, and farm enough generally to supply not only their
own wants, but those of the thousands who annually pass in caravans.   They are extremely fond of ornaments, the most common
of which is an ugly tube of the gourd thrust through the lower
lobe of the ear.   Their color is a soft ruddy brown, with a slight
infusion of black, not unlike that of a rich plum.   Impulsive by
nature, and exceedingly avaricious, they pester travelers beyond
all conception by thronging the road, jeering, quizzing, and point-

ing at them; and in camp, by intrusively forcing their way into the midst of the kit, and even into the stranger's tent. Caravans, in consequence, never enter their villages, but camp outside, generally under the big "gouty-limbed" trees, encircling their entire camp sometimes with a ring-fence of thorns to prevent any sudden attack.

To resume the thread of the journey: we found, on arrival in Ugogo, very little more food than in Usagara, for the Wagogo were mixing their small stores of grain with the monkey-bread seeds of the gouty-limbed tree. Water was so scarce in the wells at this season that we had to buy it at the normal price of country beer; and, as may be imagined where such distress in food was existing, cows, goats, sheep, and fowls were also selling at high rates.

Our mules here gave us the slip again, and walked all the way back to Marenga Mkhali, where they were found and brought back by some Wagogo, who took four yards of merikani in advance, with a promise of four more on return, for the job, their chief being security for their fidelity. This business detained us two days, during which time I shot a new variety of florikan, peculiar in having a light blue band stretching from the nose over the eye to the occiput. Each day, while we resided here, cries were raised by the villagers that the Wahŭmba were coming, and, then all the cattle out in the plains, both far and near, were driven into the village for protection.

At last, on the 26th, as the mules were brought in, I paid a hongo or tax of four barsati and four yards of chintz to the chief, and departed, but not until one of my porters, a Mhéhé, obtained a fat dog for his dinner; he had set his heart on it, and would not move until he had killed it, and tied it on to his load for the evening's repast. Passing through the next villages—a collection called Kifŭkŭro—we had to pay another small tax of two barsati and four yards of chintz to the chief. There we breakfasted, and pushed on, carrying water to a bivouac in the jungles, as the famine precluded our taking the march more easily.

Pushing on again, we cleared out of the woods, and arrived at the eastern border of the largest clearance of Ugogo, Kanyenyé. Here we were forced to halt a day, as the mules were done up, and eight of the Wanyamŭézi porters absconded, carrying with them the best part of their loads. There

To Camp in Bush, 26th.

To E. Kanyenyé, 27th.

was also another inducement for stopping here; for, after stacking the loads, as we usually did on arriving in camp, against a large gouty-limbed tree, a hungry Mgogo, on eying our guns, offered his services to show us some bicornis rhinoceros, which, he said, paid nightly visits to certain bitter pools that lay in the nullah bottoms not far off. This exciting intelligence made me inquire if it was not possible to find them at once; but, being as-

Our Camp in Ugogo.

sured that they lived very far off, and that the best chance was the night, I gave way, and settled on starting at ten, to arrive at the ground before the full moon should rise.

I set forth with the guide and two of the sheikh's boys, each carrying a single rifle, and ensconced myself in the nullah, to hide until our expected visitors should arrive, and there remained until midnight. When the hitherto noisy villagers turned into bed, the silvery moon shed her light on the desolate scene, and the Mgogo guide, taking fright, bolted. He had not, however, gone long, when, looming above us, coming over the horizon line, was the very animal we wanted.

In a fidgety manner, the beast then descended, as if he expected some danger in store—and he was not wrong; for, attaching a bit of white paper to the fly-sight of my Blissett, I approached him, crawling under cover of the banks until within eighty yards of him, when, finding that the moon shone full on his flank, I raised myself upright and planted a bullet behind his left shoulder. Thus died my first rhinoceros.

To make the most of the night, as I wanted meat for my men

to cook, as well as a stock to carry with them, or barter with the villagers for grain, I now retired to my old position, and waited again.

After two hours had elapsed, two more rhinoceros approached me in the same stealthy, fidgety way as the first one. They came even closer than the first, but, the moon having passed beyond their meridian, I could not obtain so clear a mark. Still they were big marks, and I determined on doing my best before they had time to wind us; so, stepping out, with the sheikh's boys behind me carrying the second rifle to meet all emergencies, I planted a ball in the larger one, and brought him round with a roar and whooh-whooh, exactly to the best position I could wish for receiving a second shot; but, alas! on turning sharply round for the spare rifle, I had the mortification to see that both the black boys had made off, and were scrambling like monkeys up a tree. At the same time, the rhinoceros, fortunately for me, on second consideration turned to the right-about, and shuffled away, leaving, as is usually the case when conical bullets are used, no traces of blood.

Thus ended the night's work. We now went home by dawn to apprise all the porters that we had flesh in store for them, when the two boys who had so shamelessly deserted me, instead of hiding their heads, described all the night's scenes with such capital mimicry as set the whole camp in a roar. We had all now to hurry back to the carcass before the Wagogo could find it; but, though this precaution was quickly taken, still, before the tough skin of the beast could be cut through, the Wagogo began assembling like vultures, and fighting with my men. A more savage, filthy, disgusting, but, at the same time, grotesque scene than that which followed can not be conceived. All fell to work, armed with swords, spears, knives, and hatchets, cutting and slashing, thumping and bawling, fighting and tearing, tumbling and wrestling up to their knees in filth and blood in the middle of the carcass. When a tempting morsel fell to the possession of any one, a stronger neighbor would seize and bear off the prize in triumph. All right was now a matter of pure might, and lucky it was that it did not end in a fight between our men and the villagers. These might be afterward seen, one by one, covered with blood, scampering home each with his spoil—a piece of tripe, or liver, or lights, or whatever else it might have been his fortune to get off with.

We were still in great want of men; but, rather than stop a

To Magomba's
Palace, 29th.
day, as all delays only lead to more difficulties, I pushed on to Magomba's palace with the assistance of some Wagogo carrying our baggage, each taking one cloth as his hire. The chief wazir at once came out to meet me on the way, and in an apparently affable manner, as an old friend, begged that I would live in the palace—a bait which I did not take, as I knew my friend by experience a little too well. He then, in the politest possible manner, told me that a great dearth of food was oppressing the land — so much so, that pretty cloths only would purchase grain. I now wished to settle my hongo, but the great chief could not hear of such indecent haste.

The next day, too, the chief was too drunk to listen to any one,
Halt, 30th, 1st,
and 2d.
and I must have patience. I took out this time in the jungles very profitably, killing a fine buck and doe antelope, of a species unknown. These animals are much about the same size and shape as the common Indian antelope, and, like them, roam about in large herds. The only marked difference between the two is in the shape of their horns, as may be seen by the opposite engraving; and in their color, in which, in both sexes, the Ugogo antelopes resemble the picticandata gazelle of Tibet, except that the former have dark markings on the face.

At last, after thousands of difficulties much like those I encountered in Uzaramo, the honga was settled by a pay-
To Camp in
Bush, 3d.
ment of one kisŭtŭ, one dubŭani, four yards bendéra, four yards kiniki, and three yards merikani. The wazir then thought he would do some business on his own account, and commenced work by presenting me with a pot of ghee and flour, saying at the same time "empty words did not show true love," and hoping that I would prove mine by making some slight return. To get rid of the animal, I gave him the full value of his present in cloth, which he no sooner pocketed than he had the audacity to accuse Grant of sacrilege for having shot a lizard on a holy stone, and demanded four cloths to pay atonement for this offense against the "Church." As yet, he said, the chief was not aware of the damage done, and it was well he was not; for he would himself, if I only paid him the four cloths, settle matters quietly, otherwise there would be no knowing what demands might be made on my cloth. It was necessary to get up hot temper, else there was no knowing how far he would go; so I returned him his presents, and told the sheikh, instead of giving four, to fling six cloths in his face, and tell him that the holy-stone story was

New Antelope, Ugogo.

merely a humbug, and I would take care no more white men ever
came to see him again.

Some Wanyamŭézi porters, who had been left sick here by former caravans, now wished to take service with me as far as Kazé;
but the Wagogo, hearing of their desire, frightened them off it.
A réport also at this time was brought to us that a caravan had
just arrived at our last ground, having come up from Whindi
direct by the line of the Wami River, in its upper course called
Mŭkondokŭa, without crossing a single hill all the way; I therefore sent three men to see if they had any porters to spare, as it
was said they had; but the three men, although they left their
bows and arrows behind, never came back.

Another mule died to-day. This was perplexing indeed, but
to stop longer was useless; so we pushed forward as best we
could to a pond at the western end of the district, where we found
a party of Makŭa sportsmen who had just killed an elephant.

They had lived in Ugogo one year and a half, and had killed in all seventeen elephants, half the tusks of which, as well as some portion of the flesh, they gave to Magomba for the privilege of residing there. There were many antelopes there, some of which both Grant and I shot for the good of the pot, and he also killed a crocuta hyena. From the pond we went on to the middle of a large jungle, and bivouacked for the night in a shower of rain, the second of the season.

During a fierce down-pour of rain, the porters all quivering and quaking with cold, we at length emerged from the jungle, and entered the prettiest spot in Ugogo—the populous district of Usekhé—where little hills and huge columns of granite crop out. Here we halted.

To Usekhé, 4'h.

Next day came the hongo business, which was settled by paying one dubŭani, one kitambi, one msŭtŭ, four yards merikani, and two yards kiniki; but, while we were doing it, eight porters ran away, and four fresh ones were engaged (Wanyamŭézi) who had run away from Kanyenyé.

Halt, 5th.

With one more march from this we reached the last district in Ugogo, Khoko. Here the whole of the inhabitants turned out to oppose us, imagining we had come there to revenge the Arab Mohinna, because the Wagogo attacked him a year ago, plundered his camp, and drove him back to Kazé, for having shot their old chief "Short-legs." They, however, no sooner found out who we were than they allowed us to pass on and encamp in the outskirts of the Mgŭnda Mkhali wilderness. To this position in the bush I strongly objected, on the plea that guns could be best used against arrows in the open; but none would go out in the field, maintaining that the Wagogo would fear to attack us so far from their villages as we now were, lest we might cut them off in their retreat.

To Khoko, 6th.

Hori Hori was now chief in Short-legs's stead, and affected to be much pleased that we were English, and not Arabs. He told us we might, he thought, be able to recruit all the men that we were in want of, as many Wanyamŭézi who had been left there sick wished to go to their homes; and I would only, in addition to their wages, have to pay their "hotel bills" to the Wagogo. This, of course, I was ready to do, though I knew the Wanyamŭézi had paid for themselves, as is usual, by their work in the fields of their hosts. Still, as I should be depriving these of hands, I could scarcely expect to get off for less than the value of a slave for each, and told Sheikh Said to look out for some men at once, while at the same time he laid in provisions of grain to last us eight days in the wilderness, and settle the hongo.

For this triple business I allowed three days, during which time, always eager to shoot something, either for science or the pot, I killed a bicornis rhinoceros, at a distance of five paces only, with my small 40-gauge Lancaster, as the beast stood quietly feeding in the bush; and I also shot a bitch fox of the genus *Otocyon Lalandii*, whose ill-omened cry often alarms the natives by forewarning them of danger. This was rather tame sport; but next day I had better fun.

Halt, 7th.

Starting in the early morning, accompanied by two of Sheikh Said's boys, Sŭliman and Faraj, each carrying a rifle, while I carried a shot-gun, we followed a footpath to the westward in the wilderness of Mgŭnda Mkhali. There, after walking a short while in the bush, as I heard the grunt of a buffalo close on my left, I took "Blissett" in hand, and walked to where I soon espied a large herd quietly feeding. They were quite unconscious of my approach, so I took a shot at a cow, and wounded her; then, after reloading, put a ball in a bull, and staggered him also. This caused great confusion among them; but, as none of the animals knew where the shots came from, they simply shifted about in a fidgety manner, allowing me to kill the first cow, and even fire a fourth shot, which sickened the great bull, and induced him to walk off, leaving the herd to their fate, who, considerably puzzled, began moving off also.

Halt, 8th.

I now called up the boys, and determined on following the herd down before either skinning the dead cow or following the bull, who I knew could not go far. Their footprints being well defined in the moist sandy soil, we soon found the herd again; but, as they now knew they were pursued, they kept moving on in short runs at a time, when, occasionally gaining glimpses of their large dark bodies as they forced through the bush, I repeated my shots and struck a good number, some more and some less severely. This was very provoking; for all of them, being stern shots, were not likely to kill, and the jungle was so thick I could not get a front view of them. Presently, however, one with her hind leg broken pulled up on a white-ant hill, and, tossing her horns, came down with a charge the instant I showed myself close to her. One crack of the rifle rolled her over, and gave me free scope to improve the bag, which was very soon done; for on following the spoors, the traces of blood led us up to another one as lame as the last. He then got a second bullet in the flank, and, after hobbling a little, evaded our sight and threw himself into a bush, where we no sooner arrived than he plunged head-long at us from his ambush, just, and only just, giving me time to present my small 40-gauge Lancaster.

It was a most ridiculous scene. Sŭliman by my side, with the instinct of a monkey, made a violent spring and swung himself by a bough immediately over the beast, while Faraj bolted away and left me single-gunned to polish him off. There was only one course to pursue, for in one instant more he would have been into me; so, quick as thought, I fired the gun, and, as luck would have it, my bullet, after passing through the edge of one of his horns, stuck in the spine of his neck, and rolled him over at my feet as dead as a rabbit. Now, having cut the beast's throat to make him "hilal," according to Mussulman usage, and thinking we had done enough if I could only return to the first wounded bull and settle him too, we commenced retracing our steps, and by accident came on Grant. He was passing by from another quarter, and became amused by the glowing description of my boys, who never omitted to narrate their own cowardice as an excellent tale. He begged us to go on in our course, while he would go back and send us some porters to carry home the game.

Now, tracking back again to the first point of attack, we fol-lowed the blood of the first bull, till at length I found him stand-ing like a stuck pig in some bushes, looking as if he would like to be put out of his miseries. Taking compassion, I leveled my Blissett; but, as bad luck would have it, a bough intercepted the flight of the bullet, and it went "pinging" into the air, while the big bull went off at a gallop. To follow on was no difficulty, the spoor was so good; and in ten minutes more, as I opened on a small clearance, Blissett in hand, the great beast, from the thicket on the opposite side, charged down like a mad bull, full of feroc-ity—as ugly an antagonist as ever I saw, for the front of his head was all shielded with horn. A small mound fortunately stood between us, and as he rounded it, I jumped to one side and let fly at his flank, but without the effect of stopping him; for, as quick as thought, the huge monster was at my feet, battling with the impalpable smoke of my gun, which fortunately hung so thick on the ground at the height of his head that he could not see me, though I was so close that I might, had I been possessed of a

THREE BUFFALO CHARGES IN ONE DAY. MGUNDA MKHALI.

hatchet, have chopped off his head. This was a predicament which looked very ugly, for my boys had both bolted, taking with them my guns; but suddenly the beast, evidently regarding the smoke as a phantom which could not be mastered, turned round in a bustle, to my intense relief, and galloped off at full speed, as if scared by some terrible apparition.

Oh what would I not then have given for a gun, the chance was such a good one! Still, angry though I was, I could not help laughing as the dastardly boys came into the clearance full of their mimicry, and joked over the scene they had witnessed in security, while my life was in jeopardy because they were too frightened to give me my gun. But now came the worst part of the day; for, though rain was falling, I had not the heart to relinquish my game. Tracking on through the bush, I thought every minute I should come up with the brute; but his wounds ceased to bleed, and in the confusion of the numerous tracks which scored all the forest we lost our own.

Much disappointed at this, I now proposed to make for the track we came by in the morning, and follow it down into camp; but this luxury was not destined to be our lot that night, for the rain had obliterated all our footprints of the morning, and we passed the track, mistaking it for the run of wild beasts. It struck me we had done so; but, say what I would, the boys thought they knew better; and the consequence was, that, after wandering for hours no one knew where—for there was no sun to guide us—I pulled up, and swore I would wait for the stars, else it might be our fate to be lost in the wilderness, which I did not much relish. We were all at this time "hungry as hunters," and beginning to feel very miserable from being wet through. What little ammunition I had left I fired off as signals, or made tinder of to get up a fire, but the wood would not burn. In this hapless condition the black boys began murmuring, wishing to go on, pretending, though both held opposite views, that each knew the way, for they thought nothing could be worse than their present state of discomfort.

Night with its gloom was then drawing on, heightened by thunder and lightning, which set in all around us. At times we thought we heard musketry in camp, knowing that Grant would be sure to fire signals for us; and doubtless we did so, but its sound and the thunder so much resembled one another that we distrusted our ears. At any rate, the boys mistook the west for the east; and as I thought they had done so, I stood firm to one spot, and finally lay down with them to sleep upon the cold wet ground, where we slept pretty well, being only disturbed occasionally by some animals sniffing at our feet. As the clouds broke toward morning, my obstinate boys still swore that west was east, and would hardly follow me when tracking down Venus; next up rose the moon, and then followed the sun, when, as good luck would have it, we struck on the track, and walked straight into camp.

Here every one was in a great state of excitement: Grant had been making the men fire volleys. The little sheikh was warmly congratulatory as he spoke of the numbers who had strayed away and had been lost in that wilderness; while Bombay admitted he thought we should turn up again if I did not listen to the advice of the boys, which was his only fear. Nothing as yet, I now found, had been done to further our march. The hongo, the sheikh said, had to precede every thing; yet that had not been settled, because the chief deferred it the day of our arrival, on the plea that it was the anniversary of Short-legs's death; and he also said that till then all the Wagogo had been in mourning by ceasing to wear all their brass bracelets and other ornaments, and they now wished to solemnize the occasion by feasting and renewing their finery. This being granted, the next day another pretext for delay was found by the Wahŭmba having made a raid on their cattle, which necessitated the chief and all his men turning out to drive them away; and to-day nothing could be attended to, as a party of fugitive Wanyamŭézi had arrived and put them all in a fright. These Wanyamŭézi, it then transpired, were soldiers of Manŭa Séra, "the Tippler," who was at war with the Arabs. He had been defeated at Ngŭrŭ, a district in Unyamŭézi, by the Arabs, and had sent these men to cut off the caravan route, as the best way of retaliation that lay in his power.

Halt, 9th.

At last, the tax having been settled by the payment of one dubŭani, two barsati, one sahari, six yards merikani, and three yards kiniki (not, however, until I had our tents struck, and threatened to march away if the chief would not take it), I proposed going on with the journey, for our provisions were stored. But when the loads were being lifted, I found ten more men were missing; and as nothing now could be done but throw ten loads away, which seemed too great a sacrifice to be

Change ground, 10th.

made in a hurry, I simply changed ground to show we were
ready to march, and sent my men about, either to try to induce
the fugitive Wanyamŭézi to take service with me, or else to buy
donkeys, as the chief said he had some to sell.

We had already been here too long. A report was now spread
that a lion had killed one of the chief's cows; and
the Wagogo, suspecting that our being here was the
cause of this ill luck, threatened to attack us. This no sooner
got noised over the camp than all my Wanyamŭézi porters, who
had friends in Ugogo, left to live with them, and would not come
back again even when the "storm had blown over," because they
did not like the incessant rains that half deluged the camp. The
chief, too, said he would not sell us his donkeys, lest we should
give them back to Mohinna, from whom they were taken during
his fight here. Intrigues of all sorts I could see were brewing,
possibly at the instigation of the fugitive Wanyamŭézi, who suspected we were bound to side with the Arabs—possibly from
some other cause, I could not tell what; so, to clear out of this
pandemonium as soon as possible, I issued cloths to buy double
rations, intending to cross the wilderness by successive relays in
double the ordinary number of days. I determined at the same
time to send forward two freed men to Kazé to ask Mŭsa and
the Arabs to send me out some provisions and men to meet us
half way.

Matters grew worse and worse. The sultan, now finding me
unable to move, sent a message to say if I would not
give him some better cloths to make his hongo more
respectable, he would attack my camp; and advised all the Wanyamŭézi who regarded their lives not to go near me if I resisted.
This was by no means pleasant; for the porters showed their uneasiness by extracting their own cloths from my bundles, under
the pretext that they wished to make some purchases of their
own. I ought, perhaps, to have stopped this; but I thought the
best plan was to show total indifference; so, at the same time that
they were allowed to take their cloths, I refused to comply with
the chief's request, and begged them to have no fear as long as
they saw I could hold my own ground with my guns.

The Wanyamŭézi, however, were panic-stricken, and half of
them bolted, with the kirangozi at their head, carrying off all the
double-ration cloths as well as their own. At this time, the sultan, having changed tactics, as he saw us all ready to stand on

Halt, 11th.

Halt, 12th.

the defensive, sent back his hongo; but, instead of using threats, said he would oblige us with donkeys or any thing else if we would only give him a few more pretty cloths. With this cring- ing, perfidious appeal I refused to comply, until the sheikh, still more cringing, implored me to give way, else not a single man would remain with me. I then told him to settle with the chief himself, and give me the account, which amounted to three bar- sati, two sahari, and three yards merikani; but the donkeys were never alluded to.

With half my men gone, I still ordered the march, though strongly opposed to the advice of one of old Mamba's
To Camp, 13th.
men, who was then passing by on his way to the coast, in command of his master's rear detachment. He thought it impossible for us to pull through the wilderness, with its jungle grasses and roots, depending for food only on Grant's gun and my own; still we made half way to the Mdabŭrŭ nullah, taking some of Mamba's out to camp with us, as he promised to take letters and specimens down to the coast for us, provided I paid him some cloths as ready money down, and promised some more to be paid at Zanzibar. These letters eventually reached home, but not the specimens.

The rains were so heavy that the whole country was now flooded, but we pushed on to the nullah by relays,
To Camp, 14th.
and pitched on its left bank. In the confusion of the march, however, we lost many more porters, who at the same time relieved us of their loads, by slipping off stealthily into the bush.

The fifteenth was a forced halt, as the stream was so deep and so violent we could not cross it. To make the best
Halt five days.
of this very unfortunate interruption, I now sent on two men to Kazé, with letters to Mŭsa and Sheikh Snay, both old friends on the former expedition, begging them to send me sixty men, each carrying thirty rations of grain, and some country tobacco. The tobacco was to gratify my men, who said of all things they most wanted to cheer them was something to smoke. At the same time I sent back some other men to Khoko, with cloth to buy grain for present consumption, as some of my por- ters were already reduced to living on wild herbs and white ants. I then set all the remaining men, under the directions of Bombay and Baraka, to fell a tall tree with hatchets, on the banks of the nullah, with a view to bridging it; but the tree dropped to the

wrong side, and thwarted the plan. The rain ceased on the 17th,
just as we put the rain-gauge out, which was at once interpreted
to be our Uganga, or religious charm, and therefore the cause of
its ceasing. It was the first fine day for a fortnight, so we were
only too glad to put all our things out to dry, and rejoiced to
think of the stream's subsiding. My men who went back to
Khoko for grain having returned with next to nothing—though,
of course, they had spent all the cloths—I sent back another
batch with pretty cloths, as it was confidently stated that grain
was so scarce there, nothing but the best fabrics would buy it.
This also proved a dead failure; but, although animals were very
scarce, Grant relieved our anxiety by shooting a zebra and an
antelope.

After five halts we forded the stream, middle deep, and pushed
Eight successive forward again, doing short stages of four or five miles
marches in the
Wilderness. a day, in the greatest possible confusion; for, while
Grant and I were compelled to go out shooting all day for the
pot, the sheikh and Bombay went on with the first half of the
property, and then, keeping guard over it, sent the men back
again to Baraka, who kept rear-guard, to have the rest brought
on. Order there was none; the men hated this "double work;"
all the Wanyamŭézi but three deserted, with the connivance of
the coast-men, carrying off their loads with them, under a mutual
understanding, as I found out afterward, that the coast-men were
to go shares in the plunder as soon as we reached Unyamŭézi.
The next great obstacle in this tug-and-pull wilderness-march
presented itself on the 24th, when, after the first half of the property had crossed the Mabungŭrŭ nullah, it rose in flood and cut
off the rear half. It soon, however, subsided; and the next day
we reached "the Springs," where we killed a pig and two rhinoceros. Not content, however, with this fare—notwithstanding the
whole camp had been living liberally on zebra's and antelope's
flesh every day previously—some of my coast-men bolted on to
the little settlement of Jiwa la Mkoa, contrary to orders, to purchase some grain, and in doing so increased our transport difficulties.

Pulling on in the same way again—when not actually engaged
in shooting, scolding and storming at the men, to keep them up
to the mark, and prevent them from shirking their work, which
they were forever trying to do—we arrived on the 28th at the
"Boss," a huge granite block, from the top of which the green

foliage of the forest-trees looked like an interminable cloud, soft and waving, fit for fairies to dwell upon. Here the patience of my men fairly gave way, for the village of Jiwa la Mkoa was only one long march distance from us, and they, in consequence, smelt food on in advance much sweeter than the wild game and wild grasses they had been living on; and many more of them could not resist deserting us, though they might, had we all pulled together, have gone more comfortably in, as soon as the rear property arrived next day with Baraka.

All the men who deserted on the 25th, save Johur and Mŭt-wana, now came into camp, and told us they had heard from travelers that those men who had been sent on for reliefs to Kazé were bringing us a large detachment of slaves to help us on. My men had brought no food either for us or their friends, as the cloths they took with them, "which were their own," were scarcely sufficient to purchase a meal—famines being as bad where they had been as in Ugogo. To try and get all the men together again, I now sent off a party loaded with cloths to see what they could get for us; but they returned on the 30th grinning and joking, with nothing but a small fragment of goat-flesh, telling lies by the dozens. Johur then came into camp, unconscious that Baraka by my orders had, during his absence, been inspecting his kit, where he found concealed seventy-three yards of cloth, which could only have been my property, as Johur had brought no akaba or reserve fund from the coast.

Halt three days.

The theft having been proved to the satisfaction of every one, I ordered Baraka to strip him of every thing and give him three dozen lashes; but after twenty-one had been given, the rest were remitted on his promising to turn queen's evidence, when it transpired that Mŭtwana had done as much as himself. Johur, it turned out, was a murderer, having obtained his freedom by killing his master. He was otherwise a notoriously bad character; so, wishing to make an example, as I knew all my men were robbing me daily, though I could not detect them, I had him turned out of camp. Baraka was a splendid detective, and could do every thing well when he wished it, so I sent him off now with cloths to see what he could do at Jiwa la Mkoa, and next day he returned triumphantly driving in cows and goats. Three Wanyamŭézi, also, who heard we were given to shooting wild animals continually, came with him to offer their services as porters.

As nearly all the men had now returned, Grant and I spent
New Year's Day with the first detachment at Jiwa la
Mkoa, or Round Rock—a single tembé village occupied by a few Wakimbŭ settlers, who, by their presence and domestic habits, made us feel as though we were well out of the
wood. So indeed we found it; for, although this wilderness was
formerly an entire forest of trees and wild animals, numerous Wakimbŭ, who formerly occupied the banks of the Rŭaha to the

To Jiwa la Mkoa, 1st.

The Tembé, or Mud Village, at Jiwa la Mkoa.

southward, had been driven to migrate here, wherever they could
find springs of water, by the boisterous naked pastorals the Warori.

At night three slaves belonging to Sheikh Salem bin Saif stole
into our camp, and said they had been sent by their master to
seek for porters at Kazé, as all the Wanyamŭézi porters of four
large caravans had deserted in Ugogo, and they could not move.
I was rather pleased by this news, and thought it served the merchants right, knowing, as I well did, that the Wanyamŭézi, being
naturally honest, had they not been defrauded by foreigners on
the down march to the coast, would have been honest still. Some
provisions were now obtained by sending men out to distant villages; but we still supplied the camp with our guns, killing rhinoceros, wild boar, antelope, and zebras. The last of our property did not come up till the 5th, when another thief, being caught,
got fifty lashes, under the superintendence of Baraka, to show
that punishment was only inflicted to prevent farther crime.

The next day my men came from Kazé with letters from Sheikh

Snay and Mŭsa. They had been detained there some

days after arrival, as those merchants' slaves had gone to Utambara to settle some quarrel there; but as soon as they returned, Mŭsa ordered them to go and assist us, giving them beads to find rations for themselves on the way, as the whole country about Kazé had been half starved by famines, though he did send a little rice and tobacco for me. The whole party left Kazé together; but on arrival at Tŭra the slaves said they had not enough beads and would return for some more, when they would follow my men. This bit of news was the worst that could have befallen us; my men were broken-hearted enough before, and this drove the last spark of spirit out of them. To make the best of a bad job, I now sent Bombay with two other men off to Mŭsa to see what he could do, and ordered my other men to hire Wakimbŭ from village to village. On the 7th, a nervous excitement was produced in the camp by some of my men running in and calling all to arm, as the fugitive chief Manŭa Séra was coming, with thirty armed followers carrying muskets. Such was the case; and by the time my men were all under arms, with their sword-bayonets fixed, drawn up by my tent, the veritable "Tippler" arrived; but, not liking the look of such a formidable array as my men presented, he passed on a short way, and then sent back a deputation to make known his desire of calling on me, which was no sooner complied with than he came in person, attended by a body-guard. On my requesting him to draw near and sit, his wooden stool was placed for him. He began the conversation by telling me he had heard of my distress from want of porters, and then offered to assist me with some, provided I would take him to Kazé, and mediate between him and the Arabs; for, through their unjustifiable interference in his government affairs a war had ensued, which terminated with the Arabs driving him from his possessions a vagabond. Manŭa Séra, I must say, was as fine a young man as ever I looked upon. He was very handsome, and looked, as I now saw him, the very picture of a captain of the banditti of the romances. I begged him to tell me his tale, and, in compliance, he gave me the following narrative:

"Shortly after you left Kazé for England, my old father, the late chief Fŭndi Kira, died, and by his desire I became lawful chief; for, though the son of a slave girl, and not of Fŭndi Kira's wife, such is the law of inheritance—a constitutional policy established to prevent any chance of intrigues between the sons born in legitimate wedlock. Well, after assuming the title of chief, I gave presents of ivory to all the Arabs with a liberal hand, but most so to Mŭsa, which caused great jealousy among the other merchants. Then, after this, I established a property tax on all merchandise that entered my country. Fŭndi Kira had never done so, but I did not think that any reason why I should not, especially as the Arabs were the only people who lived in my country exempt from taxation. This measure, however, exasperated the Arabs, and induced them to send me hostile messages, to the effect that, if I ever meddled with them, they would dethrone me, and place Mkisiwa, another illegitimate son, on the throne in my stead. This," Manŭa Séra continued, "I could not stand; the merchants were living on sufferance only in my country. I told them so, and defied them to interfere with my orders, for I was not a 'woman,' to be treated with contempt; and this got up a quarrel. Mkisiwa, seizing at the opportunity of the prize held out to him by the Arabs as his supporters, then commenced a system of bribery. Words led to blows; we had a long and tough fight; I killed many of their number, and they killed mine. Eventually they drove me from my palace, and placed Mkisiwa there as chief in my stead. My faithful followers, however, never deserted me; so I went to Bŭbŭga, and put up with old Maŭla there. The Arabs followed — drove me to Ngŭrŭ, and tried to kill Maŭla for having fostered me. He, however, escaped them; but they destroyed his country, and then followed me down to Ngŭrŭ. There we fought for many months, until all provisions were exhausted, when I defied them to catch me, and forced my way through their ranks. It is needless to say I have been a wanderer since; and though I wish to make friends, they will not allow it, but do all they can to hunt me to death. Ncw, as you were a friend of my father, I do hope you will patch up this war for me, which you must think is unjust."

I told Manŭa Séra I felt very much for him, and I would do my best if he would follow me to Kazé; but I knew that nothing could ever be done unless he returned to the free-trade principles of his father. He then said he had never taken a single tax from the Arabs, and would gladly relinquish his intention to do so. The whole affair was commenced in too great a hurry; but, whatever happened, he would gladly forgive all if I would use my influence to reinstate him, for by no other means could he ever get his crown back again. I then assured him that I would do what

I could to restore the ruined trade of his country, observing that, as all the ivory that went out of his country came to ours, and all imports were productions of our country also, this war injured us as well as himself. Manŭa Séra seemed highly delighted, and said he had a little business to transact in Ugogo at present, but he would overtake me in a few days. He then sent me one of my runaway porters, whom he had caught in the woods making off with a load of my beads. We then separated; and Baraka, by my orders, gave the thief fifty lashes for his double offense of theft and desertion.

On the 9th, having bought two donkeys and engaged several men, we left Jiwa la Mkoa with half our traps, and marched to Garaéswi, where, to my surprise, there were as many as twenty tembés—a recently-formed settlement of Wakimbŭ. Here we halted a day for the rear convoy, and then went on again by detachments to Zimbo, where, to our intense delight, Bombay returned to us on the 13th, triumphantly firing guns, with seventy slaves accompanying him, and with letters from Snay and Mŭsa, in which they said they hoped, if I met with Manŭa Séra, that I would either put a bullet through his head, or else bring him in a prisoner, that they might do for him, for the scoundrel had destroyed all their trade by cutting off caravans. Their fights with him commenced by his levying taxes in opposition to their treaties with his father, Fŭndi Kira, and then preventing his subjects selling them grain.

To Garaéswi, 9th.
Halt, 10th.
To Zimbo, 11th.
Halt, 12th and 13th.

Once more the whole caravan moved on; but as I had to pay each of the seventy slaves sixteen yards of cloth, by order of their masters, in the simple matter of expenditure it would have been better had I thrown ten loads away at Ugogo, where my difficulties first commenced. On arrival at Mgongo Thembo — the Elephant's Back — called so in consequence of a large granitic rock, which resembles the back of that animal, protruding through the ground—we found a clearance in the forest, of two miles in extent, under cultivation. Here the first man to meet me was the fugitive chief of Rŭbŭga, Maŭla. This poor old man—one of the honestest chiefs in the country— had been to the former expedition a host and good friend. He now gave me a cow as a present, and said he would give me ten more if I would assist him in making friends with the Arabs, who had driven him out of his country, and had destroyed all his belongings, even putting a slave to reign in his stead, though he

To Mgongo Thembo, 14th.

had committed no fault or intentional injury toward them. It was true Manŭa Séra, their enemy, had taken refuge in his palace, but that was not his fault; for, anticipating the difficulties that would arise, he did his best to keep Manŭa Séra out of it; but Manŭa Séra, being too strong for him, forced his way in. I need not say I tried to console this unfortunate victim of circumstances as best I could, inviting him to go with me to Kazé, and promising to protect him with my life if he feared the Arabs; but the old man, being too feeble to travel himself, said he would send his son with me.

Next day we pushed on a double march through the forest, and reached a nullah. As it crosses the track in a southernly direction, this might either be the head of the Kŭlŭlŭ mongo or river, which, passing through the district of Kiwélé, drains westward into the Malagarazi River, and thence into the Tanganyika, or else the most westerly tributary to the Rŭaha River, draining eastward into the sea. The plateau, however, is apparently so flat here, that nothing but a minute survey, or rather following the water-course, could determine the matter.

To Camp, 15th.

To E. Tŭra, 16th.

Then emerging from the wilderness, we came into the open cultivated district of Tŭra, or "put down" —called so by the natives because it was, only a few years ago, the first cleared space in the wilderness, and served as a good halting-station, after the normal ten days' march in the jungles, where we had now been struggling more than a month.

The whole place, once so fertile, was now almost depopulated and in a sad state of ruin, showing plainly the savage ravages of war; for the Arabs and their slaves, when they take the field, think more of plunder and slavery than the object they started on, each man of the force looking out for himself. The incentives, too, are so great—a young woman might be caught (the greatest treasure on earth), or a boy or a girl, a cow or a goat—all of them fortunes, of themselves too irresistible to be overlooked when the future is doubtful. Here Sheikh Said broke down in health of a complaint which he formerly had suffered from, and from which I at once saw he would never recover sufficiently well to be ever effective again. It was a sad misfortune, as the men had great confidence in him, being the representative of their Zanzibar government; still it could not be helped; for, as a sick man is, after all, the greatest possible impediment to a march, it was better to be rid of him than have the trouble of dragging him; so I made up my mind, as soon as we reached Kazé, I would drop him there with the Arabs. He could not be moved on the 16th, so I marched across the plain and put up in some villages on its western side. While waiting for the sheikh's arrival, some villagers at night stole several loads of beads, and ran off with them; but my men, finding the theft out in time, hunted them down, and recovered all but one load; for the thieves had thrown their loads down as soon as they found they were hotly pursued.

To W. Tŭra, 17th.

Early this morning I called all the head men of the village together, and demanded the beads to be restored to me; for, as I was living with them, they were responsible, according to the laws of the country. They acknowledged the truth and force of my demand, and said they would each give me a cow as an earnest, until their chief, who was absent, arrived. This, of course, was objected to, as the chief, in his absence, must have deputed some one to govern for him, and I expected him to settle at once, that I might proceed with the march. Then selecting five of my head men to conduct the case, with five of their elders, it was considered my losses were equivalent to thirty head of cattle. As I remitted the penalty to fifteen head, these were made over to me, and we went on with the march, all feeling delighted with the issue but the Hottentots, who, not liking the loss of the second fifteen cows, said that in Kafirland, where the laws of the country are the same as here, the whole would have been taken, and, as it was, they thought I was depriving them of their rights to beef.

Halt, 18th.

By a double march, the sheikh riding in a hammock slung on a pole, we now made Kŭalé, or "Partridge" nullah, which, crossing the road to the northward, drains these lands to the Malagarazi River, and thence into the Tanganyika Lake. Thence, having spent the night in the jungle, we next morning pushed into the cultivated district of Rŭbŭga, and put up in some half-deserted tembés, where the ravages of war were even more disgusting to witness than at Tŭra. The chief, as I have said, was a slave, placed there by the Arabs on the condition that he would allow all traders and travelers to help themselves without payment as long as they chose to reside there. In consequence of this wicked arrangement, I found it impossible to keep my men from picking and stealing. They looked upon plunder as their fortune and right, and my interference as unjustifiable.

To Camp, 19th.
To E. Rŭbŭga, 20th.

By making another morning and evening march, we then
reached the western extremity of this cultivated
opening, where, after sleeping the night, we threaded
through another forest to the little clearance of Kigŭé,
and in one more march through forest arrived in the
large and fertile district of Unyanyembé, the centre of U-n-ya-
mŭézi—the Land of the Moon—within five miles of Kazé, which
is the name of a well in the village of Tabora, now constituted
the great central slave and ivory merchants' dépôt.   My losses
up to this date (23d) were as follows: one Hottentot dead and
five returned; one freeman sent back with the Hottentots, and
one flogged and turned off; twenty-five of Sultan Majid's gardeners deserted; ninety-eight of the original Wanyamŭézi porters
deserted; twelve mules and three donkeys dead.   Besides which,
more than half of my property had been stolen; while the traveling expenses had been unprecedented, in consequence of the
severity of the famine throughout the whole length of the march.

To W. Rŭbŭga,
21st.
To Kigŭé, 22d.
To E. Unyan-
yembé, 23d.

View in Eastern Unyanyembé.

CHAPTER V.

U - N - YA - MŬÉZI.

U-N-YA-MŬÉZI—Country of the Moon—must have been one of the largest kingdoms of Africa. It is little inferior in size to England, and of much the same shape, though now, instead of being united, it is cut up into petty states. In its northern extremities it is known by the appellation U-sŭkŭma—country north; and

Myamŭézi, or Native of Unyamŭézi.

in the southern, U-takama—country south. There are no historical traditions known to the people; neither was any thing ever written concerning their country, as far as we know, until the Hindŭs, who traded with the east coast of Africa, opened commercial dealings with its people in slaves and ivory, possibly some time prior to the birth of our Savior, when, associated with their name, Men of the Moon, sprang into existence the Mountains of the Moon. These Men of the Moon are hereditarily the greatest

traders in Africa, and are the only people who, for love of barter
and change, will leave their own country as porters and go to the
coast, and they do so with as much zest as our country-folk go to
a fair. As far back as we can trace they have done this, and they
still do it as heretofore. The whole of their country ranges from
3000 to 4000 feet above the sea-level—a high plateau, studded
with little outcropping hills of granite, between which, in the valleys, there are numerous fertilizing springs of fresh water, and
rich iron ore is found in sandstone. Generally industrious—much
more so than most other negroes—they cultivate extensively,
make cloths of cotton in their own looms, smelt iron and work it
up very expertly, build tembés to live in over a large portion of
their country, but otherwise live in grass huts, and keep flocks
and herds of considerable extent.

The Wanyamŭézi, however, are not a very well-favored people in physical appearance, and are much darker than either the
Wazaramo or the Wagogo, though many of their men are handsome and their women pretty; neither are they well dressed or
well armed, being wanting in pluck and gallantry. Their wom-
en, generally, are better dressed than the men. Cloths fastened
round under the arms are their national costume, along with a
necklace of beads, large brass or copper wire armlets, and a profusion of thin circles, called sambo, made of the giraffe's tail-hairs
bound round by the thinnest iron or copper wire; while the men
at home wear loin-cloths, but in the field, or while traveling, simply hang a goatskin over their shoulders, exposing at least three
fourths of their body in a rather indecorous manner. In all other
respects they ornament themselves like the women, only, instead
of a long coil of wire wound up the arm, they content themselves
with having massive rings of copper or brass on the wrist; and
they carry for arms a spear and bow and arrows. All extract
more or less their lower incisors, and cut a ∧ between their two
upper incisors. The whole tribe are desperate smokers, and greatly given to drink.

On the 24th, we all, as many as were left of us, marched into
the merchants' dépôt, S. lat. 5° 0' 52", and E. long.
33° 1' 34",* escorted by Mŭsa, who advanced to meet

To Kazé, 24:h.

* It may be as well to remark here, that the figures, both in latitude and longitude, representing the position of Kazé, computed by Mr. Dunkin, accord with what
appeared in "Blackwood's Magazine," computed by myself, and in the R. G. S.
Journal Map, computed by Captain George.

us, and guided us into his tembé, where he begged we would reside with him until we could find men to carry our property on
to Karagŭé. He added that he would accompany us; for he
was on the point of going there when my first installment of property arrived, but deferred his intention out of respect to myself.
He had been detained at Kazé ever since I last left it in consequence of the Arabs having provoked a war with Manŭa Séra,
to which he was adverse. For a long time also he had been a
chained prisoner; as the Arabs, jealous of the favor Manŭa Séra
had shown to him in preference to themselves, basely accused
him of supplying Manŭa Séra with gunpowder, and bound him
hand and foot "like a slave." It was delightful to see old Mŭsa's
face again, and the supremely hospitable, kind, and courteous manner in which he looked after us, constantly bringing in all kind
of small delicacies, and seeing that nothing was wanting to make
us happy. All the property I had sent on in advance he had
stored away ; or rather, I should say, as much as had reached him,
for the road expenses had eaten a great hole in it.

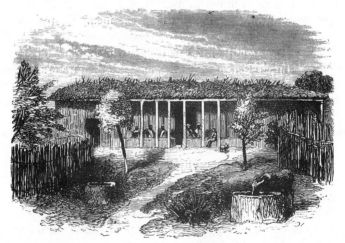

Front View of Mŭsa's Tembé at Kazé.

Once settled down into position, Sheikh Snay and the whole
conclave of Arab merchants came to call on me. They said they
had an army of four hundred slaves armed with muskets ready
to take the field at once to hunt down Manŭa Séra, who was cut-

This applies also to the position of Ujiji; at any rate, the practical differences are
so trifling that it would require a microscope to detect them on the map.

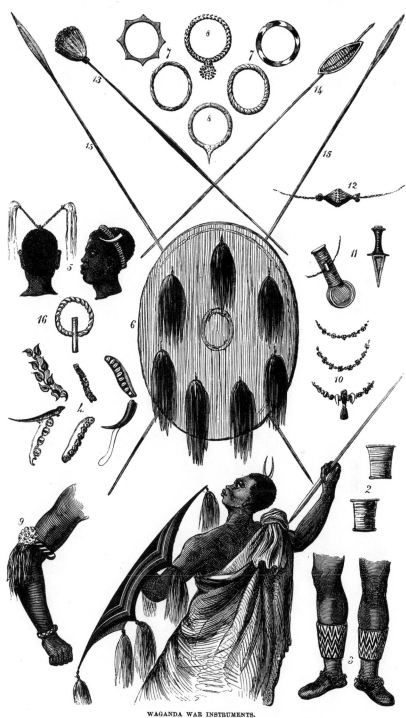

WAGANDA WAR INSTRUMENTS.

1. Warrior.	4. Men's wreaths.	9. King's amulet of beads.	12, 13, 14. Charms.
2. Ivory ornaments for legs.	5. Head ornaments.	10. Necklaces.	15. Spears.
3. King's leg ornaments.	6. Shield and spears.	11. Woman's dirk.	16. Anklet of serpent skin and bolt of wood.
	7, 8. Necklaces.		

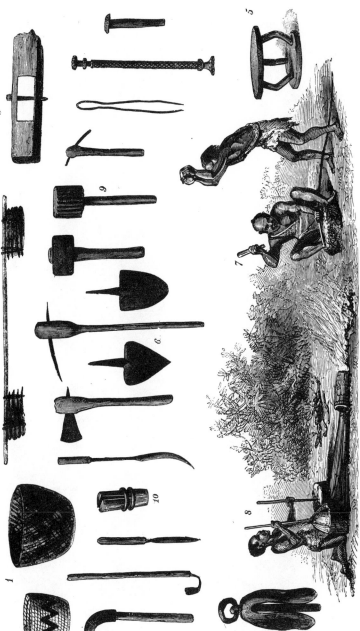

IMPLEMENTS, ETC., OF THE LAND OF THE MOON (WANYAMWÉZI).

1. Drinking-cup of hay-like grass—basket of wicker.
2. Load of hoes made of country iron.
3. Wooden stocks for criminals' legs.
4. Double-toned bell of iron.
5. Iron hoes, the *only implement* used in tilling the ground.
7. Blacksmith at his stone anvil.
8. Boy working a wooden bellows.
9. Wooden mallet for hammering bark cloths.
10. Blacksmith's hand-vice for drawing wire; the sultan's knives, gouges, hammers, hatchets, pincers, chisel, and three-legged stool.

ting their caravan road to pieces, and had just seized, by their latest reports, a whole convoy of their ammunition. I begged them strongly to listen to reason, and accept my advice as an old soldier, not to carry on their guerrilla warfare in such a headlong hurry, else they would be led a dance by Manŭa Séra, as we had been by Tantia Topee in India. I advised them to allow me to mediate between them, after telling them what a favorable interview I had had with Manŭa Séra and Maŭla, whose son was at that moment concealed in Mŭsa's tembé. My advice, however, was not wanted. Snay knew better than any one how to deal with savages, and determined on setting out as soon as his army had "eaten their beef-feast of war."

On my questioning him about the Nile, Snay still thought the N'yanza was the source of the Jub River,* as he did in our former journey, but gave way when I told him that vessels frequented the Nile, as this also coincided with his knowledge of navigators in vessels appearing on some waters to the northward of Unyoro. In a great hurry he then bade me good-by; when, as he thought it would be final, I gave him, in consideration for his former good services to the last expedition, one of the gold watches given me by the Indian government. I saw him no more, though he and all the other Arabs sent me presents of cows, goats, and rice, with a notice that they should have gone on their war-path before, only, hearing of my arrival, out of due respect to my greatness, they waited to welcome me in. Further, after doing for Manŭa Séra, they were determined to go on to Ugogo to assist Salem bin Saif and the other merchants on, during which, at the same time, they would fight all the Wagogo who persisted in taking taxes and in harassing their caravans. At the advice of Mŭsa, I sent Maŭla's son off at night to tell the old chief how sorry I was to find the Arabs so hot-headed I could not even effect an arrangement with them. It was a great pity; for Manŭa Séra was so much liked by the Wanyamŭézi, they would, had they been able, have done any thing to restore him.

Next day the non-belligerent Arabs left in charge of the station, headed by my old friends Abdŭlla and Mohinna, came to pay their respects again, recognizing in me, as they said, a "personification of their sultan," and therefore considering what they were doing only due to my rank. They

25*th* and 26*th*.

---

* The Jub is the largest river known to the Zanzibar Arabs. It debouches on the east coast north of Zanzibar, close under the equator.

regretted with myself that Snay was so hot-headed; for they themselves thought a treaty of peace would have been the best thing for them, for they were more than half ruined already, and saw no hope for the future. Then, turning to geography, I told Abdŭlla all I had written and lectured in England concerning his stories about navigators on the N'yanza, which I explained must be the Nile, and wished to know if I should alter it in any way; but he said, "Do not; you may depend it will all turn out right;" to which Mŭsa added, all the people in the north told him that when the N'yanza rose, the stream rushed with such violence it tore up islands and floated them away.

I was puzzled at this announcement, not then knowing that both the lake and the Nile, as well as all ponds, were called N'yanza; but we shall see afterward that he was right; and it was in consequence of this confusion in the treatment of distinctly different geographical features under one common name by these people that in my former journey I could not determine where the lake ended and the Nile began. Abdŭlla again—he had done so on the former journey—spoke to me of a wonderful mountain to the northward of Karagŭé, so high and steep no one could ascend it. It was, he said, seldom visible, being up in the clouds, where white matter, snow or hail, often fell. Mŭsa said this hill was in Rŭanda, a much larger country than Urŭndi; and farther, both men said, as they had said before, that the lands of Usoga and Unyoro were islands, being surrounded by water; and a salt lake, which was called N'yanza, though not the great Victoria N'yanza, lay on the other side of Unyoro, from which direction Rŭmanika, king of Karagŭé, sometimes got beads forwarded to him by Kamrasi, king of Unyoro, of a different sort from any brought from Zanzibar. Moreover, these beads were said to have been plundered from white men by the Wakidi—a stark-naked people who live up in trees—have small stools fixed on behind, always ready for sitting—wear their hair hanging down as far as the rump, all covered with cowrie-shells — suspend beads from wire attached to their ears and their lower lips—and wear strong iron collars and bracelets.

This people, I was told, are so fierce in war that no other tribe can stand against them, though they only fight with short spears. When this discourse was ended, ever perplexed about the Tanganyika being a still lake, I inquired of Mohinna and other old friends what they thought about the Marŭngŭ River: did it run into or out of the lake? and they all still adhered to its running into the lake; which, after all, in my mind, is the most conclusive argument that it does run out of the lake, making it one of a chain of lakes leading to the N'yassa, and through it by the Zambézi into the sea; for all the Arabs on the former journey said the Rŭsizi River ran out of the Tanganyika, as also the Kitangŭlé ran out of the N'yanza, and the Nile ran into it, even though Snay said he thought the Jub River drained the N'yanza. All these statements were, when literally translated into English, the reverse of what the speakers, using a peculiar Arab idiom, meant to say; for all the statements made as to the flow of rivers by the negroes—who apparently give the same meaning to "out" and "in" as we do—contradicted the Arabs in their descriptions of the direction of the flow of these rivers.

Mohinna now gave us a very graphic description of his fight with Short-legs, the late chief of Khoko. About a year ago, as he was making his way down to the coast with his ivory merchandise, on arrival at Khoko, and before his camp was fortified with a ring-fence of thorns, some of his men went to drink at a well, where they no sooner arrived than the natives began to beat them with sticks, claiming the well as their property. This commenced a row, which brought out a large body of men, who demanded a bullock at the point of their spears. Mohinna hearing this, also came to the well, and said he would not listen to their demand, but would drink as he wished, for the water was the gift of God. Words then changed to blows. All Mohinna's pagazis bolted, and his merchandise fell into the hands of the Wagogo. Had his camp been fortified, he thinks he would have been too much for his enemies; but, as it was, he retaliated by shooting Short-legs in the head, and at once bolted back to Kazé with a few slaves as followers, and his three wives.

The change that had taken place in Unyanyembé since I last left it was quite surprising. Instead of the Arabs appearing merchants, as they did formerly, they looked more like great farmers, with huge stalls of cattle attached to their houses, while the native villages were all in ruins—so much so that, to obtain corn for my men, I had to send out into the district several days' journey off, and even then had to pay the most severe famine prices for what I got. The Wanyamŭézi, I was assured, were dying of starvation in all directions; for, in addition to the war, the last rainy season had been so light, all their crops had failed.

27th and *28th.* I now gave all my men presents for the severe
trials they had experienced in the wilderness, forgetting, as I told
them, the merciless manner in which they had plundered me; but
as I gave a trifle more, in proportion, to the three sole remaining
pagazis, because they had now finished their work, my men were
all discontented, and wished to throw back their presents, saying
I did not love them, although they were " perminents," as much
as the " temperaries." They, however, gave in, after some hours
of futile arguments, on my making them understand, through
Baraka, that what they saw me give to the pagazis would, if they
reflected, only tend to prove to them that I was not a bad master
who forgot his obligations when he could get no more out of his
servants.

I then went into a long inquiry with Mŭsa about our journey
northward to Karagŭé; and as he said there were no men to be
found in or near Unyanyembé, for they were either all killed or
engaged in the war, it was settled he should send some of his head
men on to Rungŭa, where he had formerly resided, trading for
some years, and was a great favorite with the chief of the place,
by name Kiringŭana. He also settled that I might take out of
his establishment of slaves as many men as I could induce to go
with me, for he thought them more trouble than profit, hired porters being more safe; moreover, he said the plan would be of
great advantage to him, as I offered to pay both man and master
each the same monthly stipend as I gave my present men. This
was paying double, and all the heavier a burden, as the number
I should require to complete my establishment to one hundred
armed men would be sixty. He, however, very generously advised me not to take them, as they would give so much trouble,
but finally gave way when I told him I felt I could not advance
beyond Karagŭé unless I was quite independent of the natives
there—a view in which he concurred.

29th and *30th.* Jafŭ, another Indian merchant here, and copart-
ner of Mŭsa, came in from a ten days' search after grain, and described the whole country to be in the most dreadful state of famine. Wanyamŭézi were lying about dead from starvation in all
directions, and he did not think we should ever get through Usŭi,
as Sŭwarora, the chief, was so extortionate he would "tear us to
pieces;" but advised our waiting until the war was settled, when
all the Arabs would combine and go with us. Mŭsa even showed fear, but arranged, at my suggestion, that he should send some

men to Rŭmanika, informing him of our intention to visit him, and begging, at the same time, he would use his influence in preventing our being detained in Usŭi.

I may here explain that the country Uzinza was once a large kingdom, governed by a king named Rŭma, of Wahŭma blood. At his death, which took place in Dagara's time (the present Rŭmanika's father), the kingdom was contested by his two sons, Rohinda and Sŭwarora, but, at the intercession of Dagara, was divided—Rohinda taking the eastern, called Ukhanga, and Sŭwarora the western half of the country, called Usŭi. This measure made Usŭi feudatory to Karagŭé, so that much of the produce of the extortions committed in Usŭi went to Karagŭé, and therefore they were recognized, though the odium always rested on Sŭwarora, "the savage extortioner," rather than on the mild-disposed King of Karagŭé, who kept up the most amicable relations with every one who visited him.

Mŭsa, I must say, was most loud in his praises of Rŭmanika; and, on the other hand, as Mŭsa, eight years ago, had saved Rŭmanika's throne for him against an insurrection got up by his younger brother Rogéro, Rŭmanika, always regarding Mŭsa as his savior, never lost an opportunity to show his gratitude, and would have done any thing that Mŭsa might have asked him. Of this matter, however, more in Karagŭé.

31st. To-day, Jafŭ, who had lost many ivories at Khoko when Mohinna was attacked there, prepared 100 slaves, with Said bin Osman, Mohinna's brother, with a view to follow down Snay, and, combining forces, attack Hori Hori, hoping to recover their losses; for it appeared to them the time had now come when their only hope left in carrying their trade to a successful issue lay in force of arms. They would, therefore, not rest satisfied until they had reduced Khoko and Usekhé both, by actual force, to acknowledge their superiority, "feeding on them" until the Ramazan, when they would return with all the merchants detained in Ugogo, and, again combining their forces, they would fall on Usŭi, to reduce that country also.

When these men had gone, a lunatic set the whole place in commotion. He was a slave of Mŭsa's, who had wounded some men previously in his wild excesses, and had been tied up; but now, breaking loose again, he swore he would not be satisfied until he killed some "big man." His strength was so great no one could confine him, though they hunted him into a hut, where, having seized a gun and some arrows, he defied any one to put hands on him. Here, however, he was at last reduced to submission and a better state of his senses by starvation; for I must add, the African is much given to such mental fits of aberration at certain periods: these are generally harmless, but sometimes not; but they come and they go again without any visible cause.

1st. Mŭsa's men now started for Rungŭa, and promised to bring all the porters we wanted by the first day of the next moon. We found that this would be early enough, for all the members of the expedition, excepting myself, were suffering from the effects of the wilderness life—some with fever, some with scurvy, and some with ophthalmia—which made it desirable they should all have rest. Little now was done besides counting out my property, and making Sheikh Said, who became worse and worse, deliver his charge of Cafila Bashi over to Bombay for good. When it was found so much had been stolen, especially of the best articles, I was obliged to purchase many things from Mŭsa, paying 400 per cent., which he said was their value here, over the market price of Zanzibar. I also got him to have all my coils of brass and copper wire made into bracelets, as is customary, to please the northern people.

7th. To-day information was brought here that while Manŭa Séra was on his way from Ugogo to keep his appointment with me, Sheikh Snay's army came on him at Tŭra, where he was ensconced in a tembé. Hearing this, Snay, instead of attacking the village at once, commenced negotiations with the chief of the place by demanding him to set free his guest, otherwise they, the Arabs, would storm the tembé. The chief, unfortunately, did not comply at once, but begged grace for one night, saying that if Manŭa Séra was found there in the morning they might do as they liked. Of course Manŭa bolted; and the Arabs, seeing the Tŭra people all under arms ready to defend themselves the next morning, set at them in earnest, and shot, murdered, or plundered the whole of the district. Then, while Arabs were sending in their captures of women, children, and cattle, Manŭa Séra made off to a district called Dara, where he formed an alliance with its chief, Kifŭnja, and boasted he would attack Kazé as soon as the traveling season commenced, when the place would be weakened by the dispersion of the Arabs on their ivory excursions.

This startling news set the place in a blaze, and brought all the Arabs again to seek my advice; for they condemned what Snay had done in not listening to me before, and wished to know if I could not now treat for them with Manŭa Séra, which they thought could be easily managed, as Manŭa Séra himself was not only the first to propose mediation, but was actually on his way here for the purpose when Snay opposed him. I said nothing could give me greater pleasure than mediating for them, to put a stop to these horrors, but it struck me the case had now gone too far. Snay, in opposition to my advice, was bent on fighting; he could not be recalled; and unless all the Arabs were of one mind, I ran the risk of committing myself to a position I could not maintain. To this they replied that the majority were still at Kazé, all wishing for peace at any price, and that whatever terms I might wish to dictate they would agree to. Then I said, "What would you do with Mkisiwa? You have made him chief, and can not throw him over." "Oh, that," they said, "can be easily managed; for formerly, when we confronted Manŭa Séra at Ngŭrŭ, we offered to give him as much territory as his father governed, though not exactly in the same place; but he treated our message with disdain, not knowing then what a fix he was in. Now, however, as he has seen more, and wishes for peace himself, there can be no difficulty." I then ordered two of my men to go with two of Mŭsa's to acquaint Manŭa Séra with what we were about, and to know his views on the subject; but these men returned to say Manŭa Séra could not be found, for he was driven from "pillar to post" by the different native chiefs, as, wherever he went, his army ate up their stores, and brought nothing but calamities with them. Thus died this second attempted treaty. Mŭsa then told me it was well it turned out so, for Manŭa Séra would never believe the Arabs, as they had broken faith so often before, even after exchanging blood by cutting incisions in one another's legs —the most sacred bond or oath the natives know of.

As nothing more of importance was done, I set out with Grant to have a week's shooting in the district, under the guidance of an old friend, Fundi Sangoro, Mŭsa's "head gamekeeper," who assured me that the sable antelope and blanc boc, specimens of which I had not yet seen, inhabited some low swampy place called N'yama, or "Meat," not far distant, on the left bank of the Walé nullah. My companion unfortunately got fever here, and was prevented from going out, and I did little better; for, although I waded up to my middle every day, and wounded several blanc boc, I only bagged one,

Shooting at N'yama, 18th to 25th.

and should not have got even him had it not happened that some lions in the night pulled him down close to our camp, and roared so violently that they told us the story. The first thing in the morning I wished to have at them; but they took the hint of daybreak to make off, and left me only the half of the animal. I saw only one sable antelope. We all went back to Kazé, arriving there on the 24th.

25th to 13th. Days rolled on, and nothing was done in particular—beyond increasing my stock of knowledge of distant places and people, enlarging my zoological collection, and taking long series of astronomical observations—until the 13th, when the whole of Kazé was depressed by a sad scene of mourning and tears. Some slaves came in that night, having made their way through the woods from Ugogo, avoiding the track to save themselves from detection, and gave information that Snay, Jafŭ, and five other Arabs had been killed, as well as a great number of slaves. The expedition, they said, had been defeated, and the positions were so complicated nobody knew what to do. At first the Arabs achieved two brilliant successes, having succeeded in killing Hori Hori of Khoko, when they recovered their ivory, made slaves of all they could find, and took a vast number of cattle; then attacking Usekhé, they reduced that place to submission by forcing a ransom out of its people. At this period, however, they heard that a whole caravan, carrying 5000 dollars' worth of property, had been cut up by the people of Mzanza, a small district ten miles north of Usekhé; so, instead of going on to Kanyenyé to relieve the caravans which were waiting there for them, they foolishly divided their forces into three parts. Of these they sent one to take their loot back to Kazé, another to form a reserve force at Mdabŭrŭ, on the east flank of the wilderness, and a third, headed by Snay and Jafŭ, to attack Mzanza. At the first onset Snay and Jafŭ carried every thing before them, and became so excited over the amount of their loot that they lost all feelings of care or precaution.

In this high exuberance of spirits, a sudden surprise turned their momentary triumph into a total defeat; for some Wahŭmba, having heard the cries of the Wagogo, joined in their cause, and both together fell on the Arab force with such impetuosity that the former victors were now scattered in all directions. Those who could run fast enough were saved; the rest were speared to death by the natives. Nobody knew how Jafŭ fell; but Snay, after running a short distance, called one of his slaves, and begged him to take his gun, saying, "I am too old to keep up with you; keep this gun for my sake, for I will lie down here and take my chance." He never was seen again. But this was not all their misfortunes; for the slaves who brought in this information had met the first detachment, sent with the Khoko loot, at Kigŭa, where, they said, the detachment had been surprised by Manŭa Séra, who, having fortified a village with four hundred men, expecting this sort of thing, rushed out upon them, and cut them all up.

The Arabs, after the first burst of their grief was over, came to me again in a body, and begged me to assist them, for they were utterly undone. Manŭa Séra prevented their direct communication with their detachment at Mdabŭrŭ, and that again was cut off from their caravans at Kanyenyé by the Mzanza people, and, in fact, all the Wagogo; so they hoped at least I would not forsake them, which they heard I was going to do, as Manŭa Séra had also threatened to attack Kazé. I then told them, finally, that their proposals were now beyond my power, for I had a duty to perform as well as themselves, and in a day or two I should be off.

14*th* to 17*th*. On the 14th thirty-nine porters were brought in from Rungŭa by Mŭsa's men, who said they had collected one hundred and twenty, and brought them to within ten miles of this, when some travelers frightened all but thirty-nine away by telling them, "Are you such fools as to venture into Kazé now? All the Arabs have been killed, or were being cut up and pursued by Manŭa Séra." This sad disappointment threw me on my "beam-ends." For some reason or other, none of Mŭsa's slaves would take service, and the Arabs prevented theirs from leaving the place, as it was already too short of hands. To do the best under these circumstances, I determined on going to Rungŭa with what kịt could be carried, leaving Bombay behind with Mŭsa until such time as I should arrive there, and, finding more men, could send them back for the rest. I then gave Mŭsa the last of the gold watches the Indian government had given me;* and, bidding Sheikh Said take all our letters and specimens back to the coast as soon as the road was found practicable, set out on the march northward with Grant and Baraka, and all the rest of

* The two first gold watches were given away at Zanzibar.

my men who were well enough to carry loads, as well as some of
Mŭsa's head men, who knew where to get porters.

After passing Masangé and Zimbili, we put up a night in the
village of Iviri, on the northern border of Unyanyembé, and found several officers there, sent by
Mkisiwa, to enforce a levy of soldiers to take the
field with the Arabs at Kazé against Manŭa Séra;
to effect which, they walked about ringing bells, and ·
bawling out that if a certain percentage of all the inhabitants did
not muster, the village chief would be seized, and their plantations confiscated. My men all mutinied here for increase of ra-
tion allowances. To find themselves food with, I had given them
all one necklace of beads each per diem since leaving Kazé, in
lieu of cloth, which hitherto had been served out for that purpose. It was a very liberal allowance, because the Arabs never
gave more than one necklace to every three men, and that, too,
of inferior quality to what I served. I brought them to at last
by starvation, and then we went on. Dipping down into a valley
between two clusters of granitic hills, beautifully clothed with
trees and grass, studded here and there with rich plantations, we
entered the district of Usagari, and on the second day forded the
Gombé nullah again—in its upper course, called Kŭalé.

Rising again up to the main level of the plantation, we walked
into the boma of the chief of Unyambéwa, Singinya,
whose wife was my old friend the late sultana Ungŭgŭ's lady's-maid. Immediately on our entering her palace,
she came forward to meet me with the most affable air of a princess, begged I would always come to her as I did then, and sought
to make every one happy and comfortable. Her old mistress,
she said, died well stricken in years; and, as she had succeeded
her, the people of her country invited Singinya to marry her, because feuds had arisen about the rights of succession; and it was
better a prince, whom they thought best suited by birth and good
qualities, should head their warriors, and keep all in order. At
that moment Singinya was out in the field fighting his enemies;
and she was sure, when he heard I was here, that he would be
very sorry he had missed seeing me.

We next went on to the district of Ukŭmbi, and put up in a
village there, on approaching which all the villagers
turned out to resist us, supposing we were an old
enemy of theirs. They flew about brandishing their spears, and

Break ground, 17th.
To Masangé, 18th.
To Iviri, 19th.
Enter Usagari, 20th.
Cross Gombé nullah, 21st.

To Ungŭgŭ's Palace, 22d.

To Usenda, 23d.

pulling their bows in the most grotesque attitudes, alarming some of my porters so much that they threw down their loads and bolted. All the country is richly cultivated, though Indian corn at that time was the only grain ripe. The square, flat-topped tembés had now been left behind, and instead the villagers lived in small collections of grass huts, surrounded by palisades of tall poles.

Proceeding on, we put up at the small settlement of Usenda, the proprietor of which was a semi-negro Arab merchant called Sangoro. He had a large collection of women here, but had himself gone north with a view to trade in Karagŭé. Report, however, assured us that he was then detained in Usŭi by Sŭwarora, its chief, on the plea of requiring his force of musketeers to prevent the Watŭta from pillaging his country, for these Watŭta lived entirely on plunder of other people's cattle.

With one move, by alternately crossing strips of forest and cultivation, studded here and there with small hills of granite, we forded the Quandé nullah, a tributary to the Gombé, and entered the rich flat district of Mininga, where the gingerbread-palm grows abundantly. The greatest man we found here was a broken-down ivory-merchant called Sirboko, who gave us a good hut to live in. Next morning, I believe at the suggestion of my Wangŭana, with Baraka at their head, he induced me to stop there; for he said Rungŭa had been very recently destroyed by the Watŭta, and this place could afford porters better than it. To all appearance this was the case, for this district was better cultivated than any place I had seen. I also felt a certain inclination to stop, as I was dragging on sick men, sorely against my feelings; and I also thought I had better not go farther away from my rear property; but, afraid of doing wrong in not acting up to Mŭsa's directions, I called up his head men who were with me, and asked them what they thought of the matter, as they had lately come from Rungŭa. On their confirming Sirboko's story, and advising my stopping, I acceded to their recommendation, and immediately gave Mŭsa's men orders to look out for porters.

Hearing this, all my Wangŭana danced with delight; and I, fearing there was some treachery, called Mŭsa's men again, saying I had changed my mind, and wished to go on in the afternoon; but when the time came, not one of our porters could be seen. There was now no help for it; so, taking it coolly, I gave Mŭsa's

To Mininga, 24th.

men presents, begged them to look sharp in getting the men up, and trusted all would end well in the long run. Sirboko's attentions were most warm and affecting. He gave us cows, rice, and milk, with the best place he had to live in, and looked after us as constantly and tenderly as if he had been our father. It seemed quite unjust to harbor any suspicion against him.

He gave the following account of himself: He used to trade in ivory on account of some Arabs at Zanzibar. On crossing Usŭi, he once had a fight with one of the chiefs of the country and killed him; but he got through all right, because the natives, after two or three of their number had been killed, dispersed, and feared to come near his musket again. He visited Uganda when the late king Sunna was living, and even traded with Usoga; but as he was coming down from these northern countries he lost all his property by a fire breaking out in a village he stopped in, which drove him down here a ruined man. As it happened, however, he put up with the chief of this district, Ugali—Mr. Paste—at a time when the Watŭta attacked the place and drove all the inhabitants away. The chief, too, was on the point of bolting, when Sirboko prevented him by saying, "If you will only have courage to stand by me, the Watŭta shall not come near; at any rate, if they do, let us both die together." The Watŭta at that time surrounded the district, crowning all the little hills overlooking it; but, fearing the Arabs' guns might be many, they soon walked away and left them in peace. In return for this magnanimity, and feeling a great security in fire-arms, Ugali then built the large inclosure, with huts for Sirboko, we were now living in. Sirboko, afraid to return to the coast lest he should be apprehended for debt, has resided here ever since, doing odd jobs for other traders, increasing his family, and planting extensively. His agricultural operations are confined chiefly to rice, because the natives do not like it enough to be tempted to steal it.

25th to 2d. I now set to work, collecting, stuffing, and drawing, until the 2d, when Mŭsa's men came in with three hundred men, whom I sent on to Kazé at once with my specimens and letters, directing Mŭsa and Bombay to come on and join us immediately. While waiting for these men's return, one of Sirboko's slaves, chained up by him, in the most piteous manner cried out to me, " Hai Bana wangi, Bana wangi (Oh, my lord, my lord), take pity on me! When I was a free man I saw you at Uvira, on the Tanganyika Lake, when you were there; but since then the Wa-

SIRBOKO'S SLAVES CARRYING FUEL AND CUTTING RICE.

tŭta, in a fight at Ujiji, speared me all over and left me for dead, when I was seized by the people, sold to the Arabs, and have been in chains ever since. Oh, I say, Bana wangi, if you would only liberate me I would never run away, but would serve you faithfully all my life." This touching appeal was too strong for my heart to withstand, so I called up Sirboko, and told him, if he would liberate this one man to please me, he should be no loser; and the release was effected. He was then christened Farhan (Joy), and was enrolled in my service with the rest of my freed men. I then inquired if it was true the Wabembé were cannibals, and also circumcised. In one of their slaves the latter statement was easily confirmed. I was assured that he was a cannîbal; for the whole tribe of Wabembé, when they can not get human flesh otherwise, give a goat to their neighbors for a sick or dying child, regarding such flesh as the best of all. No other cannibals, however, were known of; but the Masai, and their cognates, the Wahŭmba, Watatŭrŭ, Wakasangé, Wanyaramba, and even the Wagogo and Wakimbŭ, circumcise.

On the 15th I was surprised to find Bombay come in with all my rear property and a great quantity of Mŭsa's, but without the old man. By a letter from Sheikh Said I then found that, since my leaving Kazé, the Arabs had, along with Mkisiwa, invested the position of Manŭa Séra at Kigŭé, and forced him to take flight again. Afterward the Arabs, returning to Kazé, found Mŭsa preparing to leave. Angry at this attempt to desert them, they persuaded him to give up his journey north for the present; so that at the time Bombay left, Mŭsa was engaged as public auctioneer in selling the effects of Snay, Jafŭ, and others, but privately said he would follow me on to Karagŭé as soon as his rice was cut. Adding a little advice of his own, Sheikh Said pressed me to go on with the journey as fast as possible, because all the Arabs had accused me of conspiring with Manŭa Séra, and would turn against me unless I soon got away.

2d to 30th. Disgusted with Mŭsa's vacillatory conduct, on the 22d I sent him a letter containing a bit of my mind. I had given him, as a present, sufficient cloth to pay for his porters, as well as a watch and a good sum of money, and advised his coming on at once, for the porters who had just brought in my rear property would not take pay to go on to Karagŭé; and so I was detained again, waiting while his head man went to Rungŭa to look for more. Five days after this, a party of Sangoro's arrived from

Karagŭé, saying they had been detained three months in Usŭi by Sŭwarora, who had robbed them of an enormous quantity of prop-. erty, and oppressed them so that all their porters ran away. Now, slight as this little affair might appear, it was of vital importance to me, as I found all my men shaking their heads and predicting what might happen to us when we got there; so, as a forlorn hope, I sent Baraka with another letter to Mŭsa, offering to pay as much money for fifty men carrying muskets as would buy fifty slaves, and, in addition to that, I offered to pay them what my men were receiving as servants. Next day (23d) the chief Ugali came to pay his respects to us. He was a fine-looking young man, about thirty years old, the husband of thirty wives, but he had only three children. Much surprised at the various articles composing our kit, he remarked that our "sleeping-clothes" — blankets — were much better than his royal robes; but of all things that amused him most were our picture-books, especially some birds drawn by Wolf.

Every thing still seemed going against me; for on the following day (24th) Mŭsa's men came in from Rungŭa to say the Watŭta were "out." They had just seized fifty head of cattle from Rungŭa, and the people were in such a state of alarm they dared not leave their homes and families. I knew not what to do, for there was no hope left but in what Baraka might bring; and as that even would be insufficient, I sent Mŭsa's men into Kazé, to increase the original number by thirty men more.

Patience, thank God, I had a good stock of, so I waited quietly until the 30th, when I was fairly upset by the arrival of a letter from Kazé, stating that Baraka had arrived, and had been very insolent both to Mŭsa and to Sheikh Said. The bearer of the letter was at once to go and search for porters at Rungŭa, but not a word was said about the armed men I had ordered. At the same time reports from the other side came in, to the effect that the Arabs at Kazé and Mséné had bribed the Watŭta to join them, and overrun the whole country from Ugogo to Usŭi; and, in consequence of this, all the natives on the line I should have to take were in such dread of that terrible wandering race of savages, who had laid waste in turn all the lands from N'yassa to Usŭi on their west flank, that not a soul dared leave his home. I could now only suppose that this foolish and hasty determination of the Arabs, who, quite unprepared to carry out their wicked alliance to fight, still had set every one against their own interests as well as mine, had not reached Mŭsa, so I made up my mind at once to return to Kazé, and settle all matters I had in heart with himself and the Arabs in person.

This settled, I next, in this terrible embarrassment, determined on sending back the last of the Hottentots, as all four of them, though still wishing to go on with me, distinctly said they had not the power to continue the march, for they had never ceased suffering from fever and jaundice, which had made them all yellow as guineas, save one, who was too black to change color. It felt to me as if I were selling my children, having once undertaken to lead them through the journey; but if I did not send them back then, I never could afterward, and therefore I allowed the more substantial feelings of humanity to overcome these compunctions.

Next morning, then, after giving the Tots over in charge of some men to escort them on to Kazé quietly, I set out myself with a dozen men, and the following evening I put up with Mŭsa, who told me Baraka had just left without one man, all his slaves having become afraid to go, since the news of the Arab alliance had reached Kazé. Sŭwarora had ordered his subjects to run up a line of bomas to protect his frontier, and had proclaimed his intention to kill every coast-man who dared attempt to enter Usŭi. My heart was ready to sink as I turned into bed, and I was driven to think of abandoning every body who was not strong enough to go on with me carrying a load.

March back to Kazé, 1st and 2d.

3d to 13th. Baraka, hearing I had arrived, then came back to me, and confirmed Mŭsa's words. The Arabs, too, came flocking in to beg, nay, implore me to help them out of their difficulties. Many of them were absolutely ruined, they said; others had their houses full of stores unemployed. At Ugogo those who wished to join them were unable to do so, for their porters, what few were left, were all dying of starvation; and at that moment Manŭa Séra was hovering about, shooting, both night and day, all the poor villagers in the district, or driving them away. Would to God, they said, I would mediate for them with Manŭa Séra— they were sure I would be successful—and then they would give me as many armed men as I liked. Their folly in all their actions, I said, proved to me that any thing I might attempt to do would be futile, for their alliance with the Watŭta, when they were not prepared to act, at once damned them in my eyes as fools. This they in their terror acknowledged, but said it was not past remedy, if I would join them, to counteract what had been done in that matter. Suffice it now to say, after a long conversation, arguing all the pros and cons over, I settled I would write out all the articles of a treaty of peace, by which they should be liable to have all their property forfeited on the coast if they afterward broke faith; and I begged them to call the next day and sign it.

They were no sooner gone, however, than Mŭsa assured me they had killed old Maŭla of Rŭbŭga in the most treacherous manner, as follows: Khamis, who is an Arab of most gentlemanly aspect, on returning from Ugogo attended by slaves, having heard that Maŭla was desirous of adjusting a peace, invited him, with his son, to do so. When old Maŭla came as desired, bringing his son with him, and a suitable offering of ivory and cattle, the Arab induced them both to kneel down and exchange blood with him, when, by a previously concerted arrangement, Khamis had them shot down by his slaves. This disgusting story made me quite sorry, when next day the Arabs arrived, expecting that I should attempt to help them; but, as the matter had gone so far, I asked them, in the first place, how they could hope Manŭa Séra would have any faith in them when they were so treacherous, or trust to my help, since they had killed Maŭla, who was my *protégé?* They all replied in a breath, "Oh, let the past be forgotten, and assist us now, for in you alone we can look for a preserver."

At length an armistice was agreed to; but as no one dared go to negotiate it but my men, I allowed them to take pay from the Arabs, which was settled on the 4th by ten men taking four yards of cloth each, with a promise of a feast on sweetmeats when they returned. Ex Mrs. Mŭsa, who had been put aside by her husband because she was too fat for her lord's taste, then gave me three men of her private establishment, and abused Mŭsa for being wanting in "brains." She had repeatedly advised him to leave this place and go with me, lest the Arabs, who were all in debt to him, should put him to death; but he still hung on to recover his remaining debts, a portion having been realized by the sale of Snay's and Jafŭ's effects; for every thing in the shape of commodities had been sold at the enormous price of 500 per cent. —the male slaves even fetching $100 per head, though the females went for less. The Hottentots now arrived, with many more of my men, who, seeing their old "flames," Snay's women, sold off by auction, begged me to advance them money to purchase them with, for they could not bear to see these women, who were their own when they formerly staid here, go off like cattle no one knew where. Compliance, of course, was impossible, as it would have crowded the caravan with women. Indeed, to prevent my men ever thinking of matrimony on the march, as well as to incite them on through the journey, I promised, as soon as we reached Egypt, to give them all wives and gardens at Zanzibar, provided they did not contract marriages on the road.

On the 6th, the deputation, headed by Baraka, returned triumphantly into Kazé, leading in two of Manŭa Séra's ministers —one of them a man with one eye, whom I called Cyclops—and two others, ministers of a chief called Kitambi, or Little Blue Cloth. After going a day's journey, they said they came to where Manŭa Séra was residing with Kitambi, and met with a most cheerful and kind reception from both potentates, who, on hearing of my proposition, warmly acceded to it, issued orders at once that hostilities should cease, and, with one voice, said they were convinced that, unless through my instrumentality, Manŭa Séra would never regain his possessions. Kitambi was quite beside himself, and wished my men to stop one night to enjoy his hospitality. Manŭa Séra, after reflecting seriously about the treacherous murder of old Maŭla, hesitated, but gave way when it had been explained away by my men, and said, "No; they shall go at once, for my kingdom depends on the issue, and Bana Mzungŭ (the White Lord) may get anxious if they do not return promptly." One thing, however, he insisted on, and that was, the only place he would meet the Arabs in was Unyanyembé, as it would be beneath his dignity to settle matters any where else. And farther, he specified that he wished all the transactions to take place in Mŭsa's house.

Next day, 7th, I assembled all the Arabs at Mŭsa's "court," with all my men and the two chiefs, four men attending, when Baraka, "on his legs," told them all I proposed for the treaty of peace. The Arabs gave their assent to it; and Cyclops, for Manŭa Séra, after giving a full narrative of the whole history of the war, in such a rapid and eloquent manner as would have done justice to our prime minister, said his chief was only embittered against Snay, and now Snay was killed, he wished to make friends with them. To which the Arabs made a suitable answer, adding all that they found fault with was an insolent remark which, in his wrath, Manŭa Séra had given utterance to, that their quarrel with him was owing chiefly to a scurvy jest which he had passed on them, and on the characteristic personal ceremony of initiation to their Mussulman faith. Now, however, as Manŭa Séra wished to make friends, they would abide by any thing that I might propose. Here the knotty question arose again, What territory they (the Arabs) would give to Manŭa Séra? I thought he would not be content unless he got the old place again; but as Cyclops said no, that was not, in his opinion, absolutely necessary, as the lands of Unyanyembé had once before been divided, the matter was settled on the condition that another conference should be held with Manŭa Séra himself on the subject.

I now (8th and 9th) sent these men all off again, inviting Manŭa Séra to come over and settle matters at once, if he would, otherwise I should go on with my journey, for I could not afford to wait longer here. Then, as soon as they left, I made Mŭsa order some of his men off to Rungŭa, requesting the chief of the place to send porters to Mininga to remove all our baggage over to his palace; at the same time, I begged him not to fear the Watŭta's threat to attack him, as Mŭsa would come as soon as the treaty was concluded, in company with me, to build a boma alongside his palace, as he did in former years, to be nearer his trade with Karagŭé. I should have mentioned, by the way, that Mŭsa had now made up his mind not to go farther than the borders of Usŭi with me, lest I should be "torn to pieces," and he be "held responsible on the coast." Mŭsa's men, however, whom he selected for this business, were then engaged making Mussulmans of all the Arab slave-boys, and said they would not go until they had finished, although I offered to pay the "doctor's bill," or allowance they expected to get. The ceremony, at the same time that it helps to extend their religion, as christening does ours, also stamps the converts with a mark effective enough to prevent desertion; because, after it has been performed, their own tribe would not receive them again. At last, when they did go, Mŭsa, who was suffering from a sharp illness, to prove to me that he was bent on leaving Kazé the same time as myself, began eating what he called his training pills—small dried buds of roses with alternate bits of sugar-candy. Ten of these buds, he said, eaten dry, were sufficient for ordinary cases, and he gave a very formidable description of the effect likely to follow the use of the same number boiled in rice-water or milk.

Fearful stories of losses and distress came constantly in from Ugogo by small bodies of men, who stole their way through the jungles. To-day a tremendous commotion took place in Mŭsa's tembé among all the women, as one had been delivered of still-born twins. They went about in procession, painted and adorned in the most grotesque fashion, bewailing and screeching, singing and dancing, throwing their arms and legs about as if they were drunk, until the evening set in, when they gathered a huge bundle of bulrushes, and, covering it over with a cloth, carried it up to the door of the bereaved on their shoulders, as though it had been a coffin. Then setting it down on the ground, they planted some of the rushes on either side of the entrance, and all kneeling to-gether, set to bewailing, shrieking, and howling incessantly for hours together.

After this (10th to 12th), to my great relief, quite unexpectedly, a man arrived from Usŭi conveying a present of some ivories from a great mganga or magician, named Dr. K'yengo, who had sent them to Mŭsa as a recollection from an old friend, begging at the same time for some pretty cloths, as he said he was then engaged as mtongi or caravan director, collecting together all the native caravans desirous of making a grand march to Uganda. This seemed to me a heaven-born opportunity of making friends with one who could help me so materially, and I begged Mŭsa to seal it by sending him something on my account, as I had nothing by me; but Mŭsa objected, thinking it better simply to say I was coming, and if he, K'yengo, would assist me in Usŭi, I would then give him some cloths as he wanted; otherwise, Mŭsa said, the man who had to convey it would in all probability make away with it, and then do his best to prevent my seeing K'yengo. As soon as this was settled, against my wish and opinion, a special messenger arrived from Sŭwarora to inquire of Mŭsa what truth there was in the story of the Arabs having allied themselves to the Watŭta. He had full faith in Mŭsa, and hoped, if the Arabs had no hostile intentions toward him, he, Mŭsa, would send him two men of his own, and prevail on the Arabs to send two of theirs; farther, Sŭwarora wished Mŭsa would send him a cat. A black cat was then given to the messenger for Sŭwarora, and Mŭsa sent an account of all that I had done toward effecting a peace, saying that the Arabs had accepted my views, and if he would have patience until I arrived in Usŭi, the four men required would be sent with me.

In the evening my men returned again with Cyclops, who said, for his master, that Manŭa Séra desired nothing more than peace, and to make friends with the Arabs; but as nothing was settled about deposing Mkisiwa, he could not come over here. Could the Arabs, was Manŭa Séra's rejoinder, suppose for a moment that he would voluntarily divide his dominion with one whom he regarded as his slave! Death would be preferable; and although he would trust his life in the Mzungŭ's hands if he called him again, he must know it was his intention to hunt Mkisiwa down like a wild animal, and would never rest satisfied until he was dead. The treaty thus broke down; for the same night Cyclops decamped like a thief, after brandishing an arrow which Manŭa Séra had given him to throw down as a gauntlet of defiance to fight Mkisiwa to death. After this the Arabs were too much ashamed of themselves to come near me, though invited by letter, and Mŭsa became so ill he would not take my advice and ride in a hammock, the best possible cure for his complaint; so, after being humbugged so many times by his procrastinations, I gave Sheikh Said more letters and specimens, with orders to take the Tots down to the coast as soon as practicable, and started once more for the north, expecting very shortly to hear of Mŭsa's death, though he promised to follow me the very next day or die in the attempt, and he also said he would bring on the four men required by Sŭwarora; for I was fully satisfied in my mind that he would have marched with me then had he had the resolution to do so at all.

Before I had left the district I heard that Manŭa Séra had col- To Mininga, 13th lected a mixed force of Warori, Wagogo, and Wasa- and 14th. kŭma, and had gone off to Kigŭé again, while the Arabs and Mkisiwa were feeding their men on beef before setting out to fight him. Manŭa Séra, it was said, had vast resources. His father, Fŭndi Kira, was a very rich man, and had buried vast stores of property, which no one knew of but Manŭa Séra, his heir. The Wanyamŭézi all inwardly loved him for his great generosity, and all alike thought him protected by a halo of charm-power so effective against the arms of the Arabs that he could play with them just as he liked.

On crossing Unyambéwa (14th), when I a third time put up with my old friend the sultana, her chief sent word to say he hoped I would visit him at his fighting boma to eat a cow which he had in store for me, as he could not go home and enjoy the society of his wife while the war was going on, since by so doing it was considered he " would lose strength."

On arriving at Mininga, I was rejoiced to see Grant greatly re-
Mininga, 15th to covered.　Three villagers had been attacked by two
19th.　　　　　lions during my absence.　Two of the people es-
caped, but the third was seized as he was plunging into his hut, and was dragged off and devoured by the animals.　A theft also had taken place, by which both Grant and Sirboko lost property; and the thieves had been traced over the borders of the next dis-trict.　No fear, however, was entertained about the things being recovered, for Sirboko had warned Ugali the chief, and he had promised to send his Waganga, or magicians, out to track them down, unless the neighboring chief chose to give them up.　After waiting two days, as no men came from Rungŭa, I begged Grant to push ahead on to Ukŭni, just opposite Rungŭa, with all my coast-men, while I remained behind for the arrival of Mŭsa's men and porters to carry on the rest of the kit; for I had now twenty-two in addition to men permanently enlisted, who took service on the same rate of pay as my original coast-men; though, as usual, when the order for marching was issued, a great number were found to be either sick or malingering.

Two days afterward, Mŭsa's men came in with porters, who
To Mbisŭ, 20th would not hire themselves for more than two marches,
and 21st.　　　having been forbidden to do so by their chief on ac-
count of the supposed Watŭta invasion; and for these two marches they required a quarter of the whole customary hire to Karagŭé.　Mŭsa's traps, too, I found, were not to be moved, so I saw at once Mŭsa had not kept faith with me, and there would be a fresh set of difficulties; but as every step onward was of the greatest importance—for my men were consuming my stores at a fearful pace—I paid down the beads they demanded, and next day joined Grant at Mbisŭ, a village of Ukŭni held by a small chief called Mchiméka, who had just concluded a war of two years' standing with the great chief Ukŭlima (the Digger), of Nŭnda (the Hump).　During the whole of the two years' warfare the loss was only three men on each side.　Meanwhile Mŭsa's men bolted like thieves one night, on a report coming that the chief of Unyambéwa, after concluding the war, while amusing himself with his wife, had been wounded on the foot by an arrow that fell from her hand.　The injury had at once taken a mortal turn, and the chief sent for his magicians, who said it was not the

fault of the wife; somebody else must have charmed the arrow
to cause such a deadly result. They then seized hold of their
magic horn, primed for the purpose, and allowed it to drag them
to where the culprits dwelt. Four poor men, who were convicted
in this way, were at once put to death, and the chief from that
moment began to recover.

After a great many perplexities, I succeeded in getting a kirangozi, or leader, by name Ungŭrŭé (the Pig). He had
several times taken caravans to Karaguĕ, and knew

Mbisŭ, 22d to
31st.

all the languages well, but unfortunately he afterward proved to
be what his name implied. That, however, I could not foresee;
so, trusting to him and good luck, I commenced making fresh en-
listments of porters; but they came and went in the most tanta-
lizing manner, notwithstanding I offered three times the hire that
any merchant could afford to give. Every day seemed to be
worse and worse. Some of Mŭsa's men came to get palm toddy
for him, as he was too weak to stand, and was so cold nothing
would warm him. There was, however, no message brought for
myself; and as the deputation did not come to me, I could only
infer that I was quite forgotten, or that Mŭsa, after all, had only
been humbugging me. I scarcely knew what to do. Every
body advised me to stop where I was until the harvest was over,
as no porters could be found on ahead, for Ukŭni was the last of
the fertile lands on this side of Usŭi.

Stopping, however, seemed endless; not so my supplies. I
therefore tried advancing in detachments again, sending the free
men off under Grant to Ukŭlima's, while I waited behind, keeping ourselves divided in the hopes of inducing all hands to see
the advisability of exerting themselves for the general good; as
my men, while we were all together, showed they did not care
how long they were kept doing no more fatiguing work than
chaffing each other, and feeding at my expense.

In the mean while the villagers were very merry, brewing and
drinking their pombé (beer) by turns, one house after the other
providing the treat. On these occasions, the chief—who always
drank freely, and more than any other—heading the public gath-
erings of men and women, saw the large earthen pots placed all
in a row, and the company taking long draughts from bowls
made of plaited straw, laughing as they drank, until, half-screwed,
they would begin bawling and shouting. To increase the merriment, one or two jackanapes, with zebras' manes tied over their

HARVEST IN WANYAMWÉZI, 1861.

1, 2, 3, 4. Grain. Maize, etc., stacked for the season.
5. Men with long rackets thrashing Kafir corn (sorghum).
6. Woman in the field cutting "sorghum" with a knife, and depositing it in a basket.
7. Women separating the corn from the chaff by means of a wooden pestle and mortar.
8. Woman grinding corn upon a single slab of stone.

heads, would advance with long tubes like monster bassoons, blowing with all their might, contorting their faces and bodies, and going through the most obscene and ridiculous motions to captivate their simple admirers. This, however, was only the feast; the ball then began; for the pots were no sooner emptied than five drums at once, of different sizes and tones, suspended in a line from a long horizontal bar, were beaten with fury, and all the men, women, and children, singing and clapping their hands in time, danced for hours together.

A report reached me, by some of Sirboko's men, whom he had sent to convey to us a small present of rice, that an Arab, who was crossing Msalala to our northward, had been treacherously robbed of all his arms and guns by a small district chief, whose only excuse was that the Wanyamŭézi had always traded very well by themselves until the Arabs came into the country; but now, as they were robbed of their property on account of the disturbances caused by these Arabs, they intended for the future to take all they could get, and challenged the Arabs to do the same.

My patience was beginning to suffer again, for I could not help thinking that the chiefs of the place were preventing their village men going with me in order that my presence here might ward off the Watŭta; so I called up the kirangozi, who had thirteen "Watoto," as they are called, or children of his own, wishing to go, and asked him if he knew why no other men could be got. As he could not tell me, saying some excused themselves on the plea they were cutting their corn, and others that they feared the Watŭta, I resolved at once to move over to Nŭnda; and if that place also failed to furnish men, I would go on to Usŭi or Karagŭé with what men I had, and send back for the rest of my property; for, though I could not bear the idea of separating from Grant, still the interests of old England were at stake, and demanded it.

This resolve being strengthened by the kirangozi's assurance
To Nŭnda, 31st. that the row in Msalala had shaken the few men who had half dreaded to go with me, I marched over to Nŭnda, and put up with Grant in Ukŭlima's boma, when Grant informed me that the chief had required four yards of cloth from him for having walked round a dead lioness, as he had thus destroyed a charm that protected his people against any more of these animals coming, although, fortunately, the charm could be restored again by paying four yards of cloth. Ukŭlima, howev-

er, was a very kind and good man, though he did stick the hands
and heads of his victims on the poles of his boma as a warning to

Ukŭlima's Village.

others. He kept five wives, of whom the rest paid such respect
to the elder one, it was quite pleasing to see them. A man of
considerable age, he did every thing the state or his great establishment required himself. All the men of his district clapped
their hands together as a courteous salutation to him, and the
women courtesied as well as they do at our court—a proof that
they respected him as a great potentate—a homage rarely bestow-
ed on the chiefs of other small states. Ukŭlima was also hospitable; for on one occasion, when another chief came to visit him,
he received his guest and retainers with considerable ceremony,
making all the men of the village get up a dance, which they did,
beating the drums and firing off guns like a lot of black devils
let loose.

We were not the only travelers in misfortune here, for Masŭdi,
with several other Arabs, all formed in one large caravan, had arrived at Mchiméka's, and could not advance for want of men. They told me it was the first time they
had come on this line, and they deeply regretted it, for they had
lost $5000 worth of beads by their porters running away with
their loads, and now they did not know how to proceed. Indeed, they left the coast and arrived at Kazé immediately in rear
of us, and had, like ourselves, found it as much as they could do

Halt to Nŭnda,
1st to 3d.

even to reach this, and now they were at a standstill for want of porters.

As all hopes of being able to get any more men were given up, I called on Bombay and Baraka to make arrangements for my going ahead with the best of my property as I had devised. They both shook their heads, and advised me to remain until the times improved, when the Arabs, being freed from the pressure of war, would come along and form with us a "sŭfari kŭ," or grand march, as Ukŭlima and every one else had said we should be torn to pieces in Usŭi if we tried to cross that district with so few men. I then told them again and again of the messages I had sent on to Rŭmanika in Karagŭé, and to Sŭwarora in Usŭi, and begged them to listen to me, instancing as an example of what could be done by perseverance the success of Columbus, who, opposed by his sailors' misgivings, still went on and triumphed, creating for himself immortal renown.

They gave way at last, so, after selecting all the best of my property, I formed camp at Phŭnzé, left Bombay with Grant behind, as I thought Bombay the best and most honest man I had got, from his having had so much experience, and then went ahead by myself, with the Pig as my guide and interpreter, and Baraka as my factotum. The Wagŭana then all mutinied for a cloth apiece, saying they would not lift a load unless I gave it. Of course a severe contest followed; I said, as I had given them so much before, they could not want it, and ought to be ashamed of themselves. They urged, however, they were doing double work, and would not consent to carry loads as they had done at Mgŭnda Mkhali again.

Form Camp in Phŭnzé, 3d.

Arguments were useless, for, simply because they were tired of going on, they *would* not see that as they were receiving pay every day, they therefore ought to work every day. However, as they yielded at last, by some few leaning on my side, I gave what they asked for, and went to the next village, still inefficient in men, as all the Pig's Watoto could not be collected together. This second move brought us into a small village, of which Ghiya, a young man, was chief.

Halt in Phŭnzé three days.

He was very civil to me, and offered to sell me a most charming young woman, quite the belle of the country; but, as he could not bring me to terms, he looked over my picture-books with the greatest delight, and afterward went into a discourse on geography with considerable perspicaci-

To Ghiya's, 7th.

ty, seeming fully to comprehend that if I got down the Nile it would afterward result in making the shores of the N'yanza like that of the coast at Zanzibar, where the products of his country could be exchanged, without much difficulty, for cloths, beads, and brass wire. I gave him a present; then a letter was brought to me from Sheikh Said, announcing Mŭsa's death, and the fact that Manŭa Séra was still holding out at Kigŭé; in answer to which I desired the sheikh to send me as many of Mŭsa's slaves as would take service with me, for they ought now, by the laws of the Koran, to be all free.

On packing up to leave Ghiya's, all the men of the village shut the bars of the entrance, wishing to extract some cloths from me, as I had not given enough, they said, to their chief. They soon, however, saw that we, being inside their own fort, had the best of it, and they gave way. We then pushed on to Ungŭrŭé's, another chief of the same district. Here the men and women of the place came crowding to see me, the fair sex all playfully offering themselves for wives, and wishing to know which I admired most. They were so importunate, aft-- er a time, that I was not sorry to hear an attack was made on their castle because a man of the village would not pay his dow- ry-money to his father-in-law, and this set every body flying out to the scene of action.

To Ungŭrŭé's, 8th.

After this, as Bombay brought up the last of my skulking men, I bade him good-by again, and made an afternoon-march on to Takina, in the district of Msalala, which we no sooner approached than all the inhabitants turned out and fired their arrows at us. They did no harm, however, excepting to create a slight alarm, which some neighboring villagers took advantage of to run off with two of my cows. My men followed after the thieves until these entered a boma and shut the gate in their faces. They call- ed out for the cows to be returned to them, but called in vain, as the scoundrels said, "Findings are keepings, by the laws of our country; and as we found your cows, so we will keep them." For my part, I was glad they were gone, as the Wangŭana never yet kept any thing I put under their charge; so, instead of allowing them to make a fuss the next morning, I marched straight on for M'yonga's, the chief of the district, who was famed for his infamy and great extortions, having pushed his exactions so far as to close the road.

On nearing his palace, we heard war-drums beat in every sur-

To M'yonga's, rounding village, and the kirangozi would go no far-
9th.   ther until permission was obtained from M'yonga.
This did not take long, as the chief said he was most desirous to
see a white man, never having been to the coast, though his father-in-law had, and had told him that the Wazŭngŭ were even
greater people than the sultan reigning there. On our drawing
near the palace, a small, newly-constructed boma was shown for
my residence; but as I did not wish to stop there, knowing how
anxious Grant would be to have his relief, I would not enter it,
but instead sent Baraka to pay the hongo as quickly as possible,
that we might move on again; at the same time ordering him to
describe the position both Grant and myself were in, and explain
that what I paid now was to frank both of us, as the whole of the
property was my own. Should he make any remarks about the
two cows that were stolen, I said he must know that I could not
wait for them, as my brother would die of suspense if we did not
finish the journey and send back for him quickly. Off went
Baraka with a party of men, stopping hours, of course, and firing
volleys of ammunition away. He did not return again until the
evening, when the palace-drums announced that the hongo had
been settled for one barsati, one lŭgoi, and six yards merikani.
Baraka approached me triumphantly, saying how well he had
managed the business. M'yonga did not wish to see me, because
he did not know the coast language. He was immensely pleased
with the present I had given him, and said he was much and very
unjustly abused by the Arabs, who never came this way, saying
he was a bad man. He should be very glad to see Grant, and
would take nothing from him; and, though he did not see me in
person, he would feel much affronted if I did not stop the night
there. In the mean while he would have the cows brought in,
for he could not allow any one to leave his country abused in
any way.

My men had greatly amused him by firing their guns off and
showing him the use of their sword-bayonets. I knew, as a matter of course, that if I stopped any longer I should be teased for
more cloths, and gave orders to my men to march the same instant, saying, if they did not—for I saw them hesitate—I would
give the cows to the villagers, since I knew that was the thing
that weighed on their minds. This raised a mutiny. No one
would go forward with the two cows behind; besides which, the
day was far spent, and there was nothing but jungle, they said,

beyond. The kirangozi would not show the way, nor would any man lift a load. A great confusion ensued. I knew they were telling lies, and would not enter the village, but shot the cows when they arrived, for the villagers to eat, to show them I cared for nothing but making headway, and remained out in the open all night. Next morning, sure enough, before we could get under way, M'yonga sent his prime minister to say that the king's sisters and other members of his family had been crying and tormenting him all night for having let me off so cheaply; they had got nothing to cover their nakedness, and I must pay something more. This provoked fresh squabbles. The drums had beaten and the tax was settled; I could not pay more. The kirangozi, however, said he would not move a peg unless I gave something more, else he would be seized on his way back. His "children" all said the same; and as I thought Grant would only be worsted if I did not keep friends with the scoundrel, I gave four yards more merikani, and then went on my way.

For the first few miles there were villages, but after that a long tract of jungle, inhabited chiefly by antelopes and rhinoceros. It was wilder in appearance than most parts of Unyamŭézi. In this jungle a tributary nullah to the Gombé, called Nŭrhŭngŭré, is the boundary-line between the great Country of the Moon and the kingdom of Uzinza.

CHAPTER VI.

UZINZA.

The Politics of Uzinza.—The Wahŭma.—"The Pig's" Trick.—First Taste of Usŭi Taxation.—Pillaged by Mfŭmbi.—Pillaged by Makaka.—Pillaged by Lŭmérési. —Grant stripped by M'yonga.—Stripped again by Rŭhé.—Terrors and Defections in the Camp.—Driven back to Kazé with new Tribulations and Impediments.

UZINZA, which we now entered, is ruled by two Wahŭma chieftains of foreign blood, descended from the Abys-

Cross Unyamŭézi frontier, 10th, and enter Uzinza.

sinian stock, of whom we saw specimens scattered all over Unyamŭézi, and who extended even down south as far as Fipa. Travelers see very little, however, of these Wahŭma, because, being pastorals, they roam about with their flocks and build huts as far away as they can from cultivation. Most of the small district chiefs, too, are the descendants of those who ruled in the same places before the country was invaded, and with them travelers put up and have their dealings. The dress of the Wahŭma is very simple, composed chiefly of cowhide tanned black —a few magic ornaments and charms, brass or copper bracelets, and immense numbers of sambo for stockings, which looked very awkward on their long legs. They

Mzinza, or Native of Uzinza.

smear themselves with rancid butter instead of macassar, and are, in consequence, very offensive to all but the negro, who seems, rather than otherwise, to enjoy a good sharp nose-tickler. For arms, they carry both bow and spear; more generally the latter. The Wazinza in the southern parts are so much like the Wan-

yamŭézi as not to require any especial notice; but in the north,
where the country is more hilly, they are much more energetic
and actively built. All alike live in grass-hut villages, fenced
round by bomas in the south, but open in the north. Their
country rises in high rolls, increasing in altitude as it approaches
the Mountains of the Moon, and is generally well cultivated, being subjected to more of the periodical rains than the regions we
have left, though springs are not so abundant, I believe, as they
are in the Land of the Moon, where they ooze out by the flanks
of the little granitic hills.

After tracking through several miles of low bush-jungle, we
came to the sites of some old bomas that had been destroyed by
the Watŭta not long since. Farther on, as we wished to enter a
newly-constructed boma, the chief of which was Mafŭmbŭ Wantŭ
(a Mr. Balls), we felt the effects of those ruthless marauders; for
the villagers, thinking us Watŭta in disguise, would not let us in;
for those savages, they said, had once tricked them by entering
their village, pretending to be traders carrying ivory and merchandise, while they were actually spies. This was fortunate for
me, however, as Mr. Balls, like M'yonga, was noted for his extortions on travelers. We then went on and put up in the first large
village of Bogŭé, where I wished to get porters and return for
Grant, as the place seemed to be populous. Finding, however,
that I could not get a sufficient number for that purpose, I directed those who wished for employment to go off at once and take
service with Grant.

I found many people assembled here from all parts of the district for the purpose of fighting M'yonga; but the
chief Rŭhé, having heard of my arrival, called me to
his palace, which, he said, was on my way, that he might see me,
for he never in all his life had a white man for his guest, and was
so glad to hear of my arrival that he would give orders for the
dispersing of his forces. I wished to push past him, as I might
be subjected to such calls every day; but Ungŭrŭé, in the most
piggish manner—for he was related to Rŭhé—insisted that neither
himself nor any of his children would advance one step farther
with me unless I complied with their wish, which was a simple
conformity with the laws of their country, and therefore absolute.
At length giving in, I entered Rŭhé's boma, the poles of which
were decked with the skulls of his enemies stuck upon them.
Instead, however, of seeing him myself, as he feared my evil eye,

To Rŭhé's, 11th.

I conducted the arrangements for the hongo through Baraka, in the same way as I did at M'yonga's, directing that it should be limited to the small sum of one barsati and four yards kiniki.

The drum was beaten, as the public intimation of the payment To Mihambo, of the hongo, and consequently of our release, and we 12th. went on to Mihambo, on the west border of the eastern division of Uzinza, which is called Ukhanga. It overlooks the small district of Sorombo, belonging to the great western division, known as Usŭi, and is presided over by a Sorombo chief, named Makaka, whose extortions had been so notorious that no Arabs now ever went near him. I did not wish to do so either, though his palace lay in the direct route. It was therefore agreed we should skirt round by the east of this district, and I even promised the Pig I would give him ten necklaces a day, in addition to his wages, if he would avoid all the chiefs, and march steadily ten miles every day. By doing so, we should have avoided the wandering Watŭta, whose depredations had laid waste nearly all of this country; but the designing blackguard, in opposition to my wishes, to accomplish some object of his own, chose to mislead us all, and quietly took us straight into Sorombo to Kagŭé, the boma of a sub-chief, called Mfŭmbi, where we no sooner arrived than the inhospitable brute forbade any of his subjects to sell us food until the hongo was paid, for he was not sure that we were not allied with the Watŭta to rob his country. After receiving what he called his dues—one barsati, two yards merikani, and two yards kiniki—the drums beat, and all was settled with him; but I was told the head chief Makaka, who lived ten miles to the west, and so much out of my road, had sent expressly to invite me to see him. He said it was his right I should go to him as the principal chief of the district. Moreover, he longed for a sight of a white man; for, though he had traveled all across Uganda and Usoga into Masawa, or the Masai country, as well as to the coast, where he had seen both Arabs and Indians, he had never yet seen an Englishman. If I would oblige him, he said he would give me guides to Sŭwarora, who was his mkama, or king. Of course I knew well what all this meant; and at the same time that I said I could not comply, I promised to send him a present of friendship by the hands of Baraka.

This caused a halt. Makaka would not hear of such an arrangement. A present, he said, was due to him of course, but of more importance than the present was his wish to see me. Baraka and all the men begged I would give in, as they were sure he must be a good man to send such a kind message. I strove in vain, for no one would lift a load unless I complied; so, perforce, I went there, in company, however, with Mfŭmbi, who now pretended to be great friends; but what was the result? On entering the palace, we were shown into a cowyard without a tree in it, or any shade; and no one was allowed to sell us food until a present of friendship was paid, after which the hongo would be discussed.

The price of friendship was not settled that day, however, and my men had to go supperless to bed. Baraka offered him one common cloth, and then another—all of which he rejected with such impetuosity that Baraka said his head was all on a whirl. Makaka insisted he would have a déolé, or nothing at all. I protested I had no déolés I could give him, for all the expensive cloths which I had brought from the coast had been stolen in Mgŭnda Mkhali. I had three, however, concealed at the time— which I had bought from Mŭsa, at forty dollars each—intended for the kings of Karagŭé and Uganda.

Incessant badgering went on for hours and hours, until at last Baraka, clean done with the incessant worry of this hot-headed young chief, told him, most unfortunately, he would see again if he could find a déolé, as he had one of his own. Baraka then brought one to my tent, and told me of his having bought it for eight dollars at the coast; and as I now saw I was let in for it, I told him to give it. It was given, but Makaka no sooner saw it than he said he must have another one; for it was all nonsense saying a white man had no rich cloths. Whenever he met Arabs, they all said they were poor men, who obtained all their merchandise from the white men on credit, which they refunded afterward by levying a heavy percentage on the sale of their ivory.

I would not give way that night; but next day, after fearful

Halt, 16th.
battling, the present of friendship was paid by Baraka's giving first a dubŭani, then one sahari, then one barsati, then one kisŭtŭ, and then eight yards of merikani—all of which were contested in the most sickening manner—when Baraka, fairly done up, was relieved by Makaka's saying, "That will do for friendship; if you had given the déolé quietly, all this trouble would have been saved; for I am not a bad man, as you will see." My men then had their first dinner here, after which the hongo had to be paid. This for the first time was, however,

more easily settled, because Makaka at once said he would never be satisfied until he had received, if I had really not got a déolé, exactly double in equivalents of all I had given him. This was a fearful drain on my store; but the Pig, seeing my concern, merely laughed at it, and said, "Oh, these savage chiefs are all alike here; you will have one of these taxes to pay every stage to Uyofŭ, and then the heavy work will begin; for all these men, although they assume the dignity of chief to themselves, are mere officers, who have to pay tribute to Sŭwarora, and he would be angry if they were shortcoming."

The drums as yet had not beaten, for Makaka said he would not be satisfied until we had exchanged presents, to prove that we were the best of friends. To do this last act properly, I was to get ready whatever I wished to give him, while he would come and visit me with a bullock; but I was to give him a royal salute, or the drums would not beat. I never felt so degraded as when I complied, and gave orders to my men to fire a volley as he approached my tent; but I ate the dirt with a good grace, and met the young chief as if nothing had happened. My men, however, could not fire the salute fast enough for him; for he was one of those excitable, impulsive creatures who expect others to do every thing in as great a hurry as their minds wander. The moment the first volley was fired, he said, "Now fire again, fire again; be quick, be quick! What's the use of those things?" (meaning the guns.) "We could spear you all while you are loading: be quick, be quick, I tell you." But Baraka, to give himself law, said, "No; I must ask Bana" (master) "first, as we do every thing by order; this is not fighting at all."

The men being ready, file-firing was ordered, and then the young chief came into my tent. I motioned him to take my chair, which, after he sat down upon it, I was very sorry for, as he stained the seat all black with the running color of one of the new barsati cloths he had got from me, which, to improve its appearance, he had saturated with stinking butter, and had tied round his loins. A fine-looking man of about thirty, he wore the butt-end of a large sea-shell cut in a circle, and tied on his forehead, for a coronet, and sundry small saltiana antelope horns, stuffed with magic powder, to keep off the evil eye. His attendants all fawned on him, and snapped their fingers whenever he sneezed. After passing the first compliment, I gave him a barsati, as my token of friendship, and asked him what he saw when he went to the Masai country. He assured me "that there were two lakes, and not one;" for, on going from Usoga to the Masai country, he crossed over a broad strait, which connected the big N'yanza with another one at its northeast corner. Fearfully impetuous, as soon as this answer was given, he said, "Now I have replied to your questions, do you show me all the things you have got, for I want to see every thing, and be very good friends. I did not see you the first day, because, you being a stranger, it was necessary I should first look into the magic horn to see if all was right and safe; and now I can assure you that, while I saw I was safe, I also saw that your road would be prosperous. I am indeed delighted to see you, for neither my father, nor any of my forefathers, ever were honored with the company of a white man in all their lives."

My guns, clothes, and every thing were then inspected, and begged for in the most importunate manner. He asked for the picture-books, examined the birds with intense delight—even trying to insert under their feathers his long royal finger-nails, which are grown like a Chinaman's by these chiefs, to show they have a privilege to live on meat. Then turning to the animals, he roared over each one in turn as he examined them, and called out their names. My bull's-eye lantern he coveted so much, I had to pretend exceeding anger to stop his farther importunities. He then began again begging for lucifers, which charmed him so intensely I thought I should never get rid of him. He would have one box of them. I swore I could not part with them. He continued to beg, and I to resist. I offered a knife instead, but this he would not have, because the lucifers would be so valuable for his magical observances. On went the storm, till at last I drove him off with a pair of my slippers, which he had stuck his dirty feet into without my leave. I then refused to take his bullock because he had annoyed me. On his part, he was resolved not to beat the drum; but he graciously said he would think about it if I paid another lot of cloth equal to the second déolé I ought to have given him.

I began seriously to consider whether I should have this chief shot, as a reward for his oppressive treachery, and a warning to others; but the Pig said it was just what the Arabs were subjected to in Ubéna, and they found it best to pay down at once, and do all they were ordered. If I acted rightly, I would take the bullock, and then give the cloth; while Baraka said, "We will shoot him if you give the order; only remember Grant is behind, and if you commence a row you will have to fight the whole way, for every chief in the country will oppose you."

I then told the Pig and Baraka to settle at once. They no sooner did so than the drums beat, and Makaka, in the best humor possible, came over to say I had permission to go when I liked, but he hoped I would give him a gun and a box of lucifers. This was too provoking. The perpetual worry had given Baraka a fever, and had made me feel quite sick; so I said, if he ever mentioned a gun or lucifers again, I would fight the matter out with him, for I had not come there to be bullied. He then gave way, and begged I would allow my men to fire a volley outside his boma, as the Watŭta were living behind a small line of granitic hills flanking the west of his district, and he wished to show them what a powerful force he had got with him. This was permitted; but his wisdom in showing off was turned into ridicule; for the same evening the Watŭta made an attack on his villages and killed three of his subjects, but were deterred from committing farther damage by coming in contact with my men, who, as soon as they saw the Watŭta fighting, fired their muskets off in the air and drove them away, they themselves at the same time bolting into my camp, and as usual vaunting their prowess.

I then ordered a march for the next morning, and went out in the fields to take my regular observations for latitude. While engaged in this operation, Baraka, accompanied by Wadimoyo (Heart's-stream), another of my free men, approached me in great consternation, whispering to themselves. They said they had some fearful news to communicate, which, when I heard it, they knew would deter our progress: it was of such great moment and magnitude, they thought they could not deliver it then. I said, "What nonsense! out with it at once. Are we such chickens that we can not speak about matters like men? out with it at once."

Then Baraka said, "I have just heard from Makaka that a man who arrived from Usŭi only a few minutes ago has said Sŭwarora is so angry with the Arabs that he has detained one caravan of theirs in his country, and, separating the whole of their men, has placed each of them in different bomas, with orders to his village officers that, in case the Watŭta came into his country, without farther ceremony they were to be all put to death." I said, "Oh, Baraka, how can you be such a fool? Do you not see through this humbug? Makaka only wishes to keep us here to frighten away the Watŭta; for God's sake be a man, and don't be alarmed at such phantoms as these. You always are nagging at me that Bombay is the 'big' and you are the 'small' man. Bombay would never be frightened in this silly way. Now do you reflect that I have selected you for this journey, as it would, if you succeed with me in carrying out our object, stamp you forever as a man of great fame. Pray don't give way, but do your best to encourage the men, and let us march in the morning." On this, as on other occasions of the same kind, I tried to impart confidence by explaining, in allusion to Petherick's expedition, that I had arranged to meet white men coming up from the north. Baraka at last said, " All right—I am not afraid; I will do as you desire." But as the two were walking off, I heard Wadimoyo say to Baraka, "Is he not afraid now? Won't he go back?" which, if any thing, alarmed me more than the first intelligence; for I began to think that they, and not Makaka, had got up the story.

All night Makaka's men patroled the village, drumming and shouting to keep off the Watŭta, and the next morning, instead of a march, after striking my tent, I found that the whole of my porters, the Pig's children, were not to be found. They had gone off and hidden themselves, saying they were not such fools as to go any farther, as the Watŭta were out, and would cut us up on the road. This was sickening indeed.

I knew the porters had not gone far, so I told the Pig to bring them to me, that we might talk the matter over; but, say what I would, they all swore they would not advance a step farther. Most of them were formerly men of Utămbara. The Watŭta had invaded their country and totally destroyed it, killing all their wives and their children, and despoiling every thing they held dear to them. They did not wish to rob me, and would give up their hire, but not one step more would they advance. Makaka then came forward and said, "Just stop here with me until this ill wind blows over;" but Baraka, more in a fright at Makaka than at any one else, said No; he would do any thing rather than that; for Makaka's bullying had made him quite ill. I then said to my men, " If nothing else will suit you, the best plan I can think of is to return to Mihambo in Bogŭé, and there form a dépôt, where, having stored my property, I shall give the Pig a whole load, or 63 lbs., of Mzizima beads if he will take Baraka in disguise on to Sŭwarora, and ask him to send me eighty men, while I go back to Unyanyembé to see what men I can get from the late Mŭsa's establishment, and then we might bring on Grant, and move on in a body together." At first Baraka said, "Do you wish to have us killed? Do you think, if we went to Sŭwarora's, you would ever see us back again? You would wait and wait for us, but we should never return." To which I replied, "Oh, Baraka, do not think so! Bombay, if he were here, would go in a minute. Sŭwarora by this time knows I am coming, and you may depend on it he will be just as anxious to have us in Usŭi as Makaka is to keep us here, and he can not hurt us, as Rŭmanika is over him, and also expects us." Baraka then, in the most doleful manner, said he would go if the Pig would. The Pig, however, did not like it either, but said the matter was so important he would look into the magic horn all night, and give his answer next morning as soon as we arrived at Mihambo.

On arrival at Mihambo next day, all the porters brought their pay to me, and said they would not go, for nothing would induce them to advance a step farther. I said nothing; but, with "my heart in my shoes," I gave what I thought their due for coming so far, and motioned them to be off; then calling on the Pig for his decision, I tried to argue again, though I saw it was of no use, for there was not one of my own men who wished to go on. They were unanimous in saying Usŭi was a "fire," and I had no right to sacrifice them. The Pig then finally refused, saying three loads even would not tempt him, for all were opposed to it. Of what value, he observed, would the beads be to him if his life was lost? This was crushing; the whole camp was unanimous in opposing me. I then made Baraka place all my kit in the middle of the boma, which was a very strong one, keeping out only such beads as I wished him to use for the men's rations daily, and ordered him to select a few men who would return with me to Kazé; when I said, if I could not get all the men I wanted, I would try and induce some one, who would not fear, to go on to Usŭi; failing which, I would even walk back to Zanzibar for men, as nothing in the world would ever induce me to give up the journey.

This appeal did not move him; but, without a reply, he sullenly commenced collecting some men to accompany me back to Kazé. At first no one would go; they then mutinied for more beads, announcing all sorts of grievances, which they said they were always talking over to themselves, though I did not hear them. The greatest, however, that they could get up was, that I

Marginal note: Return to Mihambo, 19th.

always paid the Wanyamŭézi "temporaries" more than they got, though "permanents." "They were the flesh, and I was the knife;" I cut and did with them just as I liked, and they could not stand it any longer. However, they had to stand it; and next day, when I brought them to reason, I gave over the charge of my tent and property to Baraka, and commenced the return with a bad hitching cough, caused by those cold easterly winds that blow over the plateau during the six dry months of the year, and which are, I suppose, the Harmattan peculiar to Africa.

Next day I joined Grant once more, and found he had collected a few Sorombo men, hoping to follow after me. I then told him all my mishaps in Sorombo, as well as of the "blue-devil" frights that had seized all my men. I felt greatly alarmed about the prospects of the expedition, scarcely knowing what I should do. I resolved at last, if every thing else failed, to make up a raft at the southern end of the N'yanza, and try to go up to the Nile in that way. My cough daily grew worse. I could not lie or sleep on either side. Still my mind was so excited and anxious that, after remaining one day here to enjoy Grant's society, I pushed ahead again, taking Bombay with me, and had breakfast at Mchiméka's.

There I found the Pig, who now said he wished he had taken my offer of beads, for he had spoken with his chief, and saw that I was right. Baraka and the Wangŭana were humbugs, and had they not opposed his going, he would have gone then; even now, he said, he wished I would take him again with Bombay. Though half inclined to accept his offer, which would have saved a long trudge to Kazé, yet, as he had tricked me so often, I felt there would be no security unless I could get some coast interpreters, who would not side with the chiefs against me as he had done. From this I went on to Sirboko's, and spent the next day with him talking over my plans. The rafting up the lake he thought a good scheme; but he did not think I should ever get through Usŭi until all the Kazé merchants went north in a body, for it was no use trying to force my men against their inclinations; and if I did not take care how I handled them, he thought they would all desert.

My cough still grew worse, and became so bad that, while mounting a hill on entering Ungŭgŭ's the second day after, I blew and grunted like a broken-winded horse, and it became so distressing I had to halt a day. In two more marches, however, I reached Kazé, and put up with Mŭsa's eldest son, Abdalla, on the 2d of July, who now was transformed from a drunken slovenly boy into the appearance of a grand swell, squatting all day as his old father used to do. The house, however, did not feel the same; no men respected him as they had done his father. Sheikh Said was his clerk and constant companion, and the Tots were well fed on his goats—at my expense, however. On hearing my fix, Abdalla said I should have men; and, what's more, he would go with me as his father had promised to do; but he had a large caravan detained in Ugogo, and for that he must wait.

At that moment Manŭa Séra was in a boma at Kigŭé, in alliance with the chief of that place; but there was no hope for him now, as all the Arabs had allied themselves with the surrounding chiefs, including Kitambi, and had invested his position by forming a line, in concentric circles, four deep, cutting off his supplies of water within it, so that they daily expected to hear of his surrendering. The last news that had reached them brought intelligence of one man killed and two Arabs wounded; while, on the other side, Manŭa Séra had lost many men, and was put to such straits that he had called out if it was the Arabs' determination to kill him he would bolt again; to which the Arabs replied it was all the same; if he ran up to the top of the highest mountain or down into hell, they would follow after and put him to death.

3d. After much bother and many disappointments, as I was assured I could get no men to help me until after the war was over, and the Arabs had been to Ugogo, and had brought up their property, which was still lying there, I accepted two men as guides—one named Bŭi, a very small creature, with very high pretensions, who was given me by Abdalla; the other, a steady old traveler, named Nasib (or Fortune), who was given me by Fŭndi Sangoro. These two slaves, both of whom knew all the chiefs and languages up to and including Uganda, promised me faithfully they would go with Bombay on to Usŭi, and bring back porters in sufficient number for Grant and myself to go on together. They laughed at the stories I told them of the terror that had seized Baraka and all the Wangŭana, and told me, as old Mŭsa had often done before, that those men, especially Baraka, had from their first leaving Kazé made up their minds they would not enter Usŭi, or go any where very far north.

I placed those men on the same pay as Bombay, and then tried to buy some beads from the Arabs, as I saw it was absolutely necessary I should increase my fast-ebbing store if I ever hoped to reach Gondokoro. The attempt failed, as the Arabs would not sell at a rate under 2000 per cent.; and I wrote a letter to Colonel Rigby, ordering up fifty armed men laden with beads and pretty cloths—which would, I knew, cost me £1000 at the least—and left once more for the north on the 5th.

Marching slowly, as my men kept falling sick, I did not reach Grant again until the 11th. His health had greatly improved, and he had been dancing with Ukŭlima, as may be seen by the accompanying woodcut. So, as I was obliged to wait for a short time to get a native guide for Bŭi, Nasib, and Bombay, who would show them a jungle-path to Usŭi, we enjoyed our leisure hours in shooting Guinea-fowls for the pot. A report then came to us that Sŭwarora had heard with displeasure that I had been endeavoring to see him, but was deterred because evil reports concerning him had been spread. This unexpected good news delighted me exceedingly; confirmed my belief that Baraka, after all, was a coward, and induced me to recommend Bombay to make his cowardice more indisputable by going on and doing what he had feared to do. To which Bombay replied, "Of course I will. It is all folly pulling up for every ill wind that blows, because, until one actually *sees* there is something in it, you never can tell among these savages, '*shaves*' are so common in Africa. Besides, a man has but one life, and God is the director of every thing." "Bravo!" said I; "we will get on as long as you keep to that way of thinking."

At length a guide was obtained, and with him came some of those men of the Pig's who returned before; for they had a great desire to go with me, but had been deterred, they said, by Baraka and the rest of my men. Seeing all this, I changed my plans again, intending, on arrival at Baraka's camp, to prevail on the whole of the party to go with me direct, which I thought they could not now refuse, since Sŭwarora had sent us an invitation. Moreover, I did not like the idea of remaining still while the three men went forward, as it would be losing time.

These separations from Grant were most annoying, but they could not be helped; so, when all was settled here, I bade him adieu—both of us saying we would do our best—and set out on my journey, thinking what a terrible thing it was I could not prevail on my men to view things as I did. Neither my experi-

GRANT DANCING WITH UKÚLIMA.

ence with native chiefs, nor my money and guns, were of any use
to me, simply because my men were such incomprehensible fools,
though many of them who had traveled before ought to have
known better.

More reports came to us about Sŭwarora, all of the most inviting nature; but nothing else worth mentioning occurred until we
reached the border of Msalala, where an officer of M'yonga's, who
said he was a bigger man than his chief, demanded a tax, which
I refused, and the dispute ended in his snatching Nasib's gun out
of his hands.   I thought little of this affair myself beyond regretting the delay which it might occasion, as M'yonga, I knew,
would not permit such usage, if I chose to go round by his palace
and make a complaint.   Both Bŭi and Nasib, however, were so
greatly alarmed, that before I could say a word they got the gun
back again by paying four yards merikani.   We had continued
bickering again, for Bŭi had taken such fright at this kind of
rough handling, and the "push-ahead" manner in which I persisted "riding over the lords of the soil," that I could hardly
drag the party along.

However, on the 18th, after breakfasting at Rŭhé's, we walked
into Mihambo, and took all the camp by surprise.   I found the
Union Jack hoisted up on a flag-staff, high above all the trees, in
the boma.   Baraka said he had done this to show the Watŭta
that the place was occupied by men with guns—a necessary precaution, as all the villages in the neighborhood had, since my departure, been visited and plundered by them.   Lŭmérési, the chief
of the district, who lived ten miles to the eastward, had been constantly pressing him to leave this post and come to his palace, as
he felt greatly affronted at our having shunned him and put up
with Rŭhé.   He did not want property, he said, but he could not
bear that the strangers had lived with his mtoto, or child, which
Rŭhé was, and yet would not live with him.   He thought Baraka's determined obstinacy on this could only be caused by the influence of the head man of the village, and threatened that if
Baraka did not come to visit him at once, he would have the head
man beheaded.   Then, shifting round a bit, he thought of ordering his subjects to starve the visitors into submission, and said
he must have a hongo equal to Rŭhé's.   To all this Baraka replied that he was merely a servant, and as he had orders to stop
where he was, he could not leave it until I came; but, to show
there was no ill feeling toward him, he sent the chief a cloth.

These first explanations over, I entered my tent, in .which Baraka had been living, and there I found a lot of my brass wires on the ground, lying scattered about. I did not like the look of this, so ordered Bombay to resume his position of factotum, and count over the kit. While this was going on, a villager came to me with a wire, and asked me to change it for a cloth. I saw at once what the game was; so I asked my friend where he got it, on which he at once pointed to Baraka. I then heard the men who were standing round us say one to another in under tones, giggling with the fun of it, "Oh, what a shame of him! Did you hear what Bana said, and that fool's reply to it? What a shame of him to tell in that way." Without appearing to know, or rather to hear, the by-play that was going on, I now said to Baraka, "How is it this man has got one of my wires, for I told you not to touch or unpack them during my absence?" To which he coolly replied, in face of such evidence, "It is not one of your wires; I never gave away one of yours; there are lots more wires besides yours in the country. The man tells a falsehood; he had the wire before, but now, seeing your cloth open, wants to exchange it." "If that is the case," I said, taking things easy, "how is it you have opened my loads and scattered the wires about in the tent?" "Oh, that was to take care of them; for I thought, if they were left outside all night with the rest of the property, some one would steal them, and I should get the blame of it."

Farther parley was useless; for, though both my wires and cloths were short, still it was better not to kick up a row, when I had so much to do to keep all my men in good temper for the journey. Baraka then, wishing to beguile me, as he thought he could do, into believing him a wonderful man for both pluck and honesty, said he had had many battles to fight with the men since I had been gone to Kazé, for there were two strong parties in the camp; those who, during the late rebellion at Zanzibar, had belonged to the Arabs that sided with Sultan Majid, and were Royalists, and those who, having belonged to the rebellious Arabs, were on the opposite side. The battle commenced, he stated, by the one side abusing the other for their deeds during that rebellion, the rebels in this sort of contest proving themselves the stronger. But he, heading the Royalist party, soon reduced them to order, though only for a short while, as from that point they turned round to open mutiny for more rations; and some of the rebels tried to kill him, which, he said, they would have done had he not settled the matter by buying some cows for them. It was on this account he had been obliged to open my loads. And now he had told me the case, he hoped I would forgive him if he had done wrong. Now the real facts of the case were these, though I did not find them out at the time: Baraka had bought some slaves with my effects, and he had had a fight with some of my men because they tampered with his temporary wife—a princess he had picked up in Phŭnzé. To obtain her hand he had given ten necklaces of *my* beads to her mother, and had agreed to the condition that he should keep the girl during the journey; and after it was over, and he took her home, he would, if his wife pleased him, give her mother ten necklaces more.

Next day Baraka told me his heart shrank to the dimensions of a very small berry when he saw whom I had brought with me yesterday, meaning Bombay, and the same porters whom he had prevented going on with me before. I said, "Pooh! nonsense; have done with such excuses, and let us get away out of this as fast as we can. Now, like a good man, just use your influence with the chief of the village, and try and get from him five or six men to complete the number we want, and then we will work round the east of Sorombo up to Usŭi, for Sŭwarora has invited us to him." This, however, was not so easy; for Lŭmérési, having heard of my arrival, sent his Wanyapara, or graybeards, to beg I would visit him. He had never seen a white man in all his life, neither had his father, nor any of his forefathers, although he had often been down to the coast; I must come and see him, as I had seen his mtoto Rŭhé. He did not want property; it was only the pleasure of my company that he wanted, to enable him to tell all his friends what a great man had lived in his house.

This was terrible: I saw at once that all my difficulties in Sorombo would have to be gone through again if I went there, and groaned when I thought what a trick the Pig had played me when I first of all came to this place; for if I had gone on then, as I wished, I should have slipped past Lŭmérési without his knowing it.

I had to get up a storm at the graybeards, and said I could not stand going out of my road to see any one now, for I had already lost so much time by Makaka's trickery in Sorombo. Bŭi then, quaking with fright at my obstinacy, said, "You must—indeed you must—give in and do with these savage chiefs as the Arabs when they travel, for I will not be a party to riding roughshod over them." Still I stuck out, and the graybeards departed to tell their chief of it. Next morning he sent them back again to say he would not be cheated out of his rights as the chief of the district. Still I would not give in, and the whole day kept "jawing" without effect, for I could get no man to go with me until the chief gave his sanction. I then tried to send Bombay off with Bŭi, Nasib, and their guide, by night; but, though Bombay was willing, the other two hung back on the old plea. In this state of perplexity, Bŭi begged I would allow him to go over to Lŭmérési and see what he could do with a present. Bŭi really now was my only stand-by, so I sent him off, and next had the mortification to find that he had been humbugged by honeyed words, as Baraka had been with Makaka, into believing that Lŭmérési was a good man, who really had no other desire at heart than the love of seeing me. His boma, he said, did not lie much out of my line, and he did not wish a stitch of my cloth. So far from detaining me, he would give me as many men as I wanted; and, as an earnest of his good intentions, he sent his copper hatchet, the badge of office as chief of the district, as a guarantee for me.

To wait here any longer after this, I knew, would be a mere waste of time, so I ordered my men to pack up that moment, and we all marched over at once to Lŭmérési's, when we put up in his boma. Lŭmérési was not in then, but, on his arrival at night, he beat all his drums to celebrate the

To Lŭmérési's, 23d.

Lŭmérési's Residence.

event, and fired a musket, in reply to which I fired three shots. The same night, while sitting out to make astronomical observations, I became deadly cold; so much so, that the instant I had taken the star to fix my position, I turned into bed, but could not get up again; for the cough that had stuck to me for a month then became so violent, heightened by fever succeeding the cold fit, that before the next morning I was so reduced I could not stand. For the last month, too, I had not been able to sleep on either side, as interior pressure, caused by doing so, provoked the cough; but now I had, in addition, to be propped in position to get any repose whatever. The symptoms, altogether, were rather alarming, for the heart felt inflamed and ready to burst, pricking and twingeing with every breath, which was exceedingly aggravated by constant coughing, when streams of phlegm and bile were ejected. The left arm felt half paralyzed, the left nostril was choked with mucus, and on the centre of the left shoulderblade I felt a pain as if some one was branding me with a hot iron. All this was constant; and, in addition, I repeatedly felt severe pains—rather paroxysms of fearful twinges—in the spleen, liver, and lungs, while during my sleep I had all sorts of absurd dreams: for instance, I planned a march across Africa with Sir Roderick Murchison; and I fancied some curious creatures, half men and half monkeys, came into my camp to inform me that Petherick was waiting in boats at the southwest corner of the N'yanza, etc., etc.

Though my mind was so weak and excited when I woke up from these trances, I thought of nothing but the march, and how I could get out of Lŭmérési's hands. He, with the most benign countenance, came in to see me the very first thing in the morning, as he said, to inquire after my health; when, to please him as much as I could, I had a guard of honor drawn up at the tent door to fire a salute as he entered; then giving him my iron camp-chair to sit upon, which tickled him much—for he was very corpulent, and he thought its legs would break down with his weight—we had a long talk, though it was as much as I could do to remember any thing, my brain was so excited and weak. Kind as he looked and spoke, he forgot all his promises about coveting my property, and scarcely got over the first salutation before he began begging for many things that he saw, and more especially for a déolé, in order that he might wear it on all great occasions, to show his contemporaries what a magnanimous man his white

visitor was. I soon lost my temper while striving to settle the
hongo. Lŭmérési would have a déolé, and I would not admit
that I had one.

23d to 31st. Next morning I was too weak to speak moderately, and roared more like a madman than a rational being, as, breaking his faith, he persisted in bullying me. The day after, I took
pills and blistered my chest all over; still Lŭmérési would not
let me alone, nor come to any kind of terms until the 25th, when
he said he would take a certain number of pretty common cloths
for his children if I would throw in a red blanket for himself. I
jumped at this concession with the greatest eagerness, paid down
my cloths on the spot, and, thinking I was free at last, ordered a
hammock to be slung on a pole, that I might leave the next day.
Next morning, however, on seeing me actually preparing to start,
Lŭmérési found he could not let me go until I increased the tax
by three more cloths, as some of his family complained that they
had got nothing. After some badgering, I paid what he asked
for, and ordered the men to carry me out of the palace before
any thing else was done, for I would not sleep another night where
I was. Lŭmérési then stood in my way, and said he would never
allow a man of his country to give me any assistance until I was
well, for he could not bear the idea of hearing it said that, after
taking so many cloths from me, he had allowed me to die in the
jungles, and dissuaded my men from obeying my orders.

In vain I appealed to his mercy, declaring that the only chance
left me of saving my life would be from the change of air in the
hammock as I marched along. He would not listen, professing
humanity while he meant plunder; and I now found he was determined not to beat the drum until I had paid him some more,
which he was to think over and settle next day. When the next
day came he would not come near me, as he said I must possess
a déolé, otherwise I would not venture on to Karagŭé; for nobody ever yet "saw" Rŭmanika without one. This suspension
of business was worse than the rows; I felt very miserable, and
became worse. At last, on my offering him any thing that he
might consider an equivalent for the déolé if he would but beat
the drums of satisfaction, he said I might consider myself his prisoner instead of his guest if I persisted in my obstinacy in not giving him Rŭmanika's déolé, and then again peremptorily ordered
all of his subjects not to assist me in moving a load. After this,
veering round for a moment on the generous tack, he offered me
a cow, which I declined.

1*st* to 4*th*. Still I rejected the offered cow until the 2d, when, finding him as dogged as ever, at the advice of my men I accept- ed it, hoping thus to please him; but it was no use, for he now said he must have two déolés, or he would never allow me to leave his palace. Every day matters got worse and worse. Mfŭm- bi, the small chief of Sorombo, came over, in an Oily-Gammon kind of manner, to say Makaka had sent him over to present his com- pliments to me, and express his sorrow on hearing that I had fallen sick here. He farther informed me that the road was closed between this and Usŭi, for he had just been fighting there, and had killed the chief Gomba, burnt down all his villages, and dis- persed all the men in the jungle, where they now resided, plun- dering every man who passed that way. This gratuitous, wick- ed, humbugging terrifier helped to cause another defeat. It was all nonsense, I knew, but both Bŭi and Nasib, taking fright, beg- ged for their discharges. In fearful alarm and anxiety, I then begged them to have patience and see the hongo settled first, for there was no necessity, at any rate, for immediate hurry; I wish- ed them to go on ahead with Bombay, as in four days they could reach Sŭwarora's. But they said they could not hear of it; they would not go a step beyond this. All the chiefs on ahead would do the same as Lŭmérési; the whole country was roused. I had not even half enough cloths to satisfy the Wasŭi; and my faith- ful followers would never consent to be witness to my being " torn to pieces."

5*th* and 6*th*. The whole day and half of the next went in dis- cussions. At last, able for the first time to sit up a little, I suc- ceeded in prevailing on Bŭi to promise he would go to Usŭi as soon as the hongo was settled, provided, as he said, I took on my- self all responsibilities of the result. This cheered me so greatly, I had my chair placed under a tree and smoked my first pipe. On seeing this, all my men struck up a dance, to the sound of the drums, which they carried on throughout the whole night, never ceasing until the evening of the next day. These protracted ca- perings were to be considered as their congratulation for my im- provement in health; for, until I got into my chair, they always thought I was going to die. They then told me, with great mirth and good mimicry, of many absurd scenes which, owing to the in- flamed state of my brain, had taken place during my interviews with Lŭmérési. Bombay at this time very foolishly told Lŭmé- rési, if he " really wanted a déolé," he must send to Grant for one. This set the chief raving. He knew there was one in my box, he said, and, unless I gave it, the one with Grant must be brought, for under no circumstances would he allow of my proceeding northward until that was given him. Bŭi and Nasib then gave me the slip, and slept that night in a neighboring boma without my knowledge.

7th to 9th. As things had now gone so far, I gave Lŭmérési the déolé I had stored away for Rŭmanika, telling him, at the same time as he took it, that he was robbing Rŭmanika, and not myself; but I hoped, now I had given it, he would beat the drums. The scoundrel only laughed as he wrapped my beautiful silk over his great broad shoulders, and said, " Yes, this will complete our present of friendship; now then for the hongo: I must have exactly double of all you have given." This Sorombo trick I attributed to the instigation of Makaka, for these savages never fail to take their revenge when they can. I had doubled back from his country, and now he was cutting me off in front. I expected as much when the oily blackguard Mfŭmbi came over from his chief to ask after my health; so, judging from my experience with Makaka, I told Lŭmérési at once to tell me what he considered his due, for this fearful haggling was killing me by inches. I had no more déolés, but would make that up in brass wire. He then fixed the hongo at fifteen masango or brass-wire bracelets, sixteen cloths of sorts, and a hundred necklaces of sami-sami or red coral beads, which was to pay for Grant as well as myself. I paid it down on the spot; the drums beat the " satisfaction," and I ordered the march with the greatest relief of mind possible.

But Bŭi and Nasib were not to be found; they had bolted. The shock nearly killed me. I had walked all the way to Kazé and back again for these men, to show mine a good example—had given them pay and treble rations, the same as Bombay and Baraka—and yet they chose to desert. I knew not what to do, for it appeared to me that, do what I would, we would never succeed; and in my weakness of body and mind I actually cried like a child over the whole affair. I would rather have died than have failed in my journey, and yet failure seemed at this juncture inevitable.

8th. As I had no interpreters, and could not go forward myself, I made up my mind at once to send back all my men, with Bombay, to Grant; after joining whom, Bombay would go back to Kazé again for other interpreters, and on his return would pick

up Grant, and bring him on here. This sudden decision set all
my men up in a flame; they swore it was no use my trying to go
on to Karagŭé; they would not go with me; they did not come
here to be killed. If I chose to lose my life, it was no business
of theirs, but they would not be witness to ·it. They all wanted
their discharge at once; they would not run away, but must have
a letter of satisfaction, and then they would go back to their
homes at Zanzibar. But when they found they lost all their arguments and could not move me, they said they would go back
for Grant, but when they had done that duty, then they would
take their leave.

10th to 15th. This business being at last settled, I wrote to
Grant on the subject, and sent all the men off who were not sick.
Thinking then how I could best cure the disease that was keeping me down, as I found the blister of no use, I tried to stick a
packing-needle, used as a seton, into my side; but, finding it was
not sharp enough, in such weak hands as mine, to go through my
skin, I got Baraka to try; and he failing too, I then made him fire
me, for the coughing was so incessant I could get no sleep at
night. I had now nothing whatever to think of but making
dodges for lying easy, and for relieving my pains, or else for cooking strong broths to give me strength, for my legs were reduced
to the appearance of pipe-sticks, until the 15th, when Baraka, in
the same doleful manner as in Sorombo, came to me and said he
had something to communicate, which was so terrible, if I heard
it I should give up the march. Lŭmérési was his authority, but
he would not tell it until Grant arrived. I said to him, "Let us
wait till Grant arrives; we shall then have some one with us who
won't shrink from whispers," meaning Bombay; and so I let the
matter drop for the time being. But when Grant came we had it
out of him, and found this terrible mystery all hung on Lŭmérési's prognostications that we never should get through Usŭi with
so little cloth.

16th to 19th. At night I had such a terrible air-catching fit, and
made such a noise while trying to fill my lungs, that it alarmed
all the camp, so much so that my men rushed into my tent to see
if I was dying. Lŭmérési, in the morning, then went on a visiting excursion into the district, but no sooner left than the chief
of Isamiro, whose place lies close to. the N'yanza, came here to
visit him (17th); but, after waiting a day to make friends with
me, he departed (18th), as I heard afterward, to tell his great Mhŭ-

ma chief, Rohinda, the ruler of Ukhanga, to which district this
state of Bogŭé belongs, what sort of presents I had given to Lŭmérési. He was, in fact, a spy whom Rohinda had sent to ascertain what exactions had been made from me, as he, being the
great chief, was entitled to the most of them himself. On Lŭmérési's return, all the men of the village, as well as mine, set up a
dance, beating the drums all day and all night.

20*th* to 21*st*. Next night they had to beat their drums for a
very different purpose, as the Watŭta, after lifting all of Makaka's
cattle in Sorombo, came hovering about, and declared they would
never cease fighting until they had lifted all those that Lŭmérési
harbored round his boma; for it so happened that Lŭmérési allowed a large party of Watosi, alias Wahŭma, to keep their cattle
in large stalls all round his boma, and these the Watŭta had now
set their hearts upon. After a little reflection, however, they
thought better of it, as they were afraid to come in at once on account of my guns.

Most gladdening news this day came in to cheer me. A large
mixed caravan of Arabs and coast-men, arriving from Karagŭé,
announced that both Rŭmanika and Sŭwarora were anxiously
looking out for us, wondering why we did not come. So great,
indeed, was Sŭwarora's desire to see us, that he had sent four men
to invite us, and they would have been here now, only that one
of them fell sick on the way, and the rest had to stop for him. I
can not say what pleasure this gave me; my fortune, I thought,
was made; and so I told Baraka, who, instead of rejoicing with
me, only shook his head at it, and pretended he did not believe
the news to be true. Without loss of time I wrote off to Grant,
and got these men to carry the letter.

Next day (22d) the Wasŭi from Sŭwarora arrived. They were
a very gentle, nice-dispositioned-looking set of men—small, but
well knit together. They advanced to my tent with much seeming grace; then knelt at my feet, and began clapping their hands
together, saying, at the same time, "My great chief, my great
chief, I hope you are well; for Sŭwarora, having heard of your
detention here, has sent us over to assure you that all those reports that have been circulated regarding his ill treatment of caravans are without foundation; he is sorry for what has happened
to deter your march, and hopes you will at once come to visit
him." I then told them all that had happened—how Grant and
myself were situated—and begged them to assist me by going off

to Grant's camp to inspire all the men there with confidence, and
bring my rear property to me; saying, as they agreed to do so,
"Here are some cloths and some beads for your expenses, and
when you return I will give you more." Baraka at once, seeing
this, told me they were not trustworthy, for at Mihambo an old
man had come there and tried to inveigle him in the same manner, but he kicked him out of the camp, because he knew he was
a touter, who wished merely to allure him with sweet words to
fleece him afterward. I then wrote to Grant another letter to be
delivered by these men.

Lŭmérési no sooner heard of the presents I had given them
than he flew into a passion, called them impostors, abused them
for not speaking to him before they came to me, and said he
would not allow them to go. High words then ensued. I said
the business was mine, and not his; he had no right to interfere,
and they should go. Still Lŭmérési was obstinate, and determined they should not, for I was his guest; he would not allow any
one to defraud me. It was a great insult to himself, if true, that
Sŭwarora should attempt to snatch me out of his house; and he
could not bear to see me take these strangers by the hand, when,
as we have seen, it took him so long to entice me to his den, and
he could not prevail over me until he actually sent his copper
hatchet.

When this breeze blew over by Lŭmérési's walking away, I
told the Wasŭi not to mind him, but to do just as I bid them.
They said they had their orders to bring me, and if Lŭmérési
would not allow them to go for Grant, they would stop where
they were, for they knew that if Sŭwarora found them delaying
long, he would send more men to look after them. There was
no peace yet, however; for Lŭmérési, finding them quietly settled down eating with my men, ordered them out of his district,
threatening force if they did not comply at once. I tried my
best for them, but the Wasŭi, fearing to stop any longer, said they
would take leave to see Sŭwarora, and in eight days more they
would come back again, bringing something with them, the sight
of which would make Lŭmérési quake. Farther words were now
useless, so I gave them more cloth to keep them up to the mark,
and sent them off. Baraka, who seemed to think this generosity
a bit of insanity, grumbled that if I had cloths to throw away it
would have been better had I disposed of them to my own men.

Next day (26th), as I was still unwell, I sent four men to Grant with inquiries how he was getting on, and a request for medicines. The messengers took four days to bring back the information that Bombay had not returned from Kazé, but that Grant, having got assistance, hoped to break ground about the 5th of next month. They brought me, at the same time, information that the Watŭta had invested Rŭhé's, after clearing off all the cattle in the surrounding villages, and had proclaimed their intention of serving out Lŭmérési next. In consequence of this, Lŭmérési daily assembled his graybeards and had councils of war in his drum-house; but, though his subjects sent to him constantly for troops, he would not assist them.

Another caravan then arrived (31st) from Karagŭé, in which I found an old friend, of half Arab breed, called Saim, who, while I was residing with Sheikh Snay at Kazé on my former expedition, taught me the way to make plantain wine. He, like the rest of the porters in the caravan, wore a shirt of fig-tree bark called mbŭgŭ. As I shall have frequently to use this word in the course of the Journal, I may here give an explanation of its meaning. The porter here mentioned told me that the people about the equator all wore this kind of covering, and made it up of numerous pieces of bark sewn together, which they stripped from the trees after cutting once round the trunk above and below, and then once more down the tree from the upper to the lower circular cutting. This operation did not kill the trees, because, if they covered the wound, while it was fresh, well over with plantain-leaves, shoots grew down from above, and a new bark came all over it. The way they softened the bark, to make it like cloth, was by immersion in water, and a good strong application of a mill-headed mallet, which ribbed it like corduroy.* Saim told me he had lived ten years in Uganda, had crossed the Nile, and had traded eastward as far as the Masai country. He thought the N'yanza was the source of the Rŭvŭma River; as the river which drained the N'yanza, after passing between Uganda and Usoga, went through Unyoro, and then all round the Tanganyika Lake into the Indian Ocean, south of Zanzibar.

* If one asked the name of a tree, and it happened to be the kind from which this cloth was made, the answer would be "mbŭgŭ." If, again, the question was as to the bark, the same answer; and the same if one saw the shirt and asked what it was. Hence I could not determine whether the word had been originally the name of the tree, of its bark, or of the article made from the bark, though I am inclined to think it is the bark, as there are many varieties of these trees, which, besides being called mbŭgŭ, had their own particular names.

Kiganda, he also said, he knew as well as his own tongue; and as I wanted an interpreter, he would gladly take service with me. This was just what I wanted—a heaven-born stroke of luck. I seized at his offer with avidity, gave him a new suit of clothes, which made him look quite a gentleman, and arranged to send him next day with a letter to Grant.

1st and 2d. A great hubbub and confusion now seized all the place, for the Watŭta were out, and had killed a woman of the place who had formerly been seized by them in war, but had since escaped and resided here. To avenge this, Lŭmérési headed his host, and was accompanied by my men; but they succeeded in nothing save in frightening off their enemies, and regaining possession of the body of the dead woman. Then another hubbub arose, for it was discovered that three Wahŭma women were missing (2d); and, as they did not turn up again, Lŭmérési suspected the men of the caravan, which left with Saim, must have taken them off as slaves. He sent for the chief of the caravan, and had him brought back to account for this business. Of course the man swore he knew nothing about the matter, while Lŭmérési swore he should stop there a prisoner until the women were freed, as it was not the first time his women had been stolen in this manner. About the same time a man of this place, who had been to Sorombo to purchase cows, came in with a herd, and was at once seized by Lŭmérési; for, during his absence, one of Lŭmérési's daughters had been discovered to be with child, and she, on being asked who was the cause of it, pointed out that man. To compensate for damage done to himself, as his daughter by this means had become reduced to half her market value, Lŭmérési seized all the cattle this man had brought with him.

3d to 10th. When two days had elapsed, one of the three missing Wahŭma women was discovered in a village close by. As she said she had absconded because her husband had ill treated her, she was flogged, to teach her better conduct. It was reported they had been seen in M'yonga's establishment; and I was at the same time informed that the husbands who were out in search of them would return, as M'yonga was likely to demand a price for them if they were claimed, in virtue of their being his rightful property under the acknowledged law of bŭni, or findings-keepings.

For the next four days nothing but wars and rumors of wars could be heard. The Watŭta were out in all directions plundering cattle and burning villages, and the Wahŭma of this place had taken such fright, they made a stealthy march with all their herds to a neighboring chief, to whom it happened that one of Lŭmérési's graybeards was on a visit. They thus caught a Tartar; for the graybeard no sooner saw them than he went and flogged them all back again, rebuking them on the way for their ingratitude to their chief, who had taken them in when they sought his shelter, and was now deserted by them on the first alarm of war.

10*th*. Wishing now to gain farther intelligence of Grant, I ordered some of my men to carry a letter to him; but they all feared the Watŭta meeting them on the way, and would not. Just then a report came in that one of Lŭmérési's sons, who had gone near the capital of Ukhanga to purchase cows, was seized by Rohinda in consequence of the Isamiro chief telling him that Lŭmérési had taken untold wealth from me, and he was to be detained there a prisoner until Lŭmérési either disgorged, or sent me on to be fleeced again. Lŭmérési, of course, was greatly perplexed at this, and sought my advice, but could get nothing out of me, for I laughed in my sleeve, and told him such was the consequence of his having been too greedy.

11*th* to 15*th*. Masŭdi with his caravan arrived from Mchiméka —Ungŭrŭé, "the Pig," who had led me astray, was, by the way, his kirangozi or caravan leader. Masŭdi told us he had suffered most severely from losses by his men running away, one after the other, as soon as they received their pay. He thought Grant would soon join me, as, the harvest being all in, the men about Rŭngŭa would naturally be anxious for service. He had had fearful work with M'yonga, having paid him a gun, some gunpowder, and a great quantity of cloth; and he had to give the same to Rŭhé, with the addition of twenty brass wires, one load of mzizima, and one load of red coral beads. This was startling, and induced me to send all the men I could prudently spare off to Grant at once, cautioning him to avoid Rŭhé's, as Lŭmérési had promised me he would not allow one other thing to be taken from me. Lŭmérési by this time was improving, from lessons on the policy of moderation which I had been teaching him; for when he tried to squeeze as much more out of Masŭdi as Rŭhé had taken, he gave way, and let him off cheaply at my intercession. He had seen enough to be persuaded that this unlimited taxation or plunder system would turn out a losing game, such

as Unyanyembé and Ugogo were at that time suffering from.
Moreover, he was rather put to shame by my saying, "Pray, who
now is biggest, Ruhé or yourself? for any one entering this country would suspect that he was, as he levies the first tax, and gives
people to understand that, by their paying it, the whole district
will be free to them; such, at any rate, he told me, and so it appears he told Masŭdi. If you are the sultan, and will take my
advice, I would strongly recommend your teaching Rŭhé a lesson
by taking from him what the Arabs paid, and giving it back to
Masŭdi."

At midnight (16th) I was startled in my sleep by the hurried
tramp of several men, who rushed in to say they were Grant's
porters—Bogŭé men who had deserted him. Grant, they said,
in incoherent, short, rapid, and excited sentences, was left by them
standing under a tree, with nothing but his gun in his hand.
All the Wangŭana had been either killed or driven away by
M'yonga's men, who all turned out and fell upon the caravan,
shooting, spearing, and plundering, until nothing was left. The
porters then, seeing Grant all alone, unable to help him, bolted
off to inform me and Lŭmérési, as the best thing they could do.
Though disbelieving the story in all its minutiæ, I felt that something serious must have happened; so, without a moment's delay,
I sent off the last of my men strong enough to walk to succor
Grant, carrying with them a bag of beads. Baraka then stepped
outside my tent, and said in a loud voice, purposely for my edifica-
tion, "There, now, what is the use of thinking any more about going to Karagŭé? I said all along it was impossible;" upon hearing
which I had him up before all the remaining men, and gave him
a lecture, saying, happen what would, I must die or go on with
the journey, for shame would not allow me to give way as Baraka
was doing. Baraka replied he was not afraid; he only meant to
imply that men could not act against impossibilities. "Impossibilities!" I said; "what is impossible? Could I not go on as a
servant with the first caravan, or buy up a whole caravan if I
liked? What is impossible? For God's sake don't try any more
to frighten my men, for you have nearly killed me already in doing so."

Next day (17th) I received a letter from Grant, narrating the
whole of his catastrophes:

"In the Jungles, near M'yonga's, 16th Sept., 1861.

"My dear Speke,—The caravan was attacked, plundered, and the men driven to the winds, while marching this morning into M'yonga's country.

" Awaking at cock-crow, I roused the camp, all anxious to re-join you; and while the loads were being packed, my attention was drawn to an angry discussion between the head men and seven or eight armed fellows sent by Sultan M'yonga, to insist on my putting up for the day in his village. They were summarily told that as *you* had already made him a present, he need not expect a visit from *me*. Adhering, I doubt not, to their master's instructions, they officiously constituted themselves our guides till we chose to strike off their path, when, quickly heading our party, they stopped the way, planted their spears, and *dared* our advance!

"This menace made us firmer in our determination, and we swept past the spears. After we had marched unmolested for some seven miles, a loud yelping from the woods excited our attention, and a sudden rush was made upon us by, say, two hundred men, who came down *seemingly* in great glee. In an instant, at the caravan's centre, they fastened upon the poor porters. The struggle was short; and with the threat of an arrow or spear at their breasts, men were robbed of their cloths and ornaments, loads were yielded and run away with before resistance could be organized; only three men of a hundred stood by me; the others, whose only *thought* was their lives, fled into the woods, where I went shouting for them. One man, little Rahan—rip as he is—stood with cocked gun, defending his load against five savages with uplifted spears. No one else could be seen. Two or three were reported killed; some were wounded. Beads, boxes, cloths, etc., lay strewed about the woods. In fact, I felt wrecked. My attempt to go and demand redress from the sultan was resisted, and, in utter despair, I seated myself among a mass of rascals' jeering round me, and insolent after the success of the day. Several were dressed in the very cloths, etc., they had stolen from my men.

"In the afternoon, about fifteen men and loads were brought me, with a message from the sultan that the attack had been a *mistake* of his subjects—that one man had had a hand cut off for it, and that all the property would be restored!

"Yours sincerely,   J. W. Grant."

Now, judging from the message sent to Grant by M'yonga, it appeared to me that his men had mistaken their chief's orders, and had gone one step beyond his intentions. It was obvious that the chief merely intended to prevent Grant from passing through or evading his district without paying a hongo, else he would not have sent his men to invite him to his palace, doubtless with instructions, if necessary, to use force. This appears the more evident from the fact of his subsequent contrition, and finding it necessary to send excuses when the property was in his hands; for these chiefs, grasping as they are, know they must conform to some kind of system, to save themselves from a general war, or the avoidance of their territory by all travelers in future. To assist Grant, I begged Lŭmérési to send him some aid in men at once; but he refused, on the plea that M'yonga was at war with him, and would kill them if they went. This was all the more provoking, as Grant, in a letter next evening, told me he could not get all his men together again, and wished to know what should be done. He had recovered all the property except six loads of beads, eighty yards of American sheeting, and many minor articles, besides what had been rifled more or less from every load. In the same letter he asked me to deliver up a Mhŭma woman to a man who came with the bearers of his missive, as she had made love to Saim at Ukŭlima's, and had bolted with my men to escape from her husband.

On inquiring into this matter, she told me her face had been her misfortune, for the man who now claimed her stole her from her parents at Ujiji, and forcibly made her his wife, but ever since had ill treated her, often thrashing her, and never giving her proper food or clothing. It was on this account she fell in love with Saim; for he, taking compassion on her doleful stories, had promised to keep her as long as he traveled with me, and in the end to send her back to her parents at Ujiji. She was a beautiful woman, with gazelle eyes, oval face, high thin nose, and fine lips, and would have made a good match for Saim, who had a good deal of Arab blood in him, and was therefore, in my opinion, much of the same mixed Shem-Hamitic breed. But, as I did not want more women in my camp, I gave her some beads, and sent her off with the messenger who claimed her, much against my own feelings. I now proposed to Grant that, as Lŭmérési's territories extended to within eight miles of M'yonga's, he should try to move over the Msalala border by relays, when I would send

some Bogŭé men to meet him; for, though Lŭmérési would not
risk sending his men into the clutches of M'yonga, he was most
anxious to have another white visitor.

20th and *21st.* I again urged Lŭmérési to help on Grant, saying it was incumbent on him to call M'yonga to account for maltreating Grant's porters, who were his own subjects, else the road
would be shut up—he would lose all the hongos he laid on caravans—and he would not be able to send his own ivory down to
the coast. This appeal had its effect: he called on his men to
volunteer, and twelve porters came forward, who no sooner left
than in came another letter from Grant, informing me that he had
collected almost enough men to march with, and that M'yonga
had returned one of the six missing loads, and promised to right
him in every thing.

Next day, however, I had from Grant two very opposite accounts—one, in the morning, full of exultation, in which he said
he hoped to reach Rŭhé's this very day, as his complement of
porters was then completed; while by the other, which came in
the evening, I was shocked to hear that M'yonga, after returning
all the loads, much reduced by rifling, had demanded as a hongo
two guns, two boxes of ammunition, forty brass wires, and 160
yards of American sheeting, in default of which he, Grant, must
lend M'yonga ten Wangŭana to build a boma on the west of his
district, to enable him to fight some Wasonga who were invading
his territory, otherwise he would not allow Grant to move from
his palace. Grant knew not what to do. He dared not part with
the guns, because he knew it was against my principle, and therefore deferred the answer until he heard from me, although all his
already collected porters were getting fidgety, and two had bolted. In this fearful fix, I sent Baraka off with strict orders to
bring Grant away at any price, except the threatened sacrifice of
men, guns, and ammunition, which I would not listen to, as one
more day's delay might end in farther exactions; at the same
time, I cautioned him to save my property as far as he could, for
it was to him that M'yonga had formerly said that what I paid
him should do for all.

Some of M'yonga's men who had plundered Grant now "caught
a Tartar." After rifling his loads of a kilyndo, or bark box of
beads, they, it appeared, received orders from M'yonga to sell a
lot of female slaves, among whom were the two Wahŭma women
who had absconded from this. The men in charge, not knowing

their history, brought them for sale into this district, where they
were instantly recognized by some of Lŭmérési's men, and brought
in to him.   The case was not examined at once, Lŭmérési happening to be absent; so, to make good their time, the men in
charge brought their beads to me to be exchanged for something
else, not knowing that both camps were mine, and that they held
my beads and not Grant's.   Of course I took them from them,
but did not give them a flogging, as I knew if I did so they
would at once retaliate upon Grant.   The poor Wahŭma women,
as soon as Lŭmérési arrived, were put to death by their husbands, because, by becoming slaves, they had broken the laws of
their race.

22*d* to 24*th*. At last I began to recover. All this exciting
news, with the prospect of soon seeing Grant, did me a world of
good; so much so, that I began shooting small birds for specimens—watching the blacksmiths as they made tools, spears, and

Blacksmith's Shop.

bracelets—and doctoring some of the Wahŭma women who came
to be treated for ophthalmia, in return for which they gave me
milk.   The milk, however, I could not boil excepting in secrecy,
else they would have stopped their donations on the plea that
this process would be an incantation or bewitchment, from which
their cattle would fall sick and dry up.   I now succeeded in getting Lŭmérési to send his Wanyapara to go and threaten M'yonga that if he did not release Grant at once, we would combine to
force him to do so.   They, however, left too late, for the hongo
had been settled, as I was informed by a letter from Grant next
day, brought to me by Bombay, who had just returned from Kazé

after six weeks' absence. He brought with him old Nasib and another man, and told me both Būi and Nasib had hidden themselves in a boma close to Lŭmérési's the day when my hongo was settled; but they bolted the instant the drums beat, and my men fired guns to celebrate the event, supposing that the noise was occasioned by our fighting with Lŭmérési. These cowards then made straight for Kazé, when Fŭndi Sangoro gave Nasib a flogging for deserting me, and made him so ashamed of his conduct that he said he would never do it again. Būi also was flogged, but, admitting himself to be a coward, was sent to the "right-about." With him Bombay also brought three new déolés, for which I had to pay $160, and news that the war with Manŭa Séra was not then over. He had effected his escape in the usual manner, and was leading the Arabs another long march after him.

Expecting to meet Grant this morning (25th), I strolled as far as my strength and wind would allow me toward Rŭhé's; but I was sold, for Rŭhé had detained him for a hongo. Lŭmérési also having heard of it, tried to interpose, according to a plan arranged between us in case of such a thing happening, by sending his officers to Rŭhé, with an order not to check my "brother's" march, as I had settled accounts for all. Later in the day, however, I heard from Grant that Rŭhé would not let him go until he paid sixteen pretty cloths, six wires, one gun, one box of ammunition, and one load of mzizima beads, coolly saying I had only given him a trifle, under the condition that, when the big caravan arrived, Grant would make good the rest. I immediately read this letter to Lŭmérési, and asked him how I should answer it, as Grant refused to pay any thing until I gave the order.

To which Lŭmérési replied, Rŭhé, "my child," could not dare to interfere with Grant after his officers arrived, and advised me to wait until the evening. At all events, if there were any farther impediments, he himself would go over there with a force and release Grant. In the evening another messenger arrived from Grant, giving a list of his losses and expenses at M'yonga's. They amounted to an equivalent of eight loads, and were as follows: 100 yards cloth, and 4600 necklaces of beads (these had been set aside as the wages paid to the porters, but, being in my custody, I had to make them good); 300 necklaces of beads stolen from the loads; one brass wire stolen; one sword-bayonet stolen; Grant's looking-glass stolen; one saw stolen; one box of ammunition stolen. Then paid in hongo 160 yards cloth; 150

necklaces; one scarlet blanket, double; one case of ammunition; ten brass wires. Lastly, there was one donkey beaten to death by the savages. This was the worst of all; for this poor brute carried me on the former journey to the southern end of the N'yanza, and, in consequence, was a great pet.

As nothing farther transpired, and I was all in the dark (26th), I wrote to Grant telling him of my interviews with Lŭmérési, and requesting him to pay nothing; but it was too late, for Grant, to my inexpressible delight, was the next person I saw; he walked into camp, and then we had a good laugh over all our misfortunes. Poor Grant, he had indeed had a most troublesome time of it. The scoundrel Rŭhé, who only laughed at Lŭmérési's orders, had stopped his getting supplies of food for himself and his men; told him it was lucky that he came direct to the palace, for full preparations had been made for stopping him had he attempted to avoid it; would not listen to any reference being made to myself; badgered and bullied over every article that he extracted; and, finally, when he found compliance with his extortionate requests was not readily granted, he beat the war-drums to frighten the porters, and ordered the caravan out of his palace, to where he said they would find his men ready to fight it out with them. It happened that Grant had just given Rŭhé a gun when my note arrived, on which they made an agreement that it was to be restored, provided that, after the full knowledge of all these transactions had reached us, it was both Lŭmérési's and my desire that it should be so.

I called Lŭmérési (27th), and begged he would show whether he was the chief or not by requiring Rŭhé to disgorge the property he had taken from me. His Wanyapara had been despised, and I had been most unjustly treated. Upon this the old chief hung down his head, and said it touched his heart more than words could tell to hear my complaint, for until I came that way no one had come, and I had paid him handsomely. He fully appreciated the good service I had done to him and his country by opening a road which all caravans for the future would follow if properly dealt with. Having two heads in a country was a most dangerous thing, but it could not be helped for the present, as his hands were too completely occupied already. There were Rohinda, the Watŭta, and M'yonga, whom he must settle with before he could attend to Rŭhé; but when he was free, then Rŭhé should know who was the chief. To bring the matter to a climax, Mrs.

Lŭmérési then said she ought to have something, because Rŭhé was her son, while Lŭmérési was only her second husband and consort, for Rŭhé was born to her by her former husband. She therefore was queen. Difficulties now commenced again (28th). All the Wangŭana struck, and said they would go no farther. I argued—they argued; they wanted more pay—I would not give more. Bombay, who appeared the only one of my men anxious to go on with Grant and myself, advised me to give in, else they would all run away, he said. I still stuck out, saying that if they did go, they should be seized on the coast and cast into jail for desertion. I had sent for fifty more men on the same terms as themselves, and nothing in the world would make me alter what had been established at the British Consulate. There all their engagements were written down in the office-book, and the consul was our judge.

29th to 4th. This shut them up, but at night two of them deserted; the Wanyamŭézi porters also deserted, and I had to find more. While this was going on, I wrote letters and packed up my specimens, and sent them back by my late valet, Rahan, who also got orders to direct Sheikh Said to seize the two men who deserted, and take them down chained to the coast when he went there. On the 4th, Lŭmérési was again greatly perplexed by his sovereign Rohinda calling on him for some cloths; he must have thirty at least, else he would not give up Lŭmérési's son. Farther, he commanded in a bullying tone that all the Wahŭma who were with Lŭmérési should be sent to him at once; adding, at the same time, if his royal mandate was not complied with as soon as he expected, he would at once send a force to seize Lŭmérési, and place another man in his stead to rule over the district.

Lŭmérési, on hearing this, first consulted me, saying his chief was displeased with him, accusing him of being too proud in having at once two such distinguished guests, and meant by these acts only to humble him. I replied, if that was the case, the sooner he allowed us to go, the better it would be for him; and, reminding him of his original promise to give me assistance on to Usŭi, said he could do so now with a very good grace.

Quite approving himself of this suggestion, Lŭmérési then gave me one of his officers to be my guide: his name was Sangizo. This man no sooner received his orders than, proud of his office as the guide of such a distinguished caravan, he set to work to find us porters. Meanwhile my Wasŭi friends, who left on the 25th of August, returned, bearing what might be called Sŭwarora's mace—a long rod of brass bound up in stick charms, and called kaquenzingiriri, "the commander of all things." This, they said, was their chief's invitation to us. Sŭwarora did not want a hongo; he only wished to see us, and sent this kaquenzingiriri to command us respect wherever we went.

5th. Without seeing us again, Lŭmérési, evidently ashamed of the power held over him by this rod of Sŭwarora's, walked off in the night, leaving word that he was on his way to Rŭhé's, to get back my gun and all the other things that had been taken from Grant. The same night a large herd of cattle was stolen from the boma without any one knowing it; so next morning, when the loss was discovered, all the Wahŭma set off on the spoor to track them down, but with what effect I never knew.

As I had now men enough to remove half our property, I made a start of it, leaving Grant to bring up the rest. To Mŭamba, *6th.* I believe I was a most miserable spectre in appearance, puffing and blowing at each step I took, with shoulder drooping, and left arm hanging like a dead log, which I was unable ever to swing. Grant, remarking this, told me then, although from a friendly delicacy he had abstained from saying so earlier, that my condition, when he first saw me on rejoining, gave him a sickening shock. Next day (7th) he came up with the rest of the property, carried by men who had taken service for that one march only.

Before us now lay a wilderness of five marches' duration, as the few villages that once lined it had all been depopulated by the Sorombo people and the Watŭta. Halt, *8th.* We therefore had to lay in rations for those days; and as no men could be found who would take service to Karagŭé, we filled up our complement with men at exorbitant wages to carry our things on to Usŭi. At this place, to our intense joy, three of Sheikh Said's boys came to us with a letter from Rigby; but, on opening it, our spirits at once fell far below zero, for it only informed us that he had sent us all kinds of nice things, and letters from home, which were packed up in boxes, and dispatched from the coast on the 30th of October, 1860.

The boys then told me that a merchant, nicknamed Msopora, had left the boxes in Ugogo, in charge of some of those Arabs who were detained there, while he went rapidly round by the south, following up the Rŭaha River to Usanga and Usenga, whence he struck across to Kazé. Sheikh Said, they said, sent his particular respects to me; he had heard of Grant's disasters with great alarm. If he could be of service, he would readily come to me; but he had dreamed three times that he saw me marching into Cairo, which, as three times were lucky, he was sure would prove good, and he begged I would still keep my nose well to the front, and push boldly on. Manŭa Séra was still in the field, and all was uncertain. Bombay then told me—he had forgotten to do so before—that when he was last at Kazé, Sheikh Said told him he was sure we would succeed if both he and myself pulled together, although it was well known no one else of my party wished to go northward.

With at last a sufficiency of porters, we all set out together, walking over a new style of country. Instead of the constantly-recurring outcrops of granite, as in Unyamŭézi, with valleys between, there were only two lines of little hills visible, one right and one left of us, a good way off; while the ground over which we were traveling, instead of being confined like a valley, rose in long high swells of sandstone formation, covered with small forest-trees, among which flowers like primroses, only very much larger, and mostly of a pink color, were frequently met with. Indeed, we ought all to have been happy together, for all my men were paid and rationed trebly—far better than they would have been if they had been traveling with any one else; but I had not paid all, as they thought, proportionably, and therefore there were constant heart-burnings, with strikes and rows every day. It was useless to tell them that they were all paid according to their own agreements—that all short-service men had a right to expect more in proportion to their work than long-service ones; they called it all love and partiality, and in their envy *would* think themselves ill used.

To Kagongo, 9*th.*

At night the kirangozi would harangue the camp, cautioning all hands to keep together on the line of march, as the Watŭta were constantly hovering about, and the men should not squabble and fight with their master, else no more white men would come this way again. On the 11th we were out of Bogŭé, in the district of Ugomba, and next march brought us into Ugombé (12th), where we crossed the Ukongo nullah, draining westward to the Malagarazi River. Here some of the porters, attempting to bolt, were intercepted by my coast-men and

To Kagéra, 10*th.*

had a fight of it, for they fired arrows, and in return the coast-men cut their bows. The whole camp, of course, was in a blaze at this; their tribe was insulted, and they would not stand it, until Bombay put down their pride with a few strings of beads, as the best means of restoring peace in the camp.

At this place we were visited by the chief of the district, Pongo Halt, 13th and 14th. (Bush-boc), who had left his palace to see us and invite us his way, for he feared we might give him the slip by going west into Uyofŭ. He sent us a cow, and said he should like some return; for Masŭdi, who had gone ahead, only gave him a trifle, professing to be our vanguard, and telling him that as soon as we came with the large caravan we would satisfy him to his heart's content. We wished for an interview, but he would not see us, as he was engaged looking into his magic horn, with an endeavor to see what sort of men we were, as none of our sort had ever come that way before.

The old sort of thing occurred again. I sent him one kitambi and eight yards of kiniki, explaining how fearfully I was reduced from theft and desertions, and begging he would have mercy; but, instead of doing so, he sent the things back in a huff, after a whole day's delay, and said he required, besides, one sahari, one kitambi, and eight yards kiniki. In a moment I sent them over, and begged he would beat the drums; but no, he thought he was entitled to ten brass wires in addition, and would accept them at his palace the next day, as he could not think of allowing us to leave his country until we had done him that honor, else all the surrounding chiefs would call him inhospitable.

Too knowing now to be caught with such chaff, I told him, To Pongo's residence, 15th. through Bombay, if he would consider the ten brass wires final, I would give them, and then go to his palace, not otherwise. He acceded to this, but no sooner got them than he broke his faith, and said he must either have more pretty cloths, or five more brass wires, and then, without doubt, he would beat the drums. A long badgering bargain ensued, at which I made all my men be present as witnesses, and we finally concluded the hongo with four more brass wires.

The drums then no sooner beat the satisfaction than the Wa-sŭi mace-bearers, in the most feeling and good-mannered possible manner, dropped down on their knees before me, and congratulated me on the cessation of this tormenting business. Feeling much freer, we now went over and put up in Pongo's palace, for

we had to halt there a day to collect more porters, as half my men
had just bolted. This was by no means an easy job, for all my
American sheeting was out, and so was the kiniki. Pongo then
for the first time showed himself, sneaking about with an escort,
hiding his head in a cloth lest our " evil eyes" might bewitch him.
Still he did us a good turn; for on the 16th he persuaded his men
to take service with us at the enormous hire of ten necklaces of
beads per man for every day's march—nearly ten times what an
Arab pays. Fowls were as·plentiful here as elsewhere, though
the people only kept them to sell to travelers, or else for cutting
them open for divining purposes by inspection of their blood and
bones.

From the frying-pan we went into the fire in crossing from
Ugombé into the district of Wanga, where we beat
up the chief N'yarŭwamba, and at once went into the
hongo business. He offered a cow to commence with, which I
would not accept until the tax was paid, and then I made my offering of two wires, one kitambi, and one kisŭtŭ. Badgering then
commenced: I must add two wires, and six makete or necklaces
of mzizima beads, the latter being due to the chief for negotiating
the tax. When this addition was paid, we should be freed by
beat of drum.

To N'yarŭ-
wamba's, 17th.

I complied at once, by way of offering a special mark of respect
and friendship, and on the reliance that he would keep his word.
The scoundrel, however, no sooner got the articles, than he said a
man had just come there to inform him that I gave Pongo ten
wires and ten cloths; he, therefore, could not be satisfied until I
added one more wire, when, without fail, he would beat the drums.
It was given, after many angry words; but it was the old story
over again—he would have one more wire and a cloth, or else
he would not allow us to proceed on the morrow. My men, this
time really provoked, said they would fight it out—a king breaking his word in that way! But, in the end, the demand had to
be paid; and at last, at 9 P.M., the drums beat the satisfaction.

From this we went on to the north end of Wanga, in front of
which was a wilderness, separating the possessions of
Rohinda from those of Sŭwarora. We put up in a
boma, but were not long ensconced there when the villagers got
up a pretext for a quarrel, thinking they could plunder us of all
our goods, and began pitching into my men. We, however,
proved more than a match for them. Our show of guns fright-

To border of
Ukhanga, 18th.

ened them all out of the place; my men then gave chase, firing off in the air, which sent them flying over the fields, and left us to do there as we liked until night, when a few of the villagers came back and took up their abode with us quietly. Next, after dark, the little village was on the alert again. The Watŭta were out marching, and it was rumored that they were bound for N'yarŭwamba's. The porters who were engaged at Pongo's now gave us the slip; we were consequently detained here next day (19th), when, after engaging a fresh set, we crossed the wilderness, and in Usŭi put up with Sŭwarora's border officer of this post, N'yamanira.

Here we were again brought to a standstill.

CHAPTER VII.

U S Ŭ I.

Taxation recommenced.—A great Doctor.—Sŭwarora Pillaging.—The Arabs.—
Conference with an Embassador from Uganda.—Disputes in Camp.—Rivalry of
Bombay and Baraka.—Departure from the inhospitable Districts.

WE were now in Usŭi, and so the mace-bearers, being on their
own ground, forgot their manners, and peremptorily
demanded their pay before they would allow us to
move one step farther. At first I tried to stave the
matter off, promising great rewards if they took us quickly on to
Sŭwarora; but they would take no alternative—their rights were
four wires each. I could not afford such a sum, and tried to beat
them down, but without effect; for they said they had it in their
power to detain us here a whole month, and they could get us
bullied at every stage by the officers of the stations. No threats
of reporting them to their chief had any effect; so, knowing that
treachery in these countries was a powerful enemy, I ordered
them to be paid. N'yamanira, the Mkŭngŭ, then gave us a goat
and two pots of pombé, begging, at the same time, for four wires,
which I paid, hoping thus to get on in the morning.

I then made friends with him, and found he was a great doctor
as well as an officer. In front of his hut he had his church or
uganga—a tree, in which was fixed a blaue boc's horn charged
with magic powder, and a zebra's hoof, suspended by a string
over a pot of water sunk in the earth below it. His badges of
office he had tied on his head; the butt of a shell, representing
the officer's badge, being fixed on the forehead, while a small
sheep's horn, fixed jauntily over the temple, denoted that he was
a magician. Wishing to try my powers in magical arts, as I
laughed at his church, he begged me to produce an everlasting
spring of water by simply scratching the ground. He, however,
drew short up, to the intense delight of my men, on my promising
that I would do so if he made one first.

At night, 22d, a steel scabbard and some cloths were extracted
from our camp, so I begged my friend, the great doctor, would

(margin note: Halt, border Usŭi, 20th and 21st.)

show us the use of his horn. This was promised, but never performed. I then wished to leave, as the Wasŭi guides, on receiving their pay, promised we should; but they deferred, on the plea
that one of them must see their chief first, and get him to frank
us through, else, they said, we shóuld be torn to pieces. I said I
thought the kaquenzingiriri could do this; but they said, "No;
Sŭwarora must be told first of your arrival, to prepare him properly for your coming; so stop here for three days with two of us,
while the third one goes to the palace and returns again; for you
know the chiefs of these countries do not feel safe until they have
had a look at the uganga."

One of them then went away, but no sooner had left than a man
named Makinga arrived to invite us on, as he said, at his adopted
brother K'yengo's request. Makinga then told us that Sŭwarora,
on first hearing that we were coming, became greatly afraid, and
said he would not let us set eyes on his country, as he was sure
we were king-dethroners; but, referring for opinion to Dr. K'yengo, his fears were overcome by the doctor assuring him that he
had seen hosts of our sort at Zanzibar; and he knew, moreover,
that some years ago we had been to Ujiji and to Ukéréwé without having done any harm in those places; and, farther, since
Mŭsa had sent word that I had done my best to subdue the war
at Unyanyembé, and had promised to do my best here, he, Sŭwarora, had been anxiously watching our movements, and longed
for our arrival. This looked famous, and it was agreed we should
move the next morning. Just then a new light broke in on my
defeat at Sorombo, for with Makinga I recognized one of my
former porters, who I had supposed was a "child" of the Pig's.
This man now-said before all my men, Baraka included, that he
wished to accept the load of mzizima I had offered the Pig if he
would go forward with Baraka and tell Sŭwarora I wanted some
porters to help me to reach him. He was not a "child" of the
Pig's, but a "child" of K'yengo's; and as Baraka would not allow
him to accept the load of mzizima, he went on to K'yengo by
himself, and told all that had happened. It was now quite clear
what motives induced Sŭwarora to send out the three Wasŭi;
but how I blessed Baraka for this in my heart, though I said
nothing about it to him, for fear of his playing some more treacherous tricks. Grant then told me Baraka had been frightened at
Mininga by a blackguard mganga, to whom he would not give a
present, into the belief that our journey would encounter some

terrible mishap; for, when the M'yonga catastrophe happened, he thought that a fulfillment of the mganga's prophecy.

I wished to move in the morning (23d), and had all hands ready, but was told by Makinga he must be settled with first. His dues for the present were four brass wires, and as many more when we reached the palace. I could not stand this: we were literally, as Mŭsa said we should be, being "torn to pieces;" so I appealed to the mace-bearers, protested that Makinga could have no claims on me, as he was not a man of Usŭi, but a native of Utambara, and brought on a row. On the other hand, as he could not refute this, Makinga swore the mace was all a pretense, and set a fighting with the Wasŭi and all the men in turn.

To put a stop to this, I ordered a halt, and called on the district officer to assist us, on which he said he would escort us on to Sŭwarora's if we would stop till next morning. This was agreed to; but in the night we were robbed of three goats, which he said he could not allow to be passed over, lest Sŭwarora might hear of it, and he would get into a scrape. He pressed us strongly to stop another day while he sought for them, but I told him I would not, as his magic powder was weak, else he would have found the scabbard we lost long before this.

At last we got under way, and, after winding through a long To Virembo's, 24th.   forest, we emerged on the first of the populous parts of Usŭi, a most convulsed-looking country, of well-rounded hills composed of sandstone. In all the parts not under cultivation they were covered with brushwood. Here the little grass-hut villages were not fenced by a boma, but were hidden in large fields of plantains. Cattle were numerous, kept by the Wahŭma, who would not sell their milk to us because we ate fowls and a bean called maharagŭé.

Happily, no one tried to pillage us here, so on we went to Vi- To Vikora's, 25th.   kora's, another officer, living at N'yakasenyé, under a sandstone hill, faced with a dike of white quartz, over which leaped a small stream of water—a seventy-feet drop—which, it is said, Sŭwarora sometimes paid homage to when the land was oppressed by drought. Vikora's father it was whom Sirboko of Mininga shot. Usually he was very severe with merchants in consequence of that act; but he did not molest us, as the messenger who went on to Sŭwarora returned here just as we arrived, to say we must come on at once, as Sŭwarora was anxious to see us, and had ordered his Wakungŭ not to molest us.

Thieves that night entered our ring-fence of thorns, and stole a cloth from off one of my men while he was sleeping.

We set down Sŭwarora, after this very polite message, "a reg-ular trump," and walked up the hill of N'yakasenyé with considerable mirth, singing his praises; but we no sooner planted ourselves on the summit than we sang a very different tune. We were ordered to stop by a huge body of men, and to pay toll.

To Kariwami's, 26th.

Sŭwarora, on second thoughts, had changed his mind, or else he had been overruled by two of his officers—Kariwami, who lived here, and Virembo, who lived two stages back, but were then with their chief. There was no help for it, so I ordered the camp to be formed, and sent Nasib and the mace-bearers at once off to the palace to express to his highness how insulted I felt as his guest, being stopped in this manner, even when I had his kaquenzingiriri with me as his authority that I was invited there as a guest. I was not a merchant who carried merchandise, but a prince like himself, come on a friendly mission to see him and Rŭmanika. I was waiting at night for the return of the messengers, and sitting out with my sextant observing the stars, to fix my position, when some daring thieves, in the dark bushes close by, accosted two of the women of the camp, pretending a desire to know what I was doing. They were no sooner told by the unsuspecting women, than they whipped off their clothes and ran away with them, allowing their victims to pass me in a state of absolute nudity. I could stand this thieving no longer. My goats and other things had been taken away without causing me much distress of mind, but now, after this shocking event, I ordered my men to shoot at any thieves that came near them.

This night one was shot, without any mistake about it; for the next morning we tracked him by his blood, and afterward heard he had died of his wound. The Wasŭi elders, contrary to my expectation, then came and congratulated us on our success. They thought us most wonderful men, and possessed of supernatural powers; for the thief in question was a magician, who until now was thought to be invulnerable. Indeed, they said Arabs with enormous caravans had often been plundered by these people; but, though they had so many more guns than ourselves, they never succeeded in killing one.

Halt, 27th.

Nasib then returned to inform us that the king had heard our complaint, and was sorry for it, but said he could not interfere with the rights of his officers. He did not wish himself to take any thing from us, and hoped we would come on to him as soon as we had satisfied his officers with the trifle they wanted. Virembo then sent us some pombé by his officers, and begged us to have patience, for he was then fleecing Masŭdi at the encamping-ground near the palace. This place was alive with thieves. During the day they lured my men into their huts by inviting them to dinner; but, when they got them, they stripped them stark-naked and let them go again, while at night they stoned our camp. After this, one more was shot dead and two others wounded.

I knew that Sŭwarora's message was all humbug, and that his officers merely kept about one per cent. of what they took from travelers, paying the balance into the royal coffers. Thinking I was now well in for a good fleecing myself, I sent Bombay off to Masŭdi's camp to tell Insangéz, who was traveling with him on a mission of his master's, old Mŭsa's son, that I would reward him handsomely if he would, on arrival at Karagŭé, get Rŭmanika to send us his mace here in the same way as Sŭwarora had done to help us out of Bogŭé, as he knew Mŭsa at one time said he would go with us to Karagŭé in person. When Bombay was gone, Virembo then deputed Kariwami to take the hongo for both at once, mildly requiring 40 wires, 80 cloths, and 400 necklaces of every kind of bead we possessed. This was, indeed, too much of a joke. ·I complained of all the losses I had suffered, and begged for mercy; but all he said, after waiting the whole day, was, "Do not stick at trifles; for, after settling with us, you will have to give as much more to Vikora, who lives down below."

Halt, 28th.

Next morning, as I said I could not by any means pay such an exorbitant tax as was demanded, Kariwami begged me to make an offer, which I did by sending him four wires. These, of course, were rejected with scorn; so, in addition, I sent an old box. That, too, was thrown back on me, as nothing short of 20 wires, 40 cloths, and 200 necklaces of all sorts of beads would satisfy him; and this I ought to be contented to pay, as he had been so moderate because I was the king's guest, and had been so reduced by robbery. I now sent six wires more, and said this was the last I could give—they were worth so many goats to me—and now, by giving them away, I should have to live on grain like a poor man, though I was a prince in my own

Halt, 29th.

country, just like Sŭwarora. Surely Sŭwarora could not permit this if he knew it; and if they would not suffice, I should have to stop here until called again by Sŭwarora. The ruffian, on hearing this, allowed the wires to lie in his hut, and said he was going away, but hoped, when he returned, I should have, as I had got no cloths, 20 wires, and 1000 necklaces of extra length, strung and all ready for him.

Just then Bombay returned flushed with the excitement of a great success. He had been in Masŭdi's camp, and had delivered my message to Insangéz. Masŭdi, he said, had been there a fortnight unable to settle his hongo, for the great Mkama had not deigned to see him, though the Arab had been daily to his palace requesting an interview. "Well," I said, "that is all very interesting, but what next? will the big king see us?" "Oh no; by the very best good fortune in the world, on going into the palace I saw Sŭwarora, and spoke to him at once; but he was, so tremendously drunk he could not understand me." "What luck was there in that?" I asked. On which Bombay said, "Oh, every body in the place congratulated me on my success in having obtained an interview with that great monarch the very first day, when Arabs had seldom that privilege under one full month of squatting; even Masŭdi had not yet seen him." To which Nasib also added, "Ah! yes—indeed it is so—a monstrous success; there is great ceremony as well as business at these courts; you will better see what I mean when you get to Uganda. These Wahŭma kings are not like those you ever saw in Unyamŭézi or any where else; they have officers and soldiers like Said Majid, the Sultan at Zanzibar." "Well," said I to Bombay, "what was Sŭwarora like?" "Oh, he is a very fine man—just as tall, and in the face very like Grant; in fact, if Grant were black you would not know the difference." "And were his officers drunk too?" "Oh yes, they were all drunk together; men were bringing in pombé all day." "And did you get drunk?" "Oh yes," said Bombay, grinning, and showing his whole row of sharp-pointed teeth, "they *would* make me drink; and then they showed me the place they assigned for your camp when you come over there. It was not in the palace, but outside, without a tree near it—any thing but a nice-looking residence." I then sent Bombay to work at the hongo business; but, after haggling till night with Kariwami, he was told he must bring fourteen brass wires, two cloths, and five mukhnai of kanyéra, or white porcelain beads, which, reduced, amounted to three hundred necklaces, else he said I might stop there for a month.

At last I settled this confounded hongo by paying seven additional wires in lieu of the cloth; and, delighted at the termination of this tedious affair, I ordered a march. Like magic, however, Vikora turned up, and said we must wait until he was settled with. His rank was the same as the others, and one bead less than I had given them he would not take. I fought all the day out, but the next morning, as he deputed the officers to take nine wires, these were given, and then we went on with the journey.

Halt, 30th.

Tripping along over the hill, we descended to a deep miry water-course, full of bulrushes, then over another hill, from the heights of which we saw Sŭwarora's palace lying down in the Uthungŭ valley, behind which again rose an-

To Uthungŭ, 31st.

Uthungŭ Valley.

other hill of sandstone, faced on the top with a dike of white quartz. The scene was very striking, for the palace inclosures, of great extent, were well laid out to give effect. Three circles of milk-bush, one within the other, formed the boma, or ring-fence. The chief's hut (I do not think him worthy the name of king, since the kingdom is divided in two) was three times as large as any of the others, and stood by itself at the farther end; while the smaller huts, containing his officers and domestics, were arranged in little groups within the circle, at certain distances apart from one another, sufficient to allow of their stalling their cattle at night.

On descending into the Uthungŭ valley, Grant, who was pre-

OUR CAMP IN THE UTHUNGŬ VALLEY.   THE WASŬI BRINGING PROVISIONS FOR SALE.

ceding the men, found Makinga opposed to the progress of the
caravan until his dues were paid. He was a stranger like ourselves, and was consequently treated with scorn, until he tried to
maintain what he called his right by pulling the loads off my
men's shoulders, whereupon Grant cowed· him into submission,
and all went on again—not to the palace, as we had supposed,
but, by the direction of the mace-bearers, to the huts of Sŭwarora's commander-in-chief, two miles from the palace; and here we
found Masŭdi's camp also. We had no sooner formed camp for
ourselves and arranged all our loads, than the eternal Vikora,
whom I thought we had settled with before we started, made a
claim for some more wire, cloth, and beads, as he had not received as much as Kariwami and Virembo. Of course I would
not listen to this, as I had paid what his men asked for, and that
was enough for me. Just then Masŭdi, with the other Arabs
who were traveling with him, came over to pay us a visit, and
inquire what we thought of the Usŭi taxes. He had just concluded his hongo to Sŭwarora by paying 80 wires, 120 yards of
cloth, and 130 lbs. of beads, while he had also paid to every
officer from 20 to 40 wires, as well as cloths and beads. On hearing of my transactions, he gave it as his opinion that I had got
off surprisingly well.

Next morning (1st) Masŭdi and his party started for Karagŭé.
They had been more than a year between this and Kazé, trying
all the time to get along. Provisions here were abundant—
hawked about by the people, who wore a very neat skin kilt
strapped round the waist, but otherwise were decorated like the
Wanyamŭézi. It was difficult to say who were of true breed
here, for the intercourse of the natives with the Wahŭma and the
Wanyamŭézi produced a great variety of facial features among
the people. Nowhere did I ever see so many men and women
with hazel eyes as at this place.

In the evening, a Uganda man, by name N'yamgundŭ, came to
pay his respects to us. He was dressed in a large skin wrapper,
made up of a number of very small antelope skins: it was as soft
as kid, and just as well sewn as our gloves. To our surprise, the
manners of the man were quite in keeping with his becoming
dress. I was enchanted with his appearance, and so were my
men, though no one could speak to him but Nasib, who told us
he knew him before. He was the brother of the dowager queen
of Uganda, and, along with a proper body of officers, he had been

sent by Mtésa, the present king of Uganda, to demand the daughter of Sŭwarora, as reports had reached his king that she was surprisingly beautiful. They had been here more than a year, during which time this beautiful virgin had died; and now Sŭwarora, fearful of the great king's wrath, consequent on his procrastinations, was endeavoring to make amends for it by sending, instead of his daughter, a suitable tribute in wires. I thought it not wonderful that we should be fleeced.

Next day (2d) Sirhid paid us a visit, and said he was the first man in the state. He certainly was a nice-looking young man, with a good deal of the Wahŭma blood in him. Flashily dressed in colored cloths and a turban, he sat down in one of our chairs as if he had been accustomed to such a seat all his life, and spoke with great suavity. I explained our difficulties as those of great men in misfortune; and, after listening to our tale, he said he would tell Sŭwarora of the way we had been plundered, and impress upon him to deal lightly with us. I said I had brought with me a few articles of European manufacture for Sŭwarora, which I hoped would be accepted if I presented them, for they were such things as only great men like his chief ever possessed. One was a five-barreled pistol, another a large block-tin box, and so forth; but, after looking at them, and seeing the pistol fired, he said, "No; you must not show these things at first, or the Mkama might get frightened, thinking them magic. I might lose my head for presuming to offer them, and then there is no knowing what might happen afterward." "Then can I not see him at once and pay my respects, for I have come a great way to obtain that pleasure?" "No," said Sirhid, "I will see him first; for he is not a man like myself, but requires to be well assured before he sees any body." "Then why did he invite me here?" "He heard that Makaka, and afterward Lŭmérési, had stopped your progress; and as he wished to see what you were like, he ordered me to send some men to you, which, as you know, I did twice. He wishes to see you, but does not like doing things in a hurry. Superstition, you know, preys on these men's minds who have not seen the world like you and myself." Sirhid then said he would ask Sŭwarora to grant us an interview as soon as possible; then, while leaving, he begged for the iron chair he had sat upon; but, hearing we did not know how to sit on the ground, and therefore could not spare it, he withdrew without any more words about it.

Virembo then said (3d) he must have some more wire and beads, as his proxy Kariwami had been satisfied with too little. I drove him off in a huff, but he soon came back again with half the hongo I had paid to Kariwami, and said he must have some cloths, or he would not have any thing. As fortune decreed it, just then Sirhid dropped in, and stopped his importunity for the time by saying that if we had possessed cloths his men must have known it, for they had been traveling with us. No sooner, however, did Virembo turn tail than the Sirhid gave us a broad hint that he usually received a trifle from the Arabs before he made an attempt at arranging the hongo with Sŭwarora. Any trifle would do, but he preferred cloth.

This was rather perplexing. Sirhid knew very well that I had a small reserve of pretty cloths, though all the common ones had been expended; so, to keep in good terms with him who was to be our intercessor, I said I would give him the last I had got if he would not tell Sŭwarora or any one else what I had done. Of course he was quite ready to undertake the condition, so I gave him two pretty cloths, and he, in return, gave me two goats. But when this little business had been transacted, to my surprise he said, "I have orders from Sŭwarora to be absent five days to doctor a sick relation of his, for there is no man in the country so skilled in medicines as myself; but, while I am gone, I will leave Karambŭlé, my brother, to officiate in my stead about taking your hongo; but the work will not commence until to-morrow, for I must see Sŭwarora on the subject myself first."

Irungŭ, a very fine-looking man of Uganda, now called on me and begged for beads. He said his king had heard of our approach, and was most anxious to see us. Hearing this, I begged him to wait here until my hongo was paid, that we might travel on to Uganda together. He said, No, he could not wait, for he had been detained here a whole year already; but, if I liked, he would leave some of his children behind with me, as their presence would intimidate Sŭwarora, and incite him to let us off quickly.

I then begged him to convey a Colt's six-chamber revolving rifle to his king, Mtésa, as an earnest that I was a prince most desirous of seeing him. No one, I said, but myself could tell what dangers and difficulties I had encountered to come this far for the purpose, and all was owing to his great fame, as the king of kings, having reached me even as far off as Zanzibar. The embassador would not take the rifle, lest his master, who had never seen such a wonderful weapon before, should think he had brought him a malign charm, and he would be in danger of losing his head. I then tried to prevail on him to take a knife and some other pretty things, but he feared them all; so, as a last chance—for I wished to send some token, by way of card or letter, for announcing my approach and securing the road—I gave him a red sixpenny pocket-handkerchief, which he accepted; and he then told me he was surprised I had come all this way round to Uganda, when the road by the Masai country was so much shorter. He told me how, shortly after the late king of Uganda, Sunna, died, and before Mtésa had been selected by the officers of the country to be their king, an Arab caravan came across the Masai as far as Usoga, and begged for permission to enter Uganda; but, as the country was disturbed by the elections, the officers of the state advised the Arabs to wait, or come again when the king was elected. I told him I had heard of this before, but also heard that those Arabs had met with great disasters, owing to the turbulence of the Masai. To which he replied, "That is true; there were great difficulties in those times, but now the Masai country was in better order; and as Mtésa was most anxious to open that line, he would give me as many men as I liked if I wished to go home that way."

This was pleasant information, but not quite new, for the Arabs had told me Mtésa was so anxious to open that route, he had frequently offered to aid them in it himself. Still it was most gratifying to myself, as I had written to the Geographical Society, on leaving Bogŭé, that if I found Petherick in Uganda, or on the northern end of the N'yanza, so that the Nile question was settled, I would endeavor to reach Zanzibar *via* the Masai country. In former days, I knew, the kings of Uganda were in the habit of sending men to Karagŭé when they heard that Arabs wished to visit them—even as many as two hundred at a time—to carry their kit; so I now begged Irungŭ to tell Mtésa that I should want at least sixty men; and then, on his promising he would be my commissioner, I gave him the beads he had begged for himself.

4th to 6th. Karambŭlé now told us to string our beads on the fibre of the mwalé-tree, which was sold here by the Wasŭi, as he intended to live in the palace for a couple of days, arranging with Sŭwarora what tax we should have to pay, after which he would come and take it from us; but we must mind and be ready, for whatever Sŭwarora said, it must be done instantly. There was no such thing as haggling with him; you must pay and be off at once, failing which, you might be detained a whole month before there would be an opportunity to speak on the subject again. Beads were then served out to all my men to be strung, a certain quantity to every khambi or mess, and our work was progressing; but next day we heard that Karambŭlé was sick, or feigning to be so, and therefore had never gone to the palace at all. On the 6th, provoked at last by the shameful manner in which we were treated, I sent word to him to say, if he did not go at once I would go myself, and force my way in with my guns, for I could not submit to being treated like a slave, stuck out here in the jungle with nothing to do but shoot for specimens, or make collections of rocks, etc. This brought on another row; for he said both Virembo and Vikora had returned their hongos, and until their tongues were quieted he could not speak to Sŭwarora.

To expedite matters (7th), as our daily consumption in camp was a tax of itself, I gave these tormenting creatures one wire, one pretty cloth, and five hundred necklaces of white beads, which were no sooner accepted than Karambŭlé, in the same way as Sirhid had done, said it would be greatly to my advantage if I gave him something worth having before he saw the Mkama. Only too glad to begin work, I gave him a red blanket, called joho, and five strings of mzizima beads, which were equal to fifty of the common white.

8th and 9th. All this time nothing but confusion reigned in camp, khambi fighting against khambi. Both men and women got drunk, while from outside we were tormented by the Wasŭi, both men and women pertinaciously pressing into our hut, watching us eat, and begging in the most shameless manner. They did not know the word bakhshish, or present; but, as bad as the Egyptians, they held out their hands, patted their bellies, and said kaniwani (my friend), until we were sick of the sound of that word. Still it was impossible to dislike these simple creatures altogether, they were such perfect children. If we threw water at them to drive them away, they came back again, thinking it fun.

Ten days now had elapsed since we came here, still nothing was done (10th), as Karambŭlé said, because Sŭwarora had been so fully occupied collecting an army to punish an officer who had refused to pay his taxes, had ignored his authority, and had set himself up as a king of the district he was appointed to superintend. After this, at midnight, Karambŭlé, in an excited manner, said he had seen Sŭwarora, and it then was appointed that not he, but Virembo, should take the royal hongo, as well as the wahinda, or princes' shares, the next morning, after which we might go as fast as we liked, for Sŭwarora was so fully occupied with his army he could not see us this time. Before, however, the hongo could be paid, I must give the Sirhid and himself twenty brass wires, three joho, three barsati, twenty strings of mzizima, and one thousand strings of white beads. They were given.

A fearful row now broke out between Bombay and Baraka (11th). Many of my men had by this time been married, notwithstanding my prohibition. Baraka, for instance, had with him the daughter of Ungŭrŭe, chief of Phŭnzé; Wadimoyo, a woman called Manamaka; Sangizo, his wife and sister; but Bombay had not got one, and mourned for a girl he had set his eyes on, unfortunately for himself letting Baraka into his confidence. This set Baraka on the *qui vive* to catch Bombay tripping; for Baraka knew he could not get her without paying a good price for her, and therefore watched his opportunity to lay a complaint against him of purloining my property, by which scheme he would, he thought, get Bombay's place as storekeeper himself. In a sly manner Bombay employed some of my other men to take five wires, a red blanket, and 500 strings of beads, to his would-be father-in-law, which, by a previously-concocted arrangement, was to be her dowry price. These men did as they were bid; but the father-in-law returned the things, saying he must have one more wire. That being also supplied, the scoundrel wanted more, and made so much fuss about it, that Baraka became conversant with all that was going on, and told me of it.

This set the whole camp in a flame, for Bombay and Baraka were both very drunk, as well as most of the other men, so that it was with great difficulty I could get hold of the rights of their stories. Bombay acknowledged he had tried to get the girl, for they had been sentimentalizing together for several days, and both alike wished to be married. Baraka, he said, was allowed to keep a wife, and his position demanded that he should have one also; but the wires were his own property, and not mine, for he was given them by the chiefs as a perquisite when I paid their hongo through him. He thought it most unjust and unfair of Baraka to call him to account in that way, but he was not surprised at it, as Baraka, from the beginning of the journey to the present moment, had always been backbiting him, to try and usurp his position. Baraka, at this, somewhat taken aback, said there was no such things as perquisites on a journey like this; for whatever could be saved from the chiefs was for the common good of all, and all alike ought to share in it—repeating words I had often expressed. Then Bombay retorted, trembling and foaming in his liquor: "I know I shall get the worst of it, for while Baraka's tongue is a yard long, mine is only an inch; but I would not have spent any wires of master's to purchase slaves with (alluding to what Baraka had done at Mihambo), nor would I for any purpose of making myself richer; but when it comes to a wife, that's a different thing."

In my heart I liked Bombay all the more for this confession, but thought it necessary to extol Baraka for his quickness in finding him out, which drove Bombay nearly wild. He wished me to degrade him if I thought him dishonest; threw himself on the ground, and kissed my feet. I might thrash him, turn him into a porter, or do any thing else that I liked with him, as long as I did not bring a charge of dishonesty against him. He could not explain himself with Baraka's long tongue opposed to him, but there were many deficiencies in my wires before he took overcharge at Bogŭé, which he must leave for settlement till the journey was over, and then, the whole question having been sifted at Zanzibar, we would see who was the most honest. I then counted all the wires over at Bombay's request, and found them complete in numbers, without those he had set aside for the dowry money. Still there was a doubt, for the wires might have been cut by him without detection, as from the commencement they were of different lengths. However, I tried to make them friends, claimed all the wires myself, and cautioned every man in the camp again that they were all losers when any thing was misappropriated; for I brought this property to pay our way with, and whatever balance was over at the end of the journey I would divide among the whole of them.

12*th* and 13*th*. When more sober, Bombay again came to crave a thousand pardons for what he had done, threw himself down at my feet, then at Grant's, kissed our toes, swore I was his Ma Bap (father and mother); he had no father or mother to teach him better; he owed all his prosperity to me; men must err sometimes; oh, if I would only forgive him—and so forth. Then, being assured that I knew he never would have done as he had if a woman's attractions had not led him astray, he went to his work again like a man, and consoled himself by taking Sangizo's sister to wife on credit instead of the old love, promising to pay the needful out of his pay, and to return her to her brother when the journey was over.

In the evening Virembo and Karambŭlé came to receive the hongo for their chief, demanding 60 wires, 160 yards merikani, 300 strings of mzizima, and 5000 strings of white beads; but they allowed themselves to be beaten down to 50 wires, 20 pretty cloths, 100 strings mzizima, and 4000 kŭtŭamnazi, or cocoa-nutleaf colored beads, my white being all done. It was too late, however, to count all the things out, so they came the next day and took them. They then said we might go as soon as we had settled with the Wahinda or Wanawami (the king's children), for Sŭwarora could not see us this time, as he was so engaged with his army; but he hoped to see us and pay us more respect when we returned from Uganda, little thinking I had sworn in my mind never to see him, or return that way again. I said to those men, I thought he was ashamed to see us, as he had robbed us so after inviting us into the country, else he was too superstitious, for he ought at least to have given us a place in his palace. They both rebutted the insinuation; and, to change the subject, commenced levying the remaining dues to the princes, which ended by my giving thirty-four wires and six pretty cloths in a lump.

Early in the morning we were on foot again, only too thankful to have got off so cheaply. Then men were appointed as guides and protectors, to look after us as far as the border. What an honor! We had come into the country drawn there by a combination of pride and avarice, and now we were leaving it in hot haste under the guidance of an escort of officers, who were in reality appointed to watch us as dangerous wizards and objects of terror. It was all the same to us, as we now only thought of the prospect of relief before us, and laughed at what we had gone through.

To Kitaré, 15th.

Rising out of the Uthungŭ valley, we walked over rolling ground, drained in the dips by miry rush rivulets. The population was thinly scattered in small groups of grass huts, where the scrub jungle had been cleared away. On the road we passed cairns, to which every passer-by contributed a stone. Of the origin of the cairns I could not gain any information, though it struck me as curious I should find them in the first country we had entered governed by the Wahŭma, as I formerly saw the same thing in the Somali country, which doubtless, in earlier days, was governed by a branch of the Abyssinians. Arrived at our camping, we were immediately pounced upon by a deputation of officers, who said they had been sent by Semamba, the officer of this district. He lived ten miles from the road; but, hearing of our approach, he had sent these men to take his dues. At first I objected to pay, lest he should afterward treat me as Virembo had done; but I gave way in the end, and paid nine wires, two chintz and two bindéra cloths, as the guides said they would stand my security against any farther molestation.

Rattling on again as merry as larks, over the same red sandstone formation, we entered a fine forest, and trended on through it at a stiff pace until we arrived at the head of a deep valley called Lohŭgati, which was so beautiful we instinctively pulled up to admire it. Deep down its well-wooded side below us was a stream, of most inviting aspect for a trout-fisher, flowing toward the N'yanza. Just beyond it the valley was clothed with fine trees and luxuriant vegetation of all descriptions, among which was conspicuous the pretty pandana palm, and rich gardens of plantains, while thistles of extraordinary size and wild indigo were the more common weeds. The land beyond that again rolled back in high undulations, over which, in the far distance, we could see a line of cones, red and bare on their tops, guttered down with white streaks, looking for all the world like recent volcanoes; and in the far background, rising higher than all, were the rich grassy hills of Karagŭé and Kishakka.

On resuming our march, a bird called khongota flew across our path; seeing which, old Nasib, beaming with joy, in his superstitious belief cried out with delight, "Ah! look at that good omen! now our journey will be sure to be prosperous." After fording the stream, we sat down to rest, and were visited by all the inhabitants, who were more naked than any people we had yet seen. All the maidens, even at the age of puberty, did not hesitate to stand boldly in front of us—for evil thoughts were not in their minds. From this we rose over a stony hill to the settlement of Vihembé, which, being the last on the Usŭi frontier, in-

duced me to give our guides three wires each, and four yards of
bindéra, which Nasib said was their proper fee.   Here Bombay's
would-be, but disappointed father-in-law sent after us to say that
he required a hongo; Sŭwarora had never given his sanction to
our quitting his country; his hongo even was not settled.   He
wished, moreover, particularly to see us; and if we did not return in a friendly manner, an army would arrest our march immediately.

CHAPTER VIII.

KARAGŬÉ.

Relief from Protectors and Pillagers.—The Scenery and Geology.—Meeting with the friendly King Rŭmanika.—His Hospitalities and Attention.—His Services to the Expedition.—Philosophical and Theological Inquiries.—The Royal Family of Karagŭé.—The M-fumbiro Mountain.—Navigation of "The Little Windermere."—The New-moon Levée.—Rhinoceros and Hippopotamus Hunting.—Measurement of a fattened Queen.—Political Polygamy.—Christmas.—Rumors of Petherick's Expedition.—Arrangements to meet it.—March to Uganda.

THIS was a day of relief and happiness. A load was removed from us in seeing the Wasŭi "protectors" depart, with the truly cheering information that we now had nothing but wild animals to contend with before reaching Karagŭé. This land is "neutral," by which is meant that it is untenanted by human beings; and we might now hope to bid adieu for a time to the scourging system of taxation to which we had been subjected.

To Vigŭra, 17th.

Gradually descending from the spur which separates the Lohŭgati valley from the bed of the Lŭérŭ lo Urigi, or Lake of Urigi, the track led us first through a meadow of much pleasing beauty, and then through a passage between the "saddle-back" domes we had seen from the heights above Lohŭgati, where a new geological

One of the Wahŭma.

formation especially attracted my notice. From the green slopes of the hills, set up at a slant, as if the central line of pressure on the dome top had weighed on the inside plates, protruded soft slabs of argillaceous sandstone, whose laminæ presented a beef-sandwich appearance, puce or purple alternating with creamy-white. Quartz and other igneous rocks were also scattered about, lying like superficial accumulations in the dips at the foot of the hills, and red sandstone conglomerate clearly indicated the presence of iron. The soil itself looked rich and red, not unlike our own fine county of Devon.

On arriving in camp we pitched under some trees, and at once were greeted by an officer sent by Rŭmanika to help us out of Usŭi. This was Kachŭchŭ, an old friend of Nasib's, who no sooner saw him than, beaming with delight, he said to us, "Now, was I not right when I told you the birds flying about on Lohŭgati Hill were a good omen? Look here what this man says: Rŭmanika has ordered him to bring you on to his palace at once, and wherever you stop a day, the village officers are instructed to supply you with food at the king's expense, for there are no taxes gathered from strangers in the kingdom of Karagŭé. Presents may be exchanged, but the name of tax is ignored." Grant here shot a rhinoceros, which came well into play to mix with the day's flour we had carried on from Vihembé.

Deluded yesterday by the sight of the broad waters of the Lŭérŭ lo Urigi, espied in the distance from the top of a hill, into the belief that we were in view of the N'yanza itself, we walked triumphantly along, thinking how well the Arabs at Kazé had described this to be a creek of the great lake; but on arrival in camp we heard from the village officer that we had been misinformed, and that it was a detached lake, but connected with the Victoria N'yanza by a passage in the hills and the Kitangŭlé River. Formerly, he said, the Urigi valley was covered with water, extending up to Uhha, when all the low lands we had crossed from Usŭi had to be ferried, and the saddle-back hills were a mere chain of islands in the water. But the country had dried up, and the Lake of Urigi became a small swamp. He farther informed us that even in the late King Dagara's time it was a large sheet of water, but the instant he ceased to exist the lake shrank to what we now saw.

Our day's march had been novel and very amusing. The hilly country surrounding us, together with the valley, brought back to recollection many happy days I had once spent with the Tartars in the Thibetian valley of the Indus—only this was more picturesque; for, though both countries are wild, and very thinly inhabited, this was greened over with grass, and dotted here and there on the higher slopes with thick bush of acacias, the haunts

of rhinoceros, both white and black; while in the flat of the valley, herds of hartebeest and fine cattle roamed about like the ki-
yang and tame yâk of Thibet. Then, to enhance all these pleasures, so different from our former experiences, we were treated
like guests by the chief of the place, who, obeying the orders of
his king, Rŭmanika, brought me presents, as soon as we arrived,
of sheep, fowls, and sweet potatoes, and was very thankful for a
few yards of red blanketing as a return, without begging for more.

The farther we went in this country the better we liked it, as
the people were all kept in good order; and the village chiefs were so civil that we could do as we liked.
After following down the left side of the valley and entering the
village, the customary presents and returns were made. Wishing
then to obtain a better view of the country, I strolled over the
nearest hills, and found the less exposed slopes well covered with
trees. Small antelopes occasionally sprang up from the grass. I
shot a florikan for the pot; and as I had never before seen white
rhinoceros, killed one now; though, as no one would eat him, I
felt sorry rather than otherwise for what I had done. When I
returned in the evening, small boys brought me sparrows for
sale; and then I remembered the stories I had heard from Mŭsa
Mzŭri, that in the whole of Karagŭé these small birds were so
numerous, the people, to save themselves from starvation, were
obliged to grow a bitter corn which the birds disliked; and so I
found it. At night, while observing for latitude, I was struck by
surprise to see a long, noisy procession pass by where I sat, led by
some men who carried on their shoulders a woman covered up in
a blackened skin. On inquiry, however, I heard she was being
taken to the hut of her espoused, where, "bundling fashion," she
would be put in bed; but it was only with virgins they took so
much trouble.

A strange but characteristic story now reached my ears. Masŭdi, the merchant who took up Insangéz, had been trying his
best to deter Rŭmanika from allowing us to enter his country by
saying we were addicted to sorcery; and had it not been for Insangéz's remonstrances, who said we were sent up by Mŭsa, our fate
would have been doubtful. Rŭmanika, it appeared, as I always
had heard, considered old Mŭsa his savior for having eight years
before quelled a rebellion, when his younger brother, Rogéro, as-
pired to the throne, while Mŭsa's honor and honesty were quite
unimpeachable. But more of this hereafter.

To Second Urigi, 19th.

Khonzé, the next place, lying in the bending concave of this
swamp lake, and facing Hangiro, was commanded by
a fine elderly man called Mŭzégi, who was chief officer during Dagara's time. He told me, with the greatest possible gravity, that he remembered well the time when a boat
could have gone from this to Vigŭra, as also when fish and crocodiles came up from the Kitangŭlé; but the old king no sooner
died than the waters dried up, which showed as plainly as words
could tell that the king had designed it, to make men remember
him with sorrow in all future ages. Our presents after this having been exchanged, the good old man, at my desire, explained
the position of all the surrounding countries, in his own peculiar
manner, by laying a long stick on the ground pointing due north
and south, to which he attached shorter ones pointing to the centre of each distant country. He thus assisted me in the protractions of the map to the countries which lie east and west of the
route.

Shortly after starting this morning we were summoned by the
last officer on the Urigi to take breakfast with him,
as he could not allow us to pass by without paying
his respects to the king's guests. He was a man of most affable
manners, and loth we should part company without one night's
entertainment at least; but, as it was a matter of necessity, he
gave us provisions to eat on the way, adding, at the same time, he
was sorry he could not give more, as a famine was then oppressing the land. We parted with reiterated compliments on both
sides; and shortly after, diving into the old bed of the Urigi,
were constantly amused with the variety of game which met our
view. On several occasions the rhinoceros were so numerous
and impudent as to contest the right of the road with us, and the
greatest sport was occasioned by our bold Wangŭana going at
them in parties of threes and fours, when, taking good care of
themselves at considerable distances, they fired their carbines all
together, and while the rhinoceros ran one way, they ran the other. While we were pitching our tents after sunset by some pools
on the plain, Dr. K'yengo arrived with the hongo of brass and
copper wires sent by Sŭwarora for the great king Mtésa, in lieu
of his daughter who died; so next morning we all marched together on to Uthenga.

Rising out of the bed of the Urigi, we passed over a low spur
of beef-sandwich clay sandstones, and descended into the close,

To Khonzé, 20th.

*To Camp Kiwé-
ra, 21st.*

To Uthenga, 22d.
rich valley of Uthenga, bound in by steep hills hanging over us more than a thousand feet high, as prettily clothed as the mountains of Scotland; while in the valley
there were not only magnificent trees of extraordinary height, but
also a surprising amount of the richest cultivation, among which
the banana may be said to prevail. Notwithstanding this apparent richness of the land, the Wanyambo, living in their small
squalid huts, seem poor. The tobacco they smoke is imported
from the coffee-growing country of Uhaiya. After arrival in the
village, who should we see but the Uganda officer Irŭngŭ! The
scoundrel, instead of going on to Uganda as he had promised to
do, conveying my present to Mtésa, had stopped here plundering
the Wanyambo, and getting drunk on their pombé, called, in
their language, *marwa*—a delicious kind of wine made from the
banana. He, of course, begged for more beads; but, not able to
trick me again, set his drummers and fifers at work, in hopes that
he would get over our feelings in that way.

Henceforth, as we marched, Irŭngŭ's drummers and fifers kept
To Rozoka, 23d.
us alive on the way. This we heard was a privilege
that Uganda Wakungŭ enjoyed both at home and
abroad, although in all other countries the sound of the drum is
considered a notice of war, unless where it happens to accompany
a dance or festival. Leaving the valley of Uthenga, we rose over
the spur of N'yamwara, where we found we had attained the delightful altitude of 5000 odd feet. Oh, how we enjoyed it! every
one feeling so happy at the prospect of meeting so soon the good
king Rŭmanika. Tripping down the greensward, we now worked our way to the Rozoka valley, and pitched our tents in the
village.

Kachŭchŭ here told us he had orders to precede us, and prepare Rŭmanika for our coming, as his king wished to know what
place we would prefer to live at—the Arab dépôt at Kufro, on
the direct line to Uganda, in his palace with himself, or outside
his inclosures. Such politeness rather took us aback; so, giving
our friend a coil of copper wire to keep him in good spirits, I
said all our pleasure rested in seeing the king; whatever honors
he liked to confer on us we should take with good grace, but one
thing he must understand, we came not to trade, but to see him
and great kings, and therefore the Arabs had no relations with
us. This little point settled, off started Kachŭchŭ in his usual
merry manner, while I took a look at the hills to see their geo-

logical formation, and found them much as before, based on streaky clay sandstones, with the slight addition of pure blue shales, and above sections of quartzose sandstone lying in flags, as well as other metamorphic and igneous rocks scattered about.

Moving on the next morning over hill and dale, we came to the junction of two roads, where Irungŭ, with his drummers, fifers, and amazon followers, took one way to Kufro, followed by the men carrying Sŭwarora's hongo, and we led off on the other, directed to the palace. The hill-tops in many places were breasted with dikes of pure white quartz, just as we had seen in Usŭi, only that here their direction tended more to the north. It was most curious to contemplate, seeing that the chief substance of the hills was a pure blue, or otherwise streaky clay sandstone, which must have been formed when the land was low, but has now been elevated, making these hills the axis of the centre of the continent, and therefore probably the oldest of all.

To Katawanga, 24th.

When within a few miles of the palace we were ordered to stop and wait for Kachŭchŭ's return; but we no sooner put up in a plantain grove, where pombé was brewing, and our men were all taking a suck at it, than the worthy arrived to call us on the same instant, as the king was most anxious to see us. The love of good beer of course made our men all too tired to march again; so I sent off Bombay with Nasib to make our excuses, and in the evening found them returning with a huge pot of pombé and some royal tobacco, which Rŭmanika sent with a notice that he intended it exclusively for our own use; for, though there was abundance for my men, there was nothing so good as what came from the palace; the royal tobacco was as sweet and strong as honey-dew, and the beer so strong it required a strong man to drink it.

After breakfast next morning we crossed the hill-spur called Weranhanjé, the grassy tops of which were 5500 feet above the sea. Descending a little, we came suddenly in view of what appeared to us a rich clump of trees, in S. lat. 1° 42′ 42″, and E. long. 31° 1′ 49″; and, 500 feet below it, we saw a beautiful sheet of water lying snugly within the folds of the hills. We were not altogether unprepared for it, as Mŭsa of old had described it, and Bombay, on his return yesterday, told us he had seen a great pond. The clump, indeed, was the palace inclosure. As to the lake, for want of a native name, I christened

To Weranhanjé, 25th.

it the Little Windermere, because Grant thought it so like our own English lake of that name. It was one of many others which, like that of Urigi, drains the moisture of the overhanging hills, and gets drained into the Victoria N'yanza through the Kitangŭlé River.

To do royal honors to the king of this charming land, I ordered my men to put down their loads and fire a volley. This was no sooner done than, as we went to the palace gate, we received an invitation to come in at once, for the king wished to see us before attending to any thing else. Now, leaving our traps outside, both Grant and myself, attended by Bombay and a few of the seniors of my Wangŭana, entered the vestibule, and, walking through extensive inclosures studded with huts of kingly dimensions, were escorted to a pent-roofed baraza, which the Arabs had built as a sort of government office, where the king might conduct his state affairs.

Here, as we entered, we saw sitting cross-legged on the ground Rŭmanika the king, and his brother Nnanaji, both of them men of noble appearance and size. The king was plainly dressed in an Arab's black choga, and wore, for ornament, dress-stockings of rich-colored beads, and neatly-worked wristlets of copper. Nnanaji, being a doctor of very high pretensions, in addition to a check cloth wrapped round him, was covered with charms. At their sides lay huge pipes of black clay. In their rear, squatting quiet as mice, were all the king's sons, some six or seven lads, who wore leather middle-coverings, and little dream-charms tied under their chins. The first greetings of the king, delivered in good Kisŭahili, were warm and affecting, and in an instant we both felt and saw we were in the company of men who were as unlike as they could be to the common order of the natives of the surrounding districts. They had fine oval faces, large eyes, and high noses, denoting the best blood of Abyssinia. Having shaken hands in true English style, which is the peculiar custom of the men of this country, the ever-smiling Rŭmanika begged us to be seated on the ground opposite to him, and at once wished to know what we thought of Karagŭé, for it had struck him his mountains were the finest in the world; and the lake, too, did we not admire it? Then laughing, he inquired—for he knew all the story—what we thought of Sŭwarora, and the reception we had met with in Usŭi. When this was explained to him, I showed him that it was for the interest of his own kingdom to keep a

check on Sŭwarora, whose exorbitant taxations prevented the
Arabs from coming to see him and bringing things from all parts
of the world. He made inquiries for the purpose of knowing
how we found our way all over the world; for on the former expedition a letter had come to him for Mŭsa, who no sooner read
it than he said I had called him and he must leave, as I was bound
for Ujiji.

This of course led to a long story, describing the world, the
proportions of land and water, and the power of ships, which conveyed even elephants and rhinoceros—in fact, all the animals in
the world—to fill our menageries at home, etc., etc., as well as
the strange announcement that we lived to the northward, and
had only come this way because his friend Mŭsa had assured me
without doubt that he would give us the road on through Uganda.   Time flew like magic, the king's mind was so quick and inquiring; but as the day was wasting away, he generously gave
us our option to choose a place for our residence in or out of his
palace, and allowed us time to select one. We found the view
overlooking the lake to be so charming, that we preferred camping outside, and set our men at once to work cutting sticks and
long grass to erect themselves sheds.

Our Camp outside the Palace.

One of the young princes—for the king ordered them all to be constantly in attendance on us—happening to see me sit on an iron chair, rushed back to his father and told him about it. This set all the royals in the palace in a state of high wonder, and ended by my getting a summons to show off the white man sitting on his throne; for of course I could only be, as all of them called me, a king of great dignity, to indulge in such state. Rather reluctantly I did as I was bid, and allowed myself once more to be dragged into court. Rŭmanika, as gentle as ever, then burst into a fresh fit of merriment, and after making sundry enlightened remarks of inquiry, which of course were responded to with the greatest satisfaction, finished off by saying, with a very expressive shake of the head, "Oh, these Wazungŭ, these Wazungŭ! they know and do every thing."

I then put in a word for myself. Since we had entered Karagŭé we never could get one drop of milk either for love or for money, and I wished to know what motive the Wahŭma had for withholding it. We had heard they held superstitious dreads, that any one who ate the flesh of pigs, fish, or fowls, or the bean called maharagŭé, if he tasted the products of their cows, would destroy their cattle, and I hoped he did not labor under any such absurd delusions. To which he replied, It was only the poor who thought so; and as he now saw we were in want, he would set apart one of his cows expressly for our use. On bidding adieu, the usual formalities of hand-shaking were gone through; and on entering camp, I found the good thoughtful king had sent us some more of his excellent beer.

The Wangŭana were now all in the highest of good-humor; for time after time goats and fowls were brought into camp by the officers of the king, who had received orders from all parts of the country to bring in supplies for his guests; and this kind of treatment went on for a month, though it did not diminish my daily expenditure of beads, as grain and plantains were not enough thought of. The cold winds, however, made the coast-men all shiver, and suspect, in their ignorance, we must be drawing close to England, the only cold place they had heard of.

26th. Hearing it would be considered indecent haste to present my tributary offering at once, I paid my morning's visit, only taking my revolving pistol, as I knew Rŭmanika had expressed a strong wish to see it. The impression it made was surprising—he had never seen such a thing in his life; so, in return for his great generosity, as well as to show I placed no value on property, not being a merchant, I begged him to accept it. We then adjourned to his private hut, which rather surprised me by the neatness with which it was kept. The roof was supported by numerous clean poles, to which he had fastened a large assortment of spears — brass-headed with iron handles, and iron-headed with wooden ones — of excellent workmanship. A large standing-screen, of fine straw-plait work, in elegant devices, partitioned off one part of the room; and on the opposite side, as mere ornaments, were placed a number of brass grapnels and small models of cows, made in iron for his amusement by the Arabs at Kufro. A little later in the day, as soon as we had done breakfast, both Rŭmanika and Nnanaji came over to pay us a visit; for they thought, as we could find our way all over the world, so we should not find much difficulty in prescribing some magic charms to kill his brother, Rogéro, who lived on a hill overlooking the Kitangŭlé. Seating them both on our chairs, which amused them intensely, I asked Rŭmanika, although I had heard before the whole facts of the case, what motives now induced him to wish the committal of such a terrible act, and brought out the whole story afresh.

Before their old father Dagara died, he had unwittingly said to the mother of Rogéro, although he was the youngest born, what a fine king he would make; and the mother, in consequence, tutored her son to expect the command of the country, although the law of the land in the royal family is the primogeniture system, extending, however, only to those sons who are born after the accession of the king to the throne.

As soon, therefore, as Dagara died, leaving the three sons alluded to, all by different mothers, a contest took place with the brothers, which, as Nnanaji held by Rŭmanika, ended in the two elder driving Rogéro away. It happened, however, that half the men of the country, either from fear or love, attached themselves to Rogéro. Feeling his power, he raised an army and attempted to fight for the crown, which it is generally admitted would have succeeded, had not Mŭsa, with unparalleled magnanimity, employed all the ivory merchandise at his command to engage the services of all the Arabs' slaves residing at Kufro to bring muskets against him. Rogéro was thus frightened away; but he went swearing that he would carry out his intentions at some future date, when the Arabs had withdrawn from the country.

Magic charms, of course, we had none; but the king would not believe it, and, to wheedle some out of us, said they would not kill their brother even if they caught him—for fratricide was considered an unnatural crime in their country—but they would merely gouge out his eyes and set him at large again, for without the power of sight he could do them no harm.

I then recommended, as the best advice I could give him for the time being, to take some strong measures against Sŭwarora and the system of taxation carried on in Usŭi. These would have the effect of bringing men with superior knowledge into the country, for it was only through the power of knowledge that good government could be obtained. Sŭwarora at present stopped eight tenths of the ivory-merchants who might be inclined to trade here from coming into the country, by the foolish system of excessive taxation he had established. Next I told him, if he would give me one or two of his children, I would have them instructed in England; for I admired his race, and believed them to have sprung from our old friends the Abyssinians, whose king, Sahéla Sélassié, had received rich presents from our queen. They were Christians like ourselves, and had the Wahŭma not lost their knowledge of God they would be so also.

A long theological and historical discussion ensued, which so pleased the king that he said he would be delighted if I would take two of his sons to England, that they might bring him a knowledge of every thing. Then turning again to the old point, his utter amazement that we should spend so much property in traveling, he wished to know what we did it for; when men had such means they would surely sit down and enjoy it. "Oh no," was the reply; "we have had our fill of the luxuries of life; eating, drinking, or sleeping have no charms for us now; we are above trade, therefore require no profits, and seek for enjoyment the run of the world. To observe and admire the beauties of creation are worth much more than beads to us. But what led us this way we have told you before; it was to see your majesty in particular, and the great kings of Africa, and at the same time to open another road to the north, whereby the best manufactures of Europe would find their way to Karagŭé, and you would get so many more guests." In the highest good-humor the king said, "As you have come to see me and see sights, I will order some boats and show you over the lake, with musicians to play before you, or any thing else that you like." Then, after looking over our pictures with intensest delight, and admiring our beds, boxes, and outfit in general, he left for the day.

In the afternoon, as I had heard from Mŭsa that the wives of the king and princes were fattened to such an extent that they could not stand upright, I paid my respects to Wazézérŭ, the king's eldest brother—who, having been born before his father ascended his throne, did not come in the line of succession—with the hope of being able to see for myself the truth of the story. There was no mistake about it. On entering the hut, I found the old man and his chief wife sitting side by side on a bench of earth strewed over with grass, and partitioned like stalls for sleeping apartments, while in front of them were placed numerous wooden pots of milk, and, hanging from the poles that supported the beehive-shaped hut, a large collection of bows six feet in length, while below them were tied an even larger collection of spears, intermixed with a goodly assortment of heavy-handed assegais. I was struck with no small surprise at the way he received me, as well as with the extraordinary dimensions, yet pleasing beauty, of the immoderately fat fair one his wife. She could not rise; and so large were her arms that between the joints the flesh hung down like large, loose-stuffed puddings. Then in came their children, all models of the Abyssinian type of beauty, and as polite in their manners as thorough-bred gentlemen. They had heard of my picture-books from the king, and all wished to see them; which they no sooner did, to their infinite delight, especially when they recognized any of the animals, than the subject was turned by my inquiring what they did with so many milk-pots. This was easily explained by Wazézérŭ himself, who, pointing to his wife, said, "This is all the product of those pots: from early youth upward we keep those pots to their mouths, as it is the fashion at court to have very fat wives."

27th. Ever anxious to push on with the journey, as I felt every day's delay only tended to diminish my means—that is, my beads and copper wire—I instructed Bombay to take the under-mentioned articles to Rŭmanika as a small sample of the products of my country;* to say I felt quite ashamed of their being so few and so poor, but I hoped he would forgive my shortcomings, as he knew I had been so often robbed on the way to him; and I

* *Rŭmanika's present.*—One block-tin box, one Raglan coat, five yards scarlet broadcloth, two coils copper wire, a hundred large blue egg-beads, five bundles best variegated beads, three bundles minute beads—pink, blue, and white.

trusted, in recollection of Mŭsa, he would give me leave to go on
to Uganda, for every day's delay was consuming my supplies.
Nnanaji, however, it was said, should get something; so, in addition to the king's present, I apportioned one out for him, and
Bombay took both up to the palace.* Every body, I was pleased
to hear, was surprised with both the quantity and quality of what
I had been able to find for them; for, after the plundering in
Ugogo, the immense consumption caused by such long delays on
the road, the fearful prices I had had to pay for my porters' wages,
the enormous taxes I had been forced to give both in Msalala
and Uzinza, besides the constant thievings in camp, all of which
was made public by the constantly-recurring tales of my men, nobody thought I had got any thing left.

Rŭmanika, above all, was as delighted as if he had come in for
a fortune, and sent to say the Raglan coat was a marvel, and the
scarlet broadcloth the finest thing he had ever seen. Nobody
but Mŭsa had ever given him such beautiful beads before, and
none ever gave with such free liberality. Whatever I wanted I
should have in return for it, as it was evident to him I had really
done him a great honor in visiting him. Neither his father nor
any of his forefathers had had such a great favor shown them.
He was alarmed, he confessed, when he heard we were coming to
visit him, thinking we might prove some fearful monsters that
were not quite human, but now he was delighted beyond all
measure with what he saw of us. A messenger should be sent
at once to the King of Uganda to inform him of our intention to
visit him, with his own favorable report of us. This was necessary according to the etiquette of the country. Without such a
recommendation our progress would be stopped by the people,
while with one word from him all would go straight; for was he
not the gatekeeper, enjoying the full confidence of Uganda? A
month, however, must elapse, as the distance to the palace of
Uganda was great; but, in the mean time, he would give me
leave to go about in his country to do and see what I liked,
Nnanaji and his sons escorting me every where. Moreover, when
the time came for my going on to Uganda, if I had not enough
presents to give the king, he would fill up the complement from
his own stores, and either go with me himself, or send Nnanaji to

---

* *Nnanaji's present.*—One déolé or gold-embroidered silk, two coils copper wire,
fifty large blue egg-beads, five bundles best variegated beads, three bundles minute
beads—pink, blue, and white.

conduct me as far as the boundary of Uganda, in order that Rogéro might not molest us on the way.   In the evening, Masŭdi, with Sangoro and several other merchants, came up from Kufro to pay us a visit of respect.

28*th* and 29*th*. A gentle hint having come to us that the king's brother, Wazézérŭ, expected a trifle in virtue of his rank, I sent him a blanket and seventy-five blue egg-beads.   These were accepted with the usual good grace of these people.   The king then, ever attentive to our position as guests, sent his royal musicians

Musicians.

to give us a tune.   The men composing the band were a mixture of Waganda and Wanyambo, who played on reed instruments made telescope fashion, marking time by hand-drums.   At first they marched up and down, playing tunes exactly like the regimental bands of the Turks, and then commenced dancing a species of "hornpipe," blowing furiously all the while.   When dismissed with some beads, Nnanaji dropped in and invited me to accompany him out shooting on the slopes of the hills overlooking the lake.   He had in attendance all the king's sons, as well as a large number of beaters, with three or four dogs.   Tripping down the greensward of the hills together, these tall, athletic princes every now and then stopped to see who could shoot farthest, and I must say I never witnessed better feats in my life.   With powerful six-feet-long bows, they pulled their arrows' heads up to the wood, and made wonderful shots in the distance.   They then placed me in position, and, arranging the field, drove the covers like men well accustomed to sport—indeed, it struck me

they indulged too much in that pleasure, for we saw nothing but
two or three montana and some diminutive antelopes, about the
size of mouse deer, and so exceedingly shy that not one was
bagged.

Returning home to the tents as the evening sky was illumined
with the red glare of the sun, my attention was attracted by observing in the distance some bold sky-scraping cones situated in
the country Rŭanda, which at once brought back to recollection
the ill-defined story I had heard from the Arabs of a wonderful
hill always covered with clouds, on which snow or hail was constantly falling.   This was a valuable discovery, for I found these
hills to be the great turn-point of the Central African watershed.
Without loss of time I set to work, and, gathering all the travelers I could in the country, protracted, from their descriptions, all
the distant topographical features set down in the map, as far
north as 3° of north latitude, as far east as 36°, and as far west as
26° of east longitude; only afterward slightly corrected, as I was
better able to connect and clear up some trifling but doubtful
points.

Indeed, I was not only surprised at the amount of information
about distant places I was enabled to get here from these men,

View of Mount Mfŭmbiro and Drainage System of the Lunæ Montes,
taken from a height of 5500 feet.

but also at the correctness of their vast and varied knowledge, as I afterward tested it by observation and the statements of others. I rely so far on the geographical information I thus received that I would advise no one to doubt the accuracy of these protractions until he has been on the spot to test them by actual inspection. About the size only of the minor lakes do I feel doubtful, more especially the Little Lŭta Nzigé, which on the former journey I heard was a salt lake, because salt was found on its shores and in one of its islands. Now, without going into any lengthy details, and giving Rŭmanika due credit for every thing—for, had he not ordered his men to give me every information that lay in their power, they would not have done so—I will merely say for the present that, while they conceived the Victoria N'yanza would take a whole month for a canoe to cross it, they thought the Little Lŭta Nzigé might be crossed in a week. The Mfŭmbiro cones in Rŭanda, which I believe reach 10,000 feet, are said to be the highest of the "Mountains of the Moon." At their base are both salt and copper mines, as well as hot springs. There are also hot springs in Mpororo, and one in Karagŭé near where Rogéro lived.

30*th.* The important business of announcing our approach to Uganda was completed by Rŭmanika appointing Kachŭchŭ to go to King Mtésa as quickly as possible, to say we were coming to visit him. He was told that we were very great men, who only traveled to see great kings and great countries; and, as such, Rŭmanika trusted we should be received with courteous respect, and allowed to roam all over the country wherever we liked, he holding himself responsible for our actions for the time being. In the end, however, we were to be restored to him, as he considered himself our father, and therefore must see that no accident befell us.

To put the royal message in proper shape, I was now requested to send some trifle by way of a letter or visiting-card; but, on taking out a Colt's revolving rifle for the purpose, Rŭmanika advised me not to send it, as Mtésa might take fright, and, considering it a charm of evil quality, reject us as bad magicians, and close his gates on us. Three bits of cotton cloth were then selected as the best thing for the purpose; and, relying implicitly on the advice of Rŭmanika, who declared his only object was to further our views, I arranged accordingly, and off went Kachŭchŭ.

To keep my friend in good-humor, and show him how well the

English can appreciate a kindness, I presented him with a hammer, a sailor's knife, a Rodgers's three-bladed penknife, a gilt letter-slip with paper and envelopes, some gilt pens, an ivory holder, and a variety of other small articles. Of each of these he asked the use, and then in high glee put it into the big block-tin box, in which he kept his other curiosities, and which I think he felt more proud of than any other possession. After this, on adjourning to his baraza, Ungŭrŭé the Pig, who had floored my march in Sorombo, and Makinga, our persecutor in Usŭi, came in to report that the Watŭta had been fighting in Usŭi, and taken six bomas, upon which Rŭmanika asked me what I thought of it, and if I knew where the Watŭta came from. I said I was not surprised to hear Usŭi had attracted the Watŭta's cupidity, for every one knew of the plundering propensities of the inhabitants, and as they became rich by their robberies, they must in turn expect to be robbed. Where the Watŭta came from nobody could tell; they were dressed something like the Zŭlŭ Kafirs of the south, but appeared to be now gradually migrating from the regions of Lake N'yassa. To this, Dr. K'yengo, who was now living with Rŭmanika as his head magician, added that, while he was living in Utambara, the Watŭta invested his boma six months; and finally, when all their cows and stores were exhausted, they killed all the inhabitants but himself, and he only escaped by the power of the charms which he carried about him. These were so powerful, that, although he lay on the ground, and the Watŭta struck at him with their spears, not one could penetrate his body.

In the evening after this, as the king wished to see all my scientific instruments, we walked down to the camp; and as he did not beg for any thing, I gave him some gold and mother-of-pearl shirt-studs to swell up his trinket-box. The same evening I made up my mind, if possible, to purchase a stock of beads from the Arabs, and sent Baraka off to Kufro to see what kind of a bargain he could make with them; for, while I trembled to think what those "bloodsuckers" would have the impudence to demand when they found me at their mercy, I felt that the beads must be bought, or the expedition would certainly come to grief.

1st and 2d. Two days after this the merchants came in a body to see me, and said their worst beads would stand me $80 per frasala, as they could realize that value in ivory on arrival at the coast. Of course no business was done, for the thing was preposterous by all calculation, being close on 2500 per cent. above Zanzibar valuation. I was "game" to give $50, but as they would not take this, I thought of dealing with Rŭmanika instead. I then gave Nnanaji, who had been constantly throwing out hints that I ought to give him a gun, as he was a great sportsmañ, a lappet of bead-work to keep his tongue quiet, and he, in return, sent me a bullock and sundry pots of pombé, which, in addition to the daily allowance sent by Rŭmanika, made all my people drunk, and so affected Baraka that one of the women—also drunk —having given him some sharp abuse, he beat her in so violent a manner that the whole drunken camp set upon him, and turned the place into a pandemonium. A row among negroes means a general rising of arms, legs, and voices; all are in a state of the greatest excitement; and each individual thinks he is doing the best to mend matters, but is actually doing his best to create confusion.

By dint of perseverance, I now succeeded in having Baraka separated from the crowd and dragged before me for justice. I found that the woman, who fully understood the jealous hatred which existed in Baraka's heart against Bombay, flirted with both of them; and, pretending to show a preference for Bombay, set Baraka against her, when from high words they came to blows, and set the place in a blaze. It was useless to remonstrate; Baraka insisted he would beat the woman if she abused him, no matter whether I thought it cowardly or not; he did not come with me expecting to be bullied in this way—the whole fault lay with Bombay—I did not do him justice—when he proved Bombay a thief at Usŭi, I did not turn him off, but now, instead, I showed the preference to Bombay by always taking him when I went to Rŭmanika. It was useless to argue with such a passionate man, so I told him to go away and cool himself before morning.

When he was gone, Bombay said there was not one man in the camp, besides his own set, who wished to go on to Egypt, for they had constant arguments among themselves about it; and while Bombay always said he would follow me wherever I led, Baraka and those who held by him abused him and his set for having tricked them away from Zanzibar, under the false hopes that the road was quite safe. Bombay said his arguments were that Bana knew better than any body else what he was about, and he would follow him, trusting to luck, as God was the disposer of all things, and men could die but once; while Baraka's arguments all rested the other way—that no one could tell what was ahead of him—Bana had sold himself to luck and the devil —but, though he did not care for his own safety, he ought not to sacrifice the lives of others—Bombay and his lot were fools for their pains in trusting to him.

. 3d. At daybreak Rŭmanika sent us word he was off to Moga-Namirinzi, a spur of a hill beyond "the Little Windermere," overlooking the Ingézi Kagéra, or river which separates Kishak-ka from Karagŭé, to show me how the Kitangŭlé River was fed by small lakes and marshes, in accordance with my expressed wish to have a better comprehension of the drainage system of the Mountains of the Moon. He hoped we would follow him, not by the land route he intended to take, but in canoes which he had ordered at the ferry below. Starting off shortly afterward, I made for the lake, and found the canoes all ready, but so small that, besides two paddlers, only two men could sit down in each. After pushing through the tall reeds with which the end of the lake is covered, we emerged in the clear open, and skirted the farther side of the water until a small strait was gained, which led us into another lake, drained at the northern end into a vast swampy plain, covered entirely with tall rushes, excepting only in a few places where bald patches expose the surface of the wa-ter, or where the main streams of the Ingézi and Luchŭro valleys cut a clear drain for themselves.

The whole scenery was most beautiful. Green and fresh, the slopes of the hills were covered with grass, with small clumps of soft cloudy-looking acacias growing at a few feet only above the water, and above them, facing over the hills, fine detached trees, and here and there the gigantic medicinal aloe. Arrived near the end of the Moga-Namirinzi Hill in the second lake, the pad-dlers splashed into shore, where a large concourse of people, headed by Nnanaji, were drawn up to receive me. I landed with all the dignity of a prince, when the royal band struck up a march, and we all moved on to Rŭmanika's frontier palace, talk-ing away in a very complimentary manner, not unlike the very polite and flowery fashion of educated Orientals.

Rŭmanika we found sitting dressed in a wrapper made of an nzoé antelope's skin, smiling blandly as we approached him. In the warmest manner possible he pressed me to sit by his side, asked how I had enjoyed myself, what I thought of his country, and if I did not feel hungry; when a picnic dinner was spread, and we all set to at cooked plantains and pombé, ending with a pipe of his best tobacco. Bit by bit Rŭmanika became more interested in geography, and seemed highly ambitious of gaining a world-wide reputation through the medium of my pen. At his invitation we now crossed over the spur to the Ingézi Kagéra side, when, to surprise me, the canoes I had come up the lake in appeared before us. They had gone out of the lake at its northern end, paddled into, and then up the Kagéra to where we stood, showing, by actual navigation, the connection of these highland lakes with the rivers which drain the various spurs of the Mountains of the Moon. The Kagéra was deep and dark, of itself a very fine stream, and, considering it was only one—and that, too, a minor one—of the various affluents which drain the mountain valleys into the Victoria N'yanza through the medium of the Kitangŭlé River, I saw at once there must be water sufficient to make the Kitangŭlé a very powerful tributary to the lake.

On leaving this interesting place, with the wide-spread information of all the surrounding countries I had gained, my mind was so impressed with the topographical features of all this part of Africa, that in my heart I resolved I would make Rŭmanika as happy as he had made me, and asked K'yengo, his doctor, of all things I possessed, what the king would like best. To my surprise, I then learned that Rŭmanika had set his heart on the revolving rifle I had brought for Mtésa—the one, in fact, which he had prevented my sending on to Uganda in the hands of Kachŭchŭ, and he would have begged me for it before had his high-minded dignity, and the principle he had established of never begging for any thing, not interfered. I then said he should certainly have it; for as strongly as I had withheld from giving any thing to those begging scoundrels who wished to rob me of all I possessed in the lower countries, so strongly now did I feel inclined to be generous with this exceptional man Rŭmanika. We then had another picnic together, and, while I went home to join Grant, Rŭmanika spent the night doing homage and sacrificing a bullock at the tomb of his father Dagara.

Instead of paddling all down the lake again, I walked over the hill, and, on crossing at its northern end, wished to shoot ducks; but the superstitious boatmen put a stop to my intended amusement by imploring me not to do so, lest the spirit of the lake should be roused to dry up the waters.

4th. Rŭmanika returned in the morning, walking up the hill,

followed by a long train of his officers, and a party of men carry-ing on their shoulders his state carriage, which consisted of a large open basket laid on the top of two very long poles. After entering his palace, I immediately called on him to thank him for the great treat he had given me, and presented him, as an earnest of what I thought, with the Colt's revolving rifle and a fair allowance of ammunition. His delight knew no bounds on becoming the proprietor of such an extraordinary weapon, and induced him to dwell on his advantages over his brother Rogéro, whose antipathy to him was ever preying on his mind. He urged me again to devise some plan for overcoming him; and, becoming more and more confidential, favored me with the fol-lowing narrative, by way of evidence how the spirits were in-clined to show all the world that he was the rightful successor to the throne: When Dagara died, and he, Nnanaji, and Rogéro, were the only three sons left in line of succession to the crown, a small mystic drum of diminutive size was placed before them by the officers of state. It was only feather weight in reality, but, being loaded with charms, became so heavy to those who were not entitled to the crown, that no one could lift it but the one per-son whom the spirits were inclined toward as the rightful success-or. Now, of all the three brothers, he, Rŭmanika, alone could raise it from the ground; and while his brothers labored hard, in vain attempting to move it, he with his little finger held it up without any exertion.

This little disclosure in the history of Karagŭé led us on to farther particulars of Dagara's death and burial, when it tran-spired that the old king's body, after the fashion of his predeces-sors, was sewn up in a cowskin, and placed in a boat floating on the lake, where it remained for three days, until decomposition set in and maggots were engendered, of which three were taken into the palace and given in charge of the heir-elect; but, instead of remaining as they were, one worm was transformed into a lion, another into a leopard, and the third into a stick. After this the body of the king was taken up and deposited on the hill Moga-Namirinzi, where, instead of putting him under ground, the people erected a hut over him, and, thrusting in five maidens and fifty cows, inclosed the doorway in such a manner that the whole of them subsequently died from starvation.

This, as may naturally be supposed, led into farther genealog-ical disclosures of a similar nature, and I was told by Rŭmanika that his grandfather was a most wonderful man; indeed, Karagué was blessed with more supernatural agencies than any other country. Rohinda the Sixth, who was his grandfather, numbered so many years that people thought he never would die; and he even became so concerned himself about it, reflecting that his son Dagara would never enjoy the benefit of his position as successor to the crown of Karagué, that he took some magic powders and charmed away his life. His remains were then taken to Moga-Namirinzi, in the same manner as were those of Dagara; but, as an improvement on the maggot story, a young lion emerged from the heart of the corpse and kept guard over the hill, from whom other lions came into existence, until the whole place has become infested by them, and has since made Karagué a power and dread to all other nations; for these lions became subject to the will of Dagara, who, when attacked by the countries to the northward, instead of assembling an army of men, assembled his lion force, and so swept all before him.

Another test was then advanced at the instigation of K'yengo, who thought Rŭmanika not quite impressive enough of his right to the throne; and this was, that each heir in succession, even after the drum dodge, was required to sit on the ground in a certain place of the country, where, if he had courage to plant himself, the land would gradually rise up, telescope-fashion, until it reached to the skies, when, if the aspirant was considered by the spirits the proper person to inherit Karagué, he would gradually be lowered again without any harm happening; but, otherwise, the elastic hill would suddenly collapse, and he would be dashed to pieces. Now Rŭmanika, by his own confession, had gone through this ordeal with marked success; so I asked him if he found the atmosphere cold when so far up aloft, and as he said he did so, laughing at the quaintness of the question, I told him I saw he had learned a good practical lesson on the structure of the universe, which I wished he would explain to me. In a state of perplexity, K'yengo and the rest, on seeing me laughing, thought something was wrong; so, turning about, they thought again, and said, "No, it must have been hot, because the higher one ascended the nearer he got to the sun."

This led on to one argument after another, on geology, geography, and all the natural sciences, and ended by Rŭmanika showing me an iron much the shape and size of a carrot. This he said was found by one of his villagers while tilling the ground,

NZOÉ ANTELOPES. LITTLE WINDERMERE, KARAGÜÉ.

buried some way down below the surface; but, dig as he would, he could not remove it, and therefore called some more men to his help. Still the whole of them united could not lift the iron, which induced them, considering there must be some magic in it, to inform the king. "Now," says Rŭmanika, "I no sooner went there and saw the iron, than, without the smallest exertion, I up-lifted the iron, and brought it here as you see it. What can such a sign mean?" "Of course that you are the rightful king," said his flatterers. "Then," said Rŭmanika, in exuberant spirits, " during Dagara's time, as the king was sitting with many other men outside his hut, a fearful storm of thunder and lightning arose, and a thunderbolt struck the ground in the midst of them, which dispersed all the men but Dagara, who calmly took up the thunderbolt and placed it in the palace. I, however, no sooner came into possession, and Rogéro began to contend with me, than the thunderbolt vanished. .How would you account for this?" The flatterers said, "It is clear as possible; God gave the thunder-bolt to Dagara as a sign he was pleased with him and his rule; but when he found two brothers contending, he withdrew it to show their conduct was wicked."

5th. Rŭmanika in the morning sent me a young male nzoé (water-boc)* which his canoe-men had caught in the high rushes at the head of the lake, by the king's order, to please me; for I had heard this peculiar animal described in such strange ways at Kazé, both by Mŭsa and the Arabs, I was desirous of having a look at one. It proved to be closely allied to a water-boc found by Livingstone on the Ngami Lake; but, instead of being striped, was very faintly spotted, and so long were its toes, it could hard-ly walk on the dry ground; while its coat, also well adapted to the moist element it lived in, was long, and of such excellent qual-ity that the natives prize it for wearing almost more than any other of the antelope tribe. The only food it would eat were the tops of the tall papyrus rushes; but, though it ate and drank free-ly, and lay down very quietly, it always charged with ferocity any person who went near it.

In the afternoon Rŭmanika invited both Grant and myself to witness his New-moon Levée, a ceremony which takes place every month with a view of ascertaining how many of his subjects are loyal. On entering his palace inclosure, the first thing we saw

* Since named by Dr. P. L. Sclater "Tragelaphus Spekii." These nzoé have been drawn by Mr. Wolff from specimens brought home by myself.

was a blaue boc's horn stuffed full of magic powder, with very
imposing effect, by K'yengo, and stuck in the ground, with its
mouth pointing in the direction of Rogéro.   In the second court
we found thirty-five drums ranged on the ground, with as many
drummers standing behind them, and a knot of young princes and

The King's New-moon Levée.

officers of high dignity waiting to escort us into the third inclosure, where, in his principal hut, we found Rŭmanika squatting on
the ground, half concealed by the portal, but showing his smiling
face to welcome us in.   His head was got up with a tiara of beads,
from the centre of which, directly over the forehead, stood a plume
of red feathers, and encircling the lower face with a fine large
white beard set in a stock or band of beads.   We were beckoned
to squat alongside Nnanaji, the master of ceremonies, and a large
group of high officials outside the porch.   Then the thirty-five
drums all struck up together in very good harmony; and when
their deafening noise was over, a smaller band of hand-drums and
reed instruments was ordered in to amuse us.

This second performance over, from want of breath only, district officers, one by one, came advancing on tiptoe, then pausing,
contorting and quivering their bodies, advancing again with a
springing gait and outspread arms, which they moved as if they
wished to force them out of their joints, in all of which actions
they held drum-sticks or twigs in their hands, swore with a maniacal voice an oath of their loyalty and devotion to their king,
backed by the expression of a hope that he would cut off their
heads if they ever turned from his enemies, and then, kneeling
before him, they held out their sticks that he might touch them.

With a constant reiteration of these scenes—the saluting at one time, the music at another—interrupted only once by a number of girls dancing something like a good rough Highland fling while the little band played, the day's ceremonies ended.

6th and 7th. During the next two days, as my men had all worn out their clothes, I gave them each thirty necklaces of beads to purchase a suit of the bark cloth called mbŭgŭ, already described. Finding the flour of the country too bitter to eat by itself, we sweetened it with ripe plantains, and made a good cake of it. The king now, finding me disinclined to fight his brother Rogéro either with guns or magic horns, asked me to give him a " doctor" or charm to create longevity ănd to promote the increase of his family, as his was not large enough to maintain the dignity of so great a man as himself. I gave him a blister, and, changing the subject, told him the history of the creation of man. After listening to it attentively, he asked what thing in creation I considered the greatest of all things in the world; for while a man at most could only live one hundred years, a tree lived many; but the earth ought to be biggest, for it never died.

I then told him again I wished one of his sons would accompany me to England, that he might learn the history of Moses, wherein he would find that men had souls which live forever, but that the earth would come to an end in the fullness of time. This conversation, diversified by numerous shrewd remarks on the part of Rŭmanika, led to his asking how I could account for the decline of countries, instancing the dismemberment of the Wahŭma in Kittara, and remarking that formerly Karagŭé included Urundi, Rŭanda, and Kishakka, which collectively were known as the kingdom of Mérŭ, governed by one man. Christian principles, I said, made us what we are, and feeling a sympathy for him made me desirous of taking one of his children to learn in the same school with us, who, on returning to him, could impart what he knew, and, extending the same by course of instruction, would doubtless end by elevating his country to a higher position than it ever knew before, etc., etc. · The policy and government of the vast possessions of Great Britain were then duly discussed, and Rŭmanika acknowledged that the power of the pen was superior to that of the sword, and the electric telegraph and steam-engine the most wonderful powers he had ever heard of.

Before breaking up, Rŭmanika wished to give me any number of ivories I might like to mention, even three or four hundred, as a lasting remembrance that I had done him the honor of visiting Karagŭé in his lifetime; for, though Dagara had given to colored merchants, he would be the first who had given to a white man. Of course this royal offer was declined with politeness; he must understand that it was not the custom of big men in my country to accept presents of value when we made visits of pleasure. I had enjoyed my residence in Karagŭé, his intellectual conversations and his kind hospitality, all of which I should record in my books to hand down to posterity; but if he would give me a cow's horn, I would keep it as a trophy of the happy days I had spent in his country. He gave me one, measuring 3 feet 5 inches in length, and 18¾ inches in circumference at the base. He then offered me a large sheet, made up of a patchwork of very small N'yéra antelope skins, most exquisitely cured and sewn. This I rejected, as he told me it had been given to himself, explaining that we prided ourselves on never parting with the gifts of a friend; and this speech tickled his fancy so much that he said he never would part with any thing I gave him.

8th and 9th. The 8th went off much in the usual way by my calling on the king, when I gave him a pack of playing-cards, which he put into his curiosity-box. He explained to me, at my request, what sort of things he would like any future visitors to bring him—a piece of gold and silver embroidery; but, before any thing else, I found he would like to have toys, such as Yankee clocks with the face in a man's stomach, to wind up behind, his eyes rolling with every beat of the pendulum; or a china-cow milk-pot, a jack-in-the-box, models of men, carriages, and horses—all animals, in fact, and railways in particular.

On the 9th I went out shooting, as Rŭmanika, with his usual politeness, on hearing my desire to kill some rhinoceros, ordered his sons to conduct the field for me. Off we started by sunrise to the bottom of the hills overlooking the head of the Little Windermere lake. On arrival at the scene of action—a thicket of acacia shrubs—all the men in the neighborhood were assembled to beat. Taking post myself, by direction, in the most likely place to catch a sight of the animals, the day's work began by the beaters driving the covers in my direction. In a very short time a fine male was discovered making toward me, but not exactly knowing where he should bolt to. While he was in this perplexity, I stole along between the bushes, and caught sight of him standing as if anchored by the side of a tree, and gave him a broadsider with Blissett, which, too much for his constitution to stand, sent him off trotting, till, exhausted by bleeding, he lay down to die, and allowed me to give him a settler.

In a minute or two afterward, the good young princes, attracted by the sound of the gun, came to see what was done. Their surprise knew no bounds; they could scarcely believe what they saw; and then, on recovering, with the spirit of true gentlemen, they seized both my hands, congratulating me on the magnitude of my success, and pointed out, as an example of it, a by-stander who showed fearful scars, both on his abdomen and at the blade of his shoulder, who they declared had been run through by one of these animals. It was, therefore, wonderful to them, they observed, with what calmness I went up to such formidable beasts.

Just at this time a distant cry was heard that another rhinoceros was concealed in a thicket, and off we set to pursue her. Arriving at the place mentioned, I settled at once I would enter with only two spare men carrying guns, for the acacia thorns were so thick that the only tracks into the thicket were runs made by these animals. Leading myself, bending down to steal in, I tracked up a run till halfway through cover, when suddenly before me, like a pig from a hole, a large female, with her young one behind her, came straight down whoof-whoofing upon me. In this awkward fix I forced myself to one side, though pricked all over with thorns in doing so, and gave her one in the head which knocked her out of my path, and induced her, for safety, to make for the open, where I followed her down and gave her another. She then took to the hills and crossed over a spur, when, following after her, in another dense thicket, near the head of a glen, I came upon three, who no sooner sighted me than all in line they charged down my way. Fortunately, at the time, my gun-bearers were with me; so, jumping to one side, I struck them all three in turn. One of them dropped dead a little way on, but the others only pulled up when they arrived at the bottom. To please myself, now I had done quite enough; but, as the princes would have it, I went on with the chase. As one of the two, I could see, had one of his fore legs broken, I went at the sounder one, and gave him another shot, which simply induced him to walk over the lower end of the hill. Then turning to the last one, which could not escape, I asked the Wanyambo to polish him off with their spears and arrows, that I might see their mode of sport. As we moved up to the animal, he kept charging with snch impetuous fury they could not go into him; so I gave him a second ball, which brought him to anchor. In this helpless state, the men set at him in earnest, and a more barbarous finale I never did witness. Every man sent his spear, assegai, or arrow into his sides, until, completely exhausted, he sank like a porcupine covered with quills. The day's sport was now ended, so I went home to breakfast, leaving instructions that the heads should be cut off and sent to the king as a trophy of what the white man could do.

10th and 11th. The next day, when I called on Rŭmanika, the spoils were brought into court, and in utter astonishment he said, "Well, this must have been done with something more potent than powder, for neither the Arabs nor Nnanaji, although they talk of their shooting powers, could have accomplished such a great feat as this. It is no wonder the English are the greatest men in the world."

Neither the Wanyambo nor the Wahŭma would eat the rhinoceros, so I was not sorry to find all the Wanyamŭézi porters of the Arabs at Kufro, on hearing of the sport, come over and carry away all the flesh. They passed by our camp half borne down with their burdens of sliced flesh, suspended from poles which they carried on their shoulders; but the following day I was disgusted by hearing that their masters had forbidden their eating "the carrion," as the throats of the animals had not been cut; and, moreover, had thrashed them soundly because they complained they were half starved, which was perfectly true, by the poor food that they got as their pay.

12th. On visiting Rŭmanika again, and going through my geographical lessons, he told me, in confirmation of Mŭsa's old stories, that in Rŭanda there existed pigmies who lived in trees, but occasionally came down at night, and, listening at the hut doors of the men, would wait until they heard the name of one of its inmates, when they would call him out, and, firing an arrow into his heart, disappear again in the same way as they came. But, more formidable even than these little men, there were monsters who could not converse with men, and never showed themselves unless they saw women pass by; then, in voluptuous excitement, they squeezed them to death. Many other similar stories were then told, when I, wishing to go, was asked if I could kill hippopotami. Having answered that I could, the king graciously said he would order some canoes for me next morning; and as I declined because Grant could not accompany me, as a terrible dis-

PRESENTING MY SPOILS TO RÚMANIKA.   HEADS OF THREE WHITE RHINOCEROS SHOT IN KARAGÜÉ.

ease had broken out in his leg, he ordered a pig-shooting party. Agreeably with this, the next day I went out with his sons, numerously attended; but, although we beat the covers all day, the rain was so frequent the pigs would not bolt.

14th. After a long and amusing conversation with Rŭmanika in the morning, I called on one of his sisters-in-law, married to an elder brother who was born before Dagara ascended the throne. She was another of those wonders of obesity, unable to stand excepting on all fours. I was desirous to obtain a good view of her, and actually to measure her, and induced her to give me facilities for doing so by offering in return to show her a bit of my naked legs and arms. The bait took as I wished it, and after getting her to sidle and wriggle into the middle of the hut, I did as I promised, and then took her dimensions, as noted below.* All of these are exact except the height, and I believe I could have obtained this more accurately if I could have had her laid on the floor. Not knowing what difficulties I should have to contend with in such a piece of engineering, I tried to get her height by raising her up. This, after infinite exertions on the part of us both, was accomplished, when she sank down again, fainting, for her blood had rushed into her head. Meanwhile, the daughter, a lass of sixteen, sat stark-naked before us, sucking at a milk-pot, on which the father kept her at work by holding a rod in his hand; for, as fattening is the first duty of fashionable female life, it must be duly enforced by the rod if necessary. I got up a bit of flirtation with missy, and induced her to rise and shake hands with me. Her features were lovely, but her body was as round as a ball.

In the evening we had another row with my head men, Baraka having accused Bombay of trying to kill him with magic. Bombay, who was so incessantly bullied by Baraka's officious attempts to form party cliques opposed to the interests of the journey, and get him turned out of the camp, indiscreetly went to one of K'yengo's men, and asked him if he knew of any medicine that would affect the hearts of the Wangŭana so as to incline them toward him; and on the sub-doctor saying Yes, Bombay gave him some beads, and bought the medicine required, which, put into a pot of pombé, was placed by Baraka's side. Baraka in the mean while got wind of the matter through K'yengo, who, misunderstanding

---

* Round the arm, 1 foot 11 inches; chest, 4 feet 4 inches; thigh, 2 feet 7 inches; calf, 1 foot 8 inches; height, 5 feet 8 inches.

the true facts of the case, said it was a charm to deprive Baraka of his life.   A court of inquiry having been convened, with all the parties concerned in attendance, K'yengo's mistake was discovered, and Bombay was lectured for his folly, as he had a thousand times before abjured his belief in such magical follies; moreover, to punish him for the future, I took Baraka, whenever I could, with me to visit the king, which, little as it might appear to others, was of the greatest consequence to the hostile parties.

15th and *16th*.   When I next called on Rŭmanika I gave him a Vautier's binocular and prismatic compass, on which he politely remarked he was afraid he was robbing me of every thing.   More compliments went round, and then he asked if it was true we could open a man's skull, look at his brains, and close it up again ; also if it was true we sailed all round the world into regions where there was no difference between night and day, and how, when we plowed the seas in such enormous vessels as would carry at once 20,000 men, we could explain to the sailors what they ought to do; for, although he had heard of these things, no one was able to explain them to him.

After all the explanations were given, he promised me a boat-hunt after the nzoé in the morning; but when the time came, as difficulties were raised, I asked him to allow us to anticipate the arrival of Kachŭchŭ, and march on to Kitangŭlé.   He answered, with his usual courtesy, That he would be very glad to oblige us in any way that we liked; but he feared that, as the Waganda were such superstitious people, some difficulties would arise, and he must decline to comply with our request.   " You must not," he added, " expect ever to find again a reasonable man like myself."   I then gave him a book on " Kafir laws," which he said he would keep for my sake, with all the rest of the presents, which he was determined never to give away, though it was usual for him to send novelties of this sort to Mtésa, king of Uganda, and Kamrasi, king of Unyoro, as a friendly recognition of their superior positions in the world of great monarchies.

17th.   Rŭmanika next introduced me to an old woman who came from the island of Gasi, situated in the Little Lŭta Nzigé. Both her upper and lower incisors had been extracted, and her upper lip perforated by a number of small holes, extending in an arch from one corner to the other.   This interesting but ugly old lady narrated the circumstances by which she had been enslaved, and then sent by Kamrasi as a curiosity to Rŭmanika, who had ever since kept her as a servant in his palace. A man from Rŭanda then told us of the Wilyanwantŭ (men-eaters), who disdained all food but human flesh; and Rŭmanika confirmed the statement. Though I felt very skeptical about it, I could not help thinking it a curious coincidence that the position they were said to occupy agreed with Petherick's Nyam Nyams (men-eaters).

Of far more interest were the results of a conversation which I had with another of Kamrasi's servants, a man of Amara, as it threw some light upon certain statements made by Mr. Leon of the people of Amara being Christians. He said they bore single holes in the centres both of their upper and lower lips, as well as in the lobes of both of their ears, in which they wear small brass rings. They live near the N'yanza—where it is connected by a strait with a salt lake, and drained by a river to the northward—in comfortable houses, built like the tembés of Unyamŭézi. When killing a cow, they kneel down in an attitude of prayer, with both hands together, held palm upward, and utter Zŭ, a word the meaning of which he did not know. I questioned him to try if the word had any trace of a Christian meaning—for instance, as a corruption of Jesu—but without success. Circumcision is not known among them, neither have they any knowledge of God or a soul. A tribe called Wakŭavi, who are white, and described as not unlike myself, often came over the water and made raids on their cattle, using the double-edged simé as their chief weapon of war. These attacks were as often resented, and sometimes led the Wamara in pursuit a long way into their enemy's country, where, at a place called Kisigŭisi, they found men robed in red cloths. Beads were imported, he thought, both from the east and from Ukidi. Associated with the countries Masau or Masai, and Usambŭrŭ, which he knew, there was a large mountain, the exact position of which he could not describe.

I took down many words of his language, and found they corresponded with the North African dialects, as spoken by the people of Kidi, Gani, and Madi. The southerners, speaking of these, would call them Wakidi, Wagani, and Wamadi, but among themselves the syllable, wa is not prefixed, as in the southern dialects, to signify people. Rŭmanika, who appeared immensely delighted as he assisted me in putting the questions I wanted, and saw me note them down in my book, was more confirmed than ever in the truth of my stories that I came from the north, and thought as the beads came to Amara, so should I be able to open the road and bring him more visitors. This he knew was his only chance of ever seeing me any more, for I swore I would never go back through Usŭi, so greatly did I feel the indignities imposed on me by Sŭwarora.

18*th.* To keep the king in good humor, I now took a table-knife, spoon, and fork to the palace, which, after their several uses were explained, were consigned to his curiosity-box. Still Rŭmanika could not understand how it was I spent so much and traveled so far, or how it happened such a great country as ours could be ruled by a woman. He asked the queen's name, how many children she had, and the mode of succession; then, when fully satisfied, led the way to show me what his father Dagara had done when wishing to know of what the centre of the earth was composed. At the back of the palace a deep ditch was cut, several yards long, the end of which was carried by a subterranean passage into the palace, where it was ended off with a cavern led into by a very small aperture. It then appeared that Dagara, having failed, in his own opinion, to arrive any nearer to the object in view, gave the excavating up as a bad job, and turned the cave into a mysterious abode, where it was confidently asserted he spent many days without eating or drinking, and turned sometimes into a young man, and then an old one, alternately, as the humor seized him.

19*th* to 22*d.* On the 19th I went fishing, but without success, for they said the fish would not take in the lake; and on the following day, as Grant's recovery seemed hopeless, for a long time at least, I went with all the young princes to see what I could do with the hippopotami in the lake, said to inhabit the small island of Conty. The party was an exceedingly merry one. We went off to the island in several canoes, and at once found an immense number of crocodiles basking in the sun, but not a single hippopotamus was in sight. The princes then, thinking me "green" at this kind of sport, said the place was enchanted, but I need not fear, for they would bring them out to my feet by simply calling out certain names, and this was no sooner done than four old and one young one came immediately in front of us. It seemed quite a sin to touch them, they looked all so innocent; but as the king wanted to try me again, I gave one a ball on the head which sent him under, never again to be seen, for on the 22d, by which time I supposed he ought to have risen inflated with gases, the king sent out his men to look out for him; but they returned to say that, while all the rest were in the old place, that one, in particular, could not be found.

On this K'yengo, who happened to be present while our interview lasted, explained that the demons of the deep were annoyed with me for intruding on their preserves without having the courtesy to commemorate the event by the sacrifice of a goat or a cow. Rŭmanika then, at my suggestion, gave Nnanaji the revolving pistol I first gave him, but not without a sharp rebuke for his having had the audacity to beg a gun of me in consideration of his being a sportsman. We then went into a discourse on astrology, when the intelligent Rŭmanika asked me if the same sun we saw one day appeared again, or whether fresh suns came every day, and whether or not the moon made different faces, to laugh at us mortals on earth.

23*d* and 24*th*. This day was spent by the king introducing me to his five fat wives, to show with what esteem he was held by all the different kings of the countries surrounding. From Mpororo—which, by-the-by, is a republic—he was wedded to Kaogéz, the daughter of Kahaya, who is the greatest chief in the country; from Unyoro he received Kaŭyangi, Kamrasi's daughter; from Nkolé, Kambiri, the late Kasiyonga's daughter; from Utŭmbi, Kirangŭ, the late Kitéimbŭa's daughter; and, lastly, the daughter of Chiŭarŭngi, his head cook.

After presenting Rŭmanika with an India-rubber band—which, as usual, amused him immensely—for the honor he had done me in showing me his wives, a party of Waziwa, who had brought some ivory from Kidi, came to pay their respects to him. On being questioned by me, they said that they once saw some men like my Wangŭana there; they had come from the north to trade, but, though they carried fire-arms, they were all killed by the people of Kidi. This was famous; it corroborated what I knew, but could not convince others of, that traders could find their way up to Kidi by the Nile. It in a manner explained also how it was that Kamrasi, some years before, had obtained some pink beads, of a variety the Zanzibar merchants had never thought of bringing into the country. Bombay was now quite convinced, and we all became transported with joy, until Rŭmanika, reflecting on the sad state of Grant's leg, turned that joy into grief by saying that the rules of Uganda are so strict that no one who is sick could enter the country. "To show," he said, "how absurd they are, your donkey would not be permitted because he has no trowsers; and you even will have to put on a gown, as your unmentionables will be considered indecorous." I now asked Rŭmanika if he would assist me in replenishing my fast-ebbing store of beads by selling tusks to the Arabs at Kufro, when for every 35 lb. weight I would give him $50 by orders on Zanzibar, and would insure him from being cheated by sending a letter of advice to our consul residing there. At first he demurred on the high-toned principle that he could not have any commercial dealings with myself; but, at the instigation of Bombay and Baraka, who viewed it in its true character, as tending merely to assist my journey in the best manner he could, without any sacrifice to dignity, he eventually yielded, and, to prove his earnestness, sent me a large tusk, with a notice that his ivory was not kept in the palace, but with his officers, and as soon as they could collect it, so soon I should get it.

Rŭmanika, on hearing that it was our custom to celebrate the birth of our Savior with a good feast of beef, sent us an ox. I immediately paid him a visit to offer the compliments of the season, and at the same time regretted, much to his amusement, that he, as one of the old stock of Abyssinians, who are the oldest Christians on record, should have forgotten this rite; but I hoped the time would come when, by making it known that his tribe had lapsed into a state of heathenism, white teachers would be induced to set it all to rights again. At this time some Wahaiya traders (who had been invited at my request by Rŭmanika) arrived. Like the Waziwa, they had traded with Kidi, and they not only confirmed what the Waziwa had said, but added that, when trading in those distant parts, they heard of Wangŭana coming in vessels to trade to the north of Unyoro; but the natives there were so savage, they only fought with these foreign traders. A man of Rŭanda now informed us that the cowrie-shells, so plentiful in that country, come there from the other or western side, but he could not tell whence they were originally obtained. Rŭmanika then told me Sŭwarora had been so frightened by the Watŭta, and their boastful threats to demolish Usŭi bit by bit, reserving him only as a titbit for the end, that he wanted a plot of ground in Karagŭé to preserve his property in.

26th, 27th, and 28th. Some other travelers from the north again informed us that they had heard of Wangŭana who attempted to

Christmas Day.

trade in Gani and Chopi, but were killed by the natives. I now assured Rŭmanika that in two or three years he would have a greater trade with Egypt than he ever could have with Zanzibar; for, when I opened the road, all those men he heard of would swarm up here to visit him. He, however, only laughed at my folly in proposing to go to a place of which all I heard was merely that every stranger who went there was killed. He began to show a disinclination to allow my going there, and though from the most friendly intention, this view was alarming, for one word from him could have ruined my projects. As it was, I feared my followers might take fright and refuse to advance with me. I thought it good policy to talk of there being many roads leading through Africa, so that Rŭmanika might see he had not got, as he thought, the sole key to the interior. I told him again of certain views I once held of coming to see him from the north up the Nile, and from the east through the Masai. He observed that, " To open either of those routes, you would require at least two hundred guns." He would, however, do something when we returned from Uganda; for, as Mtésa followed his advice in every thing, so did Kamrasi, for both held the highest opinion of him.

The conversation then turning on London, and the way men 'and carriages moved up the streets like strings of ants on their migrations, Rŭmanika said the villages in Rŭanda were of enormous extent, and the people great sportsmen, for they turned out in multitudes, with small dogs on whose necks were tied bells, and blowing horns themselves, to hunt leopards. They were, however, highly superstitious, and would not allow any strangers to enter their country ; for some years ago, when some Arabs went there, a great drought and famine set in, which they attributed to evil influences brought by them, and, turning them out of their country, said they would never admit any of their like among them again. I said, in return, I thought his Wanyambo just as superstitious, for I observed, while walking one day, that they had placed a gourd on the path, and on inquiry found they had done so to gain the sympathy of all passers-by to their crop close at hand, which was blighted, imagining that the voice of the sympathizer heard by the spirits would induce them to relent, and restore a healthy tone to the crop.

During this time an interesting case was brought before us for judgment. Two men, having married one woman, laid claim to her child, which, as it was a male one, belonged to the father. Baraka was appointed the umpire, and immediately comparing the infant's face with those of its claimants, gave a decision which all approved of but the loser. It was pronounced amid peals of laughter from my men; for, whenever any little excitement is going forward, the Wanguana all rush to the scene of action to give their opinions, and joke over it afterward.

29*th* and 30*th.* On telling Rŭmanika this story next morning, he said, "Many funny things happen in Karagŭé;", and related some domestic incidents, concluding with the moral that "Marriage in Karagŭé was a mere matter of money." Cows, sheep, and slaves have to be given to the father for the value of his daughter; but if she finds she has made a mistake, she can return the dowry-money and gain her release. The Wahŭma, although they keep slaves and marry with pure negroes, do not allow their daughters to taint their blood by marrying out of their clan. In warfare it is the rule that the wahinda, or princes, head their own soldiers, and set them the example of courage, when, after firing a few arrows, they throw their bows away, and close at once with their spears and assegais. Life is never taken in Karagŭé either for murder or cowardice, as they value so much their Wahŭma breed; but for all offenses, fines of cows are exacted according to the extent of the crime.

31*st.* Ever proud of his history since I had traced his descent from Abyssinia and King David, whose hair was as straight as my own, Rŭmanika dwelt on my theological disclosures with the greatest delight, and wished to know what difference existed between the Arabs and ourselves; to which Baraka replied, as the best means of making him understand, that while the Arabs had only one Book, we had two; to which I added, Yes, that is true in a sense; but the real merits lie in the fact that we have got the better *book,* as may be inferred from the obvious fact that we are more prosperous, and their superiors in all things, as I would prove to him if he would allow me to take one of his sons home to learn that *book;* for then he would find his tribe, after a while, better off than the Arabs are. Much delighted, he said he would be very glad to give me two boys for that purpose.

Then, changing the subject, I pressed Rŭmanika, as he said he had no idea of a God or future state, to tell me what advantage he expected from sacrificing a cow yearly at his father's grave. He laughingly replied he did not know, but he hoped he might

be favored with better crops if he did so. He also placed pombé
and grain, he said, for the same reason, before a large stone on the
hill-side, although it could not eat, or make any use of it; but the
coast-men were of the same belief as himself, and so were all the
natives. No one in Africa, as far as he knew, doubted the power
of magic and spells; and if a fox barked when he was leading an
army to battle, he would retire at once, knowing that this prog-
nosticated evil. There were many other animals, and lucky and
unlucky birds, which all believed in.

I then told him it was fortunate he had no disbelievers like us
to contend with in battle, for we, instead of trusting to luck and
such omens, put our faith only in skill and pluck, which Baraka
elucidated from his military experience in the wars in British India. Lastly, I explained to him how England formerly was as
unenlightened as Africa, and believing in the same sort of superstitions, and the inhabitants were all as naked as his skin-wearing
Wanyambo; but now, since they had grown wiser, and saw
through such impostures, they were the greatest men in the world.
He said, for the future he would disregard what the Arabs said,
and trust to my doctrines, for without doubt he had never seen
such a wise man as myself; and the Arabs themselves confirmed
this when they told him that all their beads and cloths came from
the land of the Wazŭngŭ, or white men.

1st, 2d, and 3d. The new year was ushered in by the most exciting intelligence, which drove us half wild with delight, for we
fully believed Mr. Petherick was indeed on his road up the Nile,
endeavoring to meet us. It was this: An officer of Rŭmanika's,
who had been sent four years before on a mission to Kamrasi, had
just then returned with a party of Kamrasi's who brought ivory
for sale to the Arabs at Kufro, along with a vaunting commission
to inform Rŭmanika that Kamrasi had foreign visitors as well as
himself. They had not actually come into Unyoro, but were in
his dependency, the country of Gani, coming up the Nile in vessels. They had been attacked by the Gani people, and driven
back with considerable loss both of men and property, although
they were in sailing vessels, and fired guns which even broke
down the trees on the banks. Some of their property had been
brought to him, and he, in return, had ordered his subjects not to
molest them, but allow them to come on to him. Rŭmanika enjoyed this news as much as myself, especially when I told him
of Petherick's promise to meet us, just as these men said he was

trying to do; and more especially so when I told him that if he
would assist me in trying to communicate with Petherick, the latter
would either come here himself, or send one of his men, conveying
a suitable present, while I was away in Uganda, and then,
in the end, we would all go off to Kamrasi's together.

4th. Entering warmly into the spirit of this important intelligence,
Rŭmanika inquired into its truth, and, finding no reason
to doubt it, said he would send some men back with Kamrasi's
men, if I could have patience until they were ready to go. There
would be no danger, as Kamrasi was his brother-in-law, and
would do all that he told him.

I now proposed to send Baraka, who, ashamed to cry off, said
he would go with Rŭmanika's officers if I allowed him a companion
of his own choosing, who would take care of him if he got
sick on the way otherwise he should be afraid they would leave
him to die, like a dog, in the jungles. We consoled him by assenting
to the companion he wished, and making Rŭmanika responsible
that no harm should come to him from any of the risks
which his imagination conjured up. Rŭmanika then gave him
and Ulédi, his selected companion, some sheets of mbŭgŭ, in order
that they might disguise themselves as his officers while crossing
the territories of the King of Uganda. On inquiring as to the
reason of this, it transpired that, to reach Unyoro, the party would
have to cross a portion of Uddŭ, which the late king Sunna, on
annexing that country to Uganda, had divided, not in halves, but
by alternate bands running transversely from Nkolé to the Victoria
N'yanza.

5th and *6th.* To keep Rŭmanika up to the mark, I introduced
to him Saidi, one of my men, who was formerly a slave, captured
in Walâmo, on the borders of Abyssinia, to show him, by his similarity
to the Wahŭma, how it was I had come to the conclusion
that he was of the same race. Saidi told him his tribe kept cattle
with the same stupendous horns as those of the Wahŭma; and
also that, in the same manner, they all mixed blood with milk for
their dinners, which, to his mind, confirmed my statement. At
night, as there was a partial eclipse of the moon, all the Wangŭana
marched up and down from Rŭmanika's to Nnanaji's huts,
singing and beating our tin cooking-pots to frighten off the spirit
of the sun from consuming entirely the chief object of reverence, •
the moon.

7th. Our spirits were now farther raised by the arrival of a

semi-Hindŭ-Sŭahili, named Jŭma, who had just returned from a
visit to the King of Uganda, bringing back with him a large present of ivory and slaves; for he said he had heard from the king
of our intention to visit him, and that he had dispatched officers
to call us immediately. This intelligence delighted Rŭmanika as
much as it did us, and he no sooner heard it than he said, with
ecstasies, "I will open Africa, since the white men desire it; for
did not Dagara command us to show deference to strangers?"
Then, turning to me, he added, "My only regret is, you will not
take something as a return for the great expenses you have been
put to in coming to visit me." The expense was admitted, for I
had now been obliged to purchase from the Arabs upward of
£400 worth of beads, to keep such a store in reserve for my return from Uganda as would enable me to push on to Gondokoro.
I thought this necessary, as every report that arrived from Unyamŭézi only told us of farther disasters with the merchants in that
country. Sheikh Said was there even then with my poor Hottentots, unable to convey my post to the coast.

8th to 10th. At last we heard the familiar sound of the Uganda
drum. Maŭla, a royal officer, with a large escort of smartly-
dressed men, women, and boys, leading their dogs and playing
their reeds, announced to our straining ears the welcome intelligence that their king had sent them to call us. N'yamgundŭ,
who had seen us in Usŭi, had marched on to inform the king of
our advance and desire to see him, and he, intensely delighted at
the prospect of having white men for his guests, desired no time
should be lost in our coming on. Maŭla told us that his officers
had orders to supply us with every thing we wanted while passing through his country, and that there would be nothing to pay.

One thing only now embarrassed me—Grant was worse, without hope of recovery for at least one or two months. This large
body of Waganda could not be kept waiting. To get on as fast
as possible was the only chance of ever bringing the journey to a
successful issue; so, unable to help myself, with great remorse at
another separation, on the following day I consigned my companion, with several Wangŭana, to the care of my friend Rŭmanika.
I then separated ten loads of beads and thirty copper wires for my
expenses in Uganda; wrote a letter to Petherick, which I gave to
Baraka; and gave him and his companion beads to last as money
for six months, and also a present both for Kamrasi and the Gani
chief. To Nsangéz I gave charge of my collections in natural

history, and the reports of my progress, addressed to the Geographical Society, which he was to convey to Sheikh Said at Kazé, for conveyance as far as Zanzibar.

This business concluded in camp, I started my men and went to the palace to bid adieu to Rŭmanika, who appointed Rozaro, one of his officers, to accompany me wherever I went in Uganda, and to bring me back safely again. At Rŭmanika's request, I then gave Mtésa's pages some ammunition to hurry on with to the great king of Uganda, as his majesty had ordered them to bring him, as quickly as possible, some strengthening powder, and also some powder for his gun. Then, finally, to Maŭla, also under Rŭmanika's instructions, I gave two copper wires and five bundles of beads; and, when all was completed, set out on the march, perfectly sure in my mind that before very long I should settle the great Nile problem forever; and, with this consciousness, only hoping that Grant would be able to join me before I should have to return again, for it was never supposed for a moment that it was possible I ever could go north from Uganda. Rŭmanika was the most resolute in this belief, as the kings of Uganda, ever since that country was detached from Unyoro, had been making constant raids, seizing cattle and slaves from the surrounding countries.

CHAPTER IX.

HISTORY OF THE WAHŬMA.

The Abyssinians and Gallas.—Theory of Conquest of inferior by superior Races.— The Wahŭma and the Kingdom of Kittara.—Legendary History of the Kingdom of Uganda.—Its Constitution, and the Ceremonials of the Court.

THE reader has now had my experience of several of the minor states, and has presently to be introduced to Uganda, the most powerful state in the ancient but now divided great kingdom of Kittara. I shall have to record a residence of considerable duration at the court there; and, before entering on it, I propose to state my theory of the ethnology of that part of Africa inhabited by the people collectively styled Wahŭma, otherwise Gallas or Abyssinians. My theory is founded on the traditions of the several nations, as checked by my own observation of what I saw when passing through them. It appears impossible to believe, judging from the physical appearance of the Wahŭma, that they can be of any other race than the semi-Shem-Hamitic of Ethiopia. The traditions of the imperial government of Abyssinia go as far back as the scriptural age of King David, from whom the late reigning king of Abyssinia, Sahéla Sélassié, traced his descent.

Most people appear to regard the Abyssinians as a different race from the Gallas, but, I believe, without foundation. Both alike are Christians of the greatest antiquity. It is true that, while the aboriginal Abyssinians in Abyssinia proper are more commonly agriculturists, the Gallas are chiefly a pastoral people; but I conceive that the two may have had the same relations with each other which I found the Wahŭma kings and Wahŭma herdsmen holding with the agricultural Wazinza in Uzinza, the Wanyambo in Karagŭé, the Waganda in Uganda, and the Wanyoro in Unyoro.

In these countries the government is in the hands of foreigners, who had invaded and taken possession· of them, leaving the agricultural aborigines to till the ground, while the junior members of the usurping clans herded cattle—just as in Abyssinia, or wherever the Abyssinians or Gallas have shown themselves. There a pastoral clan from the Asiatic side took the government of Abyssinia from its people and have ruled over them ever since, changing, by intermarriage with the Africans, the texture of their hair and color to a certain extent, but still maintaining a high stamp of Asiatic feature, of which a marked characteristic is a bridged instead of bridgeless nose.

It may be presumed that there once existed a foreign but compact government in Abyssinia, which, becoming great and powerful, sent out armies on all sides of it, especially to the south, southeast, and west, slave-hunting and devastating wherever they went, and in process of time becoming too great for one ruler to control. Junior members of the royal family then, pushing their fortunes, dismembered themselves from the parent stock, created separate governments, and, for reasons which can not be traced, changed their names. In this manner we may suppose that the Gallas separated from the Abyssinians, and located themselves to the south of their native land.

Other Abyssinians, or possibly Gallas—it matters not which they were or what we call them—likewise detaching themselves, fought in the Somali country, subjugated that land, were defeated to a certain extent by the Arabs from the opposite continent, and tried their hands south as far as the Jub River, where they also left many of their numbers behind. Again they attacked Omwita (the present Mombas), were repulsed, were lost sight of in the interior of the continent, and, crossing the Nile close to its source, discovered the rich pasture-lands of Unyoro, and founded the great kingdom of Kittara, where they lost their religion, forgot their language, extracted their lower incisors like the natives, changed their national name to Wahŭma, and no longer remembered the names of Hubshi or Galla, though even the present reigning kings retain a singular traditional account of their having once been half white and half black, with hair on the white side straight, and on the black side frizzly. It was a curious indication of the prevailing idea still entertained by them of their foreign extraction, that it was surmised in Unyoro that the approach of us white men into their country from both sides at once augured an intention on our part to take back the country from them. Believing, as they do, that Africa formerly belonged to Europeans, from whom it was taken by negroes with whom they had allied themselves, the Wahŭma make themselves a small residue of the original European stock driven from the land; an idea which seems natural enough when we consider that the Wahŭma are, in numbers, quite insignificant compared with the natives. Again, the princes of Unyoro are called Wawitŭ, and point to the north when asked where their country Uwitŭ is situated, doubtfully saying, when questioned about its distance, "How can we tell circumstances which took place in our forefathers' times? we only think it is somewhere near your country." Although, however, this very interesting people, the Wahŭma, delight in supposing themselves to be of European origin, they are forced to confess, on closer examination, that although they came in the first instance from the doubtful north, they came latterly from the east, as part of a powerful Wahŭma tribe, beyond Kidi, who excel in arms, and are so fierce no Kidi people, terrible in war as these too are described to be, can stand against them. This points, if our maps.are true, to the Gallas; for all pastorals in these people's minds are Wahŭma; and if we could only reconcile ourselves to the belief that the Wawitŭ derived their name from Omwita, the last place they attacked on the east coast of Africa, then all would be clear; for it must be noticed the Wakama, or kings, when asked to what race they owe their origin, invariably reply, in the first place, from princes—giving, for instance, the titles Wawitŭ in Unyoro, and Wahinda in Karagŭé—which is most likely caused by their never having been asked such a close question before, while the idiom of the language generally induces them to call themselves after the name applied to their country.

So much for ethnological conjecture. Let us now deal with the Wahŭma since they crossed the Nile and founded the kingdom of Kittara, a large tract of land bounded by the Victoria N'yanza and Kitangŭlé Kagéra or River on the south, the Nile on the east, the Little Lŭta-Nzigé Lake* on the north, and the kingdoms of Utŭmbi and Nkolé on the west.

The general name Kittara is gradually becoming extinct, and is seldom applied to any but the western portions; while the northeastern, in which the capital is situated, is called Unyoro, and the other, Uddŭ apart from Uganda, as we shall presently see.

Nobody has been able to inform us how many generations old the Wahŭma government of Unyoro is. The last three kings are Chiawambi, N'yawongo, and the present king Kamrasi. In very early times dissensions among the royal family, probably contending for the crown, such as we presume must have occurred in

* *I. e.*, Dead Locust Lake—Lŭta, dead ; Nzigé, locust.

Abyssinia, separated the parent stock, and drove the weaker to find refuge in Nkolé, where a second and independent government of Wahŭma was established. Since then, twenty generations ago, it is said the Wahŭma government of Karagŭé was established in the same manner. The conspirator Rohinda fled from Kittara to Karagŭé with a large party of Wahŭma; sought the protection of Nono, who, a Myambo, was king over the Wanyambo of that country; ingratiated himself and his followers with the Wanyambo; and, finally, designing a crown for himself, gave a feast; treacherously killed King Nono in his cups, and set himself on the throne, the first mkama or king who ruled in Karagŭé. Rohinda was succeeded by Ntaré, then Rohinda II., then Ntaré II., which order only changed with the eleventh reign, when Rŭsatira ascended the throne, and was succeeded by Mehinga, then Kaliméra, then Ntaré VII., then Rohinda.VI., then Dagara, and now Rŭmanika. During this time the Wahŭma were well south of the equator, and still destined to spread. Brothers again contended for the crown of their father, and the weaker took refuge in Uzinza, where the fourth Wahŭma government was created, and so remained under one king until the last generation, when King Rŭma died, and his two sons, Rohinda, the eldest, and Sŭwarora, contended for the crown, but divided the country between them, Rohinda taking the eastern half, and Sŭwarora the western, at the instigation of the late king Dagara of Karagŭé.

This is the most southerly kingdom of the Wahŭma, though not the farthest spread of its people, for we find the Watŭsi, who are emigrants from Karagŭé of the same stock, overlooking the Tanganyika Lake from the hills of Uhha, and tending their cattle all over Unyamŭézi under the protection of the native negro chiefs; and we also hear that the Wapoka of Fipa, south of the Rŭkwa Lake, are the same. How or when their name became changed from Wahŭma to Watŭsi no one is able to explain; but, again deducing the past from the present, we can not help suspecting that, in the same way as this change has taken place, the name Galla may have been changed from Hubshi, and Wahŭma from Gallas. But though in these southern regions the name of the clan has been changed, the princes still retain the title of Wahinda as in Karagŭé, instead of Wawitŭ as in Unyoro, and are considered of such noble breed that many of the pure negro chiefs delight in saying I am a mhinda, or prince, to the confusion of travelers, which confusion is increased by the Wahŭma habits of conforming to the regulations of the different countries they adopt.

For instance, the Wahŭma of Uganda and Karagŭé, though so close to Unyoro, do not extract their lower incisors; and though the Wanyoro only use the spear in war, the Wahŭma in Karagŭé are the most expert archers in Africa. We are thus left only the one very distinguishing mark, the physical appearance of this remarkable race, partaking even more of the phlegmatic nature of the Shemitic father than the nervous, boisterous temperament of the Hamitic mother, as a *certain* clew to their Shem-Hamitic origin.

It remains to speak of the separation of Uddŭ from Unyoro, the present kingdom of Uganda, which, to say the least of it, is extremely interesting, inasmuch as the government there is as different from the other surrounding countries as those of Europe are compared to Asia.

In the earliest times the Wahŭma of Unyoro regarded all their lands bordering on the Victoria Lake as their garden, owing to its exceeding fertility, and imposed the epithet of Wirŭ, or slaves, upon its people, because they had to supply the imperial government with food and clothing. Coffee was conveyed to the capital by the Wirŭ, also mbŭgŭ (bark cloaks), from an inexhaustible fig-tree; in short, the lands of the Wirŭ were famous for their rich productions.

Now Wirŭ in the northern dialect changes to Waddŭ in the southern; hence Uddŭ, the land of the slaves, which remained in one connected line from the Nile to the Kitangŭlé Kagéra until eight generations back, when, according to tradition, a sportsman from Unyoro, by name Uganda, came with a pack of dogs, a woman, a spear, and a shield, hunting on the left bank of Katonga valley, not far from the lake. He was but a poor man, though so successful in hunting that vast numbers of the Wirŭ flocked to him for flesh, and became so fond of him as to invite him to be their king, saying, " Of what avail to us is our present king, living so far away that when we sent him a cow as a tributary offering, that cow on the journey gave a calf, and the calf became a cow and gave another calf, and so on, and yet the present has not reached its destination?"

At first Uganda hesitated, on the plea that they had a king already; but, on being farther pressed, consented; when the people, hearing his name, said, " Well, let it be so; and for the future let this country between the Nile and Katonga be called Uganda, and let your name be Kiméra, the first king of Uganda."

The same night Kiméra stood upon a stone with a spear in his hand, and a woman and dog sitting by his side; and to this day people assert that his footprints and the mark left by his spear-end, as well as the seats of the woman and dog, are visible. The report of these circumstances soon reached the great king of Unyoro, who, in his magnificence, merely said, "The poor creature must be starving; allow him to feed there if he likes." The kings who have succeeded Kiméra are, 1. Mahanda; 2. Katéréza; 3. Chabago; 4. Simakokiro; 5. Kamanya; 6. Sunna; 7. Mtésa, not yet crowned.

These kings have all carried on the same system of government as that commenced by Kiméra, and proved themselves a perfect terror to Unyoro, as we shall see in the sequel. Kiméra, suddenly risen to eminence, grew proud and headstrong — formed a strong clan around him, whom he appointed to be his Wakungŭ, or officers—rewarded well, punished severely, and soon became magnificent. Nothing short of the grandest palace, a throne to sit upon, the largest harem, the smartest officers, the best-dressed people, even a menagerie for pleasure—in fact, only the best of every thing — would content him. Fleets of boats, not canoes, were built for war, and armies formed, that the glory of the king might never decrease. In short, the system of government, according to barbarous ideas, was perfect. Highways were cut from one extremity of the country to the other, and all rivers bridged. No house could be built without its necessary appendages for cleanliness; no person, however poor, could expose his person; and to disobey these laws was death.

After the death of Kiméra, the prosperity of Uganda never decreased, but rather improved. The clan of officers formed by him were as proud of their emancipation from slavery as the king they had created was of his dominion over them. They buried Kiméra with state honors, giving charge of the body to the late king's most favorite consort, whose duty it was to dry the corpse by placing it on a board resting on the mouth of an earthen open pot heated by fire from below. When this drying process was completed, at the expiration of three months, the lower jaw was cut out and neatly worked over with beads; the umbilical cord, which had been preserved from birth, was also worked with beads. These were kept apart, but the body was consigned to a

ARMS AND FASHIONS OF UGANDA.

1. Amulet of ivory worn by men.
2. Amulet of brass wire worn by women.
3. Bracelets of brass and copper.
4. Necklaces of beads and shells.
5. Ordinary iron wire anklet, with cow's tail hair inside.
6. Earrings of brass and beads.
7. Tobacco and pipes.
8. Doorway of village, with human skull and block of wood.
9. Bee-hive of bark.
10. Old woman boiling beer.
11. Cotton-spinner.
12. Quiver, bow, shield, etc.

tomb, and guarded ever after by this officer and a certain number of the king's next most favorite women, all of whom planted gardens for their maintenance, and were restricted from seeing the succeeding king.

By his large establishment of wives, Kiméra left a number of princes or Warangira, and as many princesses. From the warangira the wakungŭ now chose as their king the one whom they thought best suited for the government of the country; not of too high rank by the mother's side, lest their selection in his pride should kill them all, but one of low birth. The rest were placed with wives in a suite of huts, under charge of a keeper, to prevent any chance of intrigues and dissensions. They were to enjoy life until the prince elect should arrive at the age of discretion and be crowned, when all but two of the princes would be burnt to death, the two being reserved in case of accident as long as the king wanted brother companions, when one would be banished to Unyoro, and the other pensioned with suitable possessions in Uganda. The mother of the king by this measure became queen-dowager, or N'yamasoré. She halved with her son all the wives of the deceased king not stationed at his grave, taking second choice; kept up a palace only little inferior to her son's with large estates, guided the prince elect in the government of the country, and remained until the end of his minority the virtual ruler of the land; at any rate, no radical political changes could take place without her sanction. The princesses became the wives of the king; no one else could marry them.

Both mother and son had their Katikiros or commander-in-chief, also titled Kamraviona, as well as other officers of high rank. Among them, in due order of gradation, are the Ilmas, a woman who had the good fortune to have cut the umbilical cord at the king's birth; the Sawaganzi, queen's sister and king's barber; Kaggao, Pokino, Sakibobo, Kitŭnzi, and others, governors of provinces; Jumba, admiral of the fleet; Kasŭjŭ, guardian of the king's sisters; Mkŭenda, factor; Kŭnsa and Usungŭ, first and second class executioners; Mgemma, commissioner in charge of tombs; Sérŭti, brewer; Mfŭmbiro, cook; numerous pages to run messages and look after the women, and minor wakungŭ in hundreds. One Mkungŭ is always over the palace, in command of the Wanagalali, or guards, which are changed monthly; another is ever in attendance as seizer of refractory persons. There are also in the palace almost constantly the Wanangalavi, or drummers; Nsasé, pea-gourd rattlers; Milélé, flute-players; Mŭkondéri, clarionet players; also players on wooden harmonicons and lap-harps, to which the players sing accompaniments; and, lastly, men who whistle on their fingers—for music is half the amusement of these courts. Every body in Uganda is expected to keep spears, shields, and dogs, the Uganda arms and cognizance, while the wakungŭ are entitled to drums. There is also a Neptune Mgussa, or spirit, who lives in the depths of the N'yanza, communicates through the medium of his temporal mkungŭ, and guides to a certain extent the naval destiny of the king.

It is the duty of all officers, generally speaking, to attend at court as constantly as possible; should they fail, they forfeit their lands, wives, and all belongings. These will be seized and given to others more worthy of them, as it is presumed that either insolence or disaffection can be the only motive which would induce any person to absent himself for any length of time from the pleasure of seeing his sovereign. Tidiness in dress is imperatively necessary, and for any neglect of this rule the head may be the forfeit. The punishment for such offenses, however, may be commuted by fines of cattle, goats, fowls, or brass wire. All acts of the king are counted benefits, for which he must be thanked; and so every deed done to his subjects is a gift received by them, though it should assume the shape of flogging or fine; for are not these, which make better men of them, as necessary as any thing? The thanks are rendered by groveling on the ground, floundering about and whining after the manner of happy dogs, after which they rise up suddenly, take up sticks—spears are not allowed to be carried in court—make as if charging the king, jabbering as fast as tongues can rattle, and so they swear fidelity for all their lives.

This is the greater salutation; the lesser one is performed kneeling in an attitude of prayer, continually throwing open the hands, and repeating sundry words. Among them the word "n'yanzig" is the most frequent and conspicuous; and hence these gesticulations receive the general designation n'yanzig, a term which will be frequently met with, and which I have found it necessary to use like an English verb. In consequence of these salutations, there is more ceremony in court than business, though the king, ever having an eye to his treasury, continually finds some trifling fault, condemns the head of the culprit, takes his liquidation-present, if he has any thing to pay, and thus keeps up his revenue.

No one dare stand before the king while he is either standing still or sitting, but must approach him with downcast eyes and bended knees, and kneel or sit when arrived. To touch the king's throne or clothes, even by accident, or to look upon his women, is certain death. When sitting in court holding a levée, the king invariably has in attendance several women, Wabandwa, evil-eye averters or sorcerers. They talk in feigned voices raised to a shrillness almost amounting to a scream. They wear dried lizards on their heads, small goatskin aprons trimmed with little bells, diminutive shields and spears set off with cock-hackles, their functions in attendance being to administer cups of marwa (plantain wine). To complete the picture of the court, one must imagine a crowd of pages to run royal messages; they dare not walk, for such a deficiency in zeal to their master might cost their life. A farther feature of the court consists in the national symbols already referred to—a dog, two spears, and shield.

With the company squatting in a large half circle, or three sides of a square, many deep, before him, in the hollow of which .are drummers and other musicians, the king, sitting on his throne in high dignity, issues his orders for the day much to the following effect: "Cattle, women, and children are short in Uganda; an army must be formed of one to two thousand strong to plunder Unyoro. The Wasoga have been insulting his subjects, and must be reduced to subjection; for this emergency another army must be formed, of equal strength, to act by land in conjunction with the fleet. The Wahaiya have paid no tribute to his greatness ,lately, and must be taxed." For all these matters the commander-in-chief tells off the divisional officers, who are approved by the king, and the matter is ended in court. The divisional officers then find subordinate officers, who find men, and the army proceeds with its march. Should any fail with their mission, re-enforcements are sent, and the runaways, called women, are drilled with a red-hot iron until they are men no longer, and die for their cowardice. All heroism, however, insures promotion. The king receives his army of officers with great ceremony, listens to their exploits, and gives as rewards women, cattle, and command over men—the greatest elements of wealth in Uganda—with a liberal hand.

As to the minor business transacted in court, culprits are

brought in bound by officers, and reported. At once the sentence is given, perhaps awarding the most torturous, lingering death—probably without trial or investigation, and, for all the king knows, at the instigation of some one influenced by wicked spite. If the accused endeavor to plead his defense, his voice is at once drowned, and the miserable victim dragged off in the roughest manner possible by those officers who love their king, and delight in promptly carrying out his orders. Young virgins, the daughters of wakungŭ, stark naked, and smeared with grease, but holding, for decency's sake, a small square of mbŭgŭ at the upper corners in both hands before them, are presented by their fathers in propitiation for some offense, and to fill the harem. Seizing-officers receive orders to hunt down wakungŭ who have committed some indiscretions, and to confiscate their lands, wives, children, and property. An officer observed to salute informally is ordered for execution, when every body near him rises in an instant, the drums beat, drowning his cries, and the victim of carelessness is dragged off, bound by cords, by a dozen men at once. Another man, perhaps, exposes an inch of naked leg while squatting, or has his mbŭgŭ tied contrary to regulations, and is condemned to the same fate.

Fines of cows, goats, and fowls are brought in and presented; they are smoothed down by the offender's hands, and then applied to his face, to show there is no evil spirit lurking in the gift; then thanks are proffered for the leniency of the king in letting the presenter off so cheaply, and the pardoned man retires, full of smiles, to the ranks of the squatters. Thousands of cattle, and strings of women and children, sometimes the result of a victorious plundering hunt, or else the accumulated seizures from refractory wakungŭ, are brought in; for there is no more common or acceptable offering to appease the king's wrath toward any refractory or blundering officer than a present of a few young beauties, who may perhaps be afterward given as the reward of good service to other officers.

Stick-charms, being pieces of wood of all shapes, supposed to have supernatural virtues, and colored earths, endowed with similar qualities, are produced by the royal magicians. The master of the hunt exposes his spoils, such as antelopes, cats, porcupines, curious rats, etc., all caught in nets, and placed in baskets, zebra, lion, and buffalo skins being added. The fishermen bring their spoils; also the gardeners. The cutlers show knives and forks made of iron inlaid with brass and copper; the furriers, most beautifully-sewn patchwork of antelopes' skins; the habit-maker, sheets of mbŭgŭ bark-cloth; the blacksmith, spears; the maker of shields, his productions, and so forth; but nothing is ever given without rubbing it down, then rubbing the face, and going through a long form of salutation for the gracious favor the king has shown in accepting it.

When tired of business, the king rises, spear in hand, and, leading his dog, walks off without word or comment, leaving his company, like dogs, to take care of themselves.

Strict as the discipline of the exterior court is, that of the interior is not less severe. The pages all wear turbans of cord made from aloe fibres. Should a wife commit any trifling indiscretion, either by word or deed, she is condemned to execution on the spot, bound by the pages and dragged out. Notwithstanding the stringent laws for the preservation of decorum by all male attendants, stark-naked full-grown women are the valets.

On the first appearance of the new moon every month, the king shuts himself up, contemplating and arranging his magic horns— the horns of wild animals stuffed with charm-powder—for two or three days. These may be counted his Sundays or church festivals, which he dedicates to devotion. On other days he takes his women, some hundreds, to bathe or sport in ponds; or, when tired of that, takes long walks, his women running after him, when all the musicians fall in, take precedence of the party, followed by the wakungŭ and pages, with the king in the centre of the procession, separating the male company from the fair sex. On these excursions no common man dare look upon the royal procession. Should any body by chance happen to be seen, he is at once hunted down by the pages, robbed of every thing he possesses, and may count himself very lucky if nothing worse happens. Pilgrimages are not uncommon, and sometimes the king spends a fortnight yachting; but whatever he does, or wherever he goes, the same ceremonies prevail—his musicians, wakungŭ, pages, and the wives take part in all.

But the greatest of all ceremonies takes place at the time of the coronation. The prince-elect then first seeks favor from the kings of all the surrounding countries, demanding in his might and power one of each of their daughters in marriage, or else recognition in some other way, when the ilmas makes a pilgrimage to the deceased king's tomb, to observe, by the growth and other signs of certain trees and plants, what destiny awaits the king According to the prognostics, they report that he will either have to live a life of peace, or, after coronation, take the field at the head of an army to fight either east, west, or both ways, when usually the first march is on Kittara, and the second on Usoga. The mgussa's voice is also heard, but in what manner I do not know, as all communication on state matters is forbidden in Uganda. These preliminaries being arranged, the actual coronation takes place, when the king ceases to hold any farther communion with his mother. The brothers are burnt to death, and the king, we shall suppose, takes the field at the head of his army.

It is as the result of these expeditions that one half Usoga and the remaining half of Uddŭ have been annexed to Uganda.

CHAPTER X.

KARAGŬÉ AND UGANDA.

Escape from Protectors.—Cross the Kitangŭlé, the first Affluent of the Nile.—Enter
Uddŭ.—Uganda.—A rich Country.—Driving away the Devil.—A Conflict in the
Camp.—A pretending Prince.—Three Pages with a diplomatic Message from the
King of Uganda.—Crime in Uganda.

CROSSING back over the Weranhanjé spur, I put up with the
Arabs at Kufro. Here, for the first time in this part
of the world, I found good English peas growing.
Next day (11th), crossing over a succession of forks, supporters to
the main spur, we encamped at Lŭandalo. Here we were overtaken by Rozaro, who had remained behind, as I now found, to
collect a large number of Wanyambo, whom he called his children, to share with him the gratuitous living these creatures always look out for on a march of this nature.

To Kufro, 10th.

After working round the end of the great spur, while following
down the crest of a fork, we found Karagŭé separated
by a deep valley from the hilly country of Uhaiya,
famous for its ivory and coffee productions. On entering the rich
plantain gardens of Kisaho, I was informed we must halt there a
day for Maŭla to join us, as he had been detained by Rŭmanika,
who, wishing to give him a present, had summoned Rozaro's sister to his palace for that purpose. She was married to another,
and had two children by him, but that did not signify, as it was
found in time her husband had committed a fault, on account of
which it was thought necessary to confiscate all his property.

To Kisaho, 12th.

At this place all the people were in a constant state of inebri-
ety, drinking pombé all day and all night. I shot a
montana antelope, and sent its head and skin back to
Grant, accompanied with my daily report to Rŭmanika.

Halt, 13th.

Maŭla having joined me, we marched down to near the end
of the fork overlooking the plain of Kitangŭlé, the
Waganda drums beating, and whistles playing all the
way as we went along.

To Narŭeri, 14th.

We next descended from the Mountains of the Moon, and span-

To Kitangŭlé,
15th. ned a long alluvial plain to the settlement of the so-
long-heard-of Kitangŭlé, where Rŭmanika keeps his
thousands and thousands of cows. In former days the dense
green forests peculiar to the tropics, which grow in swampy places
about this plain, were said to have been stocked by vast herds of
elephants; but, since the ivory trade had increased, these animals
had all been driven off to the hills of Kisiwa and Uhaiya, or into
Uddŭ beyond the river, and all the way down to the N'yanza.

To-day we reached the Kitangŭlé Kagéra, or river, which, as I
To Ndongo, 16th. ascertained in the year 1858, falls into the Victoria
N'yanza on the west side. Most unfortunately, as we
led off to cross it, rain began to pour, so that every body and every thing was thrown into confusion. I could not get a sketch
of it, though Grant was more fortunate afterward, neither could I
measure or fathom it; and it was only after a long contest with
the superstitious boatmen that they allowed me to cross in their
canoe with my shoes on, as they thought the vessel would either
upset, or else the river would dry up, in consequence of their Nep-

Ferry on the Kitangŭlé River.

tune taking offense at me. Once over, I looked down on the noble stream with considerable pride. About eighty yards broad,
it was sunk down a considerable depth below the surface of the

land, like a huge canal, and is so deep it could not be poled by
the canoemen, while it runs at a velocity of from three to four
knots an hour.

I say I viewed it with pride, because I had formed my judgment of its being fed from high-seated springs in the Mountains
of the Moon solely on scientific geographical reasonings; and,
from the bulk of the stream, I also believed those mountains must
attain an altitude of 8000 feet* or more, just as we find they do
in Rŭanda. I thought then to myself, as I did at Rŭmanika's,
when I first viewed the Mfŭmbiro cones, and gathered all my distant geographical information there, that these highly saturated
Mountains of the Moon gave birth to the Congo as well as to the
Nile, and also to the Shiré branch of the Zambézé.

I came, at the same time, to the conclusion that all our previous
information concerning the hydrography of these regions, as well
as the Mountains of the Moon, originated with the ancient Hindŭs, who told it to the priests of the Nile; and that all those busy
Egyptian geographers, who disseminated *their* knowledge with a
view to be famous for *their* long-sightedness, in solving the deep-
seated mystery which enshrouded the source of their holy river,
were so many hypothetical humbugs. Reasoning thus, the Hindŭ
traders alone, in those days, I believed, had a firm basis to stand
upon, from their intercourse with the Abyssinians—through whom
they must have heard of the country of Amara, which they applied to the N'yanza—and with the Wanyamŭézi or men of the
Moon, from whom they heard of the Tanganyika and Karagŭé
mountains. I was all the more impressed with this belief by
knowing that the two Church missionaries, Rebmann and Erhardt,
without the smallest knowledge of the Hindŭs' map, constructed
a map of their own, deduced from the Zanzibar traders, something
on the same scale, by blending the Victoria N'yanza, Tanganyika,
and N'yassa into one; while to their triuned lake they gave the
name Moon, because the men of the Moon happened to live in
front of the central lake. And later still, Mr. Leon, another mis-
sionary, heard of the N'yanza and the country Amara, near which
he heard the Nile made its escape.

Going on with the march we next came to Ndongo, a perfect
garden of plantains. The whole country was rich—most surprisingly so. The same streaky argillaceous sandstones prevailed
as in Karagŭé. There was nothing, in fact, that would not have

* In "Blackwood's Magazine" for August, 1859.

grown here, if it liked moisture and a temperate heat. It was a perfect paradise for negroes: as fast as they sowed, they were sure of a crop without much trouble; though, I must say, they kept their huts and their gardens in excellent order.

As Maŭla would stop here, I had to halt also. The whole country along the banks of the river, and near some impenetrable forests, was alive with antelopes, principally hartebeests, but I would not fire at them until it was time to return, as the villagers led me to expect buffaloes. The consequence was, as no buffaloes were to be found, I got no sport, though I wounded a hartebeest, and followed him almost into camp, when I gave up the chase to some negroes, and amused myself by writing to Rŭmanika, to say if Grant did not reach me by a certain date, I would try to navigate the N'yanza, and return to him in boats up the Kitangŭlé River.

Halt, 17th.

We crossed over a low spur of hill extending from the mountainous kingdom of Nkolé, on our left, toward the N'yanza. Here I was shown by Nasib a village called Ngandŭ, which was the farthest trading dépôt of the Zanzibar ivory-merchants. It was established by Mŭsa Mzŭri, by the permission of Rŭmanika; for, as I shall have presently to mention, Sunna, after annexing this part of Uddŭ to Uganda, gave Rŭmanika certain bands of territory in it as a means of security against the possibility of its being wrested out of his hands again by the future kings of Unyoro. Following on Mŭsa's wake, many Arabs also came here to trade; but they were so oppressive to the Waganda that they were recalled by Rŭmanika, and obliged to locate themselves at Kufro. To the right, at the end of the spur, stretching as far as the eye could reach toward the N'yanza, was a rich, well-wooded, swampy plain, containing large open patches of water, which not many years since, I was assured, were navigable for miles, but now, like the Urigi Lake, were gradually drying up. Indeed, it appeared to me as if the N'yanza must have once washed the foot of these hills, but had since shrunk away from its original margin.

To Ngambézi, 18th.

On arrival at Ngambézi, I was immensely struck with the neatness and good arrangement of the place, as well as its excessive beauty and richness. No part of Bengal or Zanzibar could excel it in either respect; and my men, with one voice, exclaimed, "Ah! what people these Waganda are!" and passed other remarks, which may be abridged as follows: "They build their

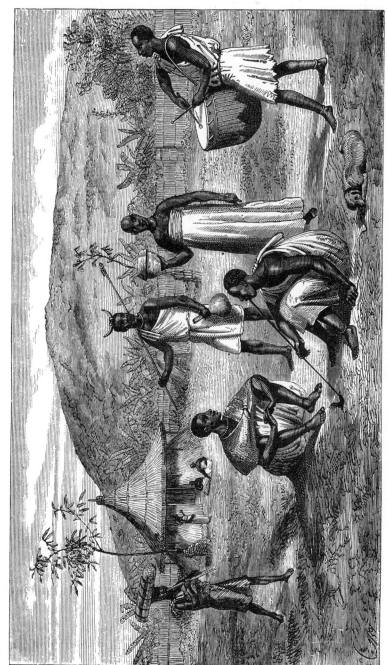

BARAZA AND RESIDENCE OF KING MTÉSA'S UNCLE—NGAMBÉZI.

huts and keep their gardens just as well as we do at Ungŭja, with screens and inclosures for privacy, a clearance in front of their establishments, and a baraza or reception-hut facing the buildings. Then, too, what a beautiful prospect it has! rich marshy plains studded with mounds, on each of which grow the umbrella cactus, or some other evergreen tree; and beyond, again, another hill-spur such as the one we have crossed over." One of King Mtésa's uncles, who had not been burnt to death by the order of the late king Sunna on his ascension to the throne, was the proprietor of this place, but unfortunately he was from home. However, his substitute gave me his baraza to live in, and brought many presents of goats, fowls, sweet potatoes, yams, plantains, sugar-cane, and Indian corn, and apologized in the end for deficiency in hospitality. I, of course, gave him beads in return.

Continuing over the same kind of ground in the next succeed-
To Semizabi, 19th.
ing spurs of the streaky red-clay sandstone hills, we put up at the residence of Isamgévi, a mkungŭ or district officer of Rŭmanika's. His residence was as well kept as Mtésa's uncle's; but, instead of a baraza fronting his house, he had a small inclosure, with three small huts in it, kept apart for devotional purposes, or to propitiate the evil spirits—in short, according to the notions of the place, a church. This officer gave me a cow and some plantains, and I, in return, gave him a wire and some beads. Many mendicant women, called by some wich-wézi, by others mabandwa, all wearing the most fantastic dresses of mbŭgŭ, covered with beads, shells, and sticks, danced before us, singing a comic song, the chorus of which was a long, shrill, rolling Coo-roo-coo-roo, coo-roo-coo-roo, delivered as they came to a standstill. Their true functions were just as obscure as the religion of the negroes generally; some called them devil-drivers, others evil-eye averters; but, whatever it was for, they imposed a tax on the people, whose minds being governed by a necessity for making some self-sacrifice to propitiate something, they could not tell what, for their welfare in the world, they always gave them a trifle in the same way as the East Indians do their fakirs.

After crossing another low swampy flat, we reached a much
To Kisŭéré, 20th.
larger group, or rather ramification, of hill-spurs pointing to the N'yanza, called Kisŭéré, and commanded by M'yombo, Rŭmanika's frontier officer. Immediately behind this, to the northward, commenced the kingdom of Unyoro; and here it was, they said, Baraka would branch off my

line on his way to Kamrasi. Maŭla's home was one march distant from this, so the scoundrel now left me to enjoy himself there, giving as his pretext for doing so that Mtésa required him, as soon as I arrived here, to send on a messenger that order might be taken for my proper protection on the line of march; for the Waganda were a turbulent set of people, who could only be kept in order by the executioner; and doubtless many, as was customary on such occasions, would be beheaded, as soon as Mtésa heard of my coming, to put the rest in a fright. I knew this was all humbug, of course, and I told him so; but it was of no use, and I was compelled to halt.

On the 23d another officer, named Maribŭ, came to me and said, Mtésa, having heard that Grant was left sick behind at Karagŭé, had given him orders to go there and fetch him, whether sick or well, for Mtésa was most anxious to see white men. Hearing this, I at once wrote to Grant, begging him to come on if he could do so, and to bring with him all the best of my property, or as much as he could of it, as I now saw there was more cunning humbug than honesty in what Rŭmanika had told me about the impossibility of our going north from Uganda, as well as in his saying sick men could not go into Uganda, and donkeys without trowsers would not be admitted there, because they were considered indecent. If he was not well enough to move, I advised him to wait there until I reached Mtésa's, when I would either go up the lake and Kitangŭlé to fetch him away, or would make the king send boats for him, which I more expressly wished, as it would tend to give us a much better knowledge of the lake.

Maŭla now came again, after receiving repeated and angry messages, and I forced him to make a move. He led me straight up to his home, a very nice place, in which he gave me a very large, clean, and comfortable hut—had no end of plantains brought for me and my men—and said, "Now you have really entered the kingdom of Uganda, for the future you must buy no more food. At every place that you stop for the day, the officer in charge will bring you plantains, otherwise your men can help themselves in the gardens, for such are the laws of the land when a king's guest travels in it. Any one found selling any thing to either yourself or your men would be punished." Accordingly, I stopped the daily issue of beads; but no sooner had I done so than all my men declared they could not

Halt, 20th to 24th.

To N'yagussa, 24th.

eat plantains. It was all very well, they said, for the Waganda
to do so, because they were used to it, but it did not·satisfy their
hunger.

Maŭla, all smirks and smiles, on seeing me order the things out
for the march, begged I would have patience, and
wait till the messenger returned from the king; it
would not take more than ten days at the most. Much annoyed
at this nonsense, I ordered my tent to be pitched. I refused all
Maŭla's plantains, and gave my men beads to buy grain again
with; and, finding it necessary to get up some indignation, said I
would not stand being chained like a dog; if he would not go on
ahead, I should go without him. Maŭla then said he would go
to a friend's and come back again. I said, if he did not, I should
go off; and so the conversation ended.

Halt, 25th.

26th. Drumming, singing, screaming, yelling, and dancing had
been going on these last two days and two nights to drive the
phépo or devil out of a village. The whole of the ceremonies
were most ludicrous. An old man and woman, smeared with
white mud, and holding pots of pombé in their laps, sat in front
of a hut, while other people kept constantly bringing them baskets full of plantain-squash, and more pots of pombé. In the court-
yard fronting them were hundreds of men and women dressed in
smart mbŭgŭs—the males wearing for turbans strings of abrus-
seeds wound round their heads, with polished boars' tusks stuck
in in a jaunty manner. These were the people who, all drunk as
fifers, were keeping up such a continual row to frighten the devil
away. In the midst of this assemblage I now found Kachŭchŭ,
Rŭmanika's representative, who went on ahead from Karagŭé
palace to tell Mtésa that I wished to visit him. With him, he
said, were two other wakungŭ of Mtésa's, who had orders to bring
on my party and Dr. K'yengo's. Mtésa, he said, was so mad to
see us, that the instant he arrived at the palace and told him we
wished to visit him, the king caused "fifty big men and four
hundred small ones" to be executed, because, he said, his subjects
were so bumptious they would not allow any visitors to come
near him, else he would have had white men before.

27th. N'yamgundŭ, my old friend at Usŭi, then came to me,
and said he was the first man to tell Mtésa of our arrival in Usŭi,
and wish to visit him. The handkerchief I had given Irungŭ at
Usŭi to present as a letter to Mtésa he had snatched away from
him, and given, himself, to his king, who no sooner received it

than he bound it round his head and said, in ecstasies of delight,
"Oh, the mzungŭ, the mzungŭ! he does indeed want to see me."
Then giving him four cows as a return letter to take to me, he
said, "Hurry off as quickly as possible and bring him here."
"The cows," said N'yamgundŭ, "have gone on to Kisŭéré by
another route, but I will bring them here; and then, as Maŭla is
taking you, I will go and fetch Grant." I then told him not to
be in such a hurry. I had turned off Maŭla for treating me like
a dog, and I would not be escorted by him again. He replied
that his orders would not be fully accomplished as long as any
part of my establishment was behind; so he would, if I wished
it, leave part of his "children" to guide me on to Mtésa's, while
he went to fetch Grant. An officer, I assured him, had just gone
on to fetch Grant, so he need not trouble his head on that score;
at any rate, he might reverse his plan, and send his children for
Grant, while he went on with me, by which means he would fully
accomplish his mission. Long arguments ensued, and I at length
turned the tables by asking who was the greatest—myself or my
children; when he said, "As I see you are the greatest, I will do
as you wish; and after fetching the cows from Kisŭéré, we will
march to-morrow at sunrise."

The sun rose, but N'yamgundŭ did not appear. I was greatly
annoyed lest Maŭla should come and try to drive
him away. I waited, restraining my impatience until noon, when, as I could stand it no longer, I ordered Bombay
to strike my tent and commence the march. A scene followed,
which brought out my commander-in-chief's temper in a rather
surprising shape. "How can we go?" said Bombay. "Strike
the tent," said I. "Who will guide us?" said Bombay. "Strike
the tent," I said again. "But Rŭmanika's men have all gone
away, and there is no one to show us the way." "Never mind;
obey my orders, and strike the tent." Then, as Bombay would
not do it, I commenced myself, assisted by some of my other men,
and pulled it down over his head, all the women who were assembled under it, and all the property. On this, Bombay flew
into a passion, abusing the men who were helping me, as there
were fires and powder-boxes under the tent. I of course had to
fly into a passion and abuse Bombay. He, in a still greater rage,
said he would pitch into the men, for the whole place would be
blown up. "That is no reason why you should abuse my men,"
I said, "who are better than you by obeying my orders. If I

To Mashondé,
28th.

choose to blow up my property, that is my look-out; and if you don't do your duty, I will blow you up also." Foaming and roaring with rage, Bombay said he would not stand being thus insulted. I then gave him a dig on the head with my fist. He squared up, and pouted like an enraged chameleon, looking savagely at me. I gave him another dig, which sent him staggering. He squared again: I gave him another; till at last, as the claret was flowing, he sulked off, and said he would not serve me any more. I then gave Nasib orders to take Bombay's post, and commence the march; but the good old man made Bombay give in, and off we went, amid crowds of Waganda, who had collected to witness this comedy, and were all digging at one another's heads, showing off in pantomime the strange ways of the white man. N'yamgundŭ then joined us, and begged us to halt only one more day, as some of his women were still at Kisŭéré; but Bombay, showing his nozzle rather flatter than usual, said, "No; I got this on account of your lies. I won't tell Bana any more of your excuses for stopping; you may tell him yourself, if you like." N'yamgundŭ, however, did not think this advisable, and so we went on as we were doing. It was the first and last time I had ever occasion to lose my dignity by striking a blow with my own hands; but I could not help it on this occasion without losing command and respect; for, although I often had occasion to award 100 and even 150 lashes to my men for stealing, I could not, for the sake of due subordination, allow any inferior officer to strike Bombay, and therefore had to do the work myself.

Skirting the hills on the left, with a large low plain to the right, we soon came on one of those numerous rush-drains that appear to me to be the last waters left of the old bed of the N'yanza. This one in particular was rather large, being 150 yards wide. It was sunk where I crossed it, like a canal, 14 feet below the plain; and what with mire and water combined, so deep, I was obliged to take off my trowsers while fording it. Once across, we sought for and put up in a village beneath a small hill, from the top of which I saw the Victoria N'yanza for the first time on this march. N'yamgundŭ delighted me much: treating me as a king, he always fell down on his knees to address me, and made all his "children" look after my comfort in camp.

We marched on again over the same kind of ground, alternately crossing rush-drains of minor importance, though provokingly

To Ukara, 29th. frequent, and rich gardens, from which, as we passed, all the inhabitants bolted at the sound of our drums, knowing well that they would be seized and punished if found gazing at the king's visitors. Even on our arrival at Ukara not one soul was visible. The huts of the villagers were shown to myself and my men without any ceremony. The Wanyambo escort stole what they liked out of them, and I got into no end of troubles trying to stop the practice; for they said the Waganda served them the same way when they went to Karagué, and they had a right to retaliate now. To obviate this distressing sort of plundering, I still served out beads to my men, and so kept them in hand a little; but they were fearfully unruly, and did not like my interference with what, by the laws of the country they considered their right.

Here I had to stop a day for some of N'yamgundŭ's women, who, in my hurry at leaving Maŭla's, were left behind. Halt, 30th. A letter from Grant was now brought to me by a very nice-looking young man, who had the skin of a leopard-cat (*F. Serval*) tied round his neck—a badge which royal personages only were entitled to wear. N'yamgundŭ, seeing this, as he knew the young man was not entitled to wear it, immediately ordered his "children" to wrench it from him. Two ruffianly fellows then seized him by his hands, and twisted his arms round and round until I thought they would come out of their sockets. Without uttering a sound, the young man resisted, until N'yamgundŭ told them to be quiet, for he would hold a court on the subject, and see if the young man could defend himself. The ruffians then sat on the ground, but still holding on to him, while N'yamgundŭ took up a long stick, and, breaking it into sundry bits of equal length, placed one by one in front of him, each of which was supposed to represent one number in line of succession to his forefathers. By this it was proved he did not branch in any way from the royal stock. N'yamgundŭ, then turning to the company, said, What would he do now to expiate his folly? If the matter was taken before Mtésa he would lose his head; was it not better he should pay one hundred cows? All agreeing to this, the young man said he would do so, and quietly allowed the skin to be untied and taken off by the ruffians.

Next day, after crossing more of those abominable rush-drains, while in sight of the Victoria N'yanza, we ascended To Méruka, 31st. the most beautiful hills, covered with verdure of all descriptions. At Méruka, where I put up, there resided some grandees, the chief of whom was the king's aunt. She sent me a goat, a hen, a basket of eggs, and some plantains, in return for which I sent her a wire and some beads. I felt inclined to stop here a month, every thing was so very pleasant. The temperature was perfect. The roads, as indeed they were every where, were as broad as our coach-roads, cut through the long grasses, straight over the hills and down through the woods in the dells —a strange contrast to the wretched tracks in all the adjacent countries. The huts were kept so clean and so neat, not a fault could be found with them—the gardens the same. Wherever I strolled I saw nothing but richness, and what ought to be wealth. The whole land was a picture of quiescent beauty, with a' boundless sea in the background. Looking over the hills, it struck the fancy at once that at one period the whole land must have been at a uniform level with their present tops, but that, by the constant denudation it was subjected to by frequent rains, it had been cut down and sloped into those beautiful hills and dales which now so much pleased the eye; for there were none of those quartz dikes I had seen protruding through the same kind of aqueous formations in Usŭi and Karagŭé, nor were there any other sorts of volcanic disturbance to distort the calm, quiet aspect of the scene.

From this, the country being all hill and dale, with miry rush-drains in the bottoms, I walked, carrying my shoes and stockings in my hands, nearly all the way. Rozaro's "children" became more and more troublesome, stealing every thing they could lay their hands upon out of the village huts we passed on the way. On arrival at Sangŭa, I found many of them had been seized by some men, who, bolder than the rest, had overtaken them while gutting their huts, and made them prisoners, demanding of me two slaves and one load of beads for their restitution. I sent my men back to see what had happened, and ordered them to bring all the men on to me, that I might see fair play. They, however, took the law into their own hands, drove off the Waganda villagers by firing their muskets, and relieved the thieves. A complaint was then laid against N'yamgundŭ by the chief officer of the village, and I was requested to halt. That I would not do, leaving the matter in the hands of the governor general, Mr. Pokino, whom I heard we should find at the next station, Masaka.

To Sangŭa, 1st.

On arrival there at the government establishment—a large collection of grass huts, separated one from the other
within large inclosures, which overspread the whole
top of a low hill—I was requested to withdraw and put up in
some huts a short distance off, and wait until his excellency, who
was from home, could come and see me; which the next day he
did, coming in state with a large number of officers, who brought
with them a cow, sundry pots of pombé, enormous sticks of sugar-cane, and a large bundle of country coffee. This grows in
great profusion all over this land in large bushy trees, the berries
sticking on the branches like clusters of holly-berries.

To Masaka, 2d.

I was then introduced, and told that his excellency was the appointed governor of all the land lying between the
Katonga and the Kitangŭlé Rivers. After the first
formalities were over, the complaint about the officers at Sangŭa
was preferred for decision, on which Pokino at once gave it
against the villagers, as they had no right, by the laws of the land,
to lay hands on a king's guest. Just then Maŭla arrived, and began to abuse N'yamgundŭ. Of course I would not stand this;
and, after telling all the facts of the case, I begged Pokino to send
Maŭla away out of my camp. Pokino said he could not do this,
as it was by the king's order he was appointed; but he put Maŭla in the background, laughing at the way he had "let the bird
fly out of his hands," and settled that N'yamgundŭ should be my
guide. I then gave him a wire, and he gave me three large
sheets of mbŭgŭ, which he said I should require, as there were so
many water-courses to cross on the road I was going. A second
day's halt was necessitated by many of my men catching fever,
probably owing to the constant crossing of those abominable rush-
drains. There was no want of food here, for I never saw such a
profusion of plantains any where. They were literally lying in
heaps on the ground, though the people were brewing pombé all
day, and cooking them for dinner every evening.

Halt, 3d and 4th.

After crossing many more hills and miry bottoms, constantly
coming in view of the lake, we reached Ugonzi, and,
after another march of the same description, came to
Kituntŭ, the last officer's residence in Uḍḍŭ. Formerly it was
the property of a Belŭch named Eseau, who came to this country
with merchandise, trading on account of Said Said, late Sultan of
Zanzibar; but, having lost it all on his way here, paying mahongo,
or taxes, and so forth, he feared returning, and instead made great

To Ugonzi, 5th.
To Kituntŭ, 6th.

POMBÉ BREWING.

friends with the late king Sunna, who took an especial fancy to him because he had a very large beard, and raised him to the rank of mkungŭ. A few years ago, however, Eseau died, and left all his family and property to a slave named Ulédi, who now, in consequence, is the border officer.

I became now quite puzzled while thinking which was the finest spot I had seen in Uddŭ, so many were exceedingly beautiful; but I think I gave the preference to this, both for its own immediate neighborhood and the long range of view it afforded of Uganda proper, the lake, and the large island, or group of islands, called Sésé, where the King of Uganda keeps one of his fleets of boats.

Halt, 7th.

Some little boys came here who had all their hair shaved off excepting two round tufts on either side of the head. They were the king's pages; and, producing three sticks, said they had brought them to me from their king, who wanted three charms or medicines. Then placing one stick on the ground before me, they said, "This one is a head which, being affected by dreams of a deceased relative, requires relief;" the second symbolized the king's desire for the accomplishment of a phenomenon to which the old phalic worship was devoted; "and this third one," they said, "is a sign that the king wants a charm to keep all his subjects in awe of him." I then promised I would do what I could when I reached the palace, but feared to do any thing in the distance. I wished to go on with the march, but was dissuaded by N'yamgundŭ, who said he had received orders to find me some cows here, as his king was most anxious I should be well fed. Next day, however, we descended into the Katonga valley, where, instead of finding a magnificent broad sheet of water, as I had been led to expect by the Arabs' account of it, I found I had to wade through a succession of rush-drains divided one from the other by islands. It took me two hours, with my clothes tucked up under my arms, to get through them all; and many of them were so matted with weeds that my feet sank down as though I trod in a bog.

To Mbŭlé, 8th.

The Waganda all said that at certain times in the year no one could ford these drains, as they all flooded; but, strangely enough, they were always lowest when most rain fell in Uganda. No one, however, could account for this singular fact. No one knew of a lake to supply the waters, nor where they came from. That they flowed into the lake there was no doubt—as I could see by the trickling waters in some few places—and they lay exactly on the equator. Rising out of the valley, I found all the country just as hilly as before, but many of the rush-drains going to northward; and in the dells were such magnificent trees they quite took me by surprise. Clean-trunked, they towered up just as so many great pillars, and then spread out their high branches like a canopy over us. I thought of the blue gums of Australia, and believed these would beat them. At the village of Mbŭlé we were gracefully received by the local officer, who brought a small present, and assured me that the king was in a nervous state of excitement, always asking after me. While speaking he trembled, and he was so restless he could never sit still.

Up and down we went on again through this wonderful country, surprisingly rich in grass, cultivation, and trees. Water-courses were as frequent as ever, though not quite so troublesome to the traveler, as they were more frequently bridged with poles or palm-tree trunks.

To Nakŭsi, 9th.

This, the next place we arrived at, was N'yamgundŭ's own residence, where I stopped a day to try and shoot buffaloes. Maŭla here had the coolness to tell me he must inspect all the things I had brought for presentation to the king, as he said it was the custom, after which he would hurry on and inform his majesty. Of course I refused, saying it was uncourteous to both the king and myself. Still he persisted, until, finding it hopeless, he spitefully told N'yamgundŭ to keep me here at least two days. N'yamgundŭ, however, very prudently told him he should obey his orders, which were to take me on as fast as he could. I then gave N'yamgundŭ wires and beads for himself and all his family round, which made Maŭla slink farther away from me than ever.

To Kibibi, 10th.

The buffaloes were very numerous in the tall grasses that lined the sides and bottoms of the hills; but, although I saw some, I could not get a shot, for the grasses, being double the height of myself, afforded them means of dashing out of view as soon as seen, and the rustling noise made while I followed them kept them on the alert. At night a hyena came into my hut, and carried off one of my goats that was tied to a log between two of my sleeping men.

Halt, 11th.

During the next march, after passing some of the most beautifully-wooded dells, in which lay small rush-lakes on the right of the road, draining, as I fancied, into the

To Nakatéma, 12th.

Victoria Lake, I met with a party of the king's gamekeepers, staking their nets all along the side of a hill, hoping to catch antelopes by driving the covers with dogs and men. Farther on, also, I came on a party driving one hundred cows, as a present from Mtésa to Rŭmanika, which the officers in charge said was their king's return for the favor Rŭmanika had done him in sending me on to him. It was in this way that great kings sent "letters" to one another.

To N'yama Goma, 13th. Next day, after going a short distance, we came on the Mwarango River, a broad rush-drain of three hundred yards' span, two thirds of which was bridged over. Until now I did not feel sure where the various rush-drains I had been crossing since leaving the Katonga valley all went to, but here my mind was made up, for I found a large volume of water going to the northward. I took off my clothes at the end of the bridge and jumped into the stream, which I found was twelve yards or so broad, and deeper than my height. I was delighted beyond measure at this very surprising fact, that I was indeed on the northern slopes of the continent, and had, to all appearance, found one of the branches of the Nile's exit from the N'yanza. I drew Bombay's attention to the current; and, collecting all the men of the country, inquired of them where the river sprang from. Some of them said, in the hills to the southward; but most of them said, from the lake. I argued the point with them; for I felt quite sure so large a body of flowing water could not be collected together in any place but the lake. They then all agreed to this view, and farther assured me it went to Kamrasi's palace in Unyoro, where it joined the N'yanza, meaning the Nile.

Pushing on again we arrived at N'yama Goma, where I found Irungŭ—the great embassador I had first met in Usŭi, with all his "children"—my enemy Makinga, and Sŭwarora's deputation with wire—altogether, a collection of one hundred souls. They had been here a month waiting for leave to approach the king's palace. Not a villager was to be seen for miles round; not a plantain remained on the trees, nor was there even a sweet potato to be found in the ground. The whole of the provisions of this beautiful place had been devoured by the king's guests, simply because he had been too proud to see them in a hurry. This was alarming, for I feared I should be served the same trick, especially as all the people said this kind of treatment was a mere matter of custom which those great kings demanded as a respect due to their dignity; and Bombay added, with laughter, they make all manner of fuss to entice one to come when in the distance, but when they have got you in their power they become haughty about it, and think only of how they can best impose on your mind the great consequence which they affect before their own people.

Here I was also brought to a standstill, for N'yamgundŭ said I must wait for leave to approach the palace. He wished to have a look at the presents I had brought for Mtésa. I declined to gratify it, taking my stand on my dignity; there was no occasion for any distrust on such a trifling matter as that, for I was not a merchant who sought for gain, but had come, at great expense, to see the king of this region. I begged, however, he would go as fast as possible to announce my arrival, explain my motive for coming here, and ask for an early interview, as I had left my brother Grant behind at Karagŭé, and found my position, for want of a friend to talk to, almost intolerable. It was not the custom of my country for great men to consort with servants, and until I saw him, and made friends, I should not be happy. I had a great deal to tell him about, as he was the father of the Nile, which river drained the N'yanza down to my country to the northward. With this message N'yamgundŭ hurried off as fast as possible.

Halt, 14th.

Next day (15th) I gave each of my men a fez cap, and a piece of red blanket to make up military jackets. I then instructed them how to form a guard of honor when I went to the palace, and taught Bombay the way nazirs were presented at courts in India. Altogether we made a good show. When this was concluded, I went with Nasib up a hill, from which we could see the lake on one side, and on the other a large range of huts said to belong to the king's uncle, the second of the late king Sunna's brothers, who was not burnt to death when he ascended the throne.

I then (16th) very much wished to go and see the escape of the Mwérango River, as I still felt a little skeptical as to its origin, whether or not it came off those smaller lakes I had seen on the road the day before I crossed the river; but no one would listen to my project. They all said I must have the king's sanction first, else people, from not knowing my object, would accuse me of practicing witchcraft, and would tell their king so. They still all maintained that the river did come out of the lake, and said, if I liked to ask the king's leave to visit the spot, then they would go and show it me. I gave way, thinking it prudent to do so, but resolved in my mind I would get Grant to see it in boats on his voyage from Karagúe. There were no Guinea-fowls to be found here, nor a fowl in any of the huts, so I requested Rozaro to hurry off to Mtésa, and ask him to send me something to eat. He simply laughed at my request, and said I did not know what I was doing. It would be as much as his life was worth to go one yard in advance of this until the king's leave was obtained. I said, rather than be starved to death in this ignominious manner, I would return to Karagúe; to which he replied, laughing, "Whose leave have you got to do that? Do you suppose you can do as you like in this country?"

Next day (17th), in the evening, N'yamgundŭ returned full of smirks and smiles, dropped on his knees at my feet, and, in company with his "children," set to n'yanzigging, according to the form of that state ceremonial already described.* In his excitement he was hardly able to say all he had to communicate. Bit by bit, however, I learned that he first went to the palace, and, finding the king had gone off yachting to the Murchison Creek, he followed him there. The king for a long while would not believe his tale that I had come, but, being assured, he danced with delight, and swore he would not taste food until he had seen me. "Oh," he said, over and over again and again, according to my informer, "can this be true? Can the white man have come all this way to see me? What a strong man he must be too, to come so quickly! Here are seven cows, four of them milch ones, as you say he likes milk, which you will give him; and there are three for yourself for having brought him so quickly. Now hurry off as fast as you can, and tell him I am more delighted at the prospect of seeing him than he can be to see me. There is no place here fit for his reception. I was on a pilgrimage which would have kept me here seven days longer; but, as I am so impatient to see him, I will go off to my palace at once, and will send word for him to advance as soon as I arrive there."

About noon the succeeding day, some pages ran in to say we

To Sunna's Kibŭga, 18th.   were to come along without a moment's delay, as their king had ordered it. He would not taste food until he saw me, so that every body might know what great respect he felt for me. In the mean while, however, he wished for some

* See p. 250.

gunpowder. I packed the pages off as fast as I could with some, and then tried myself to follow, but my men were all either sick or out foraging, and therefore we could not get under way until the evening. After going a certain distance, we came on a rush-drain, of much greater breadth even than the Mwérango, called the Moga (or river) Myanza, which was so deep I had to take off my trowsers and tuck my clothes under my arms. It flowed into the Mwérango, but with scarcely any current at all. This rush-drain, all the natives assured me, rose in the hills to the south-ward—not in the lake, as the Mwérango did—and it was never bridged over like that river, because it was always fordable. This account seemed to me reasonable; for, though so much broader in its bed than the Mwérango, it had no central, deep-flowing current. The time for judging as to their relative size, too, was favorable, as it was the height of the dry season, when most of the long grasses were burnt. When we were across this great rush-drain it was almost dark, so I gave orders to spend the night in the most favorable spot we could find. We had, how-ever, to pass the late king Sunna's kibŭga or palace before this could be done, as no eyes were allowed to dwell on the royal es-tablishments of departed kings.

One march more, and we came in sight of the king's kibŭga or
To Bandawaro-go, 19th. palace, in the province of Bandawàrogo, N. lat. 0° 21' 19'', and E. long. 32° 44' 30''. It was a magnificent sight. A whole hill was covered with gigantic huts, such as I had never seen in Africa before. I wished to go up to the palace at once, but the officers said "No, that would be considered in-decent in Uganda; you must draw up your men, and fire your guns off, to let the king know you are here; we will then show you your residence, and to-morrow you will doubtless be sent for, as the king could not now hold a levée while it is raining." I made the men fire, and then was shown into a lot of dirty huts, which, they said, were built expressly for all the king's visitors. The Arabs, when they came on their visits, always put up here, and I must do the same. At first I stuck out on my claims as a foreign prince, whose royal blood could not stand such an indig-nity. The palace was my sphere, and unless I could get a hut there, I would return without seeing the king.

In a terrible fright at my blustering, N'yamgundŭ fell at my feet, and implored me not to be hasty. The king did not under-stand who I was, and could not be spoken to then. He implored

VIEW OF KING MTÉSA'S PALACE FROM MY HUT—UGANDA.

me to be content with my lot for the present, after which the
king, when he knew all about it, would do as I liked, he was sure,
though no strangers had ever yet been allowed to reside within
the royal inclosures. I gave way to this good man's appeal, and
cleaned my hut by firing the ground, for, like all the huts in this
dog country, it was full of fleas. Once ensconced there, the king's
pages darted in to see me, bearing a message from their master,
who said he was sorry the rain prevented him from holding a
levée that day, but the next he would be delighted to see me.
Irungŭ, with all Sŭwarora's men, then came to a collection of
huts near where I was residing; and while I lay in bed that night,
Irungŭ, with all his wives, came in to see me and beg for beads.

CHAPTER XI.

PALACE, UGANDA.

Preparations for the Reception at the Court of Mtésa, King of Uganda.—The Cere-
monial.—African Diplomacy and Dignity.—Feats with the Rifle.—Cruelty, and
Wastefulness of Life.—The Pages.—The Queen-dowager of Uganda.—Her Court
Reception.—I negotiate for a Palace.—Conversations with the King and Queen.
—The Queen's grand Entertainment.—Royal Dissipation.

To-day the king sent his pages to announce his intention of
holding a levée in my honor. I prepared for my
first presentation at court, attired in my best, though
in it I cut a poor figure in comparison with the display of the

Halt, from 19th
Feb. to 7th July.

Mganda, or Native of Uganda.

dressy Waganda. They wore neat bark cloaks resembling the
best yellow corduroy cloth, crimp and well set, as if stiffened with
starch, and over that, as upper cloaks, a patchwork of small antelope skins, which I observed were sewn together as well as any

English glovers could have pieced them; while their head-dress-es, generally, were abrus turbans, set off with highly-polished boar-tusks, stick-charms, seeds, beads, or shells; and on their necks, arms, and ankles they wore other charms of wood, or small horns stuffed with magic powder, and fastened on by strings gen-erally covered with snakeskin. N'yamgundŭ and Maŭla demand-ed, as their official privilege, a first peep; and this being refused, they tried to persuade me that the articles comprising the present required to be covered with chintz, for it was considered indeco-rous to offer any thing to his majesty in a naked state. This lit-tle interruption over, the articles enumerated below* were con-veyed to the palace in solemn procession thus: With N'yamgun-dŭ, Maŭla, the pages, and myself on the flanks, the Union Jack, carried by the kirangozi guide, led the way, followed by twelve men as a guard of honor, dressed in red flannel cloaks, and carry-ing their arms sloped, with fixed bayonets; while in their rear were the rest of my men, each carrying some article as a present.

On the march toward the palace, the admiring courtiers, won-der-struck at such an unusual display, exclaimed, in raptures of astonishment, some with both hands at their mouths, and others clasping their heads with their hands, " Irungi! irungi!" which may be translated " Beautiful! beautiful!" I thought myself ev-ery thing was going on as well as could be wished; but, before entering the royal inclosures, I found, to my disagreeable surprise, that the men with Sŭwarora's hongo or offering, which consisted of more than a hundred coils of wire, were ordered to lead the procession, and take precedence of me. There was something specially aggravating in this precedence; for it will be remem-bered that these very brass wires which they saw I had myself intended for Mtésa; that they were taken from me by Sŭwarora as far back as Usŭi; and it would never do, without remon-strance, to have them boastfully paraded before my eyes in this fashion. My protests, however, had no effect upon the escorting wakungŭ. Resolving to make them catch it, I walked along as if ruminating in anger up the broad high road into a cleared square, which divides Mtésa's domain on the south from his kam-raviona's, or commander-in-chief, on the north, and then turned

---

* 1 block-tin box, 4 rich silk cloths, 1 rifle (Whitworth's), 1 gold chronometer, 1 revolver pistol, 3 rifled carbines, 3 sword-bayonets, 1 box ammunition, 1 box bullets, 1 box gun-caps, 1 telescope, 1 iron chair, 10 bundles best beads, 1 set of table-knives, spoons, and forks.

into the court. The palace or entrance quite surprised me by its extraordinary dimensions, and the neatness with which it was kept. The whole brow and sides of the hill on which we stood were covered with gigantic grass huts, thatched as neatly as so many heads dressed by a London barber, and fenced all round with the tall yellow reeds of the common Uganda tiger-grass; while within the inclosure the lines of huts were joined together, or partitioned off into courts, with walls of the same grass. It is here most of Mtésa's three or four hundred women are kept, the rest being quartered chiefly with his mother, known by the title of N'yamasoré, or queen-dowager. They stood in little groups at the doors, looking at us, and evidently passing their own remarks, and enjoying their own jokes, on the triumphal procession. At each gate as we passed, officers on duty opened and shut it for us, jingling the big bells which are hung upon them, as they sometimes are at shop doors, to prevent silent, stealthy entrance.

The first court passed, I was even more surprised to find the unusual ceremonies that awaited me. There courtiers of high dignity stepped forward to greet me, dressed in the most scrupulously neat fashions. Men, women, bulls, dogs, and goats were led about by strings; cocks and hens were carried in men's arms; and little pages, with rope turbans, rushed about, conveying messages, as if their lives depended on their swiftness, every one holding his skin cloak tightly round him lest his naked legs might by accident be shown.

This, then, was the ante-reception court; and I might have taken possession of the hut, in which musicians were playing and singing on large nine-stringed harps, like the Nubian tambira, accompanied by harmonicons. By the chief officers in waiting, however, who thought fit to treat us like Arab merchants, I was requested to sit on the ground outside in the sun with my servants. Now I had made up my mind never to sit upon the ground as the natives and Arabs are obliged to do, nor to make my obeisance in any other manner than is customary in England, though the Arabs had told me that from fear they had always complied with the manners of the court. I felt that if I did not stand up for my social position at once, I should be treated with contempt during the remainder of my visit, and thus lose the vantage-ground I had assumed of appearing rather as a prince than a trader, for the purpose of better gaining the confidence of the king. To avert overhastiness, however—for my servants began to be alarmed as I demurred against doing as I was bid—I allowed five minutes to the court to give me a proper reception, saying if it were not conceded I would then walk away.

Nothing, however, was done. My own men, knowing me, feared for me, as they did not know what a "savage" king would do in case I carried out my threat; while the Waganda, lost in amazement at what seemed little less than blasphemy, stood still as posts. The affair ended by my walking straight away home, giving Bombay orders to leave the present on the ground, and to follow me.

Although the king is said to be unapproachable excepting when he chooses to attend court—a ceremony which rarely happens—intelligence of my hot wrath and hasty departure reached him in an instant. He first, it seems, thought of leaving his toilet-room to follow me; but, finding I was walking fast and had gone far, changed his mind, and sent wakungŭ running after me. Poor creatures! they caught me up, fell upon their knees, and implored I would return at once, for the king had not tasted food, and would not until he saw me. I felt grieved at their touching appeals; but, as I did not understand all they said, I simply replied by patting my heart and shaking my head, walking, if any thing, all the faster.

On my arrival at my hut, Bombay and others came in, wet through with perspiration, saying the king had heard of all my grievances. Sŭwarora's hongo was turned out of court, and, if I desired it, I might bring my own chair with me, for he was very anxious to show me great respect, although such a seat was exclusively the attribute of the king, no one else in Uganda daring to sit on an artificial seat.

My point was gained, so I cooled myself with coffee and a pipe, and returned rejoicing in my victory, especially over Sŭwarora. After returning to the second tier of huts from which I had retired, every body appeared to be in a hurried, confused state of excitement, not knowing what to make out of so unprecedented an exhibition of temper. In the most polite manner, the officers in waiting begged me to be seated on my iron stool, which I had brought with me, while others hurried in to announce my arrival. But for a few minutes only I was kept in suspense, when a band of music, the musicians wearing on their backs long-haired goatskins, passed me, dancing as they went along like bears in a fair, and playing on reed instruments worked over with pretty beads in various patterns, from which depended leopard-cat skins, the time being regulated by the beating of long hand-drums.

The mighty king was now reported to be sitting on his throne in the state hut of the third tier. I advanced, hat in hand, with my guard of honor following, formed in "open ranks," who in their turn were followed by the bearers carrying the present. I did not walk straight up to him as if to shake hands, but went outside the ranks of a three-sided square of squatting wakungŭ, all habited in skins, mostly cowskins; some few of whom had, in addition, leopard-cat skins girt round the waist, the sign of royal blood. Here I was desired to halt and sit in the glaring sun; so I donned my hat, mounted my umbrella, a phenomenon which set them all a wondering and laughing, ordered the guard to close ranks, and sat gazing at the novel spectacle. A more theatrical sight I never saw. The king, a good-looking, well-figured, tall young man of twenty-five, was sitting on a red blanket spread upon a square platform of royal grass, incased in tiger-grass reeds, scrupulously well dressed in a new mbŭgŭ. The hair of his head was cut short, excepting on the top, where it was combed up into a high ridge, running from stem to stern like a cock's comb. On his neck was a very neat ornament—a large ring, of beautifully-worked small beads, forming elegant patterns by their various colors. On one arm was another bead ornament, prettily devised; and on the other a wooden charm, tied by a string covered with snakeskin. On every finger and every toe he had alternate brass and copper rings; and above the ankles, half way up to the calf, a stocking of very pretty beads. Every thing was light, neat, and elegant in its way; not a fault could be found with the taste of his "getting up." For a handkerchief he held a well-folded piece of bark, and a piece of gold-embroidered silk, which he constantly employed to hide his large mouth when laughing, or to wipe it after a drink of plantain wine, of which he took constant and copious draughts from neat little gourd-cups, administered by his ladies in waiting, who were at once his sisters and wives. A white dog, spear, shield, and woman—the Uganda cognizance—were by his side, as also a knot of staff officers, with whom he kept up a brisk conversation on one side; and on the other was a band of wichwézi, or lady-sorcerers, such as I have already described.

I was now asked to draw nearer within the hollow square of squatters, where leopard-skins were strewed upon the ground, and

a large copper kettle-drum, surmounted with brass bells on arching wires, along with two other smaller drums covered with
cowrie-shells, and beads of color worked into patterns, were
placed. I now longed to open conversation, but knew not the
language, and no one near me dared speak, or even lift his head
from fear of being accused of eying the women; so the king and
myself sat staring at one another for full an hour—I mute, but
he pointing and remarking with those around him on the novelty
of my guard and general appearance, and even requiring to see
my hat lifted, the umbrella shut and opened, and the guards face
about and show off their red cloaks—for such wonders had never
been seen in Uganda.

Then, finding the day waning, he sent Maŭla on an embassy to
ask me if I had seen him; and on receiving my reply, "Yes, for

King of Uganda retiring.

full one hour," I was glad to find him rise, spear in hand, lead his
dog, and walk uceremoniously away through the inclosure into

the fourth tier of huts; for this being a pure levée day, no business was transacted. The king's gait in retiring was intended to be very majestic, but did not succeed in conveying to me that impression. It was the traditional walk of his race, founded on the step of the lion; but the outward sweep of the legs, intended to represent the stride of the noble beast, appeared to me only to realize a very ludicrous kind of waddle, which made me ask Bombay if any thing serious was the matter with the royal person.

I had now to wait for some time, almost as an act of humanity; for I was told the state secret, that the king had retired to break his fast and eat for the first time since hearing of my arrival; but the repast was no sooner over than he prepared for the second act, to show off his splendor, and I was invited in, with all my men, to the exclusion of all his own officers save my two guides. Entering as before, I found him standing on a red blanket, leaning against the right portal of the hut, talking and laughing, handkerchief in hand, to a hundred or more of his admiring wives, who, all squatting on the ground outside, in two groups, were dressed in new mbŭgŭs. My men dared not advance upright, nor look upon the women, but, stooping, with lowered heads and averted eyes, came cringing after me. Unconscious myself, I gave loud and impatient orders to my guard, rebuking them for moving like frightened geese, and, with hat in hand, stood gazing on the fair sex till directed to sit and cap.

Mtésa then inquired what messages were brought from Rŭmanika; to which Maŭla, delighted with the favor of speaking to royalty, replied by saying Rŭmanika had gained intelligence of Englishmen coming up the Nile to Gani and Kidi. The king acknowledged the truthfulness of their story, saying he had heard the same himself; and both wakungŭ, as is the custom in Uganda, thanked their lord in a very enthusiastic manner, kneeling on the ground—for no one can stand in the presence of his majesty —in an attitude of prayer, and throwing out their hands as they repeated the words n'yanzig, n'yanzig, ai n'yanzig mkahma wangi, etc., etc., for a considerable time; when, thinking they had done enough of this, and heated with the exertion, they threw themselves flat upon their stomachs, and, floundering about like fish on land, repeated the same words over again and again, and rose doing the same, with their faces covered with earth; for majesty in Uganda is never satisfied till subjects have groveled before it like the most abject worms. This conversation over, after gazing at me, and chatting with his women for a considerable time, the second scene ended. The third scene was more easily arranged, for the day was fast declining. He simply moved with his train of women to another hut, where, after seating himself upon his throne, with his women around him, he invited me to approach the nearest limits of propriety, and to sit as before. Again he asked me if I had seen him, evidently desirous of indulging in his regal pride; so I made the most of the opportunity thus afforded me of opening a conversation by telling him of those grand reports I had formerly heard about him, which induced me to come all this way to see him, and the trouble it had cost me to reach the object of my desire; at the same time taking a gold ring from off my finger, and presenting it to him, I said, "This is a small token of friendship; if you will inspect it, it is made after the fashion of a dog-collar, and, being the king of metals, gold, is in every respect appropriate to your illustrious race."

He said, in return, "If friendship is your desire, what would you say if I showed you a road by which you might reach your home in one month?" Now every thing had to be told to Bombay, then to Nasib, my Kiganda interpreter, and then to either Maŭla or N'yamgundŭ, before it was delivered to the king, for it was considered indecorous to transmit any message to his majesty excepting through the medium of one of his officers. Hence I could not get an answer put in; for as all Waganda are rapid and impetuous in their conversation, the king, probably forgetting he had put a question, hastily changed the conversation and said, "What guns have you got? Let me see the one you shoot with." I wished still to answer the first question first, as I knew he referred to the direct line to Zanzibar across the Masai, and was anxious, without delay, to open the subject of Petherick and Grant; but no one dared to deliver my statement. Much disappointed, I then said, " I had brought the best shooting-gun in the world—Whitworth's rifle—which I begged he would accept, with a few other trifles; and, with his permission, I would lay them upon a carpet at his feet, as is the custom of my country when visiting sultans." He assented, sent all his women away, and had an mbŭgŭ spread for the purpose, on which Bombay, obeying my order, first spread a red blanket, and then opened each article one after the other, when Nasib, according to the usage already mentioned, smoothed them down with his dirty hands, or rubbed them

against his sooty face, and handed them to the king to show there
was no poison or witchcraft in them.   Mtésa appeared quite confused with the various wonders as he handled them, made silly
remarks, and pondered over them like a perfect child, until it was
quite dark.   Torches were then lit, and guns, pistols, powder,
boxes, tools, beads—the whole collection, in short—were tossed
together topsy-turvy, bundled into mbŭgŭs, and carried away by
the pages.   Mtésa now said, "It is late, and time to break up;
what provisions would you wish to have?"   I said, "A little of
every thing, but no one thing constantly."   "And would you like
to see me to-morrow?"   "Yes, every day."   "Then you can't to-
morrow, for I have business; but the next day come if you like.
You can now go away, and here are six pots of plantain wine for
you; my men will search for food to-morrow."

   21st. In the morning, while it rained, some pages drove in twenty cows and ten goats, with a polite metaphorical message from
their king to the effect that I had pleased him much, and he hoped
I would accept these few "chickens" until he could send more;
when both Maŭla and N'yamgundŭ, charmed with their success
in having brought a welcome guest to Uganda, never ceased
showering eulogiums on me for my fortune in having gained the
countenance of their king.   The rain falling was considered at
court a good omen, and every body declared the king mad with
delight.   Wishing to have a talk with him about Petherick and
Grant, I at once started off the wakungŭ to thank him for the
present, and to beg pardon for my apparent rudeness of yesterday,
at the same time requesting I might have an early interview with
his majesty, as I had much of importance to communicate; but
the solemn court formalities, which these African kings affect as
much as Oriental emperors, precluded my message from reaching
the king.   I heard, however, that he had spent the day receiving
Sŭwarora's hongo of wire, and that the officer who brought them
was made to sit in an empty court, while the king sat behind a
screen, never deigning to show his majestic person.   I was told,
too, that he opened conversation by demanding to know how it
happened that Sŭwarora became possessed of the wires, for they
were made by the white men to be given to himself, and Sŭwarora must therefore have robbed me of them; and it was by such
practices he, Mtésa, never could see any visitors.   The officer's
reply was, Sŭwarora would not show the white men any respect,
because they were wizards who did not sleep in houses at night,

but flew up to the tops of hills, and practiced sorcery of every abominable kind. The king to this retorted, in a truly African fashion, "That's a lie; I can see no harm in this white man; and if he had been a bad man, Rŭmanika would not have sent him on to me." At night, when in bed, the king sent his pages to say, if I desired his friendship, I would lend him one musket to make up six with what I had given him, for he intended visiting his relations the following morning. I sent three, feeling that nothing would be lost by being "open-handed."

22d. To-day the king went the round of his relations, showing the beautiful things given him by the white man—a clear proof that he was much favored by the "spirits," for neither his father nor any of his forefathers had been so recognized and distinguished by any "sign" as a rightful inheritor to the Uganda throne: an anti-Christian interpretation of omens, as rife in these dark regions now as it was in the time of King Nebuchadnezzar. At midnight the three muskets were returned, and I was so pleased with the young king's promptitude and honesty, I begged he would accept them.

23d. At noon Mtésa sent his pages to invite me to his palace. I went, with my guard of honor and my stool, but found I had to sit waiting in an ante-hut three hours with his commander-in-chief and other high officers before he was ready to see me. During this time Wasoga minstrels, playing on tambira, and accompanied by boys playing on a harmonicon, kept us amused; and a small page, with a large bundle of grass, came to me and said, "The king hopes you won't be offended if required to sit on it before him; for no person in Uganda, however high in office, is ever allowed to sit upon any thing raised above the ground, nor can any body but himself sit upon such grass as this; it is all that his throne is made of. The first day he only allowed you to sit on your stool to appease your wrath."

On consenting to do in "Rome as the Romans do," when my position was so handsomely acknowledged, I was called in, and found the court sitting much as it was on the first day's interview, only that the number of squatting wakungŭ was much diminished; and the king, instead of wearing his ten brass and copper rings, had my gold one on his third finger. This day, however, was cut out for business, as, in addition to the assemblage of officers, there were women, cows, goats, fowls, confiscations, baskets of fish, baskets of small antelopes, porcupines, and curious rats caught by his gamekeepers, bundles of mbŭgŭ, etc., etc., made by his linen-drapers, colored earths and sticks by his magician, all ready for presentation; but, as rain fell, the court broke up, and I had nothing for it but to walk about under my umbrella, indulging in angry reflections against the haughty king for not inviting me into his hut.

When the rain had ceased, and we were again called in, he was found sitting in state as before, but this time with the head of a black bull placed before him, one horn of which, knocked off, was placed alongside, while four living cows walked about the court. I was now requested to shoot the four cows as quickly as possible; but, having no bullets for my gun, I borrowed the revolving pistol I had given him, and shot all four in a second of time; but as the last one, only wounded, turned sharply upon me, I gave him the fifth and settled him. Great applause followed this *wonderful* feat, and the cows were given to my men. The king now loaded one of the carbines I had given him with his own hands, and giving it full-cock to a page, told him to go out and shoot a man in the outer court, which was no sooner accomplished than the little urchin returned to announce his success with a look of glee such as one would see in the face of a boy who had robbed a bird's nest, caught a trout, or done any other boyish trick. The king said to him, "And did you do it well?" "Oh yes, capitally." He spoke the truth, no doubt, for he dared not have trifled with the king; but the affair created hardly any interest. I never heard, and there appeared no curiosity to know, what individual human being the urchin had deprived of life.

The wakungŭ were now dismissed, and I asked to draw near, when the king showed me a book I had given to Rŭmanika, and begged for the inspiring medicine which he had before applied for through the mystic stick. The day was now gone, so torches were lit, and we were ordered to go, though as yet I had not been able to speak one word I wished to impart about Petherick and Grant; for my interpreters were so afraid of the king they dared not open their mouths until they were spoken to. The king was now rising to go, when, in great fear and anxiety that the day would be lost, I said, in Kisŭahili, "I wish you would send a letter by post to Grant, and also send a boat up to Kitangŭlé, as far as Rŭmanika's palace, 'for him, for he is totally unable to walk.". I thus attracted his notice, though he did not understand one word I uttered. The result was, that he waited for the interpretation, and replied that a post would be of no use, for no one would be responsible for the safe delivery of the message; he would send N'yamgundŭ to fetch him, but he thought Rŭmanika would not consent to his sending boats up the Kitangŭlé as far as the Little Windermere; and then, turning round with true Mganda impetuosity, he walked away without taking a word from me in exchange.

24th. Early this morning the pages came to say Mtésa desired I would send him three of my Wangŭana to shoot cows before him. This was just what I wanted. It had struck me that personal conferences with me so roused the excitable king that there was no bringing plain matters of business home to him; so, detaching seven men with Bombay, I told him, before shooting, to be sure and elicit the matter I wanted, which was, to excite the king's cupidity by telling him I had a boat full of stores, with two white men, at Gani, whom I wished to call to me if he would furnish some guides to accompany my men; and farther, as Grant could not walk, I wished boats sent for him, at least as far as the ferry on the Kitangŭlé, to which place Rŭmanika, at any rate, would slip him down in canoes. At once, on arriving, Mtésa admitted the men, and ordered them to shoot at some cows; but Bombay, obeying my orders to first have his talk out, said, No; before he could shoot he must obey master and deliver his message; which no sooner was told than the king, in a hurry, excited by the prospects of sport, impatiently said, "Very good; I will send men either by water, or overland through Kidi,* just as your master likes; only some of his men had better go with mine; but now shoot cows, shoot cows, for I want to see how the Wangŭana shoot." They shot seven, and all were given to them when they were dismissed. In the evening the pages came to ask me if I would like to shoot kites in the palace with their king; but I declined shooting any thing less than elephants, rhinoceros, or buffaloes, and even for these I would not go out unless the king went with me—a dodge, I conceived, would tend more than any other to bring us together, and so break through those ceremonial restraints of the court, which at present were stopping all plans of progression.

25th. The king invited me to shoot with him—really buffaloes —close to the palace; but, as the pages had been sent off in a

* The straight road down the Nile through Unyoro no one dared allude to at this time, as the two kings were always fighting.

THE SOURCE OF THE NILE. [1862.

hurry, without being fully instructed, I declined, on the plea that I had always been gulled and kept waiting, or treated with incivility, for hours before I obtained an interview; and as I did not wish to have any more ruptures in the palace, I proposed Bombay should go to make proper arrangements for my reception on the morrow, as, anyhow, at present I felt indisposed. The pages dreaded their master's wrath, departed for a while, and then sent another lad to tell me he was sorry to hear I felt unwell, but he hoped I would come if only for a minute, bringing my medicines with me, for he himself felt pain. That this second message was a forged one I had no doubt, for the boys had not been long enough gone; still, I packed up my medicines and went, leaving the onus, should any accident happen, upon the mischievous story-bearers.

As I anticipated, on arrival at the palace I found the king was not ready to receive me, and the pages desired me to sit with the officers in waiting until he might appear. I found it necessary to fly at once into a rage, called the pages a set of deceiving young blackguards, turned upon my heel, and walked straight back through the courts, intending to leave the palace. Every body was alarmed; information of my retreat at once reached the king, and he sent his wakungŭ to prevent my egress. These officers passed me, as I was walking hurriedly along under my umbrella, in the last court, and shut the entrance-gate in front of me. This was too much; so I stamped, and, pointing my finger, swore in every language I knew that if they did not open the gate again, as they had shut it at once, and that, too, before my face, I would never leave the spot I stood upon alive. Terror-stricken, the wakungŭ fell on their knees before me, doing as they were bid; and, to please them, I returned at once and went up to the king, who, now sitting on his throne, asked the officers how they had managed to entice me back; to which they all replied in a breath, n'yanzigging heartily, "Oh, we were so afraid—he was so terrible! but he turned at once as soon as we opened the gate." "How? what gate? tell us all about it." And when the whole story was fully narrated, the matter was thought a good joke. After pausing a little, I asked the king what ailed him, for I was sorry to hear he had been sick; but, instead of replying, he shook his head, as much as to say I had put a very uncouth question to his majesty, and ordered some men to shoot cows.

Instead of admiring this childish pastime, which in Uganda is considered royal sport, I rather looked disdainful, until, apparently disappointed at my indifference, he asked what the box I had brought contained. On being told it was the medicine he desired, he asked me to draw near, and sent his courtiers away. When only the interpreters and one confidential officer were left besides myself, he wished to know if I could apply the medicine without its touching the afflicted part. To give him confidence in my surgical skill, I moved my finger, and asked if he knew what gave it action; and on his replying in the negative, I gave him an anatomical lecture, which so pleased him, he at once consented to be operated on, and I applied a blister to him accordingly. The whole operation was rather ridiculous; for the blister, after being applied, had to be rubbed in turn on the hands and faces of both Bombay and Nasib, to show there was no evil spirit in the " doctor." Now, thought I to myself, is the right time for business, for I had the king all to myself, then considered a most fortunate occurrence in Uganda, where every man courts the favor of a word with his king, and adores him as a deity, and he, in turn, makes himself as distant as he can, to give greater effect to his exalted position. The matter, however, was merely deferred; for I no sooner told him my plans for communicating quickly with Petherick and Grant, than, after saying he desired their coming even more than myself, he promised to arrange every thing on the morrow.

26th. In the morning, as agreed, I called on the king, and found the blister had drawn nicely; so I let off the water, which Bombay called the malady, and so delighted the king amazingly. A basket of fruit, like Indian loquots, was then ordered in, and we ate them together, holding a discussion about Grant and Petherick, which ended by the king promising to send an officer by water to Kitangŭlé, and another, with two of my men, viâ Usoga and Kidi, to Gani; but as it was necessary my men should go in disguise, I asked the king to send me four mbŭgŭ and two spears; when, with the liberality of a great king, he sent me twenty sheets of the former, four spears, and a load of sun-dried fish strung on a stick in shape of a shield.

27th. At last something was done. One Uganda officer and one Kidi guide were sent to my hut by the king, as agreed upon yesterday, when I detached Mabrŭki and Bilal from my men, gave them letters and maps addressed to Petherick; and giving the officers a load of mtendé to pay their hotel bills on the way,

I gave them, at the same time, strict orders to keep by the Nile; then, having dismissed them, I called on the king to make arrangements for Grant, and to complain that my residence in Uganda was any thing but cheerful, as my hut was a mile from the palace, in an unhealthy place, where he kept his Arab visitors. It did not become my dignity to live in houses appropriated to persons in the rank of servants, which I considered the ivory-merchants to be; and as I had come only to see him and the high officers of Uganda, not seeking for ivory or slaves, I begged he would change my place of residence to the west end, when I also trusted his officers would not be ashamed to visit me, as appeared to be the case at present. Silence being the provoking resort of the king when he did not know exactly what to say, he made no answer to my appeal, but instead he began a discourse on geography, and then desired me to call upon his mother, N'yamasoré, at her palace Masorisori, vulgarly called Soli Soli, for she also required medicine; and, moreover, I was cautioned that for the future the Uganda court etiquette required I should attend on the king two days in succession, and every third day on his mother the queen-dowager, as such were their respective rights.

Till now, owing to the strict laws of the country, I had not been able to call upon any body but the king himself. I had not been able to send presents or bribes to any one, nor had any one, except the cockaded pages, by the king's order, visited me; neither was any body permitted to sell me provisions, so that my men had to feed themselves by taking any thing they chose from certain gardens pointed out by the king's officers, or by seizing pombé or plantains which they might find Waganda carrying toward the palace. This non-interventive order was part of the royal policy, in order that the king might have the full fleecing of his visitors.

To call upon the queen-mother respectfully, as it was the opening visit, I took, besides the medicine-chest, a present of eight brass and copper wire, thirty blue-egg beads, one bundle of diminutive beads, and sixteen cubits of chintz, a small guard, and my throne of royal grass. The palace to be visited lay half a mile beyond the king's, but the high road to it was forbidden me, as it is considered uncourteous to pass the king's gate without going in. So, after winding through back gardens, the slums of Bando-waroga, I struck upon the high road close to her majesty's, where every thing looked like the royal palace on a miniature scale. A large cleared space divided the queen's residence from her kamraviona's. The outer inclosures and courts were fenced with tiger-grass; and the huts, though neither so numerous nor so large, were constructed after the same fashion as the king's. Guards also kept the doors, on which large bells were hung to give alarm, and officers in waiting watched the throne-rooms. All the huts were full of women, save those kept as waiting-rooms, where drums and harmonicons were placed for amusement. On first entering, I was required to sit in a waiting-hut till my arrival was announced; but that did not take long, as the queen was prepared to receive me; and being of a more affable disposition than her son, she held rather a levée of amusement than a stiff court of show. I entered the throne-hut, as the gate of that court was thrown open, with my hat off, but umbrella held over my head, and walked straight toward her till ordered to sit upon my bundle of grass.

Her majesty—fat, fair, and forty-five—was sitting, plainly garbed in mbŭgŭ, upon a carpet spread upon the ground within a curtain of mbŭgŭ, her elbow resting on a pillow of the same bark material; the only ornaments on her person being an abrus necklace, and a piece of mbŭgŭ tied round her head, while a folding looking-glass, much the worse for wear, stood open by her side. An iron rod like a spit, with a cup on the top, charged with magic powder, and other magic wands, were placed before the entrance; and within the room, four Mabandwa sorceresses or devil-drivers, fantastically dressed, as before described, and a mass of other women, formed the company. For a short while we sat at a distance, exchanging inquiring glances at one another, when the women were dismissed, and a band of music, with a court full of wakungŭ, was ordered in to change the scene. I also got orders to draw near and sit fronting her within the hut. Pombé, the best in Uganda, was then drunk by the queen, and handed to me and to all the high officers about her, when she smoked her pipe, and bade me smoke mine. The musicians, dressed in long-haired Usoga goatskins, were now ordered to strike up, which they did, with their bodies swaying or dancing like bears in a fair. Different drums were then beat, and I was asked if I could distinguish their different tones.

The queen, full of mirth, now suddenly rose, leaving me sitting, while she went to another hut, changed her mbŭgŭ for a déolé, and came back again for us to admire her, which was no sooner done to her heart's content than a second time, by her order, the

court was cleared, and, when only three or four confidential wakungŭ were left, she took up a small fagot of well-trimmed sticks,
and, selecting three, told me she had three complaints. "This
stick," she says, "represents my stomach, which gives me much
uneasiness; this second stick my liver, which causes shooting
pains all over my body; and this third one my heart, for I get
constant dreams at night about Sunna, my late husband, and they
are not pleasant." The dreams and sleeplessness I told her was
a common widow's complaint, and could only be cured by her
majesty making up her mind to marry a second time; but, before I could advise for the bodily complaints, it would be necessary for me to see her tongue, feel her pulse, and perhaps, also,
her sides. Hearing this, the wakungŭ said, "Oh, that can never
be allowed without the sanction of the king;" but the queen, rising in her seat, expressed her scorn at the idea of taking advice
from a mere stripling, and submitted herself for examination.

I then took out two pills, the powder of which was tasted by
the wakungŭ to prove that there was no devilry in "the doctor,"
and gave orders for them to be eaten at night, restricting her
pombé and food until I saw her again. My game was now advancing, for I found through her I should get the key to an influence that might bear on the king, and was much pleased to
hear her express herself delighted with me for every thing I had
done except stopping her grog, which, naturally enough in this
great pombé-drinking country, she said would be a very trying
abstinence.

The doctoring over, her majesty expressed herself ready to inspect the honorarium I had brought for her, and the articles were
no sooner presented by Bombay and Nasib, with the usual formalities of stroking to insure their purity, than she, boiling with
pleasure, showed them all to her officers, who declared, with a
voice of most exquisite triumph, that she was indeed the most favored of queens. Then, in excellent good taste, after saying that
nobody had ever given her such treasures, she gave me, in return,
a beautifully-worked pombé sucking-pipe, which was acknowledged by every one to be the greatest honor she could pay me.

Not satisfied with this, she made me select, though against my
desire, a number of sambo, called here gundu, rings of giraffe hair
wound round with thin iron or copper wire, and worn as anklets;
and crowned all with sundry pots of pombé, a cow, and a bundle
of dried fish, of the description given in the engraving, called by

my men Samaki Kambari. This business over, she begged me
to show her my picture-books, and was so amused with them that
she ordered her sorceresses and all the other women in again to

Kambari Fish.

inspect them with her. Then began a warm and complimentary
conversation, which ended by an inspection of my rings and all
the contents of my pockets, as well as of my watch, which she
called Lŭbari—a term equivalent to a place of worship, the object
of worship itself, or the iron horn or magic pan. Still she said I
had not yet satisfied her; I must return again two days hence,
for she liked me much—excessively—she could not say how
much; but now the day was gone, I might go. With this queer
kind of adieu she rose and walked away, leaving me with my
servants to carry the royal present home.

28*th*. My whole thoughts were now occupied in devising some
scheme to obtain a hut in the palace, not only the better to maintain my dignity, and so gain superior influence in the court, but
also that I might have a better insight into the manners and customs of these strange people. I was not sorry to find the king
attempting to draw me to court, daily to sit in attendance on him,
as his officers are obliged to do all day long, in order that he
might always have a full court or escort whenever by chance he
might emerge from his palace, for it gave me an opening for as-
serting a proper position.

Instead, therefore, of going at the call of his pages this morning, I sent Bombay with some men to say that, although I was desirous of seeing him daily, I could not so expose myself to the
sun. In all other countries I received, as my right, a palace to
live in when I called on the king of the country, and unless he
gave one now I should feel slighted; moreover, I should like a
hut in the same inclosure as himself, when I could sit and converse with him constantly, and teach him the use of the things I
had given him. By Bombay's account, the king was much struck

with the force of my humble request, and replied that he should like to have Bana, meaning myself, ever by his side, but his huts were all full of women, and therefore it could not be managed; if, however, Bana would but have patience for a while, a hut should be built for him in the environs, which would be a mark of distinction he had never paid to any visitor before. Then changing the subject by inspecting my men, he fell so much in love with their little red "fez" caps, that he sent off his pages to beg me for a specimen, and, on finding them sent by the boys, he remarked, with warm approbation, how generous I was in supplying his wishes, and then, turning to Bombay, wished to know what sort of return-presents would please me best. Bombay, already primed, instantly said, "Oh, Bana, being a great man in his own country, and not thirsting for gain in ivory or slaves, would only accept such things as a spear, shield, or drum, which he could take to his own country as a specimen of the manufactures of Uganda, and a pleasing recollection of his visit to the king."

"Ah!" says Mtésa, "if that is all he wants, then indeed will I satisfy him, for I will give him the two spears with which I took all this country, and, when engaged in so doing, pierced three men with one stab.

"But, for the present, is it true what I have heard, that Bana would like to go out with me shooting?" "Oh yes, he is a most wonderful sportsman—shoots elephants and buffaloes, and birds on the wing. He would like to go out on a shooting excursion and teach you the way."

Then turning the subject, in the highest good-humor the king made centurions of N'yamgundŭ and Maŭla, my two wakungŭ, for their good service, he said, in bringing him such a valuable guest. This delighted them so much that, as soon as they could, they came back to my camp, threw themselves at my feet, and n'yanzigging incessantly, narrated their fortunes, and begged, as a great man, I would lend them some cows to present to the king as an acknowledgment for the favor he had shown them. The cows, I then told them, had come from the king, and could not go back again, for it was not the habit of white men to part with their presents; but as I felt their promotion redounded on myself, and was certainly the highest compliment their king could have paid me, I would give them each a wire to make their salaam good.

This was enough; both officers got drunk, and, beating their drums, serenaded the camp until the evening set in, when, to my utter surprise, an elderly Mganda woman was brought into camp with the commander-in-chief's metaphorical compliments, hoping I would accept her "to carry my water;" with this trifling addition, that in case I did not think her pretty enough, he hoped I would not hesitate to select which I liked from ten others, of "all colors, Wahŭma included, who, for that purpose, were then waiting in his palace.

Unprepared for this social addition in my camp, I must now confess I felt in a fix, knowing full well that nothing so offends as rejecting an offer at once, so I kept her for the time being, intending in the morning to send her back with a string of blue beads on her neck; but during the night she relieved me of my anxieties by running away, which Bombay said was no wonder, for she had obviously been seized as part of some confiscated estate, and without doubt knew where to find some of her friends.

To-day, for the first time since I have been here, I received a quantity of plantains. This was in consequence of my complaining that the king's orders to my men to feed themselves at others' expense was virtually making them a pack of thieves.

1st. I received a letter from Grant, dated 10th of February, reporting Baraka's departure for Unyoro on the 30th of January, escorted by Kamrasi's men on their return, and a large party of Rŭmanika's bearing presents as a letter from their king, while Grant himself hoped to leave Karagŭé before the end of the month. I then sent Bombay to see the queen, to ask after her health, beg for a hut in the palace inclosures, and say I should have gone myself, only I feared her gate might be shut, and I can not go backward and forward so far in the sun without a horse or an elephant to ride upon. She begged I would come next morning. A wonderful report came that the king put two tops of powder into his Whitworth rifle to shoot a cow, and the bullet not only passed through the cow, but through the court fence, then through the centre of a woman, and, after passing the outer fence, flew whizzing along no one knew where.

2d. Calling on the queen early, she admitted me at once, scolding me severely for not having come or sent my men to see her after she had taken the pills. She said they did her no good, and prevailed on me to give her another prescription. Then sending her servant for a bag full of drinking-gourds, she made me select six of the best, and begged for my watch. That, of course, I could not part with; but I took the opportunity of telling her I did not like my residence; it was not only far away from every body, but it was unworthy of my dignity. I came to Uganda to see the king and queen, because the Arabs said they were always treated with great respect; but now I could perceive those Arabs did not know what true respect means. Being poor men, they thought much of a cow or goat given gratis, and were content to live in any hovels. Such, I must inform her, was not my case. I could neither sit in the sun nor live in a poor man's hut. When I rose to leave for breakfast, she requested me to stop, but I declined, and walked away. I saw, however, there was something wrong; for Maŭla, always ordered to be in attendance when any body visits, was retained by her order to answer why I would not stay with her longer. If I wanted food or pombé, there was plenty of it in her palace, and her cooks were the cleverest in the world; she hoped I would return to see her in the morning.

3d. Our cross purposes seemed to increase; for, while I could not get a satisfactory interview, the king sent for N'yamgundŭ to ascertain why I never went to see him. I had given him good guns and many pretty things which he did not know the use of, and yet I would not visit him to explain their several uses. N'yamgundŭ told him I lived too far off, and wanted a palace. After this I walked off to see N'yamasoré, taking my blankets, a pillow, and some cooking-pots to make a day of it, and try to win the affections of the queen with sixteen cubits bindéra, three pints péké, and three pints mtendé beads, which, as Waganda are all fond of figurative language, I called a trifle for her servants.

I was shown in at once, and found her majesty sitting on an Indian carpet, dressed in a red linen wrapper with a gold border, and a box, in shape of a lady's work-box, prettily colored in divers patterns with minute beads, by her side. Her councilors were in attendance; and in the yard a band of music, with many minor wakungŭ squatting in a semicircle, completed her levée. Maŭla, on my behalf, opened conversation, in allusion to her yesterday's question, by saying I had applied to Mtésa for a palace, that I might be near enough both their majesties to pay them constant visits. She replied, in a good hearty manner, that indeed was a very proper request, which showed my good sense, and ought to have been complied with at once; but Mtésa was only a kijana or stripling, and as she influenced all the government of the country, she would have it carried into effect. Compliments were now

passed, my presents given and approved of; and the queen, thinking I must be hungry, for she wanted to eat herself, requested me
to refresh myself in another hut.   I complied, spread my bedding,
and ordered in my breakfast; but, as the hut was full of men, I
suspended a Scotch plaid, and quite eclipsed her mbŭgŭ curtain.
Reports of this magnificence at once flew to the queen, who
sent to know how many more blankets I had in my possession,
and whether, if she asked for one, she would get it.   She also desired to see my spoons, fork, and pipe—an English meerschaum,
mounted with silver; so, after breakfast, I returned to see her,
showed her the spoons and forks, and smoked my pipe, but told
her I had no blankets left but what formed my bed.   She appeared very happy and very well, did not say another word about the
blankets, but ordered a pipe for herself, and sat chatting, laughing, and smoking in concert with me.

I told her I had visited all the four quarters of the globe, and
had seen all colors of people, but wondered where she got her
pipe from, for it was much after the Rŭmish (Turkish) fashion,
with a long stick.   Greatly tickled at the flattery, she said, " We
hear men like yourself come to Amara from the other side, and
drive cattle away."   " The Gallas, or Abyssinians, who are ·tall
and fair, like Rŭmanika," I said, " might do so, for they live not
far off on the other side of Amara, but we never fight for such
paltry objects.   If cows fall into our hands when fighting, we allow our soldiers to eat them, while we take the government of the
country into our own hands."   She then said, " We hear you
don't like the Unyamŭézi route; we will open the Ukori one for
you."   " Thank your majesty," said I, in a figurative kind of
speech to please Waganda ears; and turning the advantage of the
project on her side, " You have indeed hit the right nail on the
head.   I do not like the Unyamŭézi route, as you may well
imagine when I tell you I have lost so much property there by
mere robbery of the people and their kings.   The Waganda do
not see me in a true light; but if they have patience for a year or
two, until the Ukori road is open, and trade between our respective countries shall commence, they will then see the fruits of my
advent; so much so, that every Mganda will say the first Uganda
year dates from the arrival of the first mzungŭ (white) visitor.
As one coffee-seed sown brings forth fruit in plenty, so my coming here may be considered."   All appreciated this speech, saying, " The white man, he even speaks beautifully! beautifully!

beautifully! beautifully!" and, putting their hands to their mouths, they looked askance at me, nodding their admiring approval.

The queen and her ministers then plunged into pombé and became uproarious, laughing with all their might and main. Small bugu cups were not enough to keep up the excitement of the time, so a large wooden trough was placed before the queen and filled with liquor. If any was spilled, the wakungŭ instantly fought over it, dabbing their noses on the ground, or grabbing it with their hands, that not one atom of the queen's favor might be lost; for every thing must be adored that comes from royalty, whether by design or accident. The queen put her head to the trough and drank like a pig from it, and was followed by her ministers. The band, by order, then struck up a tune called the Milélé, playing on a dozen reeds, ornamented with beads and cow-tips, and five drums, of various tones and sizes, keeping time. The musicians, dancing with zest, were led by four band-masters, also dancing, but with their backs turned to the company to show off their long, shaggy goatskin jackets, sometimes upright, at other times bending and on their heels, like the hornpipe-dancers of western countries.

It was a merry scene, but soon became tiresome; when Bombay, by way of flattery, and wishing to see what the queen's wardrobe embraced, told her, Any woman, however ugly, would assume a goodly appearance if prettily dressed; upon which her gracious majesty immediately rose, retired to her toilet-hut, and soon returned attired in a common check cloth, an abrus tiara, a bead necklace, and with a folding looking-glass, when she sat, as before, and was handed a blown-glass cup of pombé, with a cork floating on the liquor, and a napkin mbŭgŭ covering the top, by a naked virgin. For her kind condescension in assuming plain raiment, every body, of course, n'yanzigged. Next she ordered her slave girls to bring a large number of sambo (anklets), and begged me to select the best, for she liked me much. In vain I tried to refuse them: she had given more than enough for a keepsake before, and I was not hungry for property; still, I had to choose some, or I would give offense. She then gave me a basket of tobacco, and a nest of hen eggs for her "son's" breakfast. When this was over, the Mŭkondéri, another dancing-tune, with instruments something like clarionets, was ordered; but it had scarcely been struck up before a drenching rain, with strong wind, set in and spoiled the music, though not the playing—for none dared stop without an order; and the queen, instead of taking pity, laughed most boisterously over the exercise of her savage power as the unfortunate musicians were nearly beaten down by the violence of the weather.

When the rain ceased, her majesty retired a second time to her toilet-hut, and changed her dress for a puce-colored wrapper, when I, ashamed of having robbed her of so many sambo, asked her if she would allow me to present her with a little English "wool" to hang up instead of her mbŭgŭ curtain on cold days like this. Of course she could not decline, and a large double scarlet blanket was placed before her. "Oh, wonder of wonders!" exclaimed all the spectators, holding their mouths in both hands at a time—such a "pattern" had never been seen here before. It stretched across the hut, was higher than the men could reach—indeed, it was a perfect marvel; and the man must be a good one who brought such a treasure as this to Uddŭ. "And why not say Uganda?" I asked. "Because all this country is called Uddŭ. Uganda is personified by Mtésa; and no one can say he has seen Uganda until he has been presented to the king."

As I had them all in a good humor now, I complained I did not see enough of the Waganda; and as every one dressed so remarkably well, I could not discern the big men from the small; could she not issue some order by which they might call on me, as they did not dare do so without instruction, and then I, in turn, would call on them? Hearing this, she introduced me to her prime minister, chancellor of exchequer, women-keepers, hangmen, and cooks, as the first nobles in the land, that I might recognize them again if I met them on the road. All n'yanzigged for this great condescension, and said they were delighted with their guest; then producing a strip of common joho to compare it with my blanket, they asked if I could recognize it. Of course, said I, it is made in my country, of the same material, only of coarser quality, and every thing of the same sort is made in Uzungŭ. Then, indeed, said the whole company, in one voice, we do like you, and your cloth too—but you most. I modestly bowed my head, and said their friendship was my chief desire.

This speech also created great hilarity; the queen and councilors all became uproarious. The queen began to sing, and the councilors to·join in chorus; then all sang and all drank, and drank and sang, till, in their heated excitement, they turned the palace into a pandemonium; still there was not noise enough, so the band and drums were called again, and tomfool—for Uganda, like the old European monarchies, always keeps a jester—was made to sing in the gruff, hoarse, unnatural voice which he ever affects to maintain his character, and furnished with pombé when his throat was dry.

Now all of a sudden, as if a devil had taken possession of the company, the prime minister, with all the courtiers, jumped upon their legs, seized their sticks, for nobody can carry a spear when visiting, swore the queen had lost her heart to me, and running into the yard, returned, charging and jabbering at the queen; retreated and returned again, as if they were going to put an end to her for the guilt of loving me, but really to show their devotion and true love to her. The queen professed to take this ceremony with calm indifference, but her face showed that she enjoyed it. I was now getting very tired of sitting on my low stool, and begged for leave to depart, but N'yamasoré would not hear of it; she loved me a great deal too much to let me go away at this time of day, and forthwith ordered in more pombé. The same roystering scene was repeated; cups were too small, so the trough was employed; and the queen graced it by drinking, pig-fashion, first, and then handing it round to the company.

Now, hoping to produce gravity and then to slip away, I asked if my medicines had given her any relief, that I might give her more to strengthen her. She said she could not answer that question just yet; for, though the medicine had moved her copiously, as yet she had seen no snake depart from her. I told her I would give her some strengthening medicine in the morning; for the present, however, I would take my leave, as the day was far gone, and the distance home very great; but, though I dragged my body away, my heart would still remain here, for I loved her much.

This announcement took all by surprise; they looked at me and then at her, and looked again and laughed, while I rose, waved my hat, and said, "Kŭa héri, bibi" (good-by, madam). On reaching home I found Maribŭ, a mkungŭ, with a gang of men sent by Mtésa to fetch Grant from Kitangŭlé by water. He would not take any of my men with him to fetch the kit from Karagŭé, as Mtésa, he said, had given him orders to find all the means of transport; so I gave him a letter to Grant, and told him to look sharp, else Grant would have passed the Kitangŭlé before he arrived there. "Never mind," says Maribŭ, "I shall walk to the mouth of the Katonga, boat it to Sésé Island, where Mtésa keeps all his large vessels, and I shall be at Kitangŭlé in a very short time."

4th. I sent Bombay off to administer quinine to the queen; but the king's pages, who watched him making for her gateway, hurried up to him, and turned him back by force. He pleaded earnestly that I would flog him if he disobeyed my orders, but they would take all the responsibility—the king had ordered it; and then they, forging a lie, bade him run back as fast as he could, saying I wanted to see the king, but could not till his return. In this way poor Bombay returned to me half drowned in perspiration. Just then another page hurried in with orders to bring me to the palace at once, for I had not been there these four days; and while I was preparing to express the proper amount of indignation at this unceremonious message, the last impudent page began rolling like a pig upon my mbŭgŭed or carpeted floor, till I stormed and swore I would turn him out unless he chose to behave more respectfully before my majesty, for I was no peddling merchant, as he had been accustomed to see, and would not stand it; moreover, I would not leave my hut at the summons of the king, or any body else, until I chose to do so.

This expression of becoming wrath brought every one to a sense of his duty; and I then told them all I was excessively angry with Mtésa for turning back my messenger; nobody had ever dared do such a thing before, and I would never forgive the king until my medicines had been given to the queen. As for my going to the palace, it was out of the question, as I had repeatedly before told the king, unless it pleased him to give me a fitting residence near himself. In order now that full weight should be given to my expressions, I sent Bombay with the quinine to the king, in company with the boys, to give an account of all that had happened; and farther, to say I felt exceedingly distressed I could not go to see him constantly — that I was ashamed of my domicile—the sun was hot to walk in; and when I went to the palace, his officers in waiting always kept me waiting like a servant—a matter hurtful to my honor and dignity. It now rested with himself to remove these obstacles. Every body concerned in this matter left for the palace but Maŭla, who said he must stop in camp to look after Bana. Bombay no sooner arrived in the palace, and saw the king upon his throne, than Mtésa asked him why he came. "By the instructions of Bana," was his reply; "for Bana can not walk in the sun; no white man of the sultan's breed can do so."

Hearing this, the king rose in a huff, without deigning to reply, and busied himself in another court. Bombay, still sitting, waited for hours till quite tired, when he sent a boy in to say he had not delivered half my message; he had brought medicine for the queen, and as yet he had no reply for Bana. Either with haughty indifference, or else with injured pride at his not being able to command me at his pleasure, the king sent word, if medicine is brought for the queen, then let it be taken to her; and so Bombay walked off to the queen's palace. Arrived there, he sent in to say he had brought medicine, and waited without a reply till nightfall, when, tired of his charge, he gave the quinine into N'yamgundŭ's hands for delivery, and returned home. Soon after, however, N'yamgundŭ also returned to say the queen would not take the dose to-day, but hoped I would administer it personally in the morning.

While all this vexatious business had been going on in court—evidently dictated by extreme jealousy, because I showed, as they all thought, a preference for the queen—Maŭla, more than tipsy, brought a mkungŭ of some standing at court before me, contrary to all law, for as yet no Mganda, save the king's pages, had ever dared enter even the precincts of my camp. With a scowling, determined, hang-dog-looking countenance, he walked impudently into my hut, and, taking down the pombé-suckers the queen had given me, showed them with many queer gesticulations, intended to insinuate there was something between the queen and me. Among his jokes were, that I must never drink pombé excepting with these sticks; if I wanted any when I leave Uganda, to show my friends, she would give me twenty more sticks of that sort if I liked them; and, turning from verbal to practical jocularity, the dirty fellow took my common sucker out of the pot, inserted one of the queen's, and sucked at it himself, when I snatched and threw it away.

Maŭla's friend, who I imagined was a spy, then asked me whom I liked most, the mother or the son; but, without waiting to hear me, Maŭla hastily said, "The mother, the mother, of course; he does not care for Mtésa, and won't go to see him." The friend coaxingly responded, "Oh no; he likes Mtésa, and will go and see him too; won't you?" I declined, however, to answer, from fear of mistake, as both interpreters were away. Still the two went on talking to themselves, Maŭla swearing that I loved the mother most, while the friend said No, he loves the son, and asking me with anxious looks, till they found I was not to be caught by chaff, and then, both tired, walked away, the friend advising me, next time I went to court, to put on an Arab's gown, as trowsers are indecent in the estimation of every Mganda.

5th. Alarmed at having got involved in something that looked like court intrigues, I called up N'yamgundŭ; told him all that had happened yesterday, both at the two courts and with Maŭla at home, and begged him to apply to the king for a meeting of five elders, that a proper understanding might be arrived at; but, instead of doing as I desired, he got into a terrible fright, calling Maŭla, and told me if I pressed the matter in this way men would lose their lives. Meanwhile the cunning blackguard Maŭla begged for pardon; said I quite misunderstood his meaning; all he had said was that I was very fortunate, being in such favor at court, for the king and queen both equally loved me.

N'yamgundŭ now got orders to go to Karagŭé overland for Dr. K'yengo; but, dreading to tell me of it, as I had been so kind to him, he forged a falsehood, said he had leave to visit his home for six days, and begged for a wire to sacrifice to his church. I gave him what he wanted, and away he went. I then heard his servants had received orders to go overland for Grant and K'yengo; so I wrote another note to Grant, telling him to come sharp, and bring all the property by boat that he could carry, leaving what he could not behind in charge of Rŭmanika.

At noon, the plaguy little imps of pages hurried in to order the attendance of all my men fully armed before the king, as he wished to seize some refractory officer. I declined this abuse of my arms, and said I should first go and speak to the king on the subject myself, ordering the men on no account to go on such an errand; and saying this, I proceeded toward the palace, leaving instructions for those men who were not ready to follow. As the court messengers, however, objected to our going in detachments, I told Bombay to wait for the rest, and hurry on to overtake me. While lingering on the way, every minute expecting to see my men, the Wazinza, who had also received orders to seize the same officer, passed me, going to the place of attack, and, at the same time, I heard my men firing in a direction exactly opposite to the palace. I now saw I had been duped, and returned to my hut to see the issue. The boys had deceived us all. Bombay, tricked on the plea of their taking him by a short cut to the palace, suddenly found himself, with all the men, opposite the fenced gardens that had to be taken—the establishment of the recusant officer; and the boys, knowing how eager all blacks are to loot, said, "Now, then, at the houses; seize all you can, sparing nothing—men, women, or children, mbŭgŭs or cowries, all alike; for it is the order of the king;" and in an instant my men surrounded the place, fired their guns, and rushed upon the inmates. One was speared forcing his way through the fence, but the rest were taken and brought triumphantly into my camp. It formed a strange sight in the establishment of an English gentleman to see my men flushed with the excitement of their spoils, staggering under loads of mbŭgŭ, or leading children, mothers, goats, and dogs off in triumph to their respective huts. Bombay alone, of all my men, obeyed my orders, touching nothing; and when remonstrated with for having led the men, he said he could not help it; the boys had deceived him in the same way as they had tricked me.

It was now necessary that I should take some critical step in African diplomacy; so, after ordering all the seizures to be given up to Maŭla on behalf of the king, and threatening to discharge any of my men who dared retain one item of the property, I shut the door of my hut to do penance for two days, giving orders that nobody but my cook Ilmas, not even Bombay, should come near me; for the king had caused my men to sin—had disgraced their red cloth—and had inflicted on me a greater insult than I could bear. I was ashamed to show my face. Just as the door was closed, other pages from the king brought the Whitworth rifle to be cleaned, and demanded an admittance; but no one dared approach me, and they went on their way again.

6th. I still continued to do penance. Bombay, by my orders, issued from within, prepared for a visit to the king, to tell him all that had happened yesterday, and also to ascertain if the orders for sending my men on a plundering mission had really emanated from himself, when the bothering pages came again, bringing a gun and knife to be mended. My door was found shut, so they went to Bombay, asked him to do it, and told him the king desired to know if I would go shooting with him in the morning. The reply was, "No; Bana is praying to-day that Mtésa's sins might be forgiven him for having committed such an injury to him, sending his soldiers on a mission that did not become them, and without his sanction too. He is very angry about it, and

wishes to know if it was done by the king's orders." The boys
said, "Nothing can be done without the king's orders." After
farther discussion, Bombay intimated that I wished the king to
send me a party of five elderly officers to counsel with, and set all
disagreeables to rights, or I would not go to the palace again; but
the boys said there were no elderly gentlemen at court, only boys
such as themselves. Bombay now wished to go with them before
the king, to explain matters to him, and to give him all the red
cloths of my men, which I took from them, because they defiled
their uniform when plundering women and children; but the
boys said the king was unapproachable just then, being engaged
shooting cows before his women. He then wished the boys to
carry the cloth; but they declined, saying it was contrary to orders for any body to handle cloth, and they could not do it.

CHAPTER XII.

PALACE, UGANDA—*Continued.*

Continued diplomatic Difficulties.—Negro Chaffing.—The King in a new Costume.
—Adjutant and Heron Shooting at Court.—My Residence changed.—Scenes at
Court.—The Kamraviona, or Commander-in-chief.—Quarrels.—Confidential
Communications with the King.—Court Executions and Executioners.—Another
Day with the Queen.

7th. THE farce continued, and how to manage these haughty
capricious blacks puzzled my brains considerably; but I felt that
if I did not stand up now, no one would ever be treated better
hereafter. I sent Nasib to the queen to explain why I had not
been to see her. I desired to do so, because I admired her wisdom; but before I went I must first see the king, to provide
against any insult being offered to me, such as befell Bombay
when I sent him with medicine. Having dispatched him, I repaired again to the palace. In the antechamber I found a number of wakungŭ, as usual, lounging about on the ground, smoking, chatting, and drinking pombé, while Wasoga amused them
singing and playing on lap-harps, and little boys kept time on the
harmonicon.

These wakungŭ are naturally patient attendants, being well
trained to the duty; for their very lives depend upon their presenting themselves at court a certain number of months every
year, no matter from what distant part of the country they have
to come. If they failed, their estates would be confiscated, and
their lives taken unless they could escape. I found a messenger
who consented to tell the king of my desire to see him. He returned to say that the king was sleeping—a palpable falsehood.
In a huff, I walked home to breakfast, leaving my attendants,
Maŭla and Ulédi, behind to make explanations. They saw the
king, who simply asked, "Where is Bana?" And on being told
that I came, but went off again, he said, as I was informed, "That
is a lie, for had he come here to see me he would not have returned;" then rising, he walked away and left the men to follow
me.

I continued ruminating on these absurd entanglements, and the best way of dealing with them, when, lo! to perplex me still more, in ran a bevy of the royal pages to ask for mtendé beads— a whole sack of them; for the king wished to go with his women on a pilgrimage to the N'yanza. Thinking myself very lucky to buy the king's ear so cheaply, I sent Maŭla as before, adding that I considered my luck very bad, as nobody here knew my position in society, else they would not treat me as they did. My proper sphere was the palace, and unless I got a hut there, I wished to leave the country. My first desire had always been to see the king; and if he went to the N'yanza, I trusted he would allow me to go there also. The boys replied, "How can you go with his women? No one ever is permitted to see them." "Well," said I, "if I can not go to the N'yanza with him" (thinking only of the great lake, whereas they probably meant a pond in the palace inclosures, where Mtésa constantly frolics with his women), "I wish to go to Usoga and Amara, as far as the Masai; for I have no companions here but crows and vultures." They promised to take the message, but its delivery was quite another thing; for no one can speak at this court till he is spoken to, and a word put in out of season is a life lost.

On Maŭla's return, I was told the king would not believe so generous a man as Bana could have sent him so few beads; he believed most of my store must have been stolen on the road, and would ask me about that to-morrow. He intimated that for the future I must fire a gun at the waiting-hut whenever I entered the palace, so that he might hear of my arrival, for he had been up that morning, and would have been glad to see me, only the boys, from fear of entering his cabinet, had forged a lie, and deprived him of any interview with me, which he had long wished to get. This ready cordiality was as perplexing as all the rest. Could it be possible, I thought, I had been fighting with a phantom all this while, and yet the king had not been able to perceive it? At all events, now, as the key to his door had been given, I would make good use of it and watch the result. Meanwhile Nasib returned from the queen-dowager's palace without having seen her majesty, though he had waited there patiently the whole day long, for she was engaged in festivities, incessantly drumming and playing, in consequence of the birth of twins (mabassa), which had just taken place in her palace; but he was advised to return on the morrow.

8th. After breakfast I walked to the palace, thinking I had
gained all I wanted; entered, and fired guns, expecting an instant admittance; but, as usual, I was required to sit and wait;
the king was expected immediately.   All the wakungŭ talked in
whispers, and nothing was heard but the never-ceasing harps and
harmonicons.   In a little while I felt tired of the monotony, and
wished to hang up a curtain, that I might lie down in privacy and
sleep till the king was ready; but the officers in waiting forbade
this, as contrary to law, and left me the only alternative of walking up and down the court to kill time, spreading my umbrella
against the powerful rays of the sun.   A very little of that made
me fidgety and impetuous, which the Waganda noticed, and from
fear of the consequences, they began to close the gate to prevent
my walking away.   I flew out on them, told Bombay to notice
the disrespect, and shamed them into opening it again.   The king
immediately, on hearing of this, sent me pombé to keep me quiet;
but as I would not touch it, saying I was sick at heart, another
page rushed out to say the king was ready to receive me; and,
opening a side gate leading into a small open court without a
hut in it, there, to be sure, was his majesty, sitting on an Arab's
donkey-rug, propped against one page, and encompassed by four
others.

On confronting him, he motioned me to sit, which I did upon
my bundle of grass, and, finding it warm, asked leave to open my
umbrella.   He was much struck at the facility with which I
could make shade, but wondered still more at my requiring it.
I explained to him that my skin was white because I lived in a
colder country than his, and therefore was much more sensitive
to the heat of the sun than his black skin; adding, at the same
time, if it gave no offense, I would prefer sitting in the shade of
the court fence.   He had no objection, and opened conversation
by asking who it was that gave me such offense in taking my
guard from me to seize his wakungŭ.   The boy who had provoked me was then dragged in, tied by his neck and hands, when
the king asked him by whose orders he had acted in such a manner, knowing that I objected to it, and wished to speak to him on
the subject first.   The poor boy, in a dreadful fright, said he had
acted under instructions of the kamraviona: there was no harm
done, for Bana's men were not hurt.   "Well, then," said the
king, "if they were not injured, and you only did as you were
ordered, no fault rests with you; but be gone out of my sight,

for I can not bear to see you; and the kamraviona shall be taught a lesson not to meddle with my guests again until I give him authority to do so."

I now hoped, as I had got the king all by himself, and apparently in a good humor with me, that I might give him a wholesome lesson on the manners and customs of the English nation, to show how much I felt the slights I had received since my residence in Uganda; but he never lost his dignity and fussiness as a Uganda king. My words must pass through his mkungŭ, as well as my interpreter's, before they reached him; and, as he had no patience, every thing was lost, till he suddenly asked Maŭla, pretending not to know, where my hut was; why every body said I lived so far away; and when told, he said, "Oh! that is very far; he must come nearer." Still I could not say a word, his fussiness and self-importance overcoming his inquisitiveness.

Rain now fell, and the king retired by one gate, while I was shown out of another, until the shower was over. As soon as the sky was clear again, we returned to the little court, and this time became more confidential, as he asked many questions about England, such as, Whether the queen knew any thing about medicines? whether she kept a number of women as he did? and what her palace was like? which gave me an opportunity of saying I would like to see his ships, for I heard they were very numerous; and also his menagerie, said to be full of wonderful animals. He said the vessels were far off, but he would send for them; and although he once kept a large number of animals, he killed them all in practicing with his guns. The Whitworth rifle was then brought in for me to take to pieces and teach him the use of, and then the chronometer. He then inquired if I would like to go shooting. I said, "Yes, if he would accompany me— not otherwise." "Hippopotami?" "Yes; there is great fun in that, for they knock the boats over when they charge from below." "Can you swim?" "Yes." "So can I. And would you like to shoot buffalo?" "Yes, if you will go." "At night, then, I will send my keepers to look out for them. Here is a leopard-cat, with white behind its ears, and a Ndézi porcupine, of the short-quilled kind, which my people eat with great relish; and if you are fond of animals, I will give you any number of specimens, for my keepers net and bring in live animals of every kind daily; for the present, you can take this basket of porcupines home for your dinner." My men n'yanzigged; the king

walked away, giving orders for another officer to follow up the
first who went to Ukori, and bring Petherick quickly; and I
went home.

This was to be a day of varied success. When I arrived at my
hut I found a messenger sent by the queen, with a present of a
goat, called "fowls for Bana, my son," and a load of plantains,
called potatoes, waiting for me; so I gave the bearer a fundo of
mtendé beads, and told again the reasons why I had not been
able to call upon the queen, but hoped to do so shortly, as the
king had promised me a house near at hand. I doubt, however,
whether one word of my message ever reached her. That she
wanted me at her palace was evident by the present, though she
was either too proud or too cautious to say so.

At night I overheard a chat between Sangizo, a Myamŭézi, and
Ntalo, a freed man of Zanzibar, very characteristic of their way
of chaffing. Sangizo opened the battle by saying, "Ntalo, who
are you?" *N.* "A mgŭana" (freed man). *S.* "A mgŭana, indeed! then where is your mother?" *N.* "She died at Angŭja."
S. "Your mother died at Angŭja! then where is your father?"
N. "He died at Angŭja likewise." *S.* "Well, that is strange;
and where are your brothers and sisters?" *N.* "They all died
at Angŭja." *S.* (then changing the word Angŭja for Angŭza,
says to Ntalo), "I think you said your mother and father both
died at·Angŭza, did you not?" *N.* "Yes, at Angŭza." *S.* "Then
you had two mothers and two fathers—one set died at Angŭja,
and the other set at Angŭza; you are a humbug; I don't believe
you; you are no mgŭana, but a slave who has been snatched from
his family, and does not know where any of his family are. Ah!
ah! ah!" And all the men of the camp laugh together at the
wretched Ntalo's defeat; but Ntalo won't be done, so retorts by
saying, "Sangizo, you may laugh at me because I am an orphan,
but what are you? you are a savage—a mshenzi; you come from
the Mashenzi, and you wear skins, not clothes, as men do; so hold
your impudent tongue;" and the camp pealed with merry boisterous laughter again.

9th. Early in the morning, and while I was in bed, the king
sent his pages to request me to visit his royal mother, with some
specific for the itch, with which her majesty was then afflicted. I
said I could not go so far in the sun; I would wait till I received
the promised palace near her. In the mean while I prepared to
call on him. I observed, in fact, that I was an object of jealousy

between the two courts, and that, if I acted skillfully and decidedly, I might become master of the situation, and secure my darling
object of a passage northward. The boys returned, bringing a
pistol to be cleaned, and a message to say it was no use my thinking of calling on the king—that I must go to the queen immediately, for she was very ill. So far the queen won the day, but
I did not obtain my new residence, which I considered the first
step to accomplishing the greater object; I therefore put the iron
farther in the fire by saying I was no man's slave, and I should
not go until I got a house in the palace; Bombay could teach the
boys the way to clean the pistol. The pert monkeys, however,
turned up their noses at such menial service, and Ulédi was instructed in their stead.

10th. To surprise the queen, and try another dodge, I called on
her with all my dining things and bedding, to make a day of it,
and sleep the night. She admitted me at once, when I gave her
quinine, on the proviso that I should stop there all day and night
to repeat the dose, and tell her the reason why I did not come before. She affected great anger at Mtésa having interfered with
my servants when coming to see her—sympathized with me on
the distance I had to travel—ordered a hut to be cleared for me
ere night—told me to eat my breakfast in the next court—and,
rising abruptly, walked away. At noon we heard the king approaching with his drums and rattle-traps, but I still waited on
till 5 P.M., when, on summons, I repaired to the throne-hut.
Here I heard, in an adjoining court, the boisterous, explosive
laughs of both mother and son—royal shouts loud enough to be
heard a mile off, and inform the community that their sovereigns
were pleased to indulge in hilarity. Immediately afterward, the
gate between us being thrown open, the king, like a very child,
stood before us, dressed for the first time, in public, in what
Europeans would call clothes. For a cap he wore a Muscat alfia,
on his neck a silk Arab turban, fastened with a ring. Then for
a coat he had an Indian kizbow, and for trowsers a yellow woolen
doti; while in his hand, in imitation of myself, he kept running
his ramrod backward and forward through his fingers. As I advanced and doffed my hat, the king, smiling, entered the court,
followed by a budding damsel dressed in red bindera, who carried the chair I had presented to him, and two new spears.

He now took his seat for the first time upon a chair, for I had
told him, at my last interview, that all kings were expected to

bring out some new fashion, or else the world would never make progress; and I was directed to sit before him on my grass throne. Talking, though I longed to enter into conversation, was out of the question; for no one dared speak for me, and I could not talk myself; so we sat and grinned, till in a few minutes the queen, full of smirks and smiles, joined us, and sat on a mbŭgŭ. I offered the medicine-chest as a seat, but she dared not take it; in fact, by the constitution of Uganda, no one, however high in rank, not even his mother, can sit before the king. After sundry jokes, while we were all bursting with laughter at the theatrical phenomenon, the wakungŭ who were present, some twenty in number, threw themselves in line upon their bellies, and, wriggling like fish, n'yanzigged, n'goned, and demaned, and uttered other wonderful words of rejoicing—as, for instance, "Hai minangé! Hai mkama wangi!" (Oh my chief! Oh my king!)—while they continued floundering, kicking about their legs, rubbing their faces, and putting their hands upon the ground, as if the king had performed some act of extraordinary munificence by showing himself to them in that strange and new position, a thing quite enough to date a new Uganda era from.

The king, without deigning to look upon his groveling subjects, said, "Now, mother, take your medicine;" for he had been called solemnly to witness the medical treatment she was undergoing at my hands. When she had swallowed her quinine with a wry face, two very black virgins appeared on the stage holding up the double red blanket I had given the queen; for nothing, however trifling, can be kept secret from the king. The whole court was in raptures. The king signified his approval by holding his mouth, putting his head on one side, and looking askance at it. The queen looked at me, then at the blanket and her son in turn; while my men hung down their heads, fearful lest they should be accused of looking at the ladies of the court; and the wakungŭ n'yanzigged again, as if they could not contain the gratification they felt at the favor shown them. Nobody had ever brought such wonderful things to Uganda before, and all loved Bana.

Till now I had expected to vent my wrath on both together for all past grievances, but this childish, merry, homely scene—the mother holding up her pride, her son, before the state officers'—melted my heart at once. I laughed as well as they did, and said it pleased me excessively to see them both so happy together. It was well the king had broken through the old-fashioned laws of Uganda by sitting on an iron chair, and adopting European dresses, for now he was opening a road to cement his own dominions with my country. I should know what things to send that would please him. The king listened, but without replying; and said, at the conclusion, "It is late, now let us move;" and walked away, preserving famously the lion's gait. The mother also vanished, and I was led away to a hut outside, prepared for my night's residence. It was a small, newly-built hut, just large enough for my bed, with a corner for one servant; so I turned all my men away save one, ate my dinner, and hoped to have a quiet, cool night of it, when suddenly Maŭla flounced in with all his boys, lighting a fire, and they spread their mbŭgŭs for the night. In vain I pleaded I could not stand the suffocation of so many men, especially of Waganda, who eat raw plantains; and unless they turned out, I should do so, to benefit by the pure air. Maŭla said he had the queen's orders to sleep with Bana, and sleep there he would; so, rather than kick him out, which I felt inclined to do, I smoked my pipe and drank pombé all night, turning the people out and myself in, in the morning, to prepare for a small house-fight with the queen.

11th. Early in the morning, as I expected, she demanded my immediate attendance; and so the little diplomatic affair I had anticipated came on. I begin the game by intimating that I am in bed, and have not breakfasted. So at 10 A.M. another messenger arrives, to say her majesty is much surprised at my not coming. What can such conduct mean, when she arranged every thing so nicely for me after my own desire, that she might drink her medicine properly? Still I am not up; but nobody will let me rest from fear of the queen; so, to while away the time, I order Bombay to call upon her, give the quinine, and tell her all that has happened; at which she flies into a towering rage, says she will never touch medicine administered by any other hands but mine, and will not believe in one word Bombay says, either about Maŭla or the hut; for Maŭla, whose duty necessarily obliged him to take my servants before her majesty, had primed her with a lot of falsehoods on the subject; and she had a fondness for Maŭla, because he was a clever humbug and exceeding rogue; and sent Bombay back to fetch me, for nobody had ever dared disobey her mandates before.

It had now turned noon, and being ready for the visit, I went to see the queen. Determined to have her turn, she kept me waiting for a long time before she would show herself; and at last, when she came, she flounced up to her curtain, lay down in a huff, and vented her wrath, holding her head very high, and wishing to know how I could expect officers, with large establishments, to be turned out of their homes merely to give me room for one night; I ought to have been content with my fare; it was no fault of Maŭla's. I tried to explain through Nasib, but she called Nasib a liar, and listened to Maŭla who told the lies; then asked for her medicine; drank it, saying it was a small dose; and walked off in ill humor as she had come. I now made up my mind to sit till 3 P.M., hoping to see the queen again, while talking with some Kidi officers, who, contrary to the general law of the country, indulged me with some discourses on geography, from which I gathered, though their stories were rather confused, that beyond the Asŭa River, in the Galla country, there was another lake which was navigated by the inhabitants in very large vessels; and somewhere in the same neighborhood there was an exceedingly high mountain, covered with yellow dust, which the natives collected, etc., etc.

Time was drawing on, and as the queen would not appear of her own accord, I sent to request a friendly conversation with her before I left, endeavoring, as well as I could, to persuade her that the want of cordiality between us was owing to the mistakes of interpreters, who had not conveyed to her my profound sentiments of devotion. This brought her gracious corpulence out all smirks and smiles, preceded by a basket of sweet potatoes for "Bana, my son." I began conversation with a speech of courtesy, explaining how I had left my brother Grant and my great friend Rŭmanika at Karagŭé, hastening, in compliance with the invitation of the king, to visit him and herself, with the full hope of making friends in Uganda; but now I had come, I was greatly disappointed; for I neither saw half enough of their majesties, nor did any of their officers ever call upon me to converse and pass away the dreary hours. All seemed highly pleased, and complimented my speech; while the queen, turning to her officers, said, "If that is the case, I will send these men to you;" whereupon the officers, highly delighted at the prospect of coming to see me, and its consequence, a present, n'yanzigged until I thought their hands would drop off. Then her majesty, to my thorough annoyance, and before I had finished half I had to say, rose from her seat, and, showing her broad stern to the company, walked straight away. The officers then drew near me, and begged I would sleep there another night; but as they had nothing better to offer than the hut of last night, I declined, and went my way, begging them to call and make friends with me.

12*th*. Immediately after breakfast the king sent his pages in a great hurry to say he was waiting on the hill for me, and begged I would bring all my guns immediately. I prepared, thinking, naturally enough, that some buffaloes had been marked down; for the boys, as usual, were perfectly ignorant of his designs. To my surprise, however, when I mounted the hill half way to the palace, I found the king standing, dressed in a rich filigreed waistcoat, trimmed with gold embroidery, tweedling the loading-rod in his finger, and an alfia cap on his head, while his pages held his chair and guns, and a number of officers, with dogs and goats for offerings, squatting before him.

When I arrived, hat in hand, he smiled, examined my firearms, and proceeded for sport, leading the way to a high tree, on which some adjutant birds were nesting, and numerous vultures resting. This was the sport; Bana must shoot a nundo (adjutant) for the king's gratification. I begged him to take a shot himself, as I really could not demean myself by firing at birds sitting on a tree; but it was all of no use; no one could shoot as I could, and they must be shot. I proposed frightening them out with stones, but no stone could reach so high; so, to cut the matter short, I killed an adjutant on the nest, and, as the vultures flew away, brought one down on the wing, which fell in a garden inclosure.

The Waganda were for a minute all spell-bound with astonishment, when the king jumped frantically in the air, clapping his hands above his head, and singing out, "Woh, woh, woh! what wonders! Oh, Bana, Bana! what miracles he performs!" and all the wakungŭ followed in chorus. "Now load, Bana—load, and let us see you do it," cried the excited king; but, before I was half loaded, he said, "Come along, come along, and let us see the bird." Then directing the officers which way to go—for, by the etiquette of the court of Uganda, every one must precede the king—he sent them through a court where his women, afraid of the gun, had been concealed. Here the rush onward was stopped by newly-made fences, but the king roared to the officers to knock them down. This was no sooner said than done by the attendants in a body shoving on and trampling them under, as an elephant would crush small trees to keep his course. So pushing, floundering through plantain and shrub, pell-mell one upon the other, that the king's pace might not be checked, or any one come in for a royal kick or blow, they came upon the prostrate bird. "Woh, woh, woh!" cried the king again, "there he is, sure enough; come here, women—come and look what wonders!" And all the women, in the highest excitement, "woh-wohed" as loud as any of the men. But that was not enough. "Come along, Bana," said the king, "we must have some more sport;" and, saying this, he directed the way toward the queen's palace, the attendants leading, followed by the pages, then the king, next myself—for I never would walk before him—and finally the women, some forty or fifty, who constantly attended him.

To make the most of the king's good-humor, while I wanted to screen myself from the blazing sun, I asked him if he would like to enjoy the pleasures of an umbrella; and before he had time to answer, held mine over him as we walked side by side. The wakungŭ were astonished, and the women prattled in great delight; while the king, hardly able to control himself, sidled and spoke to his flatterers as if he were doubly created monarch of all he surveyed. He then, growing more familiar, said, "Now, Bana, do tell me—did you not shoot that bird with something more than common ammunition? I am sure you did, now; there was magic in it." And all I said to the contrary would not convince him. "But we will see again." "At buffaloes?" I said. "No, the buffaloes are too far off now; we will wait to go after them until I have given you a hut close by." Presently, as some herons were flying overhead, he said, "Now shoot, shoot!" and I brought a couple down right and left. He stared, and every body stared, believing me to be a magician, when the king said he would like to have pictures of the birds drawn and hung up in the palace; "but let us go and shoot some more, for it is truly wonderful." Similar results followed, for the herons were continually whirling round, as they had their nests upon a neighboring tree; and then the king ordered his pages to carry all the birds, save the vulture—which, for some reason, they did not touch—and show them to the queen.

He then gave the order to move on, and we all repaired to the palace. Arrived at the usual throne-room, he took his seat, dismissed the party of wives who had been following him, as well as the wakungŭ, received pombé from his female evil-eye averters, and ordered me, with my men, to sit in the sun facing him, till I complained of the heat, and was allowed to sit by his side. Kites, crows, and sparrows were flying about in all directions, and as they came within shot, nothing would satisfy the excited boy-king but I must shoot them, and his pages take them to the queen, till my ammunition was totally expended. He then wanted me to send for more shot; and as I told him he must wait for more until my brothers come, he contented himself with taking two or three sample grains, and ordering his ironsmiths to make some like them.

Cows were now driven in for me to kill two with one bullet; but as the off one jumped away when the gun fired, the bullet passed through the near one, then through all the courts and fences, and away no one knew where. The king was delighted, and said he must keep the rifle to look at for the night. I now asked permission to speak with him on some important matters, when he sent his women away, and listened. I said I felt anx-ious about the road on which Mabrŭki was traveling, to which I added that I had ordered him to tell Petherick to come here, or else to send property to the value of $1000; and.I felt anxious because some of the queen's officers felt doubtful about Waganda being able to penetrate Kidi. He said I need not concern my-self on that score; he was much more anxious for the white men to come here than even I was, and he would not send my men into any danger; but it was highly improper for any of his peo-ple to speak about such subjects. Then, assembling the women again, he asked me to load Whitworth for him, when he shot the remaining cow, holding the rifle in both hands close to his thigh. The feat, of course, brought forth great and uproarious congratu-lations from his women. The day thus ended, and I was dis-missed.

13th. Mabrŭki and Bilal come into camp: they returned last night; but the Waganda escort, afraid of my obtaining informa-tion of them before the king received it, kept them concealed. They had been defeated in Usoga, two marches east of Kira, at the residence of Nagozigombi, Mtésa's border officer, who gave them two bullocks, but advised their returning at once to inform the king that the independent Wasoga had been fighting with his dependent Wasoga subjects for some time, and the battle would not be over for two months or more, unless he sent an army to their assistance.

I now sent Bombay to the king to request an interview, as I had much of importance to tell him; but he could not be seen, as he was deep in the interior of the palace enjoying the society of his wives. The kamraviona, however, was found there waiting, as usual, on the mere chance of his majesty taking it into his head to come out. He asked Bombay if it was true the woman he gave me ran away; and when Bombay told him, he said, "Oh, he should have chained her for two or three days, until she became accustomed to her. residence; for women often take fright and run away in that way, believing strangers to be' cannibals." But Bombay replied, "She was not good enough for Bana; he let her go off like a dog; he wants a young and beautiful mhŭma, or none at all." "Ah! well, then, if he is so particular, he must wait a bit, for we have none on hand. What I gave him is the sort of creature we give all our guests." A Msoga was sent by the king to take the dead adjutant of yesterday out of the nest— for all Wasoga are expert climbers, which is not the case with the Waganda; but the man was attacked half way up the tree by a swarm of bees, and driven down again.

14th. After all the vexatious haggling for a house, I gained my object to-day by a judicious piece of bribery which I had intended to accomplish whenever I could. I now succeeded in sending —for I could not, under the jealous eyes in Uganda, get it done earlier—a present of fifteen pints mixed beads, twenty blue eggs, and five copper bracelets, to the commander-in-chief, as a mark of friendship. At the same time I hinted that I should like him to use his influence in obtaining for me a near and respectable resi-' dence, where I hoped he, as well as all the Waganda nobility, would call upon me; for my life in Uganda was utterly miserable, being shut up like a hermit by myself every day. The result was, that a number of huts in a large plantain garden were at once assigned to me, on the face of a hill, immediately overlooking and close to the main road. It was considered the "West End." It had never before been occupied by any visitors excepting Wahinda embassadors; and being near, and in full view of the palace, was pleasant and advantageous, as I could both hear the constant music, and see the throngs of people ever wending their way to and from the royal abodes. I lost no time in moving all my property, turning out the original occupants—in selecting the best hut for myself, giving the rest to my three officers— and ordering my men to build barracks for themselves, in street

form, from my hut to the main road. There was one thing only
left to be done: the sanitary orders of Uganda required every
man to build for himself a house of Parliament, such being the
neat and cleanly nature of the Waganda—a pattern to all other
negro tribes.

15*th*. As nobody could obtain an interview with the king yesterday, I went to the palace to-day, and fired three shots, a signal
which was at once answered from within by a double discharge
of a gun I had just lent him on his returning my rifle. In a little
while, as soon as he had time to dress, the king, walking like a
lion, sallied forth, leading his white dog, and beckoned me to follow him to the state hut, the court of which was filled with squatting men as usual, well dressed, and keeping perfect order. He
planted himself on his throne, and begged me to sit by his side.
Then took place the usual scene of a court levée, as described in
Chapter X., with the specialty, in this instance, that the son of the
chief executioner—one of the highest officers of state—was led
off for execution, for some omission or informality in his n'yanzigs, or salutes.

At this levée sundry wakungŭ of rank complained that the
Wanyambo plundered their houses at night, and rough-handled
their women, without any respect for their greatness, and, when
caught, said they were Bana's men. Bombay, who was present,
heard the complaint, and declared these were Sŭwarora's men,
who made use of the proximity of my camp to cover their own
transgressions. Then Sŭwarora's deputation, who were also present, cringed forward, n'yanzigging like Waganda, and denied the
accusation, when the king gave all warning that he would find
out the truth by placing guards on the look-out at night.

Till this time the king had not heard oné word about the defeat
of the party sent for Petherick. His kingdom might have been
lost, and he would have been no wiser; when the officer who led
Mabrŭki came forward and told him all that had happened, stating, in addition to what I heard before, that they took eighty men
with them, and went into battle three times unsuccessfully. Dismissing business, however, the king turned to me, and said he
never saw any thing so wonderful as my shooting in his life; he
was sure it was done by magic, as my gun never missed, and he
wished I would instruct him in the art. When I denied there
was any art in shooting farther than holding the gun straight, he
shook his head, and, getting me to load his revolving pistol for

him, he fired all five barrels into two cows before the multitude.
He then thought of adjutant-shooting with ball, left the court sitting, desired me to follow him, and, leading the way, went into
the interior of the palace, where only a few select officers were
permitted to follow us. The birds were wild, and as nothing was
done, I instructed him in the way to fire from his shoulder, placing the gun in position. He was shy. at first, and all the people
laughed at my handling royalty like a school-boy; but he soon
took to it very good-naturedly, when I gave him my silk neck-tie
and gold crest-ring, explaining their value, which he could not
comprehend, and telling him we gentlemen prided ourselves on
never wearing brass or copper.

He now begged hard for shot; but I told him again his only
chance of getting any lay in opening the road onward; it was on
this account, I said, I had come to see him to-day. He answered,
"I am going to send an army to Usoga to force the way from
where your men were turned back." But this, I said, would not
do for me, as I saw his people traveled like geese; not knowing
the direction of Gani, or where they were going to when sent. I
proposed that if he would call all his traveling men of experience
together, I would explain matters to them by a map I had brought;
for I should never be content till I saw Petherick.

The map was then produced. He seemed to comprehend it
immediately, and assembled the desired wakungŭ; but, to my
mortification, he kept all the conversation to himself, Waganda
fashion; spoke a lot of nonsense; and then asked his men what
they thought had better be done. The sages replied, "Oh, make
friends, and do the matter gently." But the king proudly raised
his head, laughed them to scorn, and said, "Make friends with
men who have crossed their spears with us already! Nonsense!
they would only laugh at us; the Uganda spear alone shall do
it." Hearing this bravado, the kamraviona, the pages, and the
elders, all rose to a man, with their sticks, and came charging at
their king, swearing they would carry out his wishes with their
lives. The meeting now broke up in the usual unsatisfactory,
unfinished manner, by the king rising and walking away, while I
returned with the kamraviona, who begged for ten more blue
eggs in addition to my present to make a full necklace, and told
my men to call upon him in the morning, when he would give
me any thing I wished to eat. Bombay was then ordered to describe what sort of food I lived on usually, when, Mganda fashion,

he broke a stick into ten bits, each representing a different article, and said, "Bana eat mixed food always;" and explained that stick No. 1 represented beef; No. 2, mutton; No. 3, fowl; No. 4, eggs; No. 5, fish; No. 6, potatoes; No. 7, plantains; No. 8, pombé; No. 9, butter; No. 10, flour.

16th. To-day the king was amusing himself among his women again, and not to be seen. I sent Bombay with ten blue eggs as a present for the kamraviona, intimating my desire to call upon him. He sent me a goat and ten fowls' eggs, saying he was not visible to strangers on business to-day. I inferred that he required the king's permission to receive me. This double failure was a more serious affair than a mere slight; for my cows were eaten up, and my men clamoring incessantly for food; and though they might by orders help themselves "kŭ n'yangania"—by seizing—from the Waganda, it hurt my feelings so much to witness this, that I tried from the first to dispense with it, telling the king I had always flogged my men for stealing, and now he turned them into a pack of thieves. I urged that he should either allow me to purchase rations, or else feed them from the palace as Rŭmanika did; but he always turned a deaf ear, or said that what Sunna his father had introduced it ill became him to subvert; and, unless my men helped themselves, they would die of starvation.

On the present emergency I resolved to call upon the queen. On reaching the palace, I sent an officer in to announce my arrival, and sat waiting for the reply fully half an hour, smoking my pipe, and listening to her in the adjoining court, where music was playing, and her voice occasionally rent the air with merry boisterous laughing.

The messenger returned to say no one could approach her sanctuary or disturb her pleasure at this hour; I must wait and bide my time, as the Uganda officers do. Whew! Here was another diplomatic crisis, which had to be dealt with in the usual way. "I bide my time!" I said, rising in a towering passion, and thrashing the air with my ramrod walking-stick, before all the visiting wakungŭ, "when the queen has assured me her door would always be open to me! I shall leave this court at once, and I solemnly swear I shall never set foot in it again, unless some apology be made for treating me like a dog." Then, returning home, I tied up all the presents her majesty had given me in a bundle, and calling Maŭla and my men together, told them to take them where they came from, for it ill became me to keep tokens of friendship when no friendship existed between us. I came to make friends with the queen, not to trade or take things from her —and so forth. The blackguard Maŭla, laughing, said, "Bana does not know what he is doing;' it is a heinous offense in Uganda sending presents back; nobody for their lives dare do so to the queen; her wrath would know no bounds. She will say, 'I took a few trifles from Bana as specimens of his country, but they shall all go back, and the things the king has received shall go back also, for we are all of one family;' and then won't Bana be very sorry? Moreover, wakungŭ will be killed by dozens, and lamentations will reign throughout the court to propitiate the devils who brought such disasters on them." Bombay, also in a fright, said, "Pray don't do so; you don't know these savages as we do; there is no knowing what will happen; it may defeat our journey altogether. Farther, we have had no food these four days, because row succeeds row. If we steal, you flog us; and if we ask the Waganda for food, they beat us. We don't know what to do." I was imperative, however, and said, "Maŭla must take back these things in the morning, or stand the consequences." In fact, I found that, like the organ-grinders in London, to get myself moved on I must make myself troublesome.

17th. The queen's presents were taken back by Maŭla and Nasib, while I went to see the kamraviona. Even this gentleman kept me waiting for some time to show his own importance, and then admitted me into one of his interior courts, where I found him sitting on the ground with several elders, while Wasoga minstrels played on their lap-harps, and sang songs in praise of their king, and the noble stranger who wore fine clothes and eclipsed all previous visitors. At first, on my approach, the haughty young chief, very handsome, and twenty years of age, did not raise his head; then he begged me to be seated, and even inquired after my health in a listless, condescending kind of manner, as if the exertion of talking was too much for his constitution or his rank; but he soon gave up this nonsense as I began to talk; inquired, among other things, why I did not see the Waganda at my house, when I said I should so much like to make acquaintance with them, and begged to be introduced to the company who were present.

I was now enabled to enlarge the list of topics on which it is prohibited to the Waganda to speak or act under pain of death. No one even dare ever talk about the royal pedigree, of the countries that have been conquered, or even of any neighboring countries; no one dare visit the king's guests, or be visited by them, without leave, else the king, fearing sharers in his plunder, would say, What are you plucking our goose for? Neither can any one cast his eye for a moment on the women of the palace, whether out walking or at home, lest he should be accused of amorous intentions. Beads and brass wire, exchanged for ivory or slaves, are the only article of foreign manufacture any Mganda can hold in his possession. Should any thing else be seen in his house—for instance, cloth—his property would be confiscated and his life taken.

I was now introduced to the company present, of whom one Mgéma, an elderly gentleman of great dignity, had the honor to carry Sunna, the late king; Mpungŭ, who cooked for Sunna, also ranks high in court; then Usungŭ and Kŭnza, executioners, rank very high, enjoying the greatest confidence with the king; and, finally, Jumba and Natigo, who traced their pedigree to the age of the first Uganda king. As I took down a note of their several names, each seemed delighted at finding his name written down by me; and Kŭnza, the executioner, begged as a great favor that I would plead to the king to spare his son's life, who, as I have mentioned, was ordered out to execution on the last levée day. At first I thought it necessary, for the sake of maintaining my dignity, to raise objections, and said it would ill become one of my rank to make any request that might possibly be rejected; but as the kamraviona assured me there would be no chance of failure, and every body else agreed with him, I said it would give me intense satisfaction to serve him; and the old man squeezed my hand as if overpowered with joy.

This meeting, as might be imagined, was a very dull one, because the company, being tongue-tied as regards every thing of external interest, occupied themselves solely on matters of home business, or indulged their busy tongues, Waganda fashion, in gross flattery of their "illustrious visitor." In imitation of the king, the kamraviona now went from one hut to another, requesting us to follow, that we might see all his greatness, and then took me alone into a separate court to show me his women, some five-and-twenty of the ugliest in Uganda. This, he added, was a mark of respect he had never conferred on any person before; but, fearing lest I should misunderstand his meaning, and covet any of them, he said, "Mind, they are only to be looked at."

As we retired to the other visitors, the kamraviona, in return for some courteous remarks of mine, said all the Waganda were immensely pleased with my having come to visit them; and as he heard my country is governed by a woman, what would I say if he made the Waganda dethrone her, and create me king instead. Without specially replying, I showed him a map, marking off the comparative sizes of British and Waganda possessions, and shut him up. The great kamraviona, or commander-in-chief, with all his wives, has no children, and was eager to know if my skill could avail to remove this cloud in his fortunes. He generously gave me a goat and eggs, telling my men they might help themselves to plantains from any gardens they liked beyond certain limits, provided they did not enter houses or take any thing else. He then said he was tired, and walked away without another word.

On returning home I found Nasib and Maŭla waiting for me, with all the articles that had been returned to the queen very neatly tied together. They had seen her majesty, who, on receiving my message, pretended excessive anger with her doorkeeper for not announcing my arrival yesterday—flogged him severely—inspected all the things returned—folded them again very neatly with her own hands—said she felt much hurt at the mistake which had arisen, and hoped I would forgive and forget it, as her doors would always be open to me.

I now had a laugh at my friends Maŭla and Bombay for their misgivings of yesterday, telling them I knew more of human nature than they did; but they shook their heads, and said it was all very well Bana having done it, but if Arabs or any other person had tried the same trick, it would have been another affair. "Just so," said I; "but then, don't you see, I know my value here, which makes all the difference you speak of."

18th. While walking toward the palace to pay the king a friendly visit, I met two of my men speared on the head, and streaming with blood; they had been trying to help themselves to plantains carried on the heads of Waganda; but the latter proving too strong, my people seized a boy and woman from their party as witnesses, according to Uganda law, and ran away with them, tied hand and neck together. With this addition to my attendance I first called in at the kamraviona's for justice; but, as he was too proud to appear at once, I went on to the king's, fired three shots as usual, and obtained admittance at once, when

I found him standing in a yard, dressed in cloth, with his iron chair behind him, and my double-gun loaded with half charges of powder and a few grains of iron shot, looking eagerly about for kites to fly over. His quick eye, however, readily detected my wounded men and prisoners, as also some Wazinza prisoners led in by Waganda police, who had been taken in the act of entering Waganda houses and assailing their women. Thus my men were cleared of a false stigma; and the king, while praising them, ordered all the Wazinza to leave his dominions on the morrow.

The other case was easily settled by my wounded men receiving orders to keep their prisoners till claimed, when, should any people come forward, they would be punished, otherwise their loss in human stock would be enough. The Wanguana had done quite right to seize on the highway, else they would have starved; such was the old law, and such is the present one. It was no use our applying for a change of system. At this stage of the business, the birds he was watching having appeared, the king, in a great state of excitement, said, "Shoot that kite," and then "Shoot that other;" but the charges were too light, and the birds flew away, kicking with their claws as if merely stung a little.

While this was going on, the kamraviona, taking advantage of my having opened the door with the gun, walked in to make his salutations. A blacksmith produced two very handsome spears, and a fisherman a basket of fish, from which two fish were taken out and given to me. The king then sat on his iron chair, and I on a wooden box which I had contrived to stuff with the royal grass he gave me, and so made a complete miniature imitation of his throne. The contrivance made him laugh, as much, I fancy, at his own folly in not allowing me to sit upon my portable iron stool, as at my ingenious device for carrying out my determination to sit before him like an Englishman. I wished to be communicative, and, giving him a purse of money, told him the use and value of the several coins; but he paid little regard to them, and soon put them down. The small-talk of Uganda had much more attractions to his mind than the wonders of the outer world, and he kept it up with his kamraviona until rain fell and dispersed the company.

19th. As the queen, to avoid future difficulties, desired my officers to acquaint her beforehand whenever I wished to call upon

her, I sent Nasib early to say I would call in the afternoon; but
he had to wait till the evening before he could deliver the message, though she had been drumming and playing all the day.
She then complained against my men for robbing her gardeners
on the highway, wished to know why I didn't call upon her oft-
ener, appointed the following morning for an interview, and
begged I would bring her some liver medicines, as she suffered
from constant twinges in her right side, sealing her "letter" with
a present of a nest of eggs and one fowl.

While Nasib was away, I went to the kamraviona to treat him
as I had the king. He appeared a little more affable to-day, yet
still delighted in nothing but what was frivolous. My beard, for
instance, engrossed the major part of the conversation; all the
Waganda would come out in future with hairy faces; but when
I told them that, to produce such a growth, they must wash their
faces with milk, and allow a cat to lick it off, they turned up their
noses in utter contempt.

20th. I became dead tired of living all alone, with nothing else
to occupy my time save making these notes every day in my
office letter-book, as my store of stationery was left at Karagüé.
I had no chance of seeing any visitors, save the tiresome pages,
who asked me to give or to do something for the king every day;
and my prospect was cheerless, as I had been flatly refused a visit
to Usoga until Grant should come. For want of better amusement, I made a page of Lŭgoi, a sharp little lad, son of the late
Belŭch, but adopted by Ulédi, and treated him as a son, which he
declared he wished to be, for he liked me better than Ulédi as a
father. He said he disliked Uganda, where people's lives are
taken like those of fowls; and wished to live at the coast, the
only place he ever heard of, where all the Wangŭana come from
—great *swells* in Lŭgoi's estimation. Now, with Lŭgoi dressed in
a new white pillow-case, with holes trimmed with black tape for
his head and arms to go through, a dagger tied with red bindera
round his waist, and a square of red blanket rolled on his shoulder
as a napkin for my gun to rest on, or in place of a goatskin rug
when he wished to sit down, I walked off to inquire how the
kamraviona was, and took my pictures with me.

Lŭgoi's dress, however, absorbed all their thoughts, and he was
made to take it off and put it on again as often as any fresh visitor
came to call. Hardly a word was said about any thing else; even
the pictures, which generally are in such demand, attracted but

little notice. I asked the kamraviona to allow me to draw his pet dog; when the king's sister Miengo came in and sat down, laughing and joking with me immoderately.

At first there was a demur about my drawing the dog—whether from fear of bewitching the animal or not, I can not say; but, instead of producing the pet—a beautifully-formed cream-colored dog—a common black one was brought in, which I tied in front of Miengo, and then drew both woman and dog together. After this unlawful act was discovered, of drawing the king's sister without his consent, the whole company roared with laughter, and pretended nervous excitement lest I should book them likewise. One of my men, Sangoro, did not return to camp last night from foraging; and as my men suspect the Waganda must have murdered him, I told the kamraviona, requesting him to find out; but he coolly said, "Look for him yourselves two days more, for Wangŭana often make friends with our people, and so slip away from their masters; but as they are also often murdered, provided you can not find him in that time, we will have the mganga out."

21st. Last night I was turned out of my bed by a terrible hue and cry from the quarter allotted to Rozaro and his Wanyambo companions; for the Waganda had threatened to demolish my men, one by one, for seizing their pombé and plantains, though done according to the orders of the king; and now, finding the Wanyambo nearest to the road, they set on them by moonlight with spear and club, maltreating them severely, till, with re-enforcements, the Wanyambo gained the ascendency, seized two spears and one shield as a trophy, and drove their enemies off. In the morning I sent the wakungŭ off with the trophies to the king, again complaining that he had turned my men into a pack of highwaymen, and, as I foresaw, had thus created enmity between the Waganda and them, much to my annoyance. I therefore begged he would institute some means to prevent any farther occurrence of such scenes, otherwise I would use fire-arms in self-defense.

While these men were on this mission, I went on a like errand to the queen, taking my page Lŭgoi with the liver medicine. The first object of remark was Lŭgoi, as indeed it was every where; for, as I walked along, crowds ran after the little phenomenon. Then came the liver question; and, finally, what I wanted—her complaint against my men for robbing on the road, as it gave me the opportunity of telling her the king was doing what I had been trying to undo with my stick ever since I left the coast; and I begged she would use her influence to correct these disagreeables. She told me for the future to send my men to her palace for food, and rob no more; in the mean while, here were some plantains for them. She then rose and walked away, leaving me extremely disappointed that I could not make some more tangible arrangement with her—such as, if my men came and found the gate shut, what were they to do then? there were forty-five of them; how much would she allow? etc., etc. But this was a true specimen of the method of transacting business among the royal family of Uganda. They give orders without knowing how they are to be carried out, and treat all practical arrangements as trifling details not worth attending to.

After this unsatisfactory interview I repaired to the king's, knowing the power of my gun to obtain an interview, while doubting the ability of the wakungŭ to gain an audience for me. Such was the case. These men had been sitting all day without seeing the king, and three shots opened his gate immediately to me. He was sitting on the iron chair in the shade of the court, attended by some eighty women, tweedling the loading-rod in his fingers; but as my rod appeared a better one than his, they were exchanged. I then gave him a tortoise-shell comb to comb his hair straight with, as he invariably remarked on the beautiful manner in which I dressed my hair, making me uncap to show it to his women, and afterward asked my men to bring on the affair of last night. They feared, they said, to speak on such subjects while the women were present. I begged for a private audience; still they would not speak till encouraged and urged beyond all patience. I said, in Kisŭahili, "Kbakka" (king), "my men are afraid to tell you what I want to say;" when Maŭla, taking advantage of my having engaged his attention, though the king did not understand one word I said, said of himself, by way of currying favor, " I saw a wonderful gun in Rŭmanika's hands, with six barrels; not a short one like your fiver" (meaning the revolving pistol), "but a long one, as long as my arm." "Indeed," says the king; "we must have that." A page was then sent for by Maŭla, who, giving him a bit of stick representing the gun required, told him to fetch it immediately.

The king then said to me, "What is powder made of?" I began with sulphur (kibriti), intending to explain every thing; but the word kibriti was enough for him, and a second stick was sent for kibriti, the bearer being told to hurry for his life, and fetch it. The king now ordered some high officers who were in waiting to approach. They came, almost crouching to their knees, with eyes averted from the women, and n'yanzigged for the favor of being called till they streamed with perspiration. Four young women, virgins, the daughters of these high officers, nicely dressed, were shown in as brides, and ordered to sit with the other women. A gamekeeper brought in baskets small antelopes, called mpéo— with straight horns resembling those of the saltiana, but with coats like the hog-deer of India—intended for the royal kitchen. Elderly gentlemen led in goats as commutation for offenses, and went through the ceremonies due for the favor of being relieved of so much property. Ten cows were then driven in, plundered from Unyoro, and outside, the voices of the brave army who captured them were heard n'yanzigging vehemently. Lastly, some beautifully-made shields were presented, and, because extolled, n'yanzigged over; when the king rose abruptly and walked straight away, leaving my fools of men no better off for food, or reparation for their broken heads, than if I had never gone there.

22d. I called on the queen to inquire after her health, and to know how my men were to be fed; but, without giving me time to speak, she flew at me again about my men plundering. The old story was repeated; I had forty-five hungry men, who must have food, and, unless either she or the king would make some proper provision for them, I could not help it. Again she promised to feed them, but she objected to their bearing swords, "for of what use are swords? If the Waganda don't like the Wangŭana, can swords prevail in our country?" And, saying this, she walked away. I thought to myself that she must have directed the attack upon my camp last night, and is angry at the Wangŭana swords driving her men away. At 3 P.M. I visited the king, to have a private chat, and state my grievances; but the three shots fired brought him out to levée, when animals and sundry other things were presented; and appointments of wakungŭ were made for the late gallant services of some of the men in plundering Unyoro.

The old executioner, Kŭnza, being present, I asked the king to pardon his son. Surprised, at first Mtésa said, "Can it be possible Bana has asked for this?" And when assured, in great glee he ordered the lad's release, amid shouts of laughter from every

body but the agitated father, who n'yanzigged, cried, and fell at
my feet, making a host of wonderful signs as a token of his gratitude, for his heart was too full of emotion to give utterance to his
feelings. The king then, in high good-humor, said, "You have
called on me many times without our broaching the subject of
Usoga, and perhaps you may fancy we are not exerting ourselves
in 'the matter; but my army is only now returning from war"
(meaning plundering in Unyoro), "and I am collecting another
one, which will open Usoga effectually." Before I could say
any thing, the king started up in his usual manner, inviting a select few to follow him to another court, when my medicine-chest
was inspected, and I was asked to operate for fistula on one of the
royal executioners. I had no opportunity of incurring this responsibility; for, while professing to prepare for the operation,
the king went off in a fling.

When I got home I found Sangoro, whom we thought lost or
murdered, quietly ensconced in camp. He had been foraging by
himself a long way from camp, in a neighborhood where many
of the king's women are kept; and it being forbidden ground, he
was taken up by the keepers, placed in the stocks, and fed until
to-day, when he extricated his legs by means of his sword, and
ran away. My ever-grumbling men mobbed me again, clamoring for food, saying, as they eyed my goats, I lived at ease and
overlooked their wants. In vain I told them they had fared more
abundantly than I had since we entered Uganda; while I spared
my goats to have a little flesh every day, they consumed or
squandered away the flesh of their cows as rapidly as possible,
selling the skins for pombé, which·I seldom tasted; they robbed
me as long as I had cloth or beads, and now they had all become
as fat as hogs by lifting food off the Waganda lands. As I could
not quiet them, I directed that, early next morning, Maŭla should
go to the king and Nasib to the queen, while I proposed going
to the kamraviona's to work them all three about this affair of
food.

23d. According to the plan of last night, I called early on the
kamraviona. He promised me assistance, but with an air which
seemed to say, What are the sufferings of other men to me? So
I went home to breakfast, doubting if any thing ever would be
done. As Kaggo, however, the second officer of importance, had
expressed a wish to see me, I sent Bombay to him for food, and
waited the upshot. Presently the king sent to say he wished to

see me with my compass; for the blackguard Maŭla had told him I possessed a wonderful instrument, by looking at which I could find my way all over the world. I went as requested, and found the king sitting outside the palace on my chair dressed in cloths, with my silk neckerchief and crest-ring, playing his flute in concert with his brothers, some thirty-odd young men and boys, one half of them manacled, the other half free, with an officer watching over them to see that they committed no intrigues.

We then both sat side by side in the shade of the court walls, conversed and had music by turns; for the king had invited his brothers here to please me, the first step toward winning the coveted compass. My hair must now be shown and admired, then my shoes taken off and inspected, and my trowsers tucked up to show that I am white all over. Just at this time Bombay, who had been in great request, came before us laden with plantains. This was most opportune; for the king asked what he had been about, and then the true state of the case as regards my difficulties in obtaining food were, I fancy, for the first time made known to him. In a great fit of indignation he said, "I once killed a hundred wakungŭ in a single day, and now, if they won't feed my guests, I will kill a hundred more; for I know the physic for bumptiousness." Then, sending his brothers away, he asked me to follow him into the back part of the palace, as he loved me so much he must show me every thing. We walked along under the umbrella, first looking down one street of huts, then up another, and, finally, passing the sleeping-chamber, stopped at one adjoining it. "That hut," said the king, "is the one I sleep in; no one of my wives dare venture within it unless I call her." He let me feel immediately that for the distinction conferred on me in showing me this sacred hut a return was expected. Could I after that refuse him such a mere trifle as a compass? I told him he might as well put my eyes out and ask me to walk home, as take away that little instrument, which could be of no use to him, as he could not read or understand it. But this only excited his cupidity; he watched it twirling round and pointing to the north, and looked and begged again, until, tired of his importunities, I told him I must wait until the Usoga road was open before I could part with it, and then the compass would be nothing to what I would give him. Hearing this, he reared his head proudly, and, patting his heart, said, "That is all on my shoulders; as sure as I live it shall be done; for that country has no king, and

I have long been desirous of taking it." I declined, however, to give him the instrument on the security of his promise, and he went to breakfast.

I walked off to Usungŭ to see what I could do for him in his misery. I found that he had a complication of evils entirely beyond my healing power, and among them inveterate forms of the diseases which are generally associated with civilization and its social evils. I could do nothing to cure him, but promised to do whatever was in my power to alleviate his sufferings.

24th. Before breakfast I called on poor Usungŭ, prescribing hot coffee to be drunk with milk every morning, which astonished him not a little, as the negroes only use coffee for chewing. He gave my men pombé and plantains. On my return I met a page sent to invite me to the palace. I found the king sitting with a number of women. He was dressed in European clothes, part of them being a pair of trowsers he begged for yesterday, that he might appear like Bana. This was his first appearance in trowsers, and his whole attire, contrasting strangely with his native habiliments, was in his opinion very becoming, though to me a little ridiculous; for the legs of the trowsers, as well as the sleeves of the waistcoat, were much too short, so that his black feet and hands stuck out at the extremities as an organ-player's monkey's do, while the cockscomb on his head prevented a fez cap, which was part of his special costume for the occasion, from sitting properly. This display over, the women were sent away, and I was shown into a court, where a large number of plantains were placed in a line upon the ground for my men to take away, and we were promised the same treat every day. From this we proceeded to another court, where we sat in the shade together, when the women returned again, but were all dumb, because my interpreters dared not for their lives say any thing, even on my account, to the king's women. Getting tired, I took out my sketch-book and drew Lŭbŭga, the pet, which amused the king immensely as he recognized her cockscomb.

Then twenty naked virgins, the daughters of wakungŭ, all smeared and shining with grease, each holding a small square of mbŭgŭ for a fig-leaf, marched in a line before us, as a fresh addition to the harem, while the happy fathers floundered n'yanzigging on the ground, delighted to find their darlings appreciated by the king. Seeing this done in such a quiet, mild way before all my men, who dared not lift their heads to see it, made me burst into a roar of laughter, and the king, catching the infection from me, laughed as well; but the laughing did not end there; for the pages, for once giving way to nature, kept bursting—my men chuckled in sudden gusts—while even the women, holding their mouths for fear of detection, responded—and we all laughed together. Then a sedate old dame rose from the squatting mass, ordered the virgins to right-about, and marched them off, showing their still more naked reverses. I now obtained permission for the wakungŭ to call upon me, and I fancied I only required my interpreters to speak out like men when I had any thing to say, to make my residence in Uganda both amusing and instructive; but, though the king, carried off by the prevailing good-humor of the scene we had both witnessed, supported me, I found that he had counterordered what he had said as soon as I had gone, and, in fact, no mkungŭ ever dared come near me.

25th. To-day I visited Usungŭ again, and found him better. He gave pombé and plantains for my people, but would not talk to me, though I told him he had permission to call on me.

I have now been for some time within the court precincts, and have consequently had an opportunity of witnessing court customs. Among these, nearly every day since I have changed my residence, incredible as it may appear to be, I have seen one, two,

A Queen dragged to Execution.

or three of the wretched palace women led away to execution, tied by the hand, and dragged along by one of the body-guard,

crying out, as she went to premature death, "Hai minangé!"
(Oh my lord!) "Kbakka!" (My king!) "Hai n'yawo!" (My
mother!) at the top of her voice, in the utmost despair and lam-
entation; and yet there was not a soul who dared lift hand to
save any of them, though many might be heard privately commenting on their beauty.

26*th*. To-day, to amuse the king, I drew a picture of himself
holding a levée, and proceeded to visit him. On the way I found
the high road thronged with cattle captured in Unyoro; and on
arrival at the antechamber, among the officers in waiting, Masimbi
(Mr. Cowries or Shells), the queen's uncle, and Congow, a young
general, who once led an army into Unyoro, past Kamrasi's palace. They said they had obtained leave for me to visit them,
and were eagerly looking out for the happy event. At once, on
firing, I was admitted to the king's favorite place, which, now
that the king had a movable chair to sit upon, was the shade of
the court screen. We had a chat; the picture was shown to the
women; the king would like to have some more, and gave me
leave to draw in the palace any time I liked. At the same time
he asked for my paint-box, merely to look at it. Though I repeatedly dunned him for it, I could never get it back from him
until I was preparing to leave Uganda.

27*th*. After breakfast I started on a visit to Congow; but,
finding he had gone to the king as usual, called at Masimbi's, and
he being absent also, I took advantage of my proximity to the
queen's palace to call on her majesty. For hours I was kept
waiting; firstly, because she was at breakfast; secondly, because
she was "putting on medicine;" and, thirdly, because the sun
was too powerful for her complexion; when I became tired of
her nonsense, and said, "If she does not wish to see me, she had
better say so at once, else I shall walk away; for the last time I
came I saw her but for a minute, when she rudely turned her
back upon me, and left me sitting by myself." I was told not to
be in a hurry—she would see me in the evening. This promise
might probably be fulfilled six blessed hours from the time when
it was made; but I thought to myself, every place in Uganda is
alike when there is no company at home, and so I resolved to sit
the time out, like Patience on a monument, hoping something
funny might turn up after all.

At last her majesty stumps out, squats behind my red blanket,
which is converted into a permanent screen, and says hastily, or

rather testily, "Can't Bana perceive the angry state of the weather—clouds flying about, and the wind blowing half a gale? Whenever that is the case, I can not venture out." Taking her lie without an answer, I said, I had now been fifty days or so doing nothing in Uganda; not one single visitor of my own rank ever came near me, and I could not associate with people far below her condition and mine; in fact, all I had to amuse me at home now was watching a hen lay her eggs upon my spare bed. Her majesty became genial, as she had been before, and promised to provide me with suitable society. I then told her I had desired my officers several times to ask the king how marriages were conducted in this country, as they appeared so different from ours, but they always said they dared not put such a question to him, and now I hoped she would explain it to me. To tell her I could not get any thing from the king I knew would be the surest way of eliciting what I wanted from her, because of the jealousy between the two courts; and in this instance it was fully proved, for she brightened up at once, and, when I got her to understand something of what I meant by a marriage ceremony, in high good-humor entered on a long explanation, to the following effect:

There are no such things as marriages in Uganda; there are no ceremonies attached to it. If any mkungŭ possessed of a pretty daughter committed an offense, he might give her to the king as a peace-offering; if any neighboring king had a pretty daughter, and the King of Uganda wanted her, she might be demanded as a fitting tribute. The wakungŭ in Uganda are supplied with women by the king, according to their merits, from seizures in battle abroad, or seizures from refractory officers at home. The women are not regarded as property according to the Wanyamŭézi practice, though many exchange their daughters; and some women, for misdemeanors, are sold into slavery, while others are flogged, or are degraded to do all the menial services of the house.

The wakungŭ then changed the subject by asking, If I married a black woman, would there be any offspring, and what would be their color? The company now became jovial, when the queen improvéd it by making a significant gesture, and with roars of laughter asking me if I would like to be her son-in-law, for she had some beautiful daughters, either of the Wahŭma or Waganda breed. Rather staggered at first by this awful proposal, I consulted Bombay what I should do with one if I got her. He, looking more to number one than my convenience, said, " By all means accept the offer, for if *you* don't like her, *we* should, and it would be a good means of getting her out of this land of death, for all black people love Zanzibar." The rest need not be told; as a matter of course, I had to appear very much gratified, and as the bowl went round, all became uproarious. I must wait a day or two, however, that a proper selection might be made; and when the marriage came off, I was to chain the fair one two or three days, until she became used to me, else, from mere fright, she might run away.

To keep up the spirits of the queen, though her frequent potions of pombé had well-nigh done enough, I admired her neckring, composed of copper wire, with a running inlaid twist of iron, and asked her why she wore such a wreath of vine-leaves, as I had often seen on some of the wakungŭ. On this she produced a number of rings similar to the one she wore, and taking off her own, placed it round my neck. Then, pointing to her wreath, she said, "This is the badge of a kidnapper's office: whoever wears it catches little children." I inferred that its possession, as an insignia of royalty, conferred on the bearer the power of seizure, as the great seal in this country confers power on public officers.

The queen's dinner was now announced; and, desiring me to remain where I was for a short time, she went to it. She sent me several dishes (plantain-leaves), with well-cooked beef and mutton, and a variety of vegetables, from her table, as well as a number of round moist napkins, made in the shape of wafers, from the freshly-drawn plantain fibres, to wash the hands and face with. There was no doubt now about her culinary accomplishments. I told her so when she returned, and that I enjoyed her parties all the more because they ended with a dinner. "More pombé, more pombé," cried the queen, full of mirth and glee, helping every body round in turn, and shouting and laughing at their Kiganda witticisms—making, though I knew not a word said, an amusing scene to behold—till the sun sank; and her majesty remarking it, turned to her court and said, "If I get up, will Bana also rise, and not accuse me of deserting him?" With this speech a general rising took place, and, watching the queen's retiring, I stood with my hat in hand, while all the wakungŭ fell upon their knees, and then all separated.

28*th.* I went to the palace, and found, as usual, a large levée waiting the king's pleasure to appear, among whom were the kamraviona, Masimbi, and the king's sister Miengo. I fired my gun, and got admitted at once, but none of the others could follow me save Miengo. The king, sitting on the chair with his women by his side, ordered twelve cloths, the presents of former Arab visitors, to be brought before him, and all of these I was desired to turn into European garments, like my own coats, trowsers, and waistcoats. It was no use saying I had no tailors—the thing must be done somehow; for he admired my costume exceedingly, and wished to imitate it now he had cloth enough forever to dispense with the mbŭgŭ.

As I had often begged the king to induce his men, who are all wonderfully clever artisans, to imitate the chair and other things I gave him, I now told him if he would order some of his sempsters, who are far cleverer with the needle than my men, to my camp, I would cut up some old clothes, and so teach them how to work. This was agreed to, and five cows were offered as a reward; but, as his men never came, mine had to do the job.

Maŭla then engaged the king's attention for fully an hour, relating what wonderful things Bana kept in his house, if his majesty would only deign to see them; and, for this humbug, got rewarded by a present of three women. Just at this juncture an adjutant flew overhead, and, by way of fun, I presented my gun, when the excited king, like a boy from school, jumped up, forgetting his company, and cried, " Come, Bana, and shoot the nundo; I know where he has gone: follow me." And away we went, first through one court, then through another, till we found the nundo perched on a tree, looking like a sedate old gentleman with a bald head, and very sharp, long nose. Politeness lost us the bird; for while I wished the king to shoot, he wished me to do so, from fear of missing it himself. He did not care about vultures—he could practice at them at any time; but he wanted a nundo above all things. The bird, however, took the hint and flew away.

CHAPTER XIII.

PALACE, UGANDA—*Continued.*

A Visit to a distinguished Statesman.—A Visit from the King.—Royal Sport.—The Queen's Present of Wives.—The Court Beauties and their Reverses.—Judicial Procedure in Uganda.—Buffalo-hunting.—A Musical Party.—My Medical Practice.—A Royal Excursion on the N'yanza.—The Canoes of Uganda.—A Regatta. —Rifle Practice.—Domestic Difficulties.—Interference of a Magician.—The King's Brothers.

29th. ACCORDING to appointment, I went early this morning to visit Congow. He kept me some time waiting in his outer hut, and then called me in to where I found him sitting with his women—a large group, by no means pretty. His huts are numerous, the gardens and courts all very neat and well kept. He was much delighted with my coming, produced pombé, and asked me what I thought of his women, stripping them to the waist. He assured me that he had thus paid me such a compliment as nobody else had ever obtained, since the Waganda are very jealous of one another—so much so, that any one would be killed if found staring upon a woman even in the highways. I asked him what use he had for so many women. To which he replied, "None whatever; the king gives them to us to keep up our rank, sometimes as many as one hundred together, and we either turn them into wives, or make servants of them, as we please." Just then I heard that Mkŭenda, the queen's woman-keeper, was outside waiting for me, but dared not come in, because Congow's women were all out; so I asked leave to go home to breakfast, much to the surprise of Congow, who thought I was his guest for the whole day. It is considered very indecorous in Uganda to call upon two persons in one day, though even the king or the queen should be one of them. Then, as there was no help for it —Congow could not detain me when hungry—he showed me a little boy, the only child he had, and said, with much fatherly pride, "Both the king and queen have called on me to see this fine little fellow;" and we parted to meet again some other day. Outside his gate I found Mkŭenda, who said the queen had sent

him to invite "her son" to bring her some stomach medicine in
the morning, and come to have a chat with her. With Mkŭenda
I walked home; but he was so awed by the splendor of my hut,
with its few blankets and bit of chintz, that he would not even
sit upon a cowskin, but asked if any Waganda dared venture in
there. He was either too dazzled or too timid to answer any
questions, and in a few minutes walked away again.

After this, I had scarcely swallowed my breakfast before I received a summons from the king to meet him out shooting, with
all the Wangŭana armed, and my guns; and going toward the
palace, found him with a large staff—pages and officers, as well
as women—in a plantain garden, looking eagerly out for birds,
while his band was playing. In addition to his English dress, he
wore a turban, and pretended that the glare of the sun was distressing his eyes; for, in fact, he wanted me to give him a wideawake like my own. Then, as if a sudden freak had seized
him, though I knew it was on account of Maŭla's having excited
his curiosity, he said, "Where does Bana live? lead away."
Bounding and scrambling, the wakungŭ, the women and all, went
pell-mell through every thing toward my hut. If the kamraviona
or any of the boys could not move fast enough, on account of
the crops on the fields, they were piked in the back till half
knocked over; but, instead of minding, they trotted on, n'yanzigging as if honored by a kingly poke, though treated like so many
dogs.

Arrived at the hut, the king took off his turban as I took off
my hat, and seated himself on my stool, while the kamraviona,
with much difficulty, was induced to sit upon a cowskin, and the
women at first were ordered to squat outside. Every thing that
struck the eye was much admired and begged for, though nothing so much as my wideawake and musquito-curtains; then, as
the women were allowed to have a peep in and see Bana in his
den, I gave them two sacks of beads to make the visit profitable,
the only alternative left me from being forced into inhospitality,
for no one would drink from my cup. Moreover, a present was
demanded by the laws of the country.

The king, excitedly impatient, now led the way again, shooting
hurry-scurry through my men's lines, which were much commented on as being different from Waganda hutting, on to the
tall tree with the adjutant's nest. One young bird was still living in it. There was no shot, so bullets must be fired; and the

cunning king, wishing to show off, desired me to fire simultaneously with himself. We fired, but my bullet struck the bough the nest was resting on; we fired again, and the bullet passed through the nest without touching the bird. I then asked the king to allow me to try his Whitworth, to which a little bit of stick, as a charm to secure a correct aim, had been tied below the trigger-guard. This time I broke the bird's leg, and knocked him half out of the nest; so, running up to the king, I pointed to the charm, saying, That has done it—hoping to laugh him out of the folly; but he took my joke in earnest, and he turned to his men, commenting on the potency of the charm. While thus engaged, I took another rifle and brought the bird down altogether. "Woh, woh, woh!" shouted the king; "Bana, mzungŭ, mzungŭ!" he repeated, leaping and clapping his hands, as he ran full speed to the prostrate bird, while the drums beat, and the wakungŭ followed him: "Now, is not this a wonder? but we must go and shoot another." "Where?" I said; "we may walk a long way without finding, if we have nothing but our eyes to see with. Just send for your telescope, and then I will show you how to look for birds." Surprised at this announcement, the king sent his pages flying for the instrument, and when it came I instructed him how to use it; when he could see with it, and understand its powers, his astonishment knew no bounds; and, turning to his wakungŭ, he said, laughing, "Now I do see the use of this thing I have been shutting up in the palace. On that distant tree I can see three vultures. To its right there is a hut, with a woman sitting inside the portal, and many goats are feeding all about the palace, just as large and distinct as if I was close by them."

The day was now far spent, and all proceeded toward the palace. On the way a mistletoe was pointed out as a rain-producing tree, probably because, on a former occasion, I had advised the king to grow groves of coffee-trees about his palace to improve its appearance, and supply the court with wholesome food; at the same time informing him that trees increase the falls of rain in a country, though very high ones would be dangerous, because they attract lightning. Next the guns must be fired off; and, as it would be a pity to waste lead, the king, amid thunders of applause, shot five crows, presenting his gun from the shoulder.

So ended the day's work in the field, but not at home; for I had hardly arrived there before the pages hurried in to beg for powder and shot, then caps, then cloth, and, every thing else failing, a load of beads. Such are the persecutions of this negro land: the host every day must beg something in the most shameless manner from his guest, on the mere chance of gaining something gratis, though I generally gave the king some trifle when he least expected it, and made an excuse that he must wait for the arrival of fresh stores from Gani when he asked.

30th. To fulfill my engagement with the queen, I walked off to her palace with stomach medicine, thinking we were now such warm friends all pride and distant ceremonies would be dispensed with; but, on the contrary, I was kept waiting for hours, till I sent in word to say, if she did not want medicine, I wished to go home, for I was tired of Uganda and every thing belonging to it. This message brought her to her gate, where she stood laughing till the Wahŭma girls she had promised me, one of twelve and the other a little older, were brought in and made to squat in front of us. The elder, who was in the prime of youth and beauty, very large of limb, dark in color, cried considerably; while the younger one, though very fair, had a snubby nose and everted lips, and laughed as if she thought the change in her destiny very good fun. I had now to make my selection, and took the smaller one, promising her to Bombay as soon as we arrived on the coast, where, he said, she would be considered a Hubshi or Abyssinian. But when the queen saw what I had done, she gave me the other as well, saying the little one was too young to go alone, and, if separated, she would take fright and run away. Then with a gracious bow I walked off with my two fine specimens of natural history, though I would rather have had princes, that I might have taken them home to be instructed in England; but the queen, as soon as we had cleared the palace, sent word to say she must have another parting look at her son with his wives. Still laughing, she said, "That will do; you look beautiful; now go away home;" and off we trotted, the elder sobbing bitterly, the younger laughing.

As soon as we reached home, my first inquiry was concerning their histories, of which they appeared to know but very little. The elder, whom I named Méri (plantains), was obtained by Sunna, the late king, as a wife, from Nkolé; and though she was a mere kahala, or girl, when the old king died, he was so attached to her he gave her twenty cows, in order that she might fatten up on milk after her native fashion; but on Sunna's death, when the establishment of women was divided, Méri fell to N'yamasoré's (the queen's) lot.   The lesser one, who still retains the name of Kahala, said she was seized in Unyoro by the Waganda, who took her to N'yamasoré, but what became of her father and mother she could not say.

It was now dinner-time, and as the usual sweet potatoes and goat's flesh were put upon my box-table, I asked them to dine with me, and we became great friends, for they were assured they would finally get good houses and gardens at Zanzibar; but nothing would induce either of them to touch food that had been cooked with butter.   A dish of plantains and goat-flesh was then prepared; but, though Kahala wished to eat it, Méri rejected the goat's flesh, and would not allow Kahala to taste it either; and thus began a series of domestic difficulties.   On inquiring how I could best deal with my difficult charge, I was told the Wahŭma pride was great, and their tempers so strong, they were more difficult to break in than a phŭnda or donkey, though when once tamed they became the best of wives.

31st.   I wished to call upon the queen and thank her for her charming present, but my hungry men drove me to the king's palace in search of food.   The gun-firing brought Mtésa out, prepared for a shooting trip, with his wakungŭ leading, the pages carrying his rifle and ammunition, and a train of women behind. The first thing seen outside the palace gate was a herd of cows, from which four were selected and shot at fifty paces by the king, firing from his shoulder, amid thunders of applause and handshakings of the elders.   I never saw them dare touch the king's hand before.   Then Mtésa, turning kindly to me, said, "Pray take a shot;" but I waived the offer off, saying he could kill better himself.   Ambitious of a cut above cows, the king tried his hand at some herons perched on a tree, and, after five or six attempts, hit one in the eye.   Hardly able to believe in his own skill, he stood petrified at first, and then ran madly to the fallen bird, crying "Woh, woh, woh! can this be? is it true?   Woh, woh!"   He jumped in the air, and all his men and women shouted in concert with him.   Then he rushes at me, takes both my hands —shakes, shakes—woh, woh!—then runs to his women, then to his men; shakes them all, woh-wohing, but yet not shaking or wohing half enough for his satisfaction, for he is mad with joy at his own exploit.

The bird is then sent immediately to his mother, while he retires to his palace, woh-wohing, and talking "ten to the dozen"

all the way, and boasting of his prowess. "Now, Bana, tell me
—do you not think, if two such shots as you and I were opposed
to an elephant, would he have any chance before us? I know I
can shoot—I am certain of it now. You have often asked me to
go hippopotamus shooting with you, but I staved it off until I
learned the way to shoot. Now, however, I can shoot, and that
remarkably well, too, I flatter myself. I will have at them, and
both of us will go on the lake together." The palace was now
reached; musicians were ordered to play before the king, and
wakungŭ appointments were made to celebrate the feats of the
day. Then the royal cutler brought in dinner-knives made of
iron, inlaid with squares of copper and brass, and goats and vegetables were presented as usual, when by torchlight we were dismissed, my men taking with them as many plantains as they
could carry.

1st. I staid at home all this day because the king and queen
had set it apart for looking at and arranging their horns—ma-
pembé, or fetishes, as the learned call such things—to see that
there are no imperfections in the Uganga. This was something
like an inquiry into the ecclesiastical condition of the country,
while, at the same time, it was a religious ceremony, and, as such,
was appropriate to the first day after the new moon appears.
This being the third moon by account, in pursuance of ancient
custom, all the people about court, including the king, shaved
their heads; the king, however, retaining his cockscomb, the
pages their double cockades, and the other officers their single
cockades on the back of the head, or either side, according to the
official rank of each. My men were occupied making trowsers
for the king all day, while the pages, and those sent to learn the
art of tailoring, instead of doing their duty, kept continually begging for something to present to the king.

2d. The queen, now taking a sporting fit into her head, sent
for me early in the morning, with all my men, armed, to shoot a
crested crane in her palace; but, though we were there as required, we were kept waiting till late in the afternoon, when, instead of talking about shooting, as her wakungŭ had forbidden
her doing it, she asked after her two daughters—whether they
had run away, or if they liked their new abode? I replied I was
sorry circumstances did not permit of my coming to thank her
sooner, for I felt grateful beyond measure to her for having
charmed my house with such beautiful society. I did not follow

her advice to chain either of them with iron, for I found cords of love, the only instrument white men know the use of, quite strong enough. Fascinated with this speech, she said she would give me another of a middle age between the two, expecting, as I thought, that she would thus induce me to visit her more frequently than I did her son; but, though I thanked her, it frightened me from visiting her for ages after.

She then said, with glowing pride, casting a sneer on the king's hospitality, " In the days of yore, Sunna, whenever visitors came to see him, immediately presented them with women, and, secondly, with food; for he was very particular in looking after his guests' welfare, which is not exactly what you find the case now, I presume." The rest of the business of the day consisted in applications for medicine and medical treatment, which it was difficult satisfactorily to meet.

3d. To-day Katŭmba, the king's head page, was sent to me with déolés to be made into trowsers and waistcoats, and a large sixty-dollar silk I had given him to cover the chair with. The king likes rich colors, and I was solemnly informed that he will never wear any thing but clothes like Bana.

4th. By invitation, I went to the palace at noon with guns, and found the king holding a levée, the first since the new moon, with all heads shaved in the manner I have mentioned. Soon rising, he showed the way through the palace to a pond, which is described as his bathing N'yanza, his women attending, and pages leading the way with his guns. From this we passed on to a jungle lying between the palace hill and another situated at the northern end of the lake, where wild buffaloes frequently lie concealed in the huge papyrus rushes of a miry drain; but as none could be seen at that moment, we returned again to the palace. He showed me large mounds of earth, in the shape of cocked hats, which are private observatories, from which the surrounding country can be seen. By the side of these observatories are huts, smaller than the ordinary ones used for residing in, where the king, after the exertion of "looking out," takes his repose. Here he ordered fruit to be brought—the matungŭrŭ, a crimson pod filled with acid seeds, which has only been observed growing by the rivers or waters of Uganda, and kasori, a sort of liquorice-root. He then commenced eating with us, and begging again, unsuccessfully, for my compass. I tried again to make him see the absurdity of tying a charm on Whitworth's rifle, but without

the least effect. In fact, he mistook all my answers for admiration, and asked me, in the simplest manner possible, if I would
like to possess a charm; and even when I said "No, I should be
afraid of provoking Lŭbari's" (God's) "anger if I did so," he only
wondered at my obstinacy, so thoroughly was he wedded to his
belief. He then called for his wideawake, and walked with us
into another quarter of his palace, when he entered a dressing-
hut, followed by a number of full-grown, stark-naked women, his
valets; at the same time ordering a large body òf women to sit on
one side of the entrance, while I, with Bombay, were directed to
sit on the other, waiting till he was ready to hold another levée.
From this we repaired to the great throne-hut, where all his
wakungŭ at once formed court, and business was commenced.
Among other things, an officer, by name Mbogo, or the Buffalo,
who had been sent on a wild-goose chase to look after Mr. Petherick, described a journey he had made, following down the
morning sun. After he had passed the limits of plantain-eating
men, he came upon men who lived upon meat alone, who never
wore mbŭgŭs, but either cloth or skins, and instead of the spear
they used the double-edged simé. He called the people Wasewe,
and their chief Kisawa; but the company pronounced them to be
Masawa (Masai).

After this, about eighty men were marched into the court, with
their faces blackened, and strips of plantain-bark tied on their
heads, each holding up a stick in his hand in place of a spear, under the regulation that no person is permitted to carry weapons
of any sort in the palace. They were led by an officer, who,
standing like a captain before his company, ordered them to
jump and praise the king, acting the part of fugleman himself.
Then said the king, turning to me, "Did I not tell you I had sent
many men to fight? These are some of my army returned; the
rest are coming, and will eventually, when all are collected, go in
a body to fight in Usoga." Goats and other peace-offerings were
then presented; and, finally, a large body of officers came in with
an old man, with his two ears shorn off for having been too handsome in his youth, and a young woman who, after four days'
search, had been discovered in his house. They were brought
for judgment before the king.

Nothing was listened to but the plaintiff's statement, who said
he had lost the woman four days, and, after considerable search,
had found her concealed by the old man, who was indeed old

enough to be her grandfather. From all appearances, one would have said the wretched girl had run away from the plaintiff's house in consequence of ill treatment, and had harbored herself on this decrepid old man without asking his leave; but their voices in defense were never heard, for the king instantly sentenced both to death, to prevent the occurrence of such impropriety again ; and, to make the example more severe, decreed that their lives should not be taken at once, but, being fed to preserve life as long as possible, they were to be dismembered bit by bit, as rations for the vultures, every day, until life was extinct. The dismayed criminals, struggling to be heard, in utter despair, were dragged away boisterously in the most barbarous manner, to the drowning music of the milélé and drums.

The king, in total unconcern about the tragedy he had thus enacted, immediately on their departure said, " Now, then, for shooting, Bana; let us look at your gun." It happened to be loaded, but fortunately only with powder, to fire my announcement at the palace; for he instantly placed caps on the nipples, and let off one barrel by accident, the contents of which stuck in the thatch. This created a momentary alarm, for it was supposed the thatch had taken fire; but it was no sooner suppressed than the childish king, still sitting on his throne, to astonish his officers still more, leveled the gun from his shoulder, fired the contents of the second barrel into the faces of his squatting wakungŭ, and then laughed at his own trick. In the mean while cows were driven in, which the king ordered his wakungŭ to shoot with carbines; and as they missed them, he showed them the way to shoot with the Whitworth, never missing. The company now broke up, but I still clung to the king, begging him to allow me to purchase food with beads, as I wanted it, for my establishment was always more or less in a starving state; but he only said, " Let us know what you want, and you shall always have it;" which, in Uganda, I knew from experience only meant, Don't bother me any more, but give me your spare money, and help yourself from my spacious gardens—Uganda is before you.

5th. To-day the king went on a visit to his mother, and therefore neither of them could be seen by visitors. I took a stroll toward the N'yanza, passing through the plantain-groves occupied by the king's women, where my man Sangoro had been twice taken up by the mgemma and put in the stocks. The plantain gardens were beautifully kept by numerous women, who all ran away from fright at seeing me, save one who, taken by surprise, threw herself flat on the ground, rolled herself up in her mbŭgŭ, and, kicking with her naked heels, roared murder and help, until I poked her up, and reproached her for her folly. This little incident made my fairies bolder, and, sidling up to me one by one, they sat in a knot with me upon the ground; then clasping their heads with their hands, they woh-wohed in admiration of the white man; they never in all their lives saw any thing so wonderful; his wife and children must be like him; what would not Sunna have given for such a treat? but it was destined to Mtésa's lot. What is the interpretation of this sign, if it does not point to the favor in which Mtésa is upheld by the spirits? I wished to go, but no: "Stop a little more," they said, all in a breath, or rather out of breath in their excitement; "remove the hat and show the hair; take off the shoes and tuck up the trowsers; what on earth is kept in the pockets? Oh, wonder of wonders! and the iron!" As I put the watch close to the ear of one of them, "Tick, tick, tick—woh, woh, woh"—every body must hear it; and then the works had to be seen. "Oh, fearful!" said one: "hide your faces; it is the Lŭbari. Shut it up, Bana, shut it up; we have seen enough; but you will come again and bring us beads." So ended the day's work.

6th. To-day I sent Bombay to the palace for food. Though rain fell in torrents, he found the king holding a levée, giving appointments, plantations, and women, according to merit, to his officers. As one officer, to whom only one woman was given, asked for more, the king called him an ingrate, and ordered him to be cut to pieces on the spot; and the sentence was, as Bombay told me, carried into effect; not with knives, for they are prohibited, but with slips of sharp-edged grass, after the executioners had first dislocated his neck by a blow delivered behind the head with a sharp, heavy-headed club.

No food, however, was given to my men, though the king, anticipating Bombay's coming, sent me one load of tobacco, one of butter, and one of coffee. My residence in Uganda became much more merry now, for all the women of the camp came daily to call on my two little girls, during which time they smoked my tobacco, chewed my coffee, drank my pombé, and used to amuse me with queer stories of their native land. Rozaro's sister also came, and proposed to marry me, for Maŭla, she said, was a brutal man; he killed one of his women because he did not like her, and now he had clipped one of this poor creature's ears off for trying to run away from him; and when abused for his brutality, he only replied, "It was no fault of his, as the king set the example in the country."

In the evening I took a walk with Kahala, dressed in a red scarf, and in company with Lŭgoi, to show my children off in the gardens to my fair friends of yesterday. Every body was surprised. The mgemma begged us to sit with him and drink pombé, which he generously supplied to our heart's content; wondered at the beauty of Kahala, wished I would give him a wife like her, and lamented that the king would not allow his to wear such pretty clothes. We passed on a little farther, and were invited to sit with another man, Lŭkanikka, to drink pombé and chew coffee, which we did as before, meeting with the same remarks; for all Waganda, instructed by the court, knew the art of flattery better than any people in the world, even including the French.

7*th*. In the morning, while it rained hard, the king sent to say he had started buffalo-shooting, and expected me to join him. After walking a mile beyond the palace, we found him in a plantain garden, dressed in imitation of myself, wideawake and all, the perfect picture of a snob. He sent me a pot of pombé, which I sent home to the women, and walked off for the shooting-ground, two miles farther on, the band playing in the front, followed by some hundred wakungŭ—then the pages, then the king, next myself, and finally the women—the best in front, the worst bringing up the rear, with the king's spears and shield, as also pots of pombé, a luxury the king never moves without. It was easy to see there would be no sport, still more useless to offer any remarks, therefore all did as they were bid. The broad road, like all in Uganda, went straight over hill and dale, the heights covered with high grass or plantain-groves, and the valleys with dense masses of magnificent forest-trees surrounding swamps covered with tall rushes half bridged. Proceeding on, as we came to the first water, I commenced flirtations with Mtésa's women, much to the surprise of the king and every one. The bridge was broken, as a matter of course; and the logs which composed it, lying concealed beneath the water, were toed successively by the leading men, that those who followed should not be tripped up by them. This favor the king did for me, and I, in return, for the women behind; they had never been favored in their lives with such gallantry, and therefore could not refrain from laughing, which attracted the king's notice, and set every body in a giggle; for till now no mortal man had ever dared communicate with his women.

Shortly after this we left the highway, and, turning westward, passed through a dense jungle toward the eastern shores of the Murchison Creek, cut by runnels and rivulets, where on one occasion I offered, by dumb signs, to carry the fair ones pick-a-back over, and after crossing a second myself by a floating log, offered my hand. The leading wife first fears to take it, then grows bold and accepts it; when the prime beauty, Lŭbŭga, following in her wake, and anxious to feel, I fancy, what the white man is like, with an imploring face holds out both her hands in such a captivating manner, that though I feared to draw attention by waiting any longer, I could not resist compliance. The king noticed it; but, instead of upbraiding me, passed it off as a joke, and running up to the kamraviona, gave him a poke in the ribs, and whispered what he had seen, as if it had been a secret. "Woh, woh!" says the kamraviona; "what wonders will happen next?"

We were now on the buffalo ground; but nothing could be seen save some old footprints of buffaloes, and a pitfall made for catching them. By this time the king was tired; and as he saw me searching for a log to sit upon, he made one of his pages kneel upon all fours and sat upon his back, acting the monkey in aping myself; for otherwise he would have sat on a mbŭgŭ, in his customary manner, spread on the ground. We returned, pushing along, up one way, then another, without a word, in thorough confusion, for the king delights in boyish tricks, which he has learned to play successfully. Leaving the road and plunging into thickets of tall grass, the band and wakungŭ must run for their lives, to maintain the order of march, by heading him at some distant point of exit from the jungle; while the kamraviona, leading the pages and my men, must push head first, like a herd of buffaloes, through the sharp-cutting grass, at a sufficient rate to prevent the royal walk from being impeded; and the poor women, ready to sink with exhaustion, can only be kept in their places by fear of losing their lives.

We had been out the whole day; still he did not tire of these tricks, and played them incessantly till near sundown, when we entered the palace. Then the women and wakungŭ separating from us, we—that is, the king, the kamraviona, pages, and myself —sat down to a warm feast of sweet potatoes and plantains, ending with pombé and fruit, while moist circular napkins, made in the shape of magnificent wafers out of plantain fibre, acted at once both the part of water and towel. This over, as the guns had to be emptied, and it was thought sinful to waste the bullets, four cows were ordered in and shot by the king. Thus ended the day, my men receiving one of the cows.

8th. As Mtésa was tired with his yesterday's work, and would not see any body, I took Lŭgoi and Kahala, with a bundle of beads, to give a return to the mgemma for his late treat of pombé. His household men and women were immensely delighted with us, but more so, they said, for the honor of the visit. They gave us more pombé, and introduced us to one of N'yamasoré's numerous sisters, who was equally charmed with myself and my children. The mgemma did not know how he could treat us properly, he said, for he was only a poor man; but he would order some fowls, that I might carry them away. When I refused this offer, because we came to see him, and not to rob him, he thought it the most beautiful language, and said he would bring them to the house himself. I added, I hoped he would do so in company with his wife, which he promised, though he never dared fulfill the promise; and, on our leaving, sent all his servants to escort us beyond the premises. In the evening, as the king's musicians passed the camp, I ordered them in to play the milélé, and give my men and children a treat of dancing. The performers received a bundle of beads and went away happy.

9th. I called on Congow, but found him absent, waiting on the king as usual; and the king sent for my big rifle to shoot birds with.

10th. In consequence of my having explained to the king the effect of the process of distilling, and the way of doing it, he sent a number of earthen pots and bŭgŭs of pombé that I might produce some spirits for him; but as the pots sent were not made after the proper fashion, I called at the palace, and waited all day in the hope of seeing him. No one, however, dared enter his cabinet, where he had been practicing "Uganga" all day, and so the pombé turned sour and useless. Such are the ways of Uganda all over.

11th. The king was out shooting; and as nothing else could be done, I invited Ulédi's pretty wife Gŭrikŭ to eat a mutton breakfast, and teach my child Méri not to be so proud. In this we were successful; but, whether her head had been turned, as Bombay thought, or what else, we know not; but she would neither walk nor talk, nor do any thing but lie at full length all day long, smoking and lounging in thorough indolence.

12th. I distilled some fresh pombé for the king; and taking it to him in the afternoon, fired guns to announce arrival. He was not visible, while fearful shrieks were heard from within, and presently a beautiful woman, one of the king's sisters, with cockscomb erect, was dragged out to execution, bewailing and calling on her king, the kamraviona, and mzungŭ, by turns, to save her life. Would to God I could have done it! but I did not know her crime, if crime she had committed, and therefore had to hold my tongue, while the kamraviona, and other wakungŭ present, looked on with utter unconcern, not daring to make the slightest remark. It happened that Irungŭ was present in the antechamber at this time; and as Maŭla came with my party, they had a fight in respect to their merits for having brought welcome guests to their king. Mtésa, it was argued, had given N'yamgundŭ more women and men than he did to Maŭla, because he was the first to bring intelligence of our coming, as well as that of K'yengo, and Sŭwarora's hongo to his king; while, finally, he superseded Maŭla by taking me out of his charge, and had done a farther good service by sending men on to Karagŭé to fetch both Grant and K'yengo.

Maŭla, although he had received the second reward, had literally done nothing, while Irungŭ had been years absent at Usŭi, and finally had brought a valuable hongo, yet he got less than Maŭla. This, Irungŭ said, was an injustice he would not stand; N'yamgundŭ fairly earned his reward, but Maŭla must have been tricking to get more than himself. He would get a suitable offering of wire, and lay his complaint in court the first opportunity. "Pooh! pooh! nonsense!" says Maŭla, laughing; "I will give him more wires than you, and then let us see who will win the king's ear." Upon this the two great children began collecting wire and quarreling until the sun went down, and I went home. I did not return to a quiet dinner, as I had hoped, but to meet the summons of the king. Thinking it policy to obey, I found him waiting my coming in the palace. He made apologies for not answering my gun, and tasted some spirits, resembling toddy, which I had succeeded in distilling. He imbibed it with great surprise; it was wonderful tipple; he must have some more; and, for the purpose of brewing better, would send the barrel of an old Brown Bess musket, as well as more pombé and wood in the morning.

13*th.* As nothing was done all day, I took the usual promenade in the Seraglio Park, and was accosted by a very pretty little woman, Kariana, wife of Dŭmba, who, very neatly dressed, was returning from a visit. At first she came trotting after me, then timidly paused, then advanced, and, as I approached her, stood spell-bound at my remarkable appearance. At last recovering herself, she woh-wohed with all the coquetry of a Mganda woman, and a flirtation followed; she must see my hair, my watch, the contents of my pockets—every thing; but that was not enough. I waved adieu, but still she followed. I offered my arm, showing her how to take it in European fashion, and we walked along, to the surprise of every body, as if we had been in Hyde Park rather than in Central Africa, flirting and coquetting all the way. I was surprised that no one came to prevent her forwardness; but not till I almost reached home did any one appear, and then, with great scolding, she was ordered to return— not, however, without her begging I would call in and see her on some future occasion, when she would like to give me some, pombé.

14*th.* As conflicting reports came about Grant, the king very courteously, at my request, forwarded letters to him. I passed the day in distilling pombé, and the evening in calling on Mrs. Dŭmba, with Méri, Kahala, Lŭgoi, and a troop of Wanyamŭézi women. She was very agreeable; but, as her husband was attending at the palace, could not give pombé, and instead gave my female escort sundry baskets of plantains and potatoes, signifying a dinner, and walked half way home, flirting with me as before.

15*th.* I called on the king with all the spirits I had made, as well as the saccharine residue. We found him holding a levée, and receiving his offerings of a batch of girls, cows, goats, and other things of an ordinary nature. One of the goats presented gave me an opportunity of hearing one of the strangest stories I had yet heard in this strange country: it was a fine for attempted regicide, which happened yesterday, when a boy, finding the king alone, which is very unusual, walked up to him and threatened to kill him, because, he said, he took the lives of men unjustly. The king explained by description and pantomime how the affair passed. When the youth attacked him he had in his hand the revolving pistol I had given him, and showed us, holding the weapon to his cheek, how he had presented the muzzle to the boy, which, though it was unloaded, so frightened him that he ran away. All the courtiers n'yanzigged vigorously for the condescension of the king in telling us this story. There must have been some special reason why, in a court where trifling breaches of etiquette were punished with a cruel death, so grave a crime should have been so leniently dealt with; but I could not get at the bottom of the affair. The culprit, a good-looking young fellow of sixteen or seventeen, who brought in the goat, made his n'yanzigs, stroked the goat and his own face with his hands, n'yanzigged again with prostrations, and retired.

After this scene, officers announced the startling fact that two white men had been seen at Kamrasi's, one with a beard like myself, the other smooth-faced. I jumped at this news, and said, "Of course they are there; do let me send a letter to them." I believed it to be Petherick and a companion whom I knew he was to bring with him. The king, however, damped my ardor by saying the information was not perfect, and we must wait until certain wakungŭ, whom he sent to search in Unyoro, returned.

16*th*. The regions about the palace were all in a state of commotion to-day, men and women running for their lives in all directions, followed by wakungŭ and their retainers. The cause of all this commotion was a royal order to seize sundry refractory wakungŭ, with their property, wives, concubines—if such a distinction can be made in this country—and families all together. At the palace Mtésa had a musical party, playing the flute occasionally himself. After this he called me aside, and said, "Now, Bana, I wish you would instruct me, as you have so often proposed doing, for I wish to learn every thing, though I have little opportunity for doing so." Not knowing what was uppermost in his mind, I begged him to put whatever questions he liked, and he should be answered *seriatim*, hoping to find him inquisitive on foreign matters; but nothing was more foreign to his mind: none of his countrymen ever seemed to think beyond the sphere of Uganda.

The whole conversation turned on medicines, or the cause and effects of diseases. Cholera, for instance, very much affected the land at certain seasons, creating much mortality, and vanishing again as mysteriously as it came. What brought this scourge? and what would cure it? Supposing a man had a headache, what should he take for it? or a leg-ache, or a stomach-ache, or itch—in fact, going the rounds of every disease he knew, until, exhausting the ordinary complaints, he went into particulars in which he was personally much interested; but I was unfortunately unable to prescribe medicines which produce the physical phenomenon next to his heart.

17*th*. I called upon the king by appointment, and found a large court, where the wakungŭ caught yesterday, and sentenced to execution, received their reprieve on paying fines of cattle and young damsels—their daughters. A variety of charms, among which were some bits of stick strung on leather and covered with serpent-skin, were presented and approved of. Kaggao, a large district officer, considered the second in rank here, received permission for me to call on him with my medicines. I pressed the king again to send men with mine to Kamrasi's, to call Petherick. At first he objected that they would be killed, but finally he yielded, and appointed Budja, his Unyoro embassador, for the service. Then, breaking up the court, he retired with a select party of wakungŭ, headed by the kamraviona, and opened a conversation on the subject which is ever uppermost with the king and his courtiers.

18*th*. To-day I visited Kaggao with my medicine-chest. He had a local disease, which he said came to him by magic, though a different cause was sufficiently obvious, and wanted medicine such as I gave Mkŭenda, who reported that I gave him a most wonderful draught. Unfortunately, I had nothing suitable to give my new patient, but cautioned him to have a care lest contagion should run throughout his immense establishment, and explained the whole of the circumstances to him. Still he was not satisfied; he would give me slaves, cows, or ivory, if I would only cure him. He was a very great man, as I could see, with numerous houses, numerous wives, and plenty of every thing, so that it was ill-becoming of him to be without his usual habits. Rejecting his munificent offers, I gave him a cooling dose of calomel and jalap, which he drank like pombé, and pronounced beautiful—holding up his hands, and repeating the words "Beautiful, beautiful! they are all beautiful together! There is Bana beautiful! his box is beautiful! and his medicine beautiful!" and, saying this, led us in to see his women, who at my request were grouped in war apparel, viz., a dirk fastened to the waist by many strings of colored beads. There were from fifty to sixty women present, all very ladylike, but none of them pretty. Kaggao then informed me the king had told all his wakungŭ he would keep me as his guest four months longer to see if Petherick came; and should he not by that time, he would give me an estate, stocked with men, women, and cattle, in perpetuity, so that, if I ever wished to leave Uganda, I should always have something to come back to; so I might now know what my fate was to be. Before leaving, Kaggao presented us with two cows and ten baskets of potatoes.

19th. I sent a return present of two wires and twelve fundo of beads of sorts to Kaggao, and heard that the king had gone to show himself off to his mother dressed Bana fashion. In the evening Katŭnzi, N'yamasoré's brother, just returned from the Unyoro plunder, called on me while I was at dinner. Not knowing who he was, and surprised at such audacity in Uganda, for he was the first officer who ever ventured to come near me in this manner, I offered him a knife and fork, and a share in the repast, which rather abashed him; for, taking it as a rebuff, he apologized immediately for the liberty he had taken, contrary to the etiquette of Uganda society, in coming to a house when the master was at dinner; and he would have left again had I not pressed him to remain. Katŭnzi then told me the whole army had returned from Unyoro, with immense numbers of cows, women, and children, but not men, for those who did not run away were killed fighting. He offered me a present of a woman, and pressed me to call on him.

20th. Still I found that the king would not send his wakungŭ for the Unyoro expedition, so I called on him about it. Fortunately, he asked me to speak a sentence in English, that he might hear how it sounds, and this gave me an opportunity of saying, if he had kept his promise by sending Budja to me, I should have dispatched letters to Petherick. This was no sooner interpreted than he said, if I would send my men to him with letters in the morning, he would forward them on, accompanied with an army. On my asking if the army was intended to fight, he replied in short, "First to feel the way." On hearing this, I strongly advised him, if he wished the road to be kept permanently open, to try conciliation with Kamrasi, and send him some trifling present.

Now were brought in some thirty-odd women for punishment and execution, when the king, who of late had been trying to learn Kisŭahili, in order that we might be able to converse together, asked me, in that language, if I would like to have some of these women; and if so, how many. On my replying "One,"

he begged me to take my choice, and a very pretty one was selected. God only knows what became of the rest; but the one I
selected, on reaching home, I gave to Ilmas, my valet, for a wife.
He and all the other household servants were much delighted
with this charming acquisition; but the poor girl, from the time
she had been selected, had flattered herself she was to be Bana's
wife, and became immensely indignant at the supposed transfer,
though from the first I had intended her for Ilmas, not only to
favor him for his past good services, but as an example to my
other men, as I had promised to give them all, provided they behaved well upon the journey, a "free-man's garden," with one
wife each and a purse of money, to begin a new life upon, as soon
as they reached Zanzibar. The temper of Méri and Kahala was
shown in a very forcible manner: they wanted this maid as an
addition to my family; called her into the hut and chatted till
midnight, instructing her not to wed with Ilmas; and then, in-

* View of the

stead of turning into bed as usual, they all three slept upon the
ground. My patience could stand this phase of henpecking no
longer, so I called in Manamaka, the head Myamŭézi woman,
whom I had selected for their governess, and directed her to assist Ilmas, and put them to bed "bundling."

21st. In the morning, before I had time to write letters, the
king invited me to join him at some new tank he was making between his palace and the residence of his brothers. I found him

* There being no native name for this beautiful piece of water, I christened it after Sir Roderick Murchison, the distinguished President of the Geographical Society,
to whom the expedition owed so much.

sitting with his brothers, all playing in concert on flutes. I asked him, in Kisŭahili, if he knew where Grant was. On replying in the negative, I proposed sending a letter, which he approved of; and Budja was again ordered to go with an army for Petherick.

22d. Mabrŭki and Bilal, with Budja, started to meet Petherick, and three more men, with another letter to Grant. I called on the king, who appointed the 24th instant for an excursion of three days' hippopotamus shooting on the N'yanza.

23d. To-day occurred a brilliant instance of the capricious restlessness and self-willedness of this despotic king. At noon, pages hurried in to say that he had started for the N'yanza, and wished me to follow him without delay. N'yanza, as I have mentioned, merely means a piece of water, whether a pond, river, or lake; and as no one knew which n'yanza he meant, or what project was on foot, I started off in a hurry, leaving every thing behind, and walked rapidly through gardens, over hills, and across rushy

Murchison Creek.

swamps, down the west flank of the Murchison Creek, till 3 P.M., when I found the king dressed in red, with his wakungŭ in front and women behind, traveling along in the confused manner of a pack of hounds, occasionally firing his rifle that I might know his whereabouts. He had just, it seems, mingled a little business with pleasure; for noticing, as he passed, a woman tied by the hands to be punished for some offense, the nature of which I did not learn, he took the executioner's duty on himself, fired at her, and killed her outright.

On this occasion, to test all his followers, and prove their readiness to serve him, he had started on a sudden freak for the three days' excursion on the lake one day before the appointed time, expecting every body to fall into place by magic, without the smallest regard to each one's property, feelings, or comfort. The home must be forsaken without a last adieu, the dinner untasted, and no provision made for the coming night, in order that his impetuous majesty should not suffer one moment's disappointment. The result was natural: many who would have come were nowhere to be found; my guns, bed, bedding, and note-books, as well as cooking utensils, were all left behind, and, though sent for, did not arrive till the following day.

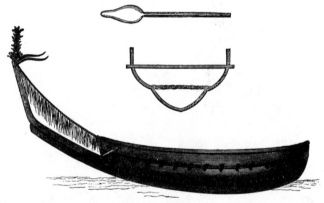

Uganda Boat.

On arrival at the mooring station no one boat was to be found, nor did any arrive until after dark, when, on the beating of drums and firing of guns, some fifty large ones appeared. They were all painted with red clay, and averaged from ten to thirty paddles, with long prows standing out like the neck of a siphon or swan, decorated on the head with the horns of the nsunnŭ (lencotis) antelope, between which was stuck upright a tuft of feathers exactly like a grenadier's plume. These arrived to convey us across the mouth of a deep rushy swamp to the royal yachting establishment, the Cowes of Uganda, distant five hours' traveling from the palace. We reached the Cowes by torchlight at 9 P.M., when the king had a picnic dinner with me, turned in with his women in great comfort, and sent me off to a dreary hut, where I had to sleep upon a grass-strewn floor. I was surprised we had to walk so far, when, by appearance, we might have boated it from the head of the creek all the way down; but, on inquiry, was informed the swampy nature of the ground at the head of the creek precluded any approach to the clear water there, and hence the long overland journey, which, though fatiguing to the unfortunate women, who had to trot the whole way behind Mtésa's four-mile-an-hour strides, was very amusing. The whole of the scenery—hill, dale, and lake—was extremely beautiful. The Wangŭana in my escort compared the view to their own beautiful poani (coast); but in my opinion it far surpassed any thing I ever saw, either from the sea or upon the coast of Zanzibar.

The king rose betimes in the morning and called me, unwashed and very uncomfortable, to picnic with him during the collection of the boats. The breakfast, eaten in the open court, consisted of sundry baskets of roast beef and plantain-squash folded in plantain-leaves. He sometimes ate with a copper knife and picker, not forked; but more usually like a dog, with both hands. The bits too tough for his mastication he would take from his mouth and give as a treat to the pages, who n'yanzigged, and swallowed them with much seeming relish. Whatever remained over was then divided by the boys, and the baskets taken to the cooks. Pombé served as tea, coffee, and beer for the king, but his guests might think themselves very lucky if they ever got a drop of it.

Cowes, 24th.

Now for the lake. Every body in a hurry falls into his place the best way he can — wakungŭ leading, and women behind. They rattle along, through plantains and shrubs, under large trees, seven, eight, and nine feet in diameter, till the beautiful waters are reached—a picture of the Rio scenery, barring that of the higher mountains in the background of that lovely place, which are here represented by the most beautiful little hills. A band of fifteen drums of all sizes, called the mazagŭzo, playing with the regularity of a lot of factory engines at work, announced the king's arrival, and brought all the boats to the shore, but not as in England, where Jack, with all the consequence of a lord at home, invites the ladies to be seated, and enjoys the sight of so many pretty faces. Here every poor fellow, with his apprehensions written in his face, leaps over the gunwale into the water, ducking his head from fear of being accused of gazing on the fair sex, which is ·death, and bides patiently his time. They were dressed in plantain-leaves, looking like grotesque Neptunes. The king, in

his red coat and wideawake, conducted the arrangements, ordering all to their proper places—the women in certain boats, the
wakungŭ and Wangŭana in others, while I sat in the same boat
with him at his feet, three women holding mbŭgŭs of pombé behind. The king's Kisŭahili now camé into play, and he was
prompt in carrying out the directions he got from myself to approach the hippopotami. But the waters were too large and the
animals too shy, so we toiled all the day without any effect, going
only once ashore to picnic; not for the women to eat—for they,
poor things, got nothing—but the king, myself, the pages, and the
principal wakungŭ. As a wind-up to the day's amusement, the
king led the band of drums, changed the men according to their
powers, put them into concert pitch, and readily detected every
slight irregularity, showing himself a thorough musician.

This day requires no remark, every thing done being the counterpart of yesterday, excepting that the king, growing bolder with me in consequence of our talking together, became more playful and familiar—amusing himself, for
instance, sometimes by catching hold of my beard as the rolling
of the boat unsteadied him.

Cowes, 25th.

We started early in the usual manner; but, after working up
and down the creek, inspecting the inlets for hippopotami, and tiring from want of sport, the king
changed his tactics, and, paddling and steering himself with a pair
of new white paddles, finally directed the boats to an island occupied by the mgussa, or Neptune of the N'yanza, not in person—
for mgussa is a spirit—but by his familiar or deputy, the great
medium who communicates the secrets of the deep to the King of
Uganda. In another sense, he might be said to be the presiding
priest of the source of the mighty Nile, and as such was, of course,
an interesting person for me to meet. The first operation on
shore was picnicking, when many large mbŭgŭs of pombé were
brought for the king; next, the whole party took a walk, winding through the trees, and picking fruit, enjoying themselves
amazingly, till, by some unlucky chance, one of the royal wives,
a most charming creature, and truly one of the best of the lot,
plucked a fruit and offered it to the king, thinking, doubtless, to
please him greatly; but he, like a madman, flew into a towering
passion, said it was the first time a woman ever had the impudence to offer him any thing, and ordered the pages to seize, bind,
and lead her off to execution.

Cowes, 26th.

These words were no sooner uttered by the king than the whole bevy of pages slipped their cord turbans from their heads, and rushed like a pack of cupid beagles upon the fairy queen, who, indignant at the little urchins daring to touch her majesty, remonstrated with the king, and tried to beat them off like flies, but was soon captured, overcome, and dragged away, crying, in the names of the kamraviona and mzungŭ (myself), for help and protection; while Lŭbŭga, the pet sister, and all the other women, clasped the king by his legs, and, kneeling, implored forgiveness for their sister. The more they craved for mercy the more brutal he became, till at last he took a heavy stick and began to belabor the poor victim on the head.

Hitherto I had been extremely careful not to interfere with any of the king's acts of arbitrary cruelty, knowing that such interference, at an early stage, would produce more harm than good. This last act of barbarism, however, was too much for my English blood to stand; and, as I heard my name, mzungŭ, imploringly pronounced, I rushed at the king, and, staying his uplifted arm, demanded from him the woman's life. Of course I ran imminent risk of losing my own in thus thwarting the capricious tyrant; but his caprice proved the friend of both. The novelty of interference even made him smile, and the woman was instantly released.

Proceeding on through the trees of this beautiful island, we next turned into the hut of the mgussa's familiar, which at the farther end was decorated with many mystic symbols—among others a paddle, the badge of his high office—and for some time we sat chatting, when pombé was brought, and the spiritual medium arrived. He was dressed wichwézi fashion, with a little white goatskin apron, adorned with numerous charms, and used a paddle for a mace or walking-stick. He was not an old man, though he affected to be so, walking very slowly and deliberately, coughing asthmatically, glimmering with his eyes, and mumbling like a witch. With much affected difficulty he sat at the end of the hut beside the symbols alluded to, and continued his coughing full half an hour, when his wife came in in the same manner, without saying a word, and assumed the same affected style. The king jokingly looked at me and laughed, and then at these strange creatures by turn, as much as to say, What do you think of them? but no voice was heard save that of the old wife, who croaked like a frog for water, and, when some was brought, croak-

ed again because it was not the purest of the lake's produce—had
the first cup changed, wetted her lips with the second, and hob-
bled away in the same manner as she came.

At this juncture the mgussa's familiar motioned the kamraviona
and several officers to draw around him, when, in a very low
tone, he gave them all the orders of the deep, and walked away.
His revelations seemed unpropitious, for we immediately repaired
to our boats and returned to our quarters.   Here we no sooner
arrived than a host of wakungŭ, lately returned from the Unyoro
war, came to pay their respects to the king: they had returned
six days or more, but etiquette had forbidden their approaching
majesty sooner.   Their successes had been great, their losses *nil*,
for not one man had lost his life fighting.   To these men the king
narrated all the adventures of the day, dwelling more particularly
on my defending his wife's life, whom he had destined for execution.   This was highly approved of by all; and they unanimous-
ly said Bana knew what he was about, because he dispenses justice like a king in his own country.

Early in the morning a great hue and cry was made because
the Wangŭana had been seen bathing in the N'yanza
naked, without the slightest regard to decency.   We
went boating as usual all day long, sometimes after hippopotami,
at others racing up and down the lake, the king and wakungŭ
paddling and steering by turns, the only break to this fatigue being when we went ashore to picnic, or the king took a turn at the
drums.   During the evening some of the principal wakungŭ were
collected to listen to an intellectual discourse on the peculiarities
of the different women in the royal establishment, and the king
in good-humor described the benefits he had derived from this
pleasant tour on the water.

Cowes, 27th.

While I was preparing my Massey's log to show the use of it
to the king, he went off boating without me; and as
the few remaining boats would not take me off be-
cause they had received no orders to do so, I fired guns, but, getting no reply, went into the country hoping to find game; but,
disappointed in that also, I spent the first half of the day with a
hospitable old lady, who treated us to the last drop of pombé in
her house—for the king's servants had robbed her of nearly every
thing—smoked her pipe with me, and chatted incessantly on the
honor paid her by the white king's visit, as well as of the horrors
of Uganda punishment, when my servants told her I saved the

Cowes, 28th.

life of one queen. Returning homeward, the afternoon was spent at a hospitable officer's, who would not allow us to depart until my men were all fuddled with pombé, and the evening setting in warned us to wend our way. On arrival at camp, the king, quite shocked with himself for having deserted me, asked me if I did not hear his guns fire. He had sent twenty officers to scour the country, looking for me every where. He had been on the lake the whole day himself, and was now amusing his officers with a little archery practice, even using the bow himself, and making them shoot by turns. A lucky shot brought forth immense applause, all jumping and n'yanzigging with delight, whether it was done by their own bows or the king's.

A shield was the mark, stuck up at only thirty paces; still they were such bad shots that they hardly ever hit it. Now tired of this slow sport, and to show his superior prowess, the king ordered sixteen shields to be placed before him, one in front of the other, and with one shot from Whitworth pierced the whole of them, the bullet passing through the bosses of nearly every one. "Ah!" says the king, strutting about with gigantic strides, and brandishing the rifle over his head before all his men, "what is the use of spears and bows? I shall never fight with any thing but guns in future." These wakungŭ, having only just then returned from plundering Unyoro, had never before seen their king in a chair, or any body sitting, as I was, by his side; and it being foreign to their notions, as well as, perhaps, unpleasant to their feelings, to find a stranger sitting higher than themselves, they complained against this outrage to custom, and induced the king to order my dethronement. The result was, as my iron stool was objectionable, I stood for a moment to see that I thoroughly understood their meaning; and then, showing them my back, walked straightway home to make a grass throne, and dodge them that way.

There was nothing for dinner last night, nothing again this morning, yet no one would go in to report this fact, as rain was falling, and the king was shut up with his women. Presently the thought struck me that the rifle, which was always infallible in gaining me a speedy admittance at the palace, might be of the same service now. I therefore shot a dove close to the royal abode, and, as I expected, roused the king at once, who sent out his pages to know what the firing was about. When told the truth—that I had been trying to shoot a dish of

Cowes, 29th.

doves for breakfast, as I could get neither meat nor drink from his kitchen—the head boy, rather guessing than understanding what was told him, distorted my message, and said to the king, as I could not obtain a regular supply of food from his house, I did not wish to accept any thing farther at his hands, but intended foraging for the future in the jungles. The king, as might be imagined, did not believe the boy's story, and sent other pages to ascertain the truth of the case, bidding them listen well, and beware of what they were about. This second lot of boys conveyed the story rightly, when the king sent me a cow. As I afterward heard, he cut off the ears of the unfortunate little mischief-maker for not making a proper use of those organs; and then, as the lad was the son of one of his own officers, he was sent home to have the sores healed. After breakfast the king called me to go boating, when I used my grass throne, to the annoyance of the attendants. This induced the king to say before them, laughing, "Bana, you see, is not to be done; he is accustomed to sit before kings, and sit he will." Then, by way of change, he ordered all the drums to embark and play upon the waters, while he and his attendants paddled and steered by turns, first up the creek, and then down nearly to the broad waters of the lake.

There was a passage this way, it was said, leading up to Usoga, but very circuitous, on account of reefs or shoals, and on the way the Kitiri island was passed; but no other Kitiri was known to the Waganda, though boats sometimes ·went coasting down the western side of the lake to Ukéréwé. The largest island on the lake is the Sésé,* off the mouth of the Katonga River, where another of the high priests of the Neptune of the N'yanza resides. The king's largest vessels are kept there, and it is famous for its supply of mbŭgŭ barks. We next went on shore to picnic, when a young hippopotamus, speared by harpoon, one pig, and a pongo or bush-boc, were presented to the king. I now advised boat-racing, which 'was duly ordered, and afforded much amusement, as the whole fifty boats formed in line, and paddled furiously to the beat of drum to the goal which I indicated.

The day was done. In great glee the king, ever much attached to the blackguard Maŭla, in consequence of his amusing stories, appointed him to the office of seizer, or chief kidnapper of wa-kungŭ; observing that, after the return of so many officers from war, much business in that line would naturally have to be done,

* Some say a group of forty islands compose Sésé.

and there was none so trustworthy now at court to carry out the king's orders. All now went to the camp; but what was my astonishment, on reaching the hut, to find every servant gone, along with the pots, pans, meat, every thing, and all in consequence of the king's having taken the drums on board, which, being unusual, was regarded as one of his delusive tricks, and a sign of immediate departure. He had told no one he was going to the N'yanza, and now it was thought he would return in the same way. I fired for my supper, but fired in vain. Boys came out, by the king's order, to inquire what I wanted, but left again without doing any thing farther.

At my request the king sent off boats to inquire after the one that left, or was supposed to have left, for Grant on Cowes, 30th. the 3d of March, and he then ordered the return home, much to my delight; for, beautiful as the N'yanza was, the want of consideration for other people's comfort, the tiring, incessant boating, all day long and every day, in the sun, as well as the king's hurry-scurry about every thing he undertook to do, without the smallest forethought, preparation, or warning, made me dream of my children, and look forward with pleasure to rejoining them. Strange as it may appear to Englishmen, I had a sort of paternal love for those little blackamoors as if they had been my offspring; and I enjoyed the simple stories that their sable visitors told me every day they came over to smoke their pipes, which they did with the utmost familiarity, helping themselves from my stores just as they liked.

Without any breakfast, we returned by the same route by which we had come, at four miles an hour, till half the way was cleared, when the king said, laughing, "Bana, are you hungry?" —a ridiculous question after twenty-four hours' starvation, which he knew full well—and led the way into a plantain-grove, where the first hut that was found was turned inside out for the king's accommodation, and picnic was prepared. As, however, he ordered my portion to be given outside with the pages', and allowed neither pombé nor water, I gave him the slip, and walked hurriedly home, where I found Kahala smirking, and apparently glad to see us, but Méri shamming ill in bed, while Manamaka, the governess, was full of smiles and conversation. She declared Méri had neither tasted food nor slept since my departure, but had been retching all the time. Dreadfully concerned at the doleful story, I immediately thought of giving relief with medicines, but neither pulse, tongue, nor any thing else indicated the slightest disorder; and, to add to these troubles, Ilmas's woman had tried during my absence to hang herself, because she would not serve as servant, but wished to be my wife; and Bombay's wife, after taking a dose of quinine, was delivered of a stillborn child.

1st. I visited the king, at his request, with the medicine-chest. He had caught a cold. He showed me several of his women grievously affected with boils, and expected me to cure them at once. I then went home, and found twenty men who had passed Grant, coming on a stretcher from Karaguĕ, without any of the

Captain Grant leaving Karague.

rear property. Méri, still persistent, rejected strengthening medicines, but said, in a confidential manner, if I would give her a goat to sacrifice to the Uganga she would recover in no time. There was something in her manner when she said this that I did not like—it looked suspicious; and I contented myself by saying, "No, I am a wiser doctor than any in these lands; if any body could cure you, that person is myself; and, farther, if I gave you a goat to sacrifice, God would be angry with both of us for our superstitious credulity; you must, therefore, say no more about it."

2*d*. The whole country around the palace was in a state of commotion to-day, from Maŭla and his children hunting down those officers who had returned from the war, yet had not paid their respects to the king at the N'yanza, because they thought they would not be justified in calling on him so quickly after their arrival. Maŭla's house, in consequence of this, was full of beef and pombé; while in his court-yard, men, women, and children, with feet in stocks, very like the old parish stocks in England, waited his pleasure, to see what demands he would make upon them as the price of their release. After anxiously watching, I found out that Méri was angry with me for not allowing Ilmas's woman to live in my house; and, to conquer my resolution against it—although I ordered it with a view to please Ilmas, for he was desperately in love with her—she made herself sick by putting her finger down her throat. I scolded her for her obstinacy. She said she was ill—it was not feigned; and if I would give her a goat to sacrifice she would be well at once; for she had looked into the magic horn already, and discovered that if I gave her a goat for that purpose it would prove that I loved her, and her health would be restored to her at once. Halloo! here was a transformation from the paternal position into that of a henpecked husband! Somebody, I smelt at once, had been tampering with my household while I was away. I commenced investigations, and after a while found out that Rozaro's sister had brought a magician belonging to her family into the hut during my absence, who had put Méri up to this trick of extorting a goat from me, in order that he might benefit by it himself, for the magician eats the sacrifice and keeps the skin.

I immediately ordered him to be seized and bound to the flag-staff, while Maŭla, Ulédi, Rozaro, and Bombay were summoned to witness the process of investigation. Rozaro flew into a passion, and tried to release the magician as soon as he saw him, affecting intense indignation that I should take the law into my own hands when one of Rŭmanika's subjects was accused, but only lost his dignity still more on being told he had acknowledged his inability to control his men so often when they had misbehaved, that I scorned to ask his assistance any longer. He took huff at this, and, as he could not help himself, walked away, leaving us to do as we liked. The charge was fully proved. The impudent magician, without leave, and contrary to all the usages of the country, had entered and set my house against itself during my absence, and had schemed to rob me of a goat. I therefore sentenced him to fifty lashes—twenty-five for the injury he had inflicted on me by working up a rebellion in my house, and the remaining twenty-five for attempting larceny—saying, as he had wanted my goat and its skin, so now, in return, I wanted his skin. These words were no sooner pronounced than the wretched Méri cried out against it, saying all the fault was hers: "Let the stick skin my back, but spare my doctor; it would kill me to see him touched."

This appeal let me see that there was something in the whole matter too deep and intricate to be remedied by my skill. I therefore dismissed her on the spot, and gave her, as a sister and free woman, to Ulédi and his pretty Mhŭma wife, giving Bombay orders to carry the sentences into execution. After walking about till after dark, on returning to the empty house I had some misgivings as to the apparent cruelty of abandoning one so helpless to the uncertainties of this wicked world. Ilmas's woman also ran away, doubtless at the instigation of Rozaro's sister, for she had been denied any farther access to the house, as being at the bottom of all this mischief.

3d. I was haunted all night by my fancied cruelty, and in the morning sent its victim, after Uganda fashion, some symbolical presents, including a goat, in token of esteem; a black blanket, as a sign of mourning; a bundle of gundŭ anklets; and a packet of tobacco, in proof of my forgiveness.

CHAPTER XIV.

PALACE, UGANDA—*Continued.*

Reception of a victorious Army at Court.—Royal Sport.—A Review of the Troops.
—Negotiations for the Opening of the Road along the Nile.—Grant's Return.—
Pillagings.—Court Marriages.—The King's Brothers.—Divinations and Sacri-
fices.—The Road granted at last.—The Preparations for continuing the Expedition.—The Departure.

I NOW received a letter from Grant to say he was coming by
boat from Kitangulé, and at once went to the palace to give the
welcome news to the king. The road to the palace I found
thronged with people; and in the square outside the entrance
there squatted a multitude of attendants, headed by the king, sitting on a cloth, dressed in his national costume, with two spears
and a shield by his side. On his right hand the pages sat waiting for orders, while on his left there was a small squatting cluster of women, headed by wichwézis, or attendant sorceresses, offering pombé. In front of the king, in form of a hollow square,
many ranks deep, sat the victorious officers, lately returned from
the war, variously dressed; the nobles distinguished by their
leopard-cat skins and dirks, the commoners by colored mbŭgŭ
and cow or antelope skin cloaks, but all their faces and arms were
painted red, black, or smoke-color. Within the square of men
immediately fronting the king, the war-arms of Uganda were arranged in three ranks; the great war-drum, covered with a leop-
ard-skin, and standing on a large carpeting of them, was placed in
advance; behind this, propped or hung on a rack of iron, were a
variety of the implements of war in common use, offensive and
defensive, as spears—of which two were of copper, the rest iron—
and shields of wood and leather; while in the last row or lot
were arranged systematically, with great taste and powerful effect,
the supernatural arms, the god of Uganda, consisting of charms
of various descriptions and in great numbers. Outside the square
again, in a line with the king, were the household arms, a very
handsome copper kettle-drum, of French manufacture, surmounted on the outer edge with pretty little brass bells depending from

swan-neck-shaped copper wire, two new spears, a painted leather shield, and magic wands of various devices, deposited on a carpet of leopard-skins—the whole scene giving the effect of true barbarous royalty in its uttermost magnificence.

Approaching, as usual, to take my seat beside the king, some slight sensation was perceptible, and I was directed to sit beyond the women. The whole ceremonies of this grand assemblage were now obvious. Each regimental commandant in turn narrated the whole services of his party, distinguishing those subs who executed his orders well and successfully from those who either deserted before the enemy or feared to follow up their success. The king listened attentively, making, let us suppose, very shrewd remarks concerning them; when to the worthy he awarded pombé, helped with gourd-cups from large earthen jars, which was n'yanzigged for vehemently; and to the unworthy, execution. When the fatal sentence was pronounced, a terrible bustle ensued, the convict wrestling and defying, while the other men seized, pulled, and tore the struggling wretch from the crowd, bound him hands and head together, and led or rather tumbled him away.

After a while, and when all business was over, the king begged me to follow him into the palace. He asked again for stimulants —a matter ever uppermost in his mind—and would not be convinced that such things can do him no possible good, but would in the end be deleterious. Grant's letter was then read to him before his women, and I asked for the dismissal of all the Wanyambo, for they had not only destroyed my peace and home, but were always getting me into disrepute by plundering the Waganda in the highways. No answer was given to this; and on walking home, I found one of the king's women at my hut, imploring protection against the Wanyambo, who had robbed and bruised her so often, she could not stand such abuse any longer.

4th. I sent Maŭla early in the morning, with the plundered woman, and desired him to request that the Wanyambo might be dismissed. He returned, saying he delivered my message, but no reply was given. I then searched for the king, and found him at his brothers' suite of huts playing the flute before them. On taking my seat, he proudly pointed to two vultures which he had shot with bullet, saying to his brothers, " There, do you see these birds? Bana shoots with shot, but I kill with bullets." To try him, I then asked for leave to go to Usoga, as Grant was so far off; but he said, "No, wait until he comes, and you shall both go together then; you fancy he is far off, but I know better. One of my men saw him coming along carried on a stretcher." I said, "No, that must be a mistake, for he told me by letter he would come by water."

Heavy rain now set in, and we got under cover; but the brothers never moved, some even sitting in the streaming gutter, and n'yanzigging whenever noticed. The eldest brother offered me his cup of pombé, thinking I would not drink it; but when he saw its contents vanishing fast, he cried "lekérow!" (hold fast!) and as I pretended not to understand him, continuing to drink, he rudely snatched the cup from my lips. Alternate concerts with the brothers, and conversation about hunting, in consequence of a bump caused by a fall when steeple-chasing, which was discovered on my forehead, ended this day's entertainment.

5th. As all the Wangŭana went foraging, I was compelled to stop at home. The king, however, sent an officer for Grant, because I would not believe in his statement yesterday that he was coming by land; and I also sent a lot of men with a litter to help him on, and bring me an answer.

6th. I went to the palace at the king's command. He kept us waiting an hour, and then passing out by a side gate, beckoned us to follow. He was dressed in European clothes, with his guns and tin box of clothes leading the way. His first question was, "Well, Bana, where are your guns? for I have called you to go shooting." "The pages never said any thing about shooting, and therefore the guns were left behind." Totally unconcerned, the king walked on to his brothers', headed by a band and attendants, who were much lauded for being ready at a moment's notice. A grand flute concert was then played, one of the younger brothers keeping time with a long hand-drum; then the band played; and dancing, and duets, and singing followed. After the usual presentations, fines, and n'yanziggings, I asked for leave to go and meet Grant by water, but was hastily told that two boats had been sent for him when we returned from the N'yanza, and that two runners, just returned from Karagué, said he was on the way not far off. The child-king then changed his dress for another suit of clothes for his brothers to admire, and I retired much annoyed, as he would neither give pombé for myself nor plantains for my men; and I was farther annoyed on my arrival at home to find the Wangŭana mobbing my hut and clamoring for food, and calling for an order to plunder if I did not give them beads, which, as the stock had run short, I could only do by their returning to Karagŭé for the beads stored there; and, even if they were obtained, it was questionable if the king would revoke his order prohibiting the sale of provisions to us.

7th. To-day I called at the queen's, but had to wait five hours in company with some attendants, to whom she sent pombé occasionally; but, after waiting for her nearly all day, they were dismissed, because excess of business prevented her seeing them, though I was desired to remain. I asked these attendants to sell me food for beads, but they declared they could not without obtaining permission. In the evening the queen stumped out of her chambers and walked to the other end of her palace, where the head or queen of the wichwézi women lived, to whom every body paid the profoundest respect. On the way I joined her, she saying, in a state of high anger, "You won't call on me now I have given you such a charming damsel: you have quite forgotten us in your love of home." Of course Méri's misdemeanor had to be explained, when she said, "As that is the case, I will give you another; but you must take Méri out of the country, else she will bring trouble on us; for, you know, I never gave girls who lived in the palace to any one in my life before, because they would tell domestic affairs not proper for common people to know." I then said my reason for not seeing her before was, that the four times I had sent messengers to make an appointment for the following day, they had been repulsed from her doors. This she would not believe, but called me a story-teller in very coarse language, until the men who had been sent were pointed out to her, and they corroborated me.

The wichwézi queen met her majesty with her head held very high, and, instead of permitting me to sit on my box of grass, threw out a bundle of grass for that purpose. All conversation was kept between the two queens; but her wichwézi majesty had a platter of clay-stone brought, which she ate with great relish, making a noise of satisfaction like a happy Guinea-pig. She threw me a bit, which, to the surprise of every body, I caught and threw into my mouth, thinking it was some confection; but the harsh taste soon made me spit it out again, to the amusement of the company. On returning home I found the king had requested me to call on him as soon as possible with the medicine-chest.

8th. Without a morsel to eat for dinner last night, or any thing this morning, we proceeded early to the palace, in great expectation that the medicines in request would bring us something; but after waiting all day till 4 P.M., as the king did not appear, leaving Bombay behind, I walked away to shoot a Guinea-fowl within earshot of the palace. The scheme was successful, for the report of the gun which killed the bird reached the king's ear, and induced him to say if Bana was present he would be glad to see him. This gave Bombay an opportunity of telling all the facts of the case, which were no sooner heard than the king gave his starving guests a number of plantains, and vanished at once, taking my page Lŭgoi with him, to instruct him in Kisŭahili (Zanzibar language).

9th. As the fruit of last night's scheme, the king sent us four goats and two cows. In great good-humor I now called on him, and found him walking about the palace environs with a carbine, looking eagerly for sport, while his pages dragged about five half-dead vultures tied in a bundle by their legs to a string. "These birds," said he, tossing his head proudly, "were all shot flying, with iron slugs, as the boys will tell you. I like the carbine very well, but you must give me a double smooth gun." This I promised to give when Grant arrived, for his good-nature in sending so many officers to fetch him.

We next tried for Guinea-fowl, as I tell him they are the game the English delight in; but the day was far spent, and none could be found. A boy then in attendance was pointed out as having seen Grant in Uddŭ ten days ago. If the statement were true, he must have crossed the Katonga. But, though told with great apparent circumspection, I did not credit it, because my men sent on the 15th ultimo for a letter to ascertain his whereabouts had not returned, and they certainly would have done so had he been so near. To make sure, the king then proposed sending the boy again with some of my men; but this I objected to as useless, considering the boy had spoken falsely. Hearing this, the king looked at the boy and then at the women in turn, to ascertain what they thought of my opinion, whereupon the boy cried. Late in the evening the sly little girl Kahala changed her cloth wrapper for a mbŭgŭ, and slipped quietly away. I did not suspect her intention, because of late she had appeared much more than ordinarily happy, behaving to me in every respect like a dutiful child to a parent. A search was made, and guns fired, in the hopes of frightening her back again, but without effect.

10th. I had promised that this morning I would teach the king the art of Guinea-fowl shooting, and when I reached the palace at 6 A.M. I found him already on the ground. He listened to the tale of the missing girl, and sent orders for her apprehension at once; then proceeding with the gun, fired eight shots successively at Guinea-birds sitting on trees, but missed them all. After this, as the birds were scared away, and both iron shot and bullets were expended, he took us to his dressing-hut, went inside himself, attended by full-grown naked women, and ordered a breakfast of pork, beef, fish, and plantains to be served me outside on the left of the entrance, while a large batch of his women sat on the right side, silently coquetting, and amusing themselves by mimicking the white man eating. Poor little Lŭgoi joined in the repast, and said he longed to return to my hut, for he was half starved here, and no one took any notice of him; but he was destined to be a royal page, for the king would not part with him. A cold fit then seized me, and as I asked for leave to go, the king gave orders for one of his wives to be flogged. The reason for this act of brutality I did not discover; but the moment the order was issued, the victim begged the pages to do it quickly, that the king's wrath might be appeased; and in an instant I saw a dozen boys tear their cord turbans from their heads, pull her roughly into the middle of the court, and belabor her with sticks, while she lay floundering about, screeching to me for protection. All I did was to turn my head away and walk rapidly out of sight, thinking it better not to interfere again with the discipline of the palace; indeed, I thought it not improbable that the king did these things sometimes merely that his guests might see his savage power. On reaching home I found Kahala standing like a culprit before my door. She would not admit, what I suspected, that Méri had induced her to run away, but said she was very happy in my house until yester-evening, when Rozaro's sister told her she was very stupid living with the mzungŭ all alone, and told her to run away; which she did, taking the direction of N'yamasoré's, until some officers finding her, and noticing beads on her neck, and her hair cut, according to the common court fashion, in slopes from a point in the forehead to the breadth of her ears, suspected her to be one of the king's women, and kept her in confinement all night, till Mtésa's men came this morning and brought her back again. As a punishment, I ordered her to live with Bombay; but my house was so dull again from want of some one to eat dinner with me, that I remitted the punishment, to her great delight.

11*th*. To-day I received letters from Grant, dated the 22d, 25th, 28th of April, and 2d of May. They were brought by my three men, with Karagŭé pease, flour, and ammunition. He was at Maŭla's house, which proved the king's boy to be correct; for the convoy, afraid of encountering the voyage on the lake, had deceived my companion and brought him on by land, like true negroes.

12*th*. I sent the three men who had returned from Grant to lay a complaint against the convoy, who had tricked him out of a pleasant voyage, and myself out of the long-wished-for survey of the lake. They carried at the same time a present of a canister of shot from me to the king. Delighted with this unexpected prize, he immediately shot fifteen birds flying, and ordered the men to acquaint me with his prowess.

13*th*. To-day the king sent me four cows and a load of butter as a return present for the shot, and allowed one of his officers, at my solicitation, to go with ten of my men to help Grant on. He also sent a message that he had just shot thirteen birds flying.

14*th*. Mabrŭki and Bilal returned with Budja and his ten children from Unyoro, attended by a deputation of four men sent by Kamrasi, who were headed by Kidgwiga. Mtésa, it now transpired, had followed my advice of making friendship with Kamrasi by sending two brass wires as a hongo instead of an army, and Kamrasi, in return, sent him two elephant tusks. Kidgwiga said Petherick's party was not in Unyoro; they had never reached there, but were lying at anchor off Gani. Two white men only had been seen—one, they said, a hairy man, the other smooth-faced; they were as anxiously inquiring after us as we were after them: they sat on chairs, dressed like myself, and had guns and every thing precisely like those in my hut. On one occasion they sent up a necklace of beads to Kamrasi, and he, in return, gave them a number of women and tusks. If I wished to go that way, Kamrasi would forward me on to their position in boats; for the land route, leading through Kidi, was a jungle of ten days, tenanted by a savage set of people, who hunt every body, and seize every thing they see.

This tract is sometimes, however, traversed by the Wanyoro and Gani people, who are traders in cows and tippet monkey-skins, stealthily traveling at night; but they seldom attempt it,

from fear of being murdered. Baraka and Ulédi, sent from Karagŭé on the 30th of January, had been at Kamrasi's palace upward of a month, applying for the road to Gani, and as they
could not get that, wished to come with Mabrŭki to me; but this
Kamrasi also refused, on the plea that, as they had come from
Karagŭé, so they must return there. Kamrasi had heard of my
shooting with Mtésa, as also of the attempt made by Mabrŭki and
Ulédi to reach Gani viâ Usoga. He had received my present of
beads from Baraka, and, in addition, took Ulédi's sword, saying,
"If you do not wish to part with it, you must remain a prisoner
in my country all your life, for you have not paid your footing."
Mabrŭki then told me he was kept waiting at a village, one hour's
walk from Kamrasi's palace, five days before they were allowed
to approach his majésty; but when they were seen, and the presents exchanged, they were ordered to pack off the following
morning, as Kamrasi said the Waganda were a set of plundering
blackguards.

This information, to say the least of it, was very embarrassing
—a mixture of good and bad. Petherick, I now felt certain, was
on the look-out for us; but his men had reached Kamrasi's, and
returned again before Baraka's arrival. Baraka was not allowed
to go on to him and acquaint him of our proximity, and the Waganda were so much disliked in Unyoro that there seemed no
hopes of our ever being able to communicate by letter. To add
to my embarrassments, Grant had not been able to survey the
lake from Kitangŭlé, nor had Usoga and the eastern side of the
lake been seen.

15th. I was still laid up with the cold fit of the 10th, which
turned into a low kind of fever. I sent Bombay to the king to
tell him the news, and ask him what he thought of doing next.
He replied that he would push for Gani direct, and sent back a
pot of pombé for the sick man.

16th. The king to-day inquired after my health, and, strange to
say, did not accompany his message with a begging request.

17th. My respite, however, was not long. At the earliest possible hour in the morning the king sent begging for things one
hundred times refused, supposing, apparently, that I had some
little reserve store which I wished to conceal from him.

18th and 19th. I sent Bombay to the palace to beg for pombé,
as it was the only thing I had an appetite for, but the king would
see no person but myself. He had broken his rifle washing-rod,

THE KING OF UGANDA REVIEWING TROOPS

and this must be mended, the pages who brought it saying that no one dared take it back to him until it was repaired. A Guinea-fowl was sent after dark for me to see, as a proof that the king was a sportsman complete.

20th. The king, going out shooting, borrowed my powder-horn. The Wangŭana mobbed the hut and bullied me for food, merely because they did not like the trouble of helping themselves from the king's garden, though they knew I had purchased their privilege to do so at the price of a gold chronometer and the best guns England could produce.

21st. I now, for the first time, saw the way in which the king collected his army together. The high roads were all thronged with Waganda warriors, painted in divers colors, with plantain-leaf bands round their heads, scanty goatskin fastened to their loins, and spears and shield in their hands, singing the tambŭré or march, ending with a repetition of the word mkavia, or monarch. They surpassed in number, according to Bombay, the troops and ragamuffins enlisted by Sultan Majid when Sayyid Swéni threatened to attack Zanzibar; in fact, he never saw such a large army collected any where.

Bombay, on going to the palace, hoping to obtain plantains for the men, found the king holding a levée, for the purpose of dispatching this said army somewhere, but where no one would pronounce. The king then, observing my men who had gone to Unyoro together with Kamrasi's, questioned them on their mission; and when told that no white men were there, he waxed wrathful, and said it was a falsehood, for his men had seen them, and could not be mistaken. Kamrasi, he said, must have hidden them somewhere, fearful of the number of guns which now surrounded him; and, for the same reason, he told lies—yes, lies; but no man living shall dare tell himself lies; and now, as he could not obtain his object by fair means, he would use arms and force it out. Then turning to Bombay, he said, "What does your master think of this business?" upon which Bombay replied, according to his instructions, "Bana wishes nothing done until Grant arrives, when all will go together." On this the king turned his back and walked away.

22d. Kitŭnzi called on me early, because he heard I was sick. I asked him why the Waganda objected to my sitting on a chair; but, to avoid the inconvenience of answering a troublesome question, without replying, he walked off, saying he heard a noise in the neighborhood of the palace which must be caused by the king ordering some persons to be seized, and his presence was so necessary he could not wait another moment. My men went for plantains to the palace and for pombé on my behalf; but the king, instead of giving them any thing, took two fez caps off their heads, keeping them to himself, and ordered them to tell Bana all his beer was done.

23d. Kidgwiga called on me to say Kamrasi so very much wanted the white men at Gani to visit him, he had sent a hongo of thirty tusks to the chief of that country in hopes that it would insure their coming to see him. He also felt sure if I went there his king would treat me with the greatest respect. This afforded an opportunity for putting in a word of reconciliation. I said that it was at my request that Mtésa sent Kamrasi a present; and so now, if Kamrasi made friends with the Waganda, there would be no difficulty about the matter.

24th. The army still thronged the highways, some going, others coming, like a swarm of ants, the whole day long. Kidgwiga paid another visit, and I went to the palace without my gun, wishing the king to fancy all my powder was done, as he had nearly consumed all my store; but the consequence was that, after waiting the whole day, I never saw him at all. In the evening pages informed me that Grant had arrived at N'yama Goma, one march only distant.

25th. I prepared twenty men, with a quarter of mutton for Grant to help him on the way, but they could not go without a native officer, lest they should be seized, and no officer would lead the way. The king came shooting close to my hut and ordered me out. I found him marching Rozaro about in custody with four other Wanyambo, who, detected plundering by Kitŭnzi, had set upon and beaten him severely. The king, pointing them out to me, said he did not like the system of plundering, and wished to know if it was the practice in Karagŭé. Of course I took the opportunity to renew my protest against the plundering system; but the king, changing the subject, told me the wazungŭ were at Gani inquiring after us, and wishing to come here. To this I proposed fetching them myself in boats, but he objected, saying he would send men first, for they were not farther off to the northward than the place he sent boats to to bring Grant. He said he did not like Unyoro, because Kamrasi hides himself like a Neptune in the Nile whenever his men go on a visit there, and instead of treating his guests with respect, he keeps them beyond the river. For this reason he had himself determined on adopting the passage by Kïdi.

I was anxious, of course, to go on with the subject thus unexpectedly opened, but, as ill luck would have it, an adjutant was espied sitting on a tree, when a terrible fuss and excitement ensued. The women were ordered one way and the attendants another, while I had to load the gun in the best way I could with the last charge and a half left in the king's pouch. Ten grains were all he would have allowed himself, reserving the residue, without reflecting that a large bird required much shot; and he was shocked to find me lavishly use the whole, and still say it was not enough.

The bird was then at a great height, so that the first shot merely tickled him, and drove him to another tree. "Woh! woh!" cried the king; "I am sure he is hit; look there, look there;" and away he rushed after the bird; down with one fence, then with another, in the utmost confusion, every body trying to keep his proper place, till at last the tree to which the bird had flown was reached, and then, with the last charge of shot, the king killed his first nundo. The bird, however, did not fall, but lay like a spread eagle in the upper branches. Wasoga were called to climb the tree and pull it down; while the king, in ecstasies of joy and excitement, rushed up and down the potato-field like a mad bull, jumping and plunging, waving and brandishing the gun above his head, while the drums beat, the attendants all woh-wohed, and the women, joining with their lord, rushed about lullalooing and dancing like insane creatures. Then began congratulations and hand-shakings, and, finally, the inspection of the bird, which, by this time, the Wasoga had thrown down. Oh! oh! what a wonder! Its wings outspread reached farther than the height of a man; we must go and show it to the brothers. Even that was not enough—we must show it to the mother; and away we all rattled as fast as our legs could carry us.

Arrived at the queen's palace, out of respect to his mother, the king changed his European clothes for a white kidskin wrapper, and then walked in to see her, leaving us waiting outside. By this time Colonel Congow, in his full-dress uniform, had arrived in the square outside, with his regiment drawn up in review order. The king, hearing the announcement, at once came out with spears and shield, preceded by the bird, and took post, standing

armed, by the entrance, encircled by his staff all squatting, when
the adjutant was placed in the middle of the company.   Before
us was a large open square, with the huts of the queen's kamraviona, or commander-in-chief beyond.   The battalion, consisting
of what might be termed three companies, each containing 200
men, being drawn up on the left extremity of the parade-ground,
received orders to march past in single file from the right of companies, at a long trot, and re-form again at the other end of the
square.

   Nothing conceivable could be more wild or fantastic than the
sight which ensued—the men all nearly naked, with goat or cat
skins depending from their girdles, and smeared with war colors
according to the taste of each individual—one half of the body
red or black, the other blue, not in regular order—as, for instance,
one stocking would be red, the other black, while the breeches
above would be the opposite colors, and so with the sleeves and
waistcoat.   Every man carried the same arms—two spears and
one shield—held as if approaching an enemy, and they thus moved
in three lines of single rank and file, at fifteen to twenty paces
asunder, with the same high action and elongated step, the ground
leg only being bent, to give their strides the greater force.   After
the men had all started, the captains of companies followed, even
more fantastically dressed; and last of all came the great Colonel
Congow, a perfect Robinson Crusoe, with his long white-haired
goatskins, a fiddle-shaped leather shield, tufted with white hair
at all six extremities, bands of long hair tied below the knees, and
a magnificent helmet, covered with rich beads of every color, in
excellent taste, surmounted with a plume of crimson feathers, from
the centre of which rose a bent stem, tufted with goathair.   Next
they charged in companies to and fro; and, finally, the senior officers came charging at their king, making violent professions of
faith and honesty, for which they were applauded.   The parade
then broke up, and all went home.

   26th. One of King Mtésa's officers now consenting to go to
N'yama Goma with some of my men, I sent Grant a quarter of
goat.   The reply brought to me was that he was very thankful
for it; that he cooked it and ate it on the spot; and begged I
would see the king, to get him released from that starving place.
Rozaro was given over to the custody of Kitŭnzi for punishment.
At the same time, the queen, having heard of the outrages committed against her brother and women, commanded that neither

Engraved by S. Hollyer, from a Photograph by Urquhart. Dingwall.

SPEKE AND GRANT AT KING MTÉSA'S LEVEE.

my men nor any of Rozaro's should get any more food at the palace; for as we all came to Uganda in one body, so all alike were, by her logic, answerable for the offense. I called∙ at the palace for explanation, but could not obtain admittance because I would not fire the gun.

27th. The king sent to say he wanted medicine to propitiate lightning. I called and described the effects of a lightning-rod, and tried to enter into the Unyoro business, wishing to go there at once myself. He objected, because he had not seen Grant, but appointed an officer to go through Unyoro on to Gani, and begged I would also send men with letters. Our talk was agreeably interrupted by guns in the distance announcing Grant's arrival, and I took my leave to welcome my friend. How we enjoyed ourselves after so much anxiety and want of one another's company I need not describe. For my part, I was only too rejoiced to see Grant could limp about a bit, and was able to laugh over the picturesque and amusing account he gave me of his own rough travels.

28th. The king in the morning sent Budja, his embassador, with Kamrasi's kidgwiga, over to me for my men and letters, to go to Kamrasi's again and ask for the road to Gani. I wished to speak to the king first, but they said they had no orders to stop for.that, and walked straight away. I sent the king a present of a double-barreled gun and ammunition, and received in answer a request that both Grant and myself would attend a levée, which he was to hold in state, accompanied by his body-guard, as when I was first presented to him. In the afternoon we proceeded to court accordingly, but found it scantily attended; and after the first sitting, which was speedily over, retired to another court, and' saw the women. Of this dumb show the king soon got tired; he therefore called for the iron chair, and entered into conversation, at first about the ever-engrossing subject of stimulants, till we changed it by asking him how he liked the gun. He pronounced it a famous weapon, which he would use intensely. We then began to talk in a general way about Sŭwarora and Rŭmanika, as well as the road through Unyamŭézi, which we hoped would soon cease to exist, and be superseded by one through Unyoro.

It will be kept in view that the hanging about at this court, and all the perplexing and irritating negotiations here described, had always one end in view—that of reaching the Nile where it pours out of the N'yanza, as I was long certain that it did. Without the consent and even the aid of this capricious barbarian I

was now talking to, such a project was hopeless. I naturally
seized every opportunity for putting in a word in the direction of
my great object, and here seemed to be an opportunity. We
now ventured on a plump application for boats that we might feel
our way to Gani by water, supposing the lake and river to be
navigable all the way; and begged Kitŭnzi might be appointed
to accompany us, in order that whatever was done might be done
all with good effect in opening up a new line of commerce, by
which articles of European manufacture might find a permanent
route to Uganda. It was "no go," however. The appeal, though
listened to and commented on, showing that it was well understood, got no direct reply. It was not my policy to make our object appear too important to ourselves, so I had to appear toler-
ably indifferent, and took the opportunity to ask for my paint-
box, which he had borrowed for a day, and had kept in his possession for months. I got no answer to that request either, but
was immediately dunned for the compass, which had been promised on Grant's arrival. Now, with a promise that the compass
would be sent him in the morning, he said he would see what
pombé his women could spare us; and, bidding good evening,
walked away.

29th. I sent Bombay with the compass, much to the delight of
the king, who no sooner saw it than he jumped and woh-wohed
with intense excitement at the treasure he had gained, said it was
the greatest present Bana had ever given him, for it was the thing
by which he found out all the roads and countries — it was, in
fact, half his knowledge; and the parting with it showed plainly
that Bana entertained an everlasting friendship for him. The
king then called Maŭla, and said, "Maŭla, indeed you have spoken
the truth; there is nothing like this instrument," etc., etc., repeating what he had already told Bombay. In the evening, the king,
accompanied by all his brothers, with iron chair and box, came
to visit us, and inspected all Grant's recently brought pictures of
the natives with great acclamation. We did not give him any
thing this time, but, instead, dunned him for the paint-box, and
afterward took a walk to my observatory hill, where I acted as
guide. On the summit of this hill the king instructed his brothers on the extent of his dominions; and as I asked where Lŭbari
or God resides, he pointed to the skies.

30th. The king at last sent the paint-box, with some birds of
his own shooting, which he wished painted. He also wanted him-

SPEKE INTRODUCES GRANT TO THE QUEEN-DOWAGER OF UGANDA.

self drawn, and all Grant's pictures copied. Then, to wind up these mild requests, a demand was made for more powder, and that all our guns be sent to the palace for inspection.

31*st.* I drew a large white and black hornbill and a green pigeon sent by himself; but he was not satisfied; he sent more birds, and wanted to see my shoes. The pages who came with the second message, however, proving impertinent, got a book flung at their heads, and a warning to be off, as I intended to see the king myself, and ask for food to keep my ever-complaining Wangŭana quiet. Proceeding to the palace, as I found Mtésa had gone out shooting, I called on the kamraviona, complained that my camp was starving, and as I had nothing left to give the king, said I wished to leave the country. Ashamed of its being supposed that his king would not give me any food because I had no more presents to give him, the kamraviona, from his own stores, gave me a goat and pombé, and said he would speak to the king on the subject.

1*st.* I drew for the king a picture of a Guinea-fowl which he shot in the early morning, and proceeded on a visit with Grant to the queen's, accompanied only by seven men, as the rest preferred foraging for themselves to the chance of picking up a few plantains at her majesty's. After an hour's waiting, the queen received us with smiles, and gave pombé and plantains to her new visitor, stating pointedly she had none for me. There was deep Uganda policy in this: it was for the purpose of treating Grant as a separate, independent person, and so obtaining a fresh hongo or tax. Laughing at the trick, I thanked her for the beer, taking it personally on my household, and told her when my property arrived from Karagŭé she should have a few more things as I promised her; but the men sent had neither brought my brother in a vessel, as they were ordered, nor did they bring my property from Karagŭé.

Still the queen was not content: she certainly expected something from Grant, if it was ever so little, for she was entitled to it, and would not listen to our being one house. Turning the subject, to put in a word for my great object, I asked her to use her influence in opening the road to Gani, as, after all, that was the best way to get new things into Uganda. Cunning as a fox, the queen agreed to this project, provided Grant remained behind, for she had not seen enough of him yet, and she would speak to her son about the matter in the morning.

This was really the first gleam of hope, and I set to putting our future operations into a shape that might lead to practical results without alarming our capricious host. I thought that while I could be employed in inspecting the river, and in feeling the route by water to Gani, Grant could return to Karagŭé by water, bringing up our rear traps, and, in navigating the lake, obtain the information he had been frustrated in getting by the machinations of his attendant Maribŭ. It was agreed to, and all seemed well; for there was much left to be done in Uganda and Usoga, if we could only make sure of communicating once with Petherick. Before going home we had some more polite conversation, during which the queen played with a toy in the shape of a cocoa du mer, studded all over with cowries: this was a sort of doll, or symbol of a baby, and her dandling it was held to indicate that she would ever remain a widow. In the evening the king returned all our rifles and guns, with a request for one of them, as also for the iron chair he sat upon when calling on us, an iron bedstead, and the Union Jack, for he did not honor us with a visit for nothing; and the head page was sent to witness the transfer of the goods, and see there was no humbug about it. It was absolutely necessary to get into a rage, and tell the head page we did not come to Uganda to be swindled in that manner, and he might tell the king I would not part with one of them.

2d. K'yengo, who came with Grant, now tried to obtain an interview with the king, but could not get admission. I had some farther trouble about the disposal of the child Méri, who said she never before had lived in a poor man's house since she was born. I thought to content her by offering to marry her to one of Rŭmanika's sons, a prince of her own breed, but she would not listen to the proposal.

3d. For days past, streams of men have been carrying fagots of fire-wood, clean-cut timber, into the palaces of the king, queen, and the kamraviona; and to-day, on calling on the king, I found him engaged having these fagots removed by Colonel Mkavia's regiment from one court into another, this being his way of ascertaining their quantity, instead of counting them. About 1600 men were engaged on this service, when the king, standing on a carpet in front of the middle hut of the first court, with two spears in his hand and his dog by his side, surrounded by his brothers and a large staff of officers, gave orders for the regiment to run to and fro in column, that he might see them well; then turning to his staff, ordered them to run up and down the regiment, and see what they thought of it. This ridiculous order set them all flying, and soon they returned, charging at the king with their sticks, dancing and jabbering that their numbers were many, he was the greatest king on earth, and their lives and services were his forever. The regiment now received orders to put down their fagots, and, taking up their own sticks in imitation of spears, followed the antics of their officers in charging and vociferating. Next, Mkavia presented five hairy Usoga goats, n'yanzigging and performing the other appropriate ceremonies. On asking the king if he had any knowledge of the extent of his army, he merely said, "How can I, when these you see are a portion of them just ordered here to carry wood?"

The regiment was now dismissed; but the officers were invited to follow the king into another court, when he complimented them on assembling so many men; they, instead of leaving well alone, foolishly replied they were sorry they were not more numerous, as some of the men lived so far away they shirked the summons; Maŭla then, ever forward in mischief, put a cap on it by saying, if he could only impress upon the Waganda to listen to his orders there would never be a deficiency. Upon which the king said, "If they fail to obey you, they disobey me; for I have appointed you as my orderly, and thereby you personify the orders of the king." Up jumped Maŭla in a moment as soon as these words were uttered, charging with his stick, then floundering and n'yanzigging as if he had been signally rewarded. I expected some piece of cruel mischief to come of all this, but the king, in his usual capricious way, suddenly rising, walked off to a third court, followed only by a select few.

Here, turning to me, he said, "Bana, I love you, because you have come so far to see me, and have taught me so many things since you have been here." Rising, with my hand to my heart, and gracefully bowing at this strange announcement—for at that moment I was full of hunger and wrath—I intimated I was much flattered at hearing it, but as my house was in a state of starvation, I trusted he would consider it. "What!" said he, "do you want goats?" "Yes, very much." The pages then received orders to furnish me with ten that moment, as the king's farm-yard was empty, and he would reimburse them as soon as more confiscations took place. But this, I said, was not enough; the Wangŭana wanted plantains, for they had received none these fifteen days. "What!" said the king, turning to his pages again, "have you given these men no plantains, as I ordered? Go and fetch them this moment, and pombé too, for Bana."

The subject then turned on the plan I had formed of going to Gani by water, and of sending Grant to Karagŭé by the lake; but the king's mind was fully occupied with the compass I had given him. He required me to explain its use, and then broke up the meeting.

4th. Viarŭngi, an officer sent by Rŭmanika to escort Grant to Uganda, as well as to apply to King Mtésa for a force to fight his brother Rogéro, called on me with Rozaro, and said he had received instructions from his king to apply to me for forty cows and two slave-boys, because the Arabs who pass through his country to Uganda always make him a present of that sort after receiving them from Mtesa. After telling him we English never give the presents they have received away to any one, and never make slaves, but free them, I laid a complaint against Rozaro for having brought much trouble and disgrace upon my camp, as well as much trouble on myself, and begged that he might be removed from my camp. Rozaro then attempted to excuse himself, but without success, and said he had already detached his residence from my camp, and taken up a separate residence with Viarŭngi, his superior officer.

I called on the king in the afternoon, and found the pages had already issued plantains for my men and pombé for myself. The king addressed me with great cordiality, and asked if I wished to go to Gani. I answered him with all promptitude, "Yes, at once, with some of his officers competent to judge of the value of all I point out to them for future purposes in keeping the road permanently open. His provoking capriciousness, however, again broke in, and he put me off till his messengers should return from Unyoro. I told him his men had gone in vain, for Budja left without my letter or my men; and, farther, that the river route is the only one that will ever be of advantage to Uganda, and the sooner it was opened up the better. I entreated him to listen to my advice, and send some of my men to Kamrasi direct, to acquaint him with my intention to go down the river in boats to him; but I could get no answer to this. Bombay then asked for cows for the Wangŭana, getting laughed at for his audacity, and the king broke up the court and walked away.

5th. I started on a visit to the queen, but half way met Congow, who informed me he had just escorted her majesty from his house, where she was visiting, to her palace. By way of a joke and feeler, I took it in my head to try, by taking a harmless rise out of Congow, whether the Nile is understood by the natives to be navigable near its exit from the N'yanza. I told him he had been appointed by the king to escort us down the river to Gani. He took the affair very seriously, delivering himself to the following purport: "Well, then, my days are numbered, for if I refuse compliance I shall lose my head; and if I attempt to pass Kamrasi's, which is on the river, I shall lose my life, for I am a marked man there, having once led an army past his palace and back again. It would be no use calling it a peaceful mission, as you propose, for the Wanyoro distrust the Waganda to such an extent, they would fly to arms at once."

Proceeding to the queen's palace, we met Mŭrondo, who had once traveled to the Masai frontier. He said it would take a month to go in boats from Kira, the most easterly district in Uganda, to Masai, where there is another N'yanza, joined by a strait to the big N'yanza, which King Mtésa's boats frequent for salt; but the same distance could be accomplished in four days overland, and three days afterward by boat. The queen, after keeping us all day waiting, sent three bunches of plantains and a pot of pombé, with a message that she was too tired to receive visitors, and hoped we would call another day.

6th. I met Pokino, the governor general of Uddŭ, in the morning's walk, who came here at the same time as Grant to visit the king, and was invited into his house to drink pombé. His badge of office is an iron hatchet, inlaid with copper and handled with ivory. He wished to give us a cow, but put it off for another day, and was surprised we dared venture into his premises without permission from the king. After this we called at the palace, just as the king was returning from a walk with his brothers. He saw us, and sent for Bana. We entered, and presented him with some pictures, which he greatly admired, looked at close and far, showed to the brothers, and inspected again. Pokino at this time came in with a number of well-made shields, and presented them groveling and n'yanzigging; but, though the governor of an important province, who had not been seen by the king for years, he was taken no more notice of than any common mkungŭ. A plan of the lake and Nile, which I brought with me to explain our projects for reaching Karagŭé and Gani, engaged the king's attention for a while, but still he would not agree to let any thing be done until his messenger returned from Unyoro. Finding him inflexible, I proposed sending a letter, arranging that his men should be under the guidance of my men after they pass Unyoro on the way to Gani; and this was acceded to, provided I should write a letter to Petherick by the morrow. I then tried to teach the king the use of the compass. To make a stand for it, I turned a drum on its head, when all the courtiers flew at me as if to prevent an outrage, and the king laughed. I found that, as the instrument was supposed to be a magic charm of very wonderful powers, my meddling with it and treating it as an ordinary movable was considered a kind of sacrilege.

7th. I wrote a letter to Petherick, but the promised wakungŭ never came for it. As K'yengo was ordered to attend court with Rŭmanika's hongo, consisting of a few wires, small beads, and a cloth I gave him, as well as a trifle from Nnanaji, I sent Bombay, in place of going myself, to remind the king of his promises for the wakungŭ to Gani, as well as for boats to Karagŭé, but a grunt was the only reply which my messenger said he obtained.

8th. Calling at the palace, I found the king issuing for a walk, and joined him, when he suddenly turned round in the rudest manner, re-entered his palace, and left me to go home without speaking a word. The capricious creature then reissued, and, finding me gone, inquired after me, presuming I ought to have waited for him.

9th. During the night, when sleeping profoundly, some person stealthily entered my hut and ran off with a box of bullets toward the palace, but on the way dropped his burden. Maŭla, on the way home, happening to see it, and knowing it must be mine, brought it back again. I staid at home, not feeling well.

10th. K'yengo paid his hongo in wire to the king, and received a return of six cows. Still at home, an invalid, I received a visit from Méri, who seemed to have quite recovered herself. Speaking of her present quarters, she said she loved Ulédi's wife very much, thinking birds of a feather ought to live together. She helped herself to a quarter of mutton, and said she would come again.

11th. To-day Viarŭngi, finding Rozaro's men had stolen thirty cows, twelve slaves, and a load of mbŭgŭ from the Waganda, laid hands on them himself for Rŭmanika, instead of giving them to King Mtésa. Such are the daily incidents among our neighbors.

12*th*. At night a box of ammunition and a bag of shot, which were placed out as a reserve present for the king, to be given on our departure, were stolen, obviously by the king's boys, and most likely by the king's orders, for he is the only person who could have made any use of them, and his boys alone know the way into the hut; besides which, the previous box of bullets was found on the direct road to the palace, while it was well known that no one dared to touch an article of European manufacture without the consent of the king.

13*th*. I sent a message to the king about the theft, requiring him, if an honest man, to set his detectives to work and ferret it out; his boys, at the same time, to show our suspicions, were peremptorily forbidden ever to enter the hut again. Twice the king sent down a hasty message to say he was collecting all his men to make a search, and, if they do not succeed, the mganga would be sent; but nothing was done. The kamraviona was sharply rebuked by the king for allowing K'yengo to visit him before permission was given, and thus defrauding the royal exchequer of many pretty things, which were brought for majesty alone. At night the rascally boys returned again to plunder, but Kahala, more wakeful than myself, heard them trying to untie the door-handle, and frightened them away in endeavoring to awaken me.

14*th* and 15*th*. Grant, doing duty for me, tried a day's penance at the palace; but, though he sat all day in the antechamber, and musicians were ordered into the presence, nobody called for him. K'yengo was sent with all his men on a wakungŭ-seizing expedition—a good job for him, as it was his perquisite to receive the major part of the plunder himself.

16*th*. I sent Kahala out of the house, giving her finally over to Bombay as a wife, because she preferred playing with dirty little children to behaving like a young lady, and had caught the itch. This was much against her wish, and the child vowed she would not leave me until force compelled her; but I had really no other way of dealing with the remnant of the awkward burden which the queen's generosity had thrown on me. K'yengo went to the palace with fifty prisoners; but as the king had taken his women to the small pond, where he has recently placed a tub canoe for purposes of amusement, they did no business.

17*th*. I took a first convalescent walk. The king, who was out shooting all day, begged for powder in the evening. Ulédi

returned from his expedition against a recusant officer at Kituntŭ,
bringing with him a spoil of ten women. It appeared that the
officer himself had bolted from his landed possessions, and as they
belonged to "the Church," or were in some way or other sacred
from civil execution, they could not be touched, so that Ulédi lost
an estate which the king had promised him. We heard that
Ilmas, wife of Majanja, who, as I already mentioned, had achieved
an illustrious position by services at the birth of the king, had
been sent to visit the late king Sŭnna's tomb, whence, after observing certain trees which were planted, and divining by mystic
arts what the future state of Uganda required, she would return
at a specific time, to order the king at the time of his coronation
either to take the field with an army, to make a pilgrimage, or to
live a life of ease at home; whichever of these courses the influence of the ordeal at the grave might prompt her to order must
be complied with by the king.

18th. I called at the palace with Grant, taking with us some
pictures of soldiers, horses, elephants, etc. We found the guard
fighting over their beef and plantain dinner. Bombay remarked

Palace Guards at Dinner—Uganda.

that this daily feeding on beef would be the lot of the Wangŭana
if they had no religious scruples about the throat-cutting of ani-

mals for food. This, I told him, was all their own fault, for they have really no religion or opinions of their own; and had they been brought up in England instead of Africa, it would have been all the other way with them as a matter of course; but Bombay replied, "We could no more throw off the Mussulman faith than you could yours." A man with a maniacal voice sang and whistled by turns. Katŭmba, the officer of the guard, saw our pictures, and, being a favorite, acquainted the king, which gained us an admittance.

We found his majesty sitting on the ground, within a hut, behind a portal, encompassed by his women, and took our seats outside. At first all was silence, till one told the king we had some wonderful pictures to show him, when in an instant he grew lively, crying, "Oh, let us see them!" and they were shown, Bombay explaining. Three of the king's wives then came in, and offered him their two virgin sisters, n'yanzigging incessantly, and beseeching their acceptance, as by that means they themselves would become doubly related to him. Nothing, however, seemed to be done to promote the union, until one old lady, sitting by the king's side, who was evidently learned in the etiquette and traditions of the court, said, "Wait and see if he embraces, otherwise you may know he is not pleased." At this announcement the girls received a hint to pass on, and the king commenced bestowing on them a series of huggings, first sitting on the lap of one, whom he clasped to his bosom, crossing his neck with hers to the right, then to the left, and, having finished with her, took post in the second one's lap, then on that of the third, performing on each of them the same evolutions. He then retired to his original position, and the marriage ceremony was supposed to be concluded, and the settlements adjusted, when all went on as before.

The pictures were again looked at and again admired, when we asked for a private interview on business, and drew the king outside. I then begged he would allow me, while his men were absent at Unyoro, to go to the Masai country, and see the Salt Lake at the northeast corner of the N'yanza, and to lend me some of his boats for Grant to fetch powder and beads from Karagŭé. This important arrangement being conceded by the king more promptly than we expected, a cow, plantains, and pombé were requested; but the cow only was given, though our men were said to be feeding on grass. Taking the king, as it appeared, in a good humor, to show him the abuses arising from the system of allowing his guests to help themselves by force upon the highways, I reported the late seizures made of thirty cows and twelve slaves by the Wanyambo; but, though surprised to hear the news, he merely remarked that there were indeed a great number of visitors in Uganda. During this one day we heard the sad voices of no less than four women, dragged from the palace to the slaughter-house.

19*th.* To follow up our success in the marching question and keep the king to his promise, I called at his palace, but found he had gone out shooting. To push my object farther, I then marched off to the queen's to bid her good-by, as if we were certain to leave next day; but, as no one would dare to approach her cabinet to apprise her of our arrival, we returned home tired and annoyed.

20*th.* The king sent for us at noon, but when we reached the palace we found he had started on a shooting tour; so, to make the best of our time, we called again upon the queen for the same purpose as yesterday, as also to get my books of birds and animals, which, taken merely to look at for a day or so, had been kept for months. After hours of waiting, her majesty appeared standing in an open gateway, beckoned us to advance, and offered pombé; then, as two or three drops of rain fell, she said she could not stand the violence of the weather, and forthwith retired without one word being obtained. An officer, however, venturing in for the books, at length I got them.

21*st.* To-day I went to the palace, but found no one; the king was out shooting again.

22*d.* We resolved to-day to try on a new political influence at the court. Grant had taken to the court of Karagué a jumping-jack, to amuse the young princes; but it had a higher destiny, for it so fascinated King Rŭmanika himself that he would not part with it, unless, indeed, Grant would make him a big one out of a tree which was handed to him for the purpose. We resolved to try the influence of such a toy on King Mtésa, and brought with us, in addition, a mask and some pictures. But, although the king took a visiting-card, the gate was never opened to us. Finding this, and the day closing, we deposited the mask and pictures on a throne, and walked away. We found that we had thus committed a serious breach of state etiquette; for the guard, as soon as they saw what we had done, seized the Wangŭana for

our offenses in defiling the royal seat, and would have bound
them had they not offered to return the articles to us.

23d. Early in the morning, hearing the royal procession marching off on a shooting excursion, we sent Bombay running after it
with the mask and pictures, to acquaint the king with our desire
to see him, and explain that we had been four days successively
foiled in attempts to find him in his palace, our object being an
eager wish to come to some speedy understanding about the appointed journeys to the Salt Lake and Karagŭé. The toys produced the desired effect; for the king stopped and played with
them, making Bombay and the pages don the mask by turns.
He appointed the morrow for an interview, at the same time ex-
cusing himself for not having seen us yesterday on the plea of
illness. In the evening Kahala absconded with another little girl
of the camp in an opposite direction from the one she took last
time; but as both of them wandered about not knowing where
to go to, and as they omitted to take off all their finery, they were
soon recognized as in some way connected with my party, taken
up, and brought into camp, where they were well laughed at for
their folly, and laughed in turn at the absurdity of their futile
venture.

24th. Hoping to keep the king to his promise, I went to the
palace early, but found he had already gone to see his brothers,
so followed him down, and found him engaged playing on a harmonicon with them. Surprised at my intrusion, he first asked
how I managed to find him out; then went on playing for a
while; but suddenly stopping to talk with me, he gave me an
opportunity of telling him I wished to send Grant off to Karagŭé,
and start myself for Usoga and the Salt Lake in the morning.
"What! going away?" said the king, as if he had never heard a
word about it before; and then, after talking the whole subject
over again, especially dwelling on the quantity of powder I had
in store at Karagŭé, he promised to send the necessary officers for
escorting us on our respective journeys in the morning.

The brothers' wives then wished to see me, and came before us,
when I had to take off my hat and shoes as usual, my ready compliance inducing the princes to pass various compliments on my
person and disposition. The brothers then showed me a stool
made of wood after the fashion of our sketching-stool, and a gun-
cover of leather, made by themselves, of as good workmanship as
is to be found in India. The king then rose, followed by his

brothers, and we all walked off to the pond. The effect of stimulants was mooted, as well as other physiological phenomena, when a second move took us to the palace by torchlight, and the king showed a number of new huts just finished, and beautifully made. Finally, he settled down to a musical concert, in which he took the lead himself. At eight o'clock, being tired and hungry, I reminded the king of his promises, and he appointed the morning to call on him for the wakungŭ, and took leave.

25th. Makinga, hearing of the intended march through Usoga, was pleased to say he would like to join my camp, and spend his time in buying slaves and ivory there. I went to the palace for the promised escort, but was no sooner announced by the pages than the king walked off into the interior of his harem, and left me no alternative but to try my luck with the kamraviona, who, equally proud with his master, would not answer my call, and so another day was lost.

26th. This morning we had the assuring intelligence from Kaddŭ that he had received orders to hold himself in readiness for a voyage to Karagŭé in twenty boats with Grant, but the date of departure was not fixed. The passage was expected to be rough, as the water off the mouth of the Kitangŭlé Kagéra (river) always runs high, so that no boats can go there except at night, when the winds of the day subside, and are replaced by the calms of night. I called at the palace, but saw nothing of the king, though the court was full of officials; and there were no less than 150 women, besides girls, goats, and various other things, seizures from refractory state officers, who, it was said, had been too proud to present themselves at court for a period exceeding propriety.

All these creatures, I was assured, would afterward be given away as return presents for the hongos or presents received from the king's visitors. No wonder the tribes of Africa are mixed breeds. Among the officers in waiting was my friend Budja, the embassador that had been sent to Unyoro with Kidgwiga, Kamrasi's deputy. He had returned three days before, but had not yet seen the king. As might have been expected, he said he had been any thing but welcomed in Unyoro. Kamrasi, after keeping him half starved and in suspense eight days, sent a message— for he would not see him—that he did not desire any communication with blackguard Waganda thieves, and therefore advised him, if he valued his life, to return by the road by which he came as speedily as possible. Turning to Congow, I playfully told him that, as the road through Unyoro was closed, he would have to go with me through Usoga and Kidi; but the gallant colonel merely shuddered, and said that would be a terrible undertaking.

27th. The king would not show, for some reason or other, and we still feared to fire guns, lest he should think our store of powder inexhaustible, and so keep us here until he had extorted the last of it. I found that the Waganda have the same absurd notion here as the Wanyambo have in Karagŭé of Kamrasi's supernatural power in being able to divide the waters of the Nile in the same manner as Moses did the Red Sea.

28th. The king sent a messenger-boy to inform us that he had just heard from Unyoro that the white men were still at Gani inquiring after us; but nothing was said of Budja's defeat. I sent Bombay immediately off to tell him we had changed our plans, and now simply required a large escort to accompany us through Usoga and Kidi to Gani, as farther delay in communicating with Petherick might frustrate all chance of opening the Nile trade with Uganda. He answered that he would assemble all his officers in the morning to consult with them on the subject, when he hoped we would attend, as he wished to further our views. A herd of cows, about eighty in number, were driven in from Unyoro, showing that the silly king was actually robbing Kamrasi at the same time that he was trying to treat with him. K'yengo informed us that the king, considering the surprising events which had lately occurred at his court, being very anxious to pry into the future, had resolved to take a very strong measure for accomplishing that end. This was the sacrifice of a child by cooking, as described in the introduction — a ceremony which it fell to K'yengo to carry out.

29th. To have two strings to my bow, and press our departure as hotly as possible, I sent first Frij off with Nasib to the queen, conveying, as a · parting present, a block-tin brush-box, a watch without a key, two sixpenny pocket-handkerchiefs, and a white towel, with an intimation that we were going, as the king had expressed his desire of sending us to Gani. Her majesty accepted the present, finding fault with the watch for not ticking like the king's, and would not believe her son Mtésa had been so hasty in giving us leave to depart, as she had not been consulted on the subject yet. Setting off to attend the king at his appointed time, I found the kamraviona already there, with a large court attendance, patiently awaiting his majesty's advent. As we were all waiting on, I took a rise out of the kamraviona by telling him I wanted a thousand men to march with me through Kidi to Gani. Surprised at the extent of my requisition, he wished to know if my purpose was fighting. I made him a present of the great principle that power commands respect, and it was to prevent any chance of fighting that we required so formidable an escort. His reply was that he would tell the king; and he immediately rose and walked away home.

K'yengo and the representatives of Usŭi and Karagŭé now arrived by order of the king to bid farewell, and received the slaves and cattle lately captured. As I was very hungry, I set off home to breakfast. Just as I had gone, the provoking king inquired after me, and so brought me back again, though I never saw him the whole day. K'yengo, however, was very communicative. He said he was present when Sunna, with all the forces he could muster, tried to take the very countries I now proposed to travel through; but, though in person exciting his army to victory, he could make nothing of it. He advised my returning to Karagŭé, when Rŭmanika would give me an escort through Nkolé to Unyoro; but, finding that did not suit my views, as I swore I would never retrace one step, he proposed my going by boat to Unyoro, following down the Nile.

This, of course, was exactly what I wanted; but how could King Mtésa, after the rebuff he had received from Kamrasi, be induced to consent to it? My intention, I said, was to try the king on the Usoga and Kidi route first, then on the Masai route to Zanzibar, affecting perfect indifference about Kamrasi; and all those failing—which of course they would—I would ask for Unyoro as a last and only resource. Still I could not see the king to open my heart to him, and therefore felt quite nonplused. "Oh," says K'yengo, "the reason why you do not see him is merely because he is ashamed to show his face, having made so many fair promises to you which he knows he never can carry out; bide your time, and all will be well." At 4 P.M., as no hope of seeing the king was left, all retired.

30th. Unexpectedly, and for reasons only known to himself, the king sent us a cow and load of butter, which had been asked for many days ago. The new moon seen last night kept the king engaged at home, paying his devotions with his magic horns or fetishes in the manner already described. The spirit of this re-ligion—if such it can be called—is not so much adoration of a

Being supreme and beneficent, as a tax to certain malignant furies
—a propitiation, in fact, to prevent them bringing evil on the
land, and to insure a fruitful harvest. It was rather ominous
that hail fell with violence, and lightning burnt down one of the
palace huts, while the king was in the midst of his propitiatory
devotions.

1st. As Bombay was ordered to the palace to instruct the king
in the art of casting bullets, I primed him well to plead for the
road, and he reported to me the results thus: First, he asked one
thousand men to go through Kidi. This the king said was impracticable, as the Waganda had tried it so often before without
success. Then, as that could not be managed, what would the
king devise himself? Bana only proposed the Usoga and Kidi
route, because he thought it would be to the advantage of Uganda.
"Oh," says the king, cunningly, "if Bana merely wishes to see
Usoga, he can do so, and I will send a suitable escort, but no
more." To this Bombay replied, "Bana never could return; he
would sooner do any thing than return—even penetrate the
Masai to Zanzibar, or go through Unyoro;" to which the king,
ashamed of his impotence, hung down his head and walked away.

In the mean while, and while this was going on at the king's
palace, I went with Grant, by appointment, to see the queen. As
usual, she kept us waiting some time, then appeared sitting by an
open gate, and invited us, together with many wakungŭ and
Wasumbŭa, to approach. Very lavish with stale sour pombé,

Waganda Officers drinking Pombé, or Plantain Wine.

she gave us all some, saving the Wasumbŭa, whom she addressed very angrily, asking what they wanted, as they have been months in the country. These poor creatures, in a desponding mood, defended themselves by saying, which was quite true, that they had left their homes in Sorombo to visit her and to trade. They had, since their arrival in the country, been daily in attendance at her palace, but never had the good fortune to see her excepting on such lucky occasions as brought the wazungŭ (white men) here, when she opened her gates to them, but otherwise kept them shut. The queen retorted, "And what have you brought me, pray? where is it? Until I touch it you will neither see me nor obtain permission to trade. Uganda is no place for idle vagabonds." We then asked for a private interview, when, a few drops of rain falling, the queen walked away, and we had orders to wait a little. During this time two boys were birched by the queen's orders, and an officer was sent out to inquire why the watch we had given her did not go. This was easily explained. It had no key; and, never losing sight of the main object, we took advantage of the opportunity to add, that if she did not approve of it, we could easily exchange it for another on arrival at Gani, provided she would send an officer with us.

The queen, squatting within her hut, now ordered both Grant and myself to sit outside and receive a present of five eggs and one cock each, saying coaxingly, "These are for my children." Then taking out the presents, she learned the way of wearing her watch with a tape guard round her neck, reposing the instrument in her bare bosom, and of opening and shutting it, which so pleased her that she declared it quite satisfactory. The key was quite a minor consideration, for she could show it to her attendants just as well without one. The towel and handkerchiefs were also very beautiful, but what use could they be put to? "Oh, your majesty, to wipe the mouth with after drinking pombé." "Of course," is the reply—"excellent; I won't use a mbŭgŭ napkin any more, but have one of these placed on my cup when it is brought to drink, and wipe my mouth with it afterward. But what does Bana want?" "The road to Gani," says Bombay for me. "The king won't see him when he goes to the palace, so now he comes here, trusting your superior influence and good-nature will be more practicable." "Oh!" says her majesty. "Bana does not know the facts of the case. My son has tried all the roads without success, and now he is ashamed to meet Bana face to face." "Then what is to be done, your majesty?" "Bana must go back to Karagŭé, and wait for a year, until my son is crowned, when he will make friends with the surrounding chiefs, and the roads will be opened." "But Bana says he will not retrace one step; he would sooner lose his life." "Oh, that's non sense; he must not be headstrong; but, before any thing more can be said, I will send a message to my son, and Bana can then go with Kaddŭ, K'yengo, and Viarŭngi, and tell all they have to say to Mtésa to-morrow, and the following day return to me, when every thing will be concluded." We all now left but Kaddŭ and some of the queen's officers, who waited for the message to her son about us. To judge from Kaddŭ, it must have been very different from what she led us to expect, as, on joining us, he said there was not the smallest chance of our getting the road we required, for the queen was so decided about it no farther argument would be listened to.

2d. Three goats were stolen, and suspicion falling on the king's cooks, who are expert foragers, we sent to the kamraviona, and asked him to order out the mganga; but his only reply was that he often loses goats in the same way. He sent us one of his own for present purposes, and gave thirty baskets of potatoes to my men. As the king held a court, and broke it up before 8 A.M., and no one would go there for fear of his not appearing again, I waited till the evening for Bombay, Kaddŭ, K'yengo, and Viarŭngi, when, finding them drunk, I went by myself, fired a gun, and was admitted to where the king was hunting Guinea-fowl. On seeing me, he took me affectionately by the hand, and, as we walked along together, he asked me what I wanted, showed me the house which was burnt down, and promised to settle the road question in the morning.

3d. With Kaddŭ, K'yengo, and Viarŭngi all in attendance, we went to the palace, where there was a large assemblage prepared for a levée, and fired a gun, which brought the king out in state. The sakibobo, or provincial governor, arrived with a body of soldiers armed with sticks, made a speech, and danced at the head of his men, all pointing sticks upward, and singing fidelity to their king.

The king then turned to me and said, "I have come out to listen to your request of last night. What is it you do want?" I said, "To open the country to the north, that an uninterrupted line of commerce might exist between England and this country

by means of the Nile. I might go round by Nkolé" (K'yengo
looked daggers at me); "but that is out of the way, and not suitable to the purpose." The queen's deputation was now ordered
to draw near, and questioned in a whisper. As K'yengo was
supposed to know all about me, and spoke fluently both in
Kiganda and Kisŭahili, he had to speak first; but K'yengo, to
every body's surprise, said, "One white man wishes to go to Kamrasi's, while the other wishes to return through Unyamŭézi."
This announcement made the king reflect; for he had been privately primed by his mother's attendants that we both wished to
go to Gani, and therefore shrewdly inquired if Rŭmanika knew
we wished to visit Kamrası, and whether he was aware we should
attempt the passage north from Uganda. "Oh yes; of course
Bana wrote to Bana Mdogo" (the little master) "as soon as he arrived in Uganda, and told him and Rŭmanika all about it."
"Wrote! what does that mean?" and I was called upon to explain. Mtésa, then seeing a flaw in K'yengo's statements, called
him a story-teller; ordered him and his party away, and bade
me draw near.

The moment of triumph had come at last, and suddenly the
road was granted! The king presently let us see the motive by
which he had been influenced. He said he did not like having
to send to Rŭmanika for every thing: he wanted his visitors to
come to him direct; moreover, Rŭmanika had sent him a message to the effect that we were not to be shown any thing out of
Uganda, and when we had done with it, were to be returned to
him. Rŭmanika, indeed! who cared about Rŭmanika? Was
not Mtésa the king of the country, to do as he liked? and we all
laughed. Then the king, swelling with pride, asked me whom I
liked best, Rŭmanika or himself—an awkward question, which I
disposed of by saying I liked Rŭmanika very much because he
spoke well, and was very communicative; but I also liked Mtésa,
because his habits were much like my own—fond of shooting and
roaming about; while he had learned so many things from my
teaching I must ever feel a yearning toward him.

With much satisfaction, I felt that my business was now done;
for Budja was appointed to escort us to Unyoro, and Jumba to
prepare us boats, that we might go all the way to Kamrasi's by
water. Viarŭngi made a petition, on Rŭmanika's behalf, for an
army of Waganda to go to Karagué, and fight the refractory
brother, Rogéro; but this was refused, on the plea that the whole

army was out fighting at the present moment. The court then broke up and we went home.

To keep the king up to the mark and seal our passage, in the evening I took a Lancaster rifle, with ammunition, and the iron chair he formerly asked for, as a parting present, to the palace, but did not find him, as he had gone out shooting with his brothers.

4th. Grant and I now called together on the king to present the rifle, chair, and ammunition, as we could not thank him in words sufficiently for the favor he had done us in granting the road through Unyoro. I said the parting gift was not half as much as I should like to have been able to give; but we hoped, on reaching Gani, to send Petherick up to him with every thing that he could desire. We regretted we had no more powder or shot, as what was intended, and actually placed out expressly to be presented on this occasion, was stolen. The king looked hard at his head page, who was once sent to get these very things now given, and then turning the subject adroitly, asked me how many cows and women I would like, holding his hand up with spread fingers, and desiring me to count by hundreds; but the reply was, Five cows and goats would be enough, for we wished to travel lightly in boats, starting from the Murchison Creek. Women were declined on such grounds as would seem rational to him. But if the king would clothe my naked men with one mbŭgŭ (bark cloth) each, and give a small tusk each to nine Wanyamŭézi porters, who desired to return to their home, the obligation would be great.

Every thing was granted without the slightest hesitation; and then the king, turning to me, said, "Well, Bana, so you really wish to go?" "Yes, for I have not seen my home for four years and upward"—reckoning five months to the year, Uganda fashion "And you can give me no stimulants?" "No." "Then you will send me some from Gani—brandy if you like; it makes people sleep sound, and gives them strength." Next we went to the queen to bid farewell, but did not see her.

On returning home I found half my men in a state of mutiny. They had been on their own account to beg for the women and cows which had been refused, saying, If Bana does not want them, we do, for we have been starved here ever since we came, and when we go for food get broken heads; we will not serve with Bana any longer; but, as he goes north, we will return to Kara-

gŭé and Unyanyembé. Bombay, however, told them they never
had fed so well in all their lives as they had in Uganda, counting
from fifty to sixty cows killed, and pombé and plantains every
day, whenever they took the trouble to forage; and for their
broken heads they invariably received a compensation in wom-
en, so that Bana had reason to regret every day spent in asking
for food for them at the palace—a favor which none but his men
received, but which they had not, as they might have done, turned
to good effect by changing the system of plundering for food in
Uganda.

5th. By the king's order we attended at the palace early. The
gun obtained us all a speedy admittance, when the king opened
conversation by saying, "Well, Bana, so you really are going?"
"Yes; I have enjoyed your hospitality for a long time, and now
wish to return to my home." "What provision do you want?"
I said, Five cows and five goats, as we sha'n't be long in Uganda;
and it is not the custom of our country, when we go visiting, to
carry any thing away with us. The king then said, "Well, I
wish to give you much, but you won't have it;" when Budja
spoke out, saying, "Bana does not know the country he has to
travel through; there is nothing but jungle and famine on the
way, and he must have cows;" on which the king ordered us
sixty cows, fourteen goats, ten loads of butter, a load of coffee and
tobacco, one hundred sheets of mbŭgŭ as clothes for my men, at
a suggestion of Bombay's, as all my cloth had been expended
even before I left Karagŭé.

This magnificent order created a pause, which K'yengo took
advantage of by producing a little bundle of peculiarly-shaped
sticks and a lump of earth, all of which have their own particular
magical powers, as K'yengo described to the king's satisfaction.
After this, Viarŭngi pleaded the cause of my mutinous followers
till I shook my finger angrily at him before the king, rebuked
him for intermeddling in other people's affairs, and told my own
story, which gained the sympathy of the king, and induced him
to say, "Supposing they desert Bana, what road do they expect
to get?" Maŭla was now appointed to go with Rozaro to Karagŭé for the powder and other things promised yesterday, while
Viarŭngi and all his party, though exceedingly anxious to get
away, had orders to remain here prisoners as a surety for the
things arriving. Farther, Kaddŭ and two other wakungŭ received
orders to go to Usŭi with two tusks of ivory to purchase gun-

powder, caps, and flints, failing which they would proceed to Unyanyembé, and even to Zanzibar, for the king must not be disappointed, and failure would cost them their lives.

Not another word was said, and away the two parties went, with no more arrangement than a set of geese—Maŭla without a letter, and Kaddŭ without any provision for the way, as if all the world belonged to Mtésa, and he could help himself from any man's garden that he liked, no matter where he was. In the evening my men made a humble petition for their discharge, even if I did not pay them, producing a hundred reasons for wishing to leave, but none which would stand a moment's argument: the fact was, they were afraid of the road to Unyoro, thinking I had not sufficient ammunition.

6th. I visited the king, and asked leave for boats to go at once; but the fleet admiral put a veto on this by making out that dangerous shallows exist between the Murchison Creek and the Kira district station, so that the boats of one place never visit the other; and, farther, if we went to Kira, we should find impracticable cataracts to the Urondogani boat-station; our better plan would therefore be to deposit our property at the Urondogani station, and walk by land up the river, if a sight of the falls at the mouth of the lake was of such material consequence to us.

Of course this man carried every thing his own way, for there was nobody able to contradict him, and we could not afford time to visit Usoga first, lest by the delay we might lose an opportunity of communicating with Petherick. Grant now took a portrait of Mtésa by royal permission, the king sitting as quietly as his impatient nature would permit. Then at home the Wanyamŭézi porters received their tusks of ivory, weighing from 16 to 50 lbs. each, and took a note besides on Rŭmanika each for twenty fundo of beads, barring one Bogŭé man, who, having lent a cloth to the expedition some months previously, thought it would not be paid him, and therefore seized a sword as security; the consequence was, his tusk was seized until the sword was returned, and he was dismissed minus his beads for having so misconducted himself. The impudent fellow then said, "It will be well for Bana if he succeeds in getting the road through Unyoro; for, should he fail, I will stand in his path at Bogŭé." Kitŭnzi offered an ivory for beads, and when told we were not merchants, and advised to try K'yengo, he said he dared not even approach K'yengo's camp lest people should tell the king of it, and accuse him of seeking for magical powers against his sovereign. Old Nasib begged for his discharge. It was granted, and he took a $50 letter on the coast, and a letter of emancipation for himself and family, besides an order, written in Kisŭahili, for ten fundo of beads on Rŭmanika, which made him very happy.

In the evening we called again at the palace with pictures of the things the king required from Rŭmanika, and a letter informing Rŭmanika what we wished done with them, in order that there might be no mistake, requesting the king to forward them after Maŭla. Just then Kaddŭ's men returned to say they wanted provisions for the way, as the Wazinza, hearing of their mission, asked them if they knew what they were about, going to a strange country without any means of paying their way. But the king, instead of listening to reason, impetuously said, "If you do not pack off at once, and bring me the things I want, every man of you shall lose his head; and as for the Wazinza, for interfering with my orders, they shall be kept here prisoners until you return."

On the way home, one of the king's favorite women overtook us, walking, with her hands clasped at the back of her head, to execution, crying "N'yawo!" in the most pitiful manner. A man was preceding her, but did not touch her; for she loved to obey the orders of her king voluntarily, and, in consequence of previous attachment, was permitted, as a mark of distinction, to walk free. Wondrous world! it was not ten minutes since we parted from the king, yet he had found time to transact this bloody piece of business.

7th. Early in the morning the king bade us come to him to say farewell. Wishing to leave behind a favorable impression, I instantly complied. On the breast of my coat I suspended the necklace the queen had given me, as well as his knife and my medals. I talked with him in as friendly and flattering a manner as I could, dwelling on his shooting, the pleasant cruising on the lake, and our sundry picnics, as well as the grand prospect there was now of opening the country to trade, by which his guns, the best in the world, would be fed with powder, and other small matters of a like nature, to which he replied with great feeling and good taste. We then all rose with an English bow, placing the hand on the heart while saying adieu; and there was a complete uniformity in the ceremonial, for, whatever I did, Mtésa, in an instant, mimicked with the instinct of a monkey.

We had, however, scarcely quitted the palace gate before the king issued himself, with his attendants and his brothers leading, and women bringing up the rear; here K'yengo and all the Wazinza joined in the procession with ourselves, they kneeling and clapping their hands after the fashion of their own country. Budja just then made me feel.very anxious by pointing out the position of Urondogani, as I thought; too far north. I called the king's attention to it, and in a moment he said he would speak to Budja in such a manner that would leave no doubts in my mind, for he liked me much, and desired to please me in all things. As the procession now drew close to our camp, and Mtésa expressed a wish to have a final look at my men, I ordered them to turn out with their arms and n'yanzig for the many favors they had received. Mtésa, much pleased, complimented them on their goodly appearance, remarking that with such a force I would have no difficulty in reaching Gani, and exhorted them to follow me through fire and water; then, exchanging adieus again, he walked ahead in gigantic strides up the hill, the pretty favorite of his harem, Lŭbŭga—beckoning and waving with her little hands, and crying "Bana! Bana!"—trotting after him conspicuous among the rest, though all showed a little feeling at the severance. We saw them no more.

CHAPTER XV.

MARCH DOWN THE NORTHERN SLOPES OF AFRICA.

Kari.—Tragic Incident there.—Renewal of Troubles.—Quarrels with the Natives.—
Reach the Nile.—Description of the Scene there.—Sport.—Church Estate.—Ascend the River to the Junction with the Lake.—Ripon Falls.—General Account
of the Source of the Nile.—Descend again to Urondogani.—The truculent Sakibobo.

7th to *11th.* With Budja appointed as the general director, a
lieutenant of the sakibobo's to furnish us with sixty cows in his
division at the first halting-place, and Kasoro (Mr. Cat), a lieutenant of Jumba's, to provide the boats at Urondogani, we started at
1 P.M. on the journey northward. The Wangŭana still grumbled,
swearing they would carry no loads, as they got no rations, and
threatening to shoot us if we pressed them, forgetting that their
food had been paid for to the king in rifles, chronometers, and
other articles, costing about $2000, and, what was more to the
point, that all the ammunition was in our hands. A
judicious threat of the stick, however, put things
right, and on we marched five successive days to Kari
—as the place was afterward named, in consequence
of the tragedy mentioned below—the whole distance
accomplished being thirty miles from the capital, through a fine
hilly country, with jungles and rich cultivation alternating. The
second march, after crossing the Katawana River, with its many
branches flowing northeast into the huge rush-drain of Lŭajerri,
carried us beyond the influence of the higher hills, and away from
the huge grasses which characterize the southern boundary of
Uganda bordering on the lake.

Each day's march to Kari was directed much in the same manner. After a certain number of hours' traveling, Budja appointed
some village of residence for the night, avoiding those which belonged to the queen, lest any rows should take place in them,
which would create disagreeable consequences with the king, and
preferring those the heads of which had been lately seized by the
orders of the king. Nevertheless, wherever we went, all the vil-

To Namavundŭ,
7th.
To Nasiré, 8th.
To Namaouja,
9th.
To Baja, 10th.
To Kari, 11th.

lagers forsook their homes, and left their houses, property, and gardens an easy prey to the thieving propensities of the escort. To put a stop to this vile practice was now beyond my power; the king allowed it, and his men were the first in every house, taking goats, fowls, skins, mbŭgŭs, cowries, beads, drums, spears, tobacco, pombé—in short, every thing they could lay their hands on—in the most ruthless manner. It was a perfect marauding campaign for them all, and all alike were soon laden with as much as they could carry.

A halt of some days had become necessary at Kari to collect the cows given by the king; and, as it is one of his most extensive pasture-grounds, I strolled with my rifle (11th) to see what new animals could be found; but no sooner did I wound a zebra than messengers came running after me to say Kari, one of my men, had been murdered by the villagers three miles off; and such was the fact. He, with others of my men, had been induced to go plundering, with a few boys of the Waganda escort, to a certain village of potters, as pots were required by Budja for making plantain wine, the first thing ever thought of when a camp is formed. On nearing the place, however, the women of the village, who were the only people visible, instead of running away, as our braves expected, commenced hullalooing, and brought out their husbands. Flight was now the only thought of our men, and all would have escaped had Kari not been slow and his musket empty. The potters overtook him, and, as he pointed his gun, which they considered a magic horn, they speared him to death, and then fled at once. Our survivors were not long in bringing the news into camp, when a party went out, and in the evening brought in the man's corpse and every thing belonging to him, for nothing had been taken.

12th. To enable me at my leisure to trace up the Nile to its exit from the lake, and then go on with the journey as quickly as possible, I wished the cattle to be collected and taken by Budja and some of my men with the heavy baggage overland to Kamrasi's. Another reason for doing so was, that I thought it advisable Kamrasi should be forewarned that we were coming by the water route, lest we should be suspected and stopped as spies by his officers on the river, or regarded as enemies, which would provoke a fight. Budja, however, objected to move until a report of Kari's murder had been forwarded to the king, lest the people, getting bumptious, should try the same trick again; and Kasoro said he would not go up the river, as he had received no orders to do so.

In this fix I ordered a march back to the palace, mentioning the king's last words, and should have gone, had not Budja ordered Kasoro to go with me. A page then arrived from the king to ask after Bana's health, carrying the Whitworth rifle as his master's card, and begging for a heavy double-barreled gun to be sent him from Gani. I called this lad to witness the agreement I had made with Budja, and told him, if Kasoro satisfied me, I would return by him, in addition to the heavy gun, a Massey's patent log. I had taken it for the navigation of the lake, and it was now of no farther use to me, but, being an instrument of complicated structure, it would be a valuable addition to the king's museum of magic charms. I added I should like the king to send me the robes of honor and spears he had once promised me, in order that I might, on reaching England, be able to show my countrymen a specimen of the manufactures of his country. The men who were with Kari were now sent to the palace, under accusation of having led him into ambush, and a complaint was made against the villagers, which we waited the reply to. As Budja forbade it, no men would follow me out shooting, saying the villagers were out surrounding our camp, and threatening destruction on any one who dared show his face; for this was not the high road to Uganda, and therefore no one had a right to turn them out of their houses and pillage their gardens.

13th. Budja lost two cows given to his party last night, and, seeing ours securely tied by their legs to trees, asked by what spells we had secured them, and would not believe our assurance that the ropes that bound them were all the medicines we knew of. One of the queen's sisters, hearing of Kari's murder, came on a visit to condole with us, bringing a pot of pombé, for which she received some beads. On being asked how many sisters the queen had, for we could not help suspecting some imposition, she replied she was the only one, till assured ten other ladies had presented themselves as the queen's sisters before, when she changed her tone, and said, "That is true, I am not the only one; but if I had told you the truth I might have lost my head." This was a significant expression of the danger of telling court secrets.

I suspected that there must be a considerable quantity of game in this district, as stake-nets and other traps were found in all the huts, as well as numbers of small antelope hoofs spitted on pipe-sticks—an ornament which is counted the special badge of the sportsman in this part of Africa. Despite, therefore, of the warnings of Budja, I strolled again with my rifle, and saw pallah, small plovers, and green antelopes with straight horns, called mpéo, the skin of which makes a favorite apron for the Mabandwa.

14*th.* I met to-day a Mhŭma cowherd in my strolls with the rifle, and asked him if he knew where the game lay. The unmannerly creature, standing among a thousand of the sleekest cattle, gruffishly replied, "What can I know of any other animals than cows?" and went on with his work as if nothing in the world could interest him but his cattle-tending. I shot a doe lencotis, called here n'sunnŭ, the first one seen upon the journey.

15*th.* In the morning, when our men went for water to the springs, some Waganda in ambush threw a spear at them, and this time caught a Tartar, for the "horns," as they called their guns, were loaded, and two of them received shot-wounds. In the evening, while we were returning from shooting, a party of Waganda, also lying in the bush, called out to know what we were about; saying, "Is it not enough that you have turned us out of our homes and plantations, leaving us to live like animals in the wilderness?" and when told we were only searching for sport, would not believe that our motive was any other than hostility to themselves.

At night one of Budja's men returned from the palace to say the king was highly pleased with the measures adopted by his wakungŭ in prosecution of Kari's affair. He hoped now, as we had cows to eat, there would be no necessity for wandering for food, but all would keep together "in one garden." At present no notice would be taken of the murderers, as all the culprits would have fled far away in their fright to escape chastisement. But when a little time had elapsed, and all would appear to have been forgotten, officers would be sent and the miscreants apprehended, for it was impossible to suppose any body could be ignorant of the white men being the guests of the king, considering they had lived at the palace so long. The king took this opportunity again to remind me that he wanted a heavy solid double gun, such as would last him all his life; and intimated that in a few days the arms and robes of honor were to be sent.

16*th.* Most of the cows for ourselves and the guides—for the king gave them also a present, ten each—were driven into camp.

We also got 50 lbs. of butter, the remainder to be picked up on the way. I strolled with the gun, and shot two zebras, to be sent to the king, as, by the constitution of Uganda, he alone can keep their royal skins.

17th. We had to halt again, as the guides had lost most of their cows, so I strolled with my rifle and shot a ndjezza doe, the first I had ever seen. It is a brown animal, a little smaller than the lencotis, and frequents much the same kind of ground.

18th. We had still to wait another day for Budja's cows, when, as it appeared all-important to communicate quickly with Petherick, and as Grant's leg was considered too weak for traveling fast, we took counsel together and altered our plans. I arranged that Grant should go to Kamrasi's direct with the property, cattle, and women, taking my letters and a map for immediate dispatch to Petherick at Gani, while I should go up the river to its source or exit from the lake, and come down again navigating as far as practicable.

At night the Waganda startled us by setting fire to the huts our men were sleeping in, but providentially did more damage to themselves than to us, for one sword only was buried in the fire, while their own huts, intended to be vacated in the morning, were burnt to the ground. To fortify ourselves against another invasion, we cut down all their plantains to make a boma or fence.

We started all together on our respective journeys; but, after the third mile, Grant turned west, to join the high road to Kamrasi's, while I went east for Urondogani, crossing the Lŭajerri, a huge rush-drain three miles broad, fordable nearly to the right bank, where we had to ferry in boats, and the cows to be swum over with men holding on to their tails. It was larger than the Katonga, and more tedious to cross, for it took no less than four hours, musquitoes in myriads biting our bare backs and legs all the while. The Lŭajerri is said to rise in the lake and fall into the Nile due south of our crossing-point. On the right bank wild buffalo are described to be as numerous as cows, but we did not see any, though the country is covered with a most inviting jungle for sport, with intermediate lays of fine grazing grass. Such is the nature of the country all the way to Urondogani, except in some favored spots, kept as tidily as in any part of Uganda, where plantains grow in the utmost luxuriance. From want of guides, and misguided by

Cross the Lŭa-
jerri, 19th.
To Kiwŭkéri,
20th.

the exclusive ill-natured Wahŭma, who were here in great numbers tending their king's cattle, we lost our way continually, so
that we did not reach the boat-station until the morning of the
21st.

Here at last I stood on the brink of the Nile.   Most beautiful
To Urondogani,   was the scene; nothing could surpass it!   It was the
21st.   very perfection of the kind of effect aimed at in a
highly-kept park; with a magnificent stream from 600 to 700
yards wide, dotted with islets and rocks, the former occupied by
fishermen's huts, the latter by sterns and crocodiles basking in
the sun, flowing between fine high grassy banks, with rich trees
and plantains in the background, where herds of the n'sunnŭ and
hartebeest could be seen grazing, while the hippopotami were
snorting in the water, and florikan and Guinea-fowl rising at our
feet.   Unfortunately, the chief district officer, Mlondo, was from
home, but we took possession of his huts—clean, extensive, and
tidily kept—facing the river, and felt as if a residence here would
do one good.   Delays and subterfuges, however, soon came to
damp our spirits.   The acting officer was sent for, and asked for
the boats; they were all scattered, and could not be collected for
a day or two; but, even if they were at hand, no boat ever went
up or down the river.   The chief was away and would be sent
for, as the king often changed his orders, and, after all, might not
mean what had been said.   The district belonged to the sakibobo,
and no representative of his had come here.   These excuses, of
course, would not satisfy us.   The boats must be collected, seven,
if there are not ten, for we must try them, and come to some understanding about them, before we march up stream, when, if the
officer values his life, he will let us have them, and acknowledge
Kasoro as the king's representative, otherwise a complaint will be
sent to the palace, for we won't stand trifling.

We were now confronting Usoga, a country which may be said
to be the very counterpart of Uganda in its richness and beauty.
Here the people use such huge iron-headed spears with short
handles, that, on seeing one to-day, my people remarked that they
were better fitted for digging potatoes than piercing men.   Elephants, as we had seen by their devastations during the last two
marches, were very numerous in this neighborhood.   Till lately,
a party from Unyoro, ivory-hunting, had driven them away.
Lions were also described as very numerous and destructive to
human life.   Antelopes were common in the jungle, and the hip-

popotami, though frequenters of the plantain garden and constantly heard, were seldom seen on land in consequence of their un-
steady habits.

The king's page again came, begging I would not forget the
gun and stimulants, and bringing with him the things I asked for
—two spears, one shield, one dirk, two leopard-cat skins, and two
sheets of small antelope skins. I told my men they ought to
shave their heads and bathe in the holy river, the cradle of Moses
—the waters of which, sweetened with sugar, men carry all the
way from Egypt to Mecca, and sell to the pilgrims. But Bombay, who is a philosopher of the Epicurean school, said, "We
don't look on those things in the same fanciful manner that you
do; we are contented with all the commonplaces of life, and look
for nothing beyond the present. If things don't go well, it is
God's will; and if they do go well, that is His will also."

22*d*. The acting chief brought a present of one cow, one goat,
and pombé, with a mob of his courtiers to pay his respects. He
promised that the seven boats, which are all the station could
muster, would be ready next day, and in the mean while a number of men would conduct me to the shooting-ground. He asked
to be shown the books of birds and animals, and no sooner saw
some specimens of Wolff's handiwork, than, in utter surprise, he
exclaimed, "I know how these are done; a bird was caught and
stamped upon the paper," using action to his words, and showing
what he meant, while all his followers n'yanzigged for the favor
of the exhibition.

In the evening I strolled in the antelope parks, enjoying the
scenery and sport excessively. A noble buck n'sunnŭ, standing
by himself, was the first thing seen this side, though a herd of
hartebeests were grazing on the Usoga banks. One bullet rolled
my fine friend over, but the rabble looking on no sooner saw the
hit than they rushed upon him and drove him off, for he was only
wounded. A chase ensued, and he was tracked by his blood,
when a pongo (bush boc) was started and divided the party. It
also brought me to another single buck n'sunnŭ, which was floored
at once, and left to be carried home by some of my men in company with Waganda, while I went on, shot a third n'sunnŭ buck,
and tracked him by his blood till dark, for the bullet had pierced
his lungs and passed out on the other side. Failing to find him
on the way home, I shot, besides florikan and Guinea-chicks, a
wonderful goatsucker, remarkable for the exceeding length of

some of its feathers floating out far beyond the rest in both wings.*
Returning home, I found the men who had charge of the dead

Goatsucker (Cosmetornis Spekii).

buck all in a state of excitement; they no sooner removed his
carcass than two lions came out of the jungle and lapped his
blood. All the Waganda ran away at once; but my braves
feared my anger more than the lions, and came off safely with
the buck on their shoulders.

23d. Three boats arrived, like those used on the Murchison
Creek, and when I demanded the rest, as well as a decisive answer
about going to Kamrasi's, the acting mkungŭ said he was afraid
accidents might happen, and he would not take me. Nothing
would frighten this pig-headed creature into compliance, though
I told him I had arranged with the king to make the Nile the
channel of communication with England. I therefore applied to
him for guides to conduct me up the river, and ordered Bombay
and Kasoro to obtain fresh orders from the king, as all future wazungŭ, coming to Uganda to visit or trade, would prefer the passage by the river. I shot another buck in the evening, as the
Waganda loved their skins, and also a load of Guinea-fowl—

* Named by Dr. P. L. Sclater *Cosmetornis Spekii.* The seventh pen feathers are
double the length of the ordinaries, the eighth double that of the seventh, and the
ninth 20 inches long. Bombay says the same bird is found in Uhiyow.

three, four, and five at a shot—as Kasoro and his boys prefer them to any thing.

24*th.* The acting officer absconded, but another man came in his place, and offered to take us on the way up the river to-mor-row, humbugging Kasoro into the belief that his road to the pal-ace would branch off from the first stage, though in reality it was here. The mkungŭ's women brought pombé, and spent the day gazing at us, till, in the evening, when I took up my rifle, one ran after Bana to see him shooč, and followed like a man; but the only sport she got was on an ant-hill, where she fixed herself some time, popping into her mouth and devouring the white ants as fast as they emanated from their cells; for, disdaining does, I missed the only pongo buck I got a shot at in my anxiety to show the fair one what she came for.

Reports came to-day of new cruelties at the palace. Kasoro improved on their off-hand manslaughter by saying that two kamravionas and two sakibobos, as well as all the old wakungŭ of Sunna's time, had been executed by the orders of King Mtésa. He told us, moreover, that if Mtésa ever has a dream that his father directs him to kill any body as being dangerous to his per-son, the order is religiously kept. I wished to send a message to Mtésa by an officer who is starting at once to pay his respects at court; but, although he received it, and promised to deliver it, Ka-soro laughed at me for expecting that one word of it would ever reach the king; for, however appropriate or important the matter might be, it was more than any body dare do to tell the king, as it would be an infringement of the rule that no one is to speak to him unless in answer to a question. My second buck of the first day was brought in by the natives, but they would not allow it to approach the hut until it had been skinned; and I found their reason to be a superstition that otherwise no others would ever be killed by the inmates of that establishment.

I marched up the left bank of the Nile, at a considerable dis-
To Isamba Rap-   tance from the water, to the Isamba Rapids, passing
ids, 25*th.*   through rich jungle and plantain gardens. Nango, an old friend, and district officer of the place, first refreshed us with a dish of plantain-squash and dried fish, with pombé. He told us he is often threatened by elephants, but he sedulously keeps them off with charms; for if they ever tasted a plantain they would never leave the garden until they had cleared it out. He then took us to see the nearest falls of the Nile—extremely

beautiful, but very confined. The water ran deep between its banks, which were covered with fine grass, soft cloudy acacias, and festoons of lilac convolvuli; while here and there, where the land had slipped above the rapids, bared places of red earth could be seen, like that of Devonshire; there, too, the waters, impeded by a natural dam, looked like a huge mill-pond, sullen and dark, in which two crocodiles, laving about, were looking out for prey. From the high banks we looked down upon a line of sloping wooded islets lying across the stream, which divide its waters, and, by interrupting them, cause at once both dam and rapids. The whole was more fairy-like, wild, and romantic than—I must confess that my thoughts took that shape—any thing I ever saw outside of a theatre. It was exactly the sort of place, in fact, where, bridged across from one side-slip to the other, on a moonlight night, brigands would assemble to enact some dreadful tragedy. Even the Wangŭana seemed spell-bound at the novel beauty of the sight, and no one thought of moving till hunger warned us night was setting in, and we had better look out for lodgings.

Start again, and after drinking pombé with Nango, when we heard that three wakungŭ had been seized at Kari in consequence of the murder, the march was recommenced, but soon after stopped by the mischievous machinations of our guide, who pretended it was too late in the day to cross the jungles on ahead, either by the road to the source or the palace, and therefore would not move till the morning; then, leaving us on the pretext of business, he vanished, and was never seen again. A small black fly, with thick shoulders and bullet-head, infests the place, and torments the naked arms and legs of the people with its sharp stings to an extent that must render life miserable to them.

To Kirindi, 26th.

After a long struggling march, plodding through huge grasses and jungle, we reached a district which I can not otherwise describe than by calling it a "Church Estate." It is dedicated in some mysterious manner to Lŭbari (Almighty), and although the king appeared to have authority over some of the inhabitants of it, yet others had apparently a sacred character, exempting them from the civil power, and he had no right to dispose of the land itself. In this territory there are small villages only at every fifth mile, for there is no road, and the lands run high again, while, from want of a guide, we often lost the track. It now transpired that Budja, when he told at the palace that

To Church Estate, 27th.

there was no road down the banks of the Nile, did so in consequence of his fear that if he sent my whole party here they would
rob these church lands, and so bring him into a scrape with the
wizards or ecclèsiastical authorities. Had my party not been under control, we could not have put up here; but on my being answerable that no thefts should take place, the people kindly consented to provide us with board and lodgings, and we found them
very obliging. One elderly man, half-witted—they said the king
had driven his senses from him by seizing his house and family
—came at once on hearing of our arrival, laughing and singing
in a loose, jaunty, maniacal manner, carrying odd sticks, shells,
and a bundle of mbŭgŭ rags, which he deposited before me, dancing and singing again, then retreating and bringing some more,
with a few plantains from a garden, which I was to eat, as kings
lived upon flesh, and "poor Tom" wanted some, for he lived with
lions and elephants in a hovel beyond the gardens, and his belly
was empty. He was precisely a black specimen of the English
parish idiot.

At last, with a good push for it, crossing hills and threading
To Ripon Falls, 28th. huge grasses, as well as extensive village plantations
lately devastated by elephants — they had eaten all
that was eatable, and what would not serve for food they had destroyed with their trunks, not one plantain nor one hut being left
entire—we arrived at the extreme end of the journey, the farthest
point ever visited by the expedition on the same parallel of latitude as King Mtésa's palace, and just forty miles east of it.

We were well rewarded; for the "stones," as the Waganda
call the falls, was by far the most interesting sight I had seen in
Africa. Every body ran to see them at once, though the march
had been long and fatiguing, and even my sketch-block was called
into play. Though beautiful, the scene was not exactly what I
expected; for the broad surface of the lake was shut out from
view by a spur of hill, and the falls, about 12 feet deep, and 400
to 500 feet broad, were broken by rocks. Still it was a sight that
attracted one to it for hours—the roar of the waters, the thousands
of passenger-fish, leaping at the falls with all their might, the Wasoga and Waganda fishermen coming out in boats and taking post
on all the rocks with rod and hook, hippopotami and crocodiles
lying sleepily on the water, the ferry at work above the falls, and
cattle driven down to drink at the margin of the lake, made, in
all, with the pretty nature of the country—small hills, grassy-top-

THE RIPON FALLS—THE NILE FLOWING OUT OF VICTORIA N'YANZA.

ped, with trees in the folds, and gardens on the lower slopes—as interesting a picture as one could wish to see.·

The expedition had now performed its functions. I saw that old Father Nile without any doubt rises in the Victoria N'yanza, and, as I had foretold, that lake is the great source of the holy river, which cradled the first expounder of our religious belief. I mourned, however, when I thought how much I had lost by the delays in the journey having deprived me of the pleasure of going to look at the northeast corner of the N'yanza to see what connection there was, by the strait so often spoken of, with it and the other lake where the Waganda went to get their salt, and from which another river flowed to the north, making " Usoga an island." But I felt I ought to be content with what I had been spared to accomplish; for I had seen full half of the lake, and had information given me of the other half, by means of which I knew all about the lake, as far, at least, as the chief objects of geographical importance were concerned.

Let us now sum up the whole and see what it is worth. Comparative information assured me that there was as much water on the eastern side of the lake as there is on the western—if any thing, rather more. The most remote waters, *or top head of the Nile*, is the southern end of the lake, situated close on the third degree of south latitude, which gives to the Nile the surprising length, in direct measurement, rolling over thirty-four degrees of latitude, of above 2300 miles, or more than one eleventh of the circumference of our globe. Now from this southern point, round by the west, to where the *great* Nile stream issues, there is only one feeder of any importance, and that is the Kitangŭlé River; while from the southernmost point, round by the east, to the strait, there are no rivers at all of any importance; for the traveled Arabs one and all aver, that from the west of the snow-clad Kilimandjaro to the lake where it is cut by the second degree, and also the first degree of south latitude, there are salt lakes and salt plains, and the country is hilly, not unlike Unyamŭézi; but they said there were no great rivers, and the country was so scantily watered, having only occasional runnels and rivulets, that they always had to make long marches in order to find water when they went on their trading journeys; and farther, those Arabs who crossed the strait when they reached Usoga, as mentioned before, during the late interregnum, crossed no river either.

There remains to be disposed of the "salt lake," which I believe is not a salt, but a fresh-water lake; and my reasons are, as before stated, that the natives call all lakes salt if they find salt beds or salt islands in such places. Dr. Krapf, when he obtained a sight of the Kenia Mountain, heard from the natives there that there was a salt lake to its northward, and he also heard that a river ran from Kenia toward the Nile. If his information was true on this latter point, then, without doubt, there must exist some connection between his river and the salt lake I have heard of, and this, in all probability, would also establish a connection between my salt lake and his salt lake, which he heard was called Baringo.* In no view that can be taken of it, however, does this unsettled matter touch the established fact that the head of the Nile is in 3° south latitude, where, in the year 1858, I discovered the head of the Victoria N'yanza to be.

I now christened the "stones" Ripon Falls, after the nobleman who presided over the Royal Geographical Society when my expedition was got up; and the arm of water from which the Nile issued, Napoleon Channel, in token of respect to the French Geographical Society, for the honor they had done me, just before leaving England, in presenting me with their gold medal for the discovery of the Victoria N'yanza. One thing seemed at first perplexing—the volume of water in the Kitangŭlé looked as large as that of the Nile; but then the one was a slow river and the other swift, and on this account I could form no adequate judgment of their relative values.

Not satisfied with my first sketch of the falls, I could not resist Ripon Falls, 29th. sketching them again; and then, as the cloudy state of the weather prevented my observing for latitude, and the officer of the place said a magnificent view of the lake could be obtained from the hill alluded to as intercepting the view from the falls, we proposed going there; but Kasoro, who had been indulged with n'sunnŭ antelope skins, and with Guinea-fowl for dinner, resisted this, on the plea that I never should be satisfied. There were orders given only to see the "stones," and if he took me to one hill I should wish to see another and another, and so on. It made me laugh, for that had been my nature all my life; but, vexed at heart, and wishing to trick the young tyrant, I asked for boats to shoot hippopotami, in the hope of reaching the hills to picnic; but boating had never been ordered,

* It is questionable whether or not this word is a corruption of Bahr (sea of) Ingo.

and he would not listen to it. "Then bring fish," I said, that I might draw them: no, that was not ordered. "Then go you to the palace, and leave me to go to Urondogani to-morrow, after I have taken a latitude;" but the willful creature would not go until he saw me under way. And as nobody would do any thing for me without Kasoro's orders, I amused the people by firing at the ferry-boat upon the Usoga side, which they defied me to hit, the distance being 500 yards; but, nevertheless, a bullet went through her, and was afterward brought by the Wasoga nicely folded up in a piece of mbŭgŭ. Bombay then shot a sleeping crocodile with his carbine, while I spent the day out watching the falls.

This day also I spent watching the fish flying at the falls, and
Ripon Falls, 30th.
felt as if I only wanted a wife and family, garden and yacht, rifle and rod, to make me happy here for life, so charming was the place. What a place, I thought to myself, this would be for missionaries! They never could fear starvation, the land is so rich; and, if farming were introduced by them, they might have hundreds of pupils. I need say no more.

In addition to the rod-and-line fishing, a number of men, armed with long heavy poles with two iron spikes, tied prong-fashion to one end, rushed to a place over a break in the falls, which tired fish seemed to use as a baiting-room, dashed in their forks, holding on by the shaft, and sent men down to disengage the pinned fish and relieve their spears. The shot they make in this manner is a blind one—only on the chance of fish being there— and therefore always doubtful in its result.

Church Estate again. As the clouds and Kasoro's willfulness
Return, 31st.
were still against me, and the weather did not give hopes of a change, I sacrificed the taking of the latitude to gain time. I sent Bombay with Kasoro to the palace, asking for the sakibobo himself to be sent with an order for five boats, five cows, and five goats, and also for a general order to go where I like, and do what I like, and have fish supplied me; "for, though I know the king likes me, his officers do not; and then, on separating, I retraced my steps to the Church Estate.

1st. To-day, after marching an hour, as there was now no need for hurrying, and a fine pongo buck, the ngubbi of Uganda, offered a tempting shot, I proposed to shoot it for the men, and breakfast in a neighboring village. This being agreed to, the animal was dispatched, and we no sooner entered the village than

we heard that n'samma, a magnificent description of antelope,
abound in the long grasses close by, and that a rogue elephant
frequents the plantains every night.   This tempting news created
a halt.   In the evening I killed a n'samma doe, an animal very
much like the Kobus Ellipsiprymnus, but without the lunated
mark over the rump; and at night, about 1 A.M., turned out to
shoot an elephant, which we distinctly heard feasting on plantains; but rain was falling, and the night so dark, he was left till
the morning.

2d. I followed up the elephant some way, till a pongo offering
an irresistible shot, I sent a bullet through him, but he was lost
after hours' tracking in the interminable large grasses.   An enormous snake, with fearful mouth and fangs, was speared by the
men.   In the evening I wounded a buck n'samma, which, after

N'samma Antelope—Uganda.

tracking till dark, was left to stiffen ere the following morning;
and just after this, on the way home, we heard the rogue elephant

crunching the branches not far off from the track; but as no one would dare follow me against the monster at this late hour, he was reluctantly left to do more injury to the gardens.

3*d*. After a warm search in the morning we found the n'samma buck lying in some water; the men tried to spear him, but he stood at bay, and took another bullet. This was all we wanted, affording one good specimen; so, after breakfast, we marched to Kirindi, where the villagers, hearing of the sport we had had, and excited with the hopes of getting flesh, begged us to halt a day.

4*th*. Not crediting the stories told by the people about the sport here, we packed to leave, but were no sooner ready than several men ran hastily in to say some fine bucks were waiting to be shot close by. This was too powerful a temptation to be withstood; so, shouldering the rifle, and followed by half the village, if not more, women included, we went to the place, but, instead of finding a buck—for the men had stretched a point to keep me at their village—we found a herd of does, and shot one at the people's urgent request.

We reached this in one stretch, and put up in our old quarters, where the women of Mlondo provided pombé, plantains, and potatoes, as before, with occasional fish, and we lived very happily till the 10th, shooting buck, Guinea-fowl, and florikan, when, Bombay and Kasoro arriving, my work began again. These two worthies reached the palace after crossing twelve considerable streams, of which one was the Lŭajerri, rising in the lake. The evening of the next day after leaving me at Kira they obtained an interview with the king immediately; for the thought flashed across his mind that Bombay had come to report our death, the Waganda having been too much for the party. He was speedily undeceived by the announcement that nothing was the matter excepting the inability to procure boats, because the officers at Urondogani denied all authority but the sakibobo's, and no one would show Bana any thing, however trifling, without an express order for it.

Irate at this announcement, the king ordered the sakibobo, who happened to be present, to be seized and bound at once, and said warmly, " Pray, who is the king, that the sakibobo's orders should be preferred to mine?" and then, turning to the sakibobo himself, asked what he would pay to be released. The sakibobo, alive to his danger, replied at once, and without the slightest hesitation, Eighty cows, eighty goats, eighty slaves, eighty mbŭgŭ, eighty

butter, eighty coffee, eighty tobacco, eighty jowari, and eighty of
all the produce of Uganda. He was then released. Bombay said
Bana wished the sakibobo to come to Urondogani, and give him
a start with five boats, five cows, and five goats; to which the
king replied, "Bana shall have all he wants; nothing shall be denied him, not even fish; but it is not necessary to send the sakibobo, as boys carry all my orders to kings as well as subjects.
Kasoro will return again with you, fully instructed in every thing,
and, moreover, both he and Budja will follow Bana to Gani."
Four days, however, my men were kept at the palace ere the king
gave them the cattle and leave to join me, accompanied with one
more officer, who had orders to find the boats at once, see us off,
and report the circumstance at court. Just as at the last interview, the king had four women, lately seized and condemned to
execution, squatting in his court. He wished to send them to
Bana, and when Bombay demurred, saying he had no authority
to take women in that way, the king gave him one, and asked
him if he would like to see some sport, as he would have the remaining women cut to pieces before him. Bombay, by his own
account, behaved with great propriety, saying Bana never wished
to see sport of that cruel kind, and it would ill become him to see
sights which his master had not. Viarŭngi sent me some tobacco, with kind regards, and said he and the Wazinza had just obtained leave to return to their homes, K'yengo alone, of all the
guests, remaining behind as a hostage until Mtésa's powder-seek-
ing wakungŭ returned. Finally, the little boy Lŭgoi had been
sent to his home. Such was the tenor of Bombay's report.

11th. The officer sent to procure boats, impudently saying there
were none, was put in the stocks by Kasoro, while other men
went to Kirindi for sailors, and down the stream for boats. On
hearing the king's order that I was to be supplied with fish, the
fishermen ran away, and pombé was no longer brewed from fear
of Kasoro.

12th. To-day we slaughtered and cooked two cows for the journey—the remaining three and one goat having been lost in the
Lŭajerri—and gave the women of the place beads in return for
their hospitality. They are nearly all Wanyoro, having been
captured in that country by King Mtésa and given to Mlondo.
They said their teeth were extracted, four to six lower incisors,
when they were young, because no Myoro would allow a person
to drink from his cup unless he conformed to that custom. The
same law exists in Usoga.

CHAPTER XVI.

BAHR EL ABIAD.

First Voyage on the Nile.—The Starting.—Description of the River and the Country.—Meet a hostile Vessel.—A naval Engagement.—Difficulties and Dangers.—Judicial Procedure.—Messages from the King of Uganda.—His Efforts to get us back.—Desertion.—The Wanyoro Troops.—Kamrasi.—Elephant-stalking.—Diabolical Possessions.

IN five boats of five planks each, tied together and calked with mbŭgŭ rags, I started with twelve Wangŭana, Kasoro and his page-followers, and a small crew, to reach Kamrasi's palace in Unyoro—goats, dogs, and kit, besides grain and dried meat, filling up the complement—but how many days it would take nobody knew. Paddles propelled these vessels, but the lazy crew were slow in the use of them, indulging sometimes in racing spurts, then composedly resting on their paddles while the gentle current drifted us along. The river, very unlike what it was from the Ripon Falls downward, bore at once the character of river and lake—clear in the centre, but fringed in most places with tall rush, above which the green banks sloped back like park lands. It was all very pretty and very interesting, and would have continued so had not Kasoro disgraced the Union Jack, turning it to piratical purposes in less than one hour.

To N'yassi, 13th.

A party of Wanyoro, in twelve or fifteen canoes, made of single tree trunks, had come up the river to trade with the Wasoga, and having stored their vessels with mbŭgŭ, dried fish, plantains cooked and raw, pombé, and other things, were taking their last meal on shore before they returned to their homes. Kasoro seeing this, and bent on a boyish spree, quite forgetting we were bound for the very ports they were bound for, ordered our sailors to drive in among them, landed himself, and sent the Wanyoro flying before I knew what game was up, and then set to pillaging and feasting on the property of those very men whom it was our interest to propitiate, as we expected them shortly to be our hosts.

The ground we were on belonged to King Mtésa, being a dependency of Uganda, and it struck me as singular that Wanyoro should be found here; but I no sooner discovered the truth than I made our boatmen disgorge every thing they had taken, called back the Wanyoro to take care of their things, and extracted a promise from Kasoro that he would not practice such wicked tricks again, otherwise we could not travel together. Getting to boat again, after a very little paddling we pulled in to shore, on the Uganda side, to stop for the night, and thus allowed the injured Wanyoro to go down the river before us. I was much annoyed by this interruption, but no argument would prevail on Kasoro to go on. This was the last village on the Uganda frontier, and before we could go any farther in boats it would be necessary to ask leave of Kamrasi's frontier officer, N'yamyonjo, to enter Unyoro. The Wanguana demanded ammunition in the most imperious manner, while I, in the same tone, refused to issue any, lest a row should take place, and they then would desert, alluding to their dastardly desertion in Msalala when Grant was attacked. If a fight should take place, I said they must flock to me at once, and ammunition, which was always ready, would be served out to them. They laughed at this, and asked, Who would stop with me when the fight began? This was making a jest of what I was most afraid of—that they would all run away.

I held a levée to decide on the best manner of proceeding.

Down the Nile and back again, 14th.

The Waganda wanted us to stop for the day and feel the way gently, arguing that etiquette demands it. Then, trying to terrify me, they said N'yamyonjo had a hundred boats, and would drive us back to a certainty if we tried to force past them, if he were not first spoken with, as the Waganda had often tried the passage and been repulsed. On the other hand, I argued that Grant must have arrived long ago at Kamrasi's, and removed all these difficulties for us; but, I said, if they would send men, let Bombay start at once by land, and we will follow in boats, after giving him time to say we are coming. This point gained after a hot debate, Bombay started at 10 A.M., and we not till 5 P.M., it being but one hour's journey by water. The frontier line was soon crossed; and then both sides of the river, Usoga as well as Unyoro, belong to Kamrasi.

I flattered myself all my walking this journey was over, and there was nothing left but to float quietly down the Nile, for Kidgwiga had promised boats, on Kamrasi's account, from Unyoro to Gani, where Petherick's vessels were said to be stationed; but this hope shared the fate of so many others in Africa. In a little while an enormous canoe, full of well-dressed and well-armed men, was seen approaching us. We worked on, and found they turned, as if afraid. Our men paddled faster, they did the same, the pages keeping time playfully by beat of drum, until at last it became an exciting chase, won by the Wanyoro by their superior numbers. The sun was now setting as we approached N'yamyonjo's. On a rock by the river stood a number of armed men, jumping, jabbering, and thrusting with their spears, just as the Waganda do. I thought, indeed, they were Waganda doing this to welcome us; but a glance at Kasoro's glassy eyes told me such was not the case, but, on the contrary, their language and gestures were threats, defying us to land.

The bank of the river, as we advanced, then rose higher, and was crowned with huts and plantations, before which stood groups and lines of men, all fully armed. Farther, at this juncture, the canoe we had chased turned broadside on us, and joined in the threatening demonstrations of the people on shore. I could not believe them to be serious—thought they had mistaken us—and stood up in the boat to show myself, hat in hand. I said I was an Englishman going to Kamrasi's, and did all I could, but without creating the slightest impression. They had heard a drum beat, they said, and that was a signal of war, so war it should be; and Kamrasi's drums rattled up both sides the river, preparing every body to arm. This was serious. Farther, a second canoe full of armed men issued out from the rushes behind us, as if with a view to cut off our retreat, and the one in front advanced upon us, hemming us in. To retreat together seemed our only chance; but it was getting dark, and my boats were badly manned. I gave the order to close together and retire, offering ammunition as an incentive, and all came to me but one boat, which seemed so paralyzed with fright it kept spinning round and round like a crippled duck.

The Wanyoro, as they saw us retreating, were now heard to say, "They are women—they are running—let us at them;" while I kept roaring to my men, "Keep together—come for powder;" and myself loaded with small shot, which even made Kasoro laugh and inquire if it was intended for the Wanyoro. "Yes, to shoot them like Guinea-fowl; and he laughed again. But confound my men! they would not keep together, and retreat with me. One of those served with ammunition went as hard as he could go up stream to be out of harm's way, and another preferred hugging the dark shade of the rushes to keeping the clear open, which I desired for the benefit of our guns. It was now getting painfully dark, and the Wanyoro were stealing on us, as we could hear, though nothing could be seen. Presently the shade-seeking boat was attacked, spears were thrown, fortunately into the river instead of into our men, and grappling-hooks were used to link the boats together. My men cried, "Help, Bana! they are killing us;" while I roared to my crew, "Go in, go in, and the victory will be ours;" but not a soul would: they were spell-bound to the place; we might have been cut up in detail; it was all the same to those cowardly Waganda, whose only action consisted in crying "N'yawo! n'yawo!"—Mother, mother, help us!

Three shots from the hooked boat now finished the action. The Wanyoro had caught a Tartar. Two of their men fell—one killed, one wounded. They were heard saying their opponents were not Waganda; it were better to leave them alone; and retreated, leaving us, totally uninjured, a clear passage up the river. But where was Bombay all this while? He did not return till after us, and then, in considerable excitement, he told his tale. He reached N'yamyonjo's village before noon, asked for the officer, but was desired to wait in a hut until the chief should arrive, as he had gone out on business; the villagers inquired, however, why we had robbed the Wanyoro yesterday, for they had laid a complaint against us. Bombay replied it was no fault of Bana's; he did every thing he could to prevent it, and returned all that the boatmen took.

These men then departed, and did not return until evening, when they asked Bombay, impudently, why he was sitting there, as he had received no invitation to spend the night; and, unless he walked off soon, they would set fire to his hut. Bombay, without the smallest intention of moving, said he had orders to see N'yamyonjo, and until he did so he would not budge. "Well," said the people, "you have got your warning, now look out for yourselves;" and Bombay, with his Waganda escort, was left again. Drums then began to beat, and men to hurry to and fro with spears and shields, until at last our guns were heard, and, guessing the cause, Bombay with his Waganda escort rushed out of the hut into the jungle, and, without daring to venture on the beaten track, through thorns and thicket worked his way back to me, lame, and scratched all over with thorns.

Crowds of Waganda, all armed as if for war, came to congratu-
Return to Kiwŭ-kéri, 15th. late us in the morning, jumping, jabbering, and shaking their spears at us, denoting a victory gained—for
we had shot Wanyoro and no harm had befallen us. "But the road," I cried, "has that been gained? I am not going to show my back. We must go again, for there is some mistake; Grant is with Kamrasi, and N'yamyonjo can not stop us. If you won't go in boats, let us go by land to N'yamyonjo's, and the boats will follow after." Not a soul, however, would stir. N'yamyonjo was described as an independent chief, who listened to Kamrasi only when he liked. He did not like strange eyes to see his se-cret lodges on the N'yanza; and if he did not wish us to go down the river, Kamrasi's orders would go for nothing. His men had now been shot; to go within his reach would be certain death. Argument was useless, boating slow, to send messages worse; so I gave in, turned my back on the Nile, and the following day (16th) came on the Lŭajerri.

Here, to my intense surprise, I heard that Grant's camp was not far off, on its return from Kamrasi's. I could not, rather would not, believe it, suspicious as it now appeared after my re-verse. The men, however, were positive, and advised my going to King Mtésa's—a ridiculous proposition, at once rejected; for I had yet to receive Kamrasi's answer to our queen about opening a trade with England. I must ascertain why he despised English-men without speaking with them, and I could not believe Kam-rasi would prove less avaricious than either Rŭmanika or Mtésa, especially as Rŭmanika had made himself responsible for our ac-tions. We slept that night near Kari, the Waganda eating two goats which had been drowned in the Lŭajerri; and the messen-ger-page, having been a third time to the palace and back again, called to ask after our welfare on behalf of his king, and remind us about the gun and brandy promised.

17th and 18th. The two following days were spent wandering about without guides, trying to keep the track Grant had taken after leaving us, crossing at first a line of small hills, then traver-sing grass and jungle, like the dâk of India. Plantain gardens were frequently met, and the people seemed very hospitably in-clined, though they complained sadly of the pages rudely rushing into every hut, seizing every thing they could lay their hands on, and even eating the food which they had just prepared for their own dinners, saying, in a mournful manner, "If it were not out of respect for you we should fight those little rascals, for it is not the king's guest nor his men who do us injury, but the king's own servants, without leave or license." I observed that special bomas or fences were erected to protect these villages against the incursions of lions. Buffaloes were about, but the villagers cautioned us not to shoot them, holding them as sacred animals; and, to judge from the appearance of the country, wild animals should abound, were it not for the fact that every Mganda seems by instinct to be a sportsman.

At last, after numerous and various reports about Grant, we
To N'yakinyama, heard his drums last night, but arrived this morning
19th.   just in time to be too late. He was on his march
back to the capital of Uganda, as the people had told us, and passed through N'yakinyama just before I reached it. What had really happened I knew not, and was puzzled to think. To insist on a treaty, demanding an answer to the queen, seemed the only chance left; so I wrote to Grant to let me know all about it, and waited the result. He very obligingly came himself, said he left Unyoro after stopping there an age asking for the road without effect, and left by the orders of Kamrasi, thinking obedience the better policy to obtain our ends. Two great objections had been raised against us; one was that we were reported to be cannibals, and the other that our advancing by two roads at once was suspicious, the more especially so as the Waganda were his enemies; had we come from Rŭmanika direct, there would have been no objection to us.

When all was duly considered, it appeared evident to me that the great king of Unyoro, "the father of all the kings," was merely a nervous, fidgety creature, half afraid of us because we were attempting his country by the unusual mode of taking two routes at once, but wholly so of the Waganda, who had never ceased plundering his country for years. As it appeared that he would have accepted us had we come by the friendly route of Kisŭéré, a farther parley was absolutely necessary, and the more especially so as now we were all together and in Uganda, which, in consequence, must relieve him from the fear of our harboring evil designs against him. No one present, however, could be prevailed on to go to him in the capacity of embassador, as the frontier officer had warned the wagéni or guests that, if they ever attempted to cross the border again, he was bound in duty, agreeably to the orders of his king, to expel them by force; therefore, should the wagéni attempt it after this warning, their first appearance would be considered a *casus belli;* and so the matter rested for the day.

To make the best of a bad bargain, and as N'yakinyama was "eaten up," we repaired to Grant's camp to consult with Budja; but Budja was found firm and inflexible against sending men to Unyoro. His pride had been injured by the rebuffs we had sustained. He would wait here three or four days as I proposed, to see what fortune sent us, if I would not be convinced that Kamrasi wished to reject us, and he would communicate with his king in the mean while, but nothing more. Here was altogether a staggerer: I would stop for three or four days, but if Kamrasi would not have us by that time, what was to be done? Would it be prudent to try Kisŭéré now Baraka had been refused the Gani route? or would it not be better still for me to sell Kamrasi altogether by offering Mtésa five hundred loads of ammunition, cloth, and beads, if he would give us a thousand Waganda as a force to pass through the Masai to Zanzibar, this property to be sent back by the escort from the coast? Kamrasi would no doubt catch it if we took this course, but it was expensive.

To Grant's Camp, 20*th.*

Thus were we ruminating, when, lo, to our delight, as if they had been listening to us, up came Kidgwiga, my old friend, who, at Mtésa's palace, had said Kamrasi would be very glad to see me, and Vittagŭra, Kamrasi's commander-in-chief, to say their king was very anxious to see us, and the Waganda might come or not, as they liked. Until now, the deputation said, Kamrasi had doubted Budja's word about our friendly intentions, but since he saw us withdrawing from his country, those doubts were removed. The N'yanswengé, they said—meaning, I thought, Petherick—was still at Gani; no English or others on the Nile ever expressed a wish to enter Unyoro, otherwise they might have done so; and Baraka had left for Karagŭé, carrying off an ivory as a present from Kamrasi.

21*st.* I ordered the march to Unyoro; Budja, however, kept brooding over the message sent to the Waganda, to the effect that they might come or not, as they liked; and considering us, with himself, to have all been treated "like dogs," begged me to give him my opinion as to what course he had better pursue; for he must, in the first instance, report the whole circumstances to the king, and could not march at once. This was a blight on our prospects, and appeared very vexatious, in the event of Budja waiting for an answer, which, considering Mtésa had ordered his wakungŭ to accompany us all the way to Gani, might stop our march altogether.

I therefore argued that Kamrasi's treatment of us was easily accounted for: he heard of us coming by two routes from an enemy's country, and was naturally suspicious of us; that had now been changed by our withdrawing, and he invited us to him. Without doubt, his commander-in-chief was never very far away, and followed on our heels. Such precaution was only natural and reasonable on Kamrasi's part, and what had been done need not alarm any one. "If you do your duty properly, you will take us at once into Unyoro, make your charge over to these men, and return or not, as you like; for in doing so you will have fulfilled both Mtésa's and Kamrasi's orders at once." "Very good," says Budja; "let it be so; for there is great wisdom in your words; but I must first send to my king, for the Waganda villagers have struck two of your men with weapons" (this had happened just before my arrival here), "and this is a most heinous offense in Uganda, which can not be overlooked. Had it been done with a common stick, it could have been overlooked; but the use of weapons is an offense, and both parties must go before the king." This, of course, was objected to on the plea that it was my own affair. I was king of the Wangŭana, and might choose to dispense with the attendance. The matter was compromised, however, on the condition that Budja should march across the border to-morrow, and wait for the return of these men and for farther orders on the Unyoro side.

The bait took. Budja lost sight of the necessity there was for his going to Gani to bring back a gun, ammunition, and some medicine—that is to say, brandy—for his king, and sent his men off with mine to tell Mtésa all our adventures—our double repulse, the intention to wait on the Unyoro side for farther orders, and the account of some Waganda having wounded my men. I added my excuses for Kamrasi, and laid a complaint against Mtésa's officers for having defrauded us out of ten cows, five goats, six butter, and sixty mbŭgŭ. It was not that we required these things, but I knew that the king had ordered them to be given to us, and I thought it right we should show that his officers, if they professed to obey his orders, had peculated. After these men had started, some friends of the villager who had been apprehended on the charge of assailing my men came and offered Budja five cows to overlook the charge; and Budja, though he could not overlook it when I pleaded for the man, asked me to recall my men. Discovering that the culprit was a queen's man, and that the affair would cause bad blood at court should the king order the man's life to be taken, I tried to do so, but things had gone too far.

Again the expedition marched on in the right direction. We reached the last village on the Uganda frontier, and there spent the night. Here Grant shot a n'sunnŭ buck. The Wangŭana mutinied for ammunition, and would not lift a load until they got it, saying, "Unyoro is a dangerous country," though they had been there before without any more than they now had in pouch. The fact was, my men, in consequence of the late issues on the river, happened to have more than Grant's men, and every man must have alike. The ringleader, unfortunately for himself, had lately fired at a dead lion, to astonish the Unyoro, and his chum had fired a salute, which was contrary to orders; for ammunition was at a low ebb, and I had done every thing in my power to nurse it. Therefore, as a warning to the others, the guns of these two were confiscated, and a caution given that any gun in future let off, either by design or accident, would be taken.

To North Frontier Station, Uganda, 22d.

To-day I felt very thankful to get across the much-vexed boundary-line, and enter Unyoro, guided by Kamrasi's deputation of officers, and so shake off the apprehensions which had teased us for so many days. This first march was a picture of all the country to its capital: an interminable forest of small trees, bush, and tall grass, with scanty villages, low huts, and dirty-looking people clad in skins; the plantain, sweet potato, sesamum, and ŭlézi (millet) forming the chief edibles, besides goats and fowls; while the cows, which are reported to be numerous, being kept, as every where else where pasture-lands are good, by the wandering, unsociable Wahŭma, are seldom seen. No hills, except a few scattered cones, disturb the level surface of the land, and no pretty views ever cheer the eye. Uganda is now entirely left behind; we shall not see its like again; for the farther one leaves the equator, and the rain-attracting influences of the Mountains of the Moon, vegetation decreases proportionately with the distance.

To South Frontier Station, Unyoro, 23d.

Fortunately, the frontier village could not feed so large a party as ours, and therefore we were compelled to move farther on, to our great delight, through the same style of forest acacia, cactus, and tall grass, to Kidgwiga's gardens, where we no sooner arrived than Mtésa's messenger-page, with a party of fifty Waganda, dropped in, in the most unexpected manner, to inquire after "his royal master's friend, Bana." The king had heard of the fight upon the river, and thought the Wanguana must be very good shots. He still trusted we would not forget the gun and ammunition, but, above all, the load of stimulants, for he desired that above all things on earth. This was the fourth message to remind us of these important matters which we had received since leaving his gracious presence, and each time brought by the same page. While the purpose of the boy's coming with so many men was not distinctly known, the whole village and camp were in a state of great agitation, Budja fearing lest the king had some fault to find with his work, and the Wanyoro deeming it a menace of war, while I was afraid they might take fright and stop our progress.

To Kidgwiga's, 24th.

But all went well in the end; Massey's log, which I have mentioned as a present I intended for Mtésa, was packed up, and the page departed with it. Some of Rŭmanika's men, who came into Unyoro with Baraka, with four of K'yengo's, were sent to call us by Kamrasi. Through Rŭmanika's men it transpired that he had stood security for our actions, else, with the many evil reports of our being cannibals and suchlike, which had preceded our coming here, we never should have gained admittance to the country. The Wanyoro, who are as squalid-looking as the Wanyamŭézi, and almost as badly dressed, now came about us to hawk ivory ornaments, brass and copper twisted wristlets, tobacco, and salt, which they exchanged for cowries, with which they purchase cows from the Waganda. As in Uganda, all the villagers forsook their huts as soon as they heard the wagéni (guests) were coming; and no one paid the least attention to the traveler save the few head men attached to the escort, or some professional traders.

25th to 28th. I had no sooner ordered the march than Vittagŭra counterordered it, and held a levée to ascertain, as he said, if the Waganda were to go back; for, though Kamrasi wished to see us, he did not want the Waganda. It was Kamrasi's orders that Budja should tell this to his "child the mkavia," meaning Mtésa; for when the Waganda came the first time to see him, three of his family died; and when they came the second time, three more died; and as this rate of mortality was quite unusual in his family circle, he could only attribute it to foul magic. The presence of people who brought such results was of course by no means desirable. This neat message elicited a declaration of the necessity of Budja's going to Gani with us, and a response from the commander-in-chief, probably to terrify the Waganda, that although Gani was only nine days' journey distant from Kamrasi's palace, the Gani people were such barbarians, they would call a straight-haired man a magician, and any person who tied his mbŭgŭ in a knot upon his shoulder, or had a full set of teeth as the Waganda have, would be surely killed by them. Finally, we must wait two days, to see if Kamrasi would see us or not. Such was Unyoro diplomacy.

An announcement of a different kind immediately followed. The king had heard that I gave a cow to Vittagŭra and Kidgwiga when they first came to me in Uganda, and wished the Wanyamŭézi to ascertain if this was true. Of course, I said they were my guests in Uganda, and if they had been wise they would have eaten their cow on the spot; what was that to Kamrasi? It was a pity he did not treat us as well who have come into his country at his own invitation, instead of keeping us starving in this gloomy wilderness, without a drop of pombé to cheer the day; why could not he let us go on? He wanted first to hear if the big mzungŭ, meaning myself, had really come yet. All fudge!

Three days were spent in simply waiting for return messages on both sides, and more might have been lost in the same way, only we amused Vittagŭra and gave him confidence by showing our pictures, looking-glass, scissors, knives, etc., when he promised a march in the morning, leaving a man behind to bring on the Wangŭana sent to Mtésa's, it being the only alternative which would please Budja; for he said there was no security for life in Unyoro, where every mkungŭ calls himself the biggest man, and no true hospitality is to be found.

The next two days took us through Chagamoyo to Kiratosi, by the aid of the compass; for the route Kamrasi's men took differed from the one which Budja knew, and he declared the Wanyoro were leading us into a trap, and would not be convinced that we were going on all right till I pulled out the compass and confirmed the Wanyoro. We were any thing but welcomed at Kiratosi, the people asking by

To Chagamoyo, 29th.
To Kiratosi, 30th.

what bad luck we had come there to eat up their crops; but in a little while they flocked to our doors and admired our traps, remarking that they believed each iron box contained a couple of white dwarfs, which we carry on our shoulders, sitting straddle-legs, back to back, and they fly off to eat people whenever they get the order.   One of these visitors happened to be the sister of one of my men, named Barŭti, who no sooner recognized her brother than, without saying a word, she clasped her head with her hands, and ran off, crying, to tell her husband what she had seen.   A spy of Kamrasi dropped the report that the Wangŭana were returning from Mtésa's, and hurried on to tell his king.

31*st*. Some Waganda hurrying in, confirmed the report of last night, and said the Wangŭana, footsore, had been left at the Uganda frontier, expecting us to return, as Mtésa, at the same time that he approved highly of my having sent men back to inform him of Kamrasi's conduct, begged we would instantly return, even if found within one march of Kamrasi's, for he had much of importance to tell his friend Bana.   The message continued to this effect: I need be under no apprehensions about the road to the coast, for he would give me as many men as I liked; and, fearing I might be short of powder, he had sent some with the Wangŭana.   Both Wangŭana were by the king given women for their services, and an old tin cartridge-box represented Mtésa's card, it being an article of European manufacture, which, if found in the possession of any Mganda, would be certain death to him. Finally, all the houses and plantains where my men were wounded had been confiscated.

When this message was fully delivered, Budja said we must return without a day's delay. I, on the contrary, called up Kidgwiga. I did not like my men having been kept prisoners in Uganda, and pronounced in public that I would not return. It would be an insult to Kamrasi my doing so, for I was now in his "house" at his own invitation. I wished Bombay would go with him (Kidgwiga) at once to his king, to say I had hoped, when I sent Budja with Mabrŭki, in the first instance, conveying a friendly present from Mtésa, which was done at my instigation, and I found Kamrasi acknowledged it by a return present, that there would be no more fighting between them. I said I had left England to visit these countries for the purpose of opening up a trade, and I had no orders to fight my way except with the force of friendship. That Rŭmanika had accepted my views Kamrasi must be fully aware by Baraka's having visited him; and that Mtésa did the same must be also evident, else he would never have ordered his men to accompany me to Gani; and I now fondly trusted that these Waganda would be allowed to go with me, when, by the influence of trade, all animosity would cease, and friendly relations be restored between the two countries.

This speech was hardly pronounced when Kajunjŭ, a fine athletic man, dropped suddenly in, nodded a friendly recognition to Budja, and wished to know what the Waganda meant by taking us back, for the king had heard of their intention last night; and when told by Budja his story, and by Kidgwiga mine, he vanished like a shadow. Budja, now turning to me, said, "If you won't go back, I shall; for the orders of Mtésa must always be obeyed, else lives will be lost; and I shall tell him that you, since leaving his country and getting your road, have quite forgotten him." "If you give such a message as that," I said, "you will tell a falsehood. Mtésa has no right to order me out of another man's house, to be an enemy with one whose friendship I desire. I am not only in honor bound to speak with Kamrasi, but I am also bound to carry out the orders of my country just as much as you are yours; moreover, I have invited Petherick to come to Kamrasi's by a letter from Karagŭé, and it would be ill-becoming in me to desert him in the hands of an enemy, as he would then certainly find Kamrasi to be if I went back now." Budja then tried the coaxing dodge, saying, "There is much reason in your words, but I am sorry you do not listen to the king, for he loves you as a brother. Did you not go about like two brothers—walking, talking, shooting, and even eating together? It was the remark of all the Waganda, and the king will be so vexed when he finds you have thrown him over. I did not tell you before, but the king says, 'How can I answer Rŭmanika if Kamrasi injures Bana? Had I known Kamrasi was such a savage, I would not have let Bana go there; and I should now have sent a force to take him away, only that some accident might arise from it by Kamrasi's taking fright; the road even to Gani shall be got by force, if necessary.'" Then, finding me still persistent, Budja turned again and threatened us with the king's power, saying, "If you choose to disobey, we will see whether you ever get the road to Gani or not; for Kamrasi is at war on all sides with his brothers, and Mtésa will ally himself with them at any moment that he wishes, and where will you be then?"

Saying this, Budja walked off, muttering that our being here would much embarrass Mtésa's actions, while my Wangŭana, who have been attentively listening, like timid hares, made up their minds to leave me, and tried, through Bombay, to obtain a final interview with me, saying they knew Mtésa's power, and disobedience to him would only end in taking away all chance of escape. In reply, I said I would not listen to them, as I had seen enough of them to know it was no use speaking with a pack of unreasonable cowards, having tried it so often before; but I sent a message requesting them, if they did desert me at last, to leave my guns; and, farther, added an intimation that, as soon as they reached the coast, they would be put into prison for three years. The scoundrels insolently said "tŭendé sétu" (let's be off), rushed to the Waganda drums, and beat the march.

1st. Early in the morning, as Budja drummed the home march, I called him up, gave him a glass rain-gauge as a letter for Mtésa, and instructed him to say I would send a man to Mtésa as soon as I had seen Kamrasi about opening the road; that I trusted he would take all the guns from the deserters and keep them for me, but the men themselves I wished transported to an island on the N'yanza, for I could never allow such scoundrels again to enter my camp. It was the effect of desertions like these that prevented any white men visiting these countries. This said, the Waganda all left us, taking with them twenty-eight Wangŭana, armed with twenty-two carbines. Among them was the wretched governess Manamaka, who had always thought me a wonderful magician, because I possessed, in her belief, an extraordinary power in inclining all the black king's hearts to me, and induced them to give the roads no one before of my color had ever attempted to use.

With a following reduced to twenty men, armed with fourteen carbines, I now wished to start for Kamrasi's, but had not even sufficient force to lift the loads. A little while elapsed, and a party of fifty Wanyoro rushed wildly into camp, with their spears uplifted, and looked for the Waganda, but found them gone. The athletic Kajunjŭ, it transpired, had returned to Kamrasi's, told him our story, and received orders to snatch us away from the Waganda by force, for the great mkamma, or king, was most anxious to see his white visitors; such men had never entered Unyoro before, and neither his father nor his father's fathers had ever been treated with such a visitation; therefore he had sent these fifty men to fall by surprise on the Waganda and secure us. But again, in a little while, about 10 A.M., Kajunjŭ, in the same wild manner, at the head of 150 warriors, with the soldier's badge—a piece of mbŭgŭ or plantain-leaf tied round their heads, and a leather sheath on their spear-heads, tufted with cow's-tail—rushed in exultingly, having found, to their delight, that there was no one left to fight with, and that they had gained an easy victory. They were certainly a wild set of ragamuffins—as different as possible from the smart, well-dressed, quick-of-speech Waganda as could be, and any thing but prepossessing to our eyes. However, they had done their work, and I offered them a cow, wishing to have it shot before them; but the chief men, probably wishing the whole animal to themselves, took it alive, saying the men were all the king's servants, and therefore could not touch a morsel.

Kamrasi expected us to advance next day, when some men would go on ahead to announce our arrival, and bring a letter which was brought with beads by Gani before Baraka's arrival here. It was shown to Baraka in the hope that he would come by the Karagŭé route, but not to Mabrŭki, because he came from Uganda. Kidgwiga informed us that Kamrasi never retaliated on Mtésa when he lifted Unyoro cows, though the Waganda keep their cattle on the border, which simply meant he had not the power of doing so. The twenty remaining Wangŭana, conversing over the sudden scheme of the deserters, proposed, on one side, sending for them, as, had they seen the Wanyoro arrive, they would have changed their minds; but the other side said, " What! those brutes who said we should all die here if we staid, and yet dared not face the danger with us, should we now give them a helping hand? Never! We told them we would share our fate with Bana, and share it we will, for God rules every thing: every man must die when his time comes."

We marched for the first time without music, as the drum is never allowed to be beaten in Unyoro except when the necessities of war demand it, or for a dance. Wan-

To Utŭti, 2d.

yamŭézi and Wanyoro, in addition to our own twenty men, carried the luggage, though no one carried more than the smallest article he could find. It was a pattern Unyoro march, of only two hours' duration. On arrival at the end, we heard that elephants had been seen close by. Grant and I then prepared our guns, and found a herd of about a hundred feeding on a plain of long grass, dotted here and there by small mounds crowned with shrub. The animals appeared to be all females, much smaller than the Indian breed; yet, though ten were fired at, none were killed, and only one made an attempt to charge. I was with the little twin Manŭa at the time, when, stealing along under cover of the high grass, I got close to the batch and fired at the largest, which sent her round roaring. The whole of them then, greatly alarmed, packed together and began sniffing the air with their uplifted trunks, till, ascertaining by the smell of the powder that their enemy was in front of them, they rolled up their trunks and came close to the spot where I was lying under a mound. My scent then striking across them, they pulled up short, lifted their heads high, and looked down sideways on us. This was a bad job. I could not get a proper front shot at the boss of any of them, and if I had waited an instant we should both have been picked up or trodden to death; so I let fly at their temples, and, instead of killing, sent the whole of them rushing away at a much faster pace than they came. After this I gave up, because I never could separate the ones I had wounded from the rest, and thought it cruel to go on damaging more. Thinking over it afterward, I came to the conclusion I ought to have put in more powder; for I had, owing to their inferior size to the Indian ones, rather despised them, and fired at them with the same charge and in the same manner as I always did at rhinoceros. Though puzzled at the strange sound of the rifle, the elephants seldom ran far, packed in herd, and began to graze again. Frij, who was always ready at spinning a yarn, told us with much gravity that two of my men, Ulédi and Wadi Hamadi, deserters, were possessed of devils (phépo) at Zanzibar. Ulédi, not wishing to be plagued by his satanic majesty's angels on the march, sacrificed a cow and fed the poor, according to the great phépo's orders, and had been exempted from it; but Wadi Hamadi, who preferred taking his chance, had been visited several times: once at Usŭi, when he was told the journey would be prosperous, only the devil wanted one man's life, and one man would fall sick; which proved true, for Hassani was murdered, and Grant fell sick in Karagŭé. The second time Wadi Hamadi saw the devil in Karagŭé, and was told one man's life would be required in Uganda, and such also was the case by Kari's murder; and a third time, in Unyoro, he was possessed, when it was said that the journey would be prosperous, but protracted.

3d. Though we stormed every day at being so shamefully neg-

THE ELEPHANTS' CHARGE.

lected and kept in the jungles, we could not get on, nor find out
the truth of our position. I asked if Kamrasi was afraid of us,
and looking into his magic horn; and was answered "No; he is
very anxious to see you, or he would not have sent six of his
highest officers to look after you, and prevent the unruly peasantry from molesting you." "Then by whose orders are we
kept here?" "By Kamrasi's." "Why does Kamrasi keep us
here?" "He thinks you are not so near, and men have gone to
tell him." "How did we come here from the last ground?"
"By Kamrasi's orders; for nothing can be done excepting by
his orders." "Then he must know we are here?" "He may
not have seen the men we sent to him; for, unless he shows in
public, no one can see him." The whole affair gave us such an
opinion of Kamrasi as induced us to think it would have served
him right had we joined Mtésa and given him a thrashing. This,
I said, was put in our power by an alliance with his refractory
brothers; but Kidgwiga only laughed and said, "Nonsense!
Kamrasi is the chief of all the countries round here—Usoga,
Kidi, Chopi, Gani, Uléga, every where; he has only to hold up
his hand and thousands would come to his assistance." Kwibéya,
the officer of the place, presented us with five fowls on the part
of the king, and some baskets of potatoes.

4th. We halted again, it was said, in order that Kwibéya might
give us all the king had desired him to present. I sent Bombay
off with a message to Kamrasi explaining every thing, and begging for an early interview, as I had much of importance to communicate, and wished, of all things, to see the letter he had from
Gani, as it must have come from our dear friends at home. Seven
goats, flour, and plantains were now brought to us; and as Kidgwiga begged for the flour without success, he flew into a fit of
high indignation because these things were given and received
without his having first been consulted. He was the big man
and appointed go-between, and no one could dispute it. This
was rather startling news to us, for Vittagŭra said he was commander-in-chief; Kajunjŭ thought himself biggest, so did Kwibéya, and even Dr. K'yengo's men justified Budja's speech.

5th and 6th. Still another halt, with all sorts of excuses. Frij,
it appeared, dreamt last night that the King of Uganda came to
fight us for not complying with his orders, and that all my men
ran away except Ulédi and himself. This, according to the interpretation of the coast, would turn out the reverse, otherwise

his head must be wrong, and, according to local science, should be set right again by actual cautery of the temples; and as Grant dreamt a letter came from Gani which I opened and ran away with, he thought it would turn out no letter at all, and therefore Kamrasi had been humbugging us. We heard that Bombay had shot a cow before Kamrasi, and would not be allowed to return until he had eaten it.

At last we made a move, but only of two hours' duration, Change ground, through the usual forest, in which elephants walked 7th. about as if it were their park. We hoped at starting to reach the palace, but found we must stop here until the king should send for us. We were informed that doubtless he was looking into his uganga, or magic horn, to discover what he had to expect from us; and he seemed as yet to have found no ground for being afraid of us. Moreover, it is his custom to keep visitors waiting on him in this way, for is he not the king of kings, the King of Kittara, which includes all the countries surrounding Unyoro?

CHAPTER XVII.

UNYORO.

Invitation to the Palace at last.—Journey to it.—Bombay's Visit to King Kamrasi.
—Our Reputation as Cannibals.—Reception at Court.—Acting the Physician
again.—Royal Mendicancy.

We halted again, but in the evening one of Dr. K'yengo's men
came to invite us to the palace. He explained that
Kamrasi was in a great rage because we only received
seven goats instead of thirty, the number he had ordered Kwibéya to give us, besides pombé and plantains without
limitation. I complained that Bombay had been shown more
respect than myself, obtaining an immediate admittance to the
king's presence. To this he gave two ready answers—that every
distinction shown my subordinate was a distinction to myself, and
that we must not expect court etiquette from savages.

To Chagŭzi, on
the left bank of
the Kafŭ River,
8th.

King Kamrasi's Palace, from my hut—Unyoro.

9th. We set off for the palace. This last march differed but
little from the others. Putting Dr. K'yengo's men in front, and

going on despite all entreaties to stop, we passed the last bit of jungle, sighted the Kidi hills, and, in a sea of swampy grass, at last we stood in front of and overlooked the great king's palace, situated N. lat. 1° 37′ 43″, and E. long.. 32° 19′ 49″, on a low tongue of land between the Kafŭ and Nile Rivers. It was a dumpy, large hut, surrounded by a host of smaller ones, and the worst royal residence we had seen since leaving Uzinza. Here Kajunjŭ, coming from behind, overtook us, and, breathless with running, in the most excited manner abused Dr. K'yengo's men for leading us on, and ordered us to stop until he saw the king, and ascertained the place his majesty wished us to reside in. Recollecting Mtésa's words that Kamrasi placed his guests on the N'yanza, I declined going to any place but the palace, which I maintained was my right, and waited for the issue, when Kajunjŭ returned with pombé, and showed us to a small, dirty set of huts beyond the Kafŭ River—the trunk of the Mwérango and N'yanza branches which we crossed in Uganda—and trusted this would do for the present, as better quarters in the palace would be looked for on the morrow.. This was a bad beginning, and caused a few of the usual anathemas in which our countrymen give vent to their irritation.

Two loads of flour, neatly packed in long strips of rush-pith, were sent for us "to consume at once," as more would be given on the morrow. To keep us amused, Kidgwiga informed us that Kamrasi and Mtésa—in fact, all the Wahŭma—came originally from a stock of the same tribe dwelling beyond Kidi. All bury their dead in the same way, under ground; but the kings are toasted first for months till they are like sun-dried meat, when the lower jaw is cut out and preserved, covered with beads. The royal tombs are put under the charge of special officers, who occupy huts erected over them. The umbilical cords are preserved from birth, and, at death, those of men are placed within the door-frame, while those of women are buried without—this last act corresponding, according to Bombay, with the custom of the Wahiyow. On the death of any of the great officers of state, the finger-bones and hair are also preserved; or, if they have died shaven, as sometimes occurs, a bit of their mbŭgŭ dress is preserved in place of the hair. Their families guard their tombs.

The story we heard at Karagŭé, about dogs with horns in Unyoro, was confirmed by Kidgwiga, who positively assured us that he once saw one in the possession of an official person, but it died.

The horn then was stuffed with magic powder, and, whenever an army was ordered for war, it was placed on the war-track for the soldiers to step over, in the same way as a child is sacrificed to insure victory in Unyamŭézi. Of the Karagŭé story, according to which all the Kidi people sleep in trees, Kidgwiga gave me a modified version. He said the bachelors alone do so, while the married folk dwell in houses. As most of these stories have some foundation in fact, we presumed that the people of Kidi sometimes mount a tree to sleep at night when traveling through their forests, where lions are plentiful, but not otherwise.

10*th*. I sent Kidgwiga with my compliments to the king, and a request that his majesty would change my residence, which was so filthy that I found it necessary to pitch a tent, and also that he would favor me with an interview after breakfast. The return was a present of twenty cows, ten cocks, two bales of flour, and two pots of pombé, to be equally divided between Grant and myself, as Kamrasi recognized in us two distinct camps, because we approached his country by two different routes—a smart method for expecting two presents from us, which did not succeed, as I thanked for all, Grant being "my son" on this occasion. The king also sent his excuses, and begged pardon for what happened to us on entering his country, saying it could not have taken place had we come from Rŭmanika direct. His fear of the Waganda gave rise to it, and he trusted we would forget and forgive. To-morrow our residence should be changed, and an interview follow, for he desired being friends with us just as much as we did with him.

At last Bombay came back. He reported that he had not been allowed to leave the palace earlier, though he pleaded hard that I expected his return; and the only excuse that he could extract from the king was, that we were coming in charge of many wakungŭ, and he had found it necessary to retard our approach in consequence of the famine at Chagŭzi. His palace proper was not here, but three marches westward: he had come here and pitched a camp to watch his brothers, who were at war with him. Bombay, doing his best to escape, or to hurry my march, replied that he was very anxious on our account, because the Waganda wished to snatch us away.

It was no doubt this hint that brought the messenger to our relief yesterday, as otherwise we might have been kept in the jungle longer. When told by Bombay of our treatment on the

Nile, the king first said he did not think we wished to see him, else we would have come direct from Rŭmanika; but when asked if Baraka's coming with Rŭmanika's officers was not sufficient to satisfy him on this point, he hung down his head and evaded the question, saying he had been the making of King Mtésa of Uganda; but he had turned out a bad fellow, and now robbed him right and left.* The Gani letter, supposed to be from Petherick, was now asked for, and a suggestion made about opening a trade with Gani, but all with the provoking result we had been so well accustomed to. No letter like that referred to had ever been received, so that Frij's interpretation about Grant's letter-dream was right; and if we wished to go to Gani, the king would send men traveling by night, for his brothers at war with him lay upon the road. As to the Uganda question, and my desiring him to make friends with Mtésa, in hopes that the influence of trade would prevent any plundering in future, he merely tossed his head. He often said he did not know what to think about his guests, now he had got them; to which Bombay, in rather successful imitation of what he had heard me say on like occasions, replied, "If you do not like them after you have seen them, cut their heads off, for they are all in your hands."

11th. With great apparent politeness Kamrasi sent in the morning to inquire how we had slept. He had "heard our cry."—an expression of regal condescension—and begged we would not be alarmed, for next morning he would see us, and after the meeting change our residence, when, should we not approve of wading to his palace, he would bridge all the swamps leading up to it; but for the present he wanted two rounds of ball cartridge—one to fire before his women, and the other before his officers and a large number of Kidi men who were there on a visit. To please this childish king, Bombay was sent with two other of my men, and no sooner arrived than a cow was placed before them to be shot. Bombay, however, thinking easy compliance would only lead to continued demands on our short store of powder, said he had no order to shoot cows, and declined. A strong debate ensued, which Bombay, by his own account, turned to advantage by saying, "What use is there in shooting cows? we have lots of meat; what we want is flour to eat with it." To which the great king

* This obviously was an allusion to the way in which the first king of Uganda was countenanced by the great king of Kittara, according to the tradition given in Chapter IX.

retorted, "If you have not got flour, that is not my fault, for I ordered your master to come slowly, and to bring provisions along with him."

Then getting impatient, as all his visitors wanted sport, he ordered the cow out again, and insisted on my men shooting at it, saying at the same time to his Kidi visitors, boastfully, "Now I will show you what devils these Wangŭana are: with fire-arms they can kill a cow with one bullet; and as they are going to Gani, I advise you not to meddle with them." The Kidi visitors said, "Nonsense; we don't believe in their power, but we will see." Irate at his defeat, Bombay gave orders to the men to fire over the cow, and told Kamrasi why he had done so—Bana would be angry with him. "Well," said the ķing of kings, "if that is true, go back to your master, tell him you have disappointed me before these men, and obtain permission to shoot the cow in the morning; after which, should you succeed, your master can come after breakfast to see me; but for the present, take him this pot of pombé."

12th. To back Bombay in what he had said, I gave him two more cartridges to shoot the cow with, and orders as well to keep Kamrasi to his word about the oft-promised interview and change of residence. He gave me the following account on his return: Upward of a thousand spectators were present when he killed the cow, putting both bullets into her, and all in a voice, as soon as they saw the effect of the shot, shouted in amazement; the Kidi visitors, all terror-stricken, crying out, as they clasped their breasts, "Oh, great king, do allow us to return to our country, for you have indeed got a new species of man with you, and we are greatly afraid!" a lot of humbug and affectation to flatter the king, which pleased him greatly. It was not sufficient, however, to make him forget his regal pride; for, though Bombay pleaded hard for our going to see him, and for a change of residence, the immovable king, to maintain the imperial state he had assuméd as "king of kings," only said, "What difference does it make whether your master sees me to-day or to-morrow? If he wants to communicate about the road to Gani, his property at Karagŭé, or his guns at Uganda, he can do so as well through the medium of my officers as with me direct, and I will send men whenever he wishes to do so. Perhaps you don't know, but I expect men from Gani every day, who took a present of slaves, ivory, and monkey-skins to the foreigners residing there, who, in the first instance, sent me a necklace of beads [showing them] by some men who wore clothes. They said white men were coming from Karagué, and requested the beads might be shown them should they do so. They left this two moons before Baraka arrived here, and I told them the white men would not come here, as I heard they had gone to Uganda."

Bombay then, finding the king very communicative, went at him for his inhospitality toward us, his turning us back from his country twice, and now, after inviting us, treating us as Sŭwarora did. On this he gave, by Bombay's account, the following curious reason for his conduct: "You don't understand the matter. At the time the white men were living in Uganda, many of the people who had seen them there came and described them as such monsters, they ate up mountains and drank the N'yanza dry; and although they fed on both beef and mutton, they were not satisfied until they got a dish of the 'tender parts' of human beings three times a day. Now I was extremely anxious to see men of such wonderful natures. I could have stood their mountain-eating and N'yanza-drinking capacities, but on no consideration would I submit to sacrifice my subjects to their appetites, and for this reason I first sent to turn them back; but afterward, on hearing from Dr. K'yengo's men that, although the white men had traveled all through their country, and brought all the pretty and wonderful things of the world there, they had never heard such monstrous imputations cast upon them, I sent a second time to call them on: these are the facts of the case. Now, with regard to your accusation of my treating them badly, it is all their own fault. I ordered them to advance slowly and pick up food by the way, as there is a famine here; but they, instead, hurried on against my wishes. That they want to see and give me presents you have told me repeatedly—so do I them; for I want them to teach me the way to shoot, and when that is accomplished I will take them to an island near Kidi, where there are some men [his refractory brothers] whom I wish to frighten away with guns; but still there is no hurry; they can come when I choose to call them, and not before." Bombay to this said, "I can not deliver such a message to Bana; I have told so many falsehoods about your saying you will have an interview to-morrow, I shall only catch a flogging," and forthwith departed.

13th. More disgusted with Kamrasi than ever, I called Kidgwiga up, and told him I was led to expect from Rŭmanika that I should find his king a good and reasonable man, which I believed, considering it was said by an unprejudiced person. Mtésa, on the contrary, told me Kamrasi treated all his guests with disrespect, sending them to the farther side of the N'yanza. I now found his enemy more truthful than his friend, and wished him to be told so. "For the future, I should never," I said, "mention his name again, but wait until his fear of me had· vanished; for he quite forgot his true dignity as a host and king in his surprise and fear, merely because we were in a hurry and desired to see him." He was reported to-day, by the way, to be drunk.

As nothing could be done yesterday in consequence of the king being in his cups, the wakungŭ conveyed my message to-day, but with the usual effect, till a diplomatic idea struck me, and I sent another messenger to say, if our residence was not changed at once, both Grant and myself had made up our minds to cut off our hair and blacken our faces, so that the king of all kings should have no more cause to fear us. Ignoring his claims to imperial rank, I maintained that his reason for ill treating us must be fear—it could be nothing else. This message acted like magic; for he fully believed we would do as we said, and disappoint him altogether of the strange sight of us as pure white men. The reply was, Kamrasi would not have us disfigured in this way for all the world; men were appointed to convey our traps to the west end at once; and Kidgwiga, Vittagŭra, and Kajunjŭ rushed over to give us the news in all haste, lest we should execute our threat, and they were glad to find us with our faces unchanged. I now gave one cow to the head of Dr. K'yengo's party, and one to the head of Rŭmanika's men, because I saw it was through their instrumentality we gained admittance in the country; and we changed residence to the west end of Chagŭzi, and found there comfortable huts close to the Kafŭ, which ran immediately between us and the palace.

Still our position in Unyoro was not a pleasant one. In a long field of grass, as high as the neck, and half under water, so that no walks could be taken, we had nothing to see but Kamrasi's miserable huts and a few distant conical hills, of which one, Udongo, we conceive, represents the Padongo of Brun-Bollet, placed by him in 1° south latitude, and 35° east longitude. We were scarcely inside our new dwelling when Kamrasi sent a cheer of two pots of pombé, five fowls, and two bunches of plantains, hoping we were now satisfied with his favor; but he damped

Change to West End, 14th.

the whole in a moment again by asking for a many-bladed knife which his officers had seen in Grant's possession. I took what he sent from fear of giving offense, but replied that I was surprised the great king should wish to see my property before seeing myself, and although I attached no more value to my property than he did to his, I could not demean myself by sending him trifles in that way. However, should he, after hearing my sentiments, still persist in asking for the knife to be sent by the hands of a black man, I would pack it up with all the things I had brought for him, and send them by a black man, judging that he liked black men more than white.

Dr. K'yengo's men then informed us that they had been twice sent with an army of Wanyoro to attack the king's brothers, on a river-island north of this about three days' journey, but each time it ended in nothing. You fancy yourself, they said, in a magnificent army, but the enemy no sooner turn out than the cowardly Wanyoro fly, and sacrifice their ally as soon as not into the hands of the opponents. They said Kamrasi would now expect us to attack them with our guns. Rionga was the head of the rebels; there were formerly five, but now only two of the brothers remained.

15th. Kamrasi, after inquiring after our health, and how we had slept, through a large deputation of head men, alluded to the knife question of yesterday, thinking it very strange that, after giving me such nice food, I should deny him the gratification of simply looking at a knife; he did not intend to keep it if it was not brought for him, but merely to look at and return it. To my reply of yesterday I added, I had been led, before entering Unyoro, to regard Kamrasi as the king of all kings—the greatest king that ever was, and one worthy to be my father; but now, as he expected me to amuse him with toys, he had lowered himself in my estimation to the position of being my child. To this the sages said, "Bana speaks beautifully, feelingly, and moderately. Of course he is displeased at seeing his property preferred before himself; all the right is on his side; we will now return and see what can be done, though none but white men in their greatness dare send such messages to our king."

Dr. K'yengo's men were now attacked by Kidgwiga for having taken a cow from me yesterday, and told they should not eat it, because both they and myself were the king's guests, and it ill became one to eat that which was given as a dinner for the other.

Fortunately, foreseeing this kind of policy, as Kamrasi had been watching our actions, I invariably gave in presents those cows which came with us from Uganda, and therefore defied any one to meddle with them. This elicited the true facts of the case. Dr. K'yengo's men had been sent to our camp to observe if any body received presents from us, as Kamrasi feared his subjects would have the fleecing of us before his turn came, and these men had reported the two cows given by me as mentioned above. Kamrasi no sooner heard of this than he took the cows and kept them himself. In their justification, Dr. K'yengo's men said that, had they not been in the country before us, Kamrasi would not have had such guests at all; for when he asked them if the Waganda reports about our cannibalism and other monstrosities were true, their head man denied it all, offered to stand security for our actions, and told the king if he found us cannibals he might make a Mohammedan of him, and sealed the statement with his oath by throwing down his shield and bow and walking over them. To this Kamrasi was said to have replied, "I will accept your statements, but you must remain with me until they come."

Kajunjŭ came with orders to say Kamrasi would seize any body found staring at us. I requested a definite answer would be given as regards Kamrasi's seeing us. Dr. K'yengo's men then said they were kept a week waiting before they could obtain an interview, while Kajunjŭ excused his king by saying, "At present the court is full of Kidi, Chopi, Gani, and other visitors, who he does not wish should see you, as some may be enemies in disguise. They are all now taking presents of cows from Kamrasi, and going to their homes, and, as soon as they are disposed of, your turn will come."

16th. We kept quiet all day, to see what effect that would have upon the king. Kidgwiga told us that, when he was a lad, Kamrasi sent him with a large party of Wanyoro to visit a king who lived close to a high mountain, two months' journey distant, to the east or southeast of this, and beg for a magic horn, as that king's doctor was peculiarly famed for his skill as a magician. The party carried with them 600 majembé (iron spades), two of which expended daily paid for their board and lodgings on the way. The horn applied for was sent by a special messenger to Kamrasi, who, in return, sent one of his horns; from which date the two kings, whenever one of them wishes to communicate with the other, sends, on the messenger's neck, the horn that had been given him, which both serves for credentials and security, as no one dare touch a mbakka with one of these horns upon his neck.

A common source of conversation among our men now was the desertion of their comrades, all fancying how bitterly they would repent it when they heard how we had succeeded, eating beef every day; and Ulédi now, in a joking manner, abused Mektŭb for having urged him to desert. He would not leave Bana, and if he had not stopped, Mektŭb would have gone, for they both served one master at Zanzibar, and therefore were like brothers; while Mektŭb, laughing over the matter as if it were a good joke, said, "I packed up my things to go, it is true, but I reflected if I got back to the coast Said Majid would only make a slave of me again." M'yinzuggi, the head of Rŭmanika's party, gave me to-day a tippet monkey-skin in return for the cow I had given him on the 14th. These men, taking their natures from their king Rŭmanika, are by far the most gentle, polite, and attentive of any black men we have traveled among.

17th. Tired and out of patience with our prison — a river of crocodiles on one side, and swamps in every other direction, while we could not go out shooting without a specific order from the king—I sent Kidgwiga and Kajunjŭ to inform Kamrasi that we could bear this life no longer. As he did not wish to see white men, our residing here could be of no earthly use. I hoped he would accept our present from Bombay, and give us leave to depart for Gani. The wakungŭ, who thought, as well as ourselves, that we were in nothing better than a prison, hurried off with the message, and soon returned with a message from their king that he was busily engaged decorating his palace to give us a triumphant reception, for he was anxious to pay us more respect than any body who had ever visited him before. We should have seen him yesterday, only that it rained; and, as a precaution against our meeting being broken up, a shed was being built. He could not hear of our leaving the country without seeing him.

18th. At last we were summoned to attend the king's levée; but the suspicious creature wished his officers to inspect the things we had brought for him before we went there. Here was another hitch. I could not submit to such disrespectful suspicions; but if he wished Bombay to convey my present to him, I saw no harm in the proposition. The king waived the point, and we all started, carrying as a present the things enumerated in the note.* The Union Jack led the way. At the ferry three shots were fired, when, stepping into ·two large canoes, we all went across the Kafŭ together, and found, to our surprise, a small hut built for the reception, low down on the opposite bank, where no strange eyes could see us.

Within this, sitting on a low wooden stool placed upon a double matting of skins—cows' below and leopards' above—on an elevated platform of grass, was the great king Kamrasi, looking, enshrouded in his mbŭgŭ dress, for all the world like a pope in state —calm and actionless. One bracelet of fine-twisted brass wire adorned his left wrist, and his hair, half an inch long, was worked up into small peppercorn-like knobs by rubbing the hand circularly over the crown of the head. His eyes were long, face narrow, and nose prominent, after the true fashion of his breed; and though a finely-made man, considerably above six feet high, he was not so large as Rŭmanika. A cowskin, stretched out and fastened to the roof, acted as a canopy to prevent dust falling, and a curtain of mbŭgŭ concealed the lower parts of the hut, in front of which, on both sides of the king, sat about a dozen head men.

This was all. We entered and took seats on our own iron stools, while Bombay placed all the presents upon the ground before the throne. As no greetings were exchanged, and all at first remained as silent as death, I commenced, after asking about his health, by saying I had journeyed six long years (by the African computation of five months in the year) for the pleasure of this meeting, coming by Karagŭé instead of by the Nile, because the "Wanya Béri" (Bari people at Gondokoro) had defeated the projects of all former attempts made by white men to reach Unyoro. The purpose of my coming was to ascertain whether his majesty would like to trade with our country, exchanging ivory for articles of European manufacture; as, should he do so, merchants would come here in the same way as they went from Zanzibar to Karagŭé. Rŭmanika and Mtésa were both anxious for trade, and I felt sorry he would not listen to my advice and make friends with Mtésa; for, unless the influence of trade was brought in to

* 1 double rifle, 1 block-tin box, 1 red blanket, 1 brown do., 10 copper wire, 4 socks full of different-colored minute beads, 2 socks full of blue and white pigeon eggs, 1 Rodgers's penknife, 2 books, 1 elastic circle, 1 red handkerchief, 1 bag guncaps, 1 pair scissors, 1 pomatum-pot, 1 quart bottle, 1 powder-flask, 7 lbs. powder, 1 dressing-case, 1 blacking-box, 1 brass lock and key, 4 brass handles, 8 brass sockets, 7 chintz, 7 bindera, 1 red bag, 1 pair glass spectacles, 1 lucifer-box.

check the Waganda from pillaging the country, nothing would do so.

Kamrasi, in a very quiet, mild manner, instead of answering the question, told us of the absurd stories which he had heard from the Waganda, said he did not believe them, else his rivers, deprived of their fountains, would have run dry; and he thought, if we did eat hills and the tender parts of mankind, we should have had enough to satisfy our appetites before we reached Unyoro. Now, however, he was glad to see that, although our hair was straight and our faces white, we still possessed hands and feet like other men.

The present was then opened, and every thing in turn placed upon the red blanket. The goggles created some mirth; so did the scissors, as Bombay, to show their use, clipped his beard; and the lucifers were considered a wonder; but the king scarcely moved or uttered any remarks till all was over, when, at the instigation of the courtiers, my chronometer was asked for and shown. This wonderful instrument, said the officers (mistaking it for my compass), was the magic horn by which the white men found their way every where. Kamrasi said he must have it; for, besides it, the gun was the only thing new to him. The chronometer, however, I said, was the only one left, and could not possibly be parted with; though, if Kamrasi liked to send men to Gani, a new one could be obtained for him.

Then changing the subject, much to my relief, Kamrasi asked Bombay, "Who governs England?" "A woman." "Has she any children?" "Yes," said Bombay, with ready impudence; "these are two of them" (pointing to Grant and myself). That settled, Kamrasi wished to know if we had any speckled cows, or cows of any peculiar color, and would we like to change four large cows for four small ones, as he coveted some of ours. This was a staggerer. We had totally failed, then, in conveying to this stupid king the impression that we were not mere traders, ready to bargain with him. We would present him with cows if we had such as he wanted, but we could not bargain. The meeting then broke up in the same chilling manner as it began, and we returned as we came, but no sooner reached home than four pots of pombé were sent us, with a hope that we had arrived all safely. The present gave great satisfaction. The Wangŭana accused Frij of having "unclean hands," because the beef had not lasted so long as it should do; it being a notable fact in Mussulman creed, that unless the man's hands are pure who cuts the throat of an animal, its flesh will not last fresh half the ordinary time.

19th. As the presents given yesterday occupied the king's mind too much for other business, I now sent to offer him one third of the guns left in Uganda, provided he would send some messengers with one of my men to ask Mtésa for them, and also the same proportion of the sixty loads of property left in charge of Rŭmanika at Karagŭé, if he would send the requisite number of porters for its removal. But of all things, I said, I most wished to send a letter to Petherick at Gani, to apprise him of our whereabouts, for he must have been four years waiting our arrival there, and by the same opportunity I would get a watch for the king. He sent us to-day two pots of pombé, one sack of salt, and what might be called a screw of butter, with an assurance that the half of every thing which came to his house—and every thing was brought from great distances in boats—he would give me; but for the present the only thing he was in need of was some medicine or stimulants. Farther, I need be under no apprehension if I did not find men at once to go on the three respective journeys; it should be all done in good time, for he loved me much, and desired to show us so much respect that his name should be celebrated for it in songs of praise until he was bowed down by years, and even after death it should be remembered.

I ascertained then that the salt, which was very white and pure, came from an island on the Little Lŭta Nzigé, about sixty miles west from the Chagŭzi palace, where the lake is said to be forty or fifty miles wide. It is the same piece of water we heard of in Karagŭé as the Little Lŭta Nzigé, beyond Utŭmbi; and the same story of Unyoro being an island circumscribed by it and the Victoria N'yanza connected by the Nile, is related here, showing that both the Karagŭé and Unyoro people, as indeed all negroes and Arabs, have the common defect in their language of using the same word for a peninsula and an island. The Waijasi—of whom we saw a specimen in the shape of an old woman, with her upper lip edged with a row of small holes, at Karagŭé—occupy a large island on this lake named Gasi, and sometimes come to visit Kamrasi. Ugungŭ, a dependency of Kamrasi's, occupies this side the lake, and on the opposite side is Ulégga; beyond which, in about 2° N. lat. and 28° E. long., is the country of Namachi; and farther west still about 2°, the Wilyanwantŭ, or cannibals, who, according to the report both here and at Karagŭé, "bury cows, but eat men." These distant people pay their homage to Kamrasi, though they have six degrees of longitude to travel over. They are, I believe, a portion of the N'yam N'yams—another name for cannibal—whose country Petherick said he entered in 1857–58. Among the other wild legends about this people, it was said that the Wilyanwantŭ, in making brotherhood, exchanged their blood by drinking at one another's veins; and, in lieu of butter with their porridge, they smear it with the fat of fried human flesh.

20th. I had intended for to-day an expedition to the lake; but Kamrasi, harboring a wicked design that we should help in an attack on his brothers, said there was plenty of time to think of that; we would only find that all the waters united go to Gani, and he wished us to be his guests for three or four months at least. Fifty Gani men had just arrived to inform him that Rionga had lately sent ten slaves and ten ivory tusks to Petherick's post, to purchase a gun; but the answer was, that a thousand times as much would not purchase a weapon that might be used against us; for our arrival with Kamrasi had been heard of, and nothing would be done to jeopardize our road.

To talk over this matter, the king invited us to meet him. We went as before, minus the flag and firing, and met a similar reception. The Gani news was talked over, and we proposed sending Bombay with a letter at once. I could get no answer; so, to pass the time, we wished to know from the king's own lips if he had prevented Baraka from going to Gani, as he had carried orders from Rŭmanika as well as from myself to visit Kamrasi, to give him fifty egg-beads, seventy necklaces of mtendé, and seventy necklaces of kŭtŭamnazi beads, and then to pass on to Gani and give its chief fifty egg-beads and forty necklaces of kŭtŭamnazi. Kamrasi replied, "I did not allow him to go, because I heard you had gone to Uganda;" and Dr. K'yengo's men happening to be present, added, " Baraka used up all the beads save forty, which he gave to Kamrasi, living upon goats all the way; and when he left, took back a tusk of ivory."

This little controversy was amusing, but did not suit Kamrasi, who had his eye on a certain valuable possession of mine. He made his approach toward it by degrees, beginning with a truly royal speech thus: "I am the king of all these countries, even including Uganda and Kidi—though the Kidi people are such savages they obey no man's orders—and you are great men also, sitting on chairs before kings; it therefore ill becomes us to talk of such trifles as beads, especially as I know if you ever return this way I shall get more from you." "Begging your majesty's pardon," I said, "the mention of beads only fell in the way of our talk like stones in a walk; our motive being to get at the truth of what Baraka did and said here, as his conduct in returning after receiving strict orders from Rŭmanika and ourselves to open the road is a perfect enigma to us. We could not have entered Unyoro at all excepting through Uganda, and we could not have put foot in Uganda without visiting its king." Without deigning to answer, Kamrasi, in the metaphorical language of a black man, said, "It would be unbecoming of me to keep secrets from you, and therefore I will tell you at once; I am sadly afflicted with a disorder which you alone can cure." "What is it, your majesty? I can see nothing in your face; it may perhaps require a private inspection." "My heart," he said, "is troubled, because you will not give me your magic horn—the thing, I mean, in your pocket, which you pulled out one day when Budja and Vittagŭra were discussing the way; and you no sooner looked at it than you said, 'That is the way to the palace.'"

So! the sly fellow has been angling for the chronometer all this time, and I can get nothing out of him until he has got it— the road to the lake, the road to Gani, every thing seemed risked on his getting my watch, a chronometer worth £50, which would be spoiled in his hands in one day. To undeceive him, and tell him it was the compass which I looked at and not the watch, I knew would only end with my losing that instrument as well; so I told him it was not my guide, but a time-keeper, made for the purpose of knowing what time to eat my dinner by. It was the only chronometer I had with me; and I begged he would have patience until Bombay returned from Gani with another, when he should have the option of taking this or the new one. "No; I must have the one in your pocket; pull it out and show it." This was done, and I placed it on the ground, saying, "The instrument is yours, but I must keep it until another one comes." "No; I must have it now, and will send it you three times every day to look at."

The watch went, gold chain and all, without any blessings following it; and the horrid king asked if I could make up another magic horn, for he hoped he had deprived us of the power of traveling, and plumed himself on the notion that the glory of opening the road would devolve upon himself. When I told him that to purchase another would cost five hundred cows, the whole party were more confirmed than ever as to its magical powers; for who in his senses would give five hundred cows for the mere gratification of seeing at what time his dinner should be eaten? Thus ended the second meeting. Kamrasi now said the Gani men would feast on beef to-morrow, and the next day be ready to start with my men for Petherick's camp. He then accompanied us to the boats, spear in hand, and saw us cross the water. Long tail-hairs of the giraffe surrounded his neck, on which little balls and other ornaments of minute beads, after the Uganda fashion, were worked. In the evening four pots of pombé and a pack of flour were brought, together with the chronometer, which was sent to be wound up—damaged of course—the seconds-hand had been dislodged.

21st. I heard from Kidgwiga that some of those Gani men now ordered to go with Bombay had actually been visiting here when the latter shot his first cow at the palace, but had gone to their homes to give information of us, and had returned again. Eager to get on with my journey, and see European faces again, I besought the king to let us depart, as our work was all finished here, since he had assured us he would like to trade with England. The N'yanswengé—meaning Petherick's party—who have hitherto been afraid to come here, would do so now, when they had seen us pass safely down, and could receive my guns and property left to come from Uganda and Karagŭé, which we ourselves could not wait for. Kamrasi, thinking me angry for his having taken the watch so rudely out of my pocket, took fright at the message, sent some of his attendants quickly back to me, requesting me to keep the instrument until another arrived, and begged I would never say I wished to leave his house again.

22d. Kamrasi sent to say Bombay was not to start to-day, but to-morrow, so we put the screw on again, and said we must go at once; if he would give us guides to Gani, we would return him his twenty cows and seven goats with pleasure. I let him understand we suspected he was keeping us here to fight his brothers, and told him he must at once know we would never lift hand against them. It was contrary to the laws of our land. "I have got no orders to enter into black men's quarrels, and my mother" (the queen), "whom I see every night in my sleep calling me home, would be very angry if she heard of it. Rŭmanika once asked me to fight his brothers Rogéro and M'yongo, but my only reply to all had been the same—I have no orders to fight with, only to make friends of, the great kings of Africa."

The game seemed now to be won. At once Kamrasi ordered Bombay to prepare for the journey. Five Wanyoro, five Chopi men, and five Gani men, were to escort him. There was no objection to his carrying arms. The moment he returned, which ought to be in little more than a fortnight, we would all go together. An earnest request was at the same time made that I would not bully him in the mean time with any more applications to depart. So Bombay and Mabrŭki, carrying their muskets, and a map and letter for Petherick, departed.

23*d* and 24*th*. Kamrasi, presuming he had gained favor in our eyes, sent, begging to know how we had slept, and said he would like us to inform him what part of his journey Bombay had this morning reached, a fact which he had no doubt must be divinable through the medium of our books. The reply was, that Bombay's luck was so good we had no doubt regarding his success; but now he had gone, and our days here were numbered, we should like to see the palace, his fat wives and children, as well as the Wanyoro's dances, and all the gayety of the place. We did not think our reception-hut by the river sufficiently dignified, and our residence here was altogether like that of prisoners—seeing no one, knowing no one. In answer to this, Kamrasi sent one pot of pombé and five fowls, begging we would not be alarmed; we should see every thing in good time, if we would but have patience, for he considered us very great men, as he was a great man himself, and we had come at his invitation. He must request, in the mean time, that we would send no more messages by his officers, as such messages are never conveyed properly. At present there was a great deal of business in the palace.

We asked for some butter, but could get none, as all the milk in the palace was consumed by the wives and children, drinking all day long, to make themselves immovably fat.

25*th*. In the morning, the commander-in-chief wished us to cast a horoscope, and see where Bombay was, and if he were getting on well. That being negatived, he told us to put our hut in order, as Kamrasi was coming to see us. Accordingly, we made every thing as smart as possible, hanging the room round with maps, horns, and skins of animals, and placed a large box, covered with a red blanket, as a throne for the king to sit upon. As he advanced, my men, forming a guard of honor, fired three shots immediately on his setting foot upon our side the river; while Frij, with his boatswain's whistle, piped the "Rogue's March," to prepare us for his majesty's approach. We saluted him, hat in hand, and, leading the way, showed him in. He was pleased to be complimentary, remarking what waséja (fine men) we were, and took his seat. We sat on smaller boxes, to appear humble, while his escort of black "swells" filled the doorway, squatting on the ground, so as to stop the light and interfere with our decorations.

After the first salutations, the king remarked the head of a n'samma buck, and handled it; then noticed my musquito-curtains hanging over the bed, and begged for them. He was told they could not be given until Bombay returned, as the musquitoes would eat us up. "But there were two," said the escort, "for we have seen one in the other hut." That was true; but were there not two white men? However, if the king wanted gauze, here was a smart gauze veil — and the veil vanished at once. The iron camp-bed was next inspected and admired; then the sextant, which was coveted and begged for, but without success, much to the astonishment of the king, as his attendants had led him to expect he would get any thing he asked for. Then the thermometers were wanted and refused; also table-knives, spoons, forks, and even cooking-pots, for we had no others, and could not part with them. The books of birds and animals had next to be seen, and, being admired, were coveted, the king offering one of the books I first gave him in exchange for one of these. In fact, he wanted to fleece us of every thing; so, to shut him up, I said I would not part with one bird for one hundred tusks of ivory; they were all the collections I had made in Africa, and if I parted with them my journey would go for nothing; but if he wanted a few drawings of birds I would do some for him: at present I wished to speak to him. "Well, what is it? we are all attention." "I wish to know positively if you would like English traders to come here regularly, as the Arabs do to trade at Karagŭé? and if so, would you give me a pembé (magic horn) as a warrant that every body may know Kamrasi, king of Unyoro, desires it?"

Kamrasi replied, "I like your proposition very much; you shall have the horn you ask for, either large or small, just as you please; and after you have gone, should we hear any English are at Gani wishing to come here, as my brothers are in the way, we will advance with spears while they approach with guns, and, between us both, my brothers must fly; for I myself will head the expedition. But, now you have had your say, I will have mine, if you will listen." " All right, your majesty; what is it?" "I am constantly stricken with fever and pains, for which I know no remedy but cautery; my children die young; my family is not large enough to uphold my dignity and station in life; in fact, I am infirm and want stimulants, and I wish you to prescribe for me, which, considering you have found your way to this, where nobody came before, must be easy to you." Two pills and a draught for the morning were given as a preliminary measure, argument being of no avail; and, to our delight, the king said it was time to go.

We jumped off our seats to show him the way, hoping our persecutions were over; but still he sat and sat, until at length, finding we did not take the hint to give him a parting present, he said, " I never visited any big man's house without taking home some trifle to show my wife and children." " Indeed, great king, then you did not come to visit us, but to beg, eh? You shall have nothing, positively nothing; for we will not have it said the king did not come to see us, but to beg." Kamrasi's face changed color; he angrily said, "Irokh togend" (let us rise and go), and forthwith walked straight out of the hut. Frij piped, but no guns fired; and as he asked the reason why, he was told it would be offensive to say we were glad he was going. The king was evidently not pleased, for no pombé came to-day.

CHAPTER XVIII.

UNYORO—*Continued.*

The Ceremonies of the New Moon.—Kamrasi's Rule and Discipline.—An Embassy from Uganda, and its Results.—The rebellious Brothers.—An African Sorcerer and his Incantations.—The Kamraviona of Unyoro.—Burial Customs.—Ethiopian Legends.—Complicated Diplomacy for our Detention.—Proposal to send Princes to England.—We get away.

26th. WE found that the palace was shut up in consequence of the new moon, seen for the first time last evening; and incessant drumming was the order of the day. Still, private interviews might be granted, and I sent to inquire after the state of the king's health. The reply was that the medicine had not been taken, and the king was very angry because nothing was given him when he took the trouble to call on us. He never called at a big man's house and left it mwiko (empty-handed) before; if there was nothing else to dispose of, could Bana not have given him a bag of beads?

To save us from this kind of incessant annoyance, I now thought it would be our best policy to mount the high horse and bully him. Accordingly, we tied up a bag of the commonest mixed beads, added the king's chronometer, and sent them to Kamrasi with a violent message that we were thoroughly disgusted with all that had happened; the beads were for the poor beggar who came to our house yesterday, not to see us, but to beg; and as we did not desire the acquaintance of beggars, we had made up our minds never to call again, nor receive any more bread or wine from the king.

This appeared to be a hit. Kamrasi, evidently taken aback, said, if he thought he should have offended us by begging, he would not have begged. He was not a poor man, for he had many cows, but he was a beggar, of course, when beads were in the question; and, having unwittingly offended, as he desired our friendship, he trusted his offense would be forgiven. On opening the chronometer, he again wrenched back the seconds-hand, and sent it for repair, together with two pots of pombé as a peace-offering. Frij, who accompanied the deputation, overheard the counselors tell their king that the Waganda were on their way back to Unyoro to snatch us away; on hearing which, the king asked his men if they would ever permit it; and, handling his spear as if for battle, said at the same time he would lose his own head before they should touch his guests. Then, turning to Frij, he said, "What would you do if they came? go back with them?" To which Frij said, "No, never, when Gani is so near; they might cut our heads off, but that is all they could do." The watch being by this time repaired, it gave me the opportunity of sending Kidgwiga back to the palace to say we trusted Kamrasi would allow Budja to come here, if only with one woman to carry his pombé, else Mtésa would take offense, form an alliance with Rionga, and surround the place with warriors, for it was not becoming in great kings to treat civil messengers like dogs.

The reply to this was, that Kamrasi was very much pleased with my fatherly wisdom and advice, and would act up to it, allowing Budja only to approach with one woman; we need, however, be under no apprehensions, for Kamrasi's power was infinite; the Gani road should be opened even at the spear's point; he had been beating the big drum in honor of us the whole day; he would not allow any beggars to come and see us, for he wanted us all to himself, and for this reason had ordered a fence to be built all round our house; but he had got no present from Grant yet, though all he wanted was his musquito-curtains, while he wished my picture-books to show his women, and be returned. We sent a picture of Mtésa as a gift, the two books to look at, and an acknowledgment that the musquito-curtains were his, only he must have patience until Bombay arrived; but his proposition about the fence we rejected with scorn. The king had been raising an army to fight Rionga—the true reason, we suspect, for the beating of the drum.

27th and 28th. There was drumming and music all day and night, and the army was being increased to a thousand men, but we poor prisoners could see nothing of it. Frij was therefore sent to inspect the armament and bring us all the news. Some of N'yamyonjo's men, seeing mine armed with carbines, became very inquisitive about them, and asked if they were the instruments which shot their men on the Nile—one in the arm, who died; the other on the top of the shoulder, who was recovering. The drums were kept in private rooms, to which a select few only were admitted.   Kamrasi conducts all business himself, awarding punishments and seeing them carried out.   The most severe instrument of chastisement is a knob-stick, sharpened at the back, like that used in Uganda, for breaking a man's neck before he is thrown into the N'yanza; but this severity is seldom resorted to, Kamrasi being of a mild disposition compared with Mtésa, whom he invariably alludes to when ordering men to be flogged, telling them that, were they in Uganda, their heads would suffer instead of their backs.   In the day's work at the palace, army collecting, ten officers were bound because they failed to bring a sufficient number of fighting men, but were afterward released on their promising to bring more.

Nothing could be more filthy than the state of the palace and all the lanes leading up to it: it was well, perhaps, that we were never expected to go there, for without stilts and respirators it would have been impracticable, such is the dirty nature of the people.   The king's cows, even, are kept in his palace inclosure, the calves actually entering the hut, where, like a farmer, Kamrasi walks among them up to his ankles in filth, and, inspecting them, issues his orders concerning them.   What has to be selected for his guests he singles out himself.

Dr. K'yengo's men, who had been sent three times into action against the refractory brothers, asked leave to return to Karagué; but the king, who did not fear for their lives when his work was to be done, would not give them leave, lest accident should befall them on the way.   We found no prejudice against eating butter among these Wahŭma, for they not only sold us some, but mixed it with porridge and ate it themselves.

29th. The king has appointed a special officer to keep our table supplied with sweet potatoes, and sent us a pot of pombé, with his excuses for not seeing us, as business was so pressing, and would continue to be so until the army marched.   Budja and Kasoro were again reported to be near with a force of fifty Waganda, prepared to snatch us away; and the king, fearing the consequences, had sent to inform Budja, that if he dared attempt to approach, he would slip us off in boats to Gani, and then fight it out with the Waganda; for his guests, since they had been handed over to him, had been treated with every possible respect.

To keep Kamrasi to his promise, as we particularly wished to hear the Uganda news, Frij was sent to inform him on my behalf

that Mtésa only wished to make friends with all the great kings
surrounding his country before his coronation took place, when his
brothers would be burnt, and he would cease to take advice from
his mother.   To treat his messengers disrespectfully could do no
good, and might provoke a war, when we should see my deserters,
joined with the Waganda, really coming in force against us;
whereas, if we saw Budja, we could satisfy him, and Mtésa too,
and obviate any such calamity.   The reply was, that Kamrasi
would arrange for our having a meeting with Budja alone if we
wished it; he did not fear my deserters siding with King Mtésa,
but he detested the Waganda, and could not bear to see them in
his country.

30*th*. At breakfast-time we heard that my old friend Kasoro
had come to our camp without permission, to the surprise of every
body, attended by all his boys, leaving Budja and his children, on
account of sickness, at the camp assigned to the Waganda, five
miles off.   Kasoro wished to speak to us, and we invited him into
the hut; but the interview could not be permitted until Kamrasi's wishes on the subject had been ascertained.   In a little
while the kamraviona, having seen Kamrasi, said we might converse with one another while his officers were present listening,
and sent a cow as a present for the Waganda.   Kasoro, with his
children, now came before us in their usual merry manner, and,
after saluting, told us how the deserters, on reaching Uganda,
begged for leave to proceed to Karagué; but Mtésa, who would
only allow two of them to approach him, abused them, saying,
"Did I not command you to take Bana to Gani at all risks?   If
there was no road by land, you were to go by water; or, if that
failed, to go under ground, or in the air above; and if he died,
you were to die with him : what, then, do you mean by deserting
him and flying here?   You shall not move a yard from this until I receive a messenger from him to hear what he has got to say
on the matter."   Mtésa would not take their arms, even at the
desire of Budja, on my behalf; for, as no messenger on my behalf came to him, he would not believe what Budja said, and
feared to touch any of our property.   The chief item of court
news was, that Mtésa had shot a buffalo which was attacking him
behind his palace, and made his wakungŭ carry the animal bodily, while life was in it, into his court.   The ammunition I wrote
for to Rŭmanika had been brought by Maŭla.

As Kasoro still remained silent with regard to Mtésa's message,

I told him we shot two of N'yamyonjo's men on our retreat up the Nile, and that Kamrasi turned us back because some miscreant Waganda had forged lies and told him we were terrible monsters, who ate hills and human flesh, and drank up all the water of the lake. He laughed, but still was silent; so I said, "What message have you brought from Mtésa?" To which, in a timid, modest kind of manner, he said, "Bana knows — what more need I say? Has he forgotten Mtésa, who loves him so?" I said, "No, indeed, I have not forgotten Mtésa; and, moreover, as I expected you back again, I have sent Bombay to bring the stimulants and all the things I promised Mtésa from Gani; in two or three days he will return." "No," said Kasoro, "that is not it; we must go to Gani with you; for Mtésa says he loves you so much he will never allow you to part from his hand until his servants have seen you safely at your homes."

I replied, "If Mtésa wishes you to see my vessels and all the wonders they contain, as far as I am concerned you may do so, and I shall be only too happy to show you a little English hospitality; but the road is in Kamrasi's hands, and his wishes must now be heard." The commander-in-chief, now content with all he had heard, went to Kamrasi to receive his orders, while I gave Kasoro a feast of porridge and salt, with pombé to wash it down, and a cow to take home with him; for the poor creatures said they were all starving, as the Wanyoro would not allow them to take a single plantain from the field until Kamrasi's permission had been given.

Kamrasi's reply now arrived; it was to the following effect: "Tell my children, the Waganda, they were never turned out of Unyoro by my orders: if they wish to go to Gani, they can do so; but, first of all, they must return to Mtésa, and ask him to deliver up all of Bana's men." I answered, "No; if any one of those scoundrels who has deserted me ever dares show his face to me again, I will shoot him like a dog. Moreover, I want Mtésa to take their guns from them, and, without taking life, to transport them all to an island on the N'yanza, where they can spend their days in growing plantains; for it is such men who prevent our traveling in the country and visiting kings." Kasoro on this said, "Mtésa will do so in a minute if you send a servant to him, but he won't if we only say you wish it."

The commander-in-chief then added, as to Kasoro's wish to accompany me, "If Mtésa will send another time one of his people whose life he wishes sacrificed on the journey, or tells us, Here is a man whom I wish you to send to Gani at all hazards, and without responsibility for his life on our part, we will be very glad to send him; but as we are at war with the Gani people continually, there will be no security for a Mganda's life there." To this I added, "Now, Kasoro, you see how it is; Kamrasi does not wish you to go to Gani, so if you take my advice you will return to Mtésa. Give this tin cartridge-box, which first came from him, back to him again, to show him you have seen me, and say, This is Bana's letter; he wishes you to transport the deserters and seize their guns. The guns, of course, I shall want again at some other time, when I will send one of my English children to visit him; for now Kamrasi has opened his country to us, and given us leave to come and purchase ivory, I never shall be very far away." I gave them three pills for Budja, blistered two of the pages, and started the whole merrily off, Kasoro asking me to send Mtésa some pretty things from England such as he never saw.

1st. Kamrasi sent his commander-in-chief to inquire after my health, and to say Budja had left in fear and trembling lest Mtésa should cut all their heads off for failing in the mission; but he had sent Kidgwiga's brother with a pot of pombé to escort the Waganda beyond his frontier, and cheer them on the way; for the tin cartridge-box, he thought, would save their lives by satisfying Mtésa they had seen me. The commander-in-chief then told me Kamrasi did not wish them to accompany me through Kidi, for the Kidi people don't like the Waganda, and, discovering their nationality by the fullness of their teeth, would bring trouble on us while trying to kill them. I said I thanked Kamrasi for his having treated the Waganda with such marked respect, in allowing them to see me, and sending them back with an escort; but I thought it would have been better if he had spoken the truth plainly out, for then I could have told them I feared to have them in company with me. In return for my civilities, the king then sent one of his Chopi officers to see me, who went four stages with Bombay, and he also sent some rich beads which he wished me to look at. They were nicely kept in a neat though very large casing of rush pith, and were those sent as a letter from Gani to inform him that we were expected to come viâ Karagué. After this, to keep us in good-humor, Kamrasi sent to inform us that some Gani men, twenty-five in number, had just arrived, and had given him a lion skin, several tippet monkey skins, and some giraffe hair, as well as a stick of copper or brass wire. Bombay was met by them on the confines of Gani.

2*d*. The king sent me a pot of pombé to-day, inquiring after my health, and saying he would like to take the medicine I gave him if I would send Frij over to administer it, but he would be ashamed to swallow pills before me. Hitherto he had not been able to take the medicine from press of business in collecting an army to fight his brothers; but as his troops would all leave for war to-day, he expected to have leisure.

In plying the kamraviona to try if we could get rid of the annoying restraints which made our residence here a sort of imprisonment, I discovered that the whole affair was not one of blunder or accident, but that we actually were prisoners thus by design. It appeared that Kamrasi's brothers, when they heard we were coming into Unyoro, murmured, and said to the king, "Why are you bringing such guests among us, who will practice all kinds of diabolical sorcery, and bring evil on us?" To which Kamrasi replied, "I have invitêd them to come, and they shall come; and if they bring evil with them, let that all fall on my shoulders, for you shall not see them." He then built a palaver-house on the banks of the Kafŭ to receive us in privately; and when we were to go to Gani, it was his intention to slip us off privately down the Kafŭ. The brothers were so thoroughly frightened, that when Kamrasi opened his chronometer before them to show them the works in motion, they turned their heads away. The large block-tin box I gave Kamrasi, as part of his hongo, was, I heard, called mzungŭ, or the white man, by him.

In the evening the beads recently brought from Gani were sent for my inspection, with an intimation that Kamrasi highly approved of them, and would like me to give him a few like them. Some of Kamrasi's spies, whom he had sent to the refractory allies of Rionga his brother, returned bringing a spear and some grass from the thatch of the hut of a Chopi chief. The removal of the grass was a piece of state policy. It was stolen by Kamrasi's orders, in order that he might spread a charm on the Chopi people, and gain such an influence over them that their spears could not prevail against the Wanyoro; but it was thought we might possess some still superior magic powder, as we had come from such a long distance, and Kamrasi would prefer to have ours. These Chopi people were leagued with the brothers, and thus kept the

KAMRASI'S MAGICIAN IN SEARCH OF THE RAIN-GAUGE.

high road to Gani, though the other half of Chopi remained loyal; and though Kamrasi continually sent armies against the refractory half which aided his brothers, they never retaliated by attacking this place.

We found, by the way, that certain drumming and harmonious accompaniments which we had been accustomed to hear all day and night were to continue for four moons, in celebration of twins born to Kamrasi since we came here.

3*d*. Kamrasi's political department was active again to-day. Some Gani officials arrived to inform him that there were two white men in the vessel spoken of as at Gani; a second vessel was coming in there, and several others were on their way. A carnelian was shown me which the Gani people gave to Kamrasi many years ago. Kamrasi expressed a wish that I would exchange magic powders with him. He had a very large variety, and would load a horn for me with all those I desired most. He wanted also medicines for longevity and perpetual strength. Those I had given him had, he said, deprived him of strength, and he felt much reduced by their effects. He would like me to go with him and attack the island his three brothers, Rionga, Wahitŭ, and Pohŭka, are in possession of. When I said I never fought with black men, he wished to know if I would not shoot them if they attacked me. My reply was, alluding to our fight in the river, "How did N'yamyonjo's men fare?" I found that Kamrasi had thirty brothers and as many sisters.

4*th*. I gave Kamrasi a bottle of quinine, which we call "strong back," and asked him, in return, for a horn containing all the powders necessary to give me the gift of tongues, so that I should be able to converse with any black men whom I might meet with. We heard that Kamrasi has called all his Gani guests to play before him, and a double shot from his Blissett rifle announced to our ears that he, in turn, was amusing them. This was the first time the gun had been discharged since he received it, and, fearing to fire it himself, he called one of my men to do it for him.

5*th*. At 9 A.M., the time for measuring the fall of rain for the last twenty-four hours, we found the rain-gauge and bottle had been removed, so we sent Kidgwiga to inform the king we wished his magicians to come at once and institute a search for it. Kidgwiga immediately returned with the necessary adept, an old man, nearly blind, dressed in strips of old leather fastened to the waist, and carrying in one hand a cow's horn primed with magic powder, carefully covered on the mouth with leather, from which dangled an iron bell. The old creature jingled the bell, entered our hut, squatted on his hams, looked first at one, then at the other; inquired what the missing things were like, grunted, moved his skinny arm round his head, as if desirous of catching air from all four sides of the hut, then dashed the accumulated air on the head of his horn, smelt it to see if all was going right, jingled the bell again close to his ear, and grunted his satisfaction; the missing articles must be found.

To carry out the incantation more effectually, however, all my men were sent for to sit in the open before the hut, when the old doctor rose, shaking the horn and tinkling the bell close to his ear. He then, confronting one of the men, dashed the horn forward as if intending to strike him on the face, then smelt the head, then dashed at another, and so on, till he became satisfied that my men were not the thieves. He then walked into Grant's hut, inspected that, and finally went to the place where the bottle had been kept. There he walked about the grass with his arm up, and jingling the bell to his ear, first on one side, then on the other, till the track of a hyena gave him the clew, and in two or three more steps he found it. A hyena had carried it into the grass and dropped it. Bravo for the infallible horn! and well done the king for his honesty in sending it! So I gave the king the bottle and gauge, which delighted him amazingly; and the old doctor, who begged for pombé, got a goat for his trouble. My men now, recollecting the powder robbery at Uganda, said King Mtésa would not send his horn when I asked for it, because he was the culprit himself.

6th. Kidgwiga told us to-day that King Kamrasi's sisters are not allowed to wed; they live and die virgins in his palace. Their only occupation in life consisted in drinking milk, of which each one consumes the produce daily of from ten to twenty cows, and hence they become so inordinately fat that they can not walk. Should they wish to see a relative, or go outside the hut for any purpose, it requires eight men to lift any of them on a litter. The brothers, too, are not allowed to go out of his reach. This confinement of the palace family is considered a state necessity, as a preventive to civil wars, in the same way as the destruction of the Uganda princes, after a certain season, is thought necessary for the preservation of peace there.

7th. In the morning the kamraviona called, on the king's behalf, to inquire after my health, and also to make some important communications. First he was to request a supply of bullets, that the king might fire a salute when Bombay returned from Gani; next, to ask for stimulative medicine, now that he had consumed all I gave him, and gone through the preliminary course; farther, to request I would spread a charm over all his subjects, so that their hearts might be inclined toward him, and they would come without calling and bow down at his feet; finally, he wished me to exchange my blood with him, that we might be brothers till death. I sent the bullets, advised him to wait a day or two for the medicine, and said there was only one charm by which he could gain the influence he required over his subjects—this was, knowledge and the power of the pen. Should he desire some of my children (meaning missionaries) to come here and instruct his, the thing would be done; but not in one year, nor even ten, for it takes many years to educate children.

As to exchanging my blood with a black man's, it was a thing quite beyond my comprehension, though Rŭmanika, I must confess, had asked me to do the same thing. The way the English make lasting friendships is done either by the expressions of their hearts, or by the exchange of some trifles as keepsakes; and now, as I had given Kamrasi some specimens of English manufacture, he might give me a horn, or any thing else he chose, which I could show to my friends, so as to keep him in recollection all my life.

The kamraviona, before leaving, said, for our information, that a robbery had occurred in the palace last night; for this morning, when Kamrasi went to inspect his mzungŭ (the block-tin box), which he had forgotten to lock, he found all his beads had been stolen. After sniffing round among the various wives, he smelt the biggest one to be the culprit, and turned the beads out of her possession. Deputies came in the evening with a pot of pombé and small screw of butter, to tell me some Gani people had just arrived, bringing information that the vessel at Gani had left to go down the river; but when intelligence reached the vessel of the approach of my men, they turned and came back again. Bombay was well feasted on the road by Kamrasi's people, receiving eight cows from one and two cows from another.

8*th* and 9*th*. We had a summons to attend at the Kafŭ palace with the medicine-chest, a few select persons only to be present. It rained so much on the 8th as to stop the visit, but we went next day. After arriving there, and going through the usual salutations, Kamrasi asked us from what stock of people we came, explaining his meaning by saying, " As we, Rŭmanika, Mtésa, and the rest of us (enumerating the kings), are wawitŭ (or princes), Uwitŭ (or the country of princes) being to the east." This interesting announcement made me quite forget to answer his question, and induced me to say, " Omwita, indeed, was the ancient name for Mombas, if you came from that place: I know all about your race for two thousand years or more. Omwita, you mean, was the last country you resided in before you came here, but originally you came from Abyssinia, the sultan of which, our great friend, is Sahéla Sélassié."

He pronounced this name laughing, and said, " Formerly our stock was half white and half black, with one side of our heads covered with straight hair, and the other side frizzly: you certainly do know every thing." The subject then turned upon medicine, and, after inspecting the chest, and inquiring into all its contents, it ended by his begging for the half of every thing. The musquito-curtains were again asked for, and refused until I should leave this. As Kamrasi was anxious I should take two of his children to England to be instructed, I agreed to do so, but said I thought it would be better if he invited missionaries to come here and educate all his family. His cattle were much troubled with sickness, dying in great numbers—could I cure them? As he again began to persecute us with begging, wanting knives and forks, etc., I advised his using ivory as money, and purchasing what he wanted from Gani. This brought out the interesting fact, the truth of which we had never reached before, that when Petherick's servant brought him one necklace of beads, and asked after us, he gave in return fourteen ivories, thirteen women, and seven mbŭgŭ cloths. One of his men accompanied the visitors back to the boats, and saw Petherick, who took the ivory and rejected the women.

10th. At 2 P.M. we were called by Kamrasi to visit him at the Kafŭ palace again, and requested to bring a lot of medicines tied up in various colored cloths, so that he might know what to select for different ailments. We repaired there as before, putting the medicines into the sextant-stand box, and found him lying at full length on the platform of his throne, with a glass-bead necklace of various colors, and a charm tied on his left arm. Nobody was allowed to be present at our interview. The medicines, four varieties, were weighed out into ten doses each, and their uses and effects explained. He begged for four bottles to put them in, till he was laughed out of it by our saying he required forty bottles; for if the powders were mixed, how could he separate them again? And to keep his mind from the begging tack, which he was getting alarmingly near, I said, "Now I have given you these things because you would insist on having them. I must also tell you they are dangerous in your hands, in consequence of your being ignorant of their properties. If you take my advice, you won't meddle with them until the two children you wish educated have learned the use of them in England; and if I have to take boys from this, I hope they will be of your family." He said, "You speak like a father to us, and we very much approve. Here is a pot of pombé; I did not give you one yesterday."

11*th.* To-day, the king having graciously granted permission, we went out shooting, but saw only a few buffalo tracks.

12*th.* The kamraviona was sent to inquire after our health, and to ascertain from me all I knew respecting the origin of Kamrasi's tribe, the distribution of countries, and the seat of the government. I sent the king a diagram, painted in various colors, with full explanations of every thing, and asked permission to send two more of my men in search of Bombay, who had now been absent twenty days. The reply was, that if Bombay did not return within four days, Kamrasi would send other men after him on the fifth day; and, in the mean time, he sent one pot of pombé as a token of his kind regard.

13*th.* The kamraviona was sent to inquire after our health, to ask for medicine for himself, and to inquire more into the origin of his race. I, on the other hand, wishing to make myself as disagreeable as possible, in order that Kamrasi might get tired of us, sent Frij to ask for fresh butter, eggs, tobacco, coffee, and fowls every day, saying I will pay their price when I reach Gani, for we were suffering from want of proper food. Kamrasi was surprised at this clamor for food, and inquired what we ate at home, that we were so different from every body else.

We heard to-day a strange story, involving the tragic fate of Budja. On coming here, he had been bewitched by Kamrasi's frontier officer, who put the charm into a pot of pombé. From the moment Budja drank it he was seized with sickness, and remained so until he reached the first station in Uganda, when he died. The facts of the bewitchment had been found out by means of the perpetrator's wives, who, from the moment the pombé was drunk, took to precipitate flight, well knowing what effects would follow, and dreading the chastisement Mtésa would bring upon their household. We heard, too, that the deserters had returned to the place they deserted from, with thirty Waganda, and a present of some cows for me.

14th. Kamrasi sent me four parcels of coffee, very neatly inclosed in rush pith.

15th. Getting more impatient, and desirous to move on at any sacrifice, I proposed giving up all claims to my muskets, as well as the present of cows from Mtésa, if Kamrasi would give us boats to Gani at once; but the reply was simply, Why be in such a hurry?

16th. The kamraviona was sent to us with a load of coffee, which Kamrasi had purchased with cowries, and to inquire how we had slept. Very badly, was the reply, because we knew Bombay would have been back long ago if Kamrasi was not concealing him somewhere, and we did not know what he was doing with deserters and Waganda. Kamrasi then wanted us to paint his mbŭgŭ cloths in different patterns and colors; but we sent him instead six packages of red-ink powder, and got abused for sauciness. He then wanted black ink, else how could he put on the red with taste; but we had none to give him. Next, he asked leave for my men to shoot cows before his Kidi visitors, which they did to his satisfaction, instructing him at the same time to fire powder with his own rifle; when, triumphant with his success, he protested he would never use any thing but guns again, and threw away his spear as useless. Bombay, we learned, had reached Gani, and ought to return in eight days.

17th and 18th. A large party of Chopi people arrived, by Kamrasi's orders, to tell the reason which induced them to apply for guns to the white men at Gani, as it appeared evident they must have wished to fight their king. The Kidi visitors got broken heads for helping themselves from the Wanyoro's fields, and when they cried out against such treatment, were told they should rob the king, if they wished to rob at all.

19th. Nothing was done because Kamrasi was dismissing his Kidi guests, 200, with presents of cows and women.

20th. Having asked Kamrasi to return my pictures, he sent the book of birds, but not of animals; and said he could not see us until a new hut was built, because the old one was flooded by the

Kafŭ, which had been rising several days. We must not, he said, talk about Bombay any more, because every body said he was detained by the N'yanswengé (Petherick's party), and would return here with the new moon. I would not accept the lie, saying, How can my "children" at Gani detain my messengers, when they have received strict orders from me by letter to send an answer quickly? It was all Kamrasi's doing, for he had either hidden Bombay, or ordered his officers to take him slowly, as he did us, stopping four days at each stage.

Frij again told me he was present when Said Said, the Sultan of Zanzibar, sent an army to assist the Wagŭnya at Amŭ, on the coast, against the incursions of the Masai. These Amŭ people have the same Wahŭma features as Kamrasi, whom they also resemble both in general physical appearance, and in many of them having circular marks, as if made by cautery, on the forehead and temples. These marks I took not to be tattooing or decorative, but as a cure for disease, cautery being a favorite remedy with both races.

The battle lasted only two days, though the Masai brought a thousand spears against the Arabs' cannon. But this was not the only battle Said Said had to fight on those grounds; for some years previously he had to subdue the Waziwa, who live on very marshy land, into respect for his sovereignty, when the battle lasted years, in consequence of the bad nature of the ground, and the trick the Waziwa had of staking the ground with spikes. The Wasŭahili, or coast-people, by his description, are the bastards or mixed breeds who live on the east coast of Africa, extending from the Somali country to Zanzibar. Their language is Kisŭahili; but there is no land Usŭahili, though people talk of going to the Sŭahili in the same vague sense as they do of going to the Mashenzi, or among the savages. The common story among the Wasŭahili at Zanzibar in regard to the government of that island was, that the Wakhadim, or aborigines of Zanzibar, did not like the oppressions of the Portuguese, and therefore allied themselves to the Arabs of Muscat—even compromising their natural birthright of freedom in government, provided the Arabs, by their superior power, would secure to them perpetual equity, peace, and justice. The senior chief, Sheikh Mŭhadim, was the mediator on their side, and without his sanction no radical changes compromising the welfare of the land could take place; the system of arbitration being that the governing Arab on the one side, and the deputy of the Wakhadim on the other, should hold conference with a screen placed between them, to obviate all attempts at favor, corruption, or bribery.

The former report of the approach of all of my men, with as many Waganda and cows for me, turned out partly false, inasmuch as only one of my men was with 102 Waganda, while the whole of the deserters were left behind in Uganda with cows; and Kamrasi hearing this, ordered all to go back again until the whole of my men should arrive.

21st. I was told how a Myoro woman, who bore twins that died, now keeps two small pots in her house, as effigies of the children, into which she milks herself every evening, and will continue to do so five months, fulfilling the time appointed by nature for suckling children, lest the spirits of the dead should persecute her. The twins were not buried as ordinary people are buried, under ground, but placed in an earthenware pot, such as the Wanyoro use for holding pombé. They were taken to the jungle and placed by a tree, with the pot turned mouth downward. Manŭa, one of my men, who is a twin, said, in Ngŭrŭ, one of the sister provinces to Unyanyembé, twins are ordered to be killed and thrown into water the moment they are born, lest droughts and famines or floods should oppress the land. Should any one attempt to conceal twins, the whole family would be murdered by the chief; but, though a great traveler, this is the only instance of such brutality Manŭa had ever witnessed in any country.

In the province of Unyanyembé, if a twin or twins die, they are thrown into water for the same reason as in Ngŭrŭ; but as their numbers increase the size of the family, their birth is hailed with delight. Still there is a source of fear there in connection with twins, as I have seen myself; for when one dies, the mother ties a little gourd to her neck as a proxy, and puts into it a trifle of every thing which she gives the living child, lest the jealousy of the dead spirit should torment her. Farther, on the death of the child, she smears herself with butter and ashes, and runs frantically about, tearing her hair and bewailing piteously; while the men of the place use toward her the foulest language, apparently as if in abuse of her person, but in reality to frighten away the demons who have robbed her nest.

22d. I sent Frij to Kamrasi to find out what he was doing with the Waganda and my deserters, as I wished to speak with their two head representatives. I also wanted some men to seek for and fetch Bombay, as I said I believed him to be tied by the leg behind one of the visible hills in Kidi. The reply was, 102 Waganda, with one of my men only, had been stationed at the village my men deserted from since the date (13th) we heard of them last. They had no cows for me, but each of the Waganda bore a log of firewood, which Mtésa had ordered them to carry until they either returned with me or brought back a box of gunpowder, in default of which they were to be all burnt in a heap with the logs they carried. Kamrasi, still acting on his passive policy, would not admit them here, but wished them to return with a message, to the effect that Mtésa had no right to hold me as his guest now I had once gone into another's hands. We were all three kings, to do with our subjects as we liked, and for this reason the deserters ought to be sent on here; but if I wished to speak to the Waganda, he would call their officer. There was no fear, he said, about Bombay; he was on his way; but the men who were escorting him were spinning out the time, stopping at every place, and feasting every day. To-morrow, he added, some more Gani people would arrive here, when we should know more about it. I still advised Kamrasi to give the road to Mtésa provided he gave up plundering the Wanyoro of women and cattle; but, if my counsel was listened to, I could get no acknowledgment that it was so.

23d and 24th. I sent to inquire what news there was of Bombay's coming, and what measures Kamrasi had taken to call the Waganda's chief officer and my deserters here, as also to beg he would send us specimens of all the various tribes that visit him, in order that we might draw them. He sent four loads of dried fish, with a request for my book of birds again, as it contains a portrait of King Mtésa, and proposed seeing us at the newly-constructed Kafú palace to-morrow, when all requests would be attended to. In the mean while, we were told that Bombay had been seen on his way returning from Gani; and the Waganda had all run away frightened, because they were told the Kidi and Chopi visitors, who had been calling on Kamrasi lately, were merely the nucleus of an army forming to drive them away and to subdue Uganda. Mtésa was undergoing the coronation formalities, and for this reason had sent the deserters to Kari's hill, giving them cows and a garden to live on, as no visitors can remain near the court while the solemnities of the coronation were going on. The thirty-odd brothers will be burnt to death, saving two or three, of which one will be sent into this country—as was the case with one of the late king Sunna's brothers, who is still in Unyoro—and the others will remain in the court with Mtésa as playfellows until the king dies, when, like Sunna's two brothers still living in Uganda, one at N'yama Goma and one at Ngambézi, they will be pensioned off. After the coronation is concluded, it is expected Mtésa will go into Kittara, on the west of Uganda, to fight first, and then, turning east, will fight with the Wasoga; but we think, if he fights any where, it will be with Kamrasi.

25th and 26th. I sent Frij to the palace to inquire after Bombay, and got the usual reply: " Why is Bana in such a hurry? He is always for doing things quickly. Tell my 'brother' to keep his mind at rest; Bombay is now on the boundary of Gani coming here, and will in due course arrive." Both Rŭmanika's men and those belonging to Dr. K'yengo asked Kamrasi's leave to return to their homes, but were refused, because the road was unsafe. "Had they not," it was said, "heard of Budja's telling Mtésa that K'yengo's children prevented the white men from returning to Uganda? and since then Mtésa had killed his frontier officer for being chicken-hearted, afraid to carry out his orders, and had appointed another in his stead, giving him strict orders to make prisoners of all foreigners who might pass that way and, farther, when some twenty Wanyoro were going to Karagŭé, they were hunted down by Mtésa's orders, and three of their number killed; for he was determined to cut off all intercourse between this country and Karagŭé. They must therefore wait till the road is safe."

Hearing this, Dr. K'yengo's men, who happened to be as well off here as any where, accepted the advice; but Rŭmanika's men said, " We are starving; we have been here too long already doing nothing, and must go, let what will happen to us." Kamrasi said, "What will be the use of your going empty-handed? I can not send cows and slaves to Rŭmanika when the road is so unsafe; you must wait a bit." But they still urged as before, and so forced the king reluctantly to acquiesce, but only on the condition that two of their head men should remain behind until some more of Rŭmanika's men came to fetch them away; in fact, as we had been accredited to him by Rŭmanika, he wanted to keep some of that king's people as a security until we were out of his hands.

27th. I sent Frij to the palace to ask once more for leave to visit the Lŭta Nzigé river-lake to the westward, and to request

KAMRASI'S FIRST LESSON IN THE BIBLE.

Kamrasi would send men to fetch my property from Karagŭé. He sent four loads of small fish and one pot of pombé, to say he would see me on the morrow, when every arrangement would be made. Late at night orders came announcing that I might write my dispatches, as sixty men were ready to start for Karagŭé.

28th. I sent one of my men with dispatches to Kamrasi, who detained him half the day, and then ordered him to call to-morrow. This being the fifteenth or twentieth time Kamrasi had disappointed me, after promising an interview, that we might have a proper understanding about every thing, and when no begging on his part was to interrupt our conversation, I sent him a threatening message, to see what effect that would have. The purport of it was, that I was afraid to send men to Karagŭé, now I had seen his disposition to make prisoners of all who visit him. Here had I been kept six weeks waiting for Bombay's return from Gani, where I only permitted him to go because I was told the journey to and fro would only occupy from eight to ten days at most. Then Rŭmanika's men, who came here with Baraka, though daily crying to get away, were still imprisoned here, without any hope before them. If I sent Msalima, he would be kept ten years on the road. If I went to the lake Lŭta Nzigé, God only knows when he would let me come back; and now, for once and for all, I wished to sacrifice all my property, and leave the countries of black kings; for what Kamrasi had done, Mtésa had done likewise, detaining the two men I detached on a friendly mission, which made me fear to send any more and inquire after my guns, lest he should seize them likewise. I would stay no longer among such people.

Kamrasi, in answer, begged I would not be afraid; there was no occasion for alarm; Bombay would be here shortly. I had promised to wait patiently for his return, and as soon as he did return I would be sent off without one day's delay, for I was not his slave, that he should use violence upon me. Rŭmanika's men, too, would be allowed to go, only that the road was unsafe, and he feared Rŭmanika would abuse him if any harm befell them.

29th. To-day I met Kamrasi at his new reception-palace on this side the Kafŭ—taking a Bible to explain all I fancied I knew about the origin and present condition of the Wahŭma branch of the Ethiopians, beginning with Adam, to show how it was the king had heard by tradition that at one time the people of his race were half white and half black. Then, proceeding with the Flood, I pointed out that the Europeans remained white, retaining Japhet's blood; while the Arabs are tawny, after Shem; and the Africans black, after Ham. And, finally, to show the greatness of the tribe, I read the 14th chapter of 2d Chronicles, in which it is written how Zerah, the Ethiopian, with a host of a thousand thousand, met the Jew Asa with a large army, in the valley of Zephathah, near Mareshah; adding to it that again, at a much later date, we find the Ethiopians battling with the Arabs in the Somali country, and with the Arabs and Portuguese at Omwita (Mombas)—in all of which places they have taken possession of certain tracts of land, and left their sons to people it.

To explain the way in which the type or physical features of people undergo great changes by interbreeding, Mtésa was instanced as having lost nearly every feature of his Mhŭma blood by the kings of Uganda having been produced, probably for several generations running, of Wagandi mothers. This amused Kamrasi greatly, and induced me to inquire how his purity of blood was maintained: "Was the King of Unyoro chosen, as in Uganda, haphazard by the chief men, or did the eldest son sit by succession on the throne?" The reply was, "The brothers fought for it, and the best man gained the crown."

Kamrasi then began counting the leaves of the Bible, an amusement that every negro that gets hold of a book indulges in; and, concluding in his mind that each page or leaf represented one year of time since the beginning of creation, continued his labor till one quarter of the way through the book, and then only shut it up on being told, if he desired to ascertain the number more closely, he had better count the words.

I begged for my picture-books, which were only lent him at his request for a few days, and then began a badgering verbal conflict: he would not return them until I drew others like them; he would not allow me to go to the Little Lŭta Nzigé, west of this, until Bombay returned, when he would send me with an army of spears to lead the way, and my men with their guns behind to protect the rear. This was for the purpose of making us his tools in his conflict with his brothers. I complained that he had, without consulting me, ordered away the men who had been sent, either to fetch me back to Uganda, or else get powder from me, although they had orders to carry out their king's desire, under the threat of being burnt with the fire-logs they carried; and

all this Kamrasi had professed to do merely out of respect for my
dignity, as I was no slave, that Mtésa should order me about. I
argued, founding on each particular in succession, that his conduct throughout was most unjustifiable, and any thing but friendly. He then produced an officer, who was to escort my man Msalima to Karagŭé, giving him orders to collect the sixty men required on the way; five of Rumanika's men could go with him,
but five must stop until other Karagŭé men came to say the road
was safe, when he would send by them the present he had prepared for Rŭmanika.

Then, turning to us, he said, "Why have you not brought the
medicine-chest and the saw? We wish to see every thing you
have got, though we do not wish to rob you." When these things
came for inspection, he coveted the saw, and discovered there
were more varieties of medicine in the chest than had been given
him. This he was told was not the case, because the papers given
him contained mixed medicines, a little being taken from every
bottle. "But there are no pills; why won't you give us pills?
We have men, women, and children who require pills as well as
you do." We were much annoyed by this dogged begging; and
as he said, "Well, if you won't give me any thing, I will go," we
at once rose, hat in hand; when, regretting the hastiness of his
speech, he begged us to be seated again, and renewed his demands.
We told him the road to Gani was the only condition on which
we would part with any more medicine; we had asked leave to
go a hundred times, and that was all we now desired. At last he
rose, and walked off in a huff; but, repenting before he reached
home, he sent us a pot of pombé, when, in return, I finished the
farce by sending him a box of pills.

30th. I gave Msalima a letter in the Kisŭahili or coast language
to convey to Rŭmanika, ordering all my property to be sent here,
his account of the things as they left him to be given to Msalima
to convey to the coast, while I sent him one pound of gunpowder
as a sort of agency fee. Msalima also took a map of all the countries we had passed, with lunar observations, and a letter to Rigby, by which he, Baraka, and Ulédi would be able to draw their
pay on arrival.

31st. I sent Frij with a letter to the king, containing an acknowledgment that, on the arrival of the rear property from Ka-
ragŭe, he would be entitled to the half of every thing, reserving
the other half for any other person I might in future send to take

them from him. He accepted the letter, and put it into his mzungŭ—the tin box I had given him. He said he would take every
care of the kit from the time ·it arrived, and would not touch his
share of it until my deputy arrived. An inhabitant of Chopi reported that he heard Bombay's gun fire the evening before he left
home, and was rewarded with the present of a cow.

1st. I purchased a small kitten, *Felis serval*, from an Unyoro
man, who requested me to give it back to him to eat if it was
likely to die, for it is considered very good food in Unyoro.

Bombay at last arrived with Mabrŭki in high glee, dressed in
cotton jumpers and drawers, presents given them by Petherick's
outpost. Petherick himself was not there. The journey to and
fro was performed in fourteen days' actual traveling, the rest of
the time being frittered away by the guides. The jemadar of the
guard said he commanded two hundred Turks, and had orders to
wait for me, without any limit as to time, until I should arrive,
when Petherick's name would be pointed out to me cut on a tree,
but as no one in camp could read my letter, they were doubtful
whether we were the party they were looking out for.

They were all armed with elephant-guns, and had killed sixteen
elephants. Petherick had gone down the river eight days' journey, but was expected to return shortly. Kamrasi would not see
Bombay immediately on his return, but sent him some pombé,
and desired an interview the following day.

2d. I sent Bombay with a farewell present to Kamrasi, consisting of one tent, one musquito-curtain, one roll of bindera or red
cotton cloth, one digester-pot, one saw, six copper wires, one box
of beads, containing six varieties of the best sort, and a request to
leave his country. Much pleased with the things, Kamrasi ordered the tent to be pitched before all his court, pointed out to
them what clever people the white people are, making iron pots
instead of earthen ones. Covetous and never satisfied, however,
instead of returning thanks, he said he was sure I must have
more beads than those I sent him ; and instead of granting the
leave asked for, said he would think about it, and send the kamraviona in the evening with his answer. This, when it came, was
any thing but satisfactory ; for we were required to stop here until the king should have prepared the people on the road for our
coming, so that they might not be surprised, or try to molest us
on the way. Kamrasi, however, returned the books of birds and
animals, requesting a picture of the King of Uganda to be drawn
for him, and gave us one pot of pombé.

3d. I sent the picture required, and an angry message to Kamrasi for breaking his word, as he promised us we should go without a day's delay; and go we must, for I could neither eat nor sleep from thinking of my home. His only reply to this was, Bana is always in a preposterous hurry. He answered that, for our gratification, he had directed a dwarf called Kimenya to be

Kimenya the Dwarf.

sent to us, and the kamraviona should follow after. Kimenya, a little old man, less than a yard high, called on us with a walking-stick higher than himself, made his salaam, and sat down very composedly. He then rose and danced, singing without invitation, and following it up with queer antics. Lastly, he performed the tambŭra, or charging-march, in imitation of wakungŭ, repeating the same words they use, and ending by a demand for simbi, or cowrie-shells, modestly saying, "I am a beggar, and want simbi; if you have not 500 to spare, you must, at any rate, give me 400."

He then narrated his fortune in life. Born in Chopi, he was sent for by Kamrasi, who first gave him two women, who died; then another, who ran away; and, finally, a distorted dwarf like himself, whom he rejected, because he thought the propagation of his pigmy breed would not be advantageous to society. Bombay then marched him back to the palace, with 500 simbi strung in necklaces round his neck. When these two had gone, the kamraviona arrived with two spears, one load of flour, and a pot of pombé, which he requested me to accept, adding that the spears were given as it was observed I had accepted some from the King of Uganda; a shield was still in reserve for me, and spears would be sent for Grant. Then, with regard to my going, Kamrasi must beg us to have patience until he had sent messengers into Kidi, requesting the natives there not to molest me on the way, for they had threatened they would do so, and, if they persisted, he would send us with a force by another route *viâ* Ugungŭ—another attempt to draw us off to fight against his brothers.

I stormed at this announcement as a breach of faith ; said I had given the king my only tent, my only digester, my only saw, my only wire, my only musquito-curtains, and my last of every thing, because he had assured me I should have to pay no more chiefs, and he would give me the road at once. If he did not intend now to fulfill his promise, I begged he would take back his spears, for I would only accept them as a farewell present. The kamraviona finding me rather warm, with the usual pertinacious duplicity of a negro, then said, " Well, let that subject drop, and consider the present Kamrasi promised you when you gave him the uganga" (meaning the watch); "Kamrasi's horn is not ready yet." This second prevarication completely set my dander up. If I did not believe in his dangers of the way before, it quite settled my opinion of the worth of his words now. I therefore tendered him what might be called the ultimatum to this effect. There was no sincerity in such haggling; I would not submit to being told lies by kings or any body else. He must take back the spears, or give us the road to-morrow; and unless the kamraviona would tell him this and bring me an answer at once, the spears should not remain in my hut during the night. Evidently in alarm, the kamraviona, with Kidgwiga and Frij in company to bear him witness, returned to the palace, telling Kamrasi that he saw we were in thorough earnest. He extracted a promise that Kamrasi would have a farewell meeting with us either to-morrow or the next day, when we should have a large escort to Petherick's boats, and the men would be able to bring back any thing that he wanted; but he could not let us go without a parting interview, such as we had at Uganda with Mtésa.

The deputation, delighted with their success and the manner in which it was effected, hurried back to me at once, and said they were so frightened themselves that they would have skulked away to their homes and not come near me if they could not have arranged matters to my satisfaction. Kamrasi would not believe I had threatened to turn out his spears until Frij testified to their statements; and he then said, "Let Bana keep the spears and drink the pombé, for I would not wish him to be a prisoner against his will." Bombay, after taking back the dwarf, met one of N'yamasoré's officers, just arrived from Uganda on some important business, and upbraided Mtésa for not having carried out my instructions. The officer in turn tried to defend Mtésa's conduct by saying he had given the deserters seventy cows and four women, as well as orders to join us quickly; but they had been delayed on the road, because wherever they went they plundered, and no one liked their company. Had we returned to Uganda, Mtésa would have given us the road through Masai, which, in their opinion, is nearer for us than this one.

This officer had been wishing to see us as much as we had been to see him; but Kamrasi would not allow him to get access to us, from fear, it was said, lest the Waganda should know where we were hidden, and enable Mtésa to send an army to come and snatch us away. As the officer said he would deliver any message I might wish to send to Uganda, I folded a visiting-card as a letter to the queen-dowager, intimating that I wished the two men whom I sent back to Mtésa to be forwarded on to Karagué; but desired that the remainder, who deserted their master in difficulty, should be placed on an island of the N'yanza, to live in exile until some other Englishmen should come to release them; that their arms should be taken from them and kept in the palace. I said farther, that should Mtésa act up to my desires, I would then know he was my friend, and other white men would not fear to enter Uganda; but if he acted otherwise, they would fear lest he should imprison them, or seize their property or their men. If these deserters escaped punishment, no white men would ever dare trust their lives with such men again. The officer said he should be afraid to deliver such a message to Mtésa direct; but he certainly would tell the queen every word of it, which would be even more efficacious.

4th. I bullied Kamrasi by telling him we must go with this moon, for the benefit of its light while crossing the Kidi wilderness; as, if we did not reach the vessels in time for seasonable departure down the Nile, we should have to wait another year for their return from Khartŭm. "What!" said Kamrasi, "does Bana forget my promised appointment that I would either see him to-day or to-morrow? I can not do so to-day, and therefore to-mor-row we will certainly meet and bid good-by." The Gani men who came with Bombay said they would escort us to their coun-try, although, as a rule, they never cross the Kidi wilderness above once in two years, from fear of the hunting natives, who make game of every body and every thing they see; in other words, they seize strangers, plunder them, and sell them as slaves. To cross that tract, the dry season is the best, when all the grass is burnt down, or from the middle of December to the end of March. I gave them a cow, and they at once killed it, and, sitting down, commenced eating her flesh raw, out of choice.

5th. The kamraviona came to inform us that the king was ready for the great interview, where we could both speak what we had at heart, for as yet he had only heard what our servants had to say; and there was a supplement to the message of the usual kind, that he would like a present of a pencil. The pencil was sent in the first place, because we did not like talking about trifles when we visited great kings.

The interview followed. It was opened on our side by our saying we had enjoyed his hospitality a great number of days, and wished to go to our homes; should he have any message to send to the great Queen of England, we should be happy to con-vey it. A long yarn then emanated from the throne. He de-fended his overcautiousness when admitting us into Unyoro. It was caused at first by wicked men who did not wish us to visit him; he subsequently saw through their representations, and now was very pleased with us as he found us. Of course he could not tie us down to stopping here against our wish, but, for safety's sake, he would like us to stop a little longer, until he could send messengers ahead, requesting the wild men in Kidi not to molest us. That state trick failing to frighten and stop us, he tried an-other, by saying, when we departed, he hoped we would leave two men with guns behind, to occupy our present camp, and so de-lude the people into the belief that merely a party of their fol-lowers, and not the white men themselves, had left his house, for the purpose of spreading terror in the minds of the people we might meet, who, not knowing the number of men behind, would naturally conclude there was a large reserve force ready to release us in case of necessity.

This foxy speech was too transparent to require one moment's reflection. In a country where men were property, the fate of one or two left behind was obvious; and had we doubted that his object was to get possession of them, his next words would have sufficiently revealed it. He said, "As you gave men to Mtésa, why would you refuse them to me?" but was checkmated on being told, "Should any of those men who deserted us in this country ever reach their homes, they will all be hung for breaking their allegiance or oath." "Well," says the king, "I have acceded to every thing you have to say; and the day after to-morrow, when I shall have had time to collect men to go with you, and selected the two princes you have promised to educate, we will meet again and say good-by; but you must give me a gun and some more medicine, as well as the powder and ball you promised after reaching the vessels." This was all acquiesced in, and we wished to take his portrait, but he would not have it done on any consideration. The kamraviona and Kidgwiga followed us home, and told Bombay the king did not wish us to leave till next moon, and then he would like us to fight his brothers on the way. This message, sent in such an underhand manner after the meeting, Bombay refused to deliver, telling them he should be afraid to do so.

6th. The kamraviona was sent to us with four loads of fish and a request for ammunition, notwithstanding every thing asked for yesterday had been refused until we reached the vessels. "Confound Kamrasi!" was the reply; "does he think we came here to trick kings that he doubts our words? We came to open the road; and, as sure as we wish it, we will send him every thing that has been promised. Why should he doubt our word more than any body else? We are not accustomed to be treated in this manner, and must beg he won't insult us any more. Then about fighting his brothers, we have already given answer that we never fight with black men; and should the king persist in it, we will never take another thing from his hands. The boys shall not go to England, neither will any other white men come this way." The kamraviona made the following answer: "But there are two more things the king wishes to know about: he has asked the question before, but forgotten the answers. Is there any medicine for women or children which will prevent the offspring from dying shortly after birth? for it is a common infirmity in this country with some women, that all their children die before they are able to walk, while others never lose a child. The other matter of inquiry was, What medicine will attach all subjects to their king? for Kamrasi wants some of that most particularly." I answered, "Knowledge of good government, attended with wisdom and justice, is all the medicine we know of; and that his boys can best learn in England, and instruct him in when they return."

7th. We went to meet Kamrasi at his Kafŭ palace to bid goodby. After all the huckstering and begging with which he had tormented us, the state he chose to assume on this occasion was very ludicrous. He sat with an air of the most solemn dignity upon his throne of skins, regarding us like mere slaves, and asking what things we intended to send to him. On being told we did not like being repeatedly reminded of our promises, he came down a little from his dignity, saying, "And what answer have you about the business on the island?" meaning the request to fight his brothers. That, of course, could not be listened to, as it was against the principles of our country. Grant's rings were then espied, and begged for, but without success. We told him it was highly improper to beg for every thing he saw, and if he persisted in it, no one would ever dare to come near him again.

Then, to change the subject, we begged K'yengo's men might be allowed to go as far as Gani with us; but no reply was given until the question was put again, with a request that the reasons might be told us for his not wishing it, as we saw great benefit would be derived to Unyoro, as the Wanyamŭézi, instead of trading merely with Karagŭé and Zanzibar, would bring their ivory through this country and barter it, thus converting Unyoro into a great commercial country; when Kamrasi said, "We don't want any more ivory in Unyoro, for the tusks are already as numerous as grass." Kidgwiga was then appointed to receive all the things we were to send back from Gani; our departure was fixed for the 9th, and the king walked away as coldly as he came, while we felt as jolly as birds released from a cage.

Floating islands of grass were seen going down the Kafŭ, reminding us of the stories told at Kazé by Mŭsa Mzŭri, of the violent manner in which, at certain seasons, the N'yanza was said to rise and rush with such velocity that islands were uprooted and carried away. In the evening a pot of pombé was brought, when the man in charge, half drunk, amused us with frantic charges, as if he were fighting with his spear; and after settling the supposed enemy, he delighted in trampling him under foot, spearing him repeatedly through and through, then wiping the blade of the spear in the grass, and finally polishing it on his tufty head, when, with a grunt of satisfaction, he shouldered arms, and walked away a hero.

8th. As the king seemed entirely to disregard our comfort on the journey, we made a request for cows, butter, and coffee ; in answer to which we only got ten cows, the other things not being procurable without delay. Twenty-four men were appointed to escort us and bring back our presents from Gani, which were to be—six carbines, with a magazine of ammunition, a large brass or iron water-pot, a hair-brush, lucifers, a dinner-knife, and any other things procurable that had never been seen in Unyoro.

Two orphan boys, seized by the king as slaves, were brought for education to England; but as they were both of the common negro breed, with nothing attractive about them, and such as no one could love but their mothers, we rejected them, fearing lest no English boys would care to play with them, and told Kamrasi that his offspring only could play with our children, and unless I got some princes of that interesting breed, no one would ever undertake to teach children brought from his country. The king was very much disappointed at this announcement; said they were his adopted children, and the only ones he could part with, for his own boys were mere balls of fat, and too small to leave home.

CHAPTER XIX.

THE MARCH TO MADI.

Sail down the Kafŭ.—The navigable Nile.—Fishing and Sporting Population.—
The Scenery on the River.—An inhospitable Governor.—Karuma Falls.—Native
Superstitions.—Thieveries.—Hospitable Reception at Koki by Chongi.

AFTER giving Kamrasi a sketching-stool, we dropped down the
Kafŭ two miles in a canoe, in order that the common
people might not see us, for the exclusive king would
not allow any eyes but his own to be indulged with the extraordinary sight of white men in Unyoro! The palace side of the
river, however, as we paddled away, was thronged with anxious
spectators, among whom the most conspicuous was the king's favorite nurse. Dr. K'yengo's men were very anxious to accompany us, even telling the king, if he would allow the road to be
opened to their countrymen, all would hongo, or pay customs-
duty, to him; but the close, narrow-minded king could not be
persuaded. Bombay here told us Kamrasi at the last moment
wished to give me some women and ivory; and when told we
never accepted any thing of that sort, wished to give them to my
head servants; but this being contrary to standing orders also,
he said he would smuggle them down to the boats for Bombay in
such a manner that I should not find it out.

To North Cha-
gŭzi, 9th.

We were now expected to march again, but, being anxious myself to see more of the river, before starting, I obtained leave to go by boat as far as the river was navigable, sending our cattle by land. To this concession was accompanied a request for a few more gun-caps, and liberty was
given us to seize any pombé which might be found coming on
the river in boats, for the supplies to the palace all come in this
manner. We then took boat again, an immense canoe, and, after
going a short distance, emerged from the Kafŭ, and found ourselves on what at first appeared a long lake, averaging from two
hundred at first to one thousand yards broad, before the day's
work was out; but this was the Nile again, navigable in this way
from Urondogani.

To Kitwara, 10th.

Both sides were fringed with the huge papyrus rush. The left one was low and swampy, while the right one—in which the Kidi people and Wanyoro occasionally hunt—rose from the water in a gently sloping bank, covered with trees and beautiful convolvuli, which hung in festoons. Floating islands, composed of rush, grass, and ferns, were continually in motion, working their way slowly down the stream, and proving to us that the Nile was in full flood. On one occasion we saw hippopotami, which our men said came to the surface because we had domestic fowls on board, supposing them to have an antipathy to that bird. Boats there were, which the sailors gave chase to; but, as they had no liquor, they were allowed to go their way, and the sailors, instead, set to lifting baskets and taking fish from the snares which fishermen, who live in small huts among the rushes, had laid for themselves.

After arrival, as we found the boatmen wished to make off, instead of carrying out their king's orders to take us to the waterfall, we seized all the paddles, and kept their tongues quiet by giving them a cow to eat. The overland route, by which Kidgwiga and the cattle went, was not so interesting, by all accounts, as the river one; for they walked the whole way through marshy ground, and crossed one drain in boats, where some savages struggled to plunder our men of their goats.

With a great deal of difficulty, and after hours of delay, we managed to get under way with two boats besides the original one; and, after an hour and a half's paddling in the laziest manner possible, the men seized two pots of pombé and pulled in to Koki, guided by a king's messenger, who said this was one of the places appointed by order to pick up recruits for the force which was to take us to Gani. We found, however, nothing but loss and disappointment—one calf stolen, and five goats nearly so. Fortunately, the thief who attempted to run off with the goats was taken by my men in the act, tied with his hands painfully tight behind his back, and left, with his face painted white, till midnight, when his comrades stole into Bombay's hut and released him. After all these annoyances, the chief officer of the place offered us a present of a goat, but was sent to the right-about in scorn. How could he be countenanced as a friend when the men under him steal from us?

The big boat gave us the slip, floating away and leaving its paddles behind. To supply its place, we took six small boats, turning my men into sailors, and going

To Koki, 11th.

To Güéni, S., 12th.

as we liked. The river still continued beautiful; but, after paddling three hours, we found it bend considerably, and narrow to
two hundred yards, the average depth being from two to three
fathoms. At the fourth hour, imagining our cattle to be far behind, we pulled in, and walked up a well-cultivated hill to Yaragonjo's, the governor of these parts. The guide, however, on first
sighting his thorn-fenced cluster of huts, regarding it apparently
with the awe and deference due to a palace, shrank from advancing, and merely pointed, till he was forced on, and in the next
minute we found ourselves confronted with the heads of the establishment. The father of the house, surprised at our unexpected manner of entrance—imagining, probably, we were the king's
sorcerers, in consequence of our hats, sent to fight "the brothers"
—without saying a word, quietly beckoned us to follow him out
of the gate by the same way as we came. Preferring, however,
to have a little talk where we were, we remained.

The eldest son, a fine young man considerably above six feet
high, with large gashes on his body received in war during late
skirmishes with the refractory brothers, now came in, did the
honors, and, on hearing of the importance of his visitors, directed
us to some huts a little distance off, where we could rest for the
night, for there was no accommodation for such a large party in the
palace. The red hill we were now on, with plantain gardens, fine
huts neatly kept, and dense grasses covering the country, reminded us of our residence in Uganda. The people seemed of a decidedly sporting order, for they kept hippopotamus-harpoons, attached to strong ropes with trimmers of pith wood, in their huts;
and outside, trophies of their toil in the shape of a pile of heads,
consisting of those of buffalo and hippopotami. The women, any
thing but pretty, wore their mbŭgŭ cut into two flounces, fastened with a drawing-string round the waist; and, in place of stockings, they bound strings of small iron beads, kept bright and shining, carefully up the leg from the ankle to the bottom of the calf.

Kidgwiga with our cattle arrived in the morning. A bundle
of cartridges, stolen from one of the men's pouches,
which we knew could only have been done by some
comrade, was discovered by stopping the rations of flesh. The
guilty person, to save detection, threw it on the road, and allowed
some of the natives to pick it up. Strange as it may appear, the
only motive for this petty theft was the hope of being able to sell
the cartridges for a trifle at Gani. Yaragonjo brought us a pres-

To Gŭéni, N.,
13th.

ent of a goat and plantains. He was sorry he sent us back yesterday from his house, and invited us to change ground to another village close by, where he would make arrangements for our receiving other boats, as the ones we had in possession must go back. Presuming this to be a very fair proposition, and thinking we would only have to walk across an elbow of land where the river bends considerably, we gave him a return-present of beads, and did as we were bid; but, after moving, it was obvious we had been sold. We had lost our former boats, and no others were near us; therefore, feeling angry with Yaragonjo, I walked back to his palace, taking the presented goat with me, as I knew that would touch the savage in the most tender part; then flaring up with the officer for treating the king's orders with contempt, as well as his guests, by sending us into the jungles like a pack of thieves, whose riddance from his presence was obviously his only intent, I gave him his goat again, and said I would have nothing more to say to him, for I should look to the king for redress.

This frightened him to such an extent that he immediately produced another and finer goat, which he begged me to accept, promising to convey all my traps to the next governor's, where there would be no doubt about our getting boats. He did not intend to deceive us, but committed an error in not informing us he had no boats of his own; and, to show his earnestness, accompanied us to the camp. Here I found the missing calf taken at Koki, and a large deputation of natives awaiting our arrival. They told me that the Koki governor had taken such fright in consequence of my anger when I refused his proffered goat, that he had traced the calf back to Kitwara, and now wished to take Kidgwiga a prisoner to Kamrasi's for having seized five cows of his, and a woman from another governor. As yet I had not heard of this piece of rough justice; and, on inquiry, found out that he had been compelled to do as he had done, because those officers, on finding we had gone ahead in boats, would not produce the complement of men required of them by the king's orders for escorting us to Gani; but now they sent the men, the woman and cows could not be returned, as they had been sent overland by the ordinary route to the ferry on the Nile.

Of course we would not listen to this reference for justice with Kamrasi, as the woman and cows were still all alive; commended Kidgwiga for carrying out his orders so well, and told the officers they had merited their punishment—as how could the affairs of government be carried on, when subordinate officers refused immediate compliance? The sub-mkungŭ of Northern Gŭéni, Kasoro, now proffered a goat and plantains, and every thing was settled for the day.

With a full complement of porters, traveling six miles through cultivation and jungle, we reached the head-quarters of Governor Kaérŭ, where all the porters threw down their loads and bolted, though we were still two miles from the post. We inquired for the boats at once, but were told they were some distance off, and we must wait here for the night. Four pots of pombé were sent us, and Kaérŭ thought we would be satisfied and conform. We suspected, however, that there was some trick at the bottom of all; so, refusing the liquor, we said, with proper emphasis, "Unless we are forwarded to the boats at once, and get them on the following morning, we can not think of receiving presents from any one. This served our purpose, for a fresh set of porters was found like magic, and traps, pombé, and all together, were forwarded to the journey's end—a snug batch of huts imbedded in large plantain cultivation surrounded by jungle, and obviously near the river, as numerous huge harpoons, intended for striking hippopotami, were suspended from the roof. Kaérŭ here presented us with a goat, and promised the boats in the morning.

To Kijumbŭra, 14th.

After fighting for the boats, we still had to wait the day for Kidgwiga and his men, who said it was all very well our pushing ahead, indifferent as to whether men were enlisted or not, but he had to prepare for the future also, as he could never recross the Kidi wilderness by himself; he must have a sufficient number of men to form his escort, and these were now grinding corn for the journey. Numerous visitors called on us here, and consequently our picture-books were in great request. We gave Kaérŭ some beads.

Halt, 15th.

After walking two miles to the boats, we entered the district of Chopi, subject to Unyoro, and went down the river, keeping the Kikungŭrŭ cone in view. On arrival at camp, Viarwanjo, the officer of the district, a very smart fellow, arrived with a large escort of spearmen, presented pombé, ordered fowls to be seized for us, and promised one boat in the morning, for he had no more disposable, and even that one he felt anxious about, lest the men on ahead should seize it.

To Koki in Chopi, 16th.

I gave Viarwanjo some beads, and dropped down the river in
his only wretched little canoe—he, with Grant and
the traps, going overland.   I caught a fever, and so
spent the night.

To Parangoni,
17th.

Here I halted to please Magamba, the governor, who is a relation of the king.   He called in great state, presented
a cow and pombé, was much pleased with the picture-
books, and wished to feast his eyes on all the wonders in the hut.
He was very communicative, also, as far as his limited knowledge
permitted.   He said the people are only a sub-tribe of the Madi ;
and the reason why the right bank of the river is preferred to the
left for traveling is, that Rionga, who lives down the river, is always on the look-out for Kamrasi's allies, with a view to kill them.
Magamba also, on being questioned, told us about Urŭri, a province of Unyoro, under the jurisdiction of Kiméziri, a noted governor, who covers his children with bead ornaments, and throws
them into the N'yanza, to prove their identity as his own true off-

Halt, *18th.*

Group of Kidi Men on a Visit to King Kamrasi.

spring; for should they sink, it stands to reason some other person must be their father; but should they float, then he recovers
them.   One of Kamrasi's cousins, Kaoroti, with his chief officer,

called on us, presenting five fowls as an honorarium. He had little to say, but begged for medicine, and when given some in a
liquid state, said his sub would like some also; then Kidgwiga's
wife, who was left behind, must have some; and as pills were
given for her, the two men must have dry medicine too, to take
home with them. Severe drain as this was on the medicine-chest,
Magamba and his wife must have both wet and dry; and even
others put in a claim, but were told they were too healthy to require physicking. Many Kidi men, dressed as in the engraving,
crossed the river to visit Kamrasi; they could not, however, pass
us without satisfying their curiosity with a look. Usually these
men despise clothes, and never deign to put any covering on except out of respect, when visiting Kamrasi. Their "sou'-wester"-
shaped wigs are made of other men's hair, as the negro hair will
not grow long enough. A message came from Ukéro, the governor general of Chopi, to request we would not go down the river in boats to-morrow, lest the Chopi ferry-men at the falls should
take fright at our strange appearance, paddle precipitately across
the river, hide their boats, and be seen no more.

We started, leaving all the traps and men to follow, and made
this place in a stride, as a whisper warned me that
Kamrasi's officers, who are as thick as thieves about
here, had made up their minds to keep us each one
day at his abode, and show us "hospitality." Such was the case,
for they all tried their powers of persuasion, which failing, they
took the alternative of making my men all drunk, and sending to
camp sundry pots of pombé. The ground on the line of march
was highly cultivated, and intersected by a deep ravine of running water, whose sundry branches made the surface very irregular. The sand-paper-tree, whose leaves resemble a cat's tongue
in roughness, and which is used in Uganda for polishing their
clubs and spear-handles, was conspicuous; but at the end of the
journey only was there any thing of much interest to be seen.
There suddenly, in a deep ravine one hundred yards below us, the
formerly placid river, up which vessels of moderate size might
steam two or three abreast, was now changed into a turbulent tor-
rent. Beyond lay the land of Kidi, a forest of mimosa-trees, rising gently away from the water in soft clouds of green. This the
governor of the place, Kija, described as a sporting-field, where
elephants, hippopotami, and buffalo are hunted by the occupants
of both sides of the river. The elephant is killed with a new.

*To Wire, over
the Karüma
Falls, 19th.*

kind of spear, with a double-edged blade a yard long, and a handle which, weighted in any way most easy, is pear-shaped.

With these instruments in their hands, some men climb into trees and wait for the herd to pass, while others drive them under. The hippopotami, however, are not hunted, but snared with lŭnda, the common tripping-trap with spike drop, which is placed in the runs of this animal, described by every South African traveler, and generally known as far as the Hametic language is spread. The Karŭma Falls, if such they may be called, are a

The Karŭma Falls—Kidi.

mere sluice or rush of water between high sienitic stones, falling in a long slope down a ten-feet drop. There are others of minor importance, and one within ear-sound, down the river, said to be very grand.

The name given to the Karŭma Falls arose from the absurd belief that Karŭma, the agent or familiar of a certain great spirit, placed the stones that break the waters in the river, and, for so doing, was applauded by his master, who, to reward his services by an appropriate distinction, allowed the stones to be called Karŭma. Near this is a tree which contains a spirit whose attributes for gratifying the powers and pleasures of either men or women who summon its influence in the form appropriate to each appear to be almost identical with that of Mahadeo's Ligna in India.

20*th*. We halted for the men to collect and lay in a store of food for the passage of the Kidi wilderness. Presents of fish, caught in baskets, were sent us by Kija. They were not bad eating, though all ground animals of the lowest order. At the Grand Falls below this, Kidgwiga informs us, the king had the heads of one hundred men, prisoners taken in war against Rionga, cut off and thrown into the river.

21*st* and 22*d*. The governor, who would not let us go until we saw him, called on the 22d with a large retinue, attended by a harpist, and bringing a present of one cow, two loads of flour, and three pots of pombé. He expected a chair to sit upon, and got a box, as at home he has a throne only a little inferior to Kamrasi's. He was very generous to Bombay on his former journey to Gani, and then said he thought the white men were all flocking this way to retake their lost country; for tradition recorded that the Wahŭma were once half black and half white, with half the hair straight and the other half curly; and how was this to be accounted for unless the country formerly belonged to white men with straight hair, but was subsequently taken by black men? We relieved his apprehensions by telling him his ancestors were formerly all white, and lived in a country beyond the salt sea, till they crossed that sea, took possession of Abyssinia, and are now generally known by the name of Hubshies and Gallas; but neither of these names was known to him.

On the east, beyond Kidi, he only knew of one clan of Wahŭma, a people who subsist entirely on meat and milk. The sportsmen of this country, like the Wanyamŭezi, plant a convolvulus of extraordinary size by the side of their huts, and pile the jawbones and horns of their spoils before, as a means of bringing good luck. This same flower, held in the hand when a man is searching for any thing that he has lost, will certainly bring him to the missing treasure. In the evening, Kidgwiga, at the head of his brave army, made one of their theatrical charges on "Bana" with spear and shield, swearing they would never desert him on the march, but would die to a man if it were necessary; and if they deserted him, then might they be deprived of their heads, or of other personal possessions not much less valuable.

Just as we were ready for crossing the river, a line of Kidi men was descried filing through the jungle on the opposite side,

To 1st Camp in Kidi, 23d. making their way for a new-moon visit to Rionga, who occasionally leads them in battle against Ukéro. The last time they fought, two men only were killed on Kamrasi's side, while nine fell on Rionga's. There was little done besides crossing, for the last cow was brought across at sunset; the ferrying-toll for the whole being one cow, besides a present of beads to the head officer. Kidgwiga's party sacrificed two kids, one on either side the river, flaying them with one long cut each down their breasts and bellies. These animals were then, spread-eagle fashion, laid on their backs upon grass and twigs, to be stepped over by the travelers, that their journey might be prosperous; and the spot selected for the ordeal was chosen in deference to the mzimŭ, or spirit—a sort of wizard or ecclesiastical patriarch, whose functions were devoted to the falls.

To 2d Camp, 24th. After a soaking night, we were kept waiting till noon for the forty porters ordered by Kamrasi, to carry our property to the vessels, wherever they might be. Only twenty-five men arrived, notwithstanding the wife and one slave belonging to a local officer, who would not supply the men required of him, were seized and confiscated by Ukéro, of Wiré. We now mustered twenty Wangŭana, twenty-five country porters, and thirty-one of Kidgwiga's "children," making a total, with ourselves, of seventy-eight souls. By a late arrival a message came from Kamrasi. Its import was, that we must defer the march, as it was reported the refractory brother Rionga harbored designs of molesting us on the way, and therefore the king conceived it prudent to clear the road by first fighting him. Without heeding this cunning advice, we made a short march across swamps, and through thick jungle and long grasses, which proved any thing but pleasant, wet and laboring hard all the way.

To 3d Camp, 25th. It was a rainy day, and we had still to toil on, fighting with the grasses. We marched up the wet margin of swamp all day, crossing the water at a fork near the end. The same jungle prevails on all sides, excluding all view; and the only signs of man's existence in these wilds lay in the meagre path, which is often lost, and an occasional hut or two, the temporary residence of the sporting Kidi people.

To 4th Camp, 26th. After toiling five miles through the same terrible grasses, and crossing swamp after swamp, we were at last rewarded by a striking view. The jungles had thinned; we found ourselves unexpectedly standing on the edge of a plateau, on the west of which, for distance interminable, lay apparently a low flat country of grass, yellowed by the sun, with a few trees or shrubs only thinly scattered over the surface; while, from fifteen to twenty miles in the rear, bearing south by west, stood conspicuously the Hill of Kisŭga, said to be situated in Chopi, not far from the refractory brothers. But this view was only for the moment; again we dived into the grasses and forced our way along. Presently elephants were seen, also buffalo; and the guide, to make the journey propitious, plucked a twig, denuded it of its leaves and branches, waved it like a wand up the line of march, muttered some unintelligible words to himself, broke it in twain, and threw the separated bits on either side of the path.

Immediately after starting, the guide ran up on an ant-hill and pointed out to us all the glories of the country round.

To 5th Camp, 27th.

In our rear we could see back upon Wiré and the Hill of Kisŭga; to the west were the same low plains of grass; east and by south, the jungles of Kidi; and to the northward, over downs of grass, the tops of some hills, which marked the neighboring village of Koki, which we were making for. Its appearance in the distance warned us that we were closing on the habitations of men, and we were told that Bombay had drunk pombé there. Then plunging through grass again over our heads, and crossing constant swamps, we arrived at a stream which drains all these lands to westward, and rested a while that the men might bathe, and also that they might set fire to the grass as a telegraph to the settlement of Koki, to apprise the people of our advance, and be ready with their pombé ere our arrival. Shortly after, toward the close of the day's work, as a solitary buffalo was seen grazing by a brook, I put a bullet through him, and allowed the savages the pleasure of dispatching him in their own wild fashion with spears.

It was a sight quite worthy of a little delay. No sooner was it observed that the huge beast could not retire, than, with springing bounds, the men, all spear in hand, as if advancing on an enemy, went top speed at him, over rise and fall alike, till, as they neared the maddened bull, he instinctively advanced to meet his assailants with the best charge his exhausted body could muster up. Wind, however, failed him soon; he knew his disadvantage, and tried to hide by plunging in the water—the worst policy he could have pursued; for the men from the bank above him soon covered him with bristling spears, and gained their victory. Now

what was to be done with this huge carcass? No one could be
induced to leave it. A cow was offered as a bribe on reaching
camp; but no, the buffalo was bigger than a cow, and must be
quartered on the spot; so, to gain our object, we went ahead, and
left the rear men to follow, thus saving a cow in rations, for we
required to slaughter one every day.

By dint of hard perseverance we accomplished ten miles over
the same downs of tall grass with occasional swamps.
We saw a herd of hartebeest, and reached at night a
place within easy run of Koki in Gani.

To 6th Camp,
28th.

Group of Gani Men.

The weather had now become fine. At length we reached the
habitations of men—a collection of conical huts on
the ridge of a small chain of granitic hills lying north-
west. As we approached the southern extremity of this chain,
knots of naked men, perched like monkeys on the granite blocks,
were anxiously watching our arrival. The guides, following the
usages of the country, instead of allowing us to mount the hill and
look out for accommodation at once, desired us to halt, and sent on
a messenger to inform Chongi, the governor general, that we were
visitors from Kamrasi, who desired he would take care of us and
forward us to our brothers. This Mercury brought forth a hearty

To Koki in Gani,
29th.

welcome; for Chongi had been appointed governor by Kamrasi of this district, which appears to have been the extreme northern limit of the originally vast kingdom of Kittara. All the *élite* of the place, covered with war-paints, and dressed, so far as their nakedness was covered at all, like clowns in a fair, charged down the hill full tilt with their spears, and, after performing their customary evolutions, mingled with our men, and invited us up the hill, where we no sooner arrived than Chongi, a very old man, attended by his familiar, advanced to receive us—one holding a white hen, the other a small gourd of pombé and a little twig.

Chongi gave us all a friendly harangue by way of greeting, and, taking the fowl by one leg, swayed it to and fro close to the ground in front of his assembled visitors. After this ceremony had been also repeated by the familiar, Chongi then took the gourd and twig, and sprinkled the contents all over us; retired to the uganga, or magic house—a very diminutive hut—sprinkled pombé over it; and, finally, spreading a cowskin under a tree, bade us sit, and gave us a jorum of pombé, making many apologies that he could not show us more hospitality, as famine had reduced his stores. What politeness in the midst of such barbarism!!! Nowhere had we seen such naked creatures, whose sole dress consisted of bead, iron, or brass ornaments, with some feathers or cowrie-beads on the head. Even the women contented themselves with a few fibres hung like tails before and behind. Some of our men, who had seen the Watŭta in Utambara, declared these savages to resemble them in every particular, save one small specialty in their costume, alluded to in the description of the Zŭlŭ Kafirs' dress. The hair of the men was dressed in the same fantastic fashion, and the women placed half gourds over the baby as it rode on its mother's back. They also, like the Kidi people, whom they much fear, carry diminutive stools to sit upon wherever they go.

Their habitat extends from this to the Asŭa River, while the Madi occupy all the country west of this meridian to the Nile, which is far beyond sight. The villages are composed of little conical huts of grass, on a framework of bamboo raised above low mud walls. There are no sultans here of any consequence, each village appointing its own chief. The granitic hills, like those of Unyamŭézi, are extremely pretty, and clad with trees, contrasting strangely with the grassy downs of indefinite extent around, which give the place, when compared with the people, the appearance of a paradise within the infernal regions. From the site of Koki we saw the hills behind which, according to Bombay, Petherick was situated with his vessels; and we also saw a nearer hill, behind which his advanced post of elephant-hunters were waiting our arrival.

I tried to ascertain if there were any prefixes, as in the South African dialects, by which one might determine the difference between the people and the country; but I was assured that both here and in the adjacent countries these people say *Chopi, Kidi, Gani, Madi, Bari*, alike for person and place, though *Jo* in their language is the equivalent for *Wa* in South Africa, and *Dano* takes the place of *Mtŭ*. All the words and system of language were wholly changed; as, for example, *Poko poko wingi bongo* means "we do not understand;" *Mazi*, "fire;" *Pi*, "water;" *Pé*, "there is none;" *Bugra*, "cow." In sound, the language of these people resembles that of the Tibet Tartars. Chongi considers himself the greatest man in the country, and of noble descent, his great-grandfather having been a Mhŭma, born at Urŭri, in Unyoro, and appointed by the then reigning king to rule over this country, and keep the Kidi people in check.

30th. We halted at the earnest solicitation of Chongi, as well as of the Chopi porters, who said they required a day to lay in grain, as the wichwézi, or mendicant sorcerers—for so they thought fit to designate Petherick's elephant-hunters—had eaten up the country all about them, and those who went before with Bombay to visit their camp could get no food.

1st. We halted again at the request of all parties, and much to the delight of old Chongi, who supplied us with abundant pombé, promised a cow, that we should not be put to any extra expense by stopping, and said that without fail he would furnish us with guides who knew a short cut across country, by which we might reach the wichwézi camp in one march, instead of going by the circuitous route which Bombay formerly took. The cow, however, never came, as the old man did not intend to give his own, and his officers refused to obey his orders in giving one of theirs.

We left Koki with difficulty, in consequence of the Chopi porters refusing to carry any loads, leaving the burden
To Mĭdŭa, 2d.
of lifting them on the country people, as they said, "We have endured all the trouble and hardships of bringing these visitors through the wilderness, and now, as they have visited you, it is your place to help them on." The consequence

was, we had to engage fresh porters at every village, each in turn saying he had done all the work which with justice fell to his lot, till at last we arrived at the borders of a jungle, where the men last engaged, feeling tired of their work, pleaded ignorance of the direct road, and turned off to the longer one, where villages and men were in abundance, thus upsetting all our plans and doubling the actual distance.

To pass the night half way was now imperative, as we had been the whole day traveling without making good much ground. From the Gani people we had, without any visible change, mingled with the Madi people, who dress in the same naked fashion as their neighbors, and use bows and arrows. Their villages were all surrounded with bomas (fences), and the country in its general aspect resembled that of Northern Unyamŭézi. At one place, the good-natured simple people, as soon as we reached their village, spread a skin, deposited a stool upon it, and placed in front two pots of pombé. At the village where we put up, however, the women and children of the head man at first all ran away, and the head man himself was very shy of us, thinking we were some unearthly creatures. He became more reconciled to us, however, when he perceived we fed like rational beings; and, calling his family in by midnight, presented us with pombé, and made many apologies for having allowed us to dine without a drop of his beer, for he was very glad to see us.

CHAPTER XX.

MADI.

Junction of the two Hemispheres.—The first Contact with Persons acquainted with European Habits.—Interruptions and Plots.—The mysterious Mahamed.—Native Revelries.—The Plundering and Tyranny of the Turks.—The Rascalities of the Ivory Trade.—Feeling for the Nile.—Taken to see a Mark left by a European.—Buffalo, Eland, and Rhinoceros Stalking.—Meet Baker.—Petherick's Arrival at Gondokoro.

AFTER receiving more pombé from the chief, and, strange to say, hot water to wash with—for he did not know how else he could show hospitality better—we started again in the same straggling manner as yesterday. In two hours we reached the palace of Piéjoko, a chief of some pretensions, and were summoned to stop and drink pombé. In my haste to meet Petherick's expedition I would listen to nothing, but pushed rapidly on, despite all entreaties to stop, both from the chief and from my porters, who, I saw clearly, wished to do me out of another day.

To Faloro, 3d.

Half my men, however, did stop there, but with the other half Grant and I went on; and, as the sun was setting, we came in sight of what we thought was Petherick's outpost, N. lat. 3° 10′ 33″, and E. long. 31° 50′ 45″. My men, as happy as we were ourselves, now begged I would allow them to fire their guns, and prepare the Turks for our reception. Crack, bang, went their carbines, and in another instant crack, bang, was heard from the northerners' camp, when, like a swarm of bees, every height and other conspicuous place was covered with men. Our hearts leaped with an excitement of joy only known to those who have escaped from long-continued banishment among barbarians once more to meet with civilized people and join old friends. Every minute increased this excitement. We saw three large red flags heading a military procession, which marched out of the camp with drums and fifes playing. I halted and allowed them to draw near. When they did so, a very black man, named Mahamed, in full Egyptian regimentals, with a curved sword, ordered his regiment to halt, and threw himself into my arms, endeavoring to hug and kiss me. Rather staggered at this unexpected manifest-

ation of affection, which was like a conjunction of the two hemispheres, I gave him a squeeze in return for his hug, but raised my
head above the reach of his lips, and asked who was his master.
"Petrik," was the reply. "And where is Petherick now?" "Oh,
he is coming." "How is it you have not got English colors,
then?" "The colors are at Debono's." "Who is Debono?"
"The same as Petrik; but come along into my camp, and let us
talk it out there;" saying which, Mahamed ordered his regiment
(a ragamuffin mixture of Nubians, Egyptians, and slaves of all
sorts, about two hundred in number) to rightabout, and we were
guided by him, while his men kept up an incessant drumming and
fifing, presenting arms, and firing, until we reached his huts, situated in a village kept exactly in the same order as that of the natives. Mahamed then gave us two beds to sit upon, and ordered
his wives to advance on their knees and give us coffee, while other men brought pombé, and prepared us a dinner of bread and
honey and mutton.

A large shed was cleared for Grant and myself, and all my
men were ordered to disperse, and chum in ones and twos with
Mahamed's men; for Mahamed said, now we had come there, his
work was finished. "If that is the case," I said, "tell us your
orders; there must be some letters." He said, "No, I have no
letters or written orders, though I have directions to take you to
Gondokoro as soon as you come. I am Debono's vakil, and am
glad you are come, for we are all tired of waiting here for you
Our business has been to collect ivory while waiting for you." I
said, "How is it Petherick has not come here to meet me? is he
married?" "Yes, he is married; and both he and his wife ride
fore-and-aft on one animal at Khartŭm." "Well, then, where is
the tree you told Bombay you would point out to us with Petherick's name on it?" "Oh, that is on the way to Gondokoro. It
was not Petherick who wrote, but some one else, who told me to
look out for your coming this way. We don't know his name,
but he said if we pointed it out to you, you would know at once."*

4th. After spending the night as Mahamed's guest, I strolled
round the place to see what it was like, and found the Turks were
all married to the women of the country, whom they had dressed
in clothes and beads. Their children were many, with a prospect
of more. Temporary marriages, however, were more common
than others, as, in addition to their slaves, they hired the daugh-

* It now also transpired that Mahamed had sent two Madi men with beads to
Kamrasi, and these we had always supposed to be Petherick's men.

ters of the villagers, who remained with them while they were
trading here, but went back to their parents when they marched

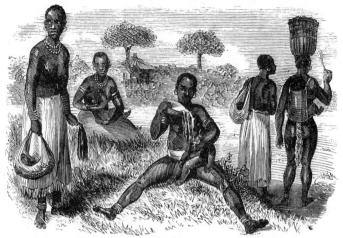

Turks' Wives and Children.

to Gondokoro.   They had also many hundreds of cattle, which it
was said they had plundered from the natives, and now used for
food, or to exchange for ivory or other purposes.   The scenery
and situation were perfect for health and beauty.   The settlement lay at the foot of small, well-wooded granitic hills, even
prettier than the outcrops of Unyamŭézi, and was intersected by
clear streams.

At noon all the rear traps arrived, with Bombay and Piéjoko
in person.   This good creature had treated Bombay very handsomely on his former journey.   He said he felt greatly disappointed at my pushing past him yesterday, as he wished to give
me a cow, but still hoped I would go over and make friends with
him.   I gave him some beads, and off he walked.   Old Chongi's
"children," who had escorted us all the way from Kamrasi's, then
took some beads and cast-off clothes for themselves and their father, and left us in good-humor.

This reduced the expedition establishment to my men and
Kidgwiga's.   With these, now, as there was no letter from Petherick, I ordered a march for the next morning, but at once met
with opposition.   Mahamed told me that there were no vessels at
Gondokoro; we must wait two months, by which time he expected they would arrive there, and some one would come to meet

him with beads. I said in answer that Petherick had promised
to have boats there all the year round, so I would not wait.
" Then," said Mahamed, " we can not go with you, for there is a
famine at this season at Gondokoro." I said, " Never mind; do
you give me an interpreter, and I will go as I am." " No," said
Mahamed, " that will not do, as the Bari people are so savage,
you could not get through them with so small a force; besides
which, just now there is a stream which can not be crossed for a
month or more."

Unable to stand Mahamed's shifting devices with equanimity
any longer, I accused him of trying to trick me in the same way
as all the common savage chiefs had done wherever I went, because they wished me to stop for their own satisfaction, quite dis-
regarding my wishes and interests; so I said I would not stop
there any longer; I would raft over the river, and find my way
through the Bari, as I had through the rest of the African savages. We talked and talked, but could make nothing of it. I
maintained that if he was commissioned to help me, he at least
could not refuse to give me a guide and interpreter; when, if I
failed in the direct route, I would try another, but go I must, as I
could not hold out any longer, being short of beads and cows. I
had just enough, but none to spare. He told me not to think of
such a thing, as he would give me all that was needful both for
myself and my men; but if I would have patience, he would collect all his officers, and the next morning would see what their
opinions were on the subject.

5th. I found that every one of Mahamed's men was against our
going to Gondokoro. They told me, in fact, with one voice, that
it was quite impossible; but they said, if I liked they would furnish me guides to escort me on ten marches to a dépôt at the farther end of the Madi country, and if I chose to wait there until
they could collect all their ivory tusks together and join us, we
would be a united party too formidable to be resisted by the Bari
people. This offer of immediate guides I of course accepted at
once, as to keep on the move was my only desire at that time;
for my men were all drunk, and Kidgwiga's were deserting. Once
more on the way, I did not despair of reaching Gondokoro by
myself. In the best good-humor now, I showed Mahamed our
picture-books; and as he said he always drilled his two hundred
men every Friday, I said I would, if he liked, command them myself. This being agreed to, all the men turned out in their best,

and, to my surprise, they not only knew the Turkish words of command, but manœuvred with some show of good training; though, as might have been expected with men of this ragamuffin stamp, all the privates gave orders as well as their captains.

When the review was over, I complimented Mahamed on the efficiency of his corps, and, retiring to my hut, as I thought I had him now in a good humor, again discussed our plans for going ahead the next day. Scarcely able to look me in the face, the humbugging scoundrel said he could not think of allowing me to go on without him, for if any accident happened he would be blamed for it. At the same time, he could not move for a few days, as he expected a party of men to arrive about the next new moon with ivory. My hurry he thought very uncalled for; for, as I had spent so many days with Kamrasi, why could I not be content to do so with him?

I was provoked beyond measure with this, as it upset all my plans. Kidgwiga's men were deserting, and I feared I should not be able to keep my promise to Kamrasi of sending him another white visitor, who would perhaps do what I had left undone, when I did not follow the connection of the Little Lŭta Nzigé with the Nile. We battled away again, and then Mahamed said there was not one man in his camp who would go with me until their crops were cut and taken in, for while residing here they grew grain for their support. We battled again, and Mahamed at last, out of patience himself, said, "Just look here, what a fix I am in," showing me a hut full of ivory. "Who," he said, "is to carry all this until the natives have got in their crops?" This, I said, so far as I was concerned, was all nonsense. I merely had asked him for a guide and interpreter, for go I must. In a huff he then absconded; and my men—those of them who were not too drunk—came and said to me, "For God's sake let us stop here. Mahamed says the road is too dangerous for us to go alone; he has promised to carry all our loads for us if we stop; and all Kamrasi's men are running away, because they are afraid to go on."

6th. Next morning I called Kidgwiga, and begged him to procure two men as guides and interpreters. He said he could not find any. I then went at Mahamed again, who first said he would give me the two men I wanted, then went off, and sent word to say he would not be visible for three days. This was too much for my patience, so I ordered all my things to be tied up in marching order, and gave out that I should leave and find out the way myself the following morning. Like an evil spirit stirred up, my preparations for going no sooner were heard of than Mahamed appeared again, and after a long and sharp contest in words, he promised us guides if I would consent to write him a note, testifying that my going was against his expressed desire.

This was done; but the next morning (7th), after our things were put out for the march, all Kidgwiga's men bolted, and no guides would take service with us. It was now obvious that, even supposing I succeeded in taking Kidgwiga to Gondokoro, he would not have a sufficient escort to come back with, unless, indeed, it happened that Englishmen might be there who might wish to carry out my investigations by penetrating to the Little Lŭta Nzigé, and to pay a visit to Kamrasi. I therefore called Kidgwiga, and after explaining these circumstances, advised him to go back to Kamrasi. He was loth to leave, he said, until his commission was fully performed; but, as I thought it advisable, he would consent. I then gave him a double gun and ammunition, as well as some very rich beads which I obtained from Mahamed's stores, to take back to Kamrasi, with orders to say that, as soon as I reached Gondokoro or Khartŭm, I would send another white man to him—not by the way I had come through Kidi, but by the left bank of the Nile; to which Kidgwiga replied, "That will do famously, for Kamrasi will change his residence soon, and come on the Nile this side of Rionga's palace, in order that he may cut in between his brother and the Turks' guns."

After this I gave a lot of rich beads to Kidgwiga for himself, and a lot also for the senior officers at the Chopi and Kamrasi's palaces, and sent the whole set off as happy as birds. When these men were gone, I tried to get up an elephant-shooting excursion due west of this, with a view to see where the Nile was, for I would not believe it was very far off, although no one as yet, since I left Chopi, either would or could tell me where the stream had gone to.

8*th*. Mahamed professed to be delighted I had made up my mind to such a scheme. He called the heads of the villages to give me all the information I sought for, and went with me to the top of a high rock, from which we could see the hills I first viewed at Chopi, sweeping round from south by east to north, which demarked the line of the Asŭa River. The Nile at that moment was, I believed, not very far off; yet, do or say what I would, every body said it was fifteen marches off, and could not be visited under a month.* It would be necessary for me to take thirty-six of Mahamed's men, besides all my own, to go there, which, he said, I was welcome to, but I should have to pay them for their services. This was a damper at once.

I knew in my mind all these reports were false, but, rather than be out of the way when the time came for marching, I agreed to wait patiently, write the history of the Wahŭma, and make collections, till Mahamed was ready, trusting that I might find some one at Gondokoro who would finish what I had left undone; or else, after arriving there, I might go up the Nile in boats and see for myself. The same evening I was attracted by the sound of drums to a neighboring village, where, by the moonlight, I found the natives were dancing. A more indecent or savage spectacle I never witnessed. The whole place was alive with naked humanity in a state of constant motion. Drawing near, I found that a number of drums were beaten by men in the centre. Next to them was a deep ring of women, half of whom carried their babies; and outside these again was a still deeper circle of men, some blowing horns, but most holding their spears erect. To the sound of the music both these rings of the opposite sexes kept jumping and sidling round and round the drummers, making the most grotesque and obscene motions to one another.

9th to 14th. Nothing of material consequence happened until the 14th, when eighty of Rionga's men brought in two slaves and thirty tusks of ivory as a present to Mahamed. Of course, I knew this was a bribe to induce Mahamed to fight with Rionga against Kamrasi; but, counting that no affair of mine, I tried to induce these men to give me some geographical information of the countries they had just left. Not one of them would come near me, for they knew I was friends with Kamrasi; and Mahamed's men, when they saw mine attempting to converse with them, abused them for "prying into other men's concerns." "These men," they said, "are our friends, and not yours; if we choose to give them presents of cloth and beads, and they give us a return in ivory, what is that to you?" Mysterious Mahamed next came to me and begged for a blanket, as he said he was going off for a few days to a dépôt where he had some ivory; and he also wanted to borrow a musket, as one of his had been burnt.

My suspicions, and even apprehensions, were now greatly ex-

* It will appear shortly that it was actually not more than two marches to the northward of Faloro.

cited. I began to think he had prevailed on me to stop here, that
I might hold the place while he went to fight Kamrasi with Rionga's men; so I begged him to listen to my advice, and not attempt to cross the Nile, "else," I said, "all his guns would be
taken from him, and his passage back cut off." At once he saw
the drift of my thought, and said he was not going toward the
Nile, but, on the contrary, he was going with Rionga's men in the
opposite direction, to a place called Paira. "If that is the case,"
I said, "why do you want a gun?" "Because there are some
other matters to settle. I shall not be long away, and my men
will take care of you while I am gone." I gave him the blanket
after this, but was too suspicious of his object to lend him a gun.

15th to 20th. I saw Mahamed march his regiment out of the
place, drums and fifes playing, colors flying, a hundred guns firing, officers riding, some of them on donkeys, and others—yes,
actually—on cows! while a host of the natives, Rionga's men included, carrying spears and bows and arrows, looked little like a
peaceful caravan of merchants, but very much resembled a band
of marauders. After this I heard they were not going to Rionga

Removing a Village—Madi.

himself, but were going to show Rionga's men the way that they
made friends with old Chongi of Koki. In reality, Chongi had

invited Mahamed to fight against an enemy of his, in whose territories immense stores of ivory were said to be buried, and the people had an endless number of cattle; for they lived by plunder, and had lifted most of old Chongi's; and this was the service on which the expedition had set off.

21st to 31st. I had constantly wondered, ever since I first came here, and saw the brutal manner in which the Turks treated the natives, that these Madi people could submit to their "Egyptian taskmasters," and therefore was not surprised now to find them pull down their huts and march off with the materials to a distant site. Every day this sort of migration continued, just as you see in the picture; and nothing more important occurred until Christmas day, when an armadillo was caught, and I heard from Mahamed's head wife that the Turks had plundered and burnt down three villages, and in all probability they would return shortly laden with ivory. This was a true anticipation; for on the 31st Mahamed came in with his triumphant army laden with ivory, and driving in five slave-girls and thirty head of cattle.

Turks tying up Ivories for the March.

1st to 3d. I now wished to go on with the journey, as I could get no true information out of these suspicious blackguards who called themselves Turks; but Mahamed postponed it until the 5th, by which time he said he would be able to collect all the men he wanted to carry his ivory. Rionga's men then departed, and Mahamed showed some signs of getting ready by ordering one dozen cows to be killed, the flesh of which was to be divided among those villagers who would carry his ivory, and the skins to be cut into thongs for binding the smaller tusks of ivory together in suitable loads.

4th and *5th.* Another specimen of Turkish barbarity came under my notice, in the head man of a village bringing a large tusk of ivory to Mahamed to ransom his daughter with, for she had been seized as a slave on his last expedition, in common with others who could not run away fast enough to save themselves from the Turks. Fortunately for both, it was thought necessary for the Turks to keep on good terms with the father as an influential man, and therefore, on receiving the tusk, Mahamed gave back the girl, and added a cow to seal their friendship.

6th to *10th.* I saw this land-pirate Mahamed take a blackmail like a negro chief. Some men who had fled from their village when Mahamed's plundering party passed by them the other day, surprised that he did not stop to sack their homes, now brought ten large tusks of ivory to him to express the gratitude they said they felt for his not having molested them. Mahamed, on finding how easy it was to get taxes in this fashion, instead of thanking them, assumed the air of the great potentate, whose clemency was abused, and told the poor creatures that, though they had done well in seeking his friendship, they had not sufficiently considered his dignity, else they would have brought double that number of tusks, for it was impossible he could be satisfied at so low a price. "What," said these poor creatures, "can we do, then, for this is all that we have got?" "Oh," says Mahamed, "if it is all you have got now in store, I will take these few for the present, but when I return from Gondokoro I expect you will bring me just as many more. Good-by, and look out for yourselves."

Tired beyond all measure with Mahamed's procrastination, as I

To Panyoro, 11th.   could not get him to start, I now started myself, much to his disgust, and went ahead again, leaving word that I would wait for him at the next place, provided he did not delay more than one day. The march led us over long rolling downs of grass, where we saw a good many antelopes feeding;

MAHAMED'S PARTY ON THE MARCH.

and after going ten miles, we came, among other villages, to one named Panyoro, in which we found it convenient to put up. At first all the villagers, thinking us Turks, bolted away with their cattle and what stores they could carry; but, after finding out who we were, they returned again, and gave us a good reception, helping us to rig up a shed with grass, and bringing a cow and some milk for our dinner.

12th. To-day I went out shooting, but, though I saw and fired at a rhinoceros, as well as many varieties of antelopes, I did not succeed in killing one head. All my men were surprised as well as myself; and the villagers who were escorting me in the hope of getting flesh, were so annoyed at their disappointment, they offered to cut my fore finger with a spear and spit on it for good luck. Joining in their talk, I told them the powder must be crooked; but, on inspecting my rifle closer, I found that the sights had been knocked on one side a little, and this created a general laugh at all in turn. Going home from the shooting, I found all the villagers bolting again with their cattle and stores, and, on looking toward Faloro, saw a party of Turks coming.

As well as I could I reassured the villagers, and brought them back again, when they said to me, " Oh, what have you done? We were so happy yesterday when we found out who you were, but now we see you have brought those men, all our hearts have sunk again; for they beat us, they make us carry their loads, and they rob us in such a manner we know not what to do." I told them I would protect them if they would keep quiet; and, when the Turks came, I told them what I had said to the head man. They were the vanguard of Mahamed's party, and said they had orders to march on as far as Apuddo with me, where we must all stop for Mahamed, who, as well as he could, was collecting men. There was a certain tree near Apuddo which was marked by an Englishman two years ago, and this, Mahamed thought, would keep us amused.

The next march brought us to Paira, a collection of villages within sight of the Nile. It was truly ridiculous; To Paira, 13th. here had we been at Faloro so long, and yet could not make out what had become of the Nile. In appearance it was a noble stream, flowing on a flat bed from west to east, and immediately beyond it were the Jbl (hills) Kŭkŭ, rising up to a height of 2000 feet above the river. Still we could not make out all until the following day, when we made a march parallel to the Nile, and arrived at Jaifi.

The Nile and Jbl Kūkū.

This was a collection of huts close to a deep nullah which
drains the central portions of Eastern Madi. At this
place the Turks killed a crocodile and ate him on the
spot, much to the amusement of my men, who immediately shook
their heads laughingly, and said, "Ewa, Allah! are these men,
then, Mussulmans? Savages in our country don't much like a
crocodile."

To Jaifi, 14th.

After crossing two nullahs we reached Apuddo, and at once I
went to see the tree said to have been cut by an Englishman some time before. There, sure enough, was
a mark, something like the letters M. I., on its bark, but not distinct enough to be ascertained, because the bark had healed up.
In describing the individual who had done this, the Turks said
he was exactly like myself, for he had a long beard, and a voice
even much resembling mine. He came thus far with Mahamed
from Gondokoro two years ago, and then returned, because he
was alarmed at the accounts the people gave of the countries to
the southward, and he did not like the prospect of having to remain a whole rainy season with Mahamed at Faloro. He knew
we were endeavoring to come this way, and directed Mahamed to
point out his name if we did so.

To Apuddo, 15th.

We took up our quarters in the village as usual, but the Turks
remained outside, and carried off all the tops of the villagers' huts
to make a camp for themselves. I rebuked them for doing so,
but was mildly told they had no huts of their own. They car-

ried no pots either for cooking their dinners, and therefore took from the villagers all that they wanted. It was a fixed custom now, they told us, and there was no use in our trying to struggle against it. If the natives were wise, they would make enough to sell; but as they would not, they must put up with their lot, for the "government" can not be balked of its ivory. Truly there seemed to be nothing but misery here; food was so scarce the villagers sought for wild berries and fruits, while the Turks helped themselves out of their half-filled bins—a small reserve store to last up to the far-distant harvest. Then, to make matters worse, all the village chiefs were at war with one another.

At night a party of warriors walked round our village, but *Halt, 16th and 17th.* feared to attack it because we were inside. Next morning the villagers turned out and killed two of the enemy; but the rest, while retreating, sang out that they would not attempt to fight until "the guns" were gone; after that, the villagers had better look out for themselves. I now proposed going on if the apina, or chief of the village, would give me a guide; but he feared to do so lest I should come to grief, and Mahamed would then be down upon him. Struggling was useless, for I had no beads to pay my way with, and my cows were now all finished; so I took the matter quietly, and went out foraging with the rifle.

18th and 19th. Antelopes were numerous, but so wild I could not get near them. On bending round homeward, however, three buffaloes, feeding in the distance, on the top of a roll of high ground beyond where we stood, were observed by the natives, who had flocked out in the hopes of getting flesh. To stalk them, I went up wind to near where I expected to find them; then bidding the natives lie down, I stole along through the grass until at last I saw three pairs of horns glistening quite close in front of me. Anxious lest they should take sudden fright, I gently raised myself, wishing to fire, but I was quite puzzled; there was no mistake about what they were; still, look from as high as I would, I could not see their bodies. The thought never struck me they were lying down in such open ground in the daytime; so, as I could not go closer without driving them off, I took a shot with my single rifle at where I judged the chest of the nearest one ought to be, and then discovered my error. In an instant all three sprang on their legs and scampered off. I began loading, but before I had half accomplished my object, those three had

mingled with the three previously seen grazing, and all six together came charging straight at me. I really thought I should
now catch a toss, if I were not trampled to death; but suddenly,
as they saw me standing, whether from fear or what else I can
not say, they changed their ferocious-looking design, swerved
round, and galloped off as fast as their legs could carry them.
This was bad luck, but Grant made up for it the next day by killing a very fine buck n'samma.

20th. I went again after the herd of six buffaloes, as I thought
one was wounded, and after walking up a long sloping hill for
three miles toward the east, I found myself at once in view of the
Nile on one hand and the long-heard-of Asŭa River on the other,
backed by hills even higher than the Jbl Kŭkŭ. The bed of the
Asŭa seemed very large, but, being far off, was not very distinct;
nor did I care to go and see it then, for at that moment, straight
in front of me, five buffaloes, five giraffes, two eland, and sundry
other antelopes, were too strong a temptation.

The place looked like a park, and I began stalking in it, first
at the eland, as I wanted to see if they corresponded with those
I shot in Usagara; but the gawky giraffes, always in the way,
gave the alarm, and drove all but two of the buffaloes away. At
these two I now went with my only rifle, leaving the servants
and savages behind. They were out in the open grass feeding
composedly, so that I stole up to within forty yards of them, and
then, in a small naked patch of ground, I waited my opportunity,
and put a ball behind the shoulder of the larger one. At the
sound of the gun, in an instant both bulls charged, but they pulled up in the same naked ground as myself, sniffing and tossing
their horns while looking out for their antagonist, who, as quick
as themselves, had thrown himself flat on the ground.

There we were, like three fools, for twenty minutes or so; one
of the buffaloes bleeding at the mouth and with a broken hind
leg, for the bullet had traversed his body, and the other turning
round and round, looking out for me, while I was anxiously
watching him, and by degrees loading my gun. When ready, I
tried a shot at the sound one, but the cap snapped and nearly be-
trayed me, for they both stared at the spot where I lay; the sound
one sniffing the air and tossing his horns, but the other bleeding
considerably. Some minutes more passed in this manner, when
they allowed me to breathe freer by walking away. I followed,
of course, but could not get a good chance; so, as the night set in,

I let them alone for the time being, to get out the following morning.

21*st* and 22*d*. At the place where I left off, I now sprang a large herd of fifty or more buffaloes, and followed them for a mile, when the wounded one, quite exhausted from the fatigue, pulled up for a charge, and allowed me to knock him over. This was glorious fun for the villagers, who cut him up on the spot and brought him home. Of course, one half the flesh was given to them, in return for which they brought us some small delicacies to show their gratitude; for, as they truly remarked, until we came to their village they never knew what it was to get a present, or any other gift but a good thrashing.

23*d*. To-day I tried the ground again, and, while walking up the hill, two black rhinoceros came trotting toward us in a very excited manner. I did not wish to fire at them, as what few bullets remained in my store I wished to reserve for better sport, and therefore, for the time being, let them alone. Presently, however, they separated; one passed in front of us, stopped to drink in a pool, and then lay down in it. Not heeding him, I walked up the hill, while the other rhinoceros, still trotting, suddenly turned round and came to drink within fifty yards of us, obstructing my path; this was too much of a joke; so, to save time, I gave him a bullet, and knocked him over. To my surprise, the natives who were with me would not touch his flesh, though pressed by me to "n'yam n'yam," or to eat. I found that they considered him an unclean beast; so, regretting I had wasted my bullet, I went farther on and startled some buffaloes.

Though I got very near them, however, a small antelope springing up in front of me scared them away, and I could not get a front shot at any of them. Thus the whole day was thrown away, for I had to return empty-handed.

24*th* to 30*th*. Grant and I, after this, kept our pot boiling by shooting three more antelopes; but nothing of consequence transpired until the 30th, when Bŭkhet, Mahamed's factotum, arrived with the greater part of the Turk's property. He then confirmed a report we had heard before, that, some few days previously, Mahamed had ordered Bŭkhet to go ahead and join us, which he attempted to do; but, on arrival at Panyoro, his party had a row with the villagers, and lost their property. Bŭkhet then returned to Mahamed and reported his defeat and losses; upon hearing which, Mahamed at once said to him, "What do you mean by returning to me empty-handed? Go back at once and recover your things, else how can I make my report at Gondokoro?" With these peremptory orders Bŭkhet went back to Panyoro, and commenced to attack it. The contest did not last long; for, after three of Bŭkhet's men had been wounded, he set fire to the villages, killed fifteen of the natives, and, besides recovering his own lost property, took one hundred cows.

31st. To-day Mahamed came in, and commenced to arrange for the march onward. This, however, was no easy matter, for the Turks alone required six hundred porters—half that number to carry their ivory, and the other half to carry their beds and bedding; while from fifty to sixty men was the most a village had to spare, and all the village chiefs were at enmity with one another. The plan adopted by Mahamed was to summon the heads of all the villages to come to him, failing which he would seize all their belongings. Then, having once got them together, he ordered them all to furnish him with so many porters a head, saying he demanded it of them, for the "great government's property" could not be left on the ground. Their separate interests must now be sacrificed, and their feuds suspended; and if he heard, on his return again, that one village had taken advantage of the other's weakness caused by their employment in his service, he would then not spare his bullets, so they might look out for themselves.

Some of the Turks, having found ninety-nine eggs in a crocodile's nest, had a grand feast. They gave us two of the eggs, which we ate, but did not like, for they had a highly musky flavor.

1st. On the 1st of February we went ahead again, with Bŭkhet and the first half of Mahamed's establishment, as a sufficient number of men could not be collected at once to move altogether. In a little while we struck on the Nile, where it was running like a fine Highland stream between the gneiss and mica-schist hills of Kŭkŭ, and followed it down to near where the Asŭa River joined it. For a while we sat here watching the water, which was greatly discolored, and floating down rushes. The river was not as full as it was when we crossed it at the Karŭma Falls, yet, according to Dr. Khoblecher's* account, it ought to have been flooding just at this time; if so, we had beaten the stream. Here we left

* Dr. Khoblecher, the founder of the Austrian Church Mission Establishment of Gondokoro, ascertained that the Nile reached its lowest level there in the middle of January.

it again as it arched round by the west, and forded the Asŭa River, a stiff rocky stream, deep enough to reach the breast when waded, but not very broad. It did not appear to me as if connected with the Victoria N'yanza, as the waters were falling, and not much discolored; whereas, judging from the Nile's condition, it ought to have been rising. No vessel ever could have gone up it, and it bore no comparison with the Nile itself. The exaggerated account of its volume, however, given by the expeditionists who were sent up the Nile by Mehemet Ali, did not surprise us, since they had mistaken its position; for we were now 3° 42′ north, and therefore had passed their "farthest point" by twenty miles.

In two hours more we reached a settlement called Madi, and found it deserted. Every man and woman had run off into the jungles from fright, and would not come back again. We wished ourselves at the end of the journey; thought any thing better than this kind of existence—living entirely at the expense of others; even the fleecings in Usŭi felt less dispiriting; but it could not be helped, for it must always exist as long as these Turks are allowed to ride roughshod over the people. The Turks, however, had their losses also; for on the way four Bari men and one Bari slave-girl slipped off with a hundred of their plundered cattle, and neither they nor the cattle could be found again. Mijalwa was here convicted of having stolen the cloth of a Turk while living in his hut when he was away at the Paira plundering, and got fifty lashes to teach him better behavior for the future.

A party of fifty men came from Labŭré, a station on ahead of this, to take service as porters, knowing that at this season the Turks always come with a large herd of plundered cattle, which they call government property, and give in payment to the men who carry their tusks of ivory across the Bari country.

Halt, 3d to 5th.

We now marched over a rolling ground, covered in some places with bush-jungle, in others with villages, where there were fine trees, resembling oaks in their outward appearance; and stopping one night at the settlement of Barwŭdi, arrived at Labŭré, where we had to halt a day for Mahamed to collect some ivory from a dépôt he had formed near by. We heard there was another ivory party collecting tusks at Obbo, a settlement in the country of Panŭquara, twenty miles east of this.

Barwŭdi, 6th; and Labŭré, 7th and 8th.

Next we crossed a nullah draining into the Nile, and, traveling over more rolling ground, flanked on the right
by a range of small hills, put up at the Madi frontier
station, Mŭgi, where we had to halt two days to collect a full complement of porters to traverse the Bari country,
the people of which are denounced as barbarians by the Turks,
because they will not submit to be bullied into carrying their
tusks for them. Here we felt an earthquake. The people would
not take beads, preferring, they said, to make necklaces and belts
out of ostrich eggs, which they cut into the size of small shirt-
buttons, and then drill a hole through their centre to string them
together. A passenger told us that three white men had just arrived in vessels at Gondokoro; and the Bari people, hearing of
our advance, instead of trying to kill us with spears, had determined to poison all the water in their country. Mahamed now
disposed of half of his herd of cows, giving them to the chiefs of
the villages in return for porters. These, he said, were all that
belonged to the government; for the half of all captures of cows,
as well as all slaves, all goats, and sheep, were allowed to the
men as part of their pay.

When all was settled, we marched, one thousand strong, to
Wurŭngi; and next day, by a double march, arrived
at Marsan, in the Bari country. I wished still to put
up in the native villages, but Mahamed so terrified
all my men, by saying these Bari would kill us in the night if
we did not all sleep together in one large camp, that we were
obliged to submit. The country, still flanked on the right by
hills, was undulating and very prettily wooded. Villages were
numerous, but as we passed them the inhabitants all fled from us
save a few men, who, bolder than the rest, would stand and look
on at us as we marched along. Both night and morning the
Turks beat their drums, and whenever they stopped to eat they
sacked the villages.

Pushing on by degrees, stopping at noon to eat, we came again
in sight of the Nile, and put up at a station called
Doro, within a short distance of the well-known hill
Rijeb, where Nile voyagers delight in cutting their names. The
country continued the same, but the grass was conspicuously becoming shorter and finer every day; so much so, that my men
all declared it was a sign of our near approach to England. After
we had settled down for the night, and the Turks had finished

To Mŭgi, 9th.
Halt, 10th and 11th.

To Wurŭngi, 12th.
To Marsan, 13th.

To Doro, 14th.

plundering the nearest villages, we heard two guns fired, and immediately afterward the whole place was alive with Bari people. Their drums were beaten as a sign that they would attack us, and the war-drums of the villages around responded by beating also. The Turks grew somewhat alarmed at this, and as darkness began to set in, sent out patrols in addition to their nightly watches. The savages next tried to steal in on us, but were soon frightened off by the patrols cocking their guns. Then, seeing themselves defeated in that tactic, they collected in hundreds in front of us, set fire to the grass, and marched up and down, brandishing ignited grass in their hands, howling like demons, and swearing they would annihilate us in the morning.

We slept the night out, nevertheless, and next morning walked in to Gondokoro, N. lat. 4° 54' 5", and E. long. 31° 46' 9", where Mahamed, after firing a salute, took us in to see a Circassian merchant, named Kŭrshid Agha. Our first inquiry was, of course, for Petherick. A mysterious silence ensued; we were informed that Mr. Debono was *the* man we had to thank for the assistance we had received in coming from Madi; and then in hot haste, after warm exchanges of greeting with Mahamed's friend, who was Debono's agent here, we took leave, to hunt up Petherick. Walking down the bank of the river—where a line of vessels was moored, and on the right hand a few sheds,

To Gondokoro, 15th.

Mission House, Gondokoro.

one half broken down, with a brick-built house representing the late Austrian Church Mission establishment—we saw hurrying

on toward us the form of an Englishman, who for one moment
we believed was the Simon Pure; but the next moment my old
friend Baker, famed for his sports in Ceylon, seized me by the
hand. A little boy of his establishment had reported our arrival,
and he in an instant came out to welcome us. What joy this
was I can hardly tell. We could not talk fast enough, so over-
whelmed were we both to meet again. Of course we were his
guests in a moment, and learned every thing that could be told.
I now first heard of the death of H. R. H. the Prince Consort,
which made me reflect on the inspiring words he made use of, in
compliment to myself, when I was introduced to him by Sir Roderick Murchison a short while before leaving England. Then
there was the terrible war in America, and other events of less
startling nature, which came on us all by surprise, as years had
now passed since we had received news from the civilized world.

Baker then said he had come up with three vessels—one dyabir
and two nuggers—fully equipped with armed men, camels, horses,
donkeys, beads, brass wire, and every thing necessary for a long
journey, expressly to look after us, hoping, as he jokingly said,
to find us on the equator in some terrible fix, that he might have
the pleasure of helping us out of it. He had heard of Mahamed's
party, and was actually waiting for him to come in, that he might
have had the use of his return-men to start with comfortably.
Three Dutch ladies,* also, with a view to assist us in the same
way as Baker (God bless them), had come here in a steamer, but
were driven back to Khartŭm by sickness. Nobody had even
dreamed for a moment it was possible we could come through.
An Italian, named Miani, had gone farther up the Nile than any
one else; and he, it now transpired, was the man who had cut his
name on the tree by Apuddo. But what had become of Petherick? He was actually trading at N'yambara, seventy miles due
west of this, though he had, since I left him in England, raised a
subscription of £1000 from those of my friends to whom this
Journal is most respectfully dedicated as the smallest return a
grateful heart can give for their attempt to succor me, when knowing the fate of the expedition was in great jeopardy.

Instead of coming up the Nile at once, as Petherick might have
done—so I was assured—he waited, while a vessel was building,
until the season had too far advanced to enable him to sail up the
river. In short, he lost the north winds at 7° north, and went

* The Baroness Miss A. van Capellan, and Mrs. and Miss Tinne.

overland to his trading dépôt at N'yambara. Previously, however, he had sent some boats up to this, under a vakil, who had his
orders to cross to his trading dépôt at N'yambara, and to work
from his trading station due south, ostensibly with a view to look
after me, though .contrary to my advice before leaving him in
England, in opposition to his own proposed views of assisting me
when he applied for help to succor me, and against the strongly
expressed opinions of every European in the same trade as himself; for all alike said they knew he would have gone to Faloro,
and pushed south from that place, had his trade on the west of
the Nile not attracted him there.

Baker now offered me his boats to go down to Khartŭm, and
asked me if there was any thing left undone which it might be
of importance for him to go on and complete, by survey or otherwise; for, although he should like to go down the river with us,
he did not wish to return home without having done something
to recompense him for the trouble and expense he had incurred
in getting up his large expedition. Of course I told him how disappointed I had been in not getting a sight of the Little Lŭta
Nzigé. I described how we had seen the Nile bending west
where we crossed in Chopi, and then, after walking down the
chord of an arc described by the river, had found it again in
Madi coming from the west, whence to the south, and as far at
least as Koshi, it was said to be navigable, probably continuing
to be so right into the Little Lŭta Nzigé. Should this be the
case, then, by building boats in Madi above the cataracts, a vast
region might be thrown open to the improving influences of navigation. Farther, I told Baker of my contract with Kamrasi, and
of the property I had left behind, with a view to stimulate any
enterprising man who might be found at this place to go there,
make good my promise, and, if found needful, claim my share of
the things, for the better prosecution of his own travels there.
This Baker at once undertook, though he said he did not want
my property; and I drew out suggestions for him how to proceed.
He then made friends with Mahamed, who promised to help him
on to Faloro, and I gave Mahamed and his men three carbines as
an honorarium.

I should now have gone down the Nile at once if the moon had
been in "distance" for fixing the longitude; but as it was not, I
had to remain until the 26th, living with Baker. Kŭrshid Agha
became very great friends with us, and, at once making a present

of a turkey, a case of wine, and cigars, said he was only sorry for his own sake that we had found a fellow-countryman, else he would have had the envied honor of claiming us as his guests, and had the pleasure of transporting us in his vessels down to Khartŭm.

The Rev. Mr. Moorlan, and two other priests of the Austrian Mission, were here on a visit from their station at Kich, to see the old place again before they left for Khartŭm; for the Austrian government, discouraged by the failure of so many years, had ordered the recall of the whole of the establishment for these regions. It was no wonder these men were recalled; for, out of twenty missionaries who, during the last thirteen years, had ascended the White River for the purpose of propagating the Gospel, thirteen had died of fever, two of dysentery, and two had retired broken in health, yet not one convert had been made by them.

The fact is, there was no government to control the population or to protect property; boys came to them, looked at their pictures, and even showed a disposition to be instructed, but there it ended; they had no heart to study when no visible returns were to be gained. One day the people would examine the books, at another throw them aside, say their stomachs were empty, and run away to look for food. The Bari people at Gondokoro were described as being more tractable than those of Kich, being of a braver and more noble nature; but they were all half starved— not because the country was too poor to produce, but because they were too lazy to cultivate. What little corn they grew they consumed before it was fully ripe, and then either sought for fish in the river or fed on tortoises in the interior, as they feared they might never reap what they sowed.

The missionaries never had occasion to complain of these blacks, and to this day they would doubtless have been kindly inclined toward Europeans, had the White Nile traders not brought the devil among them. Mr. Moorlan remembers the time when they brought food for sale; but now, instead, they turn their backs upon all foreigners, and even abuse the missionaries for having been the precursors of such dire calamities. The shell of the brick church at Gondokoro, and the cross on the top of a native-built hut in Kich, are all that will remain to bear testimony of these Christian exertions to improve the condition of these heathens. Want of employment, I heard, was the chief operative

cause in killing the poor missionaries; for, with no other resource
left them to kill time, they spent their days eating, drinking,
smoking, and sleeping, till they broke down their constitutions
by living too fast.

Mr. Moorlan became very friendly, and said he was sorry he
could not do more for us. His head-quarters were at Kich, some
way down the river, where, as we passed, he hoped at least he
might be able to show us as much attention and hospitality as lay
in his power. Musquitoes were said to be extremely troublesome
on the river, and my men begged for some clothes, as Petherick,
they said, had a store for me under the charge of his vakil. The
store-keeper was then called, and confirming the story of my men,
I begged him to give me what was my own. It then turned out
that it was all Petherick's, but he had orders to give me on account any thing that I wanted. This being settled, I took ninety-
five yards of the commonest stuff as a makeshift for musquito-
curtains for my men, besides four sailor's shirts for my head men.

On the 18th, Kŭrshid Agha was summoned by the constant fire
of musketry a mile or two down the river, and went off in his
vessels to the relief. A party of his had come across from the
N'yambara country with ivory, and on the banks of the Nile, a
few miles north of this, were engaged fighting with the natives.
He arrived just in time to settle the difficulty, and next day came
back again, having shot some of the enemy and captured their
cows. Petherick, we heard, was in a difficulty of the same kind,
upon which I proposed to go down with Baker and Grant to succor him; but he arrived in time, in company with his wife and
Dr. James Murie, to save us the trouble, and told me he had
brought a number of men with him, carrying ivory, for the purpose *now* of looking after me on the east bank of the Nile, by following its course up to the south, though he had given up all
hope of seeing me, as a report had reached him of the desertion
of my porters at Ugogo. He then offered me his dyabir, as well
as any thing else that I wanted that lay within his power to give.
Suffice it to say, I had, through Baker's generosity, at that very
moment enough and to spare; but, at his urgent request, I took
a few more yards of cloth for my men, and some cooking fat;
and, though I offered to pay for it, he declined to accept any return at my hands.

Though I naturally felt much annoyed at Petherick—for I had
hurried away from Uganda, and separated from Grant at Kari

solely to keep faith with him—I did not wish to break friendship, but dined and conversed with him, when it transpired that his vakil, or agent, who went south from the N'yambara station, came among the N'yam N'yams, and heard from them that a large river, four days' journey more to the southward, was flowing from east to west, beyond which lived a tribe of " women," who, when they wanted to marry, mingled with them in the stream and returned; and then, again, beyond this tribe of women there lived another tribe of women and dogs.   Now this may all seem a very strange story to those who do not know the negro's and Arab's modes of expression, but to me it at once came very natural, and, according to my view, could be interpreted thus: The river, running from east to west, according to the native mode of expressing direction, could be nothing but the Little Lŭta Nzigé running the opposite way, according to fact and our mode of expression.   The first tribe of women were doubtless the Wanyoro, called women by the naked tribes on this side because they wear bark coverings— an effeminate appendage, in the naked man's estimation; and the second tribe must have been in allusion to the dog-keeping Wa- ganda, who also would be considered women, as they wear bark clothes.   In my turn, I told Petherick he had missed a good thing by not going up the river to look for me; for, had he done so, he would not only have had the best ivory-grounds to work upon, but, by building a vessel in Madi above the cataracts, he would have had, in my belief, some hundred miles of navigable water to

The Nile below the Junction of the Asŭa River.

transport his merchandise. In short, his succoring petition was most admirably framed, had he stuck to it, for the welfare of both of us.*

We now received our first letters from home, and in one from Sir Roderick Murchison I found the Royal Geographical Society had awarded me their "founder's medal" for the discovery of the Victoria N'yanza in 1858.

---

* See Petherick's succoring petition, addressed to the Right Hon. Lord Ashburton, President of the Royal Geographical Society, in the Proceedings of that Society, dated the 19th of June, 1860.

CONCLUSION.

My journey down to Alexandria was not without adventure, and carried me through scenes which, in other circumstances, it might have been worth while to describe. Thinking, however, that I have already sufficiently trespassed on the patience of the reader, I am unwilling to overload my volume with any matter that does not directly relate to the solution of the great problem which I went to solve. Having now, then, after a period of twenty-eight months, come upon the tracks of European travelers, and met them face to face, I close my Journal, to conclude with a few explanations, for the purpose of comparing the various branches of the Nile with its affluents, so as to show their respective values.

The first affluent, the Bahr el Ghazal, took us by surprise; for, instead of finding a huge lake, as described in our maps, at an elbow of the Nile, we found only a small piece of water resembling a duck-pond buried in a sea of rushes. The old Nile swept through it with majestic grace, and carried us next to the Geraffe branch of the Sobat River, the second affluent, which we found flowing into the Nile with a graceful semicircular sweep and good stiff current, apparently deep, but not more than fifty yards broad.

Next in order came the main stream of the Sobat, flowing into the Nile in the same graceful way as the Geraffe, which in breadth it surpassed, but in velocity of current was inferior. The Nile by these additions was greatly increased; still, it did not assume that noble appearance which astonished us so much, *immediately after the rainy season*, when we were navigating it in canoes in Unyoro.

I here took my last lunar observations, and made its mouth N. lat. 9° 20′ 48″, E. long. 31° 24′ 0″. The Sobat has a third mouth farther down the Nile, which unfortunately was passed without my knowing it; but as it is so well known to be unimportant, the loss was not great.

Next to be treated of is the famous Blue Nile, which we found a miserable river, even when compared with the Geraffe branch of the Sobat. It is very broad at the mouth, it is true, but so shallow that our vessel with difficulty was able to come up it. It had all the appearance of a mountain stream, subject to great pe-

SPEKE'S FAITHFULS.

riodical fluctuations. I was never more disappointed than with this river; if the White River was cut off from it, its waters would all be absorbed before they could reach Lower Egypt.

The Atbara River, which is the last affluent, was more like the Blue River than any of the other affluents, being decidedly a mountain stream, which floods in the rains, but runs nearly dry in the dry season.

I had now seen quite enough to satisfy myself that the White River which issues from the N'yanza at the Ripon Falls is the true or parent Nile; for in every instance of its branching, it carried the palm with it in the distinctest manner, viewed, as all the streams were by me, in the dry season, which is the best time for estimating their relative perennial values.

Since returning to England, Dr. Murie, who was with me at Gondokoro, has also come home; and he, judging from my account of the way in which we got ahead of the flooding of the Nile between the Karŭma Falls and Gondokoro, is of opinion that the Little Lŭta Nzigé must be a great backwater to the Nile, which the waters of the Nile must have been occupied in filling during my residence in Madi; and then about the same time that I set out from Madi, the Little Lŭta Nzigé having been surcharged with water, the surplus began its march northward just about the time when we started in the same direction. For myself, I believe in this opinion, as he no sooner asked me how I could account for the phenomenon I have already mentioned of the river appearing to decrease in bulk as we descended it, than I instinctively advanced his own theory. Moreover, the same hypothesis will answer for the sluggish flooding of the Nile down to Egypt.

I hope the reader who has followed my narrative thus far will be interested in knowing how "my faithful children," for whose services I had no farther occasion, and whom I had taken so far from their own country, were disposed of. At Cairo, where we put up in Shepherd's Hotel, I had the whole of them photographed, and indulged them at the public concerts, tableau vivants, etc. By invitation, we called on the viceroy at his Rhoda Island palace, and were much gratified with the reception; for, after hearing all our stories with marked intelligence, he most graciously offered to assist me in any other undertaking which would tend to open up and develop the interior of Africa.

I next appointed Bombay captain of the "faithfuls," and gave him three photographs of all the eighteen men and three more of the four women, to give one of each to our consuls at Suez, Aden, and Zanzibar, by which they might be recognized. I also gave them increased wages, equal to three years' pay each, by orders on Zanzibar, which was one in addition to their time of service; an order for a grand "freeman's garden," to be purchased for them at Zanzibar; and an order that each one should receive ten dollars dowry money as soon as he could find a wife.

With these letters in their hands, I made arrangements with our consul, Mr. Drummond Hay, to frank them through Suez, Aden, and the Seychelles to Zanzibar.

Since then, I have heard that Captain Bombay and his party missed the Seychelles, and went on to the Mauritius, where Captain Anson, Inspector General of Police, kindly took charge of them, and made great lions of them. A subscription was raised to give them a purse of money; they were treated with tickets to the "Circus," and sent back to the Seychelles, whence they were transported by steamer to Zanzibar, and taken in charge by our lately-appointed consul, Colonel Playfair, who appears to have taken much interest in them. Farther, they all volunteered to go with me again, should I attempt to cross Africa from east to west, through the fertile zone.

1. Sikujua.   2. Kahala, alias Raziki.   3. Mzizi.   4. Faida, since married to Frij.

APPENDICES.

APPENDIX A.

NATIVE ESTABLISHMENT OF THE EXPEDITION.

These men all severally agreed, before Colonel Rigby, Sheikh Said, Bombay, and myself, to serve as my servants on the following terms, as registered in the office-books at the British Consulate, Zanzibar, on the 8th of September, 1860:

Supposing I gave Sheikh Said $500—Bombay, Baraka, and Rahan $60 each—the Wangŭana $25 each—and Sultan Majid's Watŭma gardeners $7 each, in ready money down, and promised to give them as much more on arrival in Egypt, as well as free clothes and rations on the journey, and a free passage back from Egypt to Zanzibar, then they bound themselves to follow me wherever I chose to lead them in Africa, and do any kind of duty, without hesitation, that men in such positions, while traveling with caravans, might reasonably be expected to do.

The money alluded to having been paid by me in the presence of all, the books were signed, and our compact concluded.

List of Men engaged at Zanzibar—their Pay, their Appointments, and how disposed of.

Numerical numbers.	Pay in dolls., one year advanced.	Names.	What race they belong to.	Highest appointments held by each individual.	How and where their services terminated.	No. of guns stolen by deserters.	Remarks.
1.	500	Said bin Salem	Arab	Cafila Bashi	Discharged sick at Kazé		
2.	25	Sŭlimani	Negro				Watŭma or slaves.
3.	25	Babŭ	do.	Servants to Sheikh Said	Discharged with Sheikh Said at Kazé		
4.	25	Feraj	do.				
5.	25	Yakŭt	do.				
6.	25	Yŭsuf	do.				
7.	25	Saadi	do.				
8.	60	Bombay	do.	Factotum	Paid off, Egypt		
9.	60	Baraka	do.	Commander-in-chief	Sent back, Unyoro		Wangŭana, or slaves freed.
10.	60	Rahan	do.	Valet	Sent back, Bogŭé		
11.	25	Frij	do.	Cook	Paid off, Egypt		
12.	25	Mabrŭki	do.	Valet	do.		
13.	25	Ulédi, sen	do.	do.	do.		
14.	25	Ilmasi	do.	do.	do.		
15.	25	Abédi	do.	Porter	Deserted, Bogŭé		
16.	25	Rahan	do.	do.	Deserted, Unyoro	1	
17.	25	Wadimoyo	do.	do.	do.	2	
18.	25	Wadihamadi	do.	do.	do.	3	
19.	25	Saad Allah	do.	do.	Deserted, Bogŭé		
20.	25	Tabibŭ	do.	do.	Sent back, Usugara		
21.	25	Kari	do.	do.	Murdered, Uganda		
22.	25	Matiko	do.	do.	Deserted, Unyoro	4	
23.	25	Nasibŭ	do.	do.	Left in Uganda		

LIST OF MEN ENGAGED AT ZANZIBAR—*Continued.*

Numerical numbers.	Pay in dolls., one year advanced.	Names.	What race they belong to.	Highest appointments held by each individual.	How and where their services terminated.	No. of guns stolen by deserters.	Remarks.
24.	25	Mūsa	Negro	Porter	Deserted, Unyoro	5	
25.	25	Mabrūki	do.	do.	do.	6	
26.	25	Hassani	do.	do.	Died, Kazé		
27.	25	Baraka	do.	do.	Deserted, Unyoro	7	
28.	25	Johur	do.	do.	Discharged, M'gunda Mkhali		
29.	25	Mabrūki	do.	do.	Deserted, Unyoro	8	
30.	25	Mutwané	do.	do.	Left sick, Ukuni		
31.	25	Bilal	do.	do.	Deserted, Unyoro	9	
32.	25	Othman	do.	do.	do.	10	Wangŭana, or slaves freed.
33.	25	Muftah	do.	do.	do.	11	
34.	25	Ulédi	do.	do.	do.	12	
35.	25	Jŭma	do.	do.	do.	13	
36.	25	Ulédi	do.	do.	Sent back, Unyoro		
37.	25	Mabrūki	do.	do.	Left sick, Bogŭé		
38.	25	Sirboko	do.	do.	Deserted, Unyoro	14	
39.	25	Masibŭ	do.	do.	do.	15	
40.	25	Msalima	do.	do.	Sent back, Unyoro		
41.	7	Mektŭb	do.	do.	Paid off, Egypt		
42.	7	Baraka	do.	do.	Deserted, Uzaramo		
43.	7	Kani	do.	do.	do.		
44.	7	Kirambŭ	do.	do.	do.		
45.	7	Kinanda	do.	do.	Died, Miningu		
46.	7	Mdaŕa	do.	do.	Deserted, Uzaramo		
47.	7	Mdyabŭana	do.	do.	do.		
48.	7	Ulédi	do.	Valet	Paid off, Egypt		
49.	7	Mzungŭ	do.	Porter	Deserted, Uzaramo	16	
50.	7	Thanun	do.	do.	Deserted, Ugogo		
51.	7	Kariombé	do.	do.	Deserted, coast		
52.	7	Kingunga	do.	do.	Deserted, Uzaramo		
53.	7	Matona	do.	do.	do.		
54.	7	Malini	do.	do.	Deserted, coast		Sultan Majid's Watŭma gardeners.
55.	7	Darara	do.	do.	do.		
56.	7	Khamisi	do.	do.	Deserted, Uzaramo		
57.	7	Yukŭt	do.	do.	Deserted, Unyoro	17	
58.	7	Hutibŭ	do.	do.	Deserted, coast		
59.	7	Panamba	do.	do.	do.		
60.	7	Pakarŭa	do.	do.	do.		
61.	7	Yaha	do.	do.	do.		
62.	7	Namaganga	do.	do.	Deserted, Uzaramo		
63.	7	Khamsi	do.	do.	do.		
64.	7	Wilyamanga	do.	do.	Deserted, coast		
65.	7	Mkaté	do.	Potboy	Paid off, Egypt		
66.	7	Mpŭanda	do.	Porter	Deserted, Uzaramo		
67.	7	Kirambŭ	do.	do.	Left sick, Bogŭé		
68.	7	Msaram	do.	do.	Deserted, Uzaramo		
69.	7	Kirŭmba	do.	do.	Deserted, coast		
70.	7	Kamŭna	do.	do.	do.		
71.	7	Sulamini	do.	do.	Deserted, Ugogo		
72.	7	Barŭti	do.	Under valet	Paid off, Egypt		
73.	7	Umburi	do.	Porter	do.		
74.	7	Makarani	do.	do.	Deserted, Ugogo	18	
75.	7	Ulimengo	do.	Goatherd	Paid off, Egypt		
76.	7	Khamsini	do.	Porter	do.		

LIST OF MEN ENGAGED AT ZANZIBAR (HOTTENTOTS, CAPE MOUNTED RIFLEMEN),
their Appointments, and how disposed of, etc.

Numerical numbers.	Names.	What race they belong to.	Highest appointments held by each individual.	How and where their services terminated.	No. of guns stolen by deserters.
1.	Mithalder		Corporal	Sent back, Mininga	
2.	Vandermerwe		Trumpeter	Sent back, Usagara	
3.	Adams		Private	do.	
4.	April		do.	Sent back, Mininga	
5.	Jansen		do.	Sent back, Usagara	
6.	Lemon		do.	Sent back, Mininga	
7.	Middleton		do.	do.	
8.	Peters		do.	Died, Usagara	
9.	Reyters		do.	Sent back, Usagara	
10.	Arries		do.	do.	

LIST OF MEN ENGAGED IN THE INTERIOR ON THE SAME TERMS AS THE WANGŬANA.

1.	Hassani	Negro	Porter	Murdered, Karagŭé	
2.	Sangoro	do.	do.	Deserted, Unyoro	19
3.	Ilmasi	do.	do.	do.	20
4.	Khamisi	do.	do.	do.	21
5.	Mtamani	do.	do.	Paid off, Egypt	
6.	Matagiri	do.	do.	do.	
7.	Sadiki	do.	do.	do.	
8.	Manŭa	do.	do.	do.	
9.	Nondo	do.	dq.	Sent back, Uganda	
10.	Sampti	do.	do.	Deserted, Unyamŭézi	
11.	Farhan	do.	do.	Deserted, Unyoro	
12.	Saidi	do.	do.	do.	22
13.	Chauri	do.	do.	do.	23
14.	Mijaliwa	do.	do.	Deserted, Abŭ Ahmed	
15.	Sangoro	do.	do.		
16.	Murzŭki	do.	do.	Deserted, Unyoro	24
17.	Farhan	do.	do.	Paid off, Egypt	
18.	Chongo	do.	do.	Deserted, Unyoro	
19.	Mdŭrŭ	do.	do.	do.	
20.	Pŭlimbŏfŭ	do.	do.	do.	
21.	Kŭdŭrŭ	do.	do.	do.	
22.	Fisi	do.	do.	do.	

APPENDIX B.

LIST OF PROPERTY (African money) sent forward to Kazé, to the care of Mŭsa M'zŭri, carried by 56 Pagazis, or Wanyamŭézi Porters, who were paid in advance $511, under the command of two Freed Slaves, who received $100.

FIRST LOT.

Quantity.	Measurements.	Material forming 36 Loads.	dols.	qrs.	a.
6	Frasala	Sami-Sami, or carmine beads	102	0	0
6	do.	Golabi, or pink beads	87	0	0
9	do.	Kadŭndŭgŭrŭ, or Indian red beads	49	2	0
12	do.	Langio, or blue beads	84	0	0
20	do.	Kanyéra, or white beads	110	0	0
9	do.	Mzizima, or blue circlet beads	63	0	0
		Total	495	2	0

FIRST LOT—*Continued.*

Quantity.	Measurements.		dols.	qrs.	a.
		Material forming 20 *Loads.*			
122	Bolts	Merikani, or American sheeting............	343	2	0
2	do.	Joho, or red blanketing......................	30	0	0
71	do.	Kiniki, or Indian blue stuffs.................	56	0	0
42	Pieces	Barsati, or colored cloths..........	14	0	0
5	do.	Sahari, do.	3	3	0
5	do.	Dubûani do.	3	3	0
40	Cubits	Bindéra, or Indian red stuffs................	1	2	0
16	do.	Chintz..............................	1	0	2
		Total.....................	453	2·	2

LIST OF PROPERTY (African money) taken with the Expedition, carried by 100 Pagazis, or Wanyamúézi Porters, who were paid in advance $925, under my command.

SECOND LOT.

Quantity.	Measurements.		dols.	qrs.	a.
		Material forming 59 *Loads.*			
332	Bolts	Merikani...............................	954	2	0
60	do.	Kiniki.................................	46	2	0
10	do.	Missûti, colored stuffs.......................	6	1	0
5	do.	Chintz................................	9	1	2
10	Pieces	Kisûtû..................................	4	2	0
42	do.	Barsati.................................	19	3	0
22	do.	Sahari..................................	27	3	0
25	do.	Dubûani................................	31	0	0
5	do.	Kikûi, colored stuffs.........................	4	0	0
5	do.	Khûdrangi, do.	10	0	0
2	do.	Déolé, gold embroidered	14	2	0
2	do.	Chibaya, do.	16	0	0
2	Waistcoats	Kizbao, do.	30	0	0
4	Cubits	Bindéra, do.	7	2	0
12	Caps	Kofia, Fez..............................	6	0	0
5	do.	Kofia, Surat	3	2	0
24	Bundles	Very minute beads—red, pink, white, and blue—expressly for the Wahûma kings, were concealed in these loads	48	0	0
		Total.....................	1239	0	2
		Material forming 28 *Loads.*			
10½	Frasala	Langio	84	0	0
10½	do.	Sami-Sami.....................................	178	2	0
10½	do.	Kûtûamnazi, or cocoa-nut leaf..............	94	2	0
10½	do.	Golabi.................................	157	2	0
7	do.	Mzizima.............................	21	0	0
		Total.....................	535	2	0
		Material forming 13 *Loads.*			
10½	Frasala	Brass wire.............................	90	0	0
9½	do.	Copper wire............................	130	1	0
		Total.....................	220	1	0

APPENDIX C.

LIST OF LARGE GAME BAGGED BY THE EAST AFRICAN EXPEDITION.

1860.

Sept.   Kŭsiki—One male hippopotamus.

Oct. 15.   Kidŭnda—One male and one female pallah boc, one female wart hog.

Oct. 17.   Mgéta—One male and one female brindled gnu, two male ellipsiprymna, one male pallah boc.

Oct.'25.   Zungoméro—One male and one female zebra.

Oct. 28.   Kirengŭe—One calf red antelope (?).

Nov. 3.   Makata—One male giraffe, one female ellipsiprymna. 4th. One male reduncus antelope.

Nov. 18.   Inengé—One female striped eland, one female saltiana antelope, one female red antelope (?).

Nov. 27.   East Kanyenyé—One male black rhinoceros.

Nov. 30.   West Kanyenyé—One male and one female New Ugogo antelope. Dec. 2. One male New Ugogo antelope, one male pallah boc. 3d. One female New Ugogo antelope.

Dec. 7.   Khoko—One female black rhinoceros. 8th. One male and two female buffaloes.

Dec. 12.   Wilderness—One female saltiana antelope. 18th. One male zebra, one male saltiana antelope. 20th. One male saltiana antelope. 21st. Two male zebras. 22d. One male zebra, one female wart hog. 24th. One female duyker boc. 25th. One male black rhinoceros, one male duyker boc. 27th. One female black rhinoceros, one male wart hog. 31st. One male zebra. Jan. 2, 1861. One female zebra, one male duyker boc. 3d. One male black rhinoceros. 4th. One female saltatrix antelope, one male wart hog. 6th. One male and one female zebra.

1861.

Feb. 21.   Kazé—One male blanc boc.

Aug. 25.   Ukŭni—One female bush boc.

Oct. 22.   Usŭi—One male grys boc.

Nov. 17.   Karagŭé—One (?) white rhinoceros. 19th. Two male white rhinoceros. Dec. 9. Three male white rhinoceros. Jan. 13, 1862. One male grys boc.

1862.

July 14.   Uganda—One female lencotis antelope. 16th. Two male zebras. 17th. One female ndjezza antelope. 22d. One male lencotis antelope. 24th. One male lencotis antelope. 25th. One male lencotis antelope: Aug. 1. One female nsamma antelope, one male bush boc. 3d. One male nsamma antelope. 4th. One female nsamma antelope. 15th. One male lencotis antelope.

Nov. 27.   Gani—One male buffalo.

Dec. 24.   Madi—One male bush boc. Jan. 13, 1863. One male nsamma antelope. 21st. One male buffalo. 23d. One male black rhinoceros. 28th. One female lencotis antelope. 29th. One male and one female lencotis antelope.

APPENDIX D.

LIST OF ASTRONOMICALLY FIXED STATIONS.

In offering this List of Astronomically Fixed Stations, made solely on this expedition, I wish it to be understood that the results in Latitudes and Longitudes are reductions, or rather recalculations, which have been made by Mr. E. Dunkin, Computer to the Royal Observatory, Greenwich, from my crude Observations, as it is the best security that I can produce for their accuracy. My sextants were 8-inch.

J. H. SPEKE.

Lıst of Astronomically fixed Stations—*Continued.*

No.	Station.	South Lat.	East Long.	No.	Station.	South Lat.	East Long.
1	Bagamoyo	6° 25' 59"		54	Vigūra	2° 21' 43"	
2	Bomani	6 30 44		55	1st Urigi	2 11 23	
3	Ikambūrū	6 33 49		56	Khonzé	2 5 28	
4	Kizoto	6 38 29		57	Kiwéra..........	1 59 53	
5	Kiranga Ranga	6 42 49		58	Uthenga..........	1 55 28	
6	Mūhūgūé.....	6 53 49		59	Rozoka	1 50 7	
7	Matamombo ..	7 10 39		60	Katawanga.......	1 45 53	
8	Dégé la Mhora	7 14 9		61	Rumanika's Palace	1 42 42.5	31° 1' 49"
.9	Kidúnda	7 15 39		62	Kitangūlé	1 16 40	
10	Kirūrū	7 24 34	38° 14' 0"	63	Ndongo.........	1 12 35	
11	Dūthūmi	7 24 13		64	Ngambézi	1 5 29	
12	Zungoméro....	7 26 53 5'''	37 36 45	65	Kisūéré	0 55 19	
13	Kirengūé	7 32 17		66	N'yagussa........	0 53 33	
14	Makata	7 20 37		67	Ukara...........	0 45 48	
15	Ngoto	7 13 54		68	Mérūka	0 36 2	
16	Mūhanda.....	7 9 9		69	Sangūa..........	0 30 47	
17	Mbūmi	6 56 30		70	Masaka..........	0 20 2	31 33 15
18	Manyongé.....	6 47 0		71	Kitūntū	0 7 40	
19	Rūmūma.....	6 46 29					
20	E. Ugogo....	6 31 12	35 32 4		Cross the Equator to	North Lat.	
21	W. Kanyenyé	6 23 51	35 6 10	72	Nakūsi	0 7 15	
22	Mdabūrū.....	6 21 49	34 50 8	73	Kibibi..........	0 15 0	32 9 45
23	The "Springs".	6 7 52		74	Nakatéma	0 17 55	
24	The "Boss" ...	6 3 59	34 18 30	75	N'yama Goma ...	0 17 15	
25	Jiwa la Mkoa	6 0 37		76	Mtésa's Palace....	0 21 19	32 44 30
26	Kazé.........	5 0 52	33 1 34	77	Nasirié	0 32 30	
27	S. Usagari ...	4 49 33		78	Namaouja	0 39 44	
28	Ungūgū's	4 40 19		79	Baja...........	0 47 35	
29	Mininga..∴..	4 18 34	32 39 50	80	Kari	0 51 45	
30	Mbisū........	4 3 53	32 23 15	81	Urondogani......	0 52 27	
31	Nūnda.......	3 58 59		82	Isamba.........	0 43 49	
32	Phūnzé	3 53 35		83	Kianūkka	0 53 30	
33	Takina	3 50 20		84	Kidgwiga's	1 8 6	
34	M'yonga's....	3 46 45		85	Utūti..........	1 24 53	
35	Rūhé's	3 34 24		86	Chagūzi, S.	1 36 39	
36	Mihambo.....	3 29 59		87	Kamrasi's Palace..	1 37 43	32 19 49
37	Kagūé	3 25 26		88	Kiratosi	1 19 47	
38	Makaka's.....	3 28 24		89	Kitwara	1 45 9	
39	Lūmérési's ...	3 26 10		90	Gūéni	1 52 27	
40	Mūamba	3 23 7		91	Gūtada.........	2 15 10	
41	Kagongo.....	3 19 27	32 6 30	92	5th Kidi	2 41 22	
42	Kagéra	3 14 34		93	Mūdūa	3 2 17	
43	1st Uyombé ..	3 11 4		94	Faloro..........	3 10 33	31 50 45
44	Pongo's	3 3 37		95	Panyoro	3 21 47	
45	N'yarūamba's.	3 0 58		96	Paira..........	3 25 27	
46	N. Wanga.....	2 57 43		97	Apuddo	3 34 33	
47	N'yamanira's..	2 49 27 (?)		98	Madi	3 47 15	
48	Kafumbū	2 49 34		99	Labūré	3 59 56	
49	Vikora's	2 48 44		100	Mūgi...........	4 7 1	
50	Kariwami's ..	2 47 24	31 28 40	101	Marsan.........	4 31 17	
51	Uthungū.....	2 41 33	32 28 30	102	Doro	4 42 33	
52	Kitaré.......	2 35 8		103	Gondokoro......	4 54 2	31 46 9
53	Vihembé	2 27 30		104	Mid. Sobat's Mouth	9 20 48	31 24 0

Lıst of Magnetic Variation Results, recalculated by Mr. Dunkin from my Observations between Zanzibar and Gondokoro. My compasses were small prismatic.
J. H. Speke.

Stations.	West Long.	Stations.	West Long.	Stations.	West Long.
Kirengūé.....	11° 12'	Mininga	11° 47'	Mtésa's.........	9° 59'
Mbūiga.......	12 27	Mūamba.........	11 20	Urondogani....	10 18
Mbūmi....►..	12 00	N'yamanira's...	11 0	Kamrasi's......	8 48
Ugogo, E.	11 19	Rūmanika's.....	10 58	Faloro	8 16
Mdabūrū......	11 33	Masaka..........	9 44	Gondokoro.....	8 53
Kazé.........	12 8	Kibibi............	9 28		

APPENDIX E.

HEIGHTS OF STATIONS determined by Observations of Boiling-point of Water between ZANZIBAR and GONDOKORO, recalculated by E. DUNKIN. Means of two Thermometers boiled by GRANT and myself. They are given to show the table-land formation of the interior of Africa.

STATIONS.	Feet above the Sea-level.	STATIONS.	Feet above the Sea-level.
Zanzibar................		Rŭbŭga..................	3402
Kirŭrŭ..................	262	Wali River.............	3388
Dŭthŭmi...............	391	Kazé	3564
Zungoméro	516	Iviri	3359
Kirengŭé...............	689	Usagari, S.............	3292
Mbŭiga, E.............	1068	Usagari, N.............	3413
Mbŭiga, W.............	1093	Unyambéwa	3690
Kikobogo...............	1717	Ukŭmbi.................	3489
Makata.................	1605	Mininga................	3438
Ngoto..................	1592	Mbisŭ..................	3338
Mŭhanda...............	1648	Nŭnda..................	3265
M'yombo...............	1514	Rŭhé's	3181
Mbŭmi..................	1487	Makaka's...............	3313
Mdunhwi...............	2054	Lŭmérési's.............	3354
Tzanzi..................	2474	Kagongo	3527
Manyongé..............	2959	Kagéra	3588
Rŭmŭma................	2468	Uyombé	3483
Marenga Mkhali	2848	Usŭi, S................	3989
Inengé	3633	Vikora's................	3873
E. Robého..............	4712	Kariwami's.............	3974
W. Robého	5148	Uthungŭ	4001
Marenga Mkhali ....".	2498	Kitaré.................	4204
E. Ugogo	3123	Vihembé	3563
E. Kanyenyé...........	2674	Usŭi, N.................	3487
W. Kanyenyé..........	2580	Urigi..................	3447
Usekhé.................	3329	Khonzé	3392 (?)
Khoko..................	3255	Uthenga................	3931
1st Camp in Jungle...	3408	N'yamwara Hill	4592
3d Camp in Jungle...	3511	Rŭmanika's.............	4661
Mabungŭrŭ.............	3731	Little Windermere....	3639
"The Boss"............	3702	Mtésa's................	3400
Jiwa la Mkoa	4090	Namaouja..............	3103
Mgongo Thembo......	3964	Ripon Falls*	3308 (?)
Tŭra, E...............	3691	Urondogani.............	2865 (?)
Tŭra, W...............	3597	Kamrasi's..............	2856 (?)
Kigŭé	3715	Karŭma Falls..........	2970 (?)

P.S.—There were three cataracts observed on the Nile: 1. From Ripon Falls to Urondogani; 2. From Karŭma Falls to the Little Lŭta Nzigé (?); 3. From Paira, in Madi, to near Gondokoro. The rest of the Nile was more like a long pond than a river.

This list of altitudes, as the boiling-point of water is liable to show an error of 300 feet, can only be considered as approximate to the truth. This may be clearly seen by the observations on the Nile. J. H. SPEKE.

Note.—The tables used in the reduction are deduced from Regnault's "Tables des Tensions de la Vapeur d'Eau."

Assumed mean barometer reading for level of sea, 29.92 in. EDWIN DUNKIN.

---

* On my former journey, the height of the Victoria N'yanza was made by boiling thermometer 3740 feet, as engraved on the map.

APPENDIX F.
CLIMATE OF VICTORIA N'YANZA.

CLIMATE OF THE COUNTRIES BORDERING ON THE LAKE N'YANZA, 1861-2, TABULATED FROM GRANT'S DAILY OBSERVATIONS BY FRANCIS GALTON.

Explanation: a = from the 1st to the 7th, b = " 8th " 15th, c = " 16th " 23d, d = " 24th " end.

Region	Month	Mean Temperature	Extreme Heat	Uganda maxima (Speke)	Extreme Cold	Extreme Range	Rainfall in Inches	No. of Rainy Days	Rainy Days per Month (Speke)	Days of Rain and slight Showers (Speke)	Prevalent Winds (Speke)
Karagué, 5100 feet above sea-level.	Nov. d	70	84		57	29	1.00*	3*	(12)	17	N.E.
	Dec. a	70	83		58	27	.77	4			
	b	66	78		53	26	.34	5	14	16	N.E.
	c	67	80		57	25	.32	3			
	d	69	84		57	29	1.35	2			
	Jan. a	69	82		57	27	.21	2			
	b	69	85		64	23	.89	2	14	14	N.E.
	c	68	80		57	25	.84	4			
	d	67	79		57	24	1.47	6			
	Feb. a	67	79		59	22	.96	4			
	b	69	82		58	26	1.90	3	12	12	N.E.
	c			82	59		.13	2			
	d				58		.63	3			
	Mar. a	70	80	81	62	20	.00	0			
	b	69	81		61	22	.34	3	11	21	E. by N.
	c	68	84	92	59	27	2.62	4			
	d	69	80		60	22	.98	4			
	April a	69	79	83	61	20	.84	3			
	b	65	71		60	13	4.00*	6*	18*	27	Variable.
	c			82			} 3 heavy storms (in all 8 in.*)	3*			
	d							6*			
	May a			82				4	21*	26	F. by S.
	b			82				8			
	c							5*			
	d			83							
Uganda, 3400 ft. elevation.	June a	69	79		62	19	.42	2*	8*	20	S.E.
	b	69	79		59	22	.08	3			
	c	70	78		60	20	.05	2			
	d	69	80		62	20	.05	1			
	July a	68	76		61	17	1.94	3			
Camp, 3400 ft.	b								(15)	22	S.E.
	c	76	91		64	29					
	d										
	Aug. a										
Camp, 3400 ft.	b	74	89		60	31			(14)	20	S.E.
	c										
	d										
	Sept. a										
Unyoro, 3200 ft. above sea.	b	75	86		65	23			18*	18	Variable.
	c	73	84		62	24	1.61*	3			
	d	73	80		61	21	.44	6			
	Oct. a	72	82		64	20	3.00	6			
	b	72	82		63	21	.82	4	21	27	Variable.
	c	73	82		63	21	3.48	6			
	d	74	84		65	21	1.30	5			
	Nov. a	72	83		64	21	2.20	1			
Means and Totals..		68	82		51	49	34.93	135		240	E.
Estimated value for complete year		68	82		51	49	49	178		240	E.

Notes:

Extreme Heat: These are obtained by adding 3° to the temp. at 3 P.M. No maxima were taken.

Uganda maxima, taken each fortnight by Captain Speke.

Rainfall (Uganda/Camp section): Rain seldom alluded to in note-book. (6 in.*)

Extreme Heat (Camp section): These are of doubtful value. The thermometers were hung in crowded huts. No record in note-book of any unusual heat.

The numbers marked by an asterisk * are partly, and those included in brackets ( ) are wholly deduced by proportion.

Rain chiefly falls in sudden showers and thunder-storms. The sky is either very clear, with fleeting clouds, or overcast, with low black clouds.

APPENDIX G.

LIST OF PLANTS COLLECTED BY CAPTAIN GRANT BETWEEN ZANZIBAR AND CAIRO.

THIS unique collection is the first that was ever made *by the drying process* in the interior west of Zanzibar. It has been arranged at Kew by Dr. Thomson, and is highly commended by Dr. Hooker, who regrets with myself that better facilities are not instituted for the guidance of explorers in foreign countries.   J. H. SPEKE.

N.B.—The numbers in parentheses after each species are those of Captain Grant's Note-book, and are attached to the specimens deposited in the Kew Herbarium. The native names are given within quotation marks.

I. RANUNCULACEÆ, JUSS.

1. *Clematis brachiata*, Thunb. ; Madi and Ukidi forest, 1862.   (564.)
2. *C. n. sp.*; common about waste grounds, 2½° S.   (190.)
3. *C. incisodentata*, Reich. ; Wahiyow cure headaches by smelling its dried leaves and flowers till blood comes from the nose. Uganda forests; among tall grasses. Alt. 4000 ft.   Aug., 1862.   (564.)
4. *C. sp.*; 2 ft. high; erect woody stem. The ripe feathery seeds form a white ball on the top of the flower-stalk. 1° 42' S. Feb., 1862.   (440.)
1. *Ranunculus pinnatus*, Port. ; Marenga Mkhali. 1860. Lat. 6° 44' S. Alt. 3193 ft. ; by water.

II. ANONACEÆ, JUSS.

1. *Hexalobus senegalensis*, A. D. C. ; "Imkooa;" 5 ft. circ. tree, with cedar-like wood; the Wanyamūézi color their gums and teeth with its one to two stoned drupes. 5° S. and 2° N. Dec., 1862.   (683.)
1. *Anona senegalensis*, Pers., var. ; "Mtāotāo;" 12 inch circ., and 10 ft. high tree; fruit a red edible drupe, seldom attaining perfection; wood makes good hoe-handles; Unyoro, 2° N., and Madi, 3° N. Dec., 1862.   (625½.)

III. MENISPERMACEÆ, JUSS.

1. *Chasmanthera sp.*; thick root (yellowish); Unyoro plantain-grove. Nov., 1862.

IV. NYMPHÆACEÆ.

1. *Nymphæa lotus*, L., white water-lily; flower-stalks 12 ft. long; Nile. 2° N. (622.)
2. *N. stellata*; Willd. ; "Maoongee-Oongee;" flowers and roots eaten by the Wahiyow. Karagūé Lake, R. Katonga, and Nile 2° N. Common. Flower a lilac purple, and half the size of No. 1.   (622.1.)

V. CRUCIFERÆ, JUSS.

1. *Morettia sp.*; pods curved, ¾ inch long. Great spheres of this plant (withered) were found blowing over the sandy Balama desert. 22° N. April, 1863.
1. *Sisymbrium sp.* (drawing—no specimen); flowers yellow; pods round; linear and many-seeded; stem purple on one side; leaves pinnatifid. 1° 42' S. Feb., 1862.   (446.)
1. *Senebiera Nilotica*, DC. ; smells like wild cress; Nile bank, 16¼° N. April, 1863.

VI. CAPPARIDEÆ.

1. *Gynandropsis pentaphylla*, DC. ; common near every hut; spinage is made from its leaves. 7° 27' S. and 1° 42' S.   (380.)
1. *Cleome monophylla*, L. Alt. 3900 ft. 5° 5' S., and 32° E.
1. *Polanisia oxyphylla*, DC. ; common; Mininga. 4° S. April, 1861.   (186.)
2. *P. sp.* ; common, waste grounds. 5° 1' S., and 33° E.
1. *Cadaba farinosa*, Forsk., called "Kana;" spinage is made from the leaves of this shrub at Madi. 3° N. Jan., 1863.   (746.)
1. *Physanthemum glaucum*, Kl. ; bush about Madi plains. Jan., 1863.
1. *Cratœva Adansonii*, Guill. and Perr. ; 10 ft. circ. tree; fresh shoots made into spinage, and young branches into tooth-scrubbers. 3° 15' N. Jan., 1863.   (748.)

1. *Capparis tomentosa*, Reich.; "Kowāngwee;" in famines spinage is made from its leaves; Madi plains. Jan. 25, 1863. (751.)
1. *Niebuhria ? sp.*; M'gæta River. 7° 20' S. 4 to 7 ft. high.
2. *N. sp.*; Mohonyera. 6° 55' S., and 38° 32' E.
1. *Moerua oblongifolia ?* Reich.; Kich country; Nile. 7° N. March, 1863.
1. *Boscia, sp. n.*; "M'Zazza;" moderately-sized tree, with long lanceolate leaves and terminal inflorescence; Madi. 3° N. Feb. 4, 1863. (757.)
1. *Capparideœ sp.* (drawing—no specimen); shrub; purple lines on the back of the large yellow petals; stem rose-bush appearance, covered with stiff, short, curved-down thorns. 1° 42' S. Alt. 4700 ft. April, 1862. (497.)

VII. BIXACEÆ.

1. *Flacourtia ? sp.* (leaves only); "M'seengeerra" (Kin.); slender, hazel-leaved like tree, with a few thorns; by burn; Madi. Feb., 1863.
1. *Cochlospermum n. sp.*; erect, solitary, woody; 3 to 18 in. long; stem, with large yellow flower; in bare forest; Madi. Dec. 10, 1862. (692.)

VIII. VIOLACEÆ.

1. *Ionidium sp.* Alt. 4000. Dry forest, near Simbah. 5° 26' S., 33° E.

IX. POLYGALACEÆ.

1. *Polygala sp.*; in moisture. Nov., 1862. 2° to 3° N.
2. *P. sp.*; Unyoro plateaux. 2° N. July, 1862.
3. *P. n. sp.*; erect, woody plant, on high ground; Madi. 3° N. Dec., 1862.

X. CARYOPHYLLEÆ.

1. *Polycarpœa corymbosa*, Lam.; Madi, rocks. Dec., 1862.
1. *Mollugo cerviana*, L. 7° 27' S. 37° E. Zungoméro. Oct., 1860.
2. *M. nudicaulis*, L.; weed; Zungoméro. Oct., 1860.

XI. PORTULACACEÆ.

1. *Portulaca oleracea*, L.; spinage made from its leaves, which are supposed to possess great virtue as poultices; weed. 2° N. Oct.,1862. Common. (608.)
2. *P. quadrifida*, Willd. (no specimen). (593.)
1. *Talinum cuneifolium*, Willd.; on cleared ground. 2° N. July, 1862.

XII. TAMARIXINEÆ.

1. *Tamarix gallica*, L.? "Jow" of India; Nile banks, 15° to 16° N. April, 1863. Common; not met with till these latitudes.

XIII. ELATINEÆ.

1. *Lancretia suffruticosa*, Del.; rigid plant; near cult.; Nile banks. 16° N. April 16, 1863.

XIV. DIPTEROCARPEÆ.

1. *Lophira alata*, Banks; 6 ft. circ. tree; "Meeenzerrah;" the handsomest tree seen on the route. Its leaf is used as a charm—namely, if human and buffalo blood be mixed upon its surface, and a native inoculated with the mixture, good fortune attends him. The young leaves are of a dull red color, and attain a length of 2 ft. Observed only at 3° 15' N. Dec. 10, 1862. (679.)

XV. MALVACEÆ.

1. *Sida cordifolia*, Cav.; common weed; near cult. 2° N. Aug.,1862.
2. *S. rhombifolia*, L.; common weed; near cult. 2° N. Aug.,1862.
3. *S. alba*, L.; common weed; near cult. Oct.,1862.
4. *S. (Dictyocarpus) Schimperiana*, Hochst. Alt. 5000 ft. 2° S. Karagüé Hills. Nov. 29, 1861. (163.)
1. *Abutilon muticum*, Don; about fields; Kartoum. April 2, 1863.
2. *A. sp.*; common about fields; M'bwiga 7° S. Oct.,1860.
1. *Urena lobata*, L.; "Milenda;" bark made into cordage. 2° to 3° N. Frequent. (610.)
1. *Pavonia Schimperiana*, Hochst. Alt. 5000 ft. 2° S. March, 1862. (478.)
2. *P. n. sp.*; moist rocky soil; pretty fleshy-pink flowers; Ugani and Madi. Dec. 4, 1862. Plentiful. (654.)

3. *P. macrophylla*, E. Mey.; Uganda plantain-groves. July, 1862.
1. *Hibiscus crassinervius*, Hochst.; Karagüé valleys. 2° S. Dec., 1861. (215.)
2. *H. gossypinus*, Thunb.; grassy hill slopes. Alt. 5000 ft. Nov., 1861. (162.)
3. *H. cannabinus*, L.; "Sun," cult. in India for hemp; near cornfields, Mininga. 4° 18′ S. (169.)
4. *H. heterotrichus*, E. Mey.; cordage made from its bark; among vegetation. 2° N. Oct., 1862. (586.)
5. *H. sp.*; open ground; Madi. Dec., 1862.
6. *H. sabdariffa*, L.; Roselle; cult. in Unyoro, 2° N., and Ugani, 3° N., for its seed, bark, and leaves, the bark making beautiful but short cordage; the leaves make a spinage in the Land of the Moon, called there "Tocos'was';" and the seed is eaten roasted by the Wagani. (570.)
7. *H. n. sp.*; an under-shrub; banks of the R. Kuffo, Unyoro. 2° N. Sept., 1862.
1. *Gossypium punctatum*, Sch. and Th.; 4 to 8 ft. high; perennial cotton bush planted here and there by habitations on the route. 7° 27′ S., 37½° E., and 4° N. Oct., 1860. The Wanyamüézi make a coarse heavy cloth of it; others cultivate merely enough for sewing purposes; while at 4° N. they make it into front and rear fringes for the women. Irrigation not employed in these latitudes.
1. *Eriodendron anfractuosum*, DC.; "Meesoofee;" cotton-tree, 10 ft. high, with green bark and thorns or excrescences on its bark. 7° 27′ S. and 2° N. (7½.)
1. *Adansonia digitata*, L.; Baobab; "Booyoo;" 54 ft. in circ.; rope and kilts are made from its bark, water-buckets from its gourds, and seeds mashed in water have a pleasant acid taste; dry situations. 7° S. and 2° N. (22.)
1. *Malvaceæ sp.* (drawing—no specimen); 3 to 5 ft. high; waved, tubular, grooved stem; bushy; near huts in rank cult. 1° 42′ S. April, 1862. (493.)

XVI. STERCULIACEÆ.

Sterculia tomentosa, Guill. and Per.; "M'loolooma;" 10 ft. circ. tree, whose seeds are eaten raw in dearths; cordage made from the bark of young trees; M'gunda Mkhali, and 3° N. Feb., 1863. An ice-colored gum appears on the stalk of a freshly-pulled seed-vessel. (759.)
S. sp.; shrubby tree; unburst pods (in sets of fives) are size and shape of a huge caterpillar; threads of gum appear wherever a branch is severed. The Sultan of Ukuni has his hut-lashings made from its bark, considered so good; bows made from its wood. 3° 58′ S. Sept., 28, 1861.

XVII. BYTTNERIACEÆ.

1. *Melhania Forbesii*, Planch. mss.; 3 ft. high; on bare cult. heights. 3° N. Dec., 1862. (729.)
1. *Dombeya multiflora*, Endl.; "Keenga;" 3 ft. circ. tree; leafless, but covered with blossom in Jan.; the Men of the Moon consider its wood tough and excellent for bows. 3° N. Feb. 1, 1863. Frequent. (737.)
2. *D. sp.*; same size and locality as above.
3. *D. sp.*; shrub with rich clusters of white flowers; Nile banks. 2° N. Nov., 1862.

XVIII. TILIACEÆ.

1. *Corchorus sp.* (drawing—no specimen). Each leaf has one hair (¼ inch long) on either side of its base; foot high, with smooth, shining, pink stem, which is very tough; leaves make a stringy spinage. 1°-2° N. 1862. Common. (542.)
2. *C. trilocularis*, L.; near fields. No uses. 2° N. Oct., 1862. (544.)
1. *Triumfetta annua*, L.; grows lowly among cult. 2° N. Oct. 15, 1862. (589.)
2. *T. semitriloba*, L. var.; Unyoro plantain-groves. Nov., 1862.
3. *T. rhomboidea*, L.; near fields. 5° S. 1861.
1. *Grewia, n. sp.* Shrub with snowy-white flowers; among granite rocks. Alt. 4488. 6° S., 34° E. Jan. 1, 1861.
2. *G. sp.*; shrub with delicate purplish flowers; fruit, a pea-sized, smooth, yellow, dry, one-stoned drupe; in water-cuts, Karagüé Hills. Alt. 5000. Dec., 1861. (381.)
3. *G. sp.*; "M'kōmo;" 12 ft. circ. tree; wood with a black heart resembling rosewood; uses—bows and arrows, building purposes, and ropes from bark; no insect is said to touch it; drupes, pea-size, light-colored, and pleasant-tasting. Unyanyembé, 5° S., and Madi. Dec., 1862. Spread generally. (760. 5.)

1. *Antichorus depressus*, L. fil.; near cotton fields; right bank Nile. 16° N. April 16, 1863.

XIX. ZYGOPHYLLEÆ.

1. *Tribulus terrestris*, L. 7° 27′ S., 37½ E. Oct., 1860; and 2° N., 1862.
1. *Fagonia cretica*, L.; shingle desert behind Berber. 17½° N. April 25, 1863.

XX. GERANIACEÆ.

1. *Oxalis corniculata*, L.; common near cult. Nov., 1861. (189.)
1. *Biophytum sensitivum*, DC. Alt. 3900. 5° 5′ S., and 2° N. (584.)

XXI. SIMARUBEÆ.

1. *Balanites Ægyptiaca*, Del.; "M'choonchoo;" 6 ft. circ. tree; drupe edible, and tasting like an intensely bitter date; kernels made into oil and mixed with red clay for anointing the person; bark of young trees makes strong cordage. 3° N., Jan., 1863; and frequently in other latitudes. (745.)
1. *Harrisonia sp.;* "M'ceenángo." Its boughing, thorned branches catch one's clothes in the woods. Flowers, a pink yellow. Madi. Dec., 1862. (700.)

XXII. OCHNACEÆ.

1. *Ochna sp.;* roet deeply imbedded; flower blood-red. Alt. 1700 ft. M'bumi, 6° 56′ S. Nov. 8, 1860.
2. *O. sp.* Rich pink flowers; grows in patches in light forest, Land of the Moon. Jan., 1861.
3. *O.? sp.;* ordinary-sized tree; Madi woods. Dec., 1862.

XXIII. RUTACEÆ.

1. *Citrus aurantium*, L.; cultivated by Arabs in their gardens at Unyanyembé. 5° S. 1861.

XXIV. MELIACEÆ.

1. *Trichilia emetica*, Vahl.; flowers, Jan.; grown by huts to 8 ft. circ.; the bark is used medicinally in syphilis. 3°, 4°, 5° N. Jan., 1863. (747.)
1. *Khaya ? sp.;* 10 ft. circ.; handsome tree, with small, lime-sized, four-segmented capsules; an amber-colored, glistening-fractured, tasteless, scentless gum exudes from wounds. Madi. Feb. 4, 1863. (756.)
1. *Soymida sp.;* "M'bawa;" (leaf, gum, and seed-vessel); tree 15 ft. circ., branching at 20 ft.; immense canoes are made by the Wahiyow from its trunk; a disagreeably-smelling, wax-colored gum accumulates in tears from wounds in the bark; near water. 3° N. Dec., 1862. (731.)

XXV. OLACINEÆ.

1. *Opilia celtidifolia*, Endl.; tree by water-course, unknown to our men. Madi. Jan., 1863.
1. *Ximenia Americana*, L.; "M'toondwah" (Kinyoro), and "M'peenjee" (Kisuahili); oil is extracted from the kernels, and used as an unguent; Land of the Moon, Unyoro, and Ugani. 1861, 1862, and 1863. (640.)

XXVI. CELASTRACEÆ.

1. *Gymnosporia coriacea*, Guill. and Per.; "M'thoozeea;" 30 inch circ. tree; its roots are used medicinally by women, also as a purgative. 5° S. and 3° N. Dec., 1862. Very frequent. (728.6.)
2. *G. sp.;* flowering shrub. Alt. 4800, East African chain, 6° 38′ S.

XXVII. RHAMNEÆ.

1. *Rhamnus sp.* (leaves only); shrub by water, with red, currant-sized, and colored berries, soft and sweet, with hard stone; fish are brought to the surface by throwing a mash of its leaves and berries into the water. Wanyamuézi name, "M'quæ-tæ-quætæ." 3° N. Dec., 1862. (723.)
1. *Zizyphus jujuba ?* Lam.; "M'konazee" (Kis.), "Kalembo" (Kin.); fruit nearly all stone, nauseous and woody; mashed and thrown into water brings fish to the surface; goats eat the leaves; branches made into fences. Ugani. Nov., 1862. Common every where. (638.)

XXVIII. AMPELIDEÆ.

1. *Vitis sp.*; wild vine. Usúi slopes, 2° 42′ S., Nov., 1861; and Unyoro, 2° N. (208.)
2. *V. sp.*; "M'peengee-peengee;" 3 ft. high shrub, with one-stoned, pear-shaped, deep purple, pink-spotted, edible fruit, not pleasant to the taste; neither tendrils nor thorns. Madi woods. Dec. 6, 1862. (658.)
1. *Cissus quadrangularis*, L.; "Meoleh-oleh;" spreads itself over lofty trees, Unyoro, Nov. 9, 1862. (616.)
2. *C. cyphopetala*, Fres.; climbing among shrubs, Unyoro plateaux, Nov., 1862. (389.)
3. *C. cirrhosa*, Pers.; in thicket of bushes, Karagúé, Dec., 1862.
4. *C. subdiaphana*, Steud.; climber among bushes, Unyoro forest, 1862.

XXIX. SAPINDACEÆ.

1. *Cardiospermum haliacacabum*, L.; common. 7° S. to 2° N. Leaves are made into spinage by Wahiyow. (558.)

XXX. BURSERACEÆ.

1. *Balsamodendron Africanum*, Arn.; B'dellium (resin), "M'Gazoo" (Kin.), and "Katatee" of Ugogo. Wanyamúézi boil its gum, mix it with butter, and anoint their persons. 2° S., April, 1862; and rocky heights by huts, Ugani, 3° N., Nov., 1862. Frequent. (496.)
1. *Boswellia sp.* (leaf only); 20 in. in girth, stunted 5 ft. high tree, growing locally in patches. 3° N. 1863. Amber-colored gum exudes profusely from the stem. Sp. of "Looban," or frankincense. (739.)

XXXI. ANACARDIACEÆ.

1. *Rhus villosa*, L.; thorny flowering shrub, 2° S. and 3° N. 1861 and 1862. (415.)
2. *R. sp.*; "M'sangool'a;" shrub with white-scented flowers and light foliage; not edible; wood makes tooth-scrubbers for natives, who imagine that plants for spinage can be found if its seeds are thrown about. Madi, Dec., 1862. (697.)
1. *Odina fructicosa*, Hochst.; "M'sangar'a;" lofty, elegant, thornless, 6 ft. circ. tree; wood made into posts. Madi heights, 3° N. Dec., 1862. Gum, sweet tasting; pods, glossy and a red-brown. (672.)
2. *O. Schimperi*, Hochst.; "M'oooomboo;" 3 ft. circ. tree; wood heavy; nets for game made from its roots; fruit scarcely edible. ˙5° S. to 3° N. (549.)
1. *Sclerocarya birrea*, Hochst.; "M'choowee;" grows to 12 ft. circ.; the kernels of the fruit (whose unripe sarcocarp is apple-scented) are milky and eaten like ground-nuts; leaves of young branches are notched at tips, older ones are pointed; large grain-mortars and stools are made from its red wood; forest tree; occasional. 5° S. and 3° 15′ N. (682.)
1. *Sorindeia Madagascarensis*, DC.; 8 ft. circ. tree; the 2 ft. long bunches (say 200 plums each) of sparrow-egg-sized, mango-tasting, yellow fruit, hang curiously from the main trunk and boughs like parasites; they grow also from among the leaves. Banks of rivers. 7° S. Oct., 1860. (25.)
1. *Anacardiacete??* "M'sŏŏwee;" circ. 7½ ft. Leaves compound, smelling of sweetbrier; flowers 3 in. long, erect catkins; edible bullet-sized plum; timber somewhat like deal, but heavier, and made into grain-mortars. Turah nullah, Jan. 15, 1861; and Madi, 3° N. (8.)

XXXII. LEGUMINOSEÆ.

1. *Crotalaria glauca*, Willd.; "M'cæwæ;" 3 ft. high. Plantain-groves, Unyoro, 27th Aug., 1862. The people of Madi eat its flowers, pods, and leaves as spinage. (566.)
2. *C. calycina*, Schrank; plateaux. 2° N. Oct., 1862. (573.)
3. *C. cephalotes*, Steud.; bare woods. 3° and 2° N.
4. *C. mossambicencis*, Kl.; 6 ft. high; flowers bright yellow. Zungoméro, Oct., 1862; and Nile banks, Nov., 1862.
5. *C. capensis*, Jacq.; light soil forests. Alt. 3800. 5° S.
6. *C. globifera*, Mey.; field weed. 4° 18′ S. March, 1861. (176.)
7. *C. striata*, DC.; rank cult. Alt. 3800. 5° S., 33° E.
8. *C. incana*, L.; dry soil. Right bank Nile. 5° 10′ N.
9. *C. Goréensis*, G. and P.; height 6 in. Alt. 5000. 5° S. Feb., 1862. (442.)
10. *C. n. sp.*; grows in light tufts; hills. 2° S. Dec., 1861. (397.)

11. *Crotalaria n. sp?* very handsome; fallow and grassy ground. 2° N. Aug., 1862.
12. *C. ? sp. ;* long root; near cult., 4° 18' S. April, 1861. (183.)
1. *Lupinus albus*, L. ; var. Cult., 15° N. March, 1863. Now ripe.
1. *Trifolium polystachyum*, Fres. ; E. African chain. Alt. 4700. Dec., 1860.
1. *Indigofera paucifolia*, Del. ; right bank Blue Nile, 16° N. ; used for fencing and firewood. Also Nile, 15° N.
2. *I. marginella*, Steud. ; erect stemmed ; woody. Karagŭé, March, 1862. (483.)
3. *I. pentaphylla*, L. ; Madi woods, Dec., 1862.
4. *I. stenophylla*, Guill. and Pers. ; waste ground, 3° N. Feb., 1863.
5. *I. melanotricha*, Steud. ; grassy plateaux, 2° N. (574.)
6. *I. hirsuta*, L. ; the natives do not use these indigo plants as dyes. 4° 18' S., and 2° N. (182.)
7. *I. endecaphylla*, L. ; small plant, with liquorice-tasting tapering root. Makata, 7° S. 3d Nov., 1860.
8. *I. sp. ;* growing 10 ft. high, among thorns, reeds, grasses, etc., M'Gæta River, 7° 20' S. Oct., 1860.
9. *I. ? sp. ;* bushy plant; open ground, 3° N. Dec., 1862.
1. *Psoralea plicata*, Del. Nile banks. 16th April, 1863.
1. *Tephrosia sp. ;* Uganda groves. July, 1862.
2. *T. sp. ;* creeps along the ground among luxuriant cult. 5° S., 33° E. Alt. 3800.
3. *T. sp. ;* 8 ft. to 9 ft. high. Madi burn bank, Dec., 1862.
4. *T. sp. ;* leaves small and prettily ribbed behind. 3° N. 14th Dec., 1862.
5. *T. Vogelii*, Hook. fil. ; rich white flowers, bushy, and 7 ft. high ; sometimes hedging dwellings ;. a mash of its leaves is used in destroying fish. 1° to 2° N. 1862. (587.)
6. *T. longipes*, Meisa. Karagŭé, March, 1862. Alt. 5000 ft. (487.)
7. *T. sp. ;* grows in tufts ; many-podded ; hills. 2° S. Dec., 1861. (401.)
8. *T. sp.* (drawing—no specimen); purple-flowered plant, covered with silky pubescence. 1° 42' S. Feb., 1862. (431.)
9. *T. sp.* (drawing—no specimen); stem inclining to four-cornered ; covered, as also the backs of the leaflets, with brown crooked hairs. 1° 42' S., and 0° 30' N. 1862. (432.)
1. *Sesbania Ægyptiaca*, Pers. ; tree 30 inches in girth ; herdboys use its seeds as a rattle; Indian hedge plant. 3° N. Dec., 1863. (710.)
1. *Herminiera Elaphroxylon*, Guill. and Per. The "Ambash" or pith tree of the Nile, from 3° to 8° N. Natives use its light logs to assist them when swimming across the Nile; grows so rapidly that in three years it almost choked up the channel of the R. Bahr-el-Gazelle. March, 1863.
1. *Astragalus venosus*, Hochst. ; herbaceous plant; groves, 1° N. (529.)
1. *Pisum sativum*, L. ; cult. at Karagŭé. Alt. 4000 to 5000 ft. Feb., 1862. (466.)
1. *Arachis hypogœa*, ground-nut. Cultivated to a small extent from 7° S. to 2° N. Eaten roasted, boiled, or converted into an oil. (64.)
1. *Desmodium sp. ;* 7 to 9 ft. high; sticky, mouldy stem ; abundant in grassy forests; Uganda and Unyoro. 1862. (434 and 568.)
1. *Uraria picta*, Desv. ; foot high ; rocky soil ; Madi, Dec., 1862. (666.)
1. *Alysicarpus Wallichii*, W. and A. var. ; a decoction of its leaves used along with Calophanes radicans to reduce or soothe swollen legs. Karagŭé Hills and grassy plains of Unyoro. Feb. and Sept., 1862. (435.)
1. *Smithia n. sp. ;* near cult. Mininga. 4° 18' S. (177.)
1. *Zornia diphylla*, Benth. ; in tufts, on surface rocks, Unyoro forests. Aug., 1862.
1. *Æschynomene Indica*, L. ; "M'pæcee;" "Solah" of India ; in marshes generally. 5° S. to 2° N. In Sept. (the height of the dry season, at 3° S.) this plant lies dead on the dried mud ; use, floats for nets ; erect, 7 ft. high. (127.)
2. *Æ. Schimperi ?* Hochst. ; "Kong'gōlō ;" sp. of Indian "Solah" (pith); 20 ft. high bushy tree. Waganda make their shields of its light wood ; Wanyoro use it as trimmers and door-bolts ; Wanyamŭézi as load-levers. Oct., 1862. (615.)
1. *Alhagi mauroram*, Tourn. ; thorny plant eaten by camels. Thebes, 26¼° N. May, 1863.
1. *Glycine labialis*, W. and A. ; slender climber; plateaux. 2° N. Nov., 1862.
1. *Canavalia gladiata ?* DC. ; waxy, sweet-scented, rose-pink flowers. Wanyamŭézi spin its beans as an amusement; among grasses. Chopeh, 22d Nov., 1862. (628.)
1. *Erythrina sp. ;* handsome scarlet flowering shrub, with moulded stem and slightly bent down thorns. Karagŭé, Feb., 1862. (426.)

1. *Vigna luteola*, Benth. ; "Koondé;" coarse bean, cult. by natives. 5° S. and 2° N. Karagŭé, March, 1862. (489.)
2. *V. sp.* ; creeper, with rose-colored flowers. M'gæta banks, 7° 20′ S., 38° E.
1. *Lablab vulgaris*, Savi. ; coarse bean; "Gueengueezoo" and "Maharagé;" grown on the E. coast, and Karagŭé. Feb., 1862. Leaves are dried and made into a spinage. (425.)
1. *Psophocarpus sp.* ; climber, with winged pods overhanging water, M'bwiga. Alt. 1354. 7° 24′ S.
1. *Dolichos biflorus*, L. ; small herbaceous plant. 6° 55′ S. Oct., 1860.
2. *D. ? sp.* ; Trefoil leaves. Usŭi slopes. Nov., 1861. (206.)
3. *D. ? sp.* ; resembles the "dall" of India. 2° N. Oct., 1862.
1. *Phaseolus lunatus*, L. ; Duffin bean. Kazeh. 5° S. 1860.
2. *P. Mungo*, L. ; "Moong ke dal" of India. Sown in ridges, 5° S.° Uncommon. (59 and 82.)
1. *Rhynchosia viscosa*, DC. ; near cult. Unyoro. Nov., 1862.
2. *R. sp.* ; elegant racemes of erect flowers. 2° S. Dec., 1861. (416.)
3. *R. minima*, DC. M'gæta banks, 7° 20′ S., 38° E.
1. *Pachyrhizus sp. ?* 4 ft. high, with handsome flowers. Madi woods, Jan., 1863.
1. *Cajanus Indicus*, DC. ; pigeon-peas ; "Baraz" (Kis.); or Indian "Urrur ke dall;" met with and cultivated every where ; grows to 7 ft. high ; tastes like a coarse description of field peas ; the Wahiyow strike a light by using friction with its wood and a reed. (530.)
1. *Eriosema parviflorum*, E. Mey. Karagŭé. 1862. (420.)
2. *E. n. sp.* ; stems zigzag very much ; low bush. Madi slopes, Dec.,1862.
3. *E. sp.* ; 2 ft. high, erect. Karagŭé Hills, Feb., 1862. (414.)
1. *Lonchocarpus philenoptera*, Benth. ; 5 ft. cir., rather ash-like tree, with erect clusters of handsome flowers attractive to bees. 7° S.
2. *L. laxiflorus ?* Guill. and Per. ; "Mowăleh;" 30 in. cir. tree, in lilac, sweet-scented blossom. Madi. 3° N. 13th Jan., 1863. (743.)
1. *Dalbergia melanoxylon*, Guill. and Per. ; "M'pingo" (Kis.); "M'Gembeh" (Ugogo); "M'Teendeea" (Kin.); 20 in. cir. tree ; wood considered first class, being impervious to insects ; very hard and heavy, with dull purple heart, resembling rosewood when polished ; uses—arrow-tips, wooden hammers (for beating bark cloths), rafters ; root a cure for toothache. Met with from 5° S. to 5° N. (3.)
1. *Abrus Schimperi*, Hochst. ; seemed to be a woody-climber. Madi. 3° N. 1863.
2. *A. precatorius*, L. ; found curling up a young tree. Ukuni, 4° S., Sept., 1861. Zanzibar men consider the roots boiled in grain and eaten a certain remedy for swollen testicles ; after taking it vomiting is said to ensue ; plentiful in Uganda, where the king's officers wear wreaths of its scarlet seeds. (122.)
1. *Parkinsonia aculeata*, L. ; seems to have been imported here by the Austrian Mission. Gondokoro, 5° N. 1863.
1. *Poinciana pulcherrima*, L. Zanzibar.
1. *Piliostigma Thonningii ?* Schum. ; "M'Keendambogo" (Kin.); "Keeteëmbee" (Kis.); a brushwood tree, found every where, growing like the "dâk" of India ; short lashings can be stripped from the bark ; the leaves are used to cover sores. (95.)
1. *Cassia obovata*, Coll. ; senna ; seen being collected from sand-covered fields of Kartoum, March, 1863.
2. *C. acutifolia*, Del. ; also gathered, to a smaller extent, from the sand-covered fields of Kartoum. March, 1863.
3. *C. Tora*, L. ; among grasses and near moisture. 2° N. 27th Oct., 1862. (600.)
4. *C. Occidentalis*, L. ; bush, near water, Nile banks. March, 1863.
5. *C. sp.* ; "Mcækæs'æ;" 5 ft. to 6 ft. high; outspreading, sombre, green foliaged, yellow flowering, black podded bush; seen as fencing, and common. 3° N. 12th Feb., 1863. (76.)
6. *C. sp.* ; a wild senna; near *acutifolia*, but pubescent with broader leaves. Desert valley near Korosko, 21° N. April, 1863.
7. *C. mimosoides*, L. ; foot high ; wing-like stipules remain withered on the stem after the leaves have fallen off. 2° S. and 2° N. (445.)
8. *C. sp.* (Sect. Chamæcrista); small herbaceous plant, growing locally. Alt. 1200 ft. M'bwiga, Oct., 1860.
9. *C. sp.* (drawing—no specimen); yellow flowering tree; pod 5 in. by 1 ; seeds elongate and round ; leaves thickly paired. 1° 42′ S. Feb., 1862. (430.)

10. *Cassia sp.* (drawing—no specimen); 6 ft. high shrub, with yellow flowers; pods 4 in. long, round, glossy, and brown, with green edges, crammed with flat, fig-shaped seeds; midribs red; the branches smell so nastily the natives use them to drive away musquitoes. 1° 42′ S. Alt. 5000 ft. March, 1862. (454.)

1. *Cordyla Richardi*, Planch. ; 12 ft. cir. tree; fruit large walnut size; gum in deep red bosses. 6 miles south of Gondokoro. 15th Feb., 1862.

1. *Swartzia marginata*, Benth.; "M'nyembé;" ordinary-sized tree. 3° N. 1862. (644.)

1. *Afzelia Petersiana ?* Kl.; "Makola;" 9 to 12 ft. circ. tree, branching at 10 to 25 ft. Uzaramo, Usekhe, and Unyamúézi forests; Gani and Madi, 3° N. Uses—young purple-tinted leaves are eaten as a spinage; no ropes, but drums, door-planks, quivers, and pipe-bowls are made from its light mahogany-colored wood by the Wanyamúézi; a brown, tasteless, volatile gum exudes from wounds; flowers richly perfumed. (14 and 27.)

1. *Detarium sp.;* seed only. The natives at 3° 15′ N. eat its fruit, and call the tree Bootoo. Feb., 1863. (761.)

1. *Tamarindus Indica*, L. ; "Looquájoo;" ranges from Rumuma, alt. 2700 ft., 6° 46′ S. to 3° and 4° N., in the Bari country. (124 and 541.)

1. *Novum genus* (near *Copaifera*); "M'chenga." Livingstone gives the name "Chenga" to a similar tree. Covers the Wanyamúézi forests; bark made into band-boxes, immense round stores for grain, and fibred kilts. (32.)

2. *N. genus, 2d species ?* (leaf only); "Miombo;" girth 9 ft. ; 50 ft. high, with dark green foliage; considered a first-class wood; made into rafters; flowers yield the best-flavored and whitest honey, and the bark is converted into boats, roofing, grain-bins, kilts, and m'atches; while in Uhiyow the cloth from its bark is said to bleach like sheeting. 2½° and 5½° S., 32° E. Alt. 4148. (1.)

1. *Dichrostachys nutans*, Benth. ; Shillook country. Nile banks, March, 1863.

2. *D. sp.;* flowers bottle-brush shape; one half rose-pink, contrasting beautifully with other lemon-yellow half. Bruce figures this among his Abyssinian plants. Alt. 2700. 6° 46′ S. (20.)

1. *Mimosa asperata*, L. ; thorny bush, in every swamp. 2° N., etc. (575.)

1. *Acacia Arabica*, L. ; "Soonud" (Arab.). Bagara Arabs, etc., dye their clothes with its pods. The coarse-made boats of the Upper Nile are built of its cross-grained wood, not considered durable. About 10° N. the trees measured 8 and 10 ft. in girth; those forming forests in low islands, at 12° N., measured but from 4 to 6 ft. At Muscat, this species is used in extracting spirit from the date. Seen also at Siout avenue, Nile bank, 28° N. (769.)

2. *A. Seyal ?* Del. ; "M'salla." Forests of it at 9° N. Nile left bank, March 3, 1863 ; tree stems Indian red, concealing a soft apple-green bark ; height, 12 to 18 ft. ; flat-topped, and branches much broken by wild elephants eating its legumes ; found also at 18° N., where camels eagerly fed upon it; hard, brittle gum accumulates on the trunk. (767.7.)

3. *A. sp.* (near *Seyal*)*;* "M'seekeezzee;" inner bark used as lashings for temporary huts. 2° S. and 3° N. 1861, 1862. (677.)

4. *A. sp.* (near or same as last.) A bush with pale hazel bark, scaling. Karagué valley, Dec. 6, 1861. (384.)

5. *A. eburnea ?* Willd. ; 30 ft. high ; top flat as a table. E. African chain. Alt. 4750 ft. 6° 38′ S. Dec., 1860.

6. *A. sp.* (not in flower); also "M'salla;" 10 ft. girth, with white, 2 inch long, double, bulbless thorns set closely all over the stem; inner bark made into lashings. Woods, Dec. 12, 1862. (690.5.)

7. *A. catechu ?* L. ; "M'wombweh ;" tree 20 to 30 in. girth, covered with angry, black, flattened thorns. 3° N., and Noer country, 8½° N. ; one had ripened red pods, white bark, and double black flattened thorns. March 9, 1863. No uses known except fencing. (767.8 and 756.5.)

8. *A. albida*, Del. ; "Haraz" (Arab.); leaves eaten by goats, and its bark used for curing leather. Nile bank, 15° N. March, 1863. (771.)

9. *A. sp.* Madi wood. Dec., 1862.

10. *A. sp.;* "M'footamvool'ah ;" 30 inch circ. tree; thornless, with pyramidal clusters of jasmine-scented flowers, delicate-tinted foliage, and whitish finely-striated boughs. Steaming the eyes over its boiled roots, and afterward washing the face, is considered a cure for ophthalmia by the Wanyamúézi. Madi, Feb. 4, 1863. (755.)

11. *A. pennata*, Willd. ; pea-sized, yellow, scented heads of flowers. Nov. 16,1860.
12. *A. sp.* ; "M'gongwah;" 10 to 12 ft. circ. tree, with marble-sized spots of sparkling gum ; pod contorted, dull red, 10 inches by 1½, thin as brown paper, containing ten flat, shiny seeds; uses—hatchet handles and building purposes; black as rosewood, and said to sink in water; plentiful. 5° S. (101.)
1. *Albizzia, Lebbek ;* "Lubach" (Arab.); shady, ornamental trees, planted by Government-house, Kartoom, 15½° N. April 5, 1863. (773.)
2. *A. sp.* ; "M'sangal'a;" young thornless tree, with long, uniform, boughing branches; bark brown like the mountain ash and circularly lined; used in building. Stream bank. 3° N. Feb. 10, 1863. (764.)
3. *A. rhombifolia*, Benth. ; small bushy tree; no uses. Madi. 3° N. Feb. 6,1863. (760.)
1. *Zygia sp.* (leaf only); "M'koondee ;" at 4 ft. high, measured 27 ft. in girth ; branched into noble boughs at 15 ft. ; flower, a round, pink, pendent tassel, with here and there two long pods attached; these latter are used for lashing round poisoned arrows instead of leather; fruit said to be edible ; uses—boats, drums ; wood takes a fine polish. The largest growing tree in Uhiyow. Wahiyow say it is their largest tree. 7° S. Oct. 31, 1860. (4.)
2. *Zygian sp.* ; 20 to 30 ft. high ; gracefully foliaged ; honey-sucking birds hover among its branches. 2° 41' S. Nov., 1861. (205.)

XXXIII. MYRTACEÆ.

1. *Syzygium Guineense*, DC. ; "M'sawa ;" 20 to 30 in. circ. tree; fruit edible; timber red and cross-grained. 3° N. Dec. 18, 1862. (708.)
1. *Caryophyllus aromaticus*, L. ; Clove; groves of them cult. for exportation at Zanzibar.

XXXIV. ONAGRARIÆ.

1. *Epilobium hirsutum*, L. ; willow herb; pink flowers. By edge of Marenga Mkhali stream. Alt. 3900 ft. 6° 44' S. Nov., 1860.
1. *Jussiæa villosa*, Lam. ; 4 ft. high. Marshes, 3° N., Nov., 1862 ; and Nile banks, 10° N., March, 1863.
2. *J. repens*, L. Near springs, 5° S. Flowers yellow. 2° N. Oct., 1862.
3. *J. linifolia*, Vahl. ; stem and leaves tinted red; flowers yellow. 7½° S. Oct., 1860.
4. *J. augustifolia*, Lam. Zungoméro river bank, 7½° S. Oct.,1860.
1. *Ludwirgia parviflora*, Roxb. Near moisture, Unyoro. Nov.,1862.
1. *Trapa natans*, L. ; "Singara." The Waganda gather its four-pronged nut on the shores of Victoria N'yanza; wild boars eat them. Equator and Nile, 2° N. May and Nov., 1862. (515.)

XXXV. LYTHRACEÆ.

1. *Lawsonia alba*, Lam. ; "Hin'a" or "Henna;" dye shrub. Philœ ruins, Nile, 24° N. May, 16, 1863.
1. *Nesæa erecta*, Guill.; diminutive plant; swamps. Madi. Oct., 14, 1862.
1. *Ammannia vesicatoria*, Roxb. ; in bog on Madi rocks. Dec., 1863.

XXXVI. COMBRETACEÆ.

1. *Combretum eleagnifolium*, Planch. Madi. 3° N. Dec.,1862.
2. *C. sp.* (*Terminalia hirta*, Steud.); velvet-surfaced leaf, rough underneath ; no timber. E. African chain. Alt. 4700 ft. 6° 30' S. Dec. 19, 1860. (34.)
3. *C. sp.* (like one of Kotschy's); thicket bush, with arching branches, and four-winged ovate capsules ; leaves rather linear, in whorls of fours, with shining surface, and wavy entire edges ; in water-courses. Madi. 3° N. Dec. 20, 1862. No uses. (717.)
4. *C. sp.*; "M'Landal'a;" 30 in. circ. stunted tree; abundant in all forests; fruit in bunches of four-winged, rounded capsules; leaves elliptical, alternate, crisp, and glossy. (121.5.)
5. *C. sp.* ; 5 to 6 ft. high ; shrub, with rich, port-wine colored, bottle-brush shaped flowers. Near water, among rank vegetation. 7° S., 38° E. Oct.,1860.
6. *C. sp.* ; four-winged capsules. Madi. Feb.,1863.
7. *C. sp.* ; Madi. Dec., 1862. (734.5.)
8. *C. sp.* ; no specimen; handsome creeper; stamina and corolla all of a brilliant vermilion color ; capsules five-winged ; branches boughing over, and at times

seen catching hold of and climbing up trees ; flowers like bottle-brushes on the dead-like, now leafless, stems. 5° S. Ukuney, Aug., 1861. (91.)

1. *Terminalia sp.*; "M'foof'oo;" handsome trunked tree, 10 to 12 ft. circ.; wood lemon-yellow under the bark, cutting into which a sticky juice exudes. The Arabs of Unyanyembé build their houses of this wood. Wanyamũézi tint their bark-cloths yellow with it; fruit, flat oblong, 2 by 1 in., winged all round the spherical seed; kernel as sweet as an almond. Gani. Dec. 1, 1862. (643.)

1. *Powrea sp.*; near *P. constricta.* Zanzibar. Aug., 1860.

1. *Anogeissus acuminatus*, Wall.; 4 to 6 ft. circ. tree, with airy foliage; rare. Bari country. 4° N. Feb. 13, 1863.

XXXVII. FICOIDEÆ.

1. *Trianthema crystallina;* Vahl. (not of Wight); "Ice plant." Sheep are said to fatten readily upon it. Captain Speke had seen it in the Somali country. Desert on right bank of Nile. 18° 45′ N. May 1, 1863. (776.)

XXXVIII. MELASTOMACEÆ.

1. *Osbeckia eximia*, Sond.; 4 ft. high, purple flowering plant; near water, Ukidi forest. Nov., 1862.

2. *O. Zanzibariensis*, Naud.; stem roughly-haired. Zanzibar. 1860.

1. *Argyrella incana*, Naud.; richly flowering (rose-pink) plant; by water. Karagũé, 2° S., Feb., 1862; and Ukidi, Nov., 1862. (403.)

1. *Tristemma sp.* (near *T. littorale*); rough-stemmed erect plant; surface of leaves rough as a file when rubbed reversely; uncommon. Dec., 1862. 3° N. (730.)

XXXIX. CRASSULACEÆ.

1. *Bryophyllum calycinum*, L.; very fleshy; planted by huts in Madi; said to have medicinal properties; also grows wild in dells. Dec. 1, 1862. (646.)

1. *Kalenchoe glandulosa*, Hochst.; 4 ft. high, fleshy plant. 2° S. Dec., 1861. (387.)

XL. CUCURBITACEÆ.

1. *Citrullus colocynthis*, Schrad.; Shell colocynth; "Hundhul" (Turk); from the fruit a tarry, fish-oil smelling liquid is extracted by heat, and sold at 2*d.* per pint, for smearing leather water-sacks previous to entering the desert; camels refuse its fresh-looking green leaves. Abo-Ahmed desert, 19° N. May 2, 1863. (774.)

1. *Momordica sp.* (cf. *M. Vogelii*, Planch.); climber, with rich creamy flowers and prickly round fruit. 7½° S. and 2¾° N. Nov. 26, 1862. Whole plant smelling unpleasantly. (633.)

2. *M. sp.*; Zungoméro. 7½° S. Oct., 1860.

1. *Cucurbita maxima*, Duch.; excellent pumpkin with large slightly elongated fruit; leaves, male flowers, and seeds eaten cooked. 5° S. to 2° N. Oct., 1862. (599.)

1. *Lagenaria vulgaris*, Ser.; "Booyoo;" Bottle-gourd. Drinking-cups, bottles, quivers, musical sounding-boards, etc., are all made from the fruit of this useful plant; common by habitations. (598.)

1. *Mukia scabrella*, Arn.; climber. Nile banks. March, 1863.

1. *Melothria triangularis*, Benth.; climber. Forest. 2½° N. Dec., 1862.

1. *Bryonia laciniosa*, L.; climber, with beautiful scarlet and white berries (beads like them would be vastly admired by natives at 2° N.); plant offensive to handle. Unyoro, Dec., 1862. (617.)

1. *Luffa pentandra*, Roxb.; Towel-gourd, grows wild over the garden fences. Unyanyembé, 5° S. 1861. Nile banks, 6°–9° N.

2. *L. ? sp.*; among grasses; fruit prickly. Nile, 16° N. April 16, 1863.

1. *Coccinia Indica*, W. and A.; Waganda make garlands of the leaves. Unyoro, Nov., 1862. (597.)

1. *Cucumis sativus;* common cucumber; gardens of Arabs, 5° S. Called generally "Matango." (67.)

1. *Cucurbitacea;* creeper with yellow flowers. 7° 20′ S. Oct., 1860.

2. *C. sp.*; climbs up acacias; flower, yellowish-white; leaves much divided. Noer country, 8½° N. March 9, 1863.

3. *C. sp.*; ivy-leaved creeper. 7° 20′ S. Oct., 1860.

4. *C. sp.*; climber, flowers yellow, leaves compound. Zungoméro, 7° 27′ S. Oct., 1860.

1. *Carica papaya*, L.; grown in the gardens of Arabs. 5° S. (13.)

XLI. UMBELLIFERÆ.

1. *Hydrocotyle natans*, L. ; marshes. 1° 39′ N. Alt. 3300 ft. Oct., 1862.
1. *Heteromorpha Abyssinica*, Hochst. ; flowering shrub. 2° S. Dec., 1861. (299.)
1. *Steganotœnia sp. ;* "Meonga Pembe ;" considered an evil-producing tree; with a branch in the hand, cattle or other property may be stolen without discovery, it producing unconsciousness on those to whom the property may belong; forest tree. Madi, etc. 1861–62. (639.)
1. *Lefeburia n. sp. ;* marsh, by R. Wallah. 5° S. Alt. 3800 ft.
1. *Peucedanum ? sp. ;* 6 to 7 ft. high; walking-stick thickness, tapering root. R. Kafu banks. Aug., 1862. (581.)
1. *Cachrys Abyssinica*, Hochst. ; 5 ft. high, whole plant sweetly perfumed (something like peppermint); in woods, 3° N. Nov. and Dec., 1862. (709.)

XLII. RUBIACEÆ.

1. *Coffea Arabica*, L. ; "M'wanee ;" coffee cultivated in considerable quantities on and about the equator. The trees grow 10 and 12 feet high, their boughing branches affording shade. The berry is gathered before it has completely formed, sun-dried and eaten raw as a stimulant, chiefly by the Wanyambo. The natives never drink it as we do. Alt. 4000 ft. 1° 40′ S. May, 1862. (509.)
1. *Crossopteryx febrifuga*, Afr. "M'tæloambai ;" bushy-growing tree, whose seeds roasted are used by the Wanyamuézi to fumigate their bark-cloths, or, powdered and put in grease, to form a scented pomade for the body. 5° S., 3° N. 1861– 62. (698.)
1. *Hymenodictyon sp. ;* "M'fò ;" 6 to 8 ft. high shrub, with clusters of olive-shaped, purple-brown seed-vessels, covered with gray excrescences. Madi-burn bank. Dec. 12, 1862. (686.)
1. *Sarcocephalus sp. ;* scrubby-looking tree, with 10-inch diameter rounded leaves, and rough, brown-skinned, pink-cutting, sweet apple-tasted fruit, orange size ; full of seeds. Near water, Madi woods. Dec., 1862. (690.)
1. *Mussœnda n. sp. ;* pretty shrub; the leaves next the flowers are canary yellow. In rocky places. Gani. 3° N. Dec., 1863. (669.)
1. *Vignaldia quartiṇiana ?* A. Rich. Ukidi and Madi (rocks). Dec. 11, 1862.
2. *V. sp. ;* erect plant, with deep purple flowers. 2° 41′ S. Alt. 4000. Nov., 1861. (140.)
1. *Stylocoryne sp. ;* richly flowering, jasmine-scented shrub, with evergreen leaves in whorls of threes ; by water. Karagüé, 2° S. Feb., 1862. (422.)
1. *Gardenia lutea*, Fres. ; "Kolóla ;" its roots, boiled with the flour of Andropogon sorghum and the mixture drank, is considered by the Wanyamuézi a cure for hæmaturia—blood in the bladder ; the contorted branches make an impenetrable fence. 5° S. and 3° N. 1861–63. (762.)
1. *Randia dumetorum*, Lam. ; prickly, stiff-branched shrub. 3° N. Feb. 13, 1863.
1. *Hedyotis dichotoma*. A. Rich. Karagüé and Uganda groves. 1862. (447.)
2. *H. sp. ;* Madi bogs. Dec., 1862.
3. *H. sp. ;* bushed, linear-leaved weed. 5° S., 32° E. Alt. 4000.
4. *H. (Kohautia sp.) ;* (near *pauciflorum*); very delicate lilac-colored flowers. Grows out of water, 7° 20′ S. Oct., 1860.
1. *Otomeria sp. ;* inflorescence spires up the stem, rare ; corolla pink, except the inside, which is white; stems seem eaten down by goats or cattle. Open ground, Madi, Dec. 15, 1862. (691.)
1. *Rosea sp. ;* straight thickly-growing branches, leaves opposite. 4° N. Dec., 1862.
1. *Canthium sp. ;* tree with clusters of hard several-seeded berries. Madi, Dec., 1862.
1. *Pavetta sp. ;* shrub by water, with leaves feeling like leather, and bunches of white flowers. 2° S. Nov. 29, 1861. (160.)
1. *Psychotria ? sp.* in fr. ; "M'sweet'æ ;" shrub by rocky burn, with currant-sized, sweet-tasting scarlet berries, not eaten by natives. Faloro, 3¼° N. Dec. 14, 1862. (694.)
1. *Mitracarpum sp. ;* diminutive, sandy soil, near water. Ukidi. Nov., 1862.
2. *M. sp. ;* hardy. Unyoro plateaux, Nov., 1862 ; and 5° S.
1. *Spermacoce natalensis ?* Hochst. ; low sandy ground in forest. 2° 45′ N. Nov., 1862.
2. *S. sp. ;* corolla sky-blue. Alt. 5000 ft. 2° S. Feb., 1862. (439.)
3. *S. sp. ;* low grounds about Madi. Dec., 1862.
4. *S. Ruelliœ*, DC. ; opposite leaved ; near cult., 2° N. Aug., 1862.

1. *Pentanisia sp.*; pink flowers, whole plant very milky; found growing in a sesamum field; root tuberous. 2° N. July 29, 1862. (531.)

1. *Rubia cordifolia*, L.; Red madder; clinging plant. 2° S. Dec., 1861. (383.)

1. *Rubiacea* in fruit; erect shrub, with pear-shaped leaves in whorls of threes; five-seeded seed-vessel, black, and from leaf-axles. 2° S. March 18, 1863. (481.)

2. *R.*, leaves only; bark yellow, brittle, and light as a cork; considered a remedy for swollen limbs by powdering the burnt root, and rubbing it into cuts made with a knife, while the patient sits under the tree. Madi woods, etc. 1861-63. (740.)

3. *R.*; "M'koolookootoot'oo;" edible, pleasant-tasting drupe, green gage size and color. Madi, Dec., 1862. (678.)

XLIII. LORANTHACEÆ.

1. *Loranthus Acaciæ*, Zucc.; red parasite, found growing upon Acacia seyal, Nile bank, March 29, 1863.

2. *L. sp. n.*; clove-colored parasite, found grafted on the tops of trees. Nov. 14, 1860. 2° 41' S. Alt. 4000 feet. Nov. 2, 1861. (6.)

3. *L. sp. n.*; parasite, grafted, 3 ft. long wands. 6° 47' S. Alt. 3250 feet. Nov. 14, 1861.

1. *Viscum sp.* (cf. V. tuberculatum, Rich.); mistletoe. Usúi terrace top, 2° 42' S. Alt. 4500 ft. Nov., 1861. Berries orange. (143.)

XLIV. COMPOSITÆ.

1. *Vernonia Vogeliana*, Benth.; salt-bush; burn-bank, 3° N. Dec., 1862.

2. *V. stoechadifolia*, Sch. bip.; mixed with Hygrophila spinosa, and both burnt, salt is extracted from their ashes. Forests, 2° N.; open woods, 3° N. Aug. and Dec., 1862.

3. *V. sp.*; dwarf-growing thistle; in patches on stony ground, 3° N. Dec., 1862.

4. *V. sp.*; neat slim plant, with golden florets; 2 ft. high. 1° 42' S. Dec., 1862. (408.)

5. *V. sp.*; large plant. Woods, 3° N. Dec., 1862.

6. *V. sp.*; leafy-stemmed, erect plant, with alternate leaves. Dec., 1862.

7. *V. sp.*; common. Woods, 3° N. Dec., 1862.

8. *V. sp.*; 2 ft. high; white button-like flowers; near cult., 1° 42' S. Dec., 1861. (395.)

9. *V. sp.*; weed by huts, with mauve flowers. Unyoro, Oct., 1862.

10. *V. sp.*; coarse, thick-stemmed plant, with pretty purple and white flowers. 1° 42' S. Alt. 5000 ft. Feb., 1862.

1. *Stengelia sp.?* florets white; those unblown a pale purple. 1° 42' S. Dec., 1861. (218.)

2. *S. sp.?* (same as Barter's 368); hardy bush. 2° N. Dec., 1862.

3. *S. sp.?* dwarf thistle? Madi. Dec., 1862.

1. *Elephantopus scaber*, L.; lilac flowers. Alt. 5000 ft. 1° 42' S. Feb., 1862. (444.)

1. *Ageratum conyzoides*, L.; common near fields, 2° N. Oct., 1862.

1. *Erigeron?? sp.*; beautiful plant, with round, purple button-flowers. Moist places, 4° 15' S. 1861. Salt is extracted from its ashes. (85.)

1. *Nidorella sp.*; orange-yellow flowers, erect, woody; near moisture, 7° 20' S. Oct., 1860.

1. *Sphœranthus suaveolens?* DC. "Bozeea;" blue button-flowers; mud edges of Madi burn, Dec. 18, 1862. Wanyamúézi, when troubled with ague, mash up the whole plant, add cold water, and wash the body with the mixture.

2. *S. hirtus*, Willd.; purple buttons; grows in thick tufts on cracked clay, near rice-fields. Zungoméro. Oct., 1860.

1. *Dichrocephala latifolia*, DC. E. African chain. Alt. 4700 ft. 1860.

1. *Conyza sp.* (near *C. Ægyptiaca*); greenish-yellow flowers; stem 2 to 3 ft. high; erect, but waving upward; by huts, 2° N. Oct. 15, 1862. (590.)

2. *C. sp.*; flowers yellow; 2 ft. high. 2° S. Dec., 1861. (398.)

1. *Blumea runcinata*, DC.; 4 ft. high, with bell-shaped, gracefully drooping mauve flowers; near cult., 2° N. Oct. 15, 1862. (591.)

2. *B. alata?* DC.; differs from No. 3 by its leaf edges on the stem being *entire*; bank of R. Kafu, 2° N. Oct., 1862. (611.)

3. *B. Pterodonta*, DC.; 4 to 7 ft. high; weed; by huts, 2° N. Whole plant sticky, and smelling between mint and celery. Oct. 15, 1862. (592.)

4. *B. ? sp.* Karagüé. Feb., 1862. (466.)
1. *Pluchea sp.* ; lilac-flowering 5 ft. high bush; on borders of water-cut, Kanyenyé, 6° 24' S., where the water was undrinkable from brackishness; salt extracted from its ashes. (46.)
1. *Francœuria crispa*, Cass. ; Nile, 16° N. April 16, 1863.
1. *Varthemia Arabica*, Boiss. ; Nile, 16° N. April 16, 1863.
1. *Grangea maderaspatana*, Poir. ; grows flatly; Nile bank, 14°-15° N.
1. *Poloa? sp.* ; 1 ft. high; flowers yellow; root fibrous; sandy soil, 3° N. Dec., 1862.
2. *P. ? ? sp.* ; pretty little white flowering plant, covering fallow ground. 2° N. Aug., 1862.
1. *Ambrosia maritima*, L. ; bushes of it cover the sloping clay banks of the Nile at 16° N. April 16, 1863.
1. *Eclipta erecta*, L. ; weed; white flowers. 7½° S. Oct., 1860.
1. *Wedelia sp.* ; root woody; common by roadsides. 6° S. Alt. 3800 ft.
2. *W. sp.* ; flowers and stem purple; Uganda plantain wastes, July 18, 1862. (527, No. 2.)
1. *Spilanthes Africana*, DC. ; single small yellow flower; Robeho. Alt. 4700 ft. 6° 38' S., Dec., 1860; and 2° N., Oct., 1862.
1. *Chrysanthellum Indicum*, DC. ; by cult., 2° N. Aug., 1862.
1. *Verbesina sp.* ; 1½ ft. high; flower yellow; fields, 4° 18' S. (187.)
2. *V. sp.* ; Gani, 3° N., Dec., 1862; and leaves from 1° 42' S. Dec., 1861. (448.)
3. *V. sp.* ; yellow cornflower, ½ ft. high. 1° 42' S. 1861. (406.)
4. *V. sp.* ; 3 to 4 ft. high; purple at lower part of stem; covering fallow ground, 1° 42' S. March, 1862. Sometimes roots from the stem. (448.)
1. *Bidens leucantha*, L. 1° 42' S., Dec., 1861; and 2° N., common. (394.)
1. *Ximenesia encelioides*, Cav. ; flowers yellow. 15½° N. April, 1863.
1. *Cotula Abyssinica*, Schultz ; most diminutive, with yellow flower; by a well; Nile, March, 1863.
1. *Gnaphalium sp.* (near *G. Schimperi*); large bush, with handsome clusters of soft white flowers; by water, 1° 42' S. Dec., 1861. (409.)
1. *Helichrysum sp.* (near *H. ferruginum*); everlasting yellow flowers; root woody; East Coast Range, 7° 2½' S. Oct. 30, 1860.
1. *Antennaria sp.* ; hills of Chogwe, 6° 51' S. Alt. 3000 ft. Nov. 13, 1860.
1. *Kleinia? sp.* ; diminutive, with port-wine flowers. Alt. 1750 ft. Oct., 1860.
1. *Emilia sp.* ; orange flowers, stems leafless; plantain-groves, 1° N. July, 1862.
2. *E. sagittata*, DC. ; Zanzibar, 7° 27' S., etc. ; orange flowers.
3. *E. sp.* ; 9 in. high, with orange flowers; grows bushily by cult., 1° 42' S. Feb., 1862. (464.)
1. *Senecio sp.* ; weed; Unyoro fields. Nov., 1862.
1. *Echinops sp.* ; 4 ft. high; pink-flowered, alternate-leaved thistle. 2° 41' S., and 2° N. Feb., 1861. Alt. 4200 ft. (141.)
2. *E. sp.* ; elegant plant, with bushing branches and round red flower. Madi wastes. Dec., 1862.
1. *Cullumia sp.* (near a Cape sp.); diminutive plant, 5° 5' S. Alt. 3900 ft. 1860.
2. *C. sp.* ; yellow flowering thistle; very handsome. 2° N., Aug., 1862; and 3° N., Dec., 1862.
3. *C. sp.* ; pretty plant. 4° 18' S., March, 1861. (170.)
1. *Carthamus tinctorius*, L. ; "Gartoom" (Turk); Safflower; cult. for its oil, used in burning, at Kartoom, 15½° N. Feb. 2, 1863. (778.)
1. *Arctotis? ? sp.* ; flower brightest scarlet; drooping; light-soiled open forest, 5° S., 33° E. Alt. 3800 ft.
2. *A. ? ? sp.* ; flower erect; deep scarlet; root tuberous; common, E. Equatorial Africa. 1860.
1. *Centaurea calcitrapa*, L. ; star-thistle; delicately scented; Thebes and Carnac, 26° N. Camel seen carrying away a load of it—probably for fodder. May 20, 1863.
1. *Gerbera piloselloides?* Cass. Usagara Hills, 6° 51' S. Nov. 13, 1860. Alt. 3000 ft.
1. *Dicoma sp. n.* ; pale pink pistils. 1° 42' S. 1862. (459.)
1. *Lactuca sp.* ; spinage is made of the leaves, 7½° S. ; 37° 31' E. Oct., 1860.
1. *Sonchus oleracens*, L. ; flower yellow; stem milky; by water, 1° 42' S. Feb., 1862. (407.) 2° N. April, 1862.
1. *Composita dubia*; flower yellow; root carrot-shaped. 6° 55' S. Oct., 1860.

XLV. SAPOTACEÆ.

1. *Bassia Parkii,* G. Don; Sheabutter; "Meepampa;" tree 10 to 15 ft. in girth, with bare branches, the leaves and flowers raying from their tips; general look of an oak; villagers cut away the very thick bark; milk exudes profusely, forming a hard, white, insoluble gum; timber cross-grained, cedar-colored, and too hard for the soft iron tools of natives; flowers heavily scenting the air, and covered with the honey-bee; only seen at 3° N., Dec., 1862. (650.)
1. *Chrysophyllum?* sp. (seed only); "Chenjha;" girth 10 ft.; lofty tree; fruit, green gage size, with one to three flat stones; a sweet drink is made from their pulp; wood made into spear-handles. 5° S. to 3° 15′ N.; near water. (93.)
2. *C. sp.* (near *C. Macalismontanum*); very milky; tree growing like a huge bush on the face of the rocky hills, 3° 15′ N. Dec., 1862. Leaves (chiefly at the branch-tips, where the fruit is found) silvery white underneath; ropes made from inner bark; frequent. (703.)
1. *Mimusops Kummel,* Bruce; "M'nyemvee;" lofty tree, 5 ft. in girth, bed of rocky stream, 3° 15′ N., Dec., 1862; common; fruit one-stoned, dry, but sweet-tasted; orange-yellow, and sometimes reddish.

XLVI. MYRSINEÆ:

1. *Embelia sp.;* "M'Sækær'a;" 30 inch circ. tree, whose young shoots grow straight for 10 ft., with a red-brown mould over them; fruit not edible, and small, like shot. 3° 15′ N. Dec., 1862. (695.)

XLVII. OLEACEÆ.

1. *Chionanthus?* sp.; "Meesoo;" a wild olive; handsome, lofty, tall-trunked tree, in low moist ground, 3° 15′ N., with sweet-scented white flowers; edible, large pea-sized, one-stoned drupes in clusters. Dec., 1860. (701.)

XLVIII. JASMINACEÆ.

1. *Jasminum sp.* (no specimen); in shaded nullah bed, Ukuni, 4° S. Sept., 1861. (117.)

XLIX. APOCYNEÆ.

1. *Landolphia florida?* Pal.; a tree-climber, remarkably milky, with clusters of white scented flowers, covering lofty trees. Wahiyow make playing-balls of its rubber. Natives say, if its milk be rubbed on the body, it is difficult to get it off, while that of the "M'pira," another "India-rubber," can be easily washed off. (707.)
1. *Carissa sp.;* girth 30 in.; flowers handsome; jasmine-scented; in red clusters before blooming, afterward becoming a pink-white; double, straight, inch long, pink-tipped thorns; bark, mouldy-green; banks of Little Windermere, 1° 42′ S. Dec. 3, 1861. (214.)
2. *C. sp.;* "M'fombwah;" resembling an orange-tree, but with 2 in. long, pink-pointed, double thorns, and clusters of jasmine-scented flowers; branches angle wherever the leaves and thorns are thrown out; fruit eaten by the Wanyamuézi, and its disagreeably-smelling, tasteless roots used by them to remedy coughs and chest complaints. 3° N. Dec., 1862. (688.)
1. *Adenium sp.;* 3 ft. high, scarlet-flowering bush, with swollen, rapidly-tapering branches. 4° N. Bari country. Feb. 15, 1863. (766.)
2. *A. sp.;* 1 to 2 ft. high, with rich pink flowers. 6° 55′ S. Oct., 1860.
1. *Holarrhena febrifuga?* common; jasmine-scented plant or bush. Alt. 1300 to 1500 ft. M'bwiga. Nov., 1860.

L. ASCLEPIADEÆ.

1. *Tacazzea sp.;* milky-climber, with minute red flowers, and covered with red stinging ants. 3° N., Dec., 1862; and Nile banks, 6° N., Feb., 1863. (711.)
1. *Calotropis procera,* R. Br., "Madar" of Punjab; met with 3° 15′ N., in Feb., 1863, on our entrance into the Egyptian country; not seen since 7° S.
1. *Dæmia barbata?* Klotzsch; white-flowered climber. 2° N., Nov., 1862; and 5° 10′ N., 1863.
1. *Gomphocarpus sp.* (near *G. fructicosus*); 4 to 5 ft. high bush; near recent cultivation; rare. 5° S., 33° E. 1861.
2. *G. physocarpus?* E. Meyer. (728.5.)
3. *G. sp.;* 3 ft. high; near water, 2° N., Nov., 1862. (606.)

4. *G. sp.*; very showy bushy plant; by water. Alt. 3193 ft. 6° 44' S. Nov. 16, 1860.
5. *G. sp.*; bulbous; M'bumi, 6° 44' S.
6. *G. sp.*; 4 ft. high, with carrot-shaped root; eaten medicinally by natives, and worn as a charm by those desirous of an increase to their family. 2° N. Aug., 1862. (555.)
7. *G. sp.*; Karagűé Hills. Alt. 5000 ft. Dec. 5, 1861. (216.)
1. *Leptadenia lancifolia?* Dne.; flower yellow, backs of petals green. The natives of 3° N. make spinage of its flowers and tender shoots. Jan. 26, 1863. (749.)
2. *L. pyrotechnica*, Dne.; 6 to 8 ft. high, girth 20 in.; resinous shrub in desert; 20° N., the only procurable firewood. April 29, 1863. (775.)
1. *Brachystelma n. sp.*; bushy plant, with flower a dark purple star; leaves thread-like; root edible, liquorice-tasting, garden-turnip size; rare; forests, 6° S. Jan. 1, 1861.
2. *B.? sp.* (in fruit); 9 in. high, with bulbous, tasteless, edible root. 1° 42' S. Feb., 1862. (468.)
1. *Asclepiadea? dubia;* flowering climber, in Unyoro thickets. July, 1862.

LI. LOGANIACEÆ.

1. *Strychnos sp.*; "M'phoondoo;" scrubby-looking tree, with orange-colored and sized fruit; a loose, tough skin covers the rather flat, elongated, acidulated, drop-like seeds, which are irregularly packed in a sweet-tasting yellow pulp. 6° 21' S. Woods, 3° N., Feb. 9, 1863; and 2° N. (762.5.)
2. *S. ?* (no specimen); fruit, not edible, monster orange-sized, with brittle rind, and full of yellow pulp; leaves have a distinct rib on either side of the main one, and their tips are as sharp as needles; 15 ft. high shrub, in forests, 4° S. to 2° N.

LII. GENTIANACEÆ.

1. *Octopleura loselioides*, Benth.; swamps, about 3° 15' N. Dec. 15, 1862. A Brazilian plant.

LIII. CONVOLVULACEÆ.

1. *Argyreia sp.*; "Mohambo;" 3 ft. high; delicate, mauve-colored, immense flowers; root round, 21 in. circ. Considered lucky to have the skulls of wild animals placed by it; or, with a branch in the hand, the hunter is certain of sport. Chopeh, Nov. 22, 1862, 2½° N. The large roots at first require forcing in water. (627.)
1. *Batatas edulis*, Choisy; "veeazee," sweet potato, cultivated from Zanzibar to Egypt; obtainable from the fields, or in a dried state, nearly every month in the year; make a beer from it at Bogwé. 3½° S. (173.)
2. *B. pentaphylla*, Choisy; left bank Blue Nile. 1863.
1. *Ipomœa palmata*, Forsk.; common. Nile banks, 9° N., etc. March, 1863.
2. *I. asarifolia*, R. & S.; binds down the sands of the right bank of Nile, 14½° N. March, 1863.
3. *I. reniformis*, Choisy; yellow-flowered, flatly-growing creeper; hard mud shores, Nile. Noer country, 8½° N. March 9, 1863.
4. *I. reptans*, Choisy; water convolvulus. Nile edges, 18° N. March 18, 1863; also among luxuriant vegetation, Equator, and 2° N.
5. *I. involucrata*, Beauv.; climber. Forests, 2° N. Nov., 1862.
6. *I. commatophylla?* Rich.; on and near surface rocks. Forests, 2° N. Dec., 1862.
7. *I. capitata*, Choisy; twiner among bushes. 3° 15' N. Dec., 1862.
8. *I. pterygocaulos?* Choisy. Nile banks.
9. *I. pinnata*, Hochst.; white-flowering, running plant, near moisture lying on masses of rock. 3° 15' N. Dec., 1862. (656.)
10. *I.? sp.*; very handsome; flowers large, and pale port-colored, with deep-green, long heart-shaped leaves, much impressed from below; stem slightly lactescent; climbs to 15 ft. along with the previous year's stem in seed. 2° 41' S., 1861; and 2° N., Aug. 8, 1862. (145 and 559.)
11. *I. sp.*; climber, with pinnatifid, deep-green, handsome, impressed-from-under leaves; bud purple; but *one* specimen seen. 5° 26' S. 1861.
1. *Hewittia bicolor*, W. and A. Nile banks, N. Nov., 1862.
1. *Aniseia? sp.*; leaves only; crawls flat on bare ground. 2° 41' S. Nov., 1861. (188.)

1. *Breweria malvacea*, Klotszch; erect, with pink flowers and soft silvery leaves. 2° 42′ S. (202.)
2. *B. sp.*; common near huts, Chopeh. 1° 40′ N. Nov., 1862.
1. *Evolvulus linifolius*, L.; blue flowers, growing flatly near cult., 1° 30′ N. July 29, 1862.
1. *Convolvulacea dubia* (cf. *Hygrocharis*, DC., Prod. ix., 451). Minute plant, with snow-white flowers, growing flatly on the ground in plantain-groves; rootlets come from the stem, and the seed-vessel turns into the ground after the corolla falls off. July, 1862. Equator. (529.)

LIV. SOLANACEÆ.

1. *Lycopersicum esculentum*, Don.—Tomato. 7° 27′ S.; and near swamps, 4° to 5° S. Natives surprised at our eating them. (91.)
1. *Solanum nigrum*, L.; black nightshade; scarlet-berried; leaves made into spinage. 4° 18′ S., 1° 42′ S., and 28° N.
2. *S. sp.*; common by waste fields, 5° S., 33° E. Alt. 3800 ft.
3. *S. sp.*; foot high; mauve flowers; prickly toothed leaves; stem covered with a 3 to 5 stellate pubescence, not edible. By huts, 1° 45′ N. Nov., 1862. (605.)
4. *S. Melongena*, L. Egg-plant; "Brinjall;" gardens of the Arabs, 5° S. (68½.)
1. *Withania somnifera*, Dun.; many-seeded, with scarlet berries in a loose envelope. Sultan of Ukuni, at 4° S., had its roots hung over his door in the idea that it brought him many welcome visitors; Nubians have some faith in it as a medicine; near huts, 3° 15′ N. Dec. 10, 1862. (674.)
1. *Physalis angulata;* leaves used as a vegetable; by huts, 2° N. 1862.
1. *Scopolia Datora*, Dun. (called "Thatoora"). This plant was gathered to be smoked by a man suffering from spitting blood and weak chest. They also smoke it after excessive drinking. 28° N. May 24, 1863. (779.)
1. *Nicotiana tabacum*, L.; seen cultivated from 7° S. to 4° N. Sold either as leaves, in plaited form, or manufactured into cakes, the consistence of peat; seldom or never chewed, and rarely snuffed. (185.)
2. *N. rustica*, L.; cult. at Kartoum and farther N. April 23, 1863.
1. *Capsicum frutescens*, L.; red pepper of Unyoro. Nov., 1862.
1. *Datura stramonium*, L.; thorn apple (from fig. and notes), "Nanaha;" 4 ft. high in gardens, 1° 42′ S. At the coast, mats are made from its fibre. (154.)

LV. BORAGINEÆ.

1. *Heliophytum Indicum*, DC.; 7° 20′ S. Oct., 1860.
1. *Heliotropium Europœum*, L.; near cult.; Nile banks, 16° N. April 16, 1863.
1. *Coldenia procumbens*, L.; grows flatly on baked mud. 3° 15′ N. Jan., 1863.
1. *Echium longifolium*, Del.; stings the fingers; by a well, 15° N. March, 1863.
1. *Cynoglossum micranthum*, Desf.; common, 1° 42′ S. March, 1862. (456.)

LVI. SCROPHULARIACEÆ.

1. *Doratanthera linearis*, Benth.; near cotton fields, right bank Nile, 16° N. April, 1863.
1. *Dopatrium Senegalense*, Benth.; grows in water which lies on surface rocks. 3° 15′ N. Dec., 1862.
1. *Torenia pumila*, Benth. Jan. 14, 1860, 5° 45′ S., alt. 4300 ft.; and Dec., 1861, 1° 42′ S., alt. 5500 ft. Abundant in swamps by rock; its roots, eaten with salt, are used as a gargle. (122.)
1. *Herpestes floribunda*, R. Br.; swamps, 3° 15′ N. Dec., 1862.
1. *Ilysanthes sp.;* 6 inches high; erect stem, with violet-colored flowers; among swampy grasses, 3° 15′ N. Dec., 1862.
2. *I. sp.*; bushy minute plant; on rocky ground, 3° 15′ N. Dec., 1862.
3. *I. sp.*; diminutive; flowers white, red tinted inside; by rock and water. Alt. 5500 ft. 1° 42′ S. 1861. (211.)
1. *Veronica anagallis*, L.; E. Coast Range. Alt. 4700 ft. 6° 38′ S. Dec. 19, 1860.
1. *Scoparia dulcis*, L.; common in waste ground, 5° 1′ S. Alt. 4000 ft.
1. *Ramphicarpa fistulosa*, Benth.; dries black; swamps and meadows, 3° 15′ N. Dec., 1862.
1. *Cycnium longiflorum*, E. and Zey.; flowers (both pink and white) in tufts during the very driest season; dries indigo color; E. Coast Range. Nov., 1860. Common in dry localities. (443.)

APPENDIX. 577

2. *C. sp. n.* ; "M'sweera M'dogo;" crawling, white-flowered, purple-stemmed plant
   on bare open sandy heights, 3° 15′ N. Dec. 9, 1862. Dries black; uncommon.
   Wanyamuézi, when bitten by a particular snake, cure themselves by using the
   black fibrous roots of this plant. (670.)
1. *Striga Senegalensis*, Benth. ; dries black. 2° 41′ S. Alt. 4500 ft. Nov., 1861.
   (204.)
2. *S. hermonthica*, Benth. ; field pink ; common in fallow ground. Uganda, Aug.,
   1862. (572.)
1. *Sopubia ramosa*, Hochst. ; erect, woody, pink-flowered plant in grassy plateaux.
   2° N., Oct. 20, and Dec., 1862. Wahiyow extract salt water (for cooking purposes) from its ashes; uncommon. (594.)
2. *S. sp. n.* ; flower a rich pink ; leaves in whorls of filaments ; plant woody, and
   tendency to purple ; dry ground. Alt. 5500 ft. 1° 42′ S. Dec., 1861. Uncommon. (411.)
1. *Scrophulariacea dubii generis* ; purple plant, with filiform leaves and white flowers ;
   stem smooth, shiny, and woody ; near water, 1° 42′ S. Alt. 5000 ft. Feb.,
   1862. (402.)

LVII. LENTIBULARIEAÆ.

1. *Utricularia sp.* ; yellow flowering floater ; marshes, 2° N. Aug., 1862.
2. *U. sp.* (near *U. Stellaris*). 2° N. Oct. and Nov., 1861.

LVIII. BIGNONIACEÆ.

1. *Stereospermum sp.* ; "Mololo" (Kin.) ; 3 ft. circ. tree ; in full pink-white bloom,
   3° 15′ N. Jan. 26, 1863. Seed-vessel an 18-inch long, round, purpled, silvery-
   spotted pod, like a whip-snake; sand-bees make their cocoons from its delicate
   leaves; frequent by water; wood useless. (750.)
2. *S. discolor*, R. Br. This ordinary-sized tree ornaments the hill-sides at 6°–7° S.
   with its rich blossom, perfuming the air to some distance. Alt. 1200 ft. 1860.
1. *Spathodea lœvis?* P. Beauv. (leaf only) ; Madi. Dec., 1862. Resembles *Kigelia;*
   3 ft. circ. tree, with file-surfaced, compressed, dry, serrate-edged leaves.
2. *S. sp.* (near *S. campanulata*) ; 4 ft. circ. 20 ft. high tree, with clusters of the most
   brilliant scarlet flowers tipping its densely-foliaged branches ; thornless ; in forests near springs ; about 2° N. only. Sept. 8, 1862. (571.)
3. *S. sp.* (no specimen ; from fig. and notes) ; pods 24 in. long, yellow, velvet-feeling,
   with a double row of seeds ; flowers yellow ; low grounds, 1° 42′ S. (427.)
1. *Kigelia pinnata*, DC. ; "M'sankwa" (Kin.); "Malegæa" (Kis.); every where ;
   Wanyamuézi polish their spear-handles with its leaves and sand ; they roast and
   eat its seeds in famines ; an elastic wood, used for bows. (23.)

LIX. PEDALIACEÆ.

1. *Sésamum Indicum*, L. ; "Mafoot'a;" article of food; cult. from 4° 18′ S. to 2° N.
   (more or less) for its oil, also to be eaten toasted, or to flavor potherbs. (74.)
2. *S. sp. n.* ; in rank vegetation attains a height of 8 feet, growing like the foxglove ;
   common in moist places, 5° S., 2° 41′ S. Alts. 3000 and 4000 ft. (201.)
3. *S. sp.* ; pink flowers ; 18 in. high ; in dry woods ; stunted-like ; 6° 55′ S. Alt.
   3800 ft. Mohonyera, Oct., 1860, etc.
4. *S. sp.* (near last); purple flowers ; common, 5° S. 1860.

LX. SELAGINEÆ.

1. *Hebenstreitia dentata*, L. ; Coast Range, 6° 38′ S. Alt. 4700 ft. Dec., 1860.

LXI. ACANTHACEÆ.

1. *Thunbergia atriplicifolia*, E. Mey. ; orange-yellow flowers. E. Coast Range, 6° 38′
   S. Alt. 4700 ft. Dec., 1860.
2. *T. alata*, Boj. ; twines round grasses ; uncommon, 2° N. July 29, 1862. (534.)
1. *Nelsonia tomentosa*, R. Br. ; common about waste fields, 7° 25′ S.
1. *Brilliantaisia sp.* ; 6 ft. high, 4 to 6 in. circ. ; thick-jointed, regularly-squared stem,
   with large, lilac-spotted flowers ; rare ; Uganda and Unyoro ; near cult. Sept.
   27, 1862. (583.)
2. *B. sp.* (cf. *B. Vogeliana*, Benth. ; aromatic smelling-plant, among rank vegetation
   in low grounds, 7½° S. Alt. 896 ft. 1860.
1. *Calophanes radicans?* mashed and mixed with Alysicarpus Wallichii, and hot wa-

ter added, makes a soothing wash for swòllen limbs. 2° 41′ S. ; low grounds. Feb., 1862.ᐧ (436.)

1. *Hygrophila sp. ;* erect purple stem and flowers ; calyx, after throwing off the corolla, becomes black. By water, 2° 42′ S. Feb., 1862. (404.)

2. *H. spinosa,* T. And. ; three varieties observed, all probably the same plant—one a dwarf on meadow ground, 3° 15′ N. ; 2d, 3 ft. high, near cultivation, 4° 18′ S. ; and 3d, a 10 ft. high, 10 in. circumference plant, cultivated inside the hut inclosures, 3° 15′ N., for the salt its ashes produce. (582, 589.)

1. *Ruellia patula?* Jacq. ; diminutive ; open grounds, 3° 15′ N. Dec., 1862.

2. *R. sp.* (cf. *cyanea* and *prostrata*) ; blue flowers ; stem rather woody ; growing on the steep banks of the Nile among rocks and grasses, about 2° N. Dec., 1862. Servants have eaten this plant as a spinage at Chogwe Hills, on E. coast of Africa. (665.)

1. *Phaylopsis longifolia,* Sims. ; rocky heights in shade, 3° 15′ N. Dec., 1862.

1. *Barleria sp. ;* spiny, diminutive plant ; loc. forgotten. 1860.

2. *B. sp. ;* dry ground, 7° 10′ S. Oct., 1860.

1. *Crossandra sp. ;* foot high, with pale scarlet flowers, in patches under deep shade, by water, 3° 15′ N., Dec., 1862 ; and on rocky soil of Usŭi, Nov., 1861. (685 and 135.)

1. *Lepidagathis mollis,* T. And. ; inflorescence in balls of florets at leaf-axles. 3° 15′ N. Dec., 1862.

1. *Blepharis edulis,* Pers. This was the only vegetation found on the firm sand desert behind Meroe, 16° 50′ N. April 2, 1863.

1. *Acanthus arboreus,* Forsk. var. *pubescens ;* grows from 4 to 19 ft. high ; flowers pink, and handsome ; low moist grounds generally. 2° S. to 1° N. 1861–62. (136.)

1. *Justicia blepharostegia,* E. Mey. ; rose-pink flowers. 1° 42′ S. Feb., 1862. (433.)

2. *J. ? sp.* (cf. *J. palustris*) ; by vegetation ; Unyoro, 2° N. Oct., 1862. (494 and 603.)

3. *J. sp. ;* 10 inches high ; in tufts all over the bare hills of Karagŭé ; 1° 42′ S. ; flowers yellow. Dec. 2, 1861. (213.)

4. *J. (Rostellaria) sp. ;* eaten as spinage by the Expedition, but not appreciated. 5° 50′ S. Alt. 4000 ft.

5. *J. sp. ;* woody hardy plant with white flowers ; E. Coast Range, 6° 38′ S. Alt. 4700 ft.

6. *J. neglecta?* T. And. ; climber ; common near huts, among tall grasses ; with pretty pink flowers ; 2° N. 1862.

7. *J. sp.* (near last). 7½° S. Oct., 1860.

8. *J. sp.* (near *J. anselliana*) ; among grasses of Madi swamps, 3° 15′ N. Dec., 1862.

1. *Schwabea ciliaris,* Nees. Common in low grounds, near rocks. 3° 15′ N. Dec., 1862.

1. *Dicliptera bupleuroides,* Nees ; pink-flowered, common on light stony ground, 3° 15′ N. Dec., 1862.

LXII. VERBENACEÆ.

1. *Lippia sp.* (from fig. and notes ; no specimen) ; flower diminutive and yellow. 1° 42′ S. Feb., 1862. (438.)

2. *L. sp. ;* common near cultivation, 2° N. Sept., 1862.

1. *Lantana sp.* (from fig. and notes) ; 3 to 5 ft. high ; flowers rose-pink ; ripe berries rich purple, and tasting like junipers. Karagŭé Hills, 1° 42′ S. Dec., 1861. (158.)

1. *Premna simensis?* Klotzsch ; 5° S. 1860.

1. *Clerodendron cordifolium,* Rich. ; handsome twining plant ; green calix becomes a dull purple after the corolla has fallen off. Sept. 3, 1862, and Dec., 1862. 2°–3° N. (566 and 676.)

2. *C. sp. n. ;* handsome 2 ft. high shrub, with clusters of white flowers ; young shoots have rich purple velveting over them. The Wanyambo suck their plantain wine through tubes of this shrub, calling them "Meereej'a." 1° 43′ S. Alt. 5000 ft. March, 1862. (461.)

1. *Cyclonema sp. ;* light-purple flowers ; berry black ; common on wastes, 2° 41′ S. Nov., 1861. (203.)

1. *Vitex sp.* (near one of Barter's) ; "M'thalassee ;" bush-sized, with oblong, smooth-surfaced, acrid, yellowish drupes growing from the axles of the stalked leaves, which are simple and in whorls of threes. Madi, 3° 15′ N. Feb. 5, 1863. Has a rich perfume about it. (701.6.)

2. *V. sp.* ; trunk 4 to 5 ft. circumference, with inch-long, reddish-yellow, acrid, one-stoned drupe; leaves ternate, toothed, and longly-stalked; branch bark red; wood very brittle. 3° 15′ N. Woods. Dec., 1862. (649.)

3. *V. sp.* (= 5 of Livingstone, or *V. umbrosa*, Don) "M'foo;" very handsome umbrageous tree; fruit (procurable throughout the year) a plum, date-size, damson-colored, and tasting pleasantly; difficult to clean the stone; a light wood, made into drums. Forests, 3° 58′ S.; 2½° N. Oct., 1861, 1862. (81.)

LXIII. LABIATÆ.

1. *Ocimum canum*, L. ; near cult. "Toolsie" of India. 2° N. Aug., 1862.

1. *Moschosma polystachyum*, Benth. ; Nile banks, 5° N. Feb. 28, 1863.

1. *Acrocephalus villosus*, Benth. ; 3 ft. high; honey-bee very fond of its pale lilac flowers; beds of this weed by huts, 2° N. Oct., 1862. (585.)

2. *A. sp.* ; hardy, slightly-scented plant, with flowers and bracts lilac; the midribs of the large bracteæ are green. 2° 41′ S. 1861. (139.)

3. *A. sp.* ; 2 to 3 ft. high; blue-flowered, handsome plant; the broad bracteæ are all lilac *white*, except their veins, which are green; in patches on low light soil, by water; salt is said to be extracted from its ashes. 2½° N; forest of Ukidi, Nov. 26, 1862. (632.)

1. *Plectranthus sp.* ; erect-growing plant in water-cuts of hills, 1° 42′ S. Flowers white, diminutive, with pink spots. Dec., 1861. (385.)

2. *P. sp.* ; delicate erect plant, with fibrous root. 5° S. 1860.

3. *P. sp.* ; grows in patches in flat ground near Madi burn, 3° N. Dec., 1862.

4. *P. sp.* ; loves moisture on tops and in crevices of boulders. 3° N. Dec., 1862.

1. *Coleus barbatus*, Benth. ; blue flowers and stem; leaves smell strongly of, but more richly than, ripe guavas; natives consider sitting muffled up over its burning leaves, and inhaling their smoke, an immediate cure for fever; grows in Euphorbia hedges, 4° 18′ S.; and 1° 42′ S. 1861. (73.)

2. *C. sp.* ; purple-flowered, heavy-smelling plant; by cult., 2° N. Oct. 15, 1862. (588.)

1. *Hoslundia decumbens*, Benth. Zanzibar. Sept., 1860.

1. *Pycnostachys n. sp.* ; occasionally in moist dips of forest, 2½° N. Nov., 1862.

2. *P. sp.* ; sides of the Nile; among rushes. Nov., 1862.

1. *Æolanthus n. sp.* ? showy-looking plant; in dry open ground, 5½° S. Alt. 4000 ft. 1861.

2. *Æ. sp.* ; lilac flowers growing on one side of stalk; creeps, throwing up erect stems; sweet-scented.; found on bare surface rocks, amid 2 ft. high grasses, on forest heights, 1° 42′ S. Nov., 1861. (150 and 458.)

3. *Æ. sp.* ; stem black, as if fire had scorched it. Rocks of Madi, 3° 15′ N. Dec., 1862.

4. *Æ. sp.* ; resembles No. 2; surface rocks. Aug., 1862. 2° N.

1. *Hyptis pectinata*, Poir. ; weed by the village fences, 3° 15′ N., 21st Dec., 1862, and near water, Zungoméro, 7° 27′ S., 1860. Strong aroma from the leaves. (24.)

2. *H. brevipes*, Poir. ; florets are massed in the form of a ball; low grounds, about 3° 15′ N. Dec., 1862.

3. *H. spicigera*, Lam. ; "Neeno ;" cultivated by the natives of Gani, at 3° N., as a grain, and eaten roasted by them; they also extract oil from it; seeds both black and white. Dec., 1862. Plant smells strongly.

4. *H.* ? *sp.* ; 4 ft. high; covered densely with yellow florets, and smelling like a sweet herb; rare to find leaves on the stem; dry woods of Madi, 3° 15′ N. Dec., 1862. Frequent; root deeply set in the ground. (732.)

1. *Leucas martinicensis*, R. Br. ; near fields, 4° 18′ S. 1861. (181.)

2. *L.* (§ Loxostoma) *n. sp.* ; 2 to 3 ft. high, covered with soft pubescence; flowers white. Near water, 1° 42′ S., and 3° N. Feb., 1862. (413.)

1. *Leonotis sp.* (from fig. and notes); 3 to 5 ft. high, with scarlet flowers; common by cult., 4° S. to 2° N. (423.)

1. *Labiatarum, novum genus* ; woody, straight, 4 to 6 ft. high, purple-flowered plant; on the grassy banks of Madi burn, 3° 15′ N. The four seeds are protected by an enveloping calyx, and feathered white in a beautiful manner. Frequent in forests. (705.)

LXIV. PLUMBAGINEÆ.

1. *Plumbago Zeylanica*, L. ; diminutive white flowers; seems to survive the dryest season; stem very clammy; E. Coast Range, 6° 30′ S. Alt. 4000 ft. 17th Dec., 1860.

LXV. PROTEACEÆ.

1. *Protea sp.* ; "M'zaza" (Kin.); "King'eezee" (Kihiyow); tree 20 in. in girth and 10 ft. high; leaves grow obliquely to the stems; flower sunflower size, and rich white in color, opening to the sun. Natives say where this tree is in abundance, copal is also found. Wood useless, except as a brilliant firewood; leaves make a spinage in dearths, and black ants are fond of them. Madi woods. Dec., 1862. (673.)

LXVI. SALVADORACEÆ.

1. *Salvadora Persica*, L. ; "Arāk" (Turk.); large bush; wood makes tooth-scrubbers for natives. Nile banks in any quantity at 7° N. March, 1863.

LXVII. POLYGONACEÆ.

1. *Rumex obtusifolius*, L. ; near moisture, 6° 38' S., E. Coast Range. Dec.,1860.
2. *R. Abyssinicus*, Jacq. ; grows 12 ft. high near cultivation, 2° N., among grasses. Nov.,1862. Also 1° 42' S. People of Fipa, at 8° S., are said to eat its leaves. (418 and 625.)
3. *R. Maderensis*, Lowe; 10 to 12 ft. high; in hedges; leaves much eaten away. 4° 18' S. 1861. (77.)
1. *Polygonum barbatum*, L. ; moist places, E. Coast Range. Nov., 1860.
2. *P. sp.* ; flowers and stem pink and pink-streaked; anthers blue; seeds are star-like prickles; leaf-bases sheath the stem. 1° 42' S. Feb., 1862. (437.)
3. *P. tomentosum*, Willd. Nile banks, Nov., 1862; and 8° N., March, 1863.

LXVIII. NYCTAGINEÆ.

1. *Boerhaavia sp.* (near *B. paniculata*); foot high; diminutive pink flowers, with erect purple stem and jointed branches; leaves grow flatly on the ground; root carrot-shape. The roots are eaten in famines by the Wahiyow; in cleared ground, 2° N. July, 1862. (540.)
2. *B. grandiflora*, Rich. ; straggling plant. Alt. 4700 ft. 6° 30' S.

LXIX. CHENOPODIACEÆ.

1. *Chenopodium album*, L. ; uncommon; fallow ground, 2° N. Nov.,1862. (609.)
2. *C. botrys*, L. ; 2 to 6 ft. high; smells medicinally; its leaves and flowers, pounded into flour, are applied to eruptions on the legs; extremely handsome in its bright red autumnal colors; about houses and fields, 1° 42' S., March 5, 1862; and 2° 41' S. (200 and 465.)

LXX. AMARANTACEÆ.

1. *Celosia argentea*, L. ; 4 ft. high, with salmon-colored flowers; the stem of the season falls down and takes root; near cult., Uganda, and 2° N. July, 1862. (531.)
2. *C. trigyna*, L. ; potherb; by huts. Nov., 1862.
1. *Amarantus caudatus*, L. ; Love lies bleeding; carmine flowers and pink-veined leaves; grown near huts for medicinal purposes—natives boiling the stems and leaves, washing the head with the infusion, and rubbing the powder of its charred roots into cuts made in the temples, to cure headaches. 1° 42' S., 1° to 3° N. (449.)
2. *A. blitum*, L. ; wild amaranth (no specimen; fig. and description); flowers white; 3 to 5 ft. high; near huts, in rank vegetation, 1° 42' S. and 3° N. April, 1862. (493.)
1. *Ærua lanata*, Juss. ; potherb; grows prettily over huts like an ivy, 7½° S. and 2° N. Nov., 1862, etc.
2. *Æ. Javanica*, Juss. ; on shingle desert near Berber, 17⅓° N. Not met with till in these latitudes. 14½° N. March and April, 1863.
1. *Achyranthes aspera*, L. ; about huts, 4° 18' S., March, 1863. (184.) The same (monstrous, 768); 4 to 6 ft. high; Nile edge, 7° N. Its root mashed, put in hot water, and applied as a poultice to Bombay's ear, brought a discharge, and cured him of temporary deafness.
1. *Digera arvensis*, Forsk. ; by a well, Nile bank, 17½° N. March, 1863.
1. *Amarantacearum, novum genus* ; about cornfields of Mininga, 4° 18' S. March, 1861. (179.)

LXXI. PHYTOLACCACEÆ.

1. *Phytolacca Abyssinica*, Mey.; bush with scarlet berries, whose pulp colors cloth or the fingers gamboge. 1° 42′ S. Alt. 5000 ft. Dec., 1861. (217.)

LXXII. THYMELÆACEÆ.

1. *Gnidia involucrata*, Steud.; 3 ft. high; on bare heights of Madi, 3° 15′ N. Dec., 1862.

LXXIII. EUPHORBIACEÆ.

1. *Euphorbia hypericifolia*, L.; its juices, rubbed upon a snare, are supposed to attract Guinea-fowl. 2° N. Oct., 1862. (602.)
2. *E. sp.* (*Bracteis longecaudatis*), 5 ft. high, bush growing in light soil, Unyanyembé, 5° S. 1861.
3. *E. antiquorum*, L. (no specimen); "M'toopa;" tree 3 to 4½ ft. in girth, with four to six angled 12 in. circ. boughs; common over the whole route as fences, solitary trees, etc., and dotting the bare hills of Karagué. Alt. 5000 ft. The Bari people, at 4½° N., tried to poison the running streams with its branches as we marched through; its milk is used as a glue. (151.)
4. *E. tirucalli?* L. "M'nyal'a;" a dense fence of this tree-sized bush surrounds nearly all the villages in the Land of the Moon, growing often to twenty odd feet high; a variety creeps over rocks. The milk is used for poisoning fish. 7° S. to 3½° N. (151½ and 675.)
5. *E. sp.*; 10 ft. high, bushy, with *marked* leaves; flowers small, in red panicles; drips with milk; rare; only seen at 3° 15′ N., by villages. Feb., 1862. This specimen, not having died, is now growing at Kew. (754.)
1. *Acalypha crenata*, Hochst. (=*Indica*, L.); by cult., 5° S. and 2° N. Aug., 1863. (545.)
2. *A. villicaulis*, Hochst.; pink pistils, much branched.
3. *A. sp.*; brushwood on bank of Madi burn. Dec., 1862.
4. *A. sp.*; "M'cætæ;" its wands of great length and uniform thickness, with reddish or hazel bark, are made into strong trays and baskets by the people of Unyoro, 2° N.; also by rivulets, 1° 42′ S. Nov., 1861. (161 and 625⅚.) The roots are chewed, but have no taste.
5. *A. sp.* Karagué, 1° 42′ S. Nov., 1861.
6. *A. sp.*; M'bwiga, 7° 24′ S. Alt. 1350 ft.; overhanging water.
1. *Tragia cordata*, Vahl.; "M'wavee;" nasty stinging climber, paining for a longer time than the nettle; by water in thicket, 1° 42′ S. Alt. 5000 ft. Dec. 6, 1861. (388.)
1. *Ricinus communis*, L.; castor oil; found every where near dwellings; oil for unguents or itch is expressed; no case observed of its having been used internally. The leaves have virtues among natives. (121.)
1. *Croton sp.* (near tilifolium); "M'pœfoo;" 30 in. circ. tree, with soft, beech-tree looking bark; in shady, moist ground, 3° 15′ N. Dec., 1862. Inflorescence a panicle of a half inch diameter; spherical seed-vessels, whose stalks are covered with a dry red dust; immense leaves, swelling somewhat like celery; no uses known; not common. (706.)
1. *Crozophora plicata*, A. Juss.; small pink flowers; grows flat on dry clay, Nile edges, 16° N. March 16, 1863.
1. *Jatropha sp.*; foot high; root firmly set in the ground; a yellow or gamboge color exudes at incisions, shining on paper after becoming dry; seed-vessel (unripe) with three hard-rinded seeds; uncommon; near stream, 3° 15′ N. Jan. 2, 1863. (736.)
1. *Manihot utilissima*, var. *heterophylla*; "Mahogo;" the staple food of Zanzibar people, where some kinds can be eaten raw, boiled, fried, roasted, or in flower; not met with between the equator and 15° N., 4° 18′ S., etc. (68.)
1. *Anisonema multiflorum*; by water, 3° 15′ N. Dec., 1862.
1. *Phyllanthus niruri*, L.; by dwellings, 2° N. Oct., 1862.
1. *Cluytia lanceolata*, Forsk.; shrub by water, 1° 42′ S. Feb., 1862. (421 and 479.)
1. *Briedelia sp.*; Madi, rocky heights. Feb., 1862.
2. *B. sp.*; branches have blunt thorns, and grow level and thickly; Madi burn, 3° 15′ N. Dec., 1862.
1. *Hymenocardia Heudelotii*, Planch.; 30 in. circ. tree, with brittle wood; "M'palanyonga." 3° 15′ N. Dec., 1862. (733.)

LXXIV. CERATOPHYLLEÆ.

1. *Ceratophyllum sp.*; water plant; Nile, 2° N. Oct., 1862.

LXXV. SALICINEÆ.

1. *Salix Ægyptiaca*, L.; Gherri Pass, by edge of Nile, 16° N. March, 1863.

LXXVI. ULMACEÆ.

1. *Celtis integrifolia*; "M'Læweh;" 12 ft. girth, thickly-foliaged, handsome tree. The natives of Fipa are said to make necklaces from its seeds. 3° 30' N. Feb., 1863. (753.)

LXXVII. URTICACEÆ.

1. *Urtica dioica?* L.; 3 ft. high by borders of Lake Windermere, 1° 40' S., where its 2-ft. long tapering roots are used medicinally; at 2° N. found it by habitations growing 7 ft. high. (392 and 470.)
1. *Fleurya æstuans ?* On rock under shade of tree, 3° 15' N. Dec., 1862. (703.)
1. *Cannabis sativa*, L.; "Bhang;" grows 5 ft. high near cottage dung-heaps in the Land of the Moon, where the men whoop and scream loudly while smoking it. 4° 18' S. April, 1861. (75.)
1. *Ficus sycamorus*, L.; Sycamore fig; "M'Kooyoo;" bark-cloths are sometimes made from young trees of it; found along the whole route; also in Egypt, at Schendi. April, 1863. Yields a birdlime for the natives.
2. *F. riparia*, Hochst.; leaves rounded, and dessert-plate size. (40.)
3. *F. sp.*; 12 ft. circ.; leaves lanceolate; rich, sweet, pear-shaped, half-inch diameter fruit. Jan. and Feb., 1863. (752.)
4. *F. Kotschyana?* Miq.; "M'koo;" trunk 12 to 20 ft. circ., with huge boughs; several barks can be stripped off a single individual of this genus for bark-cloths, without injuring the tree, if the bare part be for a time wrapped round with plantain leaf, or otherwise protected, until a fresh bark has grown; this tree also affords short ropes. 5° S. to 3° 30' N. (636.)
5. *F. sp. (F. glumosœ proxime affinis sed glaber)*; "M'chæræ;" 5 ft. in girth, with reddish, globular, minute figs in leaf-axles; also a bark-cloth and rope tree. 6° S. to 3° 15' N. (689.) Birdlime gathered from its trunk.
6. *F. virgata?* Roxb.; branches erect, and very rough-surfaced leaves. 3° 15' N. Dec., 1862.
1. *Planta exogena anomala dioica* (male flowers only); woody shrub; "Boss" rock, 6° 4' S. Alt. 4068 ft. Dec. 28, 1860.

LXXVIII. ORCHIDEÆ.

1. *Lissochilus sp.*; yellow-flowering plant; by water; East Coast Range. Alt. 4700 ft. 6° 38' S.
2. *L. sp.*; 5 ft. high, with yellow flowers, and unbranched, erect stem; Karagŭé, 2° 40' S. March, 1862. (463.)
1. *Angræcum? sp.*; in fruit; found upon a *Kigelia;* leaves speckled with black; each seed-vessel has a long withered appendage attached; roots uniform, with a yellow strong string in their centre. Some natives consider these parasites a remedy for ophthalmia, by mashing them in water, and washing the whole body and eyes externally with the liquid. 3° 15' N. Dec., 1862. (716.)
1. *Ansellia sp.*; found in thick clusters on lofty-stemmed trees; M'bwiga, 7° 30' S. Oct., 1860. Alt. 1200 ft. Flowers yellow; zebra-barred inside. Uhiyow men know it by the name of "Mitoōlo," and use its jointed roots medicinally.
1. *Polystachya sp.*; growing upon Angræcum; root like a small onion; linear, 6-in. long leaves. Dec., 1862. (715.)

LXXIX. SCITAMINEÆ.

1. *Amomum sp.* (leaves and seeds). The scarlet underground fruit of Uganda, and 2⅓° N. Each is the size and shape of a small plantain; four or five of those adhere to one common short stalk, growing underground at the root of the stem, until ripe, when they push up the earth like moles. The scarlet peel and an inner white membrane are thrown away, while the pulp round the apple-like seeds is *sucked*, tasting like a lime, and said to be refreshing in fevers; roots, in joints, grow creepingly, sending up and down shoots and roots. The Waganda string the fruit into necklaces. Grows 4 ft. high, in rather dry ground, among tall grasses; frequent. May, 1862. (631.)

LXXX. MUSACEÆ.

1. *Musa sapientum*, L. (no specimen); plantain; "N'deezee." The staple food of the countries one degree on either side of the equator, acres of ground being covered with its groves. There are half a dozen varieties—the boiling, baking, drying, fruit, and wine-making sorts. Uses—a chip from the stem washes the hands, and makes the wet flesh-rubber of the Waganda; thread and lashings for loads are also taken from the stem; rain is collected in the green leaves, which can be made into an ingenious temporary pipe; the dry leaves make screen-fences and sacks to hold grain or provisions; the fruit dried (from Ugigi) is like a Normandy pippin; a variety, when green and boiled, is an excellent vegetable, while another yields a wine resembling Hock in flavor; at 2° N. they cease to be grown. (12.)

2. *M. ensete?* Bruce; one specimen looking at least 10 ft. circ. and only 5 ft. high, growing outside a plantain-grove on the equator, was fruitless and wild, with huge leaves, gigantic diameter, and quite an oddity, its stem being only twice the height of its breadth, which seems the characteristic of this plant. ' Numerous smaller ones grew among rocks at 3° 15′ N. Leaves coarser than the plantain, with midrib brick-red. Its black, irregular-shaped, glossy seed is strung into necklaces, charms, and tiaras by the Waganda; no other uses known to our men; goats seem fond of the leaves. (630 and 516.5.)

LXXXI. IRIDEÆ.

1. *Gladiolus sp.*; 2 ft. high; flowers white, with pink edges, 1° 40′ S. Alt. 5000 ft. March, 1862. (473.)

2. *G. sp.*; flowers transparent horn-color; moist ground, 5° 50′ S. Alt. 4000 ft. 1861.

3. *G. sp.*; 2½ ft. high, with yellow-tinged flowers; by fences and moist places, 5° 50′ S. 1861.

4. *G. sp.*; foot high, with bright pink flowers; grows in quantities by hedges, 5° 50′ S. 1861.

LXXXII. AMARYLLIDEÆ.

1. *Crinum sp.*; umbellate bulbous lily; flower-stalk 20 to 24 inches long, with five drooping white flowers; a line of pink purple in the centre of each petal; burn bank, 3° 15′ N. Jan., 1863. Very handsome. (742.)

1. *Narcissus? sp.*; no specimen; umbellate, bulbous; 8 inches high; flowers white, with a waxy yellow corona; its leaves, tasting of onions, cooked with mashed ground-nuts, make a delicious spinage; on sandy, moist places, about 6° S. Dec., 1860. (28.)

LXXXIII. HYPOXIDEÆ.

1. *Hypoxis sp.*; height 6 ft.; bushes of it grow where springs ooze from the rock; linear leaves, from the crown only; stem 4 to 5 ft. girth at base; the branches break like a rotten stick—vitality only showing in very centre; flowers withered; seemed purple. Dec., 1860. Alt. 4068 ft. "Boss" rock, about 6° S. (782.)

2. *H. sp.*; bulbous, with yellow flower; E. of Coast Range. Oct., 1860.

LXXXIV. PONTEDERIACEÆ.

1. *Monochoria natans*, Beauv.; aquatic plant, with blue flowers; floating leaves cordate, submerged ones linear; stagnant water in bed of stream, 3° 15′ N. Dec., 1862. (726 and 727.)

2. *M. sp.*; flowers white; leaves heart-shaped; roots purple and fibrous; grows in stagnant water and mud which has lodged on rocks, 3° 15′ N. Dec., 1862. (655.)

LXXXV. LILIACEÆ.

1. *Aloe sp.* (no specimen; from fig. and notes); 12 to 15 ft. high; leaves linear, serrated, fleshy, and from the crown only; growing upon a sandstone island, Urigi valley, about 2° S. Nov., 1861. (147.)

2. *A. sp.*; inflorescence branched, flowers scarlet, with yellow tips; leaves 3 ft. long; surface marked with indistinct white streaks; their edges sharply thorned, and the juice smelling disagreeably. The Banians of the coast cut its leaves into small pieces, soak them in lime-juice, put them in the sun, and a pickle is formed. 1° S. to 2° N., etc. (613 and 429.)

1. *Sanseviera sp.* ; small clusters of flowers grow upon the erect, branchless stem ; the long leaves yield the beautiful white ropery of Uganda ; generally found on mounds of red clay thrown up by white ants. (531.)
1. *Veltheimia sp.* ; inflorescence an erect plume ; upper bells pink, lower yellow ; appears in swamps, after the first burst of the rains. Alt. 4400 ft. Natives collect its flowers for spinage ; very good, but too honey-tasting. 6° S. and 1° N. 1860–61. (31.)
1. *Allium cepa*, L. (no specimen) ; (onion) ; cult. by Arabs only at 5° S.
1. *Scilla sp.* ; small white flowers and onion-like root. 5° 5′ S. Alt. 3600 ft.
1. *Urginea? sp.* ; scaly bulb ; stem 3 ft. high, covered with white flowers, midribs of sepals brown below ; bulb tasted nauseous and bitter. The Men of the Moon roast its leaves and stalks, and cook them as spinage ; rocky ground, 3° 15′ N. Dec., 1862. (702.)
1. *Asphodelus sp.* ; common in every marsh, 6° 4′ S. Dec., 1860.
1. *Chlorophytum sp.* ; white flowers, in swamps, 5° 40′ S. Alt. 3800 ft.
1. *Asphodelea indeterminata* ; common in bogs, 5° 50′. Alt. 4000 ft.
2. *A. indeterminata* (from fig. and notes ; no specimen ; stem 3 to 4 ft. high ; flowers green, with white edges ; leaves radical. 1° 40′ S. Feb., 1862. (419.)
1. *Gloriosa virescens*, Lindl. ; clove grove, Zanzibar, etc., and 1° 40′ S. Feb., 1862. (484.)
1. *Dracaena sp.* ; "Mpopo M'weeto ;" *i. e.*, wild beetul, used as fences, growing 10 ft. high, with clusters of one-seeded berries from tips of branches ; no resemblance to beetul palm seen at Zanzibar. 2° N. Nov., 1862. (612.)
1. *Asparagus sp.* ; 4 to 5 ft. high ; very elegant, with white flowers, attractive to bees ; thorned branches. Sore eyes are said to be cured by chewing its roots with salt, and squirting the liquid into the eyes. 7° S., and in every forest ; a variety (or the same?) climbs up trees with its opposite branches. (38.)
1. *Smilax Kraussiana*, Meisn. ; "M'kolol'a ;" 3 to 4 ft. high, growing in patches in open dry forest, clinging to any support by its pair of tendrils ; stem is thorned, and dies every season ; dried leaves have a rich flavor of prunes ; roots, deeply imbedded, are stem-like, with knots showing the growth of each year. Wanyamuézi use its roots medicinally. Sept., 1861, and 3° 15′ N., Dec., 1862. (207 and 739.5.)

LXXXVI. DIOSCOREACEÆ.

1. *Dioscorea sp.* ; "Veeazee-koo ;" yam ; grown here and there on mounds ; leaves opposite, with seven reticulated veins ; stem has occasional green stumpy thorns upon it. 5° S. to 2° N. (526.)
2. *D. bulbifera*, L. ; climber, with alternate leaves, having reticulated veins, and thornless stem ; bulbs Brazil-nut size and shape ; cutting like a potato when unripe, and eating pleasantly boiled. Plantain-groves, 2° N. (151¾, and P. S. 526.)

LXXXVII. COMMELYNACEÆ.

1. *Commelyna sp.* ; sky-blue flowers ; spinage made from its leaves. Zanzibar, 1860.
2. *C. sp.* ; 15 in. high, with chocolate-colored flowers, on black soil, 5° 5′ S. Alt. 3600 ft.
3. *C. latifolia*, Hochst. (from fig. and notes ; no specimen) ; flowers blue, anthers yellow ; potherb ; every where on rich soil near huts. (491.)
1. *Cyanotis sp.* (from fig. and notes ; no specimen) ; common in moist dips of forests. (455.)
2. *C. Abyssinica*, A. Rich. 2½° N. Nov., 1862.
3. *C. longifolia*, Benth. 6° S. Alt. 3800 ft.
1. *Aneilema sp.* ; near moist sandy soil. 5° S. to 4° 18′ S. (165.)
2. *A. sp.* ; in swamps. 6° S. Alt. 3800 ft.
1. *Dithyrocarpus sp.* ; lilac-colored flowers ; common in bogs, 2½° N. Nov., 1862.

LXXXVIII. JUNCACEÆ.

1. *Flagellaria Indica*, L. ; stem inch circ. ; climbing reed ; vies in height with trees, leaf-tips having tendrils. Mgæta River, 7° 20′ S. 1860.

LXXXIX. HYDROCHARIDEÆ.

1. *Ottelia sp.* ; water-plant, with white flower just above water. 2½° N. Nile, Nov., 10, 1862. (620–5.)

2. *O. sp.* ; water-plant with frilled-edged, yard-long leaves; yellow flowers, having rather flattened stalks, much roughed, or feeling like a file. Nile, 14½° N. March 19, 1863. (770.5.)

3. *O. sp.* ; in stagnant water; flowers yellow; leaves 10 in. long; section of seed-vessel shows six spiral cells. 3° 15′ N. Dec., 1862. (696.)

1. *Hydrilla dentata?* (leaves only); grows nearly submerged, Nile, 2° N. Nov., 1862.

1. *Vallisneria sp.* ; minute water-plant; propagates from suckers. Nile edges, 14½° N. March, 1863.

XC. ALISMACEÆ.

1. *Sagittaria obtusifolia*, Roxb.; water-plant. Nile, 4° 55′ N. Feb. 22, 1863. (767.)

XCI. NAIADEÆ.

1. *Aponogeton sp.* ; grows submerged; flowers alone above water; in stagnant water collected on rocks, Ukidi forests, 2½° N. Nov., 1862.

2. *A. sp.* ; marsh-plant, with bright purple flowers, generally two on a stalk. 5° 45′ S. Alt. 4377 ft. Jan. 24, 1863.

1. *Potamogeton lucens?* L. Nile, 2° N. Nov., 1862.

XCII. ARACEÆ.

1. *Colocasia antiquorum;* "Myoog'wah;" a few plants generally round or outside the huts of Uganda and Unyoro; also cultivated on the bank of a stream at 2° S.; petioles and leaves make a potherb; Waganda use it for sore throat. (149.)

1. *Auchomanes Hookeri?* Schott; "Yal'wah;" bulb 30 in. circumference; one erect 3 ft. high-feathered stem, with curving-down thorns. Wanyamúézi eat its bulb boiled. 3° 15′ N. Dec., 1862. (712.)

1. *Amorphophallus? sp.* ; leaf only; 1 ft. high; not in flower. 2½° N. Nov., 1862.

1. *Richardia? sp.* ; leaf only; Madi bog; rare. Dec., 1862.

1. *Pistia stratiotes*, L.; in the beginning of March the Nile and Bahr Giraffe, in flood, carry down these floating rosettes in great quantities to about 13° N., beyond which scarcely one is visible; Lake Windermere and 2° N. Nov., 1862.

XCIII. PALMÆ.

1. *Phœnix sp.* ; wild date; clusters of them growing on the hill-sides, 30 and 40 ft. high, with pendent bunches of Indian red fruit; not edible; no uses. Equator and 1° 40′ S. The edible date is unknown in the countries traversed—*i. e.*, from 8° S. to 5° N.

1. *Cucos nucifera*, L. ; cocoa-nut-tree; very abundant at Zanzibar; a few on the main coast; and none in the interior; "M'nazee."

1. *Borassus Æthiopicus*, Mart. ; Deleb palm; "M'voomo;" young ones are called "Meelalla;" at 4° 18′ S.; one bare log measured 37½ ft. long, and greatest circumference 9 ft. 3 in.; the leaves furnished thatch, rope, sieves, fences, firewood, and flageolet reeds; Wanyamúézi eat the roots boiled in famines; a sweet insipid toddy is extracted; very few about the equator; plentiful in the Shillook country, 11° N., where the natives make its leaves into beautiful strong white baskets and mats for the markets on the Nile. (71.)

1. *Hyphœne Thebaica*, Mart. ; Doom palm; "Mohamma;" the people of Berber (18° N.), etc., make its leaves into coarse rope, and its trunk into beams and posts; male trees very handsomely foligaed; female naked as poles, both often branching three times; fruit eaten by donkeys as well as men; a few on the E. coast; none in the interior; first observed Feb. 28, 1863, at 6° N., where it begins to be plentiful.

2. *H. n. sp.* ; "Mizanza;" 30 ft. high; never branching; leaves much resembling the doom, but less spreading; fruit (in immense clusters, depending over the fronds that have withered) perfect ellipses, 1¼ inches long, having a shining, deep purple, brittle skin inclosing the nut, covered with a stringy, dry, yellow substance; not edible; male organs similar to, but longer than, the doom; our camel-drivers collected its green leaves to make shackles for their camels, as the fibre does not chafe the skin like the doom; one of our men had seen it growing in Mambweh, 8° or 9° S. lat. They were observed to grow in desolate valleys of desert sand, walled in with crags of slate, about 21° N. May 9, 1863. (777.)

XCIV. GRAMINEÆ.

1. *Oryza sativa*, L. ; rice; not cultivated by the natives in the interior; Arabs grow it for their own consumption, from 7° 27′ S. to 4° 18′ S. ; a small black caterpillar, appearing with the first burst of rains, is often very injurious to the young plants; irrigation was not observed.

1. *Zea mays*, L.; Indian corn; grown in ridges; plentiful from 7° 20′ to 4° S. ; but very rare as the equator is approached; and quite unknown beyond it northward to 5° N.

1. *Perotis latifolia*, Ait. ; 3 ft. high, with rich purple awns. Uganda plantain-groves, July, 1862. (527.)

1. *Andropogon sorghum;* Caffre corn; "Jowar;" "M'tama;" or "Doora;" more or less procurable along the whole route; the bitter réd variety most frequently grown; without it the African could neither have his beer nor his stirabout. This grain is used by the Waganda to assist in fermenting their plantain wine.

2. *A. eucomis*, Nees; cottony flower; marsh, 5° S. Alt. 3960 ft.

3. *A. sp.* (§ *Gymnandropogon*); stigmas rusty; stalk a pink purple; by moisture. Alt. 3600 ft. Natives in famines eat its millet. 5° 5′ S.

4. *A. sp. paniculata;* 2 ft. high. 1° 40′ S. March, 1862. (486.)

1. *Saccharum officinarum*, L. ; sugar-cane; seen only on and about the equator; the red-stalked variety most frequent; they make no farther use of it than eating the cane.

2. *S. ? sp.* (no flowers); 4 to 5 ft. high; the grass used for thatch in Uganda and Unyoro; equator, and 2° N.

1. *Cymbopogon finitimus*, Hochst. ; 6 to 7 ft. high; covering the northern sporting grounds of Uganda, 1° N. July 17, 1862. (525.)

2. *C. cymbarius*, var. ; 6 ft. high; growing richly under the shade of trees on the luxuriant rocky heights of Gani, 3° N. Dec., 1862.

3. *C. hirtus;* Nile banks, about 5° N. March, 1863.

1. *Anthistiria sp.* ; on dry sandy soil, near Tura nullah, 5° 26′ S. Alt. 3800 ft.

2. *A. imberbis*, Retz. ; 2 to 2½ ft. high; the grass that clothes and waves like corn on the treeless hills of Karagūé. Alt. 5000 to 5500 ft. Dec., 1861. Cattle are never grazed upon it. (417.)

3. *A. ciliata*, Retz. ; 2½ ft. high; growing under trees in rich low ground with great luxuriance; in famines the natives eat its grain. 5° 5′ S. Alt. 3600 ft.

1. *Pogonatherum ? sp.* (leaves only); a black spur ergot grows in its stems when in dry ground; this, or a variety, grows submerged in a perfect network, which supports a man or water boc as they plunge through it.

1. *Erianthus aureus ?* Nees; stigmas rust-colored; swamps, 5° S. Alt. 3600 ft.

1. *Vossia procera*, Griff. ; back-waters of the Nile, Nov., 1862.

1. *Manisurus granularis*, L. ; weed. 2° N. Nov., 1862.

1. *Helopus annulatus*, Nees; stigmas black. 5° 5′ S. Alt. 3600 ft.

1. *Digitaria sanguinalis*, L. ; waste grounds, Uganda. July, 1862.

2. *D. mutica ?* Forsk. ; creeping grass; stems a foot high branch from immediately above the rootlets; donkeys seek for and devour it greedily; looks a sweet grass. 1° 40′ S. March, 1862. (477.)

1. *Panicum sp.* (near *P. brizanthum*, Hochst.); grows about cult., 1° 40′ S. March, 1862. (488.)

2. *P. sp.* (near *P. brizanthum*, Hochst.); 3 feet high; 2° N., on plateaux. Nov., 1862.

3. *P. sp.* ; 3 feet high. 4° 18′ S. Alt. 3800 ft. March, 1861. (167.)

4. *P. sp.* ; grows under trees, 1° 40′ S. Dec., 1861. (400.)

5. *P. sp.* ; very handsome; 6 to 8 ft. high; near river bank; two of its dark panicles very commonly grow from one stem. 5° S. 1861.

1. *Oplismenus colonus*, L. ; Nile bank, 16° N. April, 1863.

2. *O. crus Galli*, L. ; grows along with marsh plants, its stem lying 3 or 4 feet on the ground, and then grows 6 feet high; diminutive specimens were observed to have their leaves zebra-marked (*i. e.*, with black bars at ¾-inch intervals), and pink edges; uncommon; in boggy places, 5° 16′ S., 5° 5′ S. Aug., 1862. (580.)

1. *Tricholœna sp.;* 3 feet high; by pathways; flowers handsome, and rich pink. 5° S. Alt. 3960 ft.

1. *Penicillaria spicata*, "Bajra;" seen only near the coast; not cult. in the interior.

1. *Setaria verticillata*, Beauv. ; nasty weed growing near huts, and sticking to one's clothes; cattle are said to die from eating it. (476.)

2. *S. glauca*, Beauv. ; thinly spread over the Unyanyembé forests in low ground ; brilliant golden flowers.

3. *S. aurea*, Hochst. ; by path ; liable to small round fungi, the dust of which is eaten by the natives. 2° N. Nov., 1862.

1. *Pennisetum polystachyum*, Schott ; E. Coast Range. Oct., 1860.

2. *P. Benthami*, Steud. ; "Maweengo-weengo;" 10 ft. high reed, with fox-brush flower ; by water; equator, 3° N., etc. The tall white fences round the palace, etc., and interiors of all Uganda houses, are of this reed; a strip from its bark answers all the purposes of a knife in cutting meat up; the king's victims are, we were told, cut to pieces with it. (713.)

1. *Stipa n. sp.* ; the jungle-grass about 3° 10′ N. Dec., 1862.

1. *Aristida n. sp.* ; 3 ft. high, with very elegant panicle, 4° 18′ S. May, 1861. Near cult. (164.)

1. *Sporobolus elongatus*, R. Br. ; 3 to 4 ft. high, in grassy jungles of 1° 40′ to 2° N. ; silvery-gray, span long, close panicle. (482 and 563.)

2. *S. sp.* ; boggy ground, 5° S.

1. *Arundo phragmites*, L. ; "Matætæ ;" 8 ft. high. From 4° 55′ N. to the Bahr-el Gazal (9° N.), the banks of the Nile to the horizon are a sea of this reed; at 28° N. it is diminutive, and creeps along the sand. The Waganda on the equator make their flutes from it; said to grow arm-thickness at Lake N'yassa, where it is used in making huts. (576 and 780.)

1. *Cynodon dactylon*, Pers. ; Indian Dúb grass; cattle love it; natives at 2° N. make bedding or lay their floors with it. 5° S. to 2° N. Nov.,1862.

1. *Dactyloctenium Ægyptiacum ;* grows most abundantly on waste ground, also on the flat roofs of the Arabs' houses in Unyanyembé ; natives gather the ears, dry them in the sun, beat out the grain on the rocks, grind and make stirabout of it. 5° S., etc. Feb., 1861. (10.)

1. *Microchloa setacea*, R. Br. ; stigma white; light soil, near water, 5° 5′ S.

1. *Chloris meccana*, Hochst. ; 3 to 4 ft. high ; plantain-groves, equator. July, 1862. (528.)

2. *C. sp.* ; common, by paths, 2° N. Nov., 1862.

1. *Eleusine coracana*, Gaert. ; Murwa; "oolézee ;" cult. every where in the route, sometimes in ridges, and at others broadcast; its flour, if soaked for a night in water, makes very fair unleavened cakes; a coarse beer, tasting pleasantly bitter, is made from its grain, mixed with that of doora, *i. e.*, sorghum ; natives also make stirabout of it; plantain wine fermented by it has an extra aroma imparted to it.

2. *E. Indica*, L. ; grows in tufts generally ; 2 ft. high ; by fields. As grazing for cattle the natives esteem it (though tough) more than any other species. (485.)

1. *Eragrostis megastachya*, Koch. ; in sesamum fields, 2° N., and also at 16° N. April, 1863. (582½.)

2. *E. sp.* ; right bank Nile, 16° N. April, 1863.

3. *E. ? n. sp.* ; boggy ground, 5° S. 1861.

4. *E. ? n. sp.* ; fine plant; in tufts by pathway, 2° N. Aug., 1862.

5. *E. cynosuroides*, Retz ; 3 or 4 ft. high, lining the sandy banks of the Nile; 16° to 17° N., where it is made into very coarse rope. April, 1863. (774–7.)

1. *Bambusa sp.* ; bamboo; 15 to 20 ft. high; 2 to 3 in. in circ., in thick clumps, Usagara Hills, 6½°, and not again till 3° 15′ N., where the natives construct their houses, baskets, bows, and spear-handles of it; sides of rocky streams. (37 and 719. 5.)

1. *Triticum sativum*, L. ; wheat; never met with from Zanzibar to 15½° N. (the Soudan), where it is cult. by irrigation.

XCV. CYPERACEÆ.

1. *Cyperus articulatus*, L. ; Nile edges, 2° N. Nov.,1862.

2. *C. rotundus*, L. ; 5° 6′ S. Alt. 3800 ft.

3. *C. sp.* (same from Barter); Rush; Nile edges, 2° N. Nov., 1862.

4. *C. squarrosus*, Rottb. ; on rocky heights, 3° 15′ N. Dec.,1862.

5. *C. aristatus*, Rottb. ; diminutive. 5° S., 1860; and 2° N. 1862.

6. *C. pulvinatus*, Nees ; common; in tufts; marshes, 2° N. Sept., 1862.

7. *C. mucronatus*, Rottb. ; the only vegetation within arm's-length of the bubbling from a hot spring (too hot for the hand), abundant all round it; near Zungomé-ro, 3° 33′ S.

8. *Cyperus difformis*, L. ; moist-ground ; hill-sides, 3° 15′ N. Dec., 1862.
9. *C. flavescens*, L. ; in tufts ; low rocky ground, 3° 15′ N. Dec., 1862.
10. *C. alopecuroides*, Rottb. ; "Magädee ;" 8 ft. high ; useful as thatch ; Little Windermere, 1° 40′ S. March, 1862. (480.)
11. *C. longus*, L. ; grows on cataract rocks at Gherri, 16° N., etc. ; also on the rocky edges of the R. Asŭa, 3° 40′ N. ; camels devour it greedily on arriving from the Nubian desert. (774–6.)
12. *C. denudatus*, L. 5° S. Alt. 3960 ft. Stigmas white, stem triangular.
13. *C. spherocephalus*, Vahl. ; golden-yellow flower. 6° S. Alt. 4488 ft. Jan. 1, 1861.
14. *C. lanceus*, Thunb. ; deep brown flowers. 6° S. Jan. 1, 1861.
15. *C. sp.* ; on sand, near water, 5° 6′ S. Alt. 3800 ft.
1. *Papyrus antiquorum* ; morasses, Zanzibar Island. The shallow borders of Lakes Victoria and Windermere are thickets of this rush, growing to 15 ft. high. Nile banks, 4° 56′ N. Not so much of it farther north. Uses—leaves eaten by water boc, and made into soft bedding at 1° 40′ S. Stem made into screens ; strips from the bark make beautiful fish-cruives ; and at Unyoro, a bundle of pith, cut into long strips, forms a wrapper or covers a jar. (386.)
1. *Mariscus umbellatus*, Vahl. ; hill-top. Alt. 5500 ft. 1° 40′ S. Dec., 1861. (412.)
2. *M. sp.* ; 2 ft. high ; E. Coast Range. Oct., 1860.
1. *Kyllingia sp.* ; flower white, round hill-top, by water. Dec., 1861. (410.)
2. *K. alba?* Nees. Zanzibar ; and 2° N., by moist ground. Nov., 1862.
3. *K. macrocephala?* "Keelōlo," 18 inches high ; sweetly perfumed ; roots purple ; the latter are pounded by Wanyamŭézi women, and rubbed on their bodies as a scent ; by rocky burn, 3° 15′ N. Dec. 15, 1862. (693.)
4. *K. aurea*, Nees ; common in moist woods, 6° 4′ S. Alt. 4068 ft. Dec., 1860.
1. *Fuirena umbellata?* Rottb. ; "Keekal'a." 3 ft. long ; five-sided, sharp-edged ; lodging plant on sandy edges of burn. Madi, Dec. 21, 1862. Root imbedded a foot deep. Natives extract salt from its ashes ; flowers whorl up the stem. (721.)
2. *F. pubescens*, Kunth. ; 1 ft. high. 6° S. Jan. 1, 1862.
3. *F. sp.* ; in tufts on swamps, 3° 15′ N. Dec., 1862.
1. *Isolepis saviana?* diminutive plant ; marshes, 2° N. Sept., 1862.
1. *Trichelostylis sp.* 4° 18′ S. April, 1861. (168.)
2. *T. sp.* ; 2 ft. high ; stigmas rust-colored. 4° 18′ and 5° 55′ S. Alt. 3700 ft.
1. *Abilgaardia monostachya*, Vahl. ; grassy plateaux, 2° N. Nov., 1862.
2. *A. pilosa*, Nees ; forest ; near 5° S.
1. *Scleria sp.* ; grows 7 ft. high in an erect bush, on burn side, 3° 15′ N. Fruit resembling diminutive acorns ; leaves sharp-edged. Jan., 1863.
2. *S. sp.* ; 1 ft. high ; marshes, 2° N. Aug., 1862.
3. *S. sp.* ; 6 in. high ; growing in tufts on soil the debris of rock ; seeds white, three-cornered and milky ; stem three-cornered ; fibrous roots are red-purple ; whole plant delicately scented. Dec., 1862. (668.)
1. *Diplacrum caricinum*, R. Br. ; very diminutive ; sandy soil. Dec., 1862.
1. *Antrolepis*, Welw. n. g. sp. n. ; 4 to 9 in. high ; growing like white daisies in rather moist places. Alt. 3900 ft. 5° 26′ S. Uncommon.
1. *Lipocarpha argentea*, R. Br. ; in tufts on moist ground ; below Madi rocks. (684.)

XCVI. FILICES.

1. *Asplenium furcatum*, L. 3° 15′ N. Dec., 1862.
1. *Actiniopteris radiata*, B. Jan. 11, 1861.
1. *Nephrodium propinquum*, Br. Nov., 1862.
1. *Nephrolepis tuberosa*, Pr. 3° 15′ N. Dec., 1862.
1. *Phymatodes vulgaris*, Pr. (simple frond). Zanzibar.
   P. vulgaris (pinnate frond). Zanzibar.
1. *Ceratopteris thalictroides*, Bury, in bog, Madi. Dec., 1862.
1. *Marsilia quadrifolia*, L. Nile. March 9, 1863.
1. *Lycopodium rupestre*, L. Madi. Nov., 1862.

NOTES ON OTHER PLANTS PARTLY FROM NATIVE INFORMATION.

M'bango (Kisŭahili) ; hard, heavy wood, on logs of which the bark cloths of Unyoro are beaten. (107.)

M'cherengeh (Kis.); the Wanyambo make their milk-pots from this wood, as it smells sweetly. (109.)

Chenjha (Kis.); M'Keendah (Kinyoro); (seeds only) 10 ft. circ. tree; one to three stoned edible fruit. (93.)

M'deeree (Kin.); natives cure fever from a decoction of its fibrous roots. (116.1.)

Ktannee (Kis.); its fibre made into rope. (5.)

M'Kōma (Kin.); 12 ft. circ.; black-hearted wood; made into bows, etc. (131.)

"M'Koonoongo" (Kis.); 6 ft. circ., with black, angry thorn; incised bar smells strongly of citron; rose-colored wood, used as railings, and thought most endurable; tooth-scrubbers, which induce saliva, and the steam from the boiled seeds scents clothes; its bows are esteemed, and its powdered bark yields a scarlet dye. (98, etc.)

Miloombo (Kis.); the most common of all the bark-cloth trees.

Meeleendee meela (Kis.); M'Songo (Kin.); wood made into drum-sticks and harmonicons. (120, etc.)

Moowalé (Kis.); palm, yielding the most beautiful, strong, soft fibre, made into guitar-strings, cloths, used for stringing beads, and called "ootembweh." (70.)

Mizzizeema (Unyoro); made into canoes, 45 feet long. (502.)

M'nyameet'a (Karagúé); fruit-tree; three stones in each fruit. (428.)

M'pembæzoo (Kis.); roots used as purgatives. 4° S. (112.)

M'talawanda (Kis.); walnut-colored wood; fruit edible; gun-stocks, also long handdrums of Karagúé made of it. 4° to 2° N. Large yellow deciduous flowers. (660.1.)

M'tatee (Kin.); Wanyamúézi forest tree; 12 ft. circ., with cedar-colored wood, and small edible fruit; first-rate bows. (102.)

M'teessa (Uganda); 40 to 50 ft. high; unbranched stem and not a palm. Uganda dells. (518.)

M'toondoo; Wanyamúézi forests; 12 ft. circ. Uses—drums, beams, troughs, etc., and bark made into vats for grain, planks, and rope; resembles the "Miombo;" might camp half a regiment under it; fruit flat-marble size and shape; very pleasant-tasting fig. (5 and 661.)

M'toom'wew; an ash-stick-like wood, growing in the Fipa district; its pure white kernels are worn as beads.

Uranga (Kis.); arrowroot-like, herbaceous plant, grown in Usagara; leaf, petiole, and root all eaten. (16.)

M'Vooleh (Kis.); uses—immense canoes and large purposes. (512.)

M'Yokka Yokka; an 18 ft. high tree; a decoction from the bark of its root and stem is red, tastes like quinine, and is used medicinally. (115.1.)

Yoomboo (Kis.); a tuber, resembling and tasting like Jerusalem artichokes; cult. 4° 18' S. and 1° S. (86.)

M'yézi (Kin.); palm, at Ugigi, from which an oil is extracted. (719.)

Crowfoot-shaped, straw-colored, 18 inch high vessel, with numerous arms, and centre only racket-ball size; only one found blowing about in the forest. 3½° S. (390.)

Large, handsome, densely-foliaged, sombre tree, with deep green, simple leaves, whose yellow, stoned fruit resembles in shape and taste the Loquat of India, but is smaller. Found only about the equator. (511.)

M'pembo; 12 feet in girth, with simple elliptical leaves; fruit rough, russet-brown, peach-size, tasting insipidly, with a large stone; uses—canoes, drums, etc. 7° S. 13th Nov., 1860. (2.)

Mineenga, or moosimbatee (leaf only). Leaf unequally pinnate; perhaps Leguminosæ; 12 to 20 ft. in girth; handsome-foliaged, clean-looking tree, giving out a blood-red sticky juice on incision. Uses—grain-mortars, drums, spurtles, pipebowls. The fruit mashed is considered a remedy for cough. Wood is impervious to insects, smells pleasantly, and is of a rosewood color. 4° S. and 3° 15' N. 1862-3. (33 and 686.5.)

Mosho (leaves only). Tree with simple opposite leaves. Bark can be crumbled off with the nail. Fruit, not edible, said to be one-stoned and scarlet. The roots burnt are used for fumigating wooden milk-pots—a thick, sticky, dark gum, coming off yellow on the fingers, lies under the bark; Madi rocks, 3° 15' N. 1863. (741.)

J. A. GRANT, *Captain Bengal Army.*

NOTE ON CAPTAIN GRANT'S COLLECTION OF PLANTS.

By Dr. T. THOMSON, F.R.S.

CAPTAIN GRANT having, on his return from Africa, presented his collection to the Hookerian Herbarium, the determination of the specimens was begun by Mr. Black, the curator, and was made over by him to me when he was unfortunately obliged to give it up from ill health. The collection consists of about 750 species, represented for the most part by single good specimens, carefully ticketed, with numbers attached referring to a note-book in which all essential points of habit and uses are entered.

The catalogue is based on a comparison of the specimens with the Hookerian Herbarium, and is necessarily imperfect in the present state of our knowledge of the African flora. Large collections have of late years been made in Eastern Africa by Kirk and Meller of Dr. Livingstone's expedition, and in Western Africa by Baikie, Barter, and Mann; but they are still, for the most part, undescribed. A general flora of Tropical Africa is, however, I believe, contemplated by government, on the recommendation of Sir W. Hooker.

For the present, a few general observations are all that can be made on this interesting collection. It consists in all, as already mentioned, of 750 species, collected between Zanzibar and the southern border of Egypt. Of these, 420 belong to known species, and this number might, no doubt, be increased to 450 by more careful research. We may, therefore, say that three fifths (perhaps even two thirds) of the whole are published species. Of these, two thirds at least, on a rough estimate, have been collected by previous travelers, so that not more than 80 or 100 species are quite new. Even this is probably an overestimate.

Leaving out of consideration the Egyptian plants, which were only met with at or near the north tropic, a general survey of the collection shows the great uniformity of tropical African vegetation. The small number of plants indicates a poor flora, and therefore probably a comparatively dry climate. We find in it a great number of widely-diffused tropical weeds, most of them common to India and Africa. The cultivated plants, which, it will be seen, have been carefully collected or noted, are also generally diffused.

The new plants belong, for the most part, to African genera; but there are two (*Harrisonia* and *Soymida*) which were previously only known as Indian. The *Umbelliferæ*, which are very remarkable, belong to Abyssinian types. Several Cape genera are represented, as, for instance, *Arctotis* and *Cullumia*, among thistles; *Hebenstreitia, Protea, Gnidia*. The *Melastomaceæ*, and many of the *Labiatæ*, recall the Madagascar flora; and in the *Anona, Lophira,* and *Landolphia* we have marked West African forms.

Besides a very curious new genus of *Leguminosæ*, and another of *Cyperaceæ*, which had already been sent to England by Kirk and Welwitsch, there are seemingly new and remarkable genera of *Amarantaceæ, Scrophulariaceæ, Labiatæ,* and *Asphodeleæ*, and a very curious plant, unfortunately in imperfect condition, of which the order is undeterminable without better materials.

THE END.

A CATALOG OF SELECTED
DOVER BOOKS
IN ALL FIELDS OF INTEREST

A CATALOG OF SELECTED DOVER
BOOKS IN ALL FIELDS OF INTEREST

CONCERNING THE SPIRITUAL IN ART, Wassily Kandinsky. Pioneering work by father of abstract art. Thoughts on color theory, nature of art. Analysis of earlier masters. 12 illustrations. 80pp. of text. 5⅜ × 8½. 23411-8 Pa. $3.95

ANIMALS: 1,419 Copyright-Free Illustrations of Mammals, Birds, Fish, Insects, etc., Jim Harter (ed.). Clear wood engravings present, in extremely lifelike poses, over 1,000 species of animals. One of the most extensive pictorial sourcebooks of its kind. Captions. Index. 284pp. 9 × 12. 23766-4 Pa. $12.95

CELTIC ART: The Methods of Construction, George Bain. Simple geometric techniques for making Celtic interlacements, spirals, Kells-type initials, animals, humans, etc. Over 500 illustrations. 160pp. 9 × 12. (USO) 22923-8 Pa. $9.95

AN ATLAS OF ANATOMY FOR ARTISTS, Fritz Schider. Most thorough reference work on art anatomy in the world. Hundreds of illustrations, including selections from works by Vesalius, Leonardo, Goya, Ingres, Michelangelo, others. 593 illustrations. 192pp. 7⅛ × 10¼. 20241-0 Pa. $9.95

CELTIC HAND STROKE-BY-STROKE (Irish Half-Uncial from "The Book of Kells"): An Arthur Baker Calligraphy Manual, Arthur Baker. Complete guide to creating each letter of the alphabet in distinctive Celtic manner. Covers hand position, strokes, pens, inks, paper, more. Illustrated. 48pp. 8¼ × 11.
24336-2 Pa. $3.95

EASY ORIGAMI, John Montroll. Charming collection of 32 projects (hat, cup, pelican, piano, swan, many more) specially designed for the novice origami hobbyist. Clearly illustrated easy-to-follow instructions insure that even beginning papercrafters will achieve successful results. 48pp. 8¼ × 11. 27298-2 Pa. $2.95

THE COMPLETE BOOK OF BIRDHOUSE CONSTRUCTION FOR WOOD-WORKERS, Scott D. Campbell. Detailed instructions, illustrations, tables. Also data on bird habitat and instinct patterns. Bibliography. 3 tables. 63 illustrations in 15 figures. 48pp. 5¼ × 8½. 24407-5 Pa. $1.95

BLOOMINGDALE'S ILLUSTRATED 1886 CATALOG: Fashions, Dry Goods and Housewares, Bloomingdale Brothers. Famed merchants' extremely rare catalog depicting about 1,700 products: clothing, housewares, firearms, dry goods, jewelry, more. Invaluable for dating, identifying vintage items. Also, copyright-free graphics for artists, designers. Co-published with Henry Ford Museum & Greenfield Village. 160pp. 8¼ × 11. 25780-0 Pa. $9.95

HISTORIC COSTUME IN PICTURES, Braun & Schneider. Over 1,450 costumed figures in clearly detailed engravings—from dawn of civilization to end of 19th century. Captions. Many folk costumes. 256pp. 8⅜ × 11¾. 23150-X Pa. $11.95

CATALOG OF DOVER BOOKS

STICKLEY CRAFTSMAN FURNITURE CATALOGS, Gustav Stickley and L. & J. G. Stickley. Beautiful, functional furniture in two authentic catalogs from 1910. 594 illustrations, including 277 photos, show settles, rockers, armchairs, reclining chairs, bookcases, desks, tables. 183pp. 6½ × 9¼. 23838-5 Pa. $9.95

AMERICAN LOCOMOTIVES IN HISTORIC PHOTOGRAPHS: 1858 to 1949, Ron Ziel (ed.). A rare collection of 126 meticulously detailed official photographs, called "builder portraits," of American locomotives that majestically chronicle the rise of steam locomotive power in America. Introduction. Detailed captions. xi + 129pp. 9 × 12. 27393-8 Pa. $12.95

AMERICA'S LIGHTHOUSES: An Illustrated History, Francis Ross Holland, Jr. Delightfully written, profusely illustrated fact-filled survey of over 200 American lighthouses since 1716. History, anecdotes, technological advances, more. 240pp. 8 × 10¾. 25576-X Pa. $11.95

TOWARDS A NEW ARCHITECTURE, Le Corbusier. Pioneering manifesto by founder of "International School." Technical and aesthetic theories, views of industry, economics, relation of form to function, "mass-production split" and much more. Profusely illustrated. 320pp. 6⅛ × 9¼. (USO) 25023-7 Pa. $9.95

HOW THE OTHER HALF LIVES, Jacob Riis. Famous journalistic record, exposing poverty and degradation of New York slums around 1900, by major social reformer. 100 striking and influential photographs. 233pp. 10 × 7⅞.
22012-5 Pa $10.95

FRUIT KEY AND TWIG KEY TO TREES AND SHRUBS, William M. Harlow. One of the handiest and most widely used identification aids. Fruit key covers 120 deciduous and evergreen species; twig key 160 deciduous species. Easily used. Over 300 photographs. 126pp. 5⅜ × 8½. 20511-8 Pa. $3.95

COMMON BIRD SONGS, Dr. Donald J. Borror. Songs of 60 most common U.S. birds: robins, sparrows, cardinals, bluejays, finches, more—arranged in order of increasing complexity. Up to 9 variations of songs of each species.
Cassette and manual 99911-4 $8.95

ORCHIDS AS HOUSE PLANTS, Rebecca Tyson Northen. Grow cattleyas and many other kinds of orchids—in a window, in a case, or under artificial light. 63 illustrations. 148pp. 5⅜ × 8½. 23261-1 Pa. $4.95

MONSTER MAZES, Dave Phillips. Masterful mazes at four levels of difficulty. Avoid deadly perils and evil creatures to find magical treasures. Solutions for all 32 exciting illustrated puzzles. 48pp. 8¼ × 11. 26005-4 Pa. $2.95

MOZART'S DON GIOVANNI (DOVER OPERA LIBRETTO SERIES), Wolfgang Amadeus Mozart. Introduced and translated by Ellen H. Bleiler. Standard Italian libretto, with complete English translation. Convenient and thoroughly portable—an ideal companion for reading along with a recording or the performance itself. Introduction. List of characters. Plot summary. 121pp. 5¼ × 8½.
24944-1 Pa. $2.95

TECHNICAL MANUAL AND DICTIONARY OF CLASSICAL BALLET, Gail Grant. Defines, explains, comments on steps, movements, poses and concepts. 15-page pictorial section. Basic book for student, viewer. 127pp. 5⅜ × 8½.
21843-0 Pa. $4.95

BRASS INSTRUMENTS: Their History and Development, Anthony Baines. Authoritative, updated survey of the evolution of trumpets, trombones, bugles, cornets, French horns, tubas and other brass wind instruments. Over 140 illustrations and 48 music examples. Corrected and updated by author. New preface. Bibliography. 320pp. 5⅜ × 8½. 27574-4 Pa. $9.95

HOLLYWOOD GLAMOR PORTRAITS, John Kobal (ed.). 145 photos from 1926–49. Harlow, Gable, Bogart, Bacall; 94 stars in all. Full background on photographers, technical aspects. 160pp. 8⅜ × 11¼. 23352-9 Pa. $11.95

MAX AND MORITZ, Wilhelm Busch. Great humor classic in both German and English. Also 10 other works: "Cat and Mouse," "Plisch and Plumm," etc. 216pp. 5⅜ × 8½. 20181-3 Pa. $5.95

THE RAVEN AND OTHER FAVORITE POEMS, Edgar Allan Poe. Over 40 of the author's most memorable poems: "The Bells," "Ulalume," "Israfel," "To Helen," "The Conqueror Worm," "Eldorado," "Annabel Lee," many more. Alphabetic lists of titles and first lines. 64pp. 5³⁄₁₆ × 8¼. 26685-0 Pa. $1.00

SEVEN SCIENCE FICTION NOVELS, H. G. Wells. The standard collection of the great novels. Complete, unabridged. First Men in the Moon, Island of Dr. Moreau, War of the Worlds, Food of the Gods, Invisible Man, Time Machine, In the Days of the Comet. Total of 1,015pp. 5⅜ × 8½. (USO) 20264-X Clothbd. $29.95

AMULETS AND SUPERSTITIONS, E. A. Wallis Budge. Comprehensive discourse on origin, powers of amulets in many ancient cultures: Arab, Persian, Babylonian, Assyrian, Egyptian, Gnostic, Hebrew, Phoenician, Syriac, etc. Covers cross, swastika, crucifix, seals, rings, stones, etc. 584pp. 5⅜ × 8½. 23573-4 Pa. $12.95

RUSSIAN STORIES/PYCCKNE PACCKA3bl: A Dual-Language Book, edited by Gleb Struve. Twelve tales by such masters as Chekhov, Tolstoy, Dostoevsky, Pushkin, others. Excellent word-for-word English translations on facing pages, plus teaching and study aids, Russian/English vocabulary, biographical/critical introductions, more. 416pp. 5⅜ × 8½. 26244-8 Pa. $8.95

PHILADELPHIA THEN AND NOW: 60 Sites Photographed in the Past and Present, Kenneth Finkel and Susan Oyama. Rare photographs of City Hall, Logan Square, Independence Hall, Betsy Ross House, other landmarks juxtaposed with contemporary views. Captures changing face of historic city. Introduction. Captions. 128pp. 8¼ × 11. 25790-8 Pa. $9.95

AIA ARCHITECTURAL GUIDE TO NASSAU AND SUFFOLK COUNTIES, LONG ISLAND, The American Institute of Architects, Long Island Chapter, and the Society for the Preservation of Long Island Antiquities. Comprehensive, well-researched and generously illustrated volume brings to life over three centuries of Long Island's great architectural heritage. More than 240 photographs with authoritative, extensively detailed captions. 176pp. 8¼ × 11. 26946-9 Pa. $14.95

NORTH AMERICAN INDIAN LIFE: Customs and Traditions of 23 Tribes, Elsie Clews Parsons (ed.). 27 fictionalized essays by noted anthropologists examine religion, customs, government, additional facets of life among the Winnebago, Crow, Zuni, Eskimo, other tribes. 480pp. 6⅛ × 9¼. 27377-6 Pa. $10.95

FRANK LLOYD WRIGHT'S HOLLYHOCK HOUSE, Donald Hoffmann. Lavishly illustrated, carefully documented study of one of Wright's most controversial residential designs. Over 120 photographs, floor plans, elevations, etc. Detailed perceptive text by noted Wright scholar. Index. 128pp. 9¼ × 10¾.
27133-1 Pa. $11.95

THE MALE AND FEMALE FIGURE IN MOTION: 60 Classic Photographic Sequences, Eadweard Muybridge. 60 true-action photographs of men and women walking, running, climbing, bending, turning, etc., reproduced from rare 19th-century masterpiece. vi + 121pp. 9 × 12.
24745-7 Pa. $10.95

1001 QUESTIONS ANSWERED ABOUT THE SEASHORE, N. J. Berrill and Jacquelyn Berrill. Queries answered about dolphins, sea snails, sponges, starfish, fishes, shore birds, many others. Covers appearance, breeding, growth, feeding, much more. 305pp. 5¼ × 8¼.
23366-9 Pa. $7.95

GUIDE TO OWL WATCHING IN NORTH AMERICA, Donald S. Heintzelman. Superb guide offers complete data and descriptions of 19 species: barn owl, screech owl, snowy owl, many more. Expert coverage of owl-watching equipment, conservation, migrations and invasions, etc. Guide to observing sites. 84 illustrations. xiii + 193pp. 5⅜ × 8½.
27344-X Pa. $8.95

MEDICINAL AND OTHER USES OF NORTH AMERICAN PLANTS: A Historical Survey with Special Reference to the Eastern Indian Tribes, Charlotte Erichsen-Brown. Chronological historical citations document 500 years of usage of plants, trees, shrubs native to eastern Canada, northeastern U.S. Also complete identifying information. 343 illustrations. 544pp. 6½ × 9¼.
25951-X Pa. $12.95

STORYBOOK MAZES, Dave Phillips. 23 stories and mazes on two-page spreads: Wizard of Oz, Treasure Island, Robin Hood, etc. Solutions. 64pp. 8¼ × 11.
23628-5 Pa. $2.95

NEGRO FOLK MUSIC, U.S.A., Harold Courlander. Noted folklorist's scholarly yet readable analysis of rich and varied musical tradition. Includes authentic versions of over 40 folk songs. Valuable bibliography and discography. xi + 324pp. 5⅜ × 8½.
27350-4 Pa. $7.95

MOVIE-STAR PORTRAITS OF THE FORTIES, John Kobal (ed.). 163 glamor, studio photos of 106 stars of the 1940s: Rita Hayworth, Ava Gardner, Marlon Brando, Clark Gable, many more. 176pp. 8⅜ × 11¼.
23546-7 Pa. $11.95

BENCHLEY LOST AND FOUND, Robert Benchley. Finest humor from early 30s, about pet peeves, child psychologists, post office and others. Mostly unavailable elsewhere. 73 illustrations by Peter Arno and others. 183pp. 5⅜ × 8½.
22410-4 Pa. $5.95

YEKL and THE IMPORTED BRIDEGROOM AND OTHER STORIES OF YIDDISH NEW YORK, Abraham Cahan. Film Hester Street based on Yekl (1896). Novel, other stories among first about Jewish immigrants on N.Y.'s East Side. 240pp. 5⅜ × 8½.
22427-9 Pa. $6.95

SELECTED POEMS, Walt Whitman. Generous sampling from *Leaves of Grass.* Twenty-four poems include "I Hear America Singing," "Song of the Open Road," "I Sing the Body Electric," "When Lilacs Last in the Dooryard Bloom'd," "O Captain! My Captain!"—all reprinted from an authoritative edition. Lists of titles and first lines. 128pp. 5³⁄₁₆ × 8¼.
26878-0 Pa. $1.00

THE BEST TALES OF HOFFMANN, E. T. A. Hoffmann. 10 of Hoffmann's most important stories: "Nutcracker and the King of Mice," "The Golden Flowerpot," etc. 458pp. 5⅜ × 8½. 21793-0 Pa. $8.95

FROM FETISH TO GOD IN ANCIENT EGYPT, E. A. Wallis Budge. Rich detailed survey of Egyptian conception of "God" and gods, magic, cult of animals, Osiris, more. Also, superb English translations of hymns and legends. 240 illustrations. 545pp. 5⅜ × 8½. 25803-3 Pa. $11.95

FRENCH STORIES/CONTES FRANÇAIS: A Dual-Language Book, Wallace Fowlie. Ten stories by French masters, Voltaire to Camus: "Micromegas" by Voltaire; "The Atheist's Mass" by Balzac; "Minuet" by de Maupassant; "The Guest" by Camus, six more. Excellent English translations on facing pages. Also French-English vocabulary list, exercises, more. 352pp. 5⅜ × 8½. 26443-2 Pa. $8.95

CHICAGO AT THE TURN OF THE CENTURY IN PHOTOGRAPHS: 122 Historic Views from the Collections of the Chicago Historical Society, Larry A. Viskochil. Rare large-format prints offer detailed views of City Hall, State Street, the Loop, Hull House, Union Station, many other landmarks, circa 1904–1913. Introduction. Captions. Maps. 144pp. 9⅜ × 12¼. 24656-6 Pa. $12.95

OLD BROOKLYN IN EARLY PHOTOGRAPHS, 1865–1929, William Lee Younger. Luna Park, Gravesend race track, construction of Grand Army Plaza, moving of Hotel Brighton, etc. 157 previously unpublished photographs. 165pp. 8⅞ × 11¾. 23587-4 Pa. $13.95

THE MYTHS OF THE NORTH AMERICAN INDIANS, Lewis Spence. Rich anthology of the myths and legends of the Algonquins, Iroquois, Pawnees and Sioux, prefaced by an extensive historical and ethnological commentary. 36 illustrations. 480pp. 5⅜ × 8½. 25967-6 Pa. $8.95

AN ENCYCLOPEDIA OF BATTLES: Accounts of Over 1,560 Battles from 1479 B.C. to the Present, David Eggenberger. Essential details of every major battle in recorded history from the first battle of Megiddo in 1479 B.C. to Grenada in 1984. List of Battle Maps. New Appendix covering the years 1967–1984. Index. 99 illustrations. 544pp. 6½ × 9¼. 24913-1 Pa. $14.95

SAILING ALONE AROUND THE WORLD, Captain Joshua Slocum. First man to sail around the world, alone, in small boat. One of great feats of seamanship told in delightful manner. 67 illustrations. 294pp. 5⅜ × 8½. 20326-3 Pa. $5.95

ANARCHISM AND OTHER ESSAYS, Emma Goldman. Powerful, penetrating, prophetic essays on direct action, role of minorities, prison reform, puritan hypocrisy, violence, etc. 271pp. 5⅜ × 8½. 22484-8 Pa. $5.95

MYTHS OF THE HINDUS AND BUDDHISTS, Ananda K. Coomaraswamy and Sister Nivedita. Great stories of the epics; deeds of Krishna, Shiva, taken from puranas, Vedas, folk tales; etc. 32 illustrations. 400pp. 5⅜ × 8½. 21759-0 Pa. $9.95

BEYOND PSYCHOLOGY, Otto Rank. Fear of death, desire of immortality, nature of sexuality, social organization, creativity, according to Rankian system. 291pp. 5⅜ × 8½. 20485-5 Pa. $8.95

A THEOLOGICO-POLITICAL TREATISE, Benedict Spinoza. Also contains unfinished Political Treatise. Great classic on religious liberty, theory of government on common consent. R. Elwes translation. Total of 421pp. 5⅜ × 8½. 20249-6 Pa. $8.95

CATALOG OF DOVER BOOKS

MY BONDAGE AND MY FREEDOM, Frederick Douglass. Born a slave, Douglass became outspoken force in antislavery movement. The best of Douglass' autobiographies. Graphic description of slave life. 464pp. 5⅜ × 8½.   22457-0 Pa. $8.95

FOLLOWING THE EQUATOR: A Journey Around the World, Mark Twain. Fascinating humorous account of 1897 voyage to Hawaii, Australia, India, New Zealand, etc. Ironic, bemused reports on peoples, customs, climate, flora and fauna, politics, much more. 197 illustrations. 720pp. 5⅜ × 8½.   26113-1 Pa. $15.95

THE PEOPLE CALLED SHAKERS, Edward D. Andrews. Definitive study of Shakers: origins, beliefs, practices, dances, social organization, furniture and crafts, etc. 33 illustrations. 351pp. 5⅜ × 8½.   21081-2 Pa. $8.95

THE MYTHS OF GREECE AND ROME, H. A. Guerber. A classic of mythology, generously illustrated, long prized for its simple, graphic, accurate retelling of the principal myths of Greece and Rome, and for its commentary on their origins and significance. With 64 illustrations by Michelangelo, Raphael, Titian, Rubens, Canova, Bernini and others. 480pp. 5⅜ × 8½.   27584-1 Pa. $9.95

PSYCHOLOGY OF MUSIC, Carl E. Seashore. Classic work discusses music as a medium from psychological viewpoint. Clear treatment of physical acoustics, auditory apparatus, sound perception, development of musical skills, nature of musical feeling, host of other topics. 88 figures. 408pp. 5⅜ × 8½. 21851-1 Pa. $9.95

THE PHILOSOPHY OF HISTORY, Georg W. Hegel. Great classic of Western thought develops concept that history is not chance but rational process, the evolution of freedom. 457pp. 5⅜ × 8½.   20112-0 Pa. $9.95

THE BOOK OF TEA, Kakuzo Okakura. Minor classic of the Orient: entertaining, charming explanation, interpretation of traditional Japanese culture in terms of tea ceremony. 94pp. 5⅜ × 8½.   20070-1 Pa. $3.95

LIFE IN ANCIENT EGYPT, Adolf Erman. Fullest, most thorough, detailed older account with much not in more recent books, domestic life, religion, magic, medicine, commerce, much more. Many illustrations reproduce tomb paintings, carvings, hieroglyphs, etc. 597pp. 5⅜ × 8½.   22632-8 Pa. $10.95

SUNDIALS, Their Theory and Construction, Albert Waugh. Far and away the best, most thorough coverage of ideas, mathematics concerned, types, construction, adjusting anywhere. Simple, nontechnical treatment allows even children to build several of these dials. Over 100 illustrations. 230pp. 5⅜ × 8½.   22947-5 Pa. $7.95

DYNAMICS OF FLUIDS IN POROUS MEDIA, Jacob Bear. For advanced students of ground water hydrology, soil mechanics and physics, drainage and irrigation engineering, and more. 335 illustrations. Exercises, with answers. 784pp. 6⅛ × 9¼.   65675-6 Pa. $19.95

SONGS OF EXPERIENCE: Facsimile Reproduction with 26 Plates in Full Color, William Blake. 26 full-color plates from a rare 1826 edition. Includes "The Tyger," "London," "Holy Thursday," and other poems. Printed text of poems. 48pp. 5¼ × 7.   24636-1 Pa. $4.95

OLD-TIME VIGNETTES IN FULL COLOR, Carol Belanger Grafton (ed.). Over 390 charming, often sentimental illustrations, selected from archives of Victorian graphics—pretty women posing, children playing, food, flowers, kittens and puppies, smiling cherubs, birds and butterflies, much more. All copyright-free. 48pp. 9¼ × 12¼.   27269-9 Pa. $5.95

PERSPECTIVE FOR ARTISTS, Rex Vicat Cole. Depth, perspective of sky and sea, shadows, much more, not usually covered. 391 diagrams, 81 reproductions of drawings and paintings. 279pp. 5⅜ × 8½. 22487-2 Pa. $6.95

DRAWING THE LIVING FIGURE, Joseph Sheppard. Innovative approach to artistic anatomy focuses on specifics of surface anatomy, rather than muscles and bones. Over 170 drawings of live models in front, back and side views, and in widely varying poses. Accompanying diagrams. 177 illustrations. Introduction. Index. 144pp. 8⅜ × 11¼. 26723-7 Pa. $8.95

GOTHIC AND OLD ENGLISH ALPHABETS: 100 Complete Fonts, Dan X. Solo. Add power, elegance to posters, signs, other graphics with 100 stunning copyright-free alphabets: Blackstone, Dolbey, Germania, 97 more—including many lower-case, numerals, punctuation marks. 104pp. 8⅛ × 11. 24695-7 Pa. $8.95

HOW TO DO BEADWORK, Mary White. Fundamental book on craft from simple projects to five-bead chains and woven works. 106 illustrations. 142pp. 5⅜ × 8. 20697-1 Pa. $4.95

THE BOOK OF WOOD CARVING, Charles Marshall Sayers. Finest book for beginners discusses fundamentals and offers 34 designs. "Absolutely first rate . . . well thought out and well executed."—E. J. Tangerman. 118pp. 7¾ × 10⅝. 23654-4 Pa. $5.95

ILLUSTRATED CATALOG OF CIVIL WAR MILITARY GOODS: Union Army Weapons, Insignia, Uniform Accessories, and Other Equipment, Schuyler, Hartley, and Graham. Rare, profusely illustrated 1846 catalog includes Union Army uniform and dress regulations, arms and ammunition, coats, insignia, flags, swords, rifles, etc. 226 illustrations. 160pp. 9 × 12. 24939-5 Pa. $10.95

WOMEN'S FASHIONS OF THE EARLY 1900s: An Unabridged Republication of "New York Fashions, 1909," National Cloak & Suit Co. Rare catalog of mail-order fashions documents women's and children's clothing styles shortly after the turn of the century. Captions offer full descriptions, prices. Invaluable resource for fashion, costume historians. Approximately 725 illustrations. 128pp. 8⅜ × 11¼. 27276-1 Pa. $11.95

THE 1912 AND 1915 GUSTAV STICKLEY FURNITURE CATALOGS, Gustav Stickley. With over 200 detailed illustrations and descriptions, these two catalogs are essential reading and reference materials and identification guides for Stickley furniture. Captions cite materials, dimensions and prices. 112pp. 6½ × 9¼. 26676-1 Pa. $9.95

EARLY AMERICAN LOCOMOTIVES, John H. White, Jr. Finest locomotive engravings from early 19th century: historical (1804–74), main-line (after 1870), special, foreign, etc. 147 plates. 142pp. 11⅜ × 8¼. 22772-3 Pa. $10.95

THE TALL SHIPS OF TODAY IN PHOTOGRAPHS, Frank O. Braynard. Lavishly illustrated tribute to nearly 100 majestic contemporary sailing vessels: Amerigo Vespucci, Clearwater, Constitution, Eagle, Mayflower, Sea Cloud, Victory, many more. Authoritative captions provide statistics, background on each ship. 190 black-and-white photographs and illustrations. Introduction. 128pp. 8⅞ × 11¾. 27163-3 Pa. $13.95

CATALOG OF DOVER BOOKS

EARLY NINETEENTH-CENTURY CRAFTS AND TRADES, Peter Stockham (ed.). Extremely rare 1807 volume describes to youngsters the crafts and trades of the day: brickmaker, weaver, dressmaker, bookbinder, ropemaker, saddler, many more. Quaint prose, charming illustrations for each craft. 20 black-and-white line illustrations. 192pp. 4⅜ × 6. 27293-1 Pa. $4.95

VICTORIAN FASHIONS AND COSTUMES FROM HARPER'S BAZAR, 1867–1898, Stella Blum (ed.). Day costumes, evening wear, sports clothes, shoes, hats, other accessories in over 1,000 detailed engravings. 320pp. 9⅜ × 12¼.
22990-4 Pa. $13.95

GUSTAV STICKLEY, THE CRAFTSMAN, Mary Ann Smith. Superb study surveys broad scope of Stickley's achievement, especially in architecture. Design philosophy, rise and fall of the Craftsman empire, descriptions and floor plans for many Craftsman houses, more. 86 black-and-white halftones. 31 line illustrations. Introduction. 208pp. 6½ × 9¼. 27210-9 Pa. $9.95

THE LONG ISLAND RAIL ROAD IN EARLY PHOTOGRAPHS, Ron Ziel. Over 220 rare photos, informative text document origin (1844) and development of rail service on Long Island. Vintage views of early trains, locomotives, stations, passengers, crews, much more. Captions. 8⅞ × 11¾. 26301-0 Pa. $13.95

THE BOOK OF OLD SHIPS: From Egyptian Galleys to Clipper Ships, Henry B. Culver. Superb, authoritative history of sailing vessels, with 80 magnificent line illustrations. Galley, bark, caravel, longship, whaler, many more. Detailed, informative text on each vessel by noted naval historian. Introduction. 256pp. 5⅜ × 8½. 27332-6 Pa. $6.95

TEN BOOKS ON ARCHITECTURE, Vitruvius. The most important book ever written on architecture. Early Roman aesthetics, technology, classical orders, site selection, all other aspects. Morgan translation. 331pp. 5⅜ × 8½. 20645-9 Pa. $8.95

THE HUMAN FIGURE IN MOTION, Eadweard Muybridge. More than 4,500 stopped-action photos, in action series, showing undraped men, women, children jumping, lying down, throwing, sitting, wrestling, carrying, etc. 390pp. 7⅞ × 10⅝.
20204-6 Clothbd. $24.95

TREES OF THE EASTERN AND CENTRAL UNITED STATES AND CANADA, William M. Harlow. Best one-volume guide to 140 trees. Full descriptions, woodlore, range, etc. Over 600 illustrations. Handy size. 288pp. 4½ × 6⅜.
20395-6 Pa. $5.95

SONGS OF WESTERN BIRDS, Dr. Donald J. Borror. Complete song and call repertoire of 60 western species, including flycatchers, juncoes, cactus wrens, many more—includes fully illustrated booklet. Cassette and manual 99913-0 $8.95

GROWING AND USING HERBS AND SPICES, Milo Miloradovich. Versatile handbook provides all the information needed for cultivation and use of all the herbs and spices available in North America. 4 illustrations. Index. Glossary. 236pp. 5⅜ × 8½. 25058-X Pa. $6.95

BIG BOOK OF MAZES AND LABYRINTHS, Walter Shepherd. 50 mazes and labyrinths in all—classical, solid, ripple, and more—in one great volume. Perfect inexpensive puzzler for clever youngsters. Full solutions. 112pp. 8⅛ × 11.
22951-3 Pa. $4.95

PIANO TUNING, J. Cree Fischer. Clearest, best book for beginner, amateur. Simple repairs, raising dropped notes, tuning by easy method of flattened fifths. No previous skills needed. 4 illustrations. 201pp. 5⅜ × 8½. **23267-0 Pa. $5.95**

A SOURCE BOOK IN THEATRICAL HISTORY, A. M. Nagler. Contemporary observers on acting, directing, make-up, costuming, stage props, machinery, scene design, from Ancient Greece to Chekhov. 611pp. 5⅜ × 8½. **20515-0 Pa. $11.95**

THE COMPLETE NONSENSE OF EDWARD LEAR, Edward Lear. All nonsense limericks, zany alphabets, Owl and Pussycat, songs, nonsense botany, etc., illustrated by Lear. Total of 320pp. 5⅜ × 8½. (USO) **20167-8 Pa. $6.95**

VICTORIAN PARLOUR POETRY: An Annotated Anthology, Michael R. Turner. 117 gems by Longfellow, Tennyson, Browning, many lesser-known poets. "The Village Blacksmith," "Curfew Must Not Ring Tonight," "Only a Baby Small," dozens more, often difficult to find elsewhere. Index of poets, titles, first lines. xxiii + 325pp. 5⅜ × 8¼. **27044-0 Pa. $8.95**

DUBLINERS, James Joyce. Fifteen stories offer vivid, tightly focused observations of the lives of Dublin's poorer classes. At least one, "The Dead," is considered a masterpiece. Reprinted complete and unabridged from standard edition. 160pp. 5³⁄₁₆ × 8¼. 26870-5 Pa. $1.00

THE HAUNTED MONASTERY and THE CHINESE MAZE MURDERS, Robert van Gulik. Two full novels by van Gulik, set in 7th-century China, continue adventures of Judge Dee and his companions. An evil Taoist monastery, seemingly supernatural events; overgrown topiary maze hides strange crimes. 27 illustrations. 328pp. 5⅜ × 8½. 23502-5 Pa. $7.95

THE BOOK OF THE SACRED MAGIC OF ABRAMELIN THE MAGE, translated by S. MacGregor Mathers. Medieval manuscript of ceremonial magic. Basic document in Aleister Crowley, Golden Dawn groups. 268pp. 5⅜ × 8½. **23211-5 Pa. $8.95**

NEW RUSSIAN-ENGLISH AND ENGLISH-RUSSIAN DICTIONARY, M. A. O'Brien. This is a remarkably handy Russian dictionary, containing a surprising amount of information, including over 70,000 entries. 366pp. 4½ × 6⅛. **20208-9 Pa. $9.95**

HISTORIC HOMES OF THE AMERICAN PRESIDENTS, Second, Revised Edition, Irvin Haas. A traveler's guide to American Presidential homes, most open to the public, depicting and describing homes occupied by every American President from George Washington to George Bush. With visiting hours, admission charges, travel routes. 175 photographs. Index. 160pp. 8¼ × 11. 26751-2 Pa. $10.95

NEW YORK IN THE FORTIES, Andreas Feininger. 162 brilliant photographs by the well-known photographer, formerly with *Life* magazine. Commuters, shoppers, Times Square at night, much else from city at its peak. Captions by John von Hartz. 181pp. 9¼ × 10¾. 23585-8 Pa. $12.95

INDIAN SIGN LANGUAGE, William Tomkins. Over 525 signs developed by Sioux and other tribes. Written instructions and diagrams. Also 290 pictographs. 111pp. 6⅛ × 9¼. 22029-X Pa. $3.50

ANATOMY: A Complete Guide for Artists, Joseph Sheppard. A master of figure drawing shows artists how to render human anatomy convincingly. Over 460 illustrations. 224pp. 8⅜ × 11¼. 27279-6 Pa. $10.95

MEDIEVAL CALLIGRAPHY: Its History and Technique, Marc Drogin. Spirited history, comprehensive instruction manual covers 13 styles (ca. 4th century thru 15th). Excellent photographs; directions for duplicating medieval techniques with modern tools. 224pp. 8⅜ × 11¼. 26142-5 Pa. $11.95

DRIED FLOWERS: How to Prepare Them, Sarah Whitlock and Martha Rankin. Complete instructions on how to use silica gel, meal and borax, perlite aggregate, sand and borax, glycerine and water to create attractive permanent flower arrangements. 12 illustrations. 32pp. 5⅜ × 8½. 21802-3 Pa. $1.00

EASY-TO-MAKE BIRD FEEDERS FOR WOODWORKERS, Scott D. Campbell. Detailed, simple-to-use guide for designing, constructing, caring for and using feeders. Text, illustrations for 12 classic and contemporary designs. 96pp. 5⅜ × 8½. 25847-5 Pa. $2.95

OLD-TIME CRAFTS AND TRADES, Peter Stockham. An 1807 book created to teach children about crafts and trades open to them as future careers. It describes in detailed, nontechnical terms 24 different occupations, among them coachmaker, gardener, hairdresser, lacemaker, shoemaker, wheelwright, copper-plate printer, milliner, trunkmaker, merchant and brewer. Finely detailed engravings illustrate each occupation. 192pp. 4⅝ × 6. 27398-9 Pa. $4.95

THE HISTORY OF UNDERCLOTHES, C. Willett Cunnington and Phyllis Cunnington. Fascinating, well-documented survey covering six centuries of English undergarments, enhanced with over 100 illustrations: 12th-century laced-up bodice, footed long drawers (1795), 19th-century bustles, 19th-century corsets for men, Victorian "bust improvers," much more. 272pp. 5⅜ × 8¼. 27124-2 Pa. $9.95

ARTS AND CRAFTS FURNITURE: The Complete Brooks Catalog of 1912, Brooks Manufacturing Co. Photos and detailed descriptions of more than 150 now very collectible furniture designs from the Arts and Crafts movement depict davenports, settees, buffets, desks, tables, chairs, bedsteads, dressers and more, all built of solid, quarter-sawed oak. Invaluable for students and enthusiasts of antiques, Americana and the decorative arts. 80pp. 6½ × 9¼. 27471-3 Pa. $7.95

HOW WE INVENTED THE AIRPLANE: An Illustrated History, Orville Wright. Fascinating firsthand account covers early experiments, construction of planes and motors, first flights, much more. Introduction and commentary by Fred C. Kelly. 76 photographs. 96pp. 8¼ × 11. 25662-6 Pa. $8.95

THE ARTS OF THE SAILOR: Knotting, Splicing and Ropework, Hervey Garrett Smith. Indispensable shipboard reference covers tools, basic knots and useful hitches; handsewing and canvas work, more. Over 100 illustrations. Delightful reading for sea lovers. 256pp. 5⅜ × 8½. 26440-8 Pa. $7.95

FRANK LLOYD WRIGHT'S FALLINGWATER: The House and Its History, Second, Revised Edition, Donald Hoffmann. A total revision—both in text and illustrations—of the standard document on Fallingwater, the boldest, most personal architectural statement of Wright's mature years, updated with valuable new material from the recently opened Frank Lloyd Wright Archives. "Fascinating"—*The New York Times*. 116 illustrations. 128pp. 9¼ × 10¾. 27430-6 Pa. $10.95

PHOTOGRAPHIC SKETCHBOOK OF THE CIVIL WAR, Alexander Gardner. 100 photos taken on field during the Civil War. Famous shots of Manassas, Harper's Ferry, Lincoln, Richmond, slave pens, etc. 244pp. 10⅝ × 8¼.
22731-6 Pa. $9.95

FIVE ACRES AND INDEPENDENCE, Maurice G. Kains. Great back-to-the-land classic explains basics of self-sufficient farming. The one book to get. 95 illustrations. 397pp. 5⅜ × 8½. 20974-1 Pa. $7.95

SONGS OF EASTERN BIRDS, Dr. Donald J. Borror. Songs and calls of 60 species most common to eastern U.S.: warblers, woodpeckers, flycatchers, thrushes, larks, many more in high-quality recording. Cassette and manual 99912-2 $8.95

A MODERN HERBAL, Margaret Grieve. Much the fullest, most exact, most useful compilation of herbal material. Gigantic alphabetical encyclopedia, from aconite to zedoary, gives botanical information, medical properties, folklore, economic uses, much else. Indispensable to serious reader. 161 illustrations. 888pp. 6½ × 9¼. 2-vol. set. (USO) Vol. I: 22798-7 Pa. $9.95
Vol. II: 22799-5 Pa. $9.95

HIDDEN TREASURE MAZE BOOK, Dave Phillips. Solve 34 challenging mazes accompanied by heroic tales of adventure. Evil dragons, people-eating plants, bloodthirsty giants, many more dangerous adversaries lurk at every twist and turn. 34 mazes, stories, solutions. 48pp. 8¼ × 11. 24566-7 Pa. $2.95

LETTERS OF W. A. MOZART, Wolfgang A. Mozart. Remarkable letters show bawdy wit, humor, imagination, musical insights, contemporary musical world; includes some letters from Leopold Mozart. 276pp. 5⅜ × 8½. 22859-2 Pa. $7.95

BASIC PRINCIPLES OF CLASSICAL BALLET, Agrippina Vaganova. Great Russian theoretician, teacher explains methods for teaching classical ballet. 118 illustrations. 175pp. 5⅜ × 8½. 22036-2 Pa. $4.95

THE JUMPING FROG, Mark Twain. Revenge edition. The original story of The Celebrated Jumping Frog of Calaveras County, a hapless French translation, and Twain's hilarious "retranslation" from the French. 12 illustrations. 66pp. 5⅜ × 8½.
22686-7 Pa. $3.95

BEST REMEMBERED POEMS, Martin Gardner (ed.). The 126 poems in this superb collection of 19th- and 20th-century British and American verse range from Shelley's "To a Skylark" to the impassioned "Renascence" of Edna St. Vincent Millay and to Edward Lear's whimsical "The Owl and the Pussycat." 224pp. 5⅜ × 8½.
27165-X Pa. $4.95

COMPLETE SONNETS, William Shakespeare. Over 150 exquisite poems deal with love, friendship, the tyranny of time, beauty's evanescence, death and other themes in language of remarkable power, precision and beauty. Glossary of archaic terms. 80pp. 5³⁄₁₆ × 8¼. 26686-9 Pa. $1.00

BODIES IN A BOOKSHOP, R. T. Campbell. Challenging mystery of blackmail and murder with ingenious plot and superbly drawn characters. In the best tradition of British suspense fiction. 192pp. 5⅜ × 8½. 24720-1 Pa. $5.95

CATALOG OF DOVER BOOKS

THE WIT AND HUMOR OF OSCAR WILDE, Alvin Redman (ed.). More than 1,000 ripostes, paradoxes, wisecracks: Work is the curse of the drinking classes; I can resist everything except temptation; etc. 258pp. 5⅜ × 8½. 20602-5 Pa. $5.95

SHAKESPEARE LEXICON AND QUOTATION DICTIONARY, Alexander Schmidt. Full definitions, locations, shades of meaning in every word in plays and poems. More than 50,000 exact quotations. 1,485pp. 6½ × 9¼. 2-vol. set.
Vol. I: 22726-X Pa. $16.95
Vol. 2: 22727-8 Pa. $15.95

SELECTED POEMS, Emily Dickinson. Over 100 best-known, best-loved poems by one of America's foremost poets, reprinted from authoritative early editions. No comparable edition at this price. Index of first lines. 64pp. 5³⁄₁₆ × 8¼. 26466-1 Pa. $1.00

CELEBRATED CASES OF JUDGE DEE (DEE GOONG AN), translated by Robert van Gulik. Authentic 18th-century Chinese detective novel; Dee and associates solve three interlocked cases. Led to van Gulik's own stories with same characters. Extensive introduction. 9 illustrations. 237pp. 5⅜ × 8½. 23337-5 Pa. $6.95

THE MALLEUS MALEFICARUM OF KRAMER AND SPRENGER, translated by Montague Summers. Full text of most important witchhunter's "bible," used by both Catholics and Protestants. 278pp. 6⅝ × 10. 22802-9 Pa. $11.95

SPANISH STORIES/CUENTOS ESPAÑOLES: A Dual-Language Book, Angel Flores (ed.). Unique format offers 13 great stories in Spanish by Cervantes, Borges, others. Faithful English translations on facing pages. 352pp. 5⅜ × 8½. 25399-6 Pa. $8.95

THE CHICAGO WORLD'S FAIR OF 1893: A Photographic Record, Stanley Appelbaum (ed.). 128 rare photos show 200 buildings, Beaux-Arts architecture, Midway, original Ferris Wheel, Edison's kinetoscope, more. Architectural emphasis; full text. 116pp. 8¼ × 11. 23990-X Pa. $9.95

OLD QUEENS, N.Y., IN EARLY PHOTOGRAPHS, Vincent F. Seyfried and William Asadorian. Over 160 rare photographs of Maspeth, Jamaica, Jackson Heights, and other areas. Vintage views of DeWitt Clinton mansion, 1939 World's Fair and more. Captions. 192pp. 8⅞ × 11. 26358-4 Pa. $12.95

CAPTURED BY THE INDIANS: 15 Firsthand Accounts, 1750–1870, Frederick Drimmer. Astounding true historical accounts of grisly torture, bloody conflicts, relentless pursuits, miraculous escapes and more, by people who lived to tell the tale. 384pp. 5⅜ × 8½. 24901-8 Pa. $8.95

THE WORLD'S GREAT SPEECHES, Lewis Copeland and Lawrence W. Lamm (eds.). Vast collection of 278 speeches of Greeks to 1970. Powerful and effective models; unique look at history. 842pp. 5⅜ × 8½. 20468-5 Pa. $14.95

THE BOOK OF THE SWORD, Sir Richard F. Burton. Great Victorian scholar/adventurer's eloquent, erudite history of the "queen of weapons"—from prehistory to early Roman Empire. Evolution and development of early swords, variations (sabre, broadsword, cutlass, scimitar, etc.), much more. 336pp. 6⅛ × 9¼. 25434-8 Pa. $8.95

AUTOBIOGRAPHY: The Story of My Experiments with Truth, Mohandas K. Gandhi. Boyhood, legal studies, purification, the growth of the Satyagraha (nonviolent protest) movement. Critical, inspiring work of the man responsible for the freedom of India. 480pp. 5⅜ × 8½. (USO) 24593-4 Pa. **$8.95**

CELTIC MYTHS AND LEGENDS, T. W. Rolleston. Masterful retelling of Irish and Welsh stories and tales. Cuchulain, King Arthur, Deirdre, the Grail, many more. First paperback edition. 58 full-page illustrations. 512pp. 5⅜ × 8½. 26507-2 Pa. **$9.95**

THE PRINCIPLES OF PSYCHOLOGY, William James. Famous long course complete, unabridged. Stream of thought, time perception, memory, experimental methods; great work decades ahead of its time. 94 figures. 1,391pp. 5⅜ × 8½. 2-vol. set.
Vol. I: 20381-6 Pa. **$12.95**
Vol. II: 20382-4 Pa. **$12.95**

THE WORLD AS WILL AND REPRESENTATION, Arthur Schopenhauer. Definitive English translation of Schopenhauer's life work, correcting more than 1,000 errors, omissions in earlier translations. Translated by E. F. J. Payne. Total of 1,269pp. 5⅜ × 8½. 2-vol. set.
Vol. 1: 21761-2 Pa. **$11.95**
Vol. 2: 21762-0 Pa. **$11.95**

MAGIC AND MYSTERY IN TIBET, Madame Alexandra David-Neel. Experiences among lamas, magicians, sages, sorcerers, Bonpa wizards. A true psychic discovery. 32 illustrations. 321pp. 5⅜ × 8½. (USO) 22682-4 Pa. **$8.95**

THE EGYPTIAN BOOK OF THE DEAD, E. A. Wallis Budge. Complete reproduction of Ani's papyrus, finest ever found. Full hieroglyphic text, interlinear transliteration, word-for-word translation, smooth translation. 533pp. 6½ × 9¼. 21866-X Pa. **$9.95**

MATHEMATICS FOR THE NONMATHEMATICIAN, Morris Kline. Detailed, college-level treatment of mathematics in cultural and historical context, with numerous exercises. Recommended Reading Lists. Tables. Numerous figures. 641pp. 5⅜ × 8½. 24823-2 Pa. **$11.95**

THEORY OF WING SECTIONS: Including a Summary of Airfoil Data, Ira H. Abbott and A. E. von Doenhoff. Concise compilation of subsonic aerodynamic characteristics of NACA wing sections, plus description of theory. 350pp. of tables. 693pp. 5⅜ × 8½. 60586-8 Pa. **$14.95**

THE RIME OF THE ANCIENT MARINER, Gustave Doré, S. T. Coleridge. Doré's finest work; 34 plates capture moods, subtleties of poem. Flawless full-size reproductions printed on facing pages with authoritative text of poem. "Beautiful. Simply beautiful."—*Publisher's Weekly*. 77pp. 9¼ × 12. 22305-1 Pa. **$6.95**

NORTH AMERICAN INDIAN DESIGNS FOR ARTISTS AND CRAFTS-PEOPLE, Eva Wilson. Over 360 authentic copyright-free designs adapted from Navajo blankets, Hopi pottery, Sioux buffalo hides, more. Geometrics, symbolic figures, plant and animal motifs, etc. 128pp. 8⅜ × 11. (EUK) 25341-4 Pa. **$7.95**

SCULPTURE: Principles and Practice, Louis Slobodkin. Step-by-step approach to clay, plaster, metals, stone; classical and modern. 253 drawings, photos. 255pp. 8⅛ × 11. 22960-2 Pa. **$10.95**

CATALOG OF DOVER BOOKS

THE INFLUENCE OF SEA POWER UPON HISTORY, 1660–1783, A. T. Mahan. Influential classic of naval history and tactics still used as text in war colleges. First paperback edition. 4 maps. 24 battle plans. 640pp. 5⅜ × 8½.
25509-3 Pa. $12.95

THE STORY OF THE TITANIC AS TOLD BY ITS SURVIVORS, Jack Winocour (ed.). What it was really like. Panic, despair, shocking inefficiency, and a little heroism. More thrilling than any fictional account. 26 illustrations. 320pp. 5⅜ × 8½.
20610-6 Pa. $8.95

FAIRY AND FOLK TALES OF THE IRISH PEASANTRY, William Butler Yeats (ed.). Treasury of 64 tales from the twilight world of Celtic myth and legend: "The Soul Cages," "The Kildare Pooka," "King O'Toole and his Goose," many more. Introduction and Notes by W. B. Yeats. 352pp. 5⅜ × 8½.
26941-8 Pa. $8.95

BUDDHIST MAHAYANA TEXTS, E. B. Cowell and Others (eds.). Superb, accurate translations of basic documents in Mahayana Buddhism, highly important in history of religions. The Buddha-karita of Asvaghosha, Larger Sukhavativyuha, more. 448pp. 5⅜ × 8½. ,
25552-2 Pa. $9.95

ONE TWO THREE . . . INFINITY: Facts and Speculations of Science, George Gamow. Great physicist's fascinating, readable overview of contemporary science: number theory, relativity, fourth dimension, entropy, genes, atomic structure, much more. 128 illustrations. Index. 352pp. 5⅜ × 8½.
25664-2 Pa. $8.95

ENGINEERING IN HISTORY, Richard Shelton Kirby, et al. Broad, nontechnical survey of history's major technological advances: birth of Greek science, industrial revolution, electricity and applied science, 20th-century automation, much more. 181 illustrations. ". . . excellent . . ."—Isis. Bibliography. vii + 530pp. 5⅜ × 8¼.
26412-2 Pa. $14.95

Prices subject to change without notice.

Available at your book dealer or write for free catalog to Dept. GI, Dover Publications, Inc., 31 East 2nd St., Mineola, N.Y. 11501. Dover publishes more than 500 books each year on science, elementary and advanced mathematics, biology, music, art, literary history, social sciences and other areas.